Edible Landscaping

Edible Landscaping

Text and Photographs by

Rosalind Creasy

FOR LINDA,
GREAT GARDENING!
Rosalind Creasy

Sierra Club Books

San Francisco

The Sierra Club, founded in 1892 by author and conservationist John Muir, is the oldest, largest, and most influential grassroots environmental organization in the United States. With more than a million members and supporters—and some sixty chapters across the country—we are working hard to protect our local communities, ensure an enduring legacy for America's wild places, and find smart energy solutions to stop global warming. To learn how you can participate in the Sierra Club's programs to explore, enjoy, and protect the planet, please address inquiries to Sierra Club, 85 Second Street, San Francisco, California 94105, or visit our Web site at www.sierraclub.org.

The Sierra Club's book publishing division, Sierra Club Books, has been a leading publisher of titles on the natural world and environmental issues for nearly half a century. We offer books to the general public as a nonprofit educational service in the hope that they may enlarge the public's understanding of the Sierra Club's concerns and priorities. The point of view expressed in each book, however, does not necessarily represent that of the Sierra Club. For more information on Sierra Club Books and a complete list of our titles and authors, please visit www.SierraClubBooks.org.

Published by Sierra Club Books
85 Second Street, San Francisco, CA 94105

Sierra Club Books are published in association with
Counterpoint (www.counterpointpress.com).

SIERRA CLUB, SIERRA CLUB BOOKS, and the Sierra Club design logos are registered trademarks of the Sierra Club.

Book and cover design by Linda Herman, Glyph Publishing Arts

Printed in China on acid free paper

Second Edition

Distributed by Publishers Group West
14 13 12
10 9 8 7 6 5 4

Library of Congress Cataloging-in-Publication Data

Creasy, Rosalind.
  Edible landscaping / text and photographs by Rosalind Creasy.—2nd ed.
    p. cm.
  Rev. ed. of: The complete book of edible landscaping / Rosalind Creasy. 1982.
  Includes bibliographical references and index.
  ISBN 978-1-57805-154-0 (alk. paper)
  1. Edible landscaping. 2. Plants, Edible—Dictionaries. I. Title.
  SB475.9.E35C74 2010
  712—dc22   2009052027

Preceding pages: Spring tulips and pac choi make a stunning combination (page i). A lemon tree trained over an arbor welcomes visitors to a backyard garden (page ii).

To my darling Robert and his faithful companion, Mr. X

Contents

Opposite: Apple trees, cabbages, and parsley are featured in
a four-square edible landscape in Lititz, Pennsylvania.

Opposite: Colorful containers of 'Hungarian Wax' peppers,
'Red Flame' grapes, and cilantro grace these garden steps.

Acknowledgments

The seed for this book was planted more than thirty years ago when I began writing *The Complete Book of Edible Landscaping*, published by Sierra Club Books in 1982. Thanks again to all the people who nurtured me and tended the first edition and its subsequent reprints, setting the stage for this latest work.

To say that this new edition is a labor of love is an understatement. Sharing my passion for edible landscaping is only part of it. Since I began working on this book, it has taken on a life of its own and drawn many more people into my life than I could ever have imagined. So much bounty for which to be thankful!

Thank you to my "extended family" at Sierra Club Books, with Helen Sweetland, the publisher, at the helm. Editor Linda Gunnarson was involved in developing this edition from the beginning; I haven't found the words to describe the heroic effort she has put into the project, tending to every detail with great care and keeping the entire team on track. I'm also grateful to the dynamic people that Sierra Club Books brought to the project: copyeditor extraordinaire Susan Lang, for her skillful editing and invaluable queries; Linda Herman, for the fabulous design and layouts; illustrator Jill Weissman, for the color landscape drawings; Marianne Lipanovich, for illustration coordination; Karen Stough, for proofreading; Barbara Roos, for her fine index; David Van Ness, for composition and technical expertise; and Bob Schildgen, for his wordsmithing on early chapters.

Kudos to all "my people" whose talents enhanced these pages. Marcie Hawthorne, whose black and white illustrations graced the original edition, created a number of new drawings for this edition. My gardener, Deborah Stern, who moonlights as an artist, made the bubble drawings and many of the sketches for other illustrators. Dayna Lane was alert to all the changes in botanical names, even after her temporary move to France; because of her attention to detail and record keeping, I was able to use the landscape at her Arlington, Virginia, home as a model for creating a design plan for readers.

Cathy Wilkinson Barash has been a major part of this project, moving her office from Des Moines to my kitchen table and commuting back and forth between locations. I gratefully credit her for making my thoughts and words come across more clearly, for contributing her wealth of expertise, and for locating needed photographs. She shared her gardens on Long Island and in Iowa as well as scouted edible landscapes in Iowa.

I greatly appreciate the generosity of other experts in the field for taking time to share their varied and enormous fonts of horticultural knowledge. Renee Shepherd of Renee's Garden and Rose Marie Nichols McGee of Nichols Garden Nursery, for keeping me abreast of changes in horticulture and the seed industry and for informing me about newly available varieties. Master horticulturists Jim Wilson, for imparting some of his decades of wisdom; Dr. Calvin Lamborne, for the latest information on new varieties of peas; and Roger Swain, for his vast understanding of plant hardiness as we walked around his enormous New Hampshire garden. Robert Woolley and Ed Laivo of Dave Wilson Nursery, for sharing their immense knowledge of fruit trees and for walking me through the orchards as we tasted fruit; for drilling me on the technical aspects of low chill, pruning, and rootstocks; and for answering endless questions on the flavor and ornamental virtue of each variety. Dr. Richard Merrill, for reviewing sections on basic botany, soil chemistry, and entomology, as well as helping fine-tune Appendix A.

My thanks also to the folks who shared their lists of favorite edibles: Amy Goldman, Jim Long, Debra Madison, Rose Marie Nichols McGee, Ellen Ecker Ogden, Lee Reich, and Mark Rieger.

My own gardens would never have been so exciting without the gardeners I have had through the years, including Wendy Krupnick, Joe Queirolo, Jody Main, Duncan Minalga, Rayne MacGeorge, and Deborah Stern. You'll appreciate their skills as you peruse the many photos of my garden.

Special thanks to all those who shared their gardens with me, in person and photographically: Linda Askey, Suzy Bales, Rick Bayless, Katrina Blades, Jeff and Ellen Bolch, Fanny and Don Bolen, Sherry and Jerry Cash, David Cavagnaro, Ron and Pam Clancy, David Clem, Leslie Close, Darcy Daniels, David Dodson, Kirk and Teri Doughty, Flo Gammerdinger, Amy Goldman, Dan Gray, Sandra and Andrew Hogan, Dayna Lane, Mary-Kate Mackey, Bill Melvin, David Mill, Mrs. Mullen, Nancy Ondra, Susan and Alan Patricof, Barbara Pressler, Dean Riddle, Rebecca

Opposite: Multicolored sages, chives, roses, and nasturtiums, with their many scents, enchant visitors along a front walk.

Samms and Buell Steelman, Carole Saville, William Sofield and Dennis Anderson, Ellen Spector Platt, Ton Stam, Lee Stoltzfus, Edwin and Verna Streeter, Linda Vater, David White and Robert Jakob, Wayne Winterrowd and Joe Eck, and Gene Yale. By allowing me to show what they are doing in their corners of the world, they are helping to inspire others, in different corners of the world.

My gratitude to clients who generously allowed me to design and photograph their gardens: Marcie and Daniel Hawthorne, Marilyn and David Pratt, Cheryl and Alan Rinzler, and Marva and John Warnock.

I am grateful for the time that people with "featured gardens" spent answering my sundry questions: David Cavagnaro, Ron and Pam Clancy, Leslie Close, Dayna Lane, and Dean Riddle.

My appreciation to the owners of restaurants, wineries, and inns with gardens who shared both their glorious gardens and wonderful food, notably Sinclair and Frederique Philip (and gardener Byron Cooke) at Sooke Harbour House, and Dan Barber (and garden designer Barbara Damrosch) of Blue Hill at Stone Barns.

I cannot sing high enough praise for public gardens and museum villages; our country is so blessed to have these fantastic resources to visit. Sometimes I visited these gardens on my own and other times staff members helped me find what I needed. Following are the gardens featured in the book and the staff members who helped: Chanticleer (Doug Croft), Chicago Botanic Garden, The Cloisters, Denver Botanic Gardens (Ebi Kondo), Festival Hill, Genesee Country Village & Museum (Emily Conable), Longwood Gardens, Meadowbrook Farm, Minnesota Landscape Arboretum, The New York Botanical Garden, Old Sturbridge Village (Christie White), Old Westbury Gardens (Janet Large), Seed Savers Exchange, and Van Vleck House and Gardens.

Many thanks to those who helped facilitate my travels, including Debbie Whittaker, Suzy Bales, Rose Marie Nichols McGee, Felder Rushing, Shep Ogden, and Betty Earl. Without these people showing me around their own and other gardens locally, I would have missed some of the best edible landscapes in North America. Each shared intimate knowledge of his or her plantings, climate, and varieties that work best.

Special thanks to Jane Whitfield, my one-time landscaping partner, who drove me around Oregon; Rose and Dick White, my cousins, who shepherded me to gardens to photograph; and Gina Norgard, who offered Long Island hospitality.

Enlivening the pages of this book are the works of many photographers: Charlotte Allen, Linda Askey, Karen Bussolini, Robin Bachtler Cushman, Darcy Daniels, Andrew Drake, Elena Elisseeva, Derek Fell, Adam Gibbs, Marcie Hawthorne, Noah Hawthorne, Dayna Lane, Larry Lefever, Justin Maconochie, Sylvia Martin, Mark Turner, Marc Vassallo, and Scott S. Warren. In addition to their photographs, Suzy Bales, David Cavagnaro, Saxon Holt, and Dency Kane went the extra mile to find images and locations as well as provide support. Thanks also to *Garden Gate* magazine.

This book has taken me into the new millennium, especially when it comes to digital photography. My son, Bob Creasy, provided the computer and expertise that enabled me to make the leap to digital and was always a phone call away to solve the inevitable crises that ensued. In my office, Rayne MacGeorge and Noah Hawthorne were my techies and Stacey Booth my guide through Lightroom. And the folks at Keeble & Shuchat Photography advised me on cameras, provided tips, and rush-scanned slides.

To the thousands of audience members I've spoken to over the years, your questions and comments were invaluable. Thanks for constantly challenging me and keeping me on my toes.

Gudi Riter has been the indispensable person over the past 25 years. While mainly a huge help in the office, Gudi is quick to step in and lend a hand at the drawing board, in the garden, and in the kitchen—wherever her artistry and talents are needed. She keeps everything running smoothly, and I'm truly grateful she's been at my side for so long.

And thanks to all the cheerleaders, the people who go out of their way to give me support, especially longtime friend and herb maven Carole Saville, who also acts as my personal clipping service, and Flo Gammerdinger, who weighed and counted tomatoes from her garden and generously shared her home with me. I cannot forget my neighbors on the special street where I live. The children teach me about life every day, and the adults seem to know just when an impromptu TGIF celebration is needed—thanks for sharing my enthusiasm for edibles.

Finally, heartfelt gratitude to my very special family: they believe in my dreams, sing my praises, and lift my spirits when I'm down. This supporting cast includes my son, Bob, and daughter-in-law, Julie Creasy; my daughter, Laura, and son-in-law, Joe Chavarin, and my grandchildren Alex, Jacinda, Veronica, Nani, and Chris; sisters Nancy Olds and Gail Gallagher; and brother- and sister-in-law John and Cathy Creasy. Thanks so much for being in my life.

Salvaged Douglas fir forms the posts for a patio arbor planted with four grape varieties.

Welcome to My Edible Landscape

I t has taken me almost six years to create this book. Friends and colleagues have asked why I didn't just write a traditional update of *The Complete Book of Edible Landscaping*. The answer is simple: so much has changed—in the garden, in the world in general, and in my own life—during the nearly three decades since the original edition of my book was published. This new edition, *Edible Landscaping*, reflects all of these changes.

In the following pages, I'd like to share some of my personal journey, as well as the evolution of edible landscaping, so that whether you're a seasoned gardener or new to landscaping with edibles, you'll see the creative possibilities for your own home.

A Lifelong Love of Gardening

When I was five years old, my family lived in Needham, Massachusetts, outside Boston. My father gave me my own little garden space along with three tomato seedlings, as many strawberry runners from his plants as I wanted, and a handful of 'King of the Garden' lima bean seeds (now an heirloom growing in my garden as I write). I planted the tomatoes and beans and encircled them with strawberries. I thought I could move plants as readily as furniture in my dollhouse, so nothing stayed in one place long enough to set down roots. Bless my dad, he never once suggested I stop rearranging the plants, but I don't think anything lived very long. I certainly don't remember harvesting a thing from my garden, although I do recall picking and feasting on armloads of corn, tomatoes, and beans from his. Yet what I gleaned from my own little plot was more important—my love of gardening.

Fast forward to 1966, when my late husband, Robert, our two children, and I moved from Boston to Northern California—first to an apartment and then, in 1968, to the Los Altos home where I still live. It had a very shady backyard and a front yard that was mostly lawn with a few old apricot trees. Because of the difficult growing conditions on my own property, I shared my friend's traditional backyard vegetable garden at her home—2 miles away. Living

in the San Francisco Bay Area, a melting pot of diverse cultures, my family developed a penchant for a wide variety of ethnic foods, and my passion for cooking grew alongside my love of gardening. Wanting to re-create delicious ethnic dishes at home, I began planting some unusual edibles in our joint garden, but I yearned for the convenience of gardening in my own yard.

So, even though there seemed to be an unwritten law against planting vegetables in a suburban front yard, I transformed the sunny, packed-dirt parking strip between the lawn and the street into a flower border, into which I sneaked a few spicy poblano peppers for chiles rellenos, lots of basil for pesto, cilantro for stir-fries, tarragon for béarnaise sauce, and artichoke, whose beauty made it the star of the border.

In the mid-1970s, I returned to school to take garden design classes and was soon hooked on creating beautiful gardens for my new clients—homeowners like me. Robert was a computer scientist and technical consultant, so he traveled on business to places such as Milan, Paris, Vienna, Cairo, and Taipei, and I often accompanied him. Foodwise, the travel was eye opening. In Provence, we ate salade Niçoise, replete with fingerling potatoes, haricots verts, and fresh seared tuna with tarragon vinaigrette; in Hong Kong, braised baby pac choi and mushrooms in a spicy ginger sauce; in Treviso, grilled bitter red radicchio drizzled with olive oil. These and hundreds more taste-titillating dishes completely changed my perception of vegetables and started me down the road to growing a wider range of edibles. While Robert worked with clients, I headed out to the markets, nurseries, and gardens. My most common questions to the vegetable vendors were "How do you cook it?" and "Where can I get seeds?" If I was lucky, I found a nursery and bought seeds. Back home, come harvest time, either I had recipes I obtained on my travels or I developed my own.

So much was going on in my life at this time that, when I look back, the synchronicity is astonishing. In 1973, Robert and I visited a kibbutz in Israel. The people there explained how they were "building soil" with food waste from cities so they could eventually grow their own vegetables and fruits; it took 5 to 7 years to rehabilitate the barren land before they could grow crops. That made a big

Opposite: Welcome to my garden. Herbs, showy dahlias and geraniums, and an arbor covered with cherry tomatoes beckon you into my landscape.

impression on me. Because I was working on land use studies for our county, I knew that Americans across the nation were wasting—even polluting—millions of acres of valuable agricultural soil around their homes. Where folks were growing lawns, junipers, and maybe a tree or two, they could grow a meaningful amount of food, which would be a much higher and nobler use of their soil.

I returned from Israel filled with zeal and a revised philosophy of landscaping. With the enthusiasm of youth, I was sure I could quickly change the perception of edibles in the minds of my professors and others in the landscaping field. To prove that edibles are both versatile and beautiful, I started collecting my own data, analyzing the ornamental and cultural aspects of food-bearing plants, and I began what was to become a parallel career: photography. Since homeowners and landscaping professionals were seldom exposed to edibles in a home landscape—only in farm fields and formulaic backyard vegetable gardens—they couldn't picture what I was talking about unless I showed them. So I began photographing edibles everywhere—prostrate rosemary cascading down a wall in Majorca, espaliered pears at The Cloisters in New York, and even the small apricot orchard around my local town hall.

I sought out others growing edibles: John Jeavons, who was developing his Biointensive Method for food production; members of the California Rare Fruit Growers who opened their gardens to me; and longtime community gardeners of diverse ethnic backgrounds. Dave Smith and Paul Hawken, who were testing hand tools to be sold by their new company Smith & Hawken, taught me the value of working with superior equipment. Like me, they were advocating alternatives to energy-hungry power tools. I met Helen and William Olkowski at the Bio-Integral Resource Center in Berkeley and learned about integrated pest management techniques, which enabled me to understand the science behind the organic methods being touted at the time. I soaked up information like a sponge.

In the late 1970s, I began teaching vegetable and fruit gardening in adult education programs, where I received valuable feedback from other gardeners about edibles in their ornamental gardens. My mother, a writer herself, listened to what the coursework covered and uttered the fateful words "That sounds like a book." She helped me write the proposal that I presented to Sierra Club Books, and, to grab the editors' attention, I included a jar of my homemade organic applesauce with a label that read "This does not contain…" followed by a list of more than a dozen chemicals then permitted on apples grown in California.

And so *The Complete Book of Edible Landscaping* was published in 1982. To my delight, it found an eager audience. People were anxious for something new in gardening, and many were excited that their favorite edibles could be grown in an ornamental landscape. I was soon spreading the word on landscaping with edibles by writing magazine articles and lecturing at botanical gardens and universities.

At long last, homeowners who wanted edible landscapes were seeking me out as a designer. I created a formal kitchen garden with raised beds filled with vegetables and herbs encircling a gazebo, restaurant gardens in conjunction with their chefs, urban patio herb gardens, historical restorations with edibles, and hillside gardens overflowing with Mediterranean herbs, vegetables, and fruit trees. These landscapes were generally filled with the commonly available edibles from my local nurseries and plant catalogs.

Another change in awareness was on the horizon. At speaking engagements around the country, people often came up after my talk to tell me about wonderful heirloom and antique plants. They asked, "Why didn't you mention purple string beans?" or "Where can I get apples that are red inside, like my father used to grow?" Although I joined Seed Savers Exchange in 1981, I didn't grow many heirlooms. Other lectures brought me to places like Adelma Simmons' amazing collection of herbs in Connecticut and Native Seeds/Search in Tucson, where I learned about many Native American plants. I realized that, like most other Americans, I was missing out on a whole world of incredible heirloom vegetables, herbs, and fruits.

The Evolution of My Edible Landscape

By 1984, when I started work on *Cooking from the Garden*, I wanted to create a series of trial gardens and themed landscapes in my own front yard using some of the hundreds of varieties of vegetables that few gardeners had ever seen, including red grinding corn, pink celery, and all-blue potatoes. While I was always an adventuresome cook, much of the passion behind this project was the urgent need to help save thousands of heirloom vegetable and fruit varieties that were rapidly becoming extinct. Within the pages of my new book, I could sing the praises of the

In spring of 1984, my shady backyard left no place for me to garden, so I took the leap and removed the old lawn, three dying apricot trees left over from a 1930s-era orchard, and a packed-dirt parking strip in my front yard to make way for a series of vegetable and edible-flower trial gardens and themed landscapes.

About a hundred days after ripping out the front yard, my trial garden was thriving. Zucchini varieties stand out in front, interspersed with cosmos and marigolds; eggplants line the driveway; and behind are 10 varieties of tomatoes, peppers, and greens. Nearly 100 varieties of edibles filled the beds by summer's end.

rich taste of succulent, thin-skinned heirloom tomatoes, the heady aroma and intense flavor of real paprika peppers (not that tasteless red-brown powder in a can), and the sweet decadence of roasted old-time keeper beets to both home cooks and food professionals.

With such an ambitious project in mind, I hired an experienced food gardener, Wendy Krupnick, to help me. After a contractor removed a spruce, some dying apricot trees, an old asphalt walk, and the lawn, Wendy double-dug the entire planting area, which was rock hard from years of foot traffic. We added truckloads of organic matter to the heavy clay soil and transformed the front yard into a series of garden beds. Wendy's skills didn't stop at the front door; an experienced restaurant cook, she helped me test recipes long into the evening.

In the more than 25 years since we ripped out the front yard, I have been blessed with a succession of talented gardener-cooks who were dedicated to sustainable food and my projects. They helped me remake my gardens, planting a huge diversity of edibles twice a year. Thanks to their efforts and special touches, my gardens have thrived, and my photos of their handiwork have helped me spread the word that edibles belong in home landscapes.

I also discovered that, by nature, gardening in the front yard is a communal experience. I still never know who might stop by to chat while I'm in the garden—

neighbors jogging past or drivers who get out of their cars to take a closer look. Putting in edibles draws more than a passing "Oh, that's a pretty flower." It becomes a dialogue, and sharing begins:

"What an unusual-looking tomato."

"I have lots. Would you like some?"

I knew my edible landscape was a true success when, after an open house down the street, several real estate agents asked me if I wanted to put my home on the market; it had so much curb appeal they knew they could easily sell it.

After *Cooking from the Garden* was published in 1988, my landscape received a lot of press. Baby salad greens growing in the front yard, recipes for lavender vichyssoise made from purple potatoes, neighborhood children threshing wheat on my driveway—all made good copy. To add different perspectives for my photography, I created formal paths with bricks left over from the back patio and added a welcoming arbor at the front steps.

I constantly move paths, fences, and walls. Even the plants know to keep their bags packed (I have an 'Olympiad' rose that's been moved four times). Through the years, I've redesigned the front yard about 50 times—first with trial gardens and then with themed landscapes ranging from American Gothic to Alice in Wonderland. Some landscapes showcase specific groups or types of edibles: salad greens, heirloom vegetables and flowers, Asian vegetables, Italian wild greens, spices, and even grains. All have inspired fantastic new recipes. Each of these front yard landscapes was filled with flowers that attracted both beneficial insects as well as my neighbors' attention. By changing the plantings and look of my landscape from season to season and year to year, I have managed to showcase a good portion of the vast range of edible combinations available to everyone.

Changes in the Personal and Global Landscape

Since the original edition of this book was published, my visual design style has changed, as has my design philosophy. My landscapes back then were more utilitarian, less complex, and certainly less colorful than they are today. They were more traditional, substituting edible plants, where appropriate, in an existing landscape configured with lawn, shrubs, and trees. Early on, I relied heavily on plants to dictate a design and less on paths, walls, and overhead structures. My entire yard and most of my designs for clients were on a single plane, readily seen from the street. Then, 20-odd years ago, after working on a design for an historical hacienda with numerous courtyards, I became aware of how gracious garden "rooms" can be for outdoor living—and the opportunities they offer for growing plants vertically. At that point, I created three different "rooms" in both my front and back yards and began designing more outdoor living spaces for clients. I also started using more arbors and vines in my designs.

Junipers lingered in the island between my driveway and my neighbors' because my water pressure was too low to get water there for growing edibles. In 2006, after new neighbors installed irrigation, I put in a boxwood perimeter with a central planting bed, seen here with red salvia and peppers. The next tier has 'Sunshine Blue' blueberries and strawberries; 'Pink Pearl' apple is in the top tier. My neighbors and I share the harvest. Across the driveway, trouble with parasitic nematodes spurred me to create a brick patio garden featuring large edible-filled barrels.

I had always incorporated lots of flowers and a few colorful containers here and there, but my hardscapes were subdued at first—aged wood fences, gates, and chairs; brick or stone paving; and terra-cotta or cement statues. Over the years, I began placing richly hued tiles among the paving stones, and painting walls and chairs vivid colors. Although intense colors might be a subject of debate in some garden circles, I freely paint walls purple, gates yellow, and rusted rooster ornaments brilliant red—whatever strikes my fancy. You could say I design in 3-D and Technicolor!

And my philosophy of landscaping has changed. After seeing my neighborhood children's nascent enthusiasm come alive in my gardens, I design and plant with kids in mind. Can I give them a planting bed of their own? Have I interspersed flowers for them to pick and cherry tomatoes and strawberries for them to munch on? A number of "my kids" have come back years later to tell me what a difference my edible landscape made in their lives. Some majored in environmental sciences, others shared their knowledge of plants with friends and relatives, and many still are growing edibles. Sadly, too many children nowadays have no connection to their food, the seasons, or the creatures that live in a diversified garden. I firmly believe that we owe them the gift of growing some of their own food and connecting with the earth.

Of course, the public perception of edible landscaping has changed greatly in recent decades. Today we are much more acutely aware of environmental issues, and gardeners prefer earth-friendly practices to commercial chemicals. Landscapes are freed from the lock-step lawn and shrub restrictions of the last century. Some folks expect their yards to help cut the food budget by producing a sizeable harvest of fruits and vegetables.

Now that edible landscaping has become part of the vernacular and is widely accepted, the edible plant palette has changed dramatically. People want to grow a much larger and more colorful range of edibles, so white cauliflower and yellow 'Bartlett' pear are yielding center stage to their colorful cousins. Growers are introducing new varieties of familiar edibles, bred for beauty as well as flavor. Wondrous plants have been brought in from other parts of the world—hardy kiwis (some with variegated foliage), delicious Asian pears and persimmons, spectacular mauve pomegranates, and striped lemons with pink flesh, to name a few. Cooks are demanding more diverse edibles, too: a wider range of colorful tomatoes for all uses, ever-hotter chilies, lemon and Thai basils—the list goes on and on.

Once I started inviting neighborhood children into my garden, I began creating gardens or spaces just for them. I quickly learned that pumpkins are a child's favorite crop. Here, a mother helps her son cut a small pumpkin from the vine they grew.

Antique fruits and heirloom vegetables are now mainstream. Entire companies—not just Seed Savers Exchange —are based solely on these classics. Some catalogs are devoted to edible landscaping, and others contain special edible landscaping sections. Catalog text often highlights plants as "ornamental edibles."

Today an edible landscape can be whatever you make it—from a collection of containers of salad fixings on a condo terrace to a large formal herb parterre to a cottage-style garden that comprises vegetables, herbs, fruits, and nut trees.

About This Book

I live in California, but this book and my mission extend far beyond my own yard. I write about what I have seen and experienced across the continent. I spend 3 to 4 months a year on the road, giving presentations, doing research, taking photographs, and visiting folks passionate about homegrown edibles—especially gardeners who cook and cooks who garden. They in turn introduce me to others, many of whose landscapes you will see within these pages. I have photographed throughout the United States (49 out of 50 states; for those of you wondering, North Dakota is at the top of my must-see list) and Canada to prove that people everywhere are designing imaginatively with edibles,

Here's a rarity in my gardens: a comfortable place to sit and enjoy the surrounding beauty. A patinated birdbath and large 'Tuscan Blue' rosemary set the scene; behind them you can glimpse a 'Satsuma' plum tree trunk and gray pineapple guava leaves peeking through the rosemary. Behind the chair is a dwarf 'Violette de Bordeaux' fig tree. Thymes of many flavors scent the air if you tread gently on the stepping-stones.

from Georgia to Maine, Texas to Minnesota, Ontario to British Columbia, Colorado to Oregon, and, yes, California from border to border. With this book I want you to experience the diverse ways people are incorporating edibles into existing landscapes or creating entirely new gardens. To this end, within these pages you'll find more than 300 full-color photographs taken throughout North America, as well as in my own gardens, to inspire your creativity.

Chapter 1 begins with a history of landscape design and segues into how that has influenced modern garden design and a new vision for landscaping. When I wrote the original edition of this book, I wanted to convince people to garden organically; now I assume they already do. With its strong focus on the environment, this chapter guides you toward a sustainable approach to home landscaping.

Chapter 2 is all about laying the groundwork for your edible landscape. I walk you through evaluating the physical characteristics of your property, including soil, climate, and water issues; identifying and resolving any challenges you may face; and then considering any hardscape changes or additions you may want to make.

Chapter 3 covers all the steps in making a landscape plan, from determining your wants and needs as well as your time and budget considerations, to drawing a base plan and revising it, to coming up with your final landscape design. Examples—complete with photos and landscape drawings—of how others have designed or redesigned their landscapes help illustrate your many options.

This book emphasizes landscape *design*, and five chapters are devoted to the subject. Following Chapter 4's discussion of design basics, Chapters 5 through 7 cover designing landscapes with herbs, vegetables, and fruits, berries, and nuts. Since many people, especially urban and condo dwellers, have limited space, and others have little time to devote to a large garden, Chapter 8 explores designing for small spaces. Chapters 5 through 8 each include a relevant do-it-yourself project that is easily completed in a weekend, as well as a featured garden, including a landscape drawing, to show you what others have done. All five design chapters close with a gallery of photographs showcasing even more creative ways people design with edibles.

The comprehensive Encyclopedia of Edibles and Appendix A include most of the specific plant information. The Encyclopedia—really a book in itself—provides complete horticultural and growing details, culinary uses, sources, and recommended varieties for more than 100 different edibles (some entries include more than one plant). My choice of varieties embraces standard, commonly grown plants as well as heirlooms and new disease-resistant types. Appendix A covers basic information on nearly 200 additional plants in chart form, including a number of tropicals. Over the years, some botanical names have changed and are noted. All the information within these pages is as up-to-date as possible as we head to press.

Appendix B provides information of special interest if you have a small garden space or want to grow edibles in containers. Listed here are edible plants that are especially suited for small gardens, along with key information to help you make choices that best fit your needs.

Even though this isn't primarily a gardening book, Appendix C covers the basics of planting and maintenance, and Appendix D provides information on using organic and environmentally friendly practices to control pests and diseases. The Sources and Resources and Bibliography sections direct you to sources of edible plants, seeds, and garden supplies, as well as organizations, gardens to visit for inspiration, and books to help you realize your own edible landscape vision.

As I write this, food costs are skyrocketing, the prices often reflecting the number of miles a crop travels to get to the table. By growing many of the basics ourselves— our own tomatoes, zucchini, blueberries, strawberries,

Mr. X, my 15-year-old pet rooster, heads over to check out the new young hens in the coop while I take a moment to relax in my front garden.

and greens—we save hundreds of dollars a year and help the environment. And we are seeing different models to inspire us, from vegetable gardens in the middle of the White House lawn and on the grounds of governors' mansions to city zoning changes allowing edibles in the front yard and ever-increasing numbers of home landscapes filled with gorgeous edible plants.

With all my heart, I believe that growing edibles is a connection to our vital being, hands in soil, planting seeds, marveling at how they grow, and glorying in that first juicy, sun-warmed fruit of the season. Although each step in the process is a ritual in itself, it is also part of the larger ritual of life. As Gandhi said, "To forget how to dig the earth and tend the soil is to forget ourselves."

Rosalind Creasy
Los Altos, California
January 2010

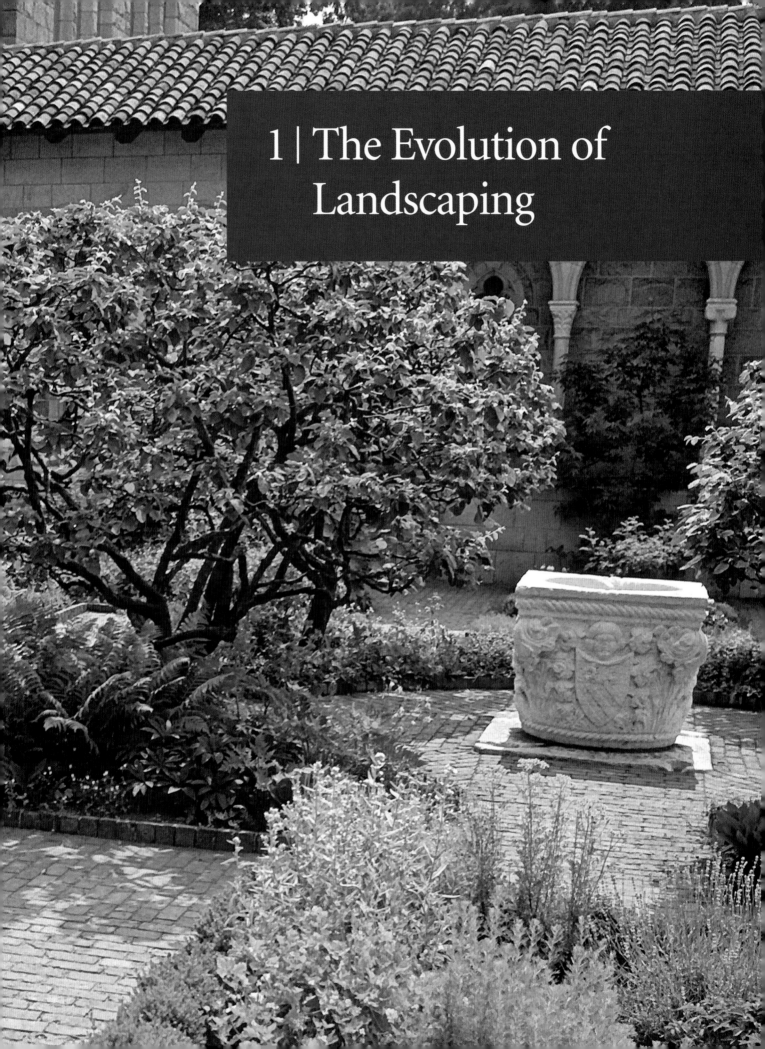

1 | The Evolution of Landscaping

Apple trees gracing front lawns in England, grapevines spilling over fences in Italy, and persimmon trees adorning entryways in Taiwan—it seemed that wherever my husband and I traveled abroad, homeowners showed off edibles in their front yards. But as we drove around North America, there was hardly an edible to be seen. Since these life-sustaining plants are so beautiful and the harvest so rewarding, why weren't they prominent in our home landscapes? It took me a few years, but my research explained a lot about the changing role of edibles in landscape design throughout history and their conspicuous absence in contemporary landscaping. A good source for more historical information is Jan and Michael Gertley's *The Art of the Kitchen Garden*.

Landscape Design Through the Ages

The first gardens, of course, were motivated by survival, not aesthetics. At the same time, our early ancestors developed an appreciation for beautiful environs. They were particularly fond of grottoes and probably used them for religious ceremonies and courtship. Exactly when the marriage of growing food and aesthetically planning garden spaces took place may be uncertain from culture to culture, but early landscape design can be traced back to a number of ancient civilizations.

In Ancient Times

The Egyptians of King Tut's era were among the first people to design a landscape—that is, to deliberately plan the grounds around a dwelling for aesthetic and utilitarian reasons. Fascinating tomb paintings from as early as 1400 B.C. show gardens of well-to-do Egyptians with pools for fish, grape-covered trellises, flower beds, and fruit-bearing trees like figs, pomegranates, and dates. They laid out formal rectangular areas surrounded by walls that offered both protection and a feeling of intimacy. The resulting pleasure gardens provided cool shade, an aesthetic ambiance, and succulent fruit—true oases in the desert.

Preceding pages: Monasteries helped preserve Roman courtyard garden traditions. The Cloisters in New York City is a re-creation of one of these gardens.

The Persians perfected the pleasure garden, weaving fragrance, pools, geometrically arranged plants and walls, fruit trees, shade from the desert sun, and imported flowers into complex garden designs that invited outdoor entertaining, dining, and lovemaking. From about 400 B.C. through the 1700s, these "paradise gardens" became increasingly elaborate, incorporating ever more intricate designs intermingling ornamental and edible plants. Weavers copied the patterns of these magnificent gardens into Persian carpets, bringing the beauty of paradise indoors year round.

Like the Egyptians and Persians (and later the Indians and Moors), the ancient Romans contributed complexity to the gardens of the Western world. Wealthy Romans created extensive villa gardens with elaborate fountains that utilized water brought from miles away via aqueducts. Roman gardens were filled with statuary and exotic plants from all parts of the empire. Although accounts of Rome's early gardens mention fruits and herbs, and much was written about agriculture, the use of edibles in ornamental gardens decreased as time went on. Later Roman gardens were devoted to ornamentation. Pliny the Younger had 500 slaves on his property on Lake Como to maintain his garden, shaping the sculptured shrubs and tending his large acreage.

Villa gardens, elaborate fountains, and topiary became consuming interests of the Romans. The showy gardens were extensions of Roman homes, created for enjoyment rather than utility or food. Some of their topiary gardens depicted entire scenes of hunting parties or fleets of ships. Imagine my empathy when I read in Anthony Huxley's *An Illustrated History of Gardening* that the writer and agronomist Columella was seriously concerned because lavish gardens were increasingly usurping valuable agricultural lands—in A.D. 1. Even earlier, other great writers and thinkers, including Horace and Cato the Younger, condemned the large estates and excesses of the Roman lifestyle. In Volume I of her classic text *A History of Garden Art*, Marie-Luise Gothein commented: "The feeling was deep-rooted in the best of [the Romans] that the dislike of agricultural life was the beginning of the end for the Roman people."

In addition to large, ostentatious topiary gardens, Roman villas also featured courtyard gardens, where many of the day's activities took place. The courtyard

The Alhambra in Granada, Spain, was constructed in the mid-1300s as a palace for Moorish rulers. Designed to reflect the pleasures of paradise, the courtyard idealizes early Persian gardens. The centerpiece is a runnel with fountains; edible citrus and roses as well as flowering trees and vines are planted on either side.

garden was the most prominent design concept to be carried over into monastery gardens, the next important development in the history of landscaping in the West.

The Medieval Era

After the fall of Rome in the fifth century, elaborate villa-style gardens disappeared from many regions. Eventually, with the spread of Christian monasteries, garden styles revived, with function the main rationale. Enclosed herb gardens with interplanted fruits and vegetables—sometimes in geometric patterns—were the norm in medieval monasteries. Common gardening practices included grafting fruit trees to produce better fruits and planting in raised beds bordered with wooden planks. Fish ponds and beehives also provided food. Only a few flowers were grown for pleasure, and the lawn—that great usurper of human energy—was institutionalized.

Grass had been grown informally near modest homes, and livestock kept it trimmed. Monastery gardens changed the way grass was used by placing lawns at the center of the

cloister to provide a soothing environment for study and meditation. The earliest practitioners of the lawn-growing art poured boiling water over an area to kill existing vegetation, then dug out the area and filled it in with pieces of turf from a nearby meadow. (No Kentucky bluegrass in seed or sod form existed in those days.) The turf was then beaten into place with wooden mallets.

The Renaissance

During the European Renaissance, pleasure gardens for the nobility and the well-to-do returned to the fore. A lot of effort was devoted to copying and elaborating on the famous villas of ancient Rome. During the fifteenth and sixteenth centuries, Renaissance pleasure gardens reached their zenith in France and Italy. These over-the-top landscapes featured acres of clipped hedges, mazes, and exotic plants from all over the world, in addition to fountains and orangeries for growing tender fruit out of season.

As the popularity of pleasure gardens grew, fruits and vegetables were relegated to kitchen gardens. The first written statement I found about this principle was in Volume II of Gothein's historical text. In laying down many ground rules for landscaping a property, Leon Battista Alberti, the influential fifteenth-century Florentine architect, dictated: "All the paths are to be bordered with box and other evergreens. Bright streams of water must run through the garden, and above all must start up unexpectedly, their source a grotto with colored shell work. Cypresses with climbing ivy must be in the pleasure garden, but fruited trees and even oaks are relegated to the kitchen garden." So fashions are made.

The Rise of the Pastoral Landscape

Between the Renaissance and the seventeenth century, formalism—the controlling hand of humans over nature—remained in vogue. André Le Nôtre's gardens at Versailles are a perfect example.

In the early 1700s a reaction against this controlled look, along with increased inspiration from Asia, prompted the English to develop a softer, more informal style of landscaping. Free, natural forms superseded straight, geometric forms. Clipped hedges became passé, considered rigid,

Prieuré Notre-Dame d'Orsan, a former monastery in central France, dates to 1107. The gardens, inspired by medieval tapestries and illuminations, were re-created according to medieval monastic concepts, combining historical design with organic crop production. They are open to the public seasonally.

pompous, and unnatural. An acceptance of nature's own forms influenced the standard of beauty. As garden historian Gothein noted in Volume II of her book, poet, essayist, and politician Joseph Addison, a strong spokesman for this new movement, stated: "For my own part, I would rather look upon a tree in all its abundance and diffusions of boughs and branches, than when it is cut and trimmed into a mathematical figure; and cannot but fancy that an orchard in flower looks infinitely more delightful than all the little labyrinths of the most finished parterre."

Eighteenth-century English landscape designs were idealized reflections of the natural landscape. They were characterized by rather tightly controlled designs contrasting open "meadows" with closed "woods." Careful attention to views and visual axes was evident throughout these landscapes, just as in medieval gardens on the Continent. These "natural" scenes echoed landscape paintings of the period: "nature" imitating art.

The shift from formal to informal and from fenced to unfenced styles took place gradually. As Hugh Johnson says in his *Principles of Gardening*: "In about 1730, William Kent 'leaped the fence.' Suddenly there was no beginning, and no end to the garden. It was all 'landskip' (in the spelling of the day) to be idealized as an earthly paradise with classical overtones."

Kent was an architect and painter who composed naturalistic pictures with sweeping lawns, water, trees, and architecture. Lancelot "Capability" Brown, the garden genius who perfected the so-called English style, succeeded him. Brown made the picturesque pastoral scene the ideal that the landed gentry strived to express in their estates: acres of rolling lawns and clumps of trees. He intended no visual excitement in these soothing scenes, as evidenced by vast acreages uninterrupted by fences or walls, and lawns that came right up to the residences.

European Edible Gardens

From the the seventeenth to nineteenth century, French and Scottish gardeners of a more practical sort were developing vegetable gardens that were both decorative and functional. Generally formal in design, they utilized clipped boxwood hedges, walks, and rectilinear patterns. Vegetables interplanted with flowers filled the beds, while espaliered fruit trees lined the walls and walkways. In addition to the wealthy upper class, the emerging middle class also cultivated these gardens. Although you can still find such gardens in Europe—Château de Villandry is the most famous—they are rare in the United States. You can't help but wonder why this style did not carry over more pervasively to America in the nineteenth and twentieth centuries, when more middle-class people came to own land and could work it to suit their own tastes.

Early American Gardens

In North America, the early colonists' first concern was survival, and therefore edible plants were a priority. Settlers grew familiar species such as apples, cabbages, lettuces, and medicinal plants brought from the Old World, as well as squash, beans, and corn introduced to them by Native Americans. Their fenced-in cottage gardens soon included flowering plants, added purely for delight. Women generally maintained these inner gardens while men cared for the livestock and acres of calorie crops such as wheat, corn, and rye.

No commercial seed companies or nurseries existed in those days, of course, so the settlers gathered mature seeds from the healthiest and tastiest vegetables, as well as the most beautiful flowers, and saved them to plant in the next growing season. They grafted fruit trees from neighbors' trees and divided and shared their perennials.

Although we have records of a few of these gardens, the garden journals of Thomas Jefferson best show the potential for diversity that was to enhance the American edible garden. This scientist-gardener noted that he grew more than 250 varieties of 89 different plant species. In the centuries that followed, wave after wave of immigrants—from the early German and Irish to today's newcomers from around the globe—would bring with them their favorite vegetables, herbs, and, in a more limited way, fruits to add to the American home landscape.

The Victorian Period

In the nineteenth century, the landscaping ideal changed again as the previous century's style of imitating the natural landscape was deemed boring and insipid. In reaction, a new school—often called the museum school—developed. The essence of this new style was eclecticism. On both sides of the Atlantic, Victorian gardeners borrowed from practically every earlier landscaping style, embellishing their grounds with lawns, statuary, metal furniture, urns, busts, pseudo-ruins, and collections of some of the new plants garnered from the great botanical expeditions around the world. Plant explorers risked life and limb to bring orchids from afar, only to have the fragile plants die in Wardian cases in the extravagant homes of

Château de Villandry is an early-twentieth-century reproduction of Louis XIV's vegetable parterre at Versailles, circa 1690. Espaliered fruit trees, flower beds, and clipped hedges surround geometric beds of ever-changing vegetables and flowers. My visit in 1984 erased any doubt I had about using edibles in my own landscape designs.

plant collectors. Edibles came into vogue if they were exotic or could be grown to fruit out of season in greenhouses. White vegetables fascinated the Victorians and, to please them, breeders created curious white pumpkins, tomatoes, and cucumbers. One-upmanship was the overriding theme permeating the Victorian age.

Following the extravagances of these Victorian gardens, a new trend took root in England: an appreciation of a plant for the form and texture of its foliage, the glorious color of its blooms, and the opportunities it offered as an element in an impressionistic picture that would live and grow. These ideas reached their peak in the horticultural writings and gardens of William Robinson and the painter Gertrude Jekyll. Both are considered the originators of the mixed herbaceous border and the informal cottage-style landscapes containing lawns, paths, and large flower beds. Robinson and Jekyll

Handsome 'Seville' sour orange trees line the streets and grace municipal buildings in the Spanish city that gave this bitter orange its name. In summer, city workers irrigate the trees with gray water. In late winter, they harvest the oranges and take them to convents, where nuns make the world-renowned marmalade.

filled beds with perennial plants chosen for their forms, textures, and leaf shapes and to provide a controlled show of color from spring through fall.

Other influences closer to home helped shape modern home landscaping styles to come. Andrew Downing and his disciples, who advocated large shade trees, expansive lawns, and a few specimen trees and shrubs, heavily impacted American landscaping after the Civil War. Later came the informal, cottage-type English landscape and interest in native plants. In the late 1800s and early 1900s, the use of foundation plantings—to conceal exposed foundations and soften the angles of houses—became popular, and by the 1950s it was a common feature in home landscape design. Limited in utility, this style provides no privacy and little design potential. Especially because it could be employed in rubber-stamp fashion by developers and contractors, it eventually became hackneyed. Homes with a mandatory "moustache" of a few shrubs around the front

entry, combined with a lawn and two street trees, became a standard sight throughout the country.

Twentieth-Century Landscapes

Fortunately, there were other trends at work as the twentieth century unfolded, including a growing cultural and horticultural exchange between Asia and the West. Despite the fact that many aspects of Asian garden designs are strongly rooted in the religions and cultures of China and Japan, many of their concepts have worked their way into American yards. It is now common to use a single boulder or a group of rocks as the focal point in a landscape, whether as a lovely accent in its own right or as a background for plants. Culturally, Americans have gained an appreciation for the beauty of gravel raked to create the appearance of ripples on a pond and learned to value the diversity of leaf textures. Pruning has risen to new levels of sophistication, accentuating the natural shape of a tree or shrub and transforming it into a living sculpture rather than a formal, clipped geometric shape. Indeed, the creative use and recycling of natural materials are two of the finest features of Eastern landscapes. Because lawns are seldom used in Asia, considering the limitless options for designs without turf frees the mind to explore alternatives.

During the rapid urbanization of the twentieth century, people generally abandoned vegetable gardens for ornamental ones except when the government encouraged growing Victory Gardens as a patriotic duty during World Wars I and II. Following World War II, many factors influenced and changed American landscaping. The rise of the suburb and subdivision resulted in smaller yards, with lawns remaining a dominant feature. Add to that the rising cost of real estate, leaving homeowners with little money for landscaping, and the shift toward large houses on small lots, leaving little space for landscaping. As more women entered the workforce, they had less time for gardening and relied more and more on convenience foods rather than produce from the garden. Pools, barbecues, and the West Coast–born phenomena of hot tubs and fire pits created new uses for yards and extended the living space to outdoor areas.

Other developments—of a more practical nature—made landscaping less labor intensive. Power mowers, blowers, tillers, and trimmers permitted us all to maintain manicured lawns and shrubs without a retinue of servants. Magazines, garden clubs, and how-to books disseminated information that reinforced the aesthetic of huge lawns and showy ornamentals. Local garden centers and big chain home improvement stores provided a wide variety of plants and chemicals to promote these trends.

Perhaps the most significant factor of all was the progress made in agriculture that "freed" people from having to grow their own food. Many Americans who left the farm for the city considered growing their own food to be straight from "Hicksville," making food gardens déclassé. For many years, professional designers and style setters discouraged the use of food-producing plants in the home landscape. In fact, as a rule, both landscape design and architectural courses snubbed edible plants.

When I took landscape design classes in the 1970s, the list of the hundreds of plants we studied included only two edibles: citrus and pineapple guava. I was discouraged from using edibles in my projects; one professor said, "We call it salad bowl gardening—and it's tacky." As

Modern Landscape Design: A Closer Look

Look out your office or living room window. Do you see a limited selection of sheared shrubs growing out of bare soil and lots of lawn? If so, you're looking at the highly popular, formulaic, modern-style landscape that is relatively affordable to install and maintain while giving the impression that it is "cared for."

One of the reasons for its pervasiveness is that an untrained landscape service or maintenance person can keep up such gardens inexpensively, if marginally, with herbicides, blowing, hedge shearing, and mowing. Since power tools are fast, a company can service more gardens in a day and charge less for the work. For many homeowners, that is easier than doing it themselves or hiring a more expensive (that is, knowledgeable) gardener for the extra time it takes to hand-weed, rake leaves, compost, mulch, and prune properly. Of course, had the garden been well thought out and designed in the first place, it would require much less care anyway.

The cumulative effect of such gardens on the environment is insidious. Instead of rolling expanses of properly pruned, lively looking, productive plants (that provide food for families and wildlife) growing in healthy soil, suburbia is replete with a mishmash of boring expanses of lawns, starved soil, and mundane gumdrop shrubs filled with dead twigs. The ground below these

plants is bald and weed free, devoid of any leaves, which are blown away every week. With them goes the wonderful, life-renewing duff that keeps the soil filled with nutrients and builds organic matter from season to season. Unfortunately, suburbanites and maintenance people are so used to seeing bare, compacted ground under trees and shrubs that they assume all is normal, and the status quo is maintained.

To break the cycle, everyone needs to take responsibility for his or her own patch of land. With your new awareness, the first change is to stop removing the precious organic matter—instead rake it into a compost or leaf pile. Better yet, let the leaves stay where they fall, adding more organic matter to the soil, and mulch, both of which encourage the soil to retain valuable moisture. If you are not your garden's caretaker, communication is key; explain what you want to the maintenance folks. If there is a language barrier, a number of Cooperative Extension Services offer classes and brochures in other languages that give earth-friendly garden alternatives. Seek out maintenance services that pride themselves on maintaining gardens without using blowers and other gas-powered tools; if you cannot find someone readily, visit the Ecological Landscaping Association website (www.ecolandscaping.org/findapro.aspx).

Blue Hill at Stone Barns (on the Rockefeller estate in Pocantico Hills, New York) is a working farm, educational center, and restaurant run by chef Dan Barber that celebrates the bond between farm and table. Barbara Damrosch, author of the classic *The Garden Primer*, designed the Dooryard Garden, laying out the beautiful rectangular beds in a classic style. Zucchini, tomatoes, and beans are so healthy they nearly flow out of the beds. Rows of apple trees invite visitors into the garden, while the magnificent antique stone barns stand guard on the sidelines.

a result, those of us who wanted to buck the trend had few design guidelines. I observed that when people did grow food-producing plants with no guidance, they often planted them in what I called the "plunk style" of landscaping: they went to the nursery, asked for a peach tree, took it home, and plunked it in the ground. No thought went into how the tree looked, only into what it would produce. Plunk landscaping has given the use of edibles a bad name among those concerned with aesthetics.

Since those days, it has become my mission to restore edibles to a prominent position in the home landscape—beyond the simple Victory Garden model—where they show off all the beauty and flavor they have to offer.

Beyond the Chemical Era

The ready availability of pesticides, fungicides, herbicides, and chemical fertilizers in the second half of the twentieth century encouraged gardeners to strive for the perfect lawn or rose, which in turn evolved into the "county fair, blue ribbon syndrome"—the relentless search for huge, flawless flowers, vegetables, and fruits. (It's a pet peeve of mine that

no one ever tastes these prizewinners; they're judged on appearance only and not on taste and nutrition.) Propped up by chemicals, breeders developed rose and peach varieties that flourished only when sprayed frequently with questionable fungicides. People planted moisture-loving bentgrass in hot, dry climates without regard for the water required to grow it. "Experts" discouraged growing nitrogen-fixing clover, instead touting "weed and feed" products that we now know pollute the soil and don't work well in most mild-winter climates. The underlying message was that we could grow anything almost anywhere—with enough water and if we bought the right chemicals.

A number of visionaries began to question this chemical approach, however. Among the most influential were J. I. Rodale and Rachel Carson. Beginning in 1942, Rodale's *Organic Farming and Gardening* magazine gave a voice to farmers and gardeners who wanted to grow food without questionable chemicals. In 1962, Carson's *Silent Spring* shocked America with its revelations about the dangers of pesticides. While seriously challenged by the establishment, these dissenting voices persisted, eventually bringing lasting changes in the way we grow our food and design our landscapes. The organic gardening movement was on its way.

A New Vision for Landscaping

When I started gardening as a new homeowner in the 1960s, among the first plants I put in were hybrid tea roses. As instructed by the nursery, I regularly sprayed them with commercial fungicides to curb mildew, blackspot, and rust. I applied herbicide to eradicate dandelions from the lawn. Over time I read *Silent Spring,* picked up a few copies of *Organic Gardening,* and joined the Sierra Club. With my growing awareness of what I was doing and the effects these practices had, I stopped them. Those roses are long gone; now I grow only disease-resistant varieties. The lawn has shrunk to a 10-by-12-foot plot, and I plant French dandelions to eat. In this case, there was no epiphany; the change occurred over several years.

Like me, the landscaping industry and many gardeners have changed from the "bend nature to my will" manner popular throughout much of the past two centuries to a much-needed "save the planet" approach. Clearly, we need to rethink some of our old ways of doing things. None of us can—or should—do it all. Fortunately, many of the necessary changes require only an awareness of our effect on the ecosystem and a change of mindset to help us make informed choices that will have a positive impact on our home, local, and global landscapes. It's important to remember, we *can* go back to basics; there were fabulous gardens before the invention of gas-powered machines and artificial chemicals, and there will still be fabulous gardens after these accouterments of modern gardening have been set aside.

Following are some of the steps we can take in facing challenges while working with our home landscapes—especially concerning soil, energy, water, and our choice of garden materials. Educating ourselves and future generations toward a more sustainable approach to landscaping will help fulfill the new vision for healthy food, healthy gardens, and a healthy planet.

Respecting the Soil

Healthy soil is a gift you receive from—and can give back to—the planet. Yet few Americans honor soil as a living entity; instead they treat it like *dirt,* with serious consequences. Some of the ongoing problems related to how we treat our soil include:

- *Contamination.* People apply millions of tons of chemical pesticides and fertilizers to their gardens. In harsh-winter areas, homeowners and municipalities spread salt on sidewalks and streets. All these chemicals kill the life in the soil.
- *Compaction.* Contractors drive heavy equipment over wet soils, and maintenance people often operate large mowers when clay soil is soggy; both compact the soil, rendering it less permeable and preventing water from percolating through.
- *Erosion.* Wind and rain erode the soil from empty, unmulched beds and slopes. All too often it ends up in lakes, contributing to algae bloom and eutrophication (a buildup of nutrients causing excess aquatic plant growth). Or it runs into streams and rivers, polluting and muddying clear water; eventually what was valuable soil ends up in the ocean in large dead zones. And airborne particles contribute to air pollution.
- *Interference with nature's renewal.* Plastic bags full of valuable leaves and lawn clippings travel to landfills, and kitchen waste churns down garbage disposals. All this biomass can be food for the compost pile, where the organic matter breaks down and returns to the soil—where it belongs—to feed microbes, plants, and consequently humankind.

There is no mistaking nutritious, well-grown root vegetables. Without healthy, well-drained soil they will be misshapen, small for their size, and pale for their variety. Here, you can see just a bit of the rich, dark soil at Seed Savers Exchange in Decorah, Iowa, that produced these gorgeous turnips, carrots, beets, and potatoes.

Experienced gardeners know that without abundant, healthy soil it's next to impossible to have a great edible garden. Healthy soil is literally alive with trillions of creatures from microbes to worms, which go about their daily lives turning organic matter, such as leaves, lawn clippings, and kitchen waste, into the elixir of life—humus.

Consider this: every time you grow something that you eat, you literally save soil. The USDA estimates that for every pound of commercially grown food that is produced, six pounds of soil are destroyed.[1] And if you grow your own edibles in soil that you have improved with your own compost and garden waste, you are actually building soil. As John Jeavons, pioneer of small-scale food production worldwide and author of *How to Grow More Vegetables and Fruits,* said so poetically, "…start with one growing bed and tend it well, and we have begun the exciting, expansive, giving process of enlivening and healing the Earth and ourselves."[2]

Saving Energy

The way that a home landscape is designed, the plants chosen, and the chemicals used—all influence the way a household uses energy. Plant placement, for example, can enhance cooling or warming of a home. When I grew up (before most people had central air conditioning), we visited my grandparents on Long Island in summer. On hot afternoons we retreated to the front porch, which was shaded by massive elms and maples. It was a social event as we shelled beans while sharing lemonade and neighborhood gossip with our relatives who lived next door. Back home, just outside Boston, a giant linden tree shaded the back of our house and an outdoor dining area, while a grape-covered arbor cooled the passage from the house to the backyard.

Incorporating climate-control techniques in the landscape still makes sense today. According to the U.S. Department of Energy, deciduous trees that shade the sunny south- and west-facing house walls can save up to $250 a year on air-conditioning costs.[3] A shaded wall may be 9 to 15 degrees cooler than the peak surface temperature of unshaded surfaces.[4] The Environmental Protection Agency (EPA) reports that evapotranspiration helps, too: a tree with a 30-foot canopy transpires 40 gallons of water a day, resulting in peak summer temperature reductions of 2 to 9 degrees.[5] The Maryland Department of Natural Resources estimates that evergreens placed to deflect winter winds can save from 10 to 50 percent on heating costs.[6]

Rethinking garden maintenance is another way to address the energy drain. For years, commercial ammonium nitrate fertilizers (made from natural gas) have been used in most home landscapes, especially on lawns; as of this writing they are outlawed in a number of counties because they pollute underground water sources. The routine use of gas-powered mowers and blowers and numerous commercial petroleum-based chemicals add up to huge amounts of energy spent needlessly. Further, gardens cared for by machines are one of the major sources of air pollution in suburban areas. *The New York Times* reported that the average gas-powered leaf blower produces as much pollution in an hour as the typical passenger vehicle during 2,000 miles of travel.[7] In addition, leaf blowers generate unsafe noise levels.[8] The lawn is far and away the energy hog of the home landscape, and I'll address that later.

Also consider the petroleum energy that can be saved on a more global scale. When I look at an ornamental garden devoid of blueberries, tomatoes, or other edibles, I see wasted energy. I know that every blueberry and tomato harvested by a home gardener saves energy, especially if cultivated organically, in comparison with commercially grown produce. No petroleum-based fertilizers and pesticides are needed to grow them, no machines to plant and harvest them, no airplanes or refrigerator trucks to transport them, no conveyor belts to move them, and no gas guzzled to drive them from store to kitchen. One statistic indicates the enormity of this issue, just in dealing with fertilizers. The University of Florida estimated that if home vegetable gardeners *only in Florida* used yard clippings and animal manures instead of inorganic nitrogen fertilizers, the energy saved would be equivalent to 684,000 to 1,368,000 gallons of diesel fuel a year.[9] Every time you grow something yourself, you save *lots* of energy.

Conserving Water

Most of the earth's water (the oceans) is salty; only about four-tenths of one percent of the fresh water is accessible to our ever-growing population. All future forecasts include water crises—due to overuse and pollution. People tend to associate a lack of water in the United States with the arid Southwest; however, wells in the north-central states are going dry from overpumping, vast sections of the South are drying up, and areas of the Midwest have underground water so polluted by agricultural runoff that it's unsafe for drinking.

Lettuce: From Field to Kitchen

Although most vegetables and fruits are water-hungry plants, growing your own is a plus for the environment. Just consider the water wasted in producing and selling commercial lettuce, for example. I cringe when I drive down Interstate 5 through the heart of California's farms and see huge plumes of water driven by 20-mile-an-hour winds overshooting the vegetable fields. What a waste, especially when thousands of acres could be on drip irrigation. Minutes after harvest, producers soak the lettuce in huge vats of water to cool it down, then wash it in more water and pack it. At the grocery store, the produce people constantly mist the lettuce to keep it fresh.

Each lettuce plant *you* grow uses dramatically less water than a commercially grown head, especially if you keep your soil rich in organic matter, mulch to maintain moisture, and use drip irrigation. When I recently caught up with John Jeavons, we talked about the efficacy of growing your own vegetables. He estimates that growing lettuce with his Biointensive Method, he uses one-quarter to one-eighth the water that the average farmer in the same climate uses.[10]

Drip tubing with in-line emitters spaced 6 inches apart is used to water lettuces and green onions. Compared with farm-raised produce, homegrown vegetables save lots of water and energy.

Reduce Use and Runoff

Since the early 1900s, the United States has been on a water-spending binge. What nature has stored drop by drop in underground aquifers over millions of years, we have used in a flood in the past century. Now, the era of unrestricted water use and interference with the water cycle is coming to a screeching halt.

Before your house was built, your yard was probably forest or grassland, and considerable amounts of rainfall soaked into the earth instead of running off. Today, rain falls on your roof and runs into gutters and then into downspouts, usually flowing undiverted into the street and eventually into storm drains. Even more rain sheets off the driveway and sloped lawn instead of soaking into the ground. With our new awareness, homeowners, contractors, and city governments are coming up with new approaches to recharge the underground water table. Many water districts put meters on homeowners' and farmers' wells to encourage them to use less water. A number of city planning departments are encouraging rainwater catchment for new homes. Metropolitan water companies are constructing percolation ponds to allow rainwater to sink in gradually and refill underground aquifers.

Above all, each of us needs to take responsibility for conserving our water supply—and that includes reducing use in our home landscapes. Many gardeners are switching to drip irrigation, adding water sensors so the irrigation does not turn on during rainfall, putting timers on sprinklers, and generally being more conscious of how they use water. And instead of letting rainwater run off their roofs, people are installing rain barrels and underground cisterns to capture it.

Reduce Polluting Practices

Americans have exacerbated the water crisis with polluting landscaping practices. High-nitrogen fertilizers and other garden chemicals (from home and commercial landscapes) percolate down into the water table contaminating it as well as running off into streams. To safeguard water supplies, more and more municipalities around the country are restricting the use of commercial fertilizers and pesticides.

More homeowners than ever before are now buying organic materials that don't pollute the groundwater. In fact, when I go into home improvement stores and nurseries, I see obviously fewer garden chemicals and petroleum-based fertilizers lining the shelves than just a few years ago. By composting and using mulch on their beds, gardeners are helping hold the water in the soil.

Rethinking Lawn Maintenance

In the early 1900s, lawns didn't consume any petroleum at all. To meet turfgrasses' high need for nitrogen, homeowners interplanted nitrogen-fixing white clover in their

The Real Cost of Lawns

A lawn area, when grown organically, can be wonderful for frolicking children, but those large, "well maintained" areas of verdure generally are the landscaping equivalents of gas guzzlers parked in the driveway. Mowers, blowers, fertilizer and pesticide runoff, habitat loss—today's lawns are primarily about wasting non-renewable resources and contributing to many of our planet's ills. Consider the following:

◆ According to NASA, in the United States lawns cover almost 32 million acres—an area the size of New England.[13]

◆ Americans spend $17.4 billion a year on everything from pesticides (70 million pounds) to lawn tractors.[14]

◆ Lawn mowing uses 300 million gallons of gas and takes about 1 billion hours annually.[15]

◆ SafeLawns.org estimates that Americans spend $5.25 billion on petroleum-based lawn fertilizers and $700 million on lawn pesticides—annually.[16]

◆ According to the EPA, running the average gas-powered lawn mower for 1 hour can create the same amount of pollution as driving a car 340 miles.[17]

◆ Nationwide, home landscape irrigation accounts for nearly one-third of all residential water use—more than 7 billion gallons per day. Lawns drink up over 50 percent of that.[18]

To determine what people could grow if they transformed a 5-by-10-foot area of lawn into a garden, I created my 100-square-foot garden (see Chapter 8). This is a late fall harvest—enough lettuces, radishes, and pac choi for an evening's dinner.

◆ Lawns require 1 inch of water a week; at that rate, using irrigation only, a 25-by 40-foot (1,000-square-foot) lawn can suck up about 625 gallons of water weekly, or approximately 10,000 gallons of water each summer.

lawns. The family got exercise pushing a mower and raking leaves, or neighborhood youngsters earned money doing such chores. Petroleum-based pesticides weren't even a twinkle in chemists' eyes, so people didn't know there was any reason not to be happy with their lawns, which, judged against artificially high modern standards, would be considered less pristine.

Well into the 1950s, people like my dad and our neighbors spread manure and compost on their lawns to renew them and prevent thatch buildup. In those days, many more people limited the size of their lawns and left adjacent space as meadows, where songbirds and fireflies could thrive. In the latter part of the twentieth century, huge, perfect, deep green lawns maintained with a roster of petrochemicals became the goal of most homeowners and maintenance companies. As a nation we were oblivious to the environmental costs.

As with the other issues we're addressing, change is happening for the good. People are starting to reduce the size of their lawns and use organic materials that are more eco-friendly. Paul Tukey of SafeLawns.org has become the national spokesperson for environmentally safe lawns,

emphasizing the effects chemicals have on people as well the environment, spreading the message through every medium, even the movie *A Chemical Reaction*.

In 2002, Canada's Quebec province passed ordinances banning the "cosmetic" use of pesticides, which it defines as "applying fungicides, herbicides, or insecticides on ornamental plantings, especially lawns."[11] A number of towns and cities elsewhere in Canada followed suit, and in 2009, the province of Ontario outlawed the use of more than 250 pesticides.[12]

For information on how you can maintain an earth-friendly lawn, visit SafeLawns.org and see *The Chemical-Free Lawn* by Warren Schultz and *The Organic Lawn Care Manual* by Paul Tukey. And, while rethinking how to maintain your lawn, you might just consider whether you want one at all (see "Lawn—or Not?" in Chapter 3).

Choosing Garden Materials

Gardeners buy all sorts of materials—from plants and fertilizers to potting soil and furniture, and from paving to fencing and more. My goal here is to help you make more informed choices when purchasing garden materials based on "net energy use"—that is, taking into consideration the energy needed to produce the material (is it mined, natural, or man-made?), the energy needed to transport it (is it local, heavy, or transported hundreds or thousands of miles?), and whether it is practical (does it work in your type of soil? do you even need it?). It's a new way of looking at what you use, and important if you are going to make educated choices on how you affect the environment—locally and globally.

Commercial Mulches and Organic Matter

Homemade compost and mulches from yard clippings and kitchen wastes are an out-and-out plus. But when you purchase these materials, it gets more complicated. First of all, there is the energy used to ship these heavy items to you. And there are other issues. For example, peat moss consists of mined plant debris from Canadian wetlands. Although the peat industry restores the bog after harvest, it takes at least a quarter century to regrow; in the meantime, habitats are lost. In Florida, cypress tree habitats are logged solely to make cypress mulch.

None of us want toxic materials in our soils, and when you grow edible plants, you need to be especially careful. While you shouldn't be paranoid, caution is warranted. Shredded recycled tires, in my opinion, have no place in any landscape, especially an edible one, as there are toxicity issues; besides that, they do not break down readily, nor do they add any organic matter to the soil. Recycled wood mulch needs to be free of toxins. For help avoiding some chemicals when you buy mulch and potting soil, look for the Mulch and Soil Council certification symbol on a package; it guarantees that no recycled lumber treated with CCA (chromated copper arsenate, used for years in pressure-treated wood) is in the material. The Council also encourages companies to use sustainable forest practices. For more information, visit www.mulchandsoilcouncil.org.

If your soil needs serious remediation or large amounts of organic matter, look for bulk organic materials, such as grape pomace, mushroom compost, pecan and peanut hulls, or sawdust, that are recycled from local industries. Or if your municipality recycles yard wastes—and *if* you can be assured the composted material is free of herbicides, weed seeds, and plant diseases—it can become a great resource, as well.

Soil Nutrients

Soil nutrients are another complex issue made simpler if you compost, and simpler still if you have a worm bin or keep chickens or rabbits. If you need to purchase a product, I recommend buying organic fertilizers, not artificial commercial fertilizers (which are made from non-renewable sources and contain salts that kill the life in the soil).

New organic products are introduced all the time. *Caveat emptor* still applies: let the buyer beware. Most products are not regulated. Read labels carefully, especially the contents; check out both the active and inactive/inert ingredients listed. "Earth friendly" and "Natural" are marketing terms, not anything certifiable, and just as meaningless as when they are used on food packages. When in doubt, look for the OMRI (Organic Materials Review Institute) designation on packaging or go to www.OMRI.org to get a list of vetted materials.

Think twice before purchasing greensand or granite dust since they are mined products that are heavy to ship; often there are local equivalents. Plus greensand is not appropriate in alkaline soils. Fertilizers made from recycled municipal sewage sludge have their advocates. I can't deny that we need to recycle sludge, but I've worked on studies that occasionally found heavy metals, drugs, and esoteric solvents in a few batches. To be safe, I don't use it in my edible gardens. While we once used ground oyster shells to neutralize alkaline soil, they have a more valuable purpose in coastal areas—dumped into the bays to create new reefs for oysters to breed.

Wood Products

For centuries wood has been a mainstay in the garden—from trellises and arbors to benches and chairs, not to mention containers and window boxes. More recently wood has been used on a larger scale for decking and building raised beds. Even when treated with chemicals or painted, wood disintegrates with time; the added stress from sun, rain, and contact with wet soil hastens its demise.

America's constant need for wood products has put pressure on forests all over the world. Two solutions have been tried: plantation forests, where the trees are replanted in vast monocultures, and certified sustainable timber, in which renewable methods are used to help maintain habitat. Neither is perfect. Plantations provide only minimum biodiversity, and the certification process for lumber is complex, expensive, and especially hard on developing nations. When you buy wood, ask for the FSC label of the Forest Stewardship Council or the SmartWood–Rediscovered Wood certificate. Go to the Rainforest Alliance website for more information on wood products: www.rainforest-alliance.org.

You can also grow and use timber bamboo in place of some wood for plant stakes, furniture, and lath; it is sustainable. Recycled plastic has entered the marketplace as another wood alternative—for fences, arbors, trellises, decking, and lumber.

Reducing Light Pollution

As you fly over urban areas at night, it's hard not to notice all the bright lights stretching across the horizon. Most of them are streetlights and commercial site lighting, but the landscaping lights around homes are contributing more and more to that pervasive glow. Astronomers were the first to be aware of light pollution, and stargazers must now travel far away from populated areas to see into the heavens.

Scientists have learned that millions of nocturnal insects and small animals are either drawn to these nighttime lights and perish or avoid the lights and stay hidden instead of feeding or looking for a mate. The light throws migratory birds off course and disrupts the mating rituals of fireflies and moths. It can even disturb the dormancy cycle of trees. According to the International Dark-Sky Association, wasted light across America uses up to 30 million barrels of oil every year. Many homeowners install permanent security lights and keep them on all night, even though research shows that motion-activated lights not only save energy but are a better crime deterrent. For the environment, the worst culprit in the home landscape is uplighting, which sends its rays unnaturally upward to highlight a tree, fountain, or other feature. For more information, see "Outdoor Lighting" in Chapter 3 and visit www.darksky.org.

Recycling

I'm adamant about reusing and repurposing materials. For decades as a landscape designer, I've had my contractors reuse the tops of fence posts in retaining walls and broken concrete as stepping-stones. The crew brings me leftover pavers, which I use when redesigning my garden. I also scavenge. My short grape stake fence was once my neighbor's taller fence. My favorite red bench had been abandoned, one leg broken, on a curb; I rescued it from the maw of a garbage truck. (For more on finding recycled materials for your own landscape projects, see "Recycled Materials" in Chapter 3.)

Now, as my grandmother would say, I'm going to get on my high horse and rant about something—namely, plastic. With all those recycling symbols stamped on plastic products and handy recycling bins supplied to us, I was lulled into thinking that we'd made great progress in recycling plastics. As it turns out, the plastics industry is anything but clean and green. The landmark 1996 Report of the Berkeley Plastics Task Force[19] raised a number of unsettling issues that we still need to address:

- Making plastics from natural gas and oil contributes 13 percent of America's toxic fumes.
- Most of our used plastic is shipped to poor countries in Asia to be sorted and melted down under conditions that would give an EPA inspector nightmares.
- Plastic cannot be melted down more than once or twice, so it will still eventually live indefinitely in landfills, along roadways, or as ocean flotsam. (The world's largest "seafill," called the Great Pacific Garbage Patch—filled with plastics in many forms and sizes and covering an area twice the size of Texas—is rotating in the waters of the northern Pacific Ocean.)
- The chasing arrows symbol on the plastic packaging pacifies us into thinking that when we "recycle" plastic, it is recycled. Yet there is no market for many of the numbered plastics, so those products are sorted out and sent to the landfill.

The obvious solution is never to buy plastic, but that's next to impossible. So, what to do? Whenever possible, I try not to purchase anything made of or packaged in plastic, but even eco-friendly hydrolyzed fish comes in a plastic bottle. Buy your garden products in bulk, such as a truckful of soil, or in the largest package size available. Choose concentrates over diluted solutions. Try not to buy new plastic. Instead, look for garden products like TerraCycle organic fertilizer—as the company says, "we sell waste [liquefied worm poop] packaged in waste [used plastic soda bottles]"—and garden furniture that contains a larger percentage of recycled plastic, so at least you help create a market for recycled plastic. Support nurseries and garden centers that recycle pots or, even better, sell plants in containers that will break down in your compost pile.

Since more and more home gardeners are now embracing organic products and methods, major suppliers are scrambling to bring recycled products to market, and dozens of companies now offer green building materials.

Recycling is the theme here. These wooden buckets started life 50 years ago as nail barrels. A friend's carpenter-father repurposed them to carry tools, and I recycled them once more to grow heirloom 'Black-Seeded Simpson' and red 'Marvel of Four Seasons' lettuces. In keeping with the theme, the buckets rest on steps made from used brick and recycled railroad ties.

Accommodating Wildlife

Today, wildlife is under siege. Americans fill up millions of square miles with homes, businesses, and agriculture—acreage once occupied by native plants and animals. Our traditional style of gardening—cleaning up every leaf and seed, killing most insects, and choosing plants that won't drop seeds or fruits—seems destined to make the situation even worse.

One autumn more than two decades ago, I didn't get around to deadheading the fluffy seed heads on my Japanese anemones. Early the following spring, I noticed a female hummingbird collecting the fuzz, then speeding to my cedar tree and adding it to her nest. Who knew those messy-looking seed heads were a hummingbird's all-time-favorite nesting material? Every year, I watch my mama hummingbirds—sometimes two or three a season—harvest the fuzz. I've told all my landscaping clients to leave their seed heads intact; sure enough, they all report back excitedly that their hummingbirds use them, too. It seems that leaving the garden a bit messy makes the neighborhood's critters much happier.

My lovely 'Angel Face' rose is a sacrificial lamb. She is very susceptible to aphids, as is my old clematis vine. Every spring, they both get covered with aphids, but I let the critters be. Soon squadrons of soldier beetles and ladybugs come in and feast. The rose and clematis may be deformed at first, but they outgrow it and look superb for the rest of the growing season. I even leave the swallowtail butterfly larvae to munch and develop on my parsley and dill—I just plant some extra for them. It's a delight to watch the fascinated neighborhood children as the larvae pupate and eventually metamorphose into elegant butterflies. Even a bug's got to eat.

My giant blackberry vine bears from June through August, and the birds sometimes help themselves to the juicy berries. I occasionally get a purple splooge on my car, but hey, it washes off. It's a small price to pay for all the joy I get watching water droplets fly when the well-fed blue jays and mockingbirds take a bath.

Some of the wildlife is less obvious. Most of the year I'm unaware of the blue-bellied lizards that populate my garden. Only during their midspring mating ritual do I see them scurrying around the garden, running out from under the bush peas and rosemary, seeking new mates, and looking for love in all the wrong places. I have to remind my gardeners when they are moving containers to take care not to hurt the tiger salamanders that also take refuge there.

For me, all the wildlife is an integral part of my landscape; I plan for them and welcome them. Driving around nearby areas with their semi-barren, modern, formal-style landscapes, I appreciate my edible landscape as my own Garden of Eden. In fact, it is certified as a wildlife habitat by the National Wildlife Federation.

For creative ideas to help you make changes in your home landscape for the benefit of wildlife, visit the websites of the Urban Wildlands Group at www.urbanwildlands.org, the National Wildlife Federation at www.nwf.org, and the Audubon Society at www.audubon.org.

Educating Ourselves and Future Generations

Even though Hillary Clinton had an herb garden that supplied the kitchen when she was First Lady, it was on the roof of the White House. Michelle Obama made headlines in 2009 when she installed a vegetable garden on the White House lawn. The publicity from that single act has drawn attention from around the world.

The Potager (designed by Ebi Kondo) at the Denver Botanic Gardens is one of a new breed of public demonstration gardens that feature edible plants—with panache. In one part of this large garden, a trellis with purple hyacinth beans and morning glories (toxic) frames a planting of chilies and variegated perennial basils. Square terra-cotta containers of eggplants mark the corners of the garden. Onions and corn grow in adjoining beds, out of view.

Permaculture

In the 1970s, Australian ecologist Bill Mollison and academic associate David Holmgren introduced permaculture, a model for sustainability. Permaculture speaks to humanity's place in an ecosystem and strives to create self-maintaining living systems that mimic Mother Earth and improve the soil- and water-holding capacity of our gardens.

Several years ago, I met Bill Melvin of Boulder, Colorado, a certified permaculture designer and contractor. In the course of our tour around his delightful garden, he shared what he considers to be the most basic principles of permaculture:

- Analyze each site individually and design a guild (a plant community in which each plant benefits the others).
- Design for efficiency: recycle, compost, capture rainwater, and use hand tools.
- Plant with a purpose: grow edible and medicinal plants, plants for structures, and plants to provide food for birds.
- Plant lots of trees to produce more biomass.
- Utilize nature's energy: sun, wind, and water.
- Be an environmental steward; share your time, food, and knowledge with others.

Institutes and classes on permaculture can be found around the globe, and there are thousands of practitioners. For more information on permaculture, consult *Edible Forest Gardens: Ecological Vision and Theory for Temperate Climate Permaculture* by

Bill Melvin of Boulder, Colorado, is part of a new breed of designers and contractors specializing in permaculture. His entry garden boasts an espaliered pear, a standard apple tree, and numerous culinary herbs and native plants. Roof gutters divert rainwater into a swale that provides moisture for his mini-orchard.

Dave Jacke with Eric Toensmeier; *Gaia's Garden: A Guide to Home-Scale Permaculture* by Toby Hemenway; and *Permaculture: A Designer's Manual* by Bill Mollison.

Today, government agencies and universities are much more aware of the environmental problems of our own making and have set in motion many institutional changes, including EPA websites for saving energy and water. Municipalities have outlawed conventional pesticides on school playgrounds and in parks, and their bans have held up in the higher courts. Local governments are educating farmers and homeowners about fertilizer runoff from lawns and fields. Currently, Cornell University, Texas A&M, and the University of California at Davis, to name a few, have websites with extensive information on biological pest controls.

Through her Edible Schoolyard Project started in 1995 in Berkeley, California, trendsetting chef and restaurateur Alice Waters has children grow, cook, and consume what they plant in their schoolyard gardens. Waters aims to cast out fast food from school cafeterias. The Vegetable Institute outside Cleveland, Ohio, is instructing children and their teachers on how to grow their own food. Many school districts throughout the country now have mandated food gardens. The next generation is being given

the gift handed down from their ancestors—how to grow and enjoy their own food.

Membership in Slow Food International, a non-profit organization founded in 1989, grew exponentially at the turn of the twenty-first century, reaching a total of more than 100,000 members in 132 countries. In the United States, Slow Food USA (www.slowfoodusa.org) "seeks to create dramatic and lasting change in the food system; reconnect Americans with the people, traditions, plants, animals, fertile soils and waters that produce our food." They are working to get real foods into school lunches.

For the first time in decades, gardeners have all the information they could ever want to grow their own food in their own edible landscapes. And non-gardeners have the written and visual inspiration to start growing some of their own food. Michael Pollan's books *The Omnivore's Dilemma* and *In Defense of Food* have done a tremendous job of awakening America to the reality of what we are consuming and defining as food. Barbara Kingsolver's best-selling *Animal, Vegetable, Miracle: A Year of Food Life* opened people's minds to the concept of eating fresh and

I designed the garden for the late chef Tom McCombie at Chez TJ in Mountain View, California in 1989. Tom trained in France under Simone Beck and was anxious to grow ample fresh herbs, edible flowers, and greens for the dishes he offered on his menu. Nowadays, the acclaimed restaurant maintains its dedication to fresh ingredients and elegant fare under the guidance of executive chef Scott Nishiyama.

local. Kitchen Gardeners International provides an online forum for kitchen gardeners worldwide to meet and further their skills and knowledge.

Farmers markets by the thousands educate cooks and gardeners. And you can visit marvelous edible landscapes at Powell Gardens near Kansas City, Missouri, as well as at the Chicago and Denver Botanic Gardens. Additional permanent displays are cropping up every year at gardens across the country.

On television, the eco-lifestyle channel Planet Green is adding to the public's awareness about the planet and the environment through programs like *Focus Earth* and *Emeril Green*. On *Living with Ed*, well-known spokesperson for environmental issues Ed Begley Jr. and his wife, Rachelle, demonstrate with humor how to live in an eco-friendly way. Visit www.planetgreen.discovery.com for the latest green information.

Reuniting Home Gardens and Kitchens

At last, food gardening is reconnecting to the kitchen—and in major ways. We are reconnecting with historic tradition but with a new appreciation for and knowledge about protecting and preserving the earth, our land, and our health.

Gardeners and cooks have been driving this groundswell. Today, women who love to cook, like Renee Shepherd and Rose Marie Nichols McGee, are involved in running retail seed companies; their bias is to choose vegetables as much for their flavor and beauty as for their productivity. Heirloom fruits and vegetables are in the mainstream; the Seed Savers Exchange in Iowa has been working for decades to preserve even more old varieties. Many seed companies and nurseries are featuring especially attractive edible plants for home landscapes.

After decades of steakhouses serving iceberg lettuce, chefs are touting seasonal and local food, leading the campaign to connect people to their food's regional birthright. Jesse Cool of Flea Street Café in Menlo Park, California, has an incredible edible garden at her home, as does Chicago's Rick Bayless of Frontera Grill and Topolobampo. Sinclair Philip of Sooke Harbour House on Vancouver Island in British Columbia, Thomas Keller of the French Laundry in Napa Valley, and Dan Barber of Blue Hill at Stone Barns in New York's Hudson Valley garner acclaim for their restaurant garden cuisine, which adds to the vibrancy of their stellar meals.

Today, eating fruits and vegetables is all about fresh, local, seasonal, and slow. There's nothing more fresh, local, seasonal, and slow than sowing, transplanting, harvesting, and eating your own luscious, sun-warmed tomatoes and strawberries.

I envision edible landscaping as the keystone of gardening in the twenty-first century. Growing your own food allows you to take responsibility for your own piece of the Earth. It builds your soil and saves precious resources, even as the aesthetic component feeds your soul. Edible landscaping is *the* new way of gardening to preserve both the integrity and beauty of our planet.

NOTES

1. John Jeavons, How to Grow More Vegetables (and Fruits, Nuts, Berries, Grains, and Other Crops) Than You Ever Thought Possible on Less Land Than You Can Imagine (Berkeley, CA: Ten Speed Press, 2006), page xi.

2. Ibid., page x.

3. www.energy.gov/news/1652.htm

4. www.energysavers.gov/your_home/landscaping/index.cfm/mytopic=11940

5. www.epa.gov/heatisland/resources/pdf/TreesandVegCompendium.pdf

6. dnr.maryland.gov/forests/publications/urban5.html

7. "Landscaping: Striking a Legal Blow for Cleaner Air," *New York Times,* November 12, 2006.

8. California EPA, Air Resources Board, www.arb.ca.gov/msprog/mailouts/msc0005/msc0005.pdf

9. edis.ifas.ufl.edu/MG323 (originally written in 1994, but reviewed in July 2009).

10. Phone conversation between Rosalind Creasy and John Jeavons, March 2009.

11. www.mindfully.org/Pesticide/2002/Canada-Bans Pesticides15nov02.htm

12. www.ene.gov.on.ca/en/news/2009/030401.php

13. earthobservatory.nasa.gov/Features/Lawn/

14. "Lawn and Disorder: A 'Natural' View of Landscaping," *USA Today,* April 11, 2002.

15. Ibid.

16. "Care for Your Lawn Naturally," *Orange County Register,* April 7, 2007.

17. outreach.tamucc.edu/aqeducinfo2.html

18. www.epa.gov/watersense/

19. www.ecologycenter.org/ptf/report1996/report1996_toc.html

2 | Laying the Groundwork

ow that I've shared my vision for a sustainable approach to landscaping, one in which you take responsibility for your piece of the planet, it's time for you to get down to the nitty-gritty of actually creating your edible landscape. Where do you start? At the beginning, by sizing up what you have to work with and considering how you might alter any of it.

The first step is to evaluate the physical characteristics of your property from soil to climate to water issues, identify any challenges, and look at possible solutions. The second step is to examine and consider possible changes to your hardscape—the permanent non-plant parts of the landscape, such as paths, fences, and retaining walls. By the end of this chapter, you'll have evaluated your property in preparation for identifying your specific needs and wants, setting your time and budget constraints, and creating a landscape plan, all of which are covered in Chapter 3.

Bear in mind that this book is not a guide to landscape construction; many good books explain the basics, from brickwork to complex sprinkler systems. Other texts cover countless ornamental plants to complete your landscape. Among the most useful books are Creative Homeowner's *Smart Guide: Home Landscaping*, Better Homes and Gardens' *New Complete Guide to Landscaping*, and the Ortho and Sunset garden books.

Preceding pages: My previously sloping lawn with a drainage problem is now a showy two-level edible landscape. *Above*: Good soil grows healthy plants. Joe Queirolo, one of my first gardeners, can determine texture and friability by running the soil through his hands. He also looks for creatures like earthworms, indicators that the soil is in good condition.

Soil: The Foundation

I cannot stress strongly enough that healthy soil is the key to a beautiful, healthy landscape. Since landscapes don't exist in isolation, by ensuring your soil's health you'll also do your part in cultivating a healthier planet.

It's staggering to think of all that is going on right under our feet. Big, strong, healthy plants grow from healthy soil—and that's not just dirt. Soil is a living substance comprising five major elements: air (primarily oxygen and nitrogen), water, living organisms (from microscopic bacteria, viruses, and fungi to larger creatures like earthworms and insects), humus (organic matter such as leaves, lawn clippings, compost, and manure, all in varying states of decay), and inorganic matter (particles of minerals and rock).

Reading the Soil

It is rare that any garden soil is perfect, yet most difficulties are readily identified and corrected. An experienced gardener learns to read the soil's health by looking at the leaves and overall growth pattern of a plant. Examine the plants on your property and ask yourself the following questions:

- *Are tree or shrub roots visible at the soil surface?*
  Roots on the soil surface often indicate a problem, usually shallow watering, not enough nutrients, or sometimes hardpan.
- *Are the plant's leaves pale overall, pale yet darkly veined, or brown edged?*
  Pale leaves usually indicate nitrogen-deficient soil. Dark-veined pale leaves often point to iron deficiency. Brown-edged leaves may be a sign of excess salt, overfertilization, or soil that has repeatedly dried out.
- *Are there a number of dead or dying plants?*
  This can indicate bad drainage, very acid or alkaline conditions, soil disease, or years of herbicide damage. To find out which is the culprit, take large samples of problem plants to a reputable nursery or your local Cooperative Extension Service for a diagnosis.

Since good soil is the foundation of a thriving and beautiful garden, all these plant and soil problems need to be addressed before you install your new landscape.

Soil Types

Since so many plant problems begin with the soil, bear with me while I take you through Soil 101. First you need to know about your soil texture (the types of particles making up your soil) because it relates to how fast your property drains and how often you have to water and fertilize. The mineral components of soil are particles of sand, silt, and clay. Everyone knows how small a grain of sand is, but it's the largest of the three kinds of particles. Sand particles range from 2 to .25mm (tiny fractions of an inch), silt particles are much smaller (.05 to .002 mm), and clay particles are as minuscule as bacteria. The size of the particles affects how different soil types perform. Because garden soils often tend to be predominately clay or sand, most gardeners concern themselves more with those particles than they do silt.

Sand feels gritty in your hand. Sandy soils have lots of pore spaces between the grains, which allow air and water to pass through easily so roots don't get waterlogged. Sandy soils warm up quickly in spring and are easy to till whether wet or dry. Since they are fast draining, they require frequent watering and fertilizing as nutrients quickly leach away.

In contrast, *clay*, sometimes called heavy soil, feels slippery and sticky between your fingers. Clay soils retain water and nutrients very well, but the pore spaces between the particles are so small that air and water cannot easily travel through. That means clay soils drain poorly, readily pack down into impervious layers, and are hard to till when either wet or dry. They also warm up slowly in spring.

The best soil for general gardening is *loam*, which contains fairly equal parts of sand, silt, and clay particles. Loamy soil is the best type of soil for growing most plants, especially the more demanding edibles, as both water and nutrients move through at a pace suitable for the majority of plants to absorb.

Soil Structure

The structure of soil (the arrangement of soil particles into aggregates, or "crumbs") is as important as texture, because the aggregates prevent the formation of rock-hard soil that crusts over and cracks. Nicely textured, friable soil is easy to work; plants thrive when their roots—and life-giving air and water—can easily penetrate the crumbs.

Billions of living creatures keep the soil alive and vital, yet we're oblivious to them. The gelatinous secretions of millions upon millions of bacteria and fungi "glue" indi-

Carrots can range from purple through red to yellow and white. For picture-perfect carrots like these, make sure the soil pH is between 5.5 and 7.5. Grow carrots in sandy soil, because in clay soil you're likely to get short, misshapen stubs. If your soil contains too much clay, cultivate carrots in raised beds.

vidual particles of soil together; these subsequently clump to one another. Air spaces between the clumps hold oxygen and carbon dioxide underground so roots can absorb the gases. Microarthropods and worms tunnel through the soil, eating and fertilizing as they go. A fungal network pervades the soil, acting like an underground railway system—transporting and storing water and nutrients. This is the soil-food web that is part of our new consciousness.

Humus

Plant and animal matter such as leaf debris, manure, and kitchen scraps—whether in nature or your compost pile—eventually break down into a complex dark brown organic substance called humus. A description of humus and its many virtues reads like those preposterous ads that promise, "Lose 10 pounds in a week!" However, in the case of humus, it really *is* a miracle worker. Just read the sales pitch:

Humus rectifies most soil structure and drainage problems, cuts down on soil erosion, helps suppress soil-dwelling disease organisms and harmful nematodes, buffers soil pH, aerates the soil, and inactivates numerous toxins such as heavy metals, herbicides, and pesticides. But wait, there's more! Humus also increases water and nutrient retention in sandy soils, keeps soil cooler in summer and warmer in winter, supplies hormones that stimulate plant growth, and—most important—provides

Okra thrives in warm, humid climates and in well-drained, fertile soils with a pH between 6 to 8—slightly acid to slightly alkaline. This dwarf red okra, 'Burgundy', grows about 4 feet tall and is well suited for the back of a flower border.

Soil pH

If you remember high school chemistry, pH is a scale that ranges from 0 (extremely acid) through 7 (neutral) and all the way to 14 (extremely alkaline). It's a logarithmic scale, which means that pH 5 is 10 times as acidic as pH 6.

Most vegetables thrive in slightly acid to neutral soil (pH 6 to 7), though members of the cabbage family prefer neutral to slightly alkaline soil (pH 7 or slightly higher). Perennial edibles are more variable. Blueberries, for example, need a very acid soil (pH 4.5 to 5.5), and plums slightly acid to somewhat alkaline soil (pH 6 to 8). When the pH is too acidic or too alkaline, some soil nutrients and minerals are chemically unavailable to the plant—tied up, so to speak.

Why should you care about all this? Because when the pH is off, your plants cannot get the nutrients they need and may starve. It also means that if you don't adjust the pH, fertilizing is a waste of time, money, and resources. When you correct the pH, the nutrients will become available to the plants and you'll be providing an ideal environment for all the creatures that live in the soil.

When creating a new garden, it's essential to check the soil pH. Get a simple test kit at a nursery or garden center. Your local Cooperative Extension Service may perform a no-frills test for a nominal fee. A professional testing is more thorough and costly but will provide a printout of the various nutrients in your soil along with suggestions on how to correct imbalances.

Some soil-testing kits and labs suggest taking samples from different areas of your property and mixing them together for analysis. I prefer to take a sample from each planting area, note where it is from, and put it in a separate bag. I've found that the soil next to my concrete foundation is alkaline because calcium leaches out of the concrete over time, yet the soil in my backyard where evergreen needles fall is acidic. If I mixed the soils together, I would get an unreliable reading.

The next step is to correct the pH if necessary. For acidic soil, raise the pH by liming the soil (some folks call it sweetening) with pelletized calcitic or dolomitic limestone. For alkaline soil, add sulfur. In both cases, follow the directions that come with the test results. Until you stabilize the pH, supplement with chelated minerals (a form that makes the minerals more available to plants).

nutrients, in slow-release form, to plants and beneficial soil organisms. Humus is, in fact, one of the few real magic bullets available to gardeners—and it's free!

Hardpan

Hardpan is a heavily packed layer of soil, usually within the top few feet, which neither roots nor water can properly penetrate. Hardpan can be a natural soil condition like caliche (a calcium carbonate layer) in the arid Southwest and shale deposits in the Northeast. Other times it is the result of human activity—especially around new houses, where building contractors compact damp soil as they drive heavy equipment over it, or where repeated use of a riding mower compresses the soil under lawn.

If the hardpan is thin, you can break it up with a digging bar. If it is thick, you'll need a professional to tear it apart with a backhoe, or you can install a French drain (a gravel- or rock-filled ditch to redirect surface water away from the area). The simplest solution may be to build raised beds.

Mineral Nutrients

Plants get the mineral nutrients they need from the soil; some nutrients occur naturally in sufficient quantity in the soil, and some have to be added. The nutrients dissolve in water and are absorbed through plant roots.

To be healthy, all plants require six major nutrients: nitrogen (N), phosphorus (P), potassium (K), calcium (Ca), magnesium (Mg), and sulfur (S). The initial three are the primary nutrients, and the remaining three secondary nutrients. Plants also require seven micronutrients: zinc, manganese, iron, boron, chlorine, copper, and molybdenum. Deficiencies—and in some cases excesses—of nutrients can lead to plant disorders and diseases.

The nutrients that are of most concern to us here are the primary ones: nitrogen, phosphorus, and potassium. Even if you only learn about nitrogen, you'll benefit your plants and garden—and the planet.

Nitrogen

As a gardener back in the 1970s, my criterion for judging a fertilizer was to check the label for nitrogen. If the percentage was high, that was a good sign. Now I know it's not so cut-and-dried. Organic fertilizers have a lower percentage of nitrogen than chemical fertilizers, but in my compost-enriched humusy soil, organic fertilizers seem to do more with less. Nitrogen nutrition is not as simple as we once thought.

What we do know is that nitrogen is critical for plant growth. A pale green or yellowish leaf color, starting on the lower or older leaves, signifies a lack of nitrogen in the soil. If the deficiency goes uncorrected, the plant will likely die because it cannibalizes itself, removing nitrogen from old leaves and sacrificing them for new leaves.

Fertilizers with nitrogen come in different forms. Organic fertilizers are made from animal or plant materials. Their nitrogen content varies; for example, blood meal can be 12 percent nitrogen, and alfalfa meal around 5 percent. Some types of fertilizers and soil amendments, such as bonemeal, leaf mold, seaweed, and compost, contain 3 percent at the most.

Most edible plants need excellent drainage and soil rich in organic matter, but their nutritional needs vary. As a rule, herbs as well as nut and fruit trees need moderate amounts of nitrogen, phosphorus, and potassium. In contrast, many vegetables, including squash, cucumbers, collards, chard, and peppers, shown here, are like high-performance athletes. Give them a diet high in nutrients, especially nitrogen, for maximum production. Beans, seen growing on a tepee, fix nitrogen in the soil, so they need less of this nutrient.

Phosphorus

This nutrient is essential for root growth, fruit development, and disease resistance. Natural sources of phosphorus include finely ground rock phosphate, bonemeal, and fishmeal. Small amounts of phosphorus occur in blood meal, wood ash, and most manures. Phosphorus doesn't move in the soil, so after you've added it a few times, there's no need to keep adding more on a regular basis. Work it well into the bottom of a planting hole, in the root zone. Side-dressing (scratching fertilizer into the soil around plants), as some books recommend, does little for the plant; also, fertilizer near the surface can run off, polluting local lakes and causing algae bloom. Highly acidic soil locks up phosphorus, but liming the soil raises the pH level and releases the available phosphorus.

Potassium

Also called potash, potassium promotes resistance to disease, cold, and drought. More potassium is available to plants in arid climates than in rainy ones. Unfortunately, a deficiency is hard to diagnose, often showing up too late to be rectified, so gardeners add potash as a preventative. Natural sources include wood ash, kelp meal, potassium sulfate, and granite dust.

Too Much of a Good Thing

Garden books usually emphasize problems associated with too little nitrogen, but too much nitrogen has a downside. It causes succulent growth that attracts aphids and other insects. The explanation is simple: excess nitrogen enlarges plant cells, but the active chemicals within the cells—which ward off pests and diseases—don't increase in volume to make up for the engorged cells; they remain relatively dilute, in effect putting out the welcome mat for pests.

Those bloated cells in fruits and vegetables have implications for human health, as well, because they contain fewer and fewer of the antioxidants and other nutrients we expect to get. According to Dr. Charles Benbrook, past executive director of the Board on Agriculture of the National Academy of Sciences, this dilution of nutrients has been going on for 40 years.

An additional concern: if overfed, some plants (including leafy greens like spinach, kale, collards, and chard) accumulate nitrogen as free nitrates. In large amounts, these are toxic to young children and anyone who is immune suppressed. The solution is grow your own fruits and vegetables and don't overfeed them.

Secondary Nutrients

Calcium, magnesium, and sulfur all have important technical functions in plant health. Calcium is a component of cell walls, magnesium is the core of the chlorophyll molecule (essential in the process of photosynthesis), and sulfur builds proteins.

There are many good sources of secondary nutrients, and some contain not just one but two of the nutrients. For example, gypsum contains calcium and sulfur, and various types of lime have both calcium and magnesium. Bonemeal and rock phosphate are other sources of calcium, and Epsom salts a magnesium source. Calcium tends to be deficient in acid soils; treat the problem by liming the soil, which raises the pH level.

Minor Nutrients

Most soils are deficient in one or more minor nutrients—zinc, manganese, iron, boron, chlorine, copper, and molybdenum. Professional soil testing gives you a heads-up on what may be lacking in your soil. Your local Cooperative Extension Service can provide general information about the soil deficits in your area.

Generally, soil that has been amended with plenty of organic matter can supply ample micronutrients. A major exception is alkaline soil, which tends to be low in iron; add chelated iron to compensate for the deficiency.

Salinity

A buildup of salts in the soil usually occurs in areas that get less than 30 to 40 inches of rain a year, or near roadways where salt is applied for ice control. If you use a salt-based de-icer on your walkways, you could be the culprit. When choosing a de-icer, read the ingredients on the package label. De-icing products generally consist of a salt (sodium or potassium chloride) or urea, both of which are bad for the soil and can damage or kill nearby plants.

The new kids on the block when it comes to de-icing are acetates, which have no known detrimental side effects. Look for CMA (calcium magnesium acetate) on the label. Although CMA is more expensive than salt, you'll save money in the long run, by protecting your plants.

Salinity is also the result of irrigating with salt-contaminated water or repeatedly adding chemical fertilizers or steer manure, both of which are high in salts. Of course, if you live by the ocean, you face the challenge of salty sea spray.

If you have a seaside garden, you need to know which edibles will and will not thrive in your salty conditions. The same holds true for a garden that abuts a road where salt is used as a winter de-icer. Cabbage will not grow well where salinity is an issue. Asparagus is the most salt-tolerant vegetable; squash, beets, and artichokes are nearly as tolerant.

Salinity is responsible for browning along leaf edges, stunted growth, poor seed germination, and less microbial activity in the soil. Prevent salt buildup by using organic fertilizers. If salinity is an issue, don't grow apples, avocados, cabbages, citrus, peaches, pears, peas, or plums, as they are especially sensitive to salts in the soil.

Soil Erosion

Erosion occurs when soil is carried off and deposited elsewhere. Although wind can be at fault, erosion usually begins when rain or irrigation water loosens soil particles. If water cannot soak into the soil—because of poor drainage, a slope, or simply too much water—it will flow and carry loose soil with it. Runoff from roofs and pavement speeds up erosion by directing large amounts of water to nearby areas that cannot absorb it quickly enough. The eroded soil ends up in low spots or flows into nearby waterways.

You can use a number of methods to control erosion on slopes: terrace the slope, install a retaining wall, plant perennials or shrubs with strong root systems to hold the soil, scatter straw or lay down woven coir fabric until vegetation fills in, place netted rolls of straw at the bottom of newly planted slopes, or replace sprinklers with drip irrigation.

Here are ways to keep empty garden beds from eroding: plant a cover crop such as winter rye in autumn and turn it under in spring, practice no-till gardening, or leave the previous season's spent plants in place and plant in the stubble the next season.

For those of you who want to dig deeper into the intricacies of soil, there's lots of great information in *The Gardener's Table* by Richard Merrill and Joe Ortiz, *Secrets to Great Soil* by Elizabeth P. Stell, *Rodale's Ultimate Encyclopedia of Organic Gardening*, and *Roots Demystified* by Robert Kourik.

Soil Amendments, Fertilizers, and Mulches

None of us can afford to think about soil amendments, fertilizers, and mulches in the way we might have a few decades or even a few years ago. It's not enough to consider whether they do an adequate job or, in the case of mulches, look appealing in the landscape. It's not even enough to just think organic.

In my opinion, it's time to go beyond focusing only on what our own plants need or what pleases us or our pocketbooks and start thinking about what's good for the planet. That means thinking about the origin of a product—whether it is natural (and if it is a limited or unlimited resource) or manufactured—and also how far it has to travel to get to us.

I have long addressed gardening from an environmental perspective, and I'm glad to see others now doing the same. Unfortunately, many books and websites use buzzwords like "all-natural," "sustainable," and "green" without thinking them through or more as a marketing ploy than a researched fact. Some authentic information is out there, but you need to sift through everything else to ferret it out. It may help you to know that the information I'm giving you has been well tested—during three decades of growing hundreds of vegetables, fruits, berries, and nuts in my own garden, as well as working with and sharing knowledge with other leaders in the field.

The products I describe here I chose because they do the job while creating the least disruption to the environment. Most will also have less impact on your budget—for example, homemade compost costs you nothing except a little labor.

Soil Amendments

Many people freely interchange the words "soil amendment" and "fertilizer." Technically speaking, fertilizers supply nutrients whereas soil amendments improve soil texture and structure and help build up microbial activity—although, as a bonus, they may also provide some nutrients.

Home-Based (DIY) Soil Amendments

This is a category of my own creation, comprising materials available right in your own (or your neighbor's) backyard:

Compost: In Appendix C, I delve into compost in detail—all its virtues and how to make it. Suffice it to say, compost has rightly earned the moniker "black gold" as the most useful and beneficial soil amendment (and mulch).

Green manure: Grow cover crops such alfalfa, clover, and vetch (legumes) as well as buckwheat and ryegrass; next season, before they set seed, till them under to decay. It's especially important to sow these crops in newly developed properties before planting lawns or gardens; also sow them in existing vegetable gardens and orchards. Find seeds at Bountiful Gardens, Harmony Farm and Garden Supply, Johnny's Selected Seeds, Nichols Garden Nursery, and Peaceful Valley Farm & Garden Supply.

Leaf mold: With autumn comes leaf fall. Too many people bag their leaves and set them on the curb to be hauled away. Instead, pile them into a corner to rot over time. To speed up the process, run over the leaves several times with a lawn mower, make a pile, and wet thoroughly. Come spring you'll discover a much smaller pile of rich-smelling, humus-rich leaf mold.

As a bonus, all of these home-based soil amendments are free—there for the taking—and, if handled properly, a plus for the environment. They have not been shipped over oceans on large freighters or trucked to your local garden center, and they don't require that you burn any fuel driving to get them. The net energy use for items in this category is nearly zero.

Your Soil: What Type? Amendments?

The fist test is a quick, down and dirty way to find out what type of soil you have. (Do not perform this test if your soil is very wet or completely dry.) Place a palm-size chunk of soil in your hand, close your fingers, and make a gentle fist. Open your hand and lightly poke at the soil clump to find out what type of soil you have:

- *Sand.* Clump crumbles completely with little pressure.
- *Clay.* Clump holds its shape, retaining the imprint of your palm and fingers.
- *Loam.* Clump may hold together but is not compacted; may break into several discrete clusters.

If you determine that your soil is primarily sand or clay, you'll need to add substantial amounts of organic matter. Sandy soils require organic matter to hold moisture and nutrients so that both are available to plants. Clay soils need organic matter so that air and water can move through the soil—meaning the soils will drain better and won't be as prone to compaction. In the lucky event your soil is loam, then generally little remediation is needed.

Plant-Based Soil Amendments

These two products are also called soil conditioners; they expand greatly when soaked in water, slowly releasing moisture to plant roots. They are often used for moisture retention in soilless potting mixes. Both have the ability to loosen hard clay soils and bind sandy soils. However, both are shipped long distances, and, as noted in Chapter 1, peat bogs take at least a quarter century to regrow.

Coir: A by-product of the coconut industry, coir is the sterilized coarse fiber from the outer shell of a coconut. Often sold in "bricks," coir resists compacting and does not crust when dry.

Peat moss: Also called sphagnum peat moss, this material is harvested from peat bogs in Canada, dried, and shipped to garden centers. Its low pH makes it an appealing soil amendment for growing acid-loving plants like cranberries and blueberries. Once dry, peat moss is challenging to re-wet.

Fertilizers

Personally, I liken fertilizing the garden to feeding my family. I would never give them a steady diet of canned protein drinks, multivitamin pills, and powdered fiber instead of real nutrients: fresh fruits, vegetables, whole grains, eggs, and fish. I know that real food contains a trove of health-giving pectins, fiber, antioxidants, and enzymes our bodies need that are not in those products. Commercial chemical fertilizers contain only the nutritional salts that plants need, though they are not used efficiently by either the plants or the life in the soil. These salts can even burn tender root hairs. To make matters worse, much leaches away, contaminating waterways.

In contrast, a varied diet of organic fertilizers from compost (for humus, enzymes, bioactivity, plant hormones, and so much more), kelp powder (for trace elements and plant growth hormones), hydrolyzed fish and fish emulsion (for nitrogen as well as various amino acids), and minerals duplicates nature's way. They release their nutrients slowly and evenly and are less likely to leach away.

It's not necessary to apply nutrients on a set schedule. Using materials as needed to correct deficiencies and not as a precautionary measure "just in case" saves money and resources.

For organization's sake, I have put each of the many organic fertilizers into one of the following three categories: plant based, animal based, and mineral based. If

Many folks don't produce enough compost for their needs, so packaged compost is a good substitute. Avoid buying wet bags or those on top of a pile in the hot sun. Use compost to amend the soil or as a mulch. For heavy feeders like zucchini and peppers, mix in some all-purpose organic fertilizer.

you have questions about whether a product is organic, visit www.omri.org.

Plant-Based Fertilizers

Generally, these fertilizers provide nitrogen and sometimes potassium. Farmers grow some of these plants solely for organic fertilizers, while others—like corn gluten—are simply waste products of another industry.

Alfalfa meal (2.5-1-1): The meal consists of ground and dried alfalfa; a pellet form is also available. In addition to supplying primary nutrients, alfalfa meal contains some trace minerals. This fertilizer is beneficial to soil organisms and contains a plant growth regulator that results in larger flowers as well as increased cold tolerance.

Corn gluten meal (10-0-0): A by-product of corn refining sold as an organic pre-emergent herbicide or weed blocker, corn gluten meal also makes a good fertilizer, as it breaks down quickly, releasing its 10 percent nitrogen. **Caution:** Do not sow seeds for 6 weeks after applying corn gluten meal.

Cottonseed meal (6-2-1): This slow-release fertilizer—the waste product after ginning cotton and pressing the seeds for oil—can acidify soil in addition to supplying nutrients. Look for organic cottonseed meal, as cotton is one of the most heavily pesticide-sprayed crops and some is genetically modified.

Kelp and seaweed (1-0-5): Excellent sources of trace minerals and amino acids that enhance soil microbial activity, these algae are sold in meal or liquid form. Work the meal into the soil; use the liquid as a foliar feed. They are renewable resources harvested off both coasts, so check the origin of products for the one closest to you. "Cold-pressed" on the label indicates a higher biologic activity.

Soybean meal (7-2-1): This is a ground-up leftover of soybeans after the oil has been extracted (mechanically or with a solvent). Look for organic versions.

Animal-Based Fertilizers

Some folks, especially strict vegetarians and vegans, choose to avoid any animal by-products in their gardens. So if you fall into that category, you'll want to stay away from these fertilizers, by-products of the meat- and fish-processing and dairy industries.

Blood meal (12-1.3-0.7): This high-nitrogen powder from slaughterhouses can burn plants if applied too heavily. In addition to using petroleum energy in the drying process, blood meal attracts dogs and other animals to dig in the soil.

Bonemeal (3-15-0): Steamed, ground-up bones from slaughterhouses, bonemeal is high (22 percent) in calcium. It releases its nutrients slowly and reduces soil acidity. This fertilizer is irresistible to some dogs.

Fish products: By-products of the fish industry come in numerous forms, all of them good N-P-K sources. For years fish emulsion (steamed and fermented fish waste) was the benchmark, but hydrolyzed fish (the technical name is fish hydrosolates) is slowly replacing it. Hydrolyzed fish doesn't smell as bad, and some products readily flow through drip irrigation without clogging. Cold processing leaves natural organic compounds

In my book, chicken manure is as valuable as a chicken's eggs, since it nourishes plants that eventually feed me and is available year round. The chicken coop, in the background at left, has squash climbing up the side. I scoop out the manure every 2 weeks, age it in a recycled-plastic compost bin, and mix it into the soil before planting. See how well everything is growing: zucchini, strawberries (mulched with straw to keep them clean), two bean tepees, and, at the back, tomatoes towering over their extra-high supports.

intact (look for names like Eco-Nutrients, Neptune, and MultiBloom). Fishmeal is ground fish waste with oils removed and dried at high temperatures; it is a good soil amendment but not easily soluble. Fish powder is heat-dried, water-soluble fish matter.

Manures: Farm animal excrement is a good soil amendment, though often high in salts. The N-P-K content varies widely. Look for manure locally—free for the taking or at low cost. Do not use any manure fresh, but rather let it age and rot. Horse manure often comes with weed seeds and may be high in salts. Commercially available cow manure is high in salts, usually contains antibiotics, and typically sits exposed to the elements in feedlots, where it loses a lot of nutrients. If you have chickens, you can't do better than your own chicken manure, as long as you let it age before adding it to the soil.

N-P-K

By law, labels on all commercial fertilizers must indicate the percentage by weight of each of the three primary nutrients they contain: nitrogen (N), phosphorus (P), and potassium (K). A synthetic formulation labeled 20-20-20 means that the product contains 20 percent nitrogen, 20 percent phosphorus, and 20 percent potassium. Labeling also includes information about nutrients' sources and the presence of micronutrients. The nitrogen may be in the form of ammonium sulfate or urea, for instance, and the product may also contain other nutrients such as iron or zinc. Although organic fertilizers generally have lower numbers than chemical fertilizers, those numbers don't fully reflect potency, as the organic fertilizers fortify plants with many other life-giving substances. They also feed soil microbes, which in turn feed plants when they decay.

Mineral-Based Fertilizers

I cannot underscore enough how important a detailed soil analysis is. There is no need to add any fertilizers unless the soil is deficient. As noted earlier in this chapter, if the soil pH is off, certain minerals will be unavailable. When adding rock minerals, first mix plenty of organic matter into the soil and then work the minerals into the root zone.

Chilean nitrate (16-0-0; sodium nitrate, nitrate of soda): The only rock mineral nitrogen fertilizer, Chilean nitrate is mined in the Atacama Desert in Chile. Apply it just before planting; nitrogen will be available almost immediately. Do not use it in low-rainfall areas of the Southwest where soils are alkaline, as it raises soil pH and sodium levels.

Epsom salts (magnesium sulfate): The effects of this highly soluble, fast-acting source of magnesium last for up to two growing seasons. Use it in magnesium-deficient soils; it's also good for container-grown plants and magnesium-hungry plants like roses, tomatoes, peppers, and potatoes.

Granite dust: A by-product of quarry activity, granite dust releases potassium slowly, lasting 5 or more years in the soil. It works best when used in conjunction with compost.

Greensand (0-0-3; glauconite, iron potassium silicate): Mined in New Jersey from ancient sea deposits, greensand takes years to release potassium. It is effective only in acidic soils.

Lime: Add lime to acidic soil to raise the pH level. Choose a form of lime suited to the amount of magnesium in your soil. *Dolomitic limestone* (50 percent calcium carbonate, 40 percent magnesium carbonate) is mined worldwide. Use it in soils with low to medium magnesium levels; it lasts 3 to 4 years. *Pelletized calcitic limestone*, also mined around the world, is good in soils with adequate magnesium because it contains high amounts of calcium and very little, if any, magnesium. It lasts 3 to 4 years. *Oyster shell limestone* (75 percent calcium, 10 percent magnesium) is best in soils with high magnesium levels.

Rock phosphate: This finely ground rock is high in phosphorus, calcium, and micronutrients, supplying long-lasting benefits. Nearly insoluble in water, rock phosphate needs microbial action and slightly acid conditions (ideally pH 6.2) for slow release of the phosphorus. To provide the right conditions, mix manure into the soil several months before applying rock phosphate. Because phosphorus does not move in the soil, it's crucial to incorporate rock phosphate at root depth. *Colloidal,* or *soft rock, phosphate*, which is mined in Florida, contains colloidal clay; use it only in sandy soils.

Sulfur: This fertilizer lowers soil pH and also supplies the nutrient sulfur. Apply it in spring or summer when soil-dwelling bacteria are active. Mix sulfur well into the soil to avoid hardpan.

Sul-Po-Mag (langbeinite, a mineral containing sulfur, potassium, and magnesium): Mined in New Mexico, this short-term fertilizer consisting of 22 percent potassium (readily available) lasts for up to 6 months. Apply it in spring or during the growing season to supply all three nutrients; use it in low-magnesium soils.

Bioactivators

If your soil has been repeatedly treated with artificial fertilizers, herbicides, and pesticides, no doubt it is deficient in microbial life and can use a boost. Sterilized potting mixes, too, need some added life so they can hold nutrients and slowly release them to your plants. Harmony Farm and Peaceful Valley are sources offering a large selection of bioactivators.

Compost tea: See "Compost Tea" in Appendix D. Make it from your own compost.

Legume inoculants: Commercial nitrogen-fixing bacteria are specific for members of the pea family (including green beans, peas, and soybeans). Add the appropriate ones to new plantings of legumes, especially when growing them in fresh potting soil.

Mycorrhizae: These fungi, which occur naturally in the forest duff (acid soil), form a symbiotic relationship with 90 percent of plants' roots. Their presence is necessary for the healthy growth of woody plants.

Worm castings: Whenever possible, use your own worm castings while they are still wet; they have more bioactivity than heat-dried commercial castings. See "Vermiculture: Worm Composting" in Appendix C.

Sterilized seed-starting mixes used to start seeds in containers have little microbial life. Without a bioactivator, seed-starting can be challenging as there is little to help feed plants unless you keep adding fertilizer. I use worm castings (worm poop) and toss them into the mix before I sow the seeds. My success rate is high.

Mulches

A mulch is a top-dressing applied to the soil surface to conserve moisture, control weeds, prevent compaction or erosion, and moderate soil temperature. It can be an organic material, such as compost, pine needles, or grass clippings, which gradually decomposes and feeds the soil; a natural material that does not break down, such as gravel, shells, or sand; or a manufactured substance, such as plastic.

When vegetable gardens were far from the house and screened from view, the odor and appearance of mulch were inconsequential. But for an edible landscape, foul-smelling, spoiled hay near a front walk or ugly black plastic bordering the patio just won't do. Mulches can be utilitarian and also enhance the appearance of the landscape. For example, shredded oak leaf mulch and well-rotted and screened compost are attractive.

Availability of the following recommended mulches varies from region to region. Most are products you have to purchase. See "Mulching" in Appendix C for how to use these materials.

Bark: Packaged tree bark is available regionally, usually shredded or as small, medium, or large chips. Avoid dyed bark. Look for the Mulch & Soil Council seal.

Cocoa hulls: This handsome mulch breaks down fairly quickly and smells like chocolate. **Caution:** Cocoa hulls can be toxic to dogs.

Compost: Well-aged compost, screened and spread around landscape areas, is pleasing to the eye. Since most of us don't produce enough compost to fill our mulching needs, give priority to new fruit trees and annual flowers and vegetables.

Grass clippings: Apply no more than an inch of fresh clippings at a time; otherwise they form an impermeable mat. Use only herbicide- and pesticide-free clippings.

Gravel or rock chips: Many different types, sizes, and colors of rock mulch are available. They do not break down or improve soil structure. Pea gravel works well as a cooling mulch under herbs in a hot, humid climate. Although most types are good-looking, the large ones are a challenge to rake—a particular problem under fruit trees when decaying fruits and dropped or diseased leaves need to be removed.

Newspaper: Recycle and save money by laying down four to six sheets of wet newspaper. Make sure the sheets overlap or weeds will squeeze their way through. Some folks shred their junk mail (black and white only) and wet it in the same way. Top with a thin layer of any attractive mulch.

Nut hulls: Depending on where you live, nut hulls (hazelnuts, peanuts, pecans, and others) may be available free or at low cost from processing plants. Because of their coarse consistency, they are better around trees and shrubs than around annual vegetables or on pathways. Do not use walnut hulls—the juglone in them inhibits most plant growth.

Pine needles: This mulch gives an informal look; it is ideal for woodland or acid-loving plants and perfect under strawberries to keep them from rotting on the ground. Pine needles acidify the soil when they break down.

Regional mulches: These mulches are available only in certain parts of the country and generally are not packaged or shipped to other areas. In the Midwest, soak ground corncobs in water before applying. In the South, mix peanut hulls with a weightier mulch or risk them blowing away. Bagasse, available in the warmer regions of the South, is fibrous sugar cane residue that decomposes quickly and lowers soil pH.

Rubber (recycled tires): Although this is a recycled material, I don't think it should be used near edible plants because of possible toxins. Besides, the rubber does not break down over time, and it gets hot in the daytime.

Sand: Use builders sand, not beach sand (unless rinsed well to remove salt). In moist climates, mulch with an inch of sand around Mediterranean herbs to prevent rotting.

Sawdust: Apply well-aged sawdust 2 or 3 inches deep around edibles. When using fresh sawdust, mix it well with an organic, nitrogen-rich fertilizer like blood meal before spreading near edibles; otherwise microbes will use available soil nitrogen as they break down the sawdust, starving the plants. Use this plant-starving effect to your advantage to prevent weed growth on garden paths; apply 3 to 4 inches of raw sawdust on the paths to discourage weeds for several years. Years later, when the sawdust is well composted, it can be added to the garden bed.

To me, compost is a neutral-looking mulch; it does its job without making any color or texture statement. It lets the plants be the stars of the garden and provides a handsome backdrop to any leaf regardless of shape, size, or color. Before long, the pepper and zucchini plants pictured here will cover the mulch completely.

Long Islanders David White and Robert Jakob planted a grapevine outside their kitchen window that enhances the views from both indoors and out. As practical as it is beautiful, the vine shades the west-facing wall in summer. In fall, yellow leaves send their glow into the room. In winter, the bare vines let in sunlight and a bit of warmth to help lower fuel bills.

Climate: Getting Along with Mother Nature

Climate has a huge effect on your landscape. During the growing season your skies might be predominantly sunny or overcast, your property subject to strong winds or light breezes, or your weather quite rainy, bone-dry, or somewhere in between. Whatever your climate, you'll be more successful growing edibles if you respect Mother Nature and take advantage of her benefits and lessen any of her drawbacks.

Sun can be a plus or a minus. In South Florida, your goal would be to reduce solar radiation; in Toronto, you would want to take full advantage of it. You would want to capitalize on cool breezes near the ocean, but block hot, drying winds in an arid, inland location. Rainfall is another vital issue. While all of us need to conserve water, anyone in a dry climate must plan around saving

and recycling water and designing plantings that are drought tolerant. In a wet climate, keeping rainstorms from damaging your landscape is key.

Sun and Shade

Is your yard sunny, shady, or in-between? Since most edible plants need full sun, it's important to know how much sun your garden area actually receives; track the sun throughout the year. For instance, in spring—before deciduous trees leaf out—you may have a lovely sunny spot that is perfect for early greens or other fast-growing plants. In summer, plants in very hot climates do better with some early afternoon shade.

Because the sun's energy is so important to hard-working edible plants, let's define the terms so you'll be talking the same language as the seed packets, reference books, and the Encyclopedia section of this book when you plan your garden.

Full sun: more than 6 hours of direct, unfiltered sunlight a day, including at least 2 hours in the peak time when the sun is overhead (from 10 a.m. to 2 p.m.)

Partial shade: 4 to 6 hours of sun a day, not a lot at midday; or lightly dappled sun off and on with some full sun

Full shade: basically little full sun, no more than a few hours, or heavily dappled sunlight all day

Trees to Modify Climate

South-facing walls are exposed to the sun most of the day, and west-facing ones in the afternoon when the sun's rays are most intense. You want to prevent the hot summer sun from striking these walls—and windows—and heating them. Shading a south- or west-facing window in the middle of summer can actually lower the inside temperature by 15 to 20 degrees. In moderate climates, deciduous shade trees make sense. When in full leaf in summer, they shade the house, and when bare in winter, the sun's rays warm the house (see the illustrations). In the hottest climates where year-round protection is needed, consider evergreen trees instead.

Other Climate Control Methods

In very hot areas, plan for a cool, north-facing patio. Where temperatures soar, dark-colored masonry walks and patios absorb heat, so avoid locating them near the house unless you can shade them in summer. In tropical climates, consider awnings or constructed overhangs that are 3 feet or more deep; they will create shade and allow you to keep windows and doors open during the cooling afternoon rains.

Garden Shadows

Are you aware that sun patterns change with the seasons? I sure am. When I first started gardening as an adult, I planted tomatoes against the south-facing wall in full sun—in April. By June they were leggy and pale; because of the roof overhang, they were in full shade. To avoid future mistakes, my husband, an astronomy buff, taught me a helpful trick to predict the sun's pattern from season to season.

Go outside at midnight at the full moon; the moon shadows you see are approximately where the sun's shadows will fall at noon 6 months later. For example, when you check the full moon's shadow in December, you'll have an excellent idea of where noontime shadows will be in June.

A computer landscaping program can predict the shadows even more precisely—useful if you live in the cold north, where midnight in winter months can be rather off-putting.

Wind

Do you know which direction the prevailing wind comes from in summer? In winter? Wind direction information is necessary in your planning process, to shield your house from blustery winter winds and to direct summer breezes to a patio. Local weather bureaus can give general information, but your own observations are more useful.

Cold winter winds generally come from the north or west; check your own property as hills and bodies of water alter the patterns. Keep in mind that with a 32°F outside temperature, you need twice as much fuel to heat the house when the wind is blowing at 12 miles an hour than at 3 miles.

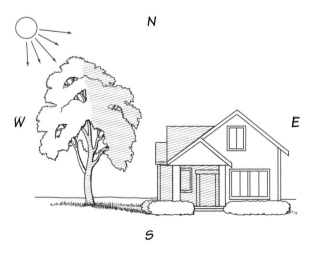

Deciduous shade trees planted near the west- or south-facing wall of a house can dramatically cool the home in summer.

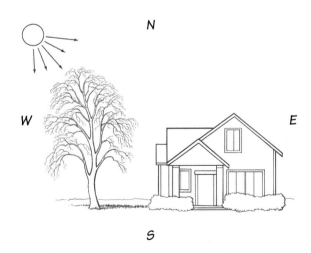

In winter, the sun shines through the leafless branches, warming the house.

Wind doesn't affect just your comfort and your home's fuel consumption; some edible plants are especially sensitive to wind and should be planted in a sheltered spot, such as near the house. Kiwi plants dry out and the vines get tangled; banana leaves can shred and the heavy fruiting stalk can fall over, bringing the plant right up out of the ground. In hot, dry climates tomato plants are better trained along the ground rather than trellised so they don't get wind burned and lose some of their foliage.

Windbreaks

Plant evergreens on the north and west sides of the house to guard against chilling winter winds. Avoid evergreens on the south-facing side—except in the hottest climates or as a windbreak—as they create year-round shade. Properly placed windbreaks redirect prevailing winds (see the illustration), saving up to 30 percent on your heating bill. If your property is subject to strong sea breezes or other gusty summer winds, a windbreak will work for you during the warm months, too. On the other hand, if summer brings gentle winds, use hedges and shrub borders to funnel them into the patio or house.

Protective Berms

Another way to buffer cold winds is to build earthen berms (large mounds of earth) on the north and west

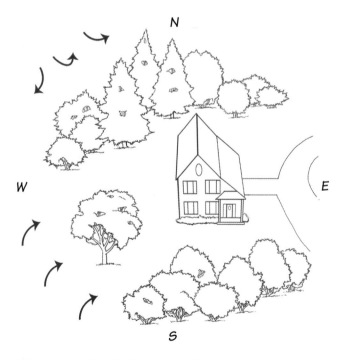

Well-placed windbreaks divert cold winds in winter, and they direct breezes to cool the house in summer.

sides of your house. Avoid erosion by making the slope ratio no greater than 3:2 (meaning, 3 feet wide for every 2 feet in height). Then plant the berms with strong-rooted ground covers.

Rainfall

No matter where you live, you must factor in your annual rainfall and learn how to manage it to benefit your landscape. Rainfall varies in different parts of the country, and often in different parts of a region. It even varies on different sides of hills and mountains. In much of the East and in the Midwest, precipitation in the form of rain or snow comes year round; in the Southwest the amount and timing of rain depend on whether a particular area has a Mediterranean climate, characterized by winter rains and dry summers, or a monsoon climate, noted for heavy summer rains that often cause flash floods.

The two considerations are how to save what you receive and how to best make use of it—both are addressed here. And, of course, you need to consider controlling water pollution, as discussed in Chapter 1 and earlier in this chapter under fertilizer issues. If you and your neighbors have wells or septic tanks, remember to keep at least 50 feet away from them when directing water running off your roof or building a rain garden.

Roof Runoff

Much of the rain in suburban areas is wasted and ends up in storm drains instead of recharging the water table. Controlling roof runoff is dependent on breaking the "roof to stream connection," that is, diverting excess water so it can sink into the earth rather than flowing into and possibly contaminating streams.

However you plan to move water from the roof, always direct it away from the house or you risk undermining the foundation, causing mold, wood rot, and seepage into the basement, just for starters. Remember that water really does seek the lowest point. Check your property for drainage problems: Are there places where water stands for a few days at a time? Do your downspouts empty out onto a patio and make the surface slippery? Is the basement wet after a storm?

The ideal solution is to direct runoff from downspouts to an area where it can be absorbed or to plants that need the water. A flexible downspout that unrolls in the rain is inexpensive and easy to install. It becomes, in effect, an extension of the roof downspout, diverting roof water 6 or 8 feet away from the house.

Connecting one or more rain barrels to downspouts is a simple way to store rainwater. Rain barrels are available in a range of sizes. To calculate how much water you can collect from your roof (the area that is diverted from a downspout to the rain barrel), visit www.gardeners.com/Rain-Barrel-How-To/5497,default,pg.html.

Of course, the way you use a rain barrel depends on your climate. In an area like mine in California, rain (when it comes) is concentrated in the rainy season, generally in winter. There is no way I can have enough rain barrels to catch all the rain and ration it throughout the dry season. So, after I have used all the stored rain, I fill the barrels with water that I collect indoors—water that would otherwise go down the drain while I wait for hot water in the sink or shower. I often end up filling a large basin or tub with water when I clean greens, wash vegetables in the garden, or rinse items in the set tub; that water, too, can go into the barrel and be used to water my container plants. In much of the East and Midwest, rain or snow falls year round, so it is much easier to use that water as you need it for the garden.

Drainage Systems

Some homeowners put what are variously called catch basins, dry wells, or French drains a distance from the house. These drainage systems hold large amounts of storm water in large gravel wells or big plastic tanks and let the water flow slowly out into a drain field or boggy area, where it will recharge the water table. For more information on these systems, consult a local landscape contractor. Before putting in a system, check out any local ordinances and codes you need to follow. For many more ways to save water visit www.epa.gov/watersense/where.htm.

Rain Gardens

When storm drains and gutter systems were created to keep house foundations dry, no one thought of the consequences of flushing untreated water into our streams and didn't realize rainwater is needed to recharge the underground water tables. So today our underground water sources are not properly recharging, and untreated roof and driveway pollutants end up in our waterways.

Rain gardens to the rescue! Create an area to collect rainwater runoff and plant it with non-invasive, native, water-tolerant plants that filter the runoff and release it slowly into the ground. By reducing the volume and velocity of storm water runoff, a rain garden reduces soil erosion, creates a habitat for dragonflies and other native

Use rain barrels (singly or connected) to store water for a sunny day. Set each barrel on bricks or another support if you want to fit a watering can under the spigot rather than attach a hose to it or dip a container into the barrel. Place screening over the top to keep out mosquitoes, roof debris, and leaves.

creatures, filters fine particulates, and captures and neutralizes fertilizers and toxins that pollute waterways. The microbes necessary to break down pollutants in the runoff are attracted to the space and help detoxify the soil before the rainwater percolates into the water table. A rain garden typically retains 30 percent more water than a lawn—although the garden should hold water for only 3 to 4 days to avoid mosquitoes breeding.

Rain gardens are now well researched and becoming mainstream. Well-documented and climate-specific information is available, especially online, from many Cooperative Extension Services as well as the Brooklyn Botanic Garden, the New England Wildflower Society, and www.raingardens.org.

Oasis Planting

When I design a yard in an arid climate, I can't rely on rain to water plants—and I certainly don't want to create a landscape that depends heavily on irrigation.

Instead I apply a concept that dates back to the early Egyptians and plant an oasis. This lets me include water-loving plants like blueberries, strawberries, citrus, and most vegetables primarily near the house, where the blossoms, foliage, and fruits are certain to be seen and appreciated. I plant the rest of the landscape with drought-resistant edibles, such as figs, almonds, pomegranates, and Mediterranean herbs, and xeriphytic native material. Siting the oasis near the house makes watering quick and efficient; it is simple to design an irrigation system that waters only those plants that need it.

Hardscape: The Structural Elements of the Landscape

The hardscape—the man-made elements in your garden, including structures and surfaces—is basic to any landscape plan, framing the picture you want to create. Patios increase usable outdoor space, built-in planter boxes add interest, and walls provide privacy. Let's look at the range of structural elements—common and unusual—and how they affect your planning.

Surface Areas

Although rainwater needs to go back into the ground to recharge our dwindling resources, we needn't give up our driveways, patios, or walkways. Instead, we can make these surfaces more permeable, enabling water to percolate down into the soil. Solutions are all around us, if we just think outside the traditional paved box.

Brick set in sand is a time-honored paving method that allows water to soak in between the bricks, unlike with brick set on concrete. Likewise, gravel or broken clamshell walks and drives are much more absorbent than concrete. Check out newer materials, including interlocking pavers with gravel between them, hollow concrete pavers with space for grass to grow, and that wonderful new oxymoron—porous concrete.

Before you call a contractor or hightail it to the nearest DIY store, be aware that these porous surfaces must be used judiciously. Do not use a water-permeable surface material near the house (for patios, walks, and drives) where water could percolate under the foundation or into the basement. You must have good drainage *away* from the house.

Driveways

Sometimes you need large surfaced areas (extra parking spaces or turnaround areas for cars) where permeability is extremely important. For best results, start with a deep layer of drain rock to act as a reservoir, allowing water to flow slowly into the ground. Top it with interlocking paving stones with gravel between them, such as Eco-Stone, or precast concrete forms like turf blocks with holes for gravel or ground covers. Types containing plants stand up to occasional car traffic. Other pavers take regular car traffic but may not withstand heavy trucks. All of these permeable materials work best on a flat area. When using a power mower or snowblower, wear protective gear to avoid flying gravel. In cold-winter areas, the blocks are subject to frost heaving as the ground freezes and thaws.

Check your local Yellow Pages or go online for paving contractors and suppliers. For information on many of the new materials, visit Scottsdale Arizona's Green Building Program at www.scottsdaleaz.gov/greenbuilding.asp.

Patios

Because patios are used extensively for family recreation, you want a level surface to accommodate chairs and tables. There's a wide range of suitable materials, including recycled cobblestones, broken concrete, and native stone.

In most areas of North America, site a patio on the south side of the house so it will be warm in spring and fall. The patio can warm a south-facing wall with reflected heat during winter. In summer, provide shade with deciduous trees and arbors to keep you cool while you're on the patio and prevent the wall from heating up in the summer sun. In the hottest climates, such as South Florida, site a patio in a cooler location that can be used year round. In cool-summer climates, plan for fencing or hedges to protect the patio from chilling winds.

Paths and Walkways

Paved paths are a necessity if you want to keep your feet clean and dry as you move from one part of the yard to another. Suitable choices include porous concrete pavers described in "Driveways," broken concrete, cobblestones, stepping-stones, and wood chips. Solid concrete or brick in mortar may be necessary for heavily traveled front walks and pathways where equipment such as snowblowers could hurl loose paving material into the air.

Structures

Structures play an important role in a landscape. Some are for utility—a storage shed or a greenhouse—while others, like a grape arbor with a wonderful swing hanging from it, are for beauty. You can make outbuildings purely func-

This front yard in the Pacific Northwest showcases a number of sustainable features, including terracing to prevent rain and irrigation water runoff. The upper terrace is easier to mow than the steep hill was. The gravel driveway and steps planted with herbs let rainwater percolate into the water table, and a handsome planter box accommodates edibles, such as these sculptural Brussels sprouts and red cabbages.

tional and hide them from view or choose to incorporate them as attractive focal points in your edible landscape.

Arbors and Gazebos

Both types of structures are usually made of wood. An arbor provides upright supports for climbing vines while defining or framing a view. A gazebo—an airy, freestanding, roofed structure—can bring a touch of drama or whimsy to a landscape as a focal point. Use either to support grapes, kiwis, hops, or pole beans. An arbored walk can help shade south- and west-facing walls.

Fences and Walls

Fences and walls are both utilitarian and versatile—as windbreaks, privacy screens, and protection from intruders. They also define spaces, exclude or contain animals, and provide limits for children. Vines and shrubs soften most fences and walls, altering their appearance. For example, a chain-link fence bordering a dog run is strictly utilitarian. Adding a coat of black paint completely changes its character and makes the fence almost disappear. Train some runner beans on the outside of the fence and it becomes a beautiful addition to the landscape.

Generally, fences are constructed of wire or wood, whereas walls are masonry. Although both contribute greatly to the beauty of the garden, they can be expensive. Use sustainable bamboo, or recycle used barn lumber and grape stakes for fences. A charming idea borrowed from Asia is to weave gnarled branches into a rustic gate. Recycled wall materials include stone, used brick, and broken concrete. Search the Internet for sources for environmentally friendly paints and finishes to give structures a new look.

Hedges

If you're wondering why hedges are in this section since they aren't man-made, it's because they're permanent structural elements—living walls and fences, if you will, that serve the same purpose. There are a number of benefits to using hedges: they cost considerably less than walls or fences, they don't absorb heat in warm climates, and they can provide luscious food. However, hedges require more upkeep, especially if you want a formal, clipped appearance.

Although you're likely to think of large plants for hedging, sometimes all you need is a visual divider between two areas. Numerous plants fit that bill—from blueberries to asparagus (during the growing season). Hedges can be extremely informal and thorny—effective barriers to intruders (human and four legged) and a haven for birds. See "Hedges" in Chapter 4 for lists of edible plants you can use.

A recycled concrete retaining wall creates a strong line for the collection of antique washtubs by the rustic barn on this Wisconsin property. The wall's rough texture contrasts with the smooth lawn, adding drama. Raised beds with carrots, onions, tomatoes, and lettuces connect the barn to the house, out of view.

Retaining Walls

A retaining wall holds back the soil on a hillside or slope. Although you can use standard concrete blocks to make a low retaining wall, a more sustainable approach employs native stone, recycled wood, or broken concrete. Since a retaining wall affects the area's drainage, use decorative drainage rock to carry water away from the bottom of the wall. A retaining wall with plants spilling over the top adds exciting lines and interest to a yard. Because drainage is so good at the top of the wall, your plant choices are almost limitless. At the bottom of the wall, however, you are limited to plants that tolerate soggy soil, such as cranberries. For a retaining wall more than 2½ feet high, call in a professional engineer.

Patio Covers

In most areas, the ideal patio cover provides shade in summer and lets the sun pour through in winter. An overhang of at least 8 feet effectively shades a south-facing wall. A wood arbor positioned over the patio and attached to the house usually needs a building permit and must be designed by an architect to make it safe. Train deciduous grapes, hops, or kiwis to cover the arbor. Another option is to set up metal poles and cover the area with canvas; it's easy to disassemble in fall or winter.

The type of patio cover you choose will depend on where you live. In a cold-winter area, avoid creating a dense, permanent top. A removable cover or one that lets the sun's rays penetrate will warm the house wall and brighten the home's interior in winter. In areas where the patio is in use throughout the year, such as Florida, Hawaii, and the low desert, choose a dense lath covering.

Water Features

Water instills a sense of serenity in a landscape. Its calming sound masks surrounding urban noise and turns the garden into a welcoming retreat. For me, water gives a landscape a sense of place. Even a small fountain transports me to luscious gardens I've visited in Spain, Italy, and Mexico. And for the great enjoyment that small water gardens and recirculating fountains provide, the amount of energy and other resources they consume is negligible.

Adding a swimming pool will change your lifestyle. A pool—with plenty of deck space—becomes a gathering place for a weekly barbecue and pool parties. Tight on space? A narrow lap pool is an investment in your family's health, especially when surrounded by beautiful edible plants to inspire swimmers to go one more lap.

This water feature is the focal point in Carole Saville's Los Angeles herb garden. Elevated sides provide a shelf for rosemary and thyme topiaries. The tall, large-leaved plant against the house, just to the left of the toxic datura with its white, trumpet-shaped flowers, is hoja santa, a Mexican specialty. Spaces between the pavers catch rainwater in winter and anchor low-growing herbs such as thyme, violets, and creeping oregano.

Decorative Water Features

You can craft a small spill fountain from an endless array of recycled materials: old copper plumbing equipment, stacked flowerpots, or a collection of native fieldstone. You'll need a source of power to run the pump of a recirculating water feature. Solar-powered features are not yet perfected, but the technology is improving, so check them out. Small ponds and fountains are simple enough to install. Sunset's *Water Gardens* and Ortho's *Creating Water Gardens* are good resources.

Edibles work well as part of a small decorative pond; lotus, watercress, and water chestnuts are especially appropriate. Consult the "Water Plants" section in Chapter 4 for a complete listing of edibles for water gardens.

Swimming Pools

Planning for a swimming pool is beyond the scope of this book. Look into earth-friendly alternatives like natural swimming pools, although they require 20 percent more surface area for plants to filter and clean the water. For standard pools, plan for a retractable pool cover to cut evaporation; in cold climates, choose a dark color for pool finish to absorb heat; and consider solar pool equipment. To avoid bee stings when kids are running around the pool deck and splashing in the water, don't grow edible plants that attract bees. Instead, try cabbages, beets, lettuces, bamboo, figs, and French tarragon.

For more information on natural pools, consult the book *Natural Swimming Pools: Inspiration for Harmony with Nature* by Michael Littlewood and search online.

Once you've evaluated your soil, climate, and hardscape, and carefully considered any problems and solutions, you'll be well on your way to creating the perfect plan for your landscape. Don't skimp on this initial phase—remember, you're laying important groundwork.

3 | Creating a Landscape Plan

Now that you've evaluated the physical characteristics of your landscape, including your soil, climate, and hardscape, it's time to decide what you want and then move forward with a landscape plan. In addition to helping you identify your needs and how to create a landscape for the enjoyment of family and friends, this chapter guides you through a reality check of how much time, money, and effort you're willing to spend on installing and maintaining the landscape. I'll walk you step by step through creating a landscape plan, including examples of what some folks have done to change their outdoor space. By the end of this chapter, you'll be ready to put together your own edible landscape plan.

What You Want: Planning for Enjoyment and Utility

Whether you're updating an existing landscape or creating an entirely new one, there's a lot of planning involved. You need to consider not only your own vision for the yard but also what your family members want

Preceding pages: Dozens of edibles thrive in Ron and Pam Clancy's British Columbia backyard. *Above*: Port Orchard, Washington, home-owners Kirk and Teri Doughty wanted edibles, but their children wanted a lawn for play. Designer David Tubberville's solution was to terrace one side of the grassy slope with raised beds for vegetables.

and need. Take into account current needs—play areas for children, for example—and how they might change 10 years down the road when accessibility for a parent or older relative living with you may be necessary.

Making the Most of Your Outdoor Space

Consider how you want to use your outdoor space. For instance, if you enjoy entertaining friends, you may want a large patio area near the kitchen with a low sitting wall and perhaps an outdoor barbecue. All yards need a compost area as well as a general utility area for storing items such as garbage cans and patio furniture; the primary goal in siting these, of course, is to make them unobtrusive yet accessible.

When you're about to change your home landscape, whether it's a complete redesign or the addition of a new garden area, there are a number of questions to chew on, including:

- Are there ways to enhance outdoor living, like a door from the master bedroom onto a sheltered deck or private garden? Or a pass-through window from the kitchen to the patio?
- Do you want to add an outdoor barbeque or kitchen or an area spacious enough to allow you to entertain large groups, such as for family reunions or charity events?
- Do you need a small storage place for cushions, toys, and other items used outdoors on a daily basis?
- Would you like a separate garden shed to store tools, soil, stakes, and pots, or a small greenhouse to start seedlings?
- Do you want a quiet corner for meditation, maybe surrounded by bamboo, or some other peaceful retreat, such as a gazebo?

As you and your family ponder these questions, look at your property from all angles. Think about how the features of your outdoor space could be rearranged to best suit everyone's needs and desires.

Family Considerations

It's important to take the entire family into consideration when creating or redesigning your home landscape. Here are some issues to think about:

- How is the family going to use the yard?
- Do you need to view the space from indoors to supervise children?
- Are there young children who would enjoy sandboxes and climbing structures?
- Do you need lawn space as a base for a play area—from a wading pool for toddlers to a badminton or croquet court for teens and adults?
- Are wheelchair access and raised beds for gardening needed—now or in the future?

Family dynamics can change over the years, and your outdoor space should keep pace with any changes. For example, when a lawn area is no longer needed for small children as a play area, it can be transformed into a vegetable garden. A wood sandbox can become a raised bed for a specimen fruit tree.

Pets

Most families have a pet or two, and it pays to factor in their impact on the garden before starting a design. Dogs and cats demand the most attention. Rabbits and outdoor bird pets such as guinea hens and chickens have needs to consider, as well.

Dogs

Most dogs love freshly dug soil, especially if it's amended with bonemeal or blood meal, and they dig and wreak havoc on new plants. Provide temporary fencing until the area fills in. Some dogs, like poodles and Maltese, are polite and usually stay on paths. On the other hand, retrievers and other hunting dogs are famous for plowing through plantings instead of going around them. Some dogs are great deterrents to marauding deer, woodchucks, and raccoons. A small proportion of dogs develop a taste for tomatoes and soft fruits.

Planter boxes 2 feet high, permanent fences, and low-voltage electric collars in combination with a perimeter system are all possible disincentives to misbehaving dogs, as is training the dog and owner. Hygiene is important in an edible garden to control diseases and for the aesthetics. Train your dog to relieve itself in a designated area of the yard that is easily cleaned up.

Cats

I've had cats that didn't hunt birds and ones that did; because of declining bird populations, any future feline I may have will live indoors only. Cats not only hunt

Remember to plan your garden for both activities and quiet time. While this small corner of the garden provides food for the table and flowers for the house, it also includes a bench perfect for reading a book or sitting contentedly while observing nature.

birds, they use newly dug garden soil as a latrine. I cover new beds with bird netting or floating row covers until the plants fill in. On the positive side, cats control rodents around the compost pile and fruit trees.

Outdoor Birds

The most compatible outdoor birds for an edible landscape are free-ranging guinea fowl, though they can be very noisy. Guinea fowl control many pests, including Japanese beetles, grubs, and deer ticks, and they consume weed seeds. These African natives generally leave your edible plants alone. They lay small eggs that taste similar to chicken eggs, and you generally care for them as you would chickens (see sidebar on the next page).

Rabbits

Rabbits by nature consume many greens and young edible plants, so if you allow your bunny to run free outdoors during the day, you must either fence your vegetables or grow them in raised boxes; any fences and

Chickens: Enriching the Garden

My chickens are a constant source of joy to me and the neighborhood children, who come by almost daily to feed them or get an occasional egg for breakfast. Here, my grandson Alex Chavarin and my young neighbor Kate Eng meet my new 10-week-old hens—a blond Buff Orpington, a dark Cuckoo Marin, and a rare Red Star.

Although you may not have thought about raising chickens in your yard, now's the time to start thinking about it. Their very presence animates the garden, even if they aren't allowed loose in it—it's amazing how quickly chickens defoliate most greens. My chickens are champion recyclers, providing a steady supply of high-quality manure. In fact, some experts say that chicken manure is the richest of all manures in plant growth enzymes. My chickens feast on stale tortillas, weeds, old bean vines, sun-scalded tomatoes, and more. With a coop in my front yard, a parade of neighborhood children come to feed them.

I raise chickens for their eggs. A few hens supply the tastiest and most nutritious eggs imaginable—fresh every day. Store-bought eggs pale by comparison to the rich golden orange yolks (full of omega-3s) in my girls' eggs. Most layers produce nearly an egg a day from spring through fall; four hens are plenty for an average family.

Before introducing a flock of chickens into your neighborhood, check the local ordinances. Talk to your neighbors, especially those closest to the proposed coop site, and let them know there will be some noise. Keeping those folks in fresh eggs generally makes up for the loud squawks that inevitably emanate from the coop.

FYI, a rooster is not necessary for egg production. At night I move my rooster, Mr. X, to a dog carrier in the garage. The evening I forgot to bring him in, we made the local newspaper's police blotter: "Disturbance at 5:05 a.m. in North Los Altos." Obviously someone wasn't happy.

Consider raising heritage chickens. In addition to their beautiful plumage, many of these breeds are more domesticated and people friendly than modern commercial breeds. Some are endangered; by raising such chickens you can help keep a breed alive. McMurray Hatchery in Webster City, Iowa, offers one of the largest selections of heritage breeds.

For more information, see *Raising Small Livestock: A Practical Handbook* by Jerome D. Belanger and visit www.organicchickens.homestead.com and www.motherearthnews.com.

---

boxes should be at least 18 inches tall. Rabbits can safely hop around and eat weeds around fruit trees and forage among established perennials and most herbs without damaging plants. Protect your pet at night in a hutch. The hutch floor collects the animal's manure, which can be added to the compost pile to age.

Activities

Many people think of their home landscape primarily as a place where they can simply and unashamedly relax. If you feel this way, plan an informal, cottage-style garden, which doesn't need meticulous attention. This type of garden often attracts creatures that actually help you unwind—for example, a pair of robins looking for worms or a hummingbird sipping nectar from pineapple sage blossoms. Maybe you want to grow a specialty garden such as a collection of old rose varieties, medicinal plants, or raw materials for dyes; the options are limitless. Clearly, you'll need to plan for such a space and the kind of gardening activities you'll be engaged in.

When planning your landscape, it's also important to figure out how people move around in the area and get from one point to another. Note the routes you and your family regularly take as the landscape exists now. Think seriously about what kinds of paths you need and where to put them. Do you need a wide path for a wheelchair or to maneuver a garden cart? Make sure a path is going to work before you install it. As a test, mark it out with a garden hose or string, leave it in place for a day or two, and then make any adjustments based on your comings and goings. Think practically. If you put in an aesthetic but arbitrary curve in a front walk, people will inevitably walk the shortest line, ignoring the path.

In general, keep in mind that there are edible landscapes for all seasons and all tastes. You are creating a space for you and your family to enjoy and one that meets all of your needs.

What the Planet Needs: Planning Globally

In the past, when planning a landscape, a designer and homeowner concentrated only on the desires of that one homeowner's family while meeting municipal and county zoning requirements. Now we all think more globally. Will the runoff from a proposed lawn pollute a river or lake and eventually end up in the ocean? If outdoor lighting around a patio and security lights are planned, will they disrupt the mating patterns of fireflies and throw migrating birds off course? How much energy goes into producing and shipping exotic paving stones from thousands of miles away? The next section speaks to these pressing issues and offers many creative alternatives.

Lawn—or Not?

Given all the environmental problems a lawn creates (see Chapter 1), ask yourself if you really want one. Are your children going to be grown and moving out in a few years so that open play areas aren't really needed? Do you want to spend valuable weekend time—or pay for—mowing, weeding, watering, and fertilizing?

If you decide that your lawn is a waste of money and resources, you have hundreds of redesign options. For example, you can craft an area of paving stones with thyme or alpine strawberries growing in between, plant a geometric mini-orchard of fruit trees, or create a series of raised beds for vegetables and flowers around a small decorative playhouse.

However, if you do want some lawn, select a grass variety suited to your climate and location—one that grows well and requires the least amount of water and fertilizer—and restrict it to level ground. Choosing the right grass species for your yard is a complex task. To make an informed choice, see *The Organic Lawn Care Manual* by Paul Tukey, visit SafeLawns.org, or consult your local Cooperative Extension Service.

Outdoor Lighting

Outdoor lighting sets a mood, adds a sense of security, and welcomes visitors to your home and landscape. Despite its advantages, outdoor lighting contributes significantly to the ever-growing problem of light pollution. Uplighting—with its beams aiming skyward—is the most unnatural and least desirable type of lighting. Avoid spotlighting with high-intensity lights, as well.

Low-voltage lighting is readily available and inexpensive, and installation is a simple DIY project. Select fixtures that direct light downward. Solar lighting has improved but has yet to live up to its promise. As of this writing, some solar-powered systems don't last more than a year or so. In addition, they don't store enough energy during the short days of fall and winter to stay lit for much of the long nights. Yet the technology is constantly improving, so keep an eye out for new lighting systems, including ones that employ LEDs and have NiMH battery support for longer lighting cycles as well as other systems still on the horizon.

Solar lighting or motion-activated lights alongside steps often solve safety issues. For security, well-placed motion detectors that turn on selected outdoor lights by doors and windows for a short time save energy and may

Fritz Haeg's Edible Estates

Fritz Haeg, a landscape architect, artist, and founder of Edible Estates—a project dedicated to replacing front lawns with productive edible landscapes—is outspoken about the way Americans garden and explores the social aspects of an edible yard. In his book *Edible Estates: Attack on the Front Lawn*, Haeg observes, "When we plant a front lawn, we avoid considering where or how we live. We grow an unnatural monoculture, a generally unwelcoming space that isolates us from everything around us. In contrast, when we plant an organic, diverse, and productive Edible Estate in our front yard, we reconnect to our food, our environment, and our neighbors. Suddenly we are forced to ask more thoughtful questions about where and how we live."

Fritz encourages potential Estate gardeners to consider how they will relate not only to the garden but also to the people living around them, by asking such questions as: Does the front yard invite neighbors into a dialogue, or close them out? Could the front yard become a demonstration garden with edibles that provide pleasure for people who live around us as well as be inviting to neighborhood children? Since a front yard garden is by nature more public, can we maintain it at a level that's acceptable to our neighbors? Is there a welcoming location in the yard to relax and chat with neighbors and enjoy the fruits of the new garden?

be more of a deterrent to intruders than leaving outdoor lights on all night.

Holiday lighting—the old-fashioned, large white lights—has its bonuses in mild-winter climates. When frosts threaten, these lights have saved my plants many times; I keep them on all night to protect tender citrus and avocados from damage when temperatures below 30°F are predicted. While they raise the temperature around the foliage only a few degrees, that is often enough to protect the plants from heavy damage. In cold climates, where frosts are heavier and long lasting, and for most landscape lighting in mild-winter areas, use energy-saving, lower-voltage LED lights.

Recycled Materials

Many recycled items, such as wood rounds cut from dead tree trunks, used bricks, and whiskey barrels, are useful and attractive garden elements, providing a pleasant change from stepping-stones that have been trucked long distances, standard patio concrete, and plastic pots.

Some recycled materials are free, but note that most dumps no longer allow scavenging; you must get your hands on the materials before they end up there. Community trash days can sometimes yield treasures, and check out www.freecycle.org for other possibilities.

The Idea Garden at Longwood Gardens in Pennsylvania inspires homeowners to think of new ways to use their landscape. Here a semicircular dome made of recycled saplings and twigs creates a cozy place to sit and read to children or to eat a quick snack. The cherry tomatoes growing on the structure are a mere arm's length away.

Recycled lumber makes great wood for garden projects. Even your partly rotten 4-by-4-foot fence posts are salvageable; cut off the useless portions and make planter boxes or retaining walls from the rest. Lumberyards have plenty of wood scraps. Some give these away or charge a nominal fee. Others are starting to sell recycled wood; look for the SmartWood–Rediscovered Wood certificate.

One of the most versatile recycling materials, particularly useful in informal gardens, is broken concrete. You can't beat the price; it's usually yours for the taking. You can find broken concrete at construction sites. Since contractors have to cart it away and then pay a dump fee, they are often delighted to have someone use it. If you live nearby, they may even deliver it, but be aware that you may end up with some rubble you'll need to dispose of.

To make use of recycled concrete, set the interesting shapes in sand and soil, with low ground covers planted in between for a water-permeable patio. Or stack the pieces to create a wall, and plant the pockets with a variety of herbs. When selecting concrete, be discriminating. Not all concrete pieces are created equal; some are too thin and pulverize, while others are oil stained. Large pieces are the most versatile. Some landscape contractors use commercial stains to give the concrete a more uniform look. Small pieces and rubble can come in handy for solving drainage problems.

Some recycled materials, while not free, are demonstrably less expensive than new items, especially at flea markets, Goodwill and Salvation Army stores, and garage sales. Visit a local Habitat for Humanity ReStore. They accept donations of new and resalable used building materials and sell them at greatly reduced prices at over 500 stores around the country. For more information, visit www.habitat.org/cd/env/restore.aspx.

While at least as expensive as virgin wood, faux lumber made from recycled plastic is growing in popularity. It requires no staining and lasts for decades. It has little strength, however, and so is not usable for posts and joists, but it makes good planking for decks and the sides of planter boxes. Trex is the best-known brand. Orcaboard manufactures faux lumber items such as tables, planters, and storage benches, using locally recycled plastic (not sent to Asia and recycled under questionable circumstances). Visit www.ciwmb.ca.gov/Plastic/Recycled/Lumber and National Geographic's www.thegreenguide.com for "new" recycled products and suppliers.

While recycling usually saves you money, when it comes to items such as used brick, resurfaced old growth timber, and antiques, the prices range from the ridiculous to the sublime. To find just the right garden accents to give your yard more character—such as Victorian newel posts as gateposts, old tiles to cover a sitting wall, or a boat hatch cover as a garden table—seek out architectural salvage firms that sell materials from old houses as well as stores that recycle marine items.

Wildlife Gardening

Watching with a neighbor's son as a ladybug pupa hatches and its wing covers turn from white to red and black is memorable. On the other hand, watching a squirrel go through my ripe plum tree dropping 10 plums for every plum it eats makes me crazy. We all encounter some conflicts with critters, and you'll find information to help mitigate wildlife problems in Appendix D.

I have just a quarter-acre, yet at least 10 different bird families nest in my yard. Every spring hundreds of bees of all types buzz around the flowers, lizards nest in the ground in my back garden, and swallowtails lay eggs in my dill. Attracting wildlife to my garden is something I value. Your garden, too, can be an ark that provides refuge for migratory birds, caterpillars, native pollinators, and amphibians, so many of which are in trouble.

Include water in one form or another in your landscape. Plan for birdbaths, a marshy low spot planted with native bog-loving plants, or a small pond to attract wildlife. Some come to drink, others, like frogs and dragonflies, to breed and hunt, and still others to bathe. Use mosquito control rings (*Bt* var. *israelensis* available at garden centers) or mosquito fish to kill any mosquito larvae in features with standing water.

Animals need a supply of leaves, nectar, pollen, fruits, seeds, and nuts to thrive. Choose plants native to your area; they are better adapted to your local climate and feed many native species. Monarch butterflies specifically need milkweed to eat; hummingbirds are more generic and sip from a host of flowers, native or exotic. Numerous books and websites are devoted to native plants; also check out www.abnativeplants.com.

Include a selection of evergreens in your plantings to give winter protection for birds. Native junipers, live oaks, and pines work well, and their berries and acorns are a nutritional powerhouse bonus. Thorny plants like blackberries and large roses protect nestlings from cats and skunks. Leave a small area of tall grasses and wildflowers along your property line where lightning bugs can hang out and beneficial insects can hide.

Honeybees are attracted to most culinary herbs, including this exotic and tasty heirloom chive from Mongolia. Plant edibles with small single or compound flowers to attract pollinators such as bees and butterflies.

A few more suggestions: Generally, an informal garden style is much more inviting to wildlife than a manicured yard. Plants that spread and touch one another provide a safe journey for fledgling birds and space for nests. Cut down on pest control products—even *Btk* (*Bt* var. *kurstaki*), which is considered benign, kills cutworms and butterfly larvae alike.

The National Wildlife Federation offers guidance for beginning wildlife gardeners. Your yard can qualify as a wildlife habitat—if it provides food, water, and shelter and is free of toxic chemicals. Register your yard as a certified wildlife habitat at www.nwf.org/backyard wildlifehabitat.

Reality Strikes: Time, Money, and Restrictions

It's exciting to conjure up your new edible landscape and imagine all the wonderful things you can do, but eventually you have to make some hard decisions. From years of design experience with my clients, I have learned that it pays to be realistic. It's important for you to sit down with your family and discuss each person's wants and needs and then prioritize. Note those changes that will make the most positive impact with the least outlay of time and money.

Time and Effort

How much time are you willing to spend maintaining your edible landscape? Do you have the time to prune, feed, mulch, and spray throughout the year—or would you rather hire someone to take care of your landscape? Are you keen to pick and process a large harvest of cherries, apricots, or blackberries?

Look up the edibles you want to grow in the Encyclopedia and check the effort scale for each one. In late summer I easily spend 5 hours a week picking and preserving the summer harvest from my ambitious garden. For me, this is fun and worth the effort, but you may not have as much time—and that's okay. As tempting as it may be to create the most bodacious edible landscape ever, or try 12 different heirloom tomato plants, nothing is more disheartening than seeing fruits and vegetables rotting on the vine because you didn't have time to harvest them. I always advise my clients to start small; it's easier to add than to subtract.

Do you like manicured gardens, or do you find enthusiastic cottage-style gardens more appealing? The average manicured garden with a lawn requires at least 3 to 4 hours a week during the growing season for raking, weeding, mowing, and trimming. If you decide to hire a gardener, perhaps this high-maintenance option won't be a problem.

In contrast to manicured gardens, informal ones with minimal lawn demand only an hour or so a week for a little pruning, trimming, and weeding. Still, even a low-maintenance garden doesn't really live up to its name until after the first two summers—the time it takes for most plants to become established and fill in.

Budget

For most landscaping projects, plants represent less than 10 percent of the total cost. Fences, patios, large arbors, sprinkler systems, and earthmoving—all can be expensive. Three young fruit trees might amount to $150; a slate patio (installation and materials) can cost $20,000; and you can move up to six figures for a swimming pool and gazebo connected by an allée of espaliered fruit trees.

You can save money by doing some of the work yourself. Certain projects only take muscle or time. Here are a few ways to help keep your budget in line:

- Measure your property and make a base plan on paper (see "The Base Plan: Your Starting Point").
- Do your own deconstruction work, such as removing sod, clearing brush and weeds, breaking down old brick walls, and tearing out PVC irrigation systems.
- Dig any drainage ditches, rototill the soil, and add and mix in amendments.
- If you're handy, consider doing simple projects such as building planter boxes and assembling prefabricated sheds. Both are ideal weekend DIY projects.
- After the contractor is done with the installation of the hardscape and large plants, such as trees, do the rest of the planting yourself.

I recommend hiring a trained professional to do some projects. In my experience, pouring and smoothing large areas of concrete takes skill to get it even and to have it drain properly, and a talented brick or stonemason is worth every penny spent.

Before embarking on any money-saving project, take your health into consideration. If you spend most of your time tapping on a computer keyboard, some of the work might be too much of a strain on your body, especially your back. Ask for help with heavy lifting from friends or family, or hire someone for specific jobs.

A further way to trim your budget is to get the best cost estimate possible from a contractor. When assessing contractors, make sure they are licensed and that you see their work and obtain recommendations. And honestly ask yourself whether you're really fussy about how the paving joints line up or the quality of the materials the contractor uses. Some folks are satisfied with a journeyman's job and others are unhappy if the job done isn't the very highest quality with every detail perfect. As in the rest of life, you get what you pay for. When comparing estimates, make sure that you are not comparing apples and oranges, that the work quality and the tasks required are equal. And remember, the lowest bid may not be the best bid. Some contractors make up for a low bid by cutting corners and pushing you to include more upgrades.

Construction, Digging, and Zoning Restrictions

There are many legal restrictions on what you can do to your land, and some projects require one or more permits. Before you start a major overhaul of your yard, check with your local building authority. It may be a county or municipal building or planning department; names vary throughout the country. Townhouses and condos often have covenants and restrictions on what you are allowed to do on your property. Some homeowner associations require lawn and uniform plantings from building to building and specifically forbid edibles. These edicts are slowly fading away, and governing boards, if given up-to-date information, often change the rules. Most areas have laws governing the placement of retaining walls, patio covers, and setbacks for pools, fences, and arbors.

Whether you are planning a large home improvement job or planting a large tree, call 811 before you start digging. A call to 811 gets your underground utility lines marked—for free—and eliminates potentially hazardous errors. Visit www.call811.com for more info.

The Base Plan: Your Starting Point

Once you have a rough idea of what you want and how much time, effort, and budget you can devote to it, you're ready to create a base plan by measuring your property, existing structures, utilities, and plantings, and either drawing it to scale on paper or entering it into a landscaping program on your computer. A base plan provides an accurate graphic representation of your property and its existing features (both man-made and natural)—a "before" snapshot, so to speak.

Having everything correctly documented in a clear manner can avoid costly mistakes during the installation phase. It also allows you to convey your ideas clearly to others, such as a designer or contractor and especially any municipal officials whose certification you may need. Once you have a base plan, you can refer to it to expedite any future changes to your landscape, especially if you are doing a project piecemeal over time.

Base Plan Preparations

Check to see if you have an architect's drawing, developer's plat, or deed map from the relevant planning department that includes a drawing of your house and property. A topographical map, if you can find one, is helpful in determining any slopes. After ascertaining that the drawing or map is accurate, check whether it has been photocopied and reduced. If so, recalculate the scale; otherwise all the measurements will be incorrect.

You will need some basic supplies, the most important of which is graph paper. Most properties of less than 80 by 60 feet fit on a standard 8½-by-11-inch sheet of ⅛-inch graph paper (8 squares measure 1 inch; each square is equivalent to 1 foot). This type of paper allows you to use a ruler to measure distances instead of having to count squares (1 inch represents 8 feet). For larger or complex jobs, use big sheets of drawing paper. Drafting supply houses carry 17-by-22-inch architect's vellum with a ⅛-inch grid, which will accommodate most suburban lots; larger sizes of paper are available. If your yard covers more than a quarter-acre, scale the drawing to ¹⁄₁₆ inch (or less) to the foot, in order to fit the drawing on paper of a manageable size. Tracing paper is helpful in developing a plan for any size property.

A notebook, ruler, pencil, stiff piece of smooth cardboard or board, and 100-foot measuring tape as well as masking or painter's tape round out the supplies necessary. Include colored pencils if you want to test different flower and foliage colors in your plan.

Better Homes and Gardens' *New Complete Guide to Landscaping* gives detailed instructions on measuring your property and slopes and handling any complicated situations. It also covers a lot of construction how-to and includes building projects.

Creating the Base Plan

Measuring and drawing to scale all the features of your yard might seem like a chore, but the end product is invaluable as you proceed. Don't be intimidated. Putting your yard on paper is one of those jobs that is more difficult to explain than to do.

Even if you have all the property documentation mentioned earlier, it's a good idea to take some basic measurements to be sure everything is up-to-date, including additions to the house, easements, or property line changes.

Measuring your yard is much easier to do with two people. Tape the graph paper or vellum to the cardboard. Measure and then draw the property lines on the paper. Include the house in relation to the property lines as well as major permanent structures such as walks, fences, driveways, walls, and telephone poles. If you have a septic tank, don't forget to indicate it as well as its drain field.

Use a dotted line to indicate overhanging structures such as eaves, porch roofs, and patio covers that shade plants and limit their height. Note all first-floor windows, doors, and porch stairs to avoid placing plants in front of them. Locate and record all utility lines, such as sewer, water, gas, cable, and electrical, to avoid disturbing them and risking injury during construction. Locate and record all major trees and shrubs you want to keep.

Locate the house downspouts, and notice if water collects on the ground there; mark hose bibs on the plan, too. Note if there are any areas in the yard with bad drainage and indicate them on the plan. If your yard has a slope, approximate where it begins and ends as well as its angle. For yards with a gentle slope, that's all you need; steep slopes require professional guidance.

Now step back and take a look at the adjoining properties. Note features that you don't want to see and should be screened, such as a neighbor's windows or camper, and those that you want to enjoy, such as a distant steeple or surrounding woods.

Determine which direction is north by using a GPS or compass, or by finding your house on a local street map; indicate north in the margin of the plan. Your property's exposure to the sun's path is important when incorporating energy-saving features like shading a hot south-facing wall. And, of course, exposure is critical in making the right plant choices.

Once the base plan is complete, make at least two copies. Put the original in a safe place in case you need it in the future. Use one copy to trace over when you create your bubble drawings (explained later in this chapter), and use the second copy for the final design for the yard. You will need a third copy if you plan to install an irrigation system or outdoor lighting. On that copy draw the location of any underground wiring or irrigation pipes and valves so you can easily find them if repairs are needed.

Choosing a Design: The Lane Landscape as a Model

Take a walk around your property with fresh eyes and view it as if you were a potential homebuyer. What non-plant features would you want to change? Do you really like the color of the house or is it time for a paint makeover? If you swapped that window in the family room for a door leading into the yard, would that create an enjoyable usable space? How about a fence or hedge to screen off your neighbor's basketball hoop or garbage can area?

With your new plans and changes in mind, you're ready to focus on the edibles for your landscape and consider which fruits and vegetables you like best. Where on your property could you grow them? Which varieties taste best and look most attractive?

To help you conceptualize the entire process, I'm going to share with you the experience of my naturalist friend and longtime right-hand woman, Dayna Lane, when she moved from California to Arlington, Virginia. You can follow, step by step, what Dayna did to transform a typical suburban property into an exciting edible landscape and certified wildlife habitat.

Dayna Lane's Arlington, Virginia, house is typical of the 1950s, with a lawn in front and shrubs against the house. The sloping lawn is hard to mow and rainwater runs off, but the south-facing exposure and lack of street trees makes the space ideal for edibles.

Taking Inventory

In addition to putting her base plan on paper, Dayna had taken inventory of her property. Arlington is in Zone 7. The temperature rarely drops below 10°F in winter; however, it gets hot and humid in summer. The house faces south on a somewhat busy street. There are no street trees to block the sun—a positive factor, in her case, for putting in edibles. Although the soil appeared good, there was a layer of clay about a foot down that required attention. The sloped front lawn was hard to mow and water, and the backyard needed a privacy screen and had poor drainage.

The Want List

Dayna's grown son, Adam, who was living with her at the time, became an integral part of her planning. As a stonemason, he could provide the hardscape and the artistic touches she wanted. Well schooled in environmental science and botany, Dayna made it very clear that there were global issues she wanted to address in her vision for her property:

- Live in a 100 percent organic edible landscape that would inspire others, with ample harvest to share
- Grow flowers for a balanced ecosystem and to attract beneficial insects
- Create wildlife habitat using as many native plants as possible
- Remediate backyard drainage and front lawn issues

In addition she wanted the following features:

- Rain garden
- More welcoming front yard
- Play area for visiting grandchildren
- Compost area
- Patio for entertaining
- Decorative pond
- Privacy from the house behind hers
- One-car garage

Like most of us, Dayna had too many items on her want list. Because of time and budget constraints, Dayna knew that the overall installation would take at least 5 years, probably more. That was reason enough to draw up a plan—so the project could progress in an orderly manner.

Bubble Drawings

Although Dayna is a longtime gardener, she makes no claim to being a designer. Therefore, she chose the time-honored way for working out the best use of her property: making several simple bubble drawings. Her first drawing documented the existing challenges in her yard, showing the problem areas as ovals or circles (hence the name "bubble drawing"). The next two bubble drawings were variations showing different possible layouts incorporating various items from Dayna's want list. Doing two different drawings helped Dayna conceptualize the plan. After looking over each bubble drawing, Dayna listed its pros and cons. Going through this process led her to a final landscape design.

Assessing the Existing Challenges

Starting with a copy of her base plan, Dayna laid a sheet of tracing paper over it and, for the first bubble drawing, circled the existing challenges she determined when she took inventory, as shown in the accompanying illustration.

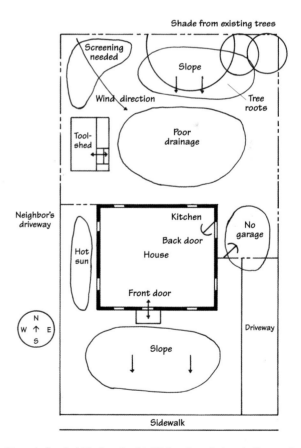

Dayna's first bubble drawing highlights the existing challenges. Rainwater runs downhill toward the house, creating a muddy mess. Backyard trees produce heavy shade and invasive roots. The west side in back needs screening. The sloping front lawn is a nuisance to mow.

Rethinking the Landscape: Dayna's First Go-Round

Working from her want list, Dayna made her first bubble plan (see illustration) and listed all its positive and negative aspects. The major pros were:

- Garage protects the car.
- French drain solves backyard drainage problems.
- Front yard patio provides a sheltered sunny place to sit on cool days.
- Cool patio for midsummer is close to the kitchen with adjacent lawn for children.

And the cons:

- Garage takes up a lot of space and eats up the majority of the landscaping budget.
- Fenced front patio needs a stabilizing retaining wall, zoning regulations may limit the fence height, and the enclosed patio is not a welcoming entry.
- No room exists for even a few fruit trees.

Dayna quickly discovered that her want list and initial bubble drawing needed tweaking. The simple process of listing positives and negatives made her realize she had to make some important changes.

Rethinking the Landscape: Dayna's Second Go-Round

Dayna then made another bubble drawing (see illustration). She could see with a keener eye what would and would not work for her landscape while keeping in mind her greater environmental goals.

Once again Dayna mulled over the plan and wrote out its positive attributes, which in this case were many. In addition to most of her global environmental issues, they included:

- Front yard with edible beds not only solves the problem of a sloped lawn, but eliminates a mowing problem.
- Retaining wall, new steps, and offset front walk update and add style to the property.

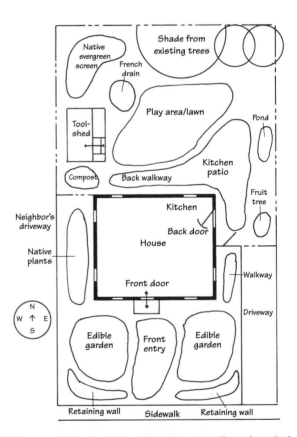

In her first go-round, Dayna included a garage at the end of the driveway, moved the entry walk from the sidewalk to the driveway, and added a small vegetable garden in back and a private patio with a retaining wall and fence as well as a pond in front.

In her second go-round, Dayna kept the entry walkway from the house to the front sidewalk, added a stone retaining wall to contain the slope abutting the sidewalk on both sides of the walk, and created two edible gardens in the front yard—one on each side of the walkway.

Five years after its creation, Dayna's edible landscape is well on its way to becoming her dream garden. Adam's fine stonework adds style: the steps are finished on either side with a decorative stone retaining wall topped by a pedestal. The planting to the left of the stairs includes strawberries, variegated Cuban oregano, the last spring lettuces, young pepper plants, and a young blueberry bush. On the right, two large plantings of strawberries hold the the hill in place, while blueberries, basil, and peppers are off to a good start.

- French drain solves much of the drainage problem, and evergreens in the back left corner help screen the neighbors' houses.
- Backyard walkway allows easy access to compost area from kitchen and helps prevent rainwater from draining under the house.
- Backyard patio is in shade in the heat of the summer, and new pond with waterfall adds to the cooling effect and masks noise from neighbors.

This time, the negative aspects were limited. The few trade-offs were well worth it in Dayna's mind and were ones she could live with:

- Rain garden is out.
- Pond in backyard mandates adult supervision of young children.
- Front yard patio is out.
- Garage is out.

This bubble drawing became the basis of the master plan for Dayna's landscaping project. This process of trying out different approaches is a worthwhile exercise for anyone who is planning a landscape, whether you're working with a professional or on your own. As you can see, you may change your mind about your priorities as you look at the pros and cons.

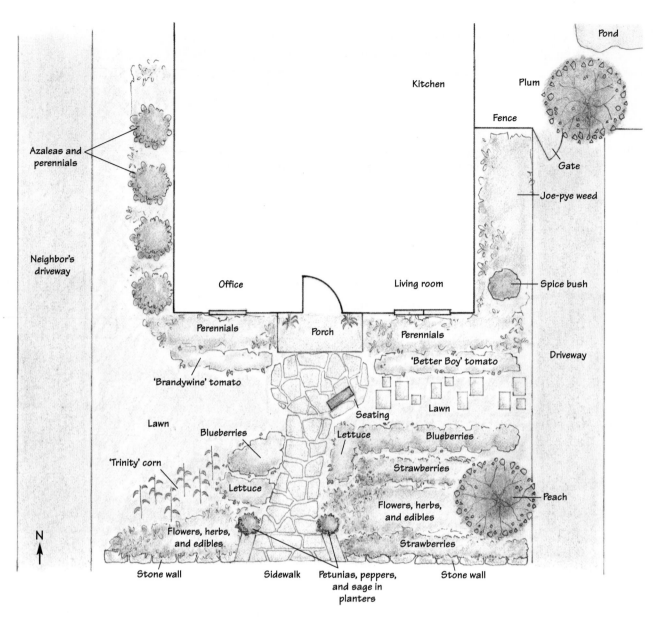

Pond

Kitchen

Plum

Fence

Gate

Azaleas and perennials

Joe-pye weed

Neighbor's driveway

Office

Living room

Spice bush

Perennials

Porch

Perennials

Driveway

'Brandywine' tomato

'Better Boy' tomato

Lawn

Seating

Lawn

Blueberries

Lettuce

Blueberries

'Trinity' corn

Strawberries

Lettuce

Peach

Flowers, herbs, and edibles

Flowers, herbs, and edibles

N

Strawberries

Stone wall

Sidewalk

Petunias, peppers, and sage in planters

Stone wall

The overview of Dayna Lane's front yard shows, starting at street level, the retaining wall that holds the garden in place. Broad, welcoming stairs lead to the offset front walkway. Behind the retaining walls, the slightly sloped beds on either side are now filled with edible plants and flowers to attract beneficial insects. Stepping-stones connect the driveway with the front walkway. A small lawn behind the left bed tapers down to the neighbor's driveway.

When you are making your own bubble drawings, you may find that it takes you five or six tries—or if you're lucky, only two—until you happen on the one that is just right. And remember, nothing is cast in stone; you can always make changes along the way.

The Final Landscape Plan

Dayna's landscape has taken well over 5 years to install and is still evolving. During the first few years, she planted fruit trees with help from her grandchildren: a plum in the backyard by the kitchen and a peach in the

front yard. Dayna removed large sections of grass from the front yard, and the children planted strawberries, mesclun mix, carrots, and flowers. Adam built the stone steps and wall and planted honeydew melons, which flourished in the sunny front beds, as have tomatoes, peppers, basil, and eggplants. The blueberries lining the entry walk and edible beds will eventually grow to form a hedge.

Adam's planned garden wedding motivated him to finish the stonework and the backyard patios. Adam and his bride were married near the pond. The waterfall provided the wedding music, and the flower girl sprinkled colorful petals freshly picked from Dayna's flower garden.

Looking Back

All in all, Dayna is pleased with the changes she and Adam made. If she were starting over, instead of planting northern blueberry varieties, she would plant southern highbush varieties more suited to her sunny, hot front yard. She has yet to harvest more than three ripe peaches because of the abundance of squirrels in her neighborhood. After innumerable tactics to deter the rodents, Dayna is ready to take out the tree. The plum tree, on the other hand, is so full of fruit every summer that she has extra to share with friends, family, and squirrels. Initially, the strawberries produced plentiful berries, but after 4 years, the harvest dwindled and the plants were struggling; it was time to pull them out and add lots of compost to the soil and replant. As Dayna said, "Of course it's a learning process—that's part of gardening."

The Clancy Landscape

Ron and Pam Clancy live in the cool humid climate (Zone 7b) of Vancouver, British Columbia, Canada, where summer temperatures hover in the 70s and winter temperatures rarely dip below 10°F. Their 1950s house is on a corner lot with a small north-facing front yard and a narrow growing strip outside the eastern fence. The house needed an update that included a new drainage system around the perimeter, which would involve major excavation, including digging up most of the backyard. While most people would look on this as a problem, the Clancys saw it as the excuse they needed to renovate a backyard thicket dominated by an overgrown cedar and a dying cherry tree—the chance of a lifetime to put in their dream garden and even add two greenhouses so they could start seedlings and grow some frost-sensitive plants. Ron and Pam both love to garden, and as vegetarians they were motivated to grow lots of edibles.

The Landscape Plan

Once the Clancys decided what they wanted, the project got under way. The contractor brought in a backhoe and removed almost everything from the backyard except the carport and a few shrubs on the west side. They added a deck at the back of the house and designed a sunken greenhouse as a lean-to structure against the back of the house at basement level.

When work on the house was done, Ron and Pam roughed out plans for the paths and laid them out—full-size—on the ground to see how they would look. They chose concrete for the paths as it would offer easy, dry access to every part of the backyard—even in their soggy winters—plus it would be easy to add a raised curb to hold soil in mounded beds. Concrete absorbs heat during the day, raising the ambient soil temperature a few degrees, and it is relatively inexpensive.

When the paths were in place, the contractor poured a slab for the garden greenhouse and built fencing and other vertical structures—an entry arbor, heavy-duty wire trellises along the top of the fence for kiwifruit, support systems for raspberries, and espalier wires and posts for apples. The many vertical structures gave the

A grape arbor welcomes visitors entering from the alley and is flanked by beds of cucumbers, leeks, and flowers—to cut and to attract beneficial insects. Staked tomatoes are in front of a bed with a floating row cover. The Clancys' deck is screened by espaliered apples, providing privacy.

landscape more dimension, and once the plants filled in, they would serve to divide some of the areas into individual garden rooms.

After all the construction, the Clancys were left with subsoil that consisted mostly of sand and rocks, not a recipe for growing great edibles. The next step was to enrich the soil with lots of mushroom compost, work it in, and mound some of the beds. Once the beds were prepared, planting began.

Looking Back

I spoke with Ron and Pam Clancy almost a decade after their landscape renovation. Removing two large trees opened the area to the sun and warmth, and fixing the drainage problems allowed the soil to dry out more quickly. Ron said, "Growing vegetables used to be a struggle. The soil wasn't great, and we had lots of weeds. With the concrete paths, no one steps in the beds, so there is no need to dig and fluff up the soil every planting season." And the beds warm up and are more workable early in the season.

Unlike their former tangle of plants, an abundance of well-grown annuals, perennials, and vines now fill the Clancys' backyard. The greenhouses have been a boon to their productivity. The lean-to lets them enjoy the luxury of fresh bay leaves and citrus. The freestanding greenhouse allows them to start seeds early to get a jump on the season and provides the extra heat that makes all the difference for eggplants, basil, and peppers. Pam loves that they can eat fresh out of the garden throughout the summer, "with ample harvest to put up for winter." And there is still plenty to share with neighbors—especially kiwis.

The Clancys have had a few problems. A peach tree didn't make it, and two apples have been replaced—one with a grapevine and the other with an olive tree.

This view of the Clancy back garden features the long kiwi trellis that sits atop a tall wooden fence. Crosspieces are bolted to the fence posts and wires are strung between the crosspieces to support the heavy vines. In the foreground is an espaliered apple trained on wires that are strung between posts. Cutting flowers fill the rest of the corner and add color to this mostly green scene.

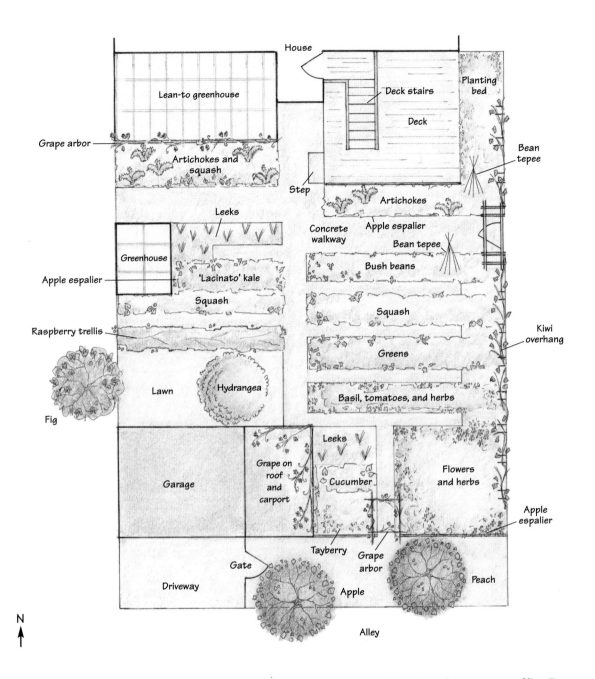

House

Lean-to greenhouse

Grape arbor

Artichokes and squash

Deck stairs

Deck

Planting bed

Bean tepee

Step

Artichokes

Apple espalier

Bean tepee

Leeks

Concrete walkway

Greenhouse

'Lacinato' kale

Bush beans

Apple espalier

Squash

Squash

Raspberry trellis

Greens

Kiwi overhang

Lawn

Hydrangea

Basil, tomatoes, and herbs

Fig

Leeks

Garage

Grape on roof and carport

Cucumber

Flowers and herbs

Apple espalier

Tayberry

Gate

Grape arbor

Peach

Driveway

Apple

N

Alley

The paths are the dominant design feature in the Clancy landscape; their symmetry provides unity and a strong sense of line. Ron and Pam planned generous paths—the main one is 4 feet wide, and smaller ones among the vegetable beds are 18 inches across. Three major trellises support grapes and kiwis, and posts and wire structures support espaliered apple trees. A mini-greenhouse built on a slab on the west side of the yard was positioned so it doesn't block the view of the garden from the new deck.

Pam said that raccoons have been decimating the grapes trained up the carport, and I suggested going to a Mexican grocery store to purchase powdered hot chilies and sprinkling the powder on the ground around the grapevine to discourage the critters.

The changes the Clancys made to their landscape transformed the muddy, dreary space that used to surround their house into an inviting, bounteous area with ample room for them to enjoy year round.

The Close Landscape

Leslie Close and her husband, Chuck, a well-known painter, live part-time in a lovely secluded cottage in Bridgehampton (Zone 6) on the east end of Long Island. When Leslie and Chuck first moved to the property, there was a slope in the front yard that was too steep and windy to plant easily. Initially, Leslie cut the garden into the grade and essentially leveled and lowered it several

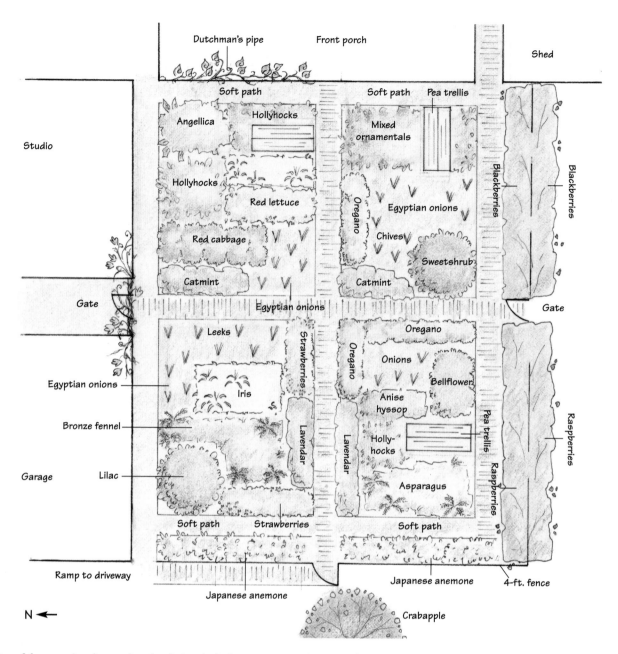

Dutchman's pipe   Front porch   Shed

Soft path   Soft path   Pea trellis

Studio

Angellica   Hollyhocks   Mixed ornamentals

Hollyhocks   Egyptian onions   Blackberries   Blackberries

Oregano

Red lettuce   Chives

Red cabbage   Sweetshrub

Gate   Catmint   Catmint   Gate

Egyptian onions

Egyptian onions   Leeks   Oregano

Oregano

Strawberries   Onions

Bronze fennel   Iris   Bellflower

Anise hyssop

Lavender   Lavendar   Holly-hocks

Garage

Lilac   Pea trellis   Raspberries

Asparagus   Raspberries

Soft path   Strawberries   Soft path

Ramp to driveway   Japanese anemone   4-ft. fence

Japanese anemone

N ←

Crabapple

One of the most time-honored garden designs is the four-square, seen here in Leslie and Chuck Close's front yard, which can work in many styles, formal or informal. Creating the design and connecting the beds with the house are wood walkways, which allow Chuck to access the garden in his wheelchair. The garden abuts the house on one side and the studio and garage on the adjacent side, protecting it from wind. A fence with rabbit wire on the two exposed sides helps keep the critters out.

feet. The front yard garden was a simple four-square design, intersected by paths.

Then in 2002, major house renovations, which included the addition of a wing—with an art studio for Chuck—at a right angle to the front of the house, necessitated removing all the plants from the front yard and replanting them after construction was finished. This was a great opportunity for them to rethink the garden design and make it better fit their needs.

The Landscape Plan

The new wing abutted what had been the north side of the garden, protecting it from winds and keeping it warmer. Leslie added a fence along the unprotected side and the front of the garden to keep marauding critters out. The wood walkways that make the garden wheelchair-accessible for Chuck also complement the wood-shingled house and give structure to the garden. Leslie, also an artist, gave the beds a simple geometric pattern

The view from Leslie and Chuck Close's driveway sets a scene of serenity. This sophisticated garden has evolved through years of knowledgeable editing and loving care, giving it a sense of timelessness. In another month, hollyhocks, which are allowed to grow where they set seed, will add subtle exclamations of color. The weathered wood and the soft hues of the herbs, including bronze fennel and lavender, add to the delicate beauty.

and then pulled all the plantings together by using the many soft greens of the vegetables and herbs, to which she added flowering ornamentals in pastel shades of blue, creamy white, and yellow. The effect is soothing yet lively.

Every year this charming entry garden starts out with a formal look, but by midsummer the lines of the garden disappear with all the overflowing abundance. Leslie loves to cook, so much of what she grows ends up on their plates. The beds overflow with salad greens, peas, leeks, beets, beans, cabbages, and clusters of herbs growing in ever-changing patterns; and perennials abound, strawberries stretch out of their beds, hops cling to the house wall, blackberries grow along the path and screen off the compost pile, and neat rows of asparagus form a filmy backdrop for flowering irises, peonies, and hollyhocks.

Seeds of some of the plants growing in the front entry garden now also grow happily in the meadow in back of their house. Angelica, lemon balm, oregano, and fennel with some added natives, including echinacea and goldenrod, all foster beneficial insects and provide a home for rabbits and other wildlife.

Looking Back

When I caught up with Leslie, she was excited about gardening in her new space. "I can't imagine anything more wonderful to do," she said. "It's spiritual, physical, intellectual, aesthetic, sensual. I feel tied to the basic process of life."

Leslie considers her garden a living scrapbook; each plant has its special memories. Like one of her sources of inspiration, Thomas Jefferson, she maintains a garden journal so she has a record of the garden day by day and year by year. Leslie glories in her exuberant and welcoming front garden—a living and productive work of art.

Now that you've seen what other gardeners have done with their properties—from major tearing out and renovation to updates and additions—you're ready to tackle your own yard. Chapter 4 will take you through the basics of landscape design, and Chapters 5 through 8 will guide you through the details of designing with specific groups of edibles and in small spaces.

4 | Design Basics

Many years ago I participated on a panel for an edible landscaping seminar with several other landscape designers. At that time—with self-centered naiveté—I thought we all approached the subject as I did. I conjure up mental images of how I want a client's landscape to appear, as if I were looking at a series of photographs. I analyze each version, note what part of the design works and what does not, and come up with a final plan.

While two of the designers on the panel used a similar approach, I was surprised that the other two had different methods. One considered himself a kinesthetic designer. His background was in sculpture. As he walked through a client's yard, he "felt" how spaces opened up or closed down and noted the differences in temperatures and fragrances. When he chose materials and plants he was acutely aware of their shapes and textures. He showed a photo of a great undulating bench that worked into a slope and around a patio. He said that the existing space had felt exposed and uninviting; his bench now embraced it. The other designer said she had trouble visualizing a potential garden, so she went to a nursery and moved plants and furniture around until she found a pleasing configuration.

Whichever technique you choose, this chapter will help you design a special place for you and your family and transform a simple food garden into a bountiful edible landscape. Go beyond the visual and include some of the other senses, especially smell and sound. The intoxicating fragrance of ripening strawberries, the buzz of bees pollinating blossoms, and late afternoon breezes swishing through a small stand of bamboo are enthralling. In arid climates especially, a small fountain creates a soothing sound and has the psychological cooling effect of a large lawn. Of course, since this book is about designing with edibles, the sense of taste is all-important.

Preceding pages: This stunning view beckons me to the garden. My potting bench breaks up the expanse of blue wall and holds containers of herbs, handy to the kitchen. *Above*: Establishing a strong line in a garden creates a sense of place. Even wheat has style when grown in arcs rather than straight rows; the circular rows are intriguing. A wheat patch can be designed as a labyrinth or a maze—even a meditation walk.

Design Principles

As a designer, I try to remember two things: First, landscape design is an art, not a science, and—as in any art—the rules are meant to be broken. Second, a healthy plant growing in healthy soil in the right exposure and climate is always a thing of beauty.

Visualize your yard as a three-dimensional, outdoor room. Think of walls, fences, hedges, and planting groups as vertical dividers to create enclosed spaces and privacy. Whether made of concrete, lawn, or ground covers, the interesting and pleasing patterns of the "floor" of the garden provide the surface for various activities. Trees and arbors or trellises covered with vines offer shade and privacy, forming the "ceiling." Circulation patterns are important in outdoor rooms; walks, steps, and ramps provide access for both people and equipment.

The following sections discuss the most important design principles to help you create the garden of your dreams.

Unity

The goal of a good design is to unify a space and to lead the viewer's eye rather than allowing it to dart randomly about the landscape. A unified landscape has defined lines (paths, patios, or raised beds) combined with a thoughtful arrangement of contrasting textures and colors. A yard devoid of unity is simply a hodgepodge or a collection of plants, such as a farmer's orchard or a backyard full of rare fruits that delight the homeowner's palate. I have no argument with collectors' gardens; in fact, I enjoy them and they give pleasure in a thousand ways. But for me, without visual unity you may call it a garden, but it isn't a landscape.

Line

The most important tool in a designer's bag of tricks is the use of line—either to lead the viewer's eye from one place to another or to delineate an area. The line may be totally visible, like a clean-edged brick path, or intermittent, as when broken by lingonberries spilling over the path edge. It may even be invisible—just sensed—as with wild rice growing along the edge of a pond hiding the true hard boundary. Whether the line is visible or sensed, curved or rectangular, or one- or multidimensional, it guides the eye, saying, "follow me."

However, line by itself does not a landscape make. Although stripes down the middle of a highway and rows of vegetables in a field are lines, they have little visual appeal. An eye-pleasing line connects areas, leads to something of interest, or is a noteworthy shape in itself. A cornfield can be pretty boring, but create a spiral path through it, and you have grace and mystery. Is it a labyrinth for meditation or a corn maze? What's at the middle of the spiral? It can be beautiful and magical—a delight for both mind and eye.

You can also create line with the color, texture, and form or shape of plants. A curved line of mounded, frilly-leaved, chartreuse lettuces or a row of upright blueberry shrubs in blazing fall color leads the eye as reliably as a brick path. Spiral, geometric, gently curving, and zigzagging—all purposeful lines have their virtues in a landscape design.

Scale

A good design utilizes relative scale to achieve harmony among plants and the hardscape in proportion to the space they occupy. Remember that plants have different growth patterns and can change radically in appearance over time. A young pine in a 5-gallon container may be perfect in a small yard, but the mature 50-foot

Scale is especially important in small gardens as large plants or ornaments can easily overwhelm the area. Here, a simple container of small-leaved creeping lemon thyme sits atop a miniature column and draws the eye, creating a focal point in a dainty entry garden. 'Blue Wave' petunias bordered with dusty miller surround the column.

tree could overwhelm the space. Gemlike alpine plants stay small and are just right in a jewel-box setting; in a border with larger plants, they are insignificant and overlooked. Even a relatively large lovage plant does nothing to enhance a two-story blank wall, and a small cottage loses its intimate character if 20-foot formal yews grow at its corners.

Scale is also important when choosing garden structures. Massive walls around a small yard make it seem smaller. Likewise, a 3-foot-high white picket fence around a stately colonial house adds little and looks like an afterthought.

Balance

Concentrate on balancing the various elements of your landscape in the areas most commonly seen, such as the view from the street, from your living room or kitchen window, or from your outdoor living area. Imagine a vertical axis through the middle of the area. For a formal landscape, create mirror-image symmetry around this axis. For instance, plant a row of matching shrubs, trees, or planters on either side of the walk or entryway. Clipped hedges, espaliered fruit trees against brick walls, and an allée of shading pecan trees also provide formal balance while giving a sense of stateliness and stability. However, avoid too much repetition of plants and structure, which can make a yard seem stiff and dull.

For an informal space, create a striking asymmetrical, yet pleasing, visual balance of plants and structures. For example, a wide cluster of shrubs or a gazebo can balance a large tree, and an ample swath of ground cover can balance a large section of patio. Informal balance gives a feeling of movement and interest. However, too much movement can produce an agitated, confused feeling.

Simplicity

When designing a landscape, I always err on the side of simplicity, as the natural course of a garden is to get more and more complex. We all tend to add to a garden rather than subtract; if you start with a simple, disciplined design and elaborate it over time, the final result will be a joy, not a jumble.

Certain plants or interesting structures and decorative gates or pottery are intended to stand out in the landscape, and the limited use of such accents adds variety. Plants used as accents (interest plants) usually have some outstanding feature—the graceful, pendulous form of a weeping 'Santa Rosa' plum, the brilliant spring display of white flowers on a pear tree, or the bright fall foliage of a serviceberry. But be careful: too many stunning plants and dramatic urns and birdbaths competing for attention can bring more chaos than comfort.

When I was a child, my grandmother had a friend called Mrs. Johnson. Whenever Mrs. Johnson went out,

Go Formal or Informal

Designers use a variety of strategies to achieve formality or informality. Here are a few tips for planning your own garden:

FORMAL

- ◆ Create beds with geometric shapes.
- ◆ Install straight or circular paths, with intersections to draw the eye in.
- ◆ Use brick, stone, or stucco walls or tall clipped hedges (for example, currant, barberry, viburnum, or citrus) to surround the garden or serve as a backdrop.
- ◆ Edge each bed with clipped low-growing plants, such as dwarf boxwood, rosemary, germander, or dwarf English lavender.
- ◆ Place one or more plants of the same variety in the same location in each bed to tighten the design.
- ◆ Line paths with brick or stone on sand, gravel, or lawn grasses.
- ◆ Draw the eye in with one or two focal points (plants in containers, birdbaths, statuary, topiary, showy edibles with unusual

foliage, or espaliered fruit) in the center of the garden, at the end of long paths, or in the middle of each bed.

INFORMAL

- ◆ Create beds with free-form shapes.
- ◆ Impart an overall sense of abundance by planting herbs and flowers close enough so the mature plants will rub shoulders.
- ◆ Interplant vegetables and annual herbs with loose, heirloom varieties of flowers in a range of colors.
- ◆ Line paths with shredded bark, wood chips, compost, or indigenous stone.
- ◆ Allow self-seeding annual vegetables, herbs, and flowers to come up in beds and then remove ones you don't want (edit the plants).
- ◆ Break up long borders with a few creeping herbs planted along the edges of the paths.

In Amy Goldman's Rhinebeck, New York, garden, hardy kiwi vines cover a large formal pergola that separates the stepped herb garden from the lawn and back garden. The symmetry of large sedums, petunias, and matching containers on each side of the steps reflects classic formality. Fieldstone walls, steps, and columns repeated throughout the garden unify the space, and the clipped boxwood tightens the effect.

she would wear a large hat with flowers, a colorful scarf, two or three bracelets, numerous strings of beads, a polka-dot blouse, and, of course, lace gloves. When I was tempted to overdress, my grandmother would admonish me with, "That's too much Johnson!" The temptation we all have is to use too many interest plants and have a yard with "too much Johnson."

Formal and Informal Design

Landscape designs are generally categorized as formal or informal (aka naturalistic). A formal garden has a strong sense of order and control. It includes at least some of these elements: strong geometric lines, symmetry, closely clipped hedges, topiary, precision-cut lawn, straight paths, neat flowering plants with no spent flower heads, deep green foliage, geometrically espaliered fruits, or classical statuary and fountains. A formal design requires a considerable amount of time and energy to maintain.

An informal garden incorporates free-flowing lines, asymmetry, and plants growing in their natural forms. Billowing plants may intermix and spill over the boundaries, softening the lines. A few controlled elements, such as well-placed clipped hedges or a swath of manicured lawn—even an occasional geometric bed—contrast nicely with the loose lines. Fallen leaves on the ground, large blowsy shrubs with room for a bird's nest, and a few seed heads here and there are all at home in this type

This informal, cottage-style bed showcases an interplanting of herbs surrounding two hardy kiwi vines trained on the portico over an entry to Sooke Harbour House, a 3-acre resort located on Vancouver Island in British Columbia. Its five-star restaurant takes full advantage of the gardens, in which almost every plant is edible.

of garden. Even a few chewed leaves are forgiven. An informal design begets a more laissez-faire, less labor-intensive style.

Levels: Creating Dimension

Imagine two gardens with the same plant material—all sorts of wonderful edibles. In the first landscape, everything is planted on level ground. Like driving on a flat, straight road, the effect is tedious. Now, picture the second garden with a planter or two, a small gazebo, some trellises, and raised vegetable beds. These different levels make it more dynamic and inviting.

There are several methods for adding dimension. The simplest is to incorporate a variety of containers in different sizes, either clustered or integrated into the landscape. Container sizes, shapes, and materials as well as placement are virtually limitless. You can create dis-

tinct levels with steps that take you from one area to another, or install large planter boxes to add drama. And don't forget about window boxes; they draw the eye to yet another level.

Raised beds not only add a level but are ideal for edibles. Those of us who are not as flexible as we once were can easily plant, weed, and harvest plants in raised beds. In addition, each bed can be custom filled with soil that works best for the specific plants you want to grow. In cold-winter regions, you get a head start on planting because in spring raised beds warm up more quickly than the surrounding soil.

Other Considerations

In addition to the design principles discussed above, there are other design approaches that can be used to create appealing edible landscapes—in all seasons.

Consider the Off-Season

Since gardening year round is not possible in most areas, it's important to consider what the landscape looks like in the off-season when it is not burgeoning with edible bounty. That's when the hardscape—the bones of the garden—really comes into play, adding vitality to the dormant landscape. Be sure to include distinct geometric shapes or curving lines that are impressive on their own. In areas with long winters, evergreens—especially those with blue or bronze foliage—add color to an otherwise bleak landscape. Form and shape take center stage in cold-winter areas as well as regions where scorching summer is the dormant season. Include a small arbor or a raised area for a bird-bath; the shapes of the beds also add interest. An off-season edible landscape is much more interesting than the typical ornamental plot with brown lawn and a few foundation shrubs.

Unify with a Theme

Many designers use a theme as a unifying force to pull landscape elements together, especially to harmonize with the architecture of the house. The theme may be cultural (French or Spanish style), horticultural (featuring native plants or collections of exotic edibles), or functional (oriented around an entertaining area or a specialized food-production garden). While ornamental themes, such as native flowering plants or a collec-

tion of hydrangeas, have many devotees, remember that I'm addressing edible themes that span a wide range of possibilities—limited only by your taste and budget.

Harmonize with Surroundings

Well-designed landscapes are in harmony with the surrounding land. When visiting Las Vegas, I found it very unsettling to see elaborate gardens—replete with lawn and clipped hedges—that ended abruptly against desert scrub. The goal is a graceful transition between the landscaped property and its environs regardless of the character of those surroundings.

The great Italian and Asian landscape designers took advantage of their surroundings, incorporating the views into their designs, thus the term "borrowed landscape." For example, if there is a venerable cherry tree on a neighboring property, include it in the design. The same holds true for a view of some dusky hills in the distance; borrowing objects from surrounding areas draws the viewer out of the immediate vicinity, making a small garden appear larger. Integrate the borrowed feature into the landscape by leading the eye to it with a path or expanse of lawn or other lines.

Sun and shadow impart their own special qualities to a landscape. As the sun travels through the sky, it highlights different objects. High noon produces the harshest lighting, whereas early morning and late afternoon light are magical. The soft golden tones of morning

Author Suzy Bales' glorious moon gate transforms a simple orchard space into an invitation to stroll and enjoy the glories of a Long Island spring. The center of the rounded gate focuses your eye on the star of the moment—the apple blossoms. The carpet of spring-blooming flowers broadens the garden's appeal.

Again the moon gate performs its magic, this time in winter. Its sculptural shape, made even more dramatic by a dusting of snow, begs you to focus on the drama found in the bones of the landscape. The shadows on the snow and the bare branches of espaliered apples contrast with the snowy white scene.

This backyard seating area next to the energy-saving dark-bottomed swimming pool is in Arizona but would be lovely anywhere. Yet it's the borrowed landscape—the hills—that makes it absolutely breathtaking, an inspiration to swim more laps. Note that the homeowners planted the fig where it does not obstruct the view.

sun streaming through the translucent chartreuse leaves of a persimmon tree in spring have a memorable charm, as does the sun setting through the bare branches of a butternut tree and tracing designs in shadows on snow or lawn in late afternoon in winter.

Add the Element of Surprise

An optional—yet fun—element to consider is surprise. Meandering paths and hidden views pique a person's interest and curiosity. Add a treat at the end of a path, say, a circle of dwarf fruit trees where children can hide, and you have a delightful surprise. A scarecrow made of terra-cotta pots is whimsical, and not at all what one expects a scarecrow to be—plus it lasts far longer than its straw counterpart.

Guidelines for Edible Plant Selection

Your choice of plants is determined by local growing conditions. These questions are addressed within each entry in the Encyclopedia. (For non-edible, ornamental plants, the best guides are specialized reference books, your local Cooperative Extension Service, or a well-informed local nursery.) When choosing the plants, ask yourself: first, does the plant produce something I actually want to eat and, second, what does the plant look like (size, form, leaf texture, and color)?

Size

The single biggest mistake all garden designers make—professionals and amateurs alike—is underestimating the eventual size of plants, especially in foundation plantings. Plants can quickly cover windows or look completely out of scale for the space. That innocent walnut tree you purchased in its little container can shoot up to 30 feet tall before you know it, shading everything around it.

Conversely, a fully grown plant might prove too small to serve its intended purpose. Common quince, for example, rarely grows tall enough to shade the south wall of a two-story house. Therefore, it is important to consider the probable growth habits of plants—both height and width—before making your final selections.

Form

Form (shape) is the most obvious characteristic of most plants. The most common form among woody edible plants is rounded, like that of apples, almonds, peaches, persimmons, and citrus. Another typical shape is upright, as seen in currants, raspberries, bamboos, ginger, and pears. Some plants, such as pomegranates, highbush blueberries, and certain types of plums, are rather vase or fountain shaped, while others, including thyme, lowbush blueberries, and cranberries, have a matlike form. Thoughtful pruning accentuates the generalized plant shape. Prune a plum tree to highlight its natural vase shape or shear a citrus to make it completely round.

Some plants, both edible and purely ornamental, are considered interest plants (also called accent or specimen plants) for their striking form alone. Included among these attention-grabbers are the pawpaw with its pyramidal form, and an old fig tree or grapevine with its gnarled appearance. Such forms dominate the area where they grow; give them ample space so they can be enjoyed as the focal points they deserve to be.

Texture

Texture describes the coarseness or fineness of a plant—the size and shape of the leaves and the spacing between them. Big, bold banana leaves, which often grow more than 6 feet long, and dainty, narrow, ½-inch-long fernlike leaves of asparagus, with their almost wispy appearance, exemplify the two texture extremes. Fine-textured plants work particularly well in small gardens. Coarse-textured plants, which give a bold look and substance, make a superb foil for large structures. They are also associated with a tropical look.

Color

Color is the most versatile design tool for an edible landscape; inexpensive and, unlike concrete patios or wooden arbors, color doesn't require a large commitment of time, money, skilled labor, or building inspections. If I don't like the look of lots of red flowers and yellow containers, I simply change the dominant colors for the next season and go with another combination.

Plants add color to the landscape in a variety of ways—multihued flowers, showy fruit, or vivid seasonal foliage—but only for a relatively short period. The leaves, in every hue and intensity of green, help tie the design together—from the rich deep green of strawberry leaves through the bright light green of lettuce to the gray-green of sage. Green becomes the neutral color against which you see all the other colors in a landscape. The possibilities are almost limitless. For example, you can choose between the gray-green herbs and members of the blue-green cabbage family or the celebratory yellow-greens of endives and fruit trees in spring to unify your different colors.

After choosing the basic foliage hues, add colors with trees, shrubs, and herbaceous plants that bloom at different times of the year. I limit myself to two or three basic colors in simultaneous bloom; other gardeners like a full palette, a riot of many colors. It's all about individual taste.

Edible Plants for All Your Landscape Needs

Once you have determined the structures and paving surfaces, you are ready to choose the plants. Herein lies the true subtlety of the landscaper's art. The first step is to make a list of edibles you like most and that grow well in your climate. As you take stock of them, note their cultural needs (sun versus shade, moist or dry soil). Be aware of their overall form; the size, shape, and color of their foliage; and the flowers or fruit they produce (if any).

Go online to find out, for example, if that apple variety you like comes in different sizes. Perhaps you will

Working with Color

For well over two decades, my muralist friend Marcie Hawthorne has been sharing her extensive knowledge of color. I've taken some of her ideas and come up with theories of my own while creating gardens. Here are a few of our observations:

- Decide whether you want subdued tones or intense bright shades.
- For a soft romantic look, combine subtle pastel-colored blooms with silver-leaved plants, or emphasize white flowers.
- To create energy and richness in a garden, use complementary colors (opposite each other on the color wheel)—purple and yellow, blue and orange, or red and green.
- For a calm and restful effect, consider a monochromatic color scheme (variations on a single hue adjacent on the color wheel), such as pink and maroon.
- Try to limit your color choices to three—plus green.
- Create a sense of place by using traditional color combinations, like pastel colors for England (from its cottage gardens), yellow and rich blue for France, and the many shades of greens as well as burgundy foliage for the Pacific Northwest. For a southwestern feel, look to the warm sunset colors of orange and yellow; add some blue or lavender to represent the early evening sky.
- Restate plant or flower color with another element: a colorful chair or trellis, a fancy enamel container or two, painted wooden stakes, or rusty old buckets. Live dangerously: paint your old white picket fence a cheery deep yellow to add panache.

Always on the lookout for new and creative ways to design with edible plants, I purchased an inexpensive wood trellis, sawed off the legs, painted it, laid it on the ground, and transplanted a young Bibb lettuce into each square. This little area stopped traffic when visitors came up my main walk; everyone wanted a closer look.

My favorite color combinations are deep blue, bright red, and silver; plum with chartreuse and peach; pink, lavender, and light yellow; burgundy and coral; and plum, bright red-orange, and yellow. But remember, the only person you really have to please is yourself.

Learn more about the subtleties of working with color from Kevin McCloud's books, in particular, *Choosing Colours*.

Vegetable gardens transform into elegant parterres when you incorporate design principles. At The Digger's Club Nursery near Melbourne, Australia, 'Ruby' chard, savoy cabbages, basil, and parsley intermingle with red salvia and yellow marigolds. Note the arrangement of six triangular beds around the focal statue. Finely textured grass contrasts with large-leaved chard and cabbages, creating dynamic lines. Using mostly red and green (opposites on the color wheel), with yellow as an accent, tightly unifies the garden and results in a vibrant landscape.

come upon a new introduction with similar fruit and gorgeous flowers. Plant breeders are becoming much more aware of edibles in landscaping and are adding new varieties.

Be sure to note the mature size of the plants you are considering. If, like many people, your sense of garden space is a bit off, place a hose or string on the ground to mark the boundary of a full-grown plant in its intended space. Have someone hold a pole or broom in the air to indicate how tall the plant will grow; then step back and see if it really fits in. You may need to update your plant list. Then consider the final look of the garden. These tips can help you make the best choices:

- To counteract the somber effect of plants with dark green or gray leaves (especially near a gray or dark-colored house), add a few plants with bright green

foliage and/or ones with variegated leaves. Also, consider edibles with bright fall foliage and/or vibrant fruit.

- Limit lots of large-leaved plants to sizeable areas or a garden with a tropical theme. But keep in mind that a few big plants can add drama. For example, a triangular planting of 'Giant Purple' mustard around a fountain or a dwarf banana in a large container delights the eye.

- Select a few favorite plants and use them in quantity to tie a planting together.

- Set off a special plant with adjacent plantings of contrasting form and/or foliage color. Make a dark-leaved plum a more striking focal point with a large planting of lime-colored or variegated herbs in front of it. Emphasize a showy green and white variegated elderberry with a tightly clipped hedge of medium green boxwood. Contrast always adds drama.

- Look through magazines and books for design inspiration. Get ideas from a walk or drive around your neighborhood; check out other people's yards.

Of course, you can always choose to grow inedible rhododendrons with your blueberries and cranberries, or plant inedible red salvia beside your dwarf apple. Innumerable combinations of inedible ornamentals and edibles are possible. My goal is to convince you to plan for edibles first and then find ornamentals that thrive in similar conditions.

The following sections describe categories of plants based on their landscaping uses, with lists of suitable edibles. These lists are not all-inclusive; see the entries in the Encyclopedia and Appendix A for the complete range.

Although I won't be discussing strictly ornamental plants, I know you'll want to include some. There are multitudes of sources showing which ornamentals to use in each category.

Ground Covers

Ground covers are low-growing plants used to cover fairly large areas. Some, like chamomile, grow only to 6 inches or so and creep along the ground. They generally are grown between stepping-stones to allow for weeding and walking. Others, like lowbush blueberry and trailing rosemary, grow from a foot to 3 or 4 feet tall and form undulating mounds.

Use all ground covers as substitutes for an entire lawn or portions of the lawn. Include edible ground covers on slopes where mowing is difficult and water runs off, or among trees and shrubs where lawn grows poorly. Some, like alpine strawberries, creeping mint, oca, sweet woodruff, and wintergreen, tolerate or prefer some shade. With the exception of chamomile, which takes light foot traffic, none of the edible ground covers can be walked on.

Choose from among the many following edible species of ground covers:

Alpine strawberry	*Peanut (temporary cover)*
Blueberry (lowbush)	*Rosemary (trailing types)*
Chamomile	*Sweet potato (temporary cover)*
Cranberry	
Lingonberry	*Sweet woodruff*
Mint (creeping types)	*Thyme*
Natal plum (dwarf)	*Wintergreen*
Oca	

Safety First: Know What Not to Eat

Before you start, remember that when you are growing food plants in your landscape and eating food straight from the plant, you must be aware of the poisonous ornamentals. I teach children in my garden to always check with an adult before eating something from the yard. Know that *parts of* some edible plants are poisonous—rhubarb leaves and potato leaves, for instance. Check the Encyclopedia for specific information on each plant, and please, **never eat anything you can't identify as safe and edible.**

Common Poisonous Ornamentals

COMMON NAME	BOTANICAL NAME
Azalea	*Rhododendron* spp.
Bleeding heart	*Dicentra* spp.
Boxwood	*Buxus* spp.
Buttercup family (anemone, clematis, delphinium, ranunculus)	Ranunculaceae
Castor bean	*Ricinus communis*
Cherry laurel	*Prunus laurocerasus*
Daffodil	*Narcissus* spp.
Daphne	*Daphne* spp.
Foxglove	*Digitalis* spp.
Hydrangea	*Hydrangea* spp.
Ivy	*Hedera* spp.
Lantana	*Lantana* spp.
Lily-of-the-valley	*Convallaria majalis*
Mountain laurel	*Kalmia latifolia*
Oleander	*Nerium oleander*
Privet	*Ligustrum* spp.
Ranunculus	*Ranunculus* spp.
Rhododendron	*Rhododendron* spp.
Sweet pea	*Lathyrus* spp.
Vinca (periwinkle, myrtle)	*Vinca* spp.
Wisteria	*Wisteria* spp.
Yew	*Taxus* spp.

Herbaceous Borders

Include herbaceous border plants in a perennial or annual border; they combine well with both flowering and foliage plants. Such borders are especially beautiful next to walks, driveways, walls, and patios, where you can appreciate the plants up close. You can also use these versatile edibles to break up large expanses of lawn or ground cover.

The edibles listed below are fairly easy to incorporate without changing a conventional border planting:

Alpine strawberry
Amaranth
Angelica
Anise hyssop
Artichoke
Arugula (perennial)
Asparagus
Basil
Beet
Borage
Broccoli
Cabbage
Cantaloupe (bush)
Cardoon

Celery
Chamomile (German)
Chard (colorful ones)
Chives
Collards
Corn
Cucumber (bush or on trellis)
Edible flowers
Eggplant
Endive
Escarole
Fennel
Kale

Lavender
Lettuce
Licorice
Lovage
Marjoram
Mitsuba
Mizuna
Mustard
Nasturtium
Okra
Orach
Oregano
Papaloquelite
Parsley
Pea
Peanut

Pepper
Poppy (breadseed)
Rhubarb
Rosemary
Safflower
Sage
Scented geranium
Sea kale
Shallot
Shungiku
Squash (summer)
Tarragon (Mexican)
Tomato (bush types)
Yacon

In Hayefield—her Bucks County, Pennsylvania, garden—garden designer Nancy Ondra created two colorful beds that combine edibles with traditional ornamentals and border a handsome gravel path. The repeating patterns of 'Bull's Blood' beet, curly parsley, and 'Lemon Gem' marigold give rhythm to the space. Also featured are 'Golden Delicious' pineapple sage as well as 'Yellow Pear' and 'Sweet 100' tomatoes.

Shrub Borders

Plants in this category are generally compact; most are woody shrubs that don't die down in winter, such as blueberries, but a few are leafy herbaceous plants like rhubarb. For the most impact, choose plants that include a diversity of foliage types and colors. Utilize them—if short enough—in a foundation planting, or combine them with ground covers. Create islands of shrubbery surrounded by lawn.

These edible plants work well in a shrub border—next to a walkway, woodland, or driveway:

Apple (dwarf)   *Natal plum*
Artichoke   *Pineapple guava*
Blueberry   *Pomegranate*
Bush cherry   *Quince (flowering)*
Bush plum   *Salal*
Cardoon   *Sea berry*
Citrus (dwarf)   *Sweet bay*
Currant   *Tea*
Gooseberry

While visiting the Alaska State Fair in Palmer, I sought out the permanent edible demonstration garden. I was excited to see all sorts of edible plants that would be perfect for an informal hedge: blueberry bushes, black and white currants, many different gooseberry varieties, and especially a lot of showy red currants, like those pictured here.

Hedges

A hedge is defined as a continuous, closely spaced line of one type of plant, which creates a boundary around a property or defines a specific area. Use a hedge to screen a view, create a barrier, or direct the eye toward a major focal point like a statue. It can be either sheared or unsheared.

A sheared hedge is a formation of plants pruned to a definite geometrical shape and usually associated with a formal landscape. Such hedges can be used as borders or barriers. (An edible hedge plant that is heavily clipped yields much less fruit.)

An informal hedge should not be sheared; instead, prune it lightly. Thin out stems and head back wayward branches to encourage the plant to develop its natural form. Use unclipped hedges to define boundaries, for windbreaks, or as privacy screens. In addition, you can utilize trees, such as carob, filbert, or full-size citrus, as large hedges.

Choose from the following edibles for hedges:

SHEARED HEDGES

Bush cherry   *Rosemary (upright*
Carob   *varieties)*
Citrus   *Salal*
Filbert   *Surinam cherry*
Natal plum   *Sweet bay*
Olive   *Tea*
Pineapple guava

UNSHEARED HEDGES

Apple (dwarf)   *Gooseberry*
Asparagus   *Pomegranate*
Bamboo   *Quince*
Beach plum   *Rose (hip-forming*
Blueberry   *varieties)*
Bush cherry   *Rosemary (upright*
Bush plum   *varieties)*
Citrus (dwarf)   *Salal*
Currant   *Surinam cherry*
Elderberry   *Sweet bay*
Tea

Barrier and Boundary Plants

Barrier and boundary plants are dense, compact shrubs—some thorny—that are used to define boundary lines or to divert traffic from an area. Once thorny plantings are established, they are impenetrable, even by dogs and children. Choose your edible barrier and boundary plants from the list below:

THORNLESS BARRIERS

Bamboo   *Pineapple guava*
Carob   *Rosemary (upright*
Elderberry   *varieties)*
Mandarin orange   *Salal*
Orange

Rugosa roses perform triple duty: they make a formidable barrier against intruders, provide vibrant pink roses that perfume the air, and set showy orange hips, as shown here, that are packed with vitamin C and make fantastic tea and jelly.

THORNY BARRIERS

Brambleberry
Gooseberry
Lemon
Lime
Natal plum
Prickly pear
Rose (hip-forming varieties)

Foundation Plants

For eons, the plantings adjacent to and nearby houses and barns overflowed with useful plants such as rhubarb, berry bushes, and culinary and medicinal herbs. In America in the twentieth century, foundation plantings—mostly of non-edible evergreens—became the pervasive style that was used to disguise a raised foundation. Unfortunately, this type of landscaping became so insidious that it led to abuses, including poorly chosen plants that grow to 20 feet tall, obliterating the house, or equally inferior choices that resemble a boring mustache of similar shrubs.

A properly chosen foundation plant is a shrub, large perennial, or small tree used to soften the right angles of a house and highlight the front door. Intermix deciduous and evergreen shrubs to give the planting a pleasing form in winter. Choose from among the edibles listed below:

DECIDUOUS

Artichoke
Blueberry
Bush cherry
Currant
Gooseberry
Rhubarb
Rose (hip-forming varieties)
Surinam cherry

EVERGREEN

Chilean guava
Natal plum
Rosemary
Salal
Sweet bay
Tea

Vines and Climbers

Climbers generally have long vigorous stems that wend their way upward by twining around a support or by sending out tendrils to hold themselves up. Use these plants to cover fences, arbors, and trellises; filter the sun's glare; shade a south- or west-facing wall; or provide privacy for outdoor living. In addition, edible plants with pliable limbs, which are usually considered freestanding trees, such as figs and citrus, function in the same way when trained over or along an arbor.

Annual climbers, primarily warm-season plants, are valuable temporary privacy screens, hiding the view from the street or a neighbor's condominium patio. Combine them with magenta morning glories or red-flowered cardinal vines to give more color and attract hummingbirds. Use flexible materials as a sling to support large fruits such as squash and pumpkins.

The following edible plants can be trained on a trellis or arbor:

ANNUAL VINES AND CLIMBERS

Bean (pole)

Bitter melon

Cantaloupe (vining types)

Chayote

Cucumber (vining types)

Hyacinth bean

Jicama

Malabar spinach

Nasturtium (vining types)

Pea (vining types)

Pumpkin (small- and medium-fruited types best)

Runner bean

Squash (vining types; small- and medium-fruited types best)

Tomato (indeterminate types, especially cherry tomatoes)

PERENNIAL VINES AND CLIMBERS

Grape

Hops

Kiwi

Passion fruit

Screens and Windbreaks

Plant a tree or shrub with dense foliage and a relatively large growth habit as a screen to block a view or as a windbreak. Site it to divert winter winds or funnel summer breezes into windows or across a patio area. Both deciduous and evergreen plants can be used in this way. For small screens, see the "Hedges" section earlier in this chapter. The following edible plants are suitable for large screens and windbreaks:

Bamboo

Carob

Cherry

Chestnut

Citrus

Elderberry

Hickory

Loquat

Mango

Maple

Scarlet runner beans are graceful and productive plants—perfect edible ornamentals. A dark green trellis supports them in my front entry garden. When I grow them, I usually include other red-flowered plants to highlight the runner beans' bright blossoms. Enjoy the crunchy flowers, fresh young beans, or dried beans.

Olive

Pecan

Pineapple guava

Pine nut

Pomegranate

Sea grape

Sweet bay

Walnut

Hedgerows

Traditionally, people planted untrimmed hedgerows (a mixture of trees and shrubs) to separate or define fields or property. Edibles planted in classic hedgerows provide food for people as well as sustenance and welcome shelter for native and migratory birds, insects, and small mammals. Thick shrubs and low-branching fruiting trees are the most suitable. Create a habitat by including a few evergreens for winter protection, thorny plants for security from predators, and native shrubs to attract resident pollinators. The following plants produce edible fruit and grow well when planted in clusters or rows; as a bonus, most are easy to maintain:

Beach plum
Bush cherry
Chestnut
Cornelian cherry
Crabapple
Elderberry
Juniper
Loquat
Medlar
Mulberry
Nanking cherry
Olive
Pawpaw
Persimmon (American)
Pineapple guava
Pomegranate
Quince (flowering)
Rose (hip-forming
    varieties)
Sea berry
Sea grape
Serviceberry
Strawberry tree

Many edible plants—such as native serviceberry, elderberry, and beach plum—are good choices for a hedgerow, offering ample edibles for people and wildlife. Add sea berry, a hardy shrub from Central Asia, to your list. A striking plant with narrow silver leaves, it bears huge sprays of highly nutritious gold berries in fall.

Espaliers

The art of espalier creates living sculptures in the landscape. Espalier is a pruning method in which a plant is trained to grow in a single plane—usually flat against a building, trellis, or other structure but sometimes as a freestanding screen or hedge. You can train the branches to a formal geometric shape or leave them in an informal pattern. This technique is most often used with woody plants—trees and shrubs—and it can be used with vines, as well. Most fruit trees can be trained in this fashion.

If you plan to espalier, be aware that it requires extra effort. Espaliers are particularly valuable for small gardens and limited spaces, where they can serve as screens or focal points. See Chapter 7 for information on how to use espaliers and to see a variety of shapes. The following edible plants are well suited to be espaliered:

Almond
Apple
Apricot
Cherry
Citrus
Currant
Fig
Gooseberry
Grape
Loquat
Nectarine
Olive
Peach
Pear
Persimmon
Pineapple guava
Plum
Pomegranate
Quince
Surinam cherry
Tea

Large Trees

I classify a tree as large if it grows to at least 30 feet tall. Such trees are excellent for providing summer shade and lending a stately feeling to large yards and woodland areas. The following large trees produce edible fruits, nuts, or leaves:

Avocado
Butternut
Cherry
Chestnut
Hickory
Mango
Pecan
Pine nut
Pistachio
Sweet bay
Walnut

Lawn Trees

Lawn trees are deep rooted, so they are tolerant of lawn irrigation and don't compete for moisture and fertilizer. Few trees are suitable as they must have a clean habit; debris from trees that routinely shed leaves, seed heads, flowers, or bark could smother the underlying grass. Shade from lawn trees should be light or dappled enough so grass can grow beneath them. Most fruit trees do not perform well in a lawn because they cannot compete for water and nutrients and are prone to diseases if nicked by a mower or trimmer. The following trees grow fairly well in a lawn and produce an edible treat for the kitchen:

Jujube
Maple

Colorful Fall Foliage

After a long hot summer, the greenery of many trees and shrubs loses its vibrancy; the leaves have a tired green appearance. As the days begin to cool and fall is in the air, it is refreshing to see bold color return; some trees, shrubs, and vines put on a spectacular show, their foliage turning from green to many shades of yellow, orange, and red. The fall foliage on the following edibles enlivens your garden as well as providing for your table:

Apricot	*Medlar*
Blueberry	*Pear (some varieties)*
Fig	*Persimmon*
Gooseberry	*Pomegranate*
Grape	*Serviceberry*
Maple	*Walnut*

Interest Plants

An interest plant (sometimes called a specimen or accent plant) is one with a particularly striking form, foliage, flowers, or fruit, making it an effective focal point. Some plants, such as fig or grape, are attention grabbing throughout all four seasons. Others have the potential to be interest plants if pruned in a special way, such as an espalier, or if a special variety with unusual foliage is chosen or the plant has colorful fruit produced over a fairly long season. Some of the showiest edibles are listed here:

PLANT	INTEREST
All espaliered plants	*Form*
Apricot	*Flowers, fruit, fall foliage*
Artichoke	*Form, gray foliage*
Bamboo	*Form*
Banana	*Dramatic leaves and form*
Bush plum	*White flowers, red fruit*
Cherry	*White flowers, red fruit, interesting bark*

'Fuyu' persimmon is among the most beautiful edible plants. Chartreuse leaves in spring turn orange in the fall, followed by deep orange fruits in early winter. Unlike many persimmon varieties, 'Fuyu' flesh is sweet and crisp when the fruit first ripens. Weeks later when the flesh softens, I use the fruit in smoothies and persimmon pudding.

PLANT	INTEREST
Citrus	*Fragrant flowers, fruit*
Currant (some varieties)	*Red fruit*
Fig	*Dramatic leaves and gnarled form*
Grape	*Form, fall color*
Hops (gold variety)	*Leaves*
Japanese plum	*Coral flowers*
Jujube	*Weeping form*
Kiwi	*Leaf pattern, form*
Loquat	*Dramatic form, fuzzy leaves, fruit*
Lotus	*Dramatic leaves, pink flowers*
Medlar	*White flowers, foliage, fall color*
Mulberry (some varieties)	*Weeping form*
Natal plum	*White flowers, red fruit*
Olive	*Gray foliage, gnarled form*
Persimmon	*Spring and fall foliage, orange fruit, bark*
Pineapple	*Dramatic succulent*
Pineapple guava	*Magenta flowers, gray foliage, bark*
Plum (weeping or red-leaved varieties)	*Form or wine red leaf color*
Pomegranate	*Red flowers, fall foliage, red fruit*
Prickly pear	*Yellow or pink flowers, sculptured form, fruit*

Many tropical edibles—including lemongrass, a popular ingredient in South Asian curries—will grow in North America. Plant lemongrass in containers; in cold-winter climates bring it indoors before the first autumn frost.

PLANT	INTEREST
Rosemary	Form, blue flowers
Sea berry	Silver foliage, orange fruit
Sea grape	Dramatic leaves and form
Sea kale	Dramatic form, gray leaves
Serviceberry	White flowers, fall foliage

Tropical and Other Tender Edibles

These plants are valuable for gardeners in tropical and semi-tropical climates as well as for those in colder climates who want to use the large dramatic leaves and form to give a tropical style to the garden or greenhouse.

The following edibles are all quite tender (hardy in Zones 10 and 11) and require protection in the winter:

Avocado	Lemongrass
Bamboo	Litchi
Banana	Loquat
Carambola	Mango
Chayote	Medlar
Cherimoya	Monstera
Citrus	Papaya
Coconut palm	Pepino
Date palm	Pineapple
Fig	Sea grape
Galangal	Surinam cherry
Ginger	Taro
Hoja santa	

Flowering Edibles

Flowering plants, with their showy displays, are often used as interest plants. Each of the plants listed here is edible and produces showy blooms; the flower colors recorded for each are the most common for that particular plant. (Note that inclusion on this list does not indicate that the flowers themselves are edible; see the "Edible Flowers" section later in this chapter for information on edible flowers.)

PLANT	FLOWER COLOR
Almond	White, pink
Apple	White, pink
Apricot	White, pink
Artichoke	Lavender
Bean (some varieties)	White, purple, red
Blueberry	White, pink
Borage	Blue, white
Bush cherry	White, pink
Bush plum	White, pink
Caper	Pink, white
Cardoon	Lavender
Cherry	White
Chestnut	White
Chives	Lavender, white
Eggplant	Lavender
Elderberry	White, pink
Jerusalem artichoke	Yellow
Kiwi	White
Lotus	Pink
Nasturtium	Orange to red

PLANT	FLOWER COLOR
Natal plum	*White*
Nectarine (larger-flowered varieties)	*Pink*
Okra	*White, yellow*
Passion vine	*Mauve*
Peach (larger-flowered varieties)	*Pink*
Pineapple guava	*Maroon with pink*
Plum	*White, pink*
Pomegranate	*Red, orange*
Prickly pear	*Yellow, orange*
Quince	*White, light pink, coral*
Rose (hip-forming varieties)	*White, rose, pink*
Rosemary	*Blue, lavender, pink*
Runner bean	*Red, white, bicolor*
Saffron	*Mauve*
Sage	*Purple, red, white*
Strawberry	*White, pink*
Tea	*White, pink*

Cardoon blossoms, very similar to those of artichoke, are among the showiest in the plant world. Allow the flower spikes to develop and you'll be rewarded with these gorgeous purple blooms. These giant thistles are amazingly fragrant and attract scores of native bees.

Edibles with Showy Fruit and Flower Buds

Some edible plants have especially attractive flowers and, in some cases, like purple cauliflower, spectacular flower buds. These effects are fleeting but special when they occur. Choose the edible plants listed here to add some seasonal color to your landscape:

Apple (some varieties)
Apricot
Banana (red varieties)
Blueberry
Cauliflower (purple varieties)
Cherry
Citrus (most varieties)
Cranberry
Currants (red varieties)
Eggplant
Elderberry
Loquat
Mango (most varieties)
Natal plum
Nectarine
Pear (some varieties)
Pepper (most varieties)
Persimmon
Pomegranate
Rose (some varieties)
Sea berry
Squash (most varieties)
Tomato (most varieties)

Edible Plants with Colorful Foliage

To add life to an otherwise monochromatic design, interplant with edibles that have showy red veins or red to purple leaves. Spice it up and unify the area with burgundy containers. For a really flamboyant design, plant dozens of red tulips, scarlet runner beans, and/or red currants to emphasize the rosy tones. Edible plants with gold or lime green leaves, such as golden lemon thyme and chartreuse lettuces, light up a dark garden; heighten their impact by including some yellow- to green-leaved ornamentals like lime-colored coleus, feverfew, or even yellow-needled junipers. Enhance and dramatize the near fluorescence of these plants by interspersing them with bronze, deep pink, or sunset orange.

At the other end of the spectrum, silver-leaved plants calm a garden and help create an oasis. Intermingle them with pastel pink, lavender, and blue to soothe your sometimes-hectic life—and for a cool, refreshing scene in hot-summer areas.

EDIBLES WITH GOLD TO LIME FOLIAGE
Anise hyssop 'Golden Jubilee'
Bamboo
Basil
Celery 'Chinese Golden'
Chard 'Bright Yellow', 'Golden Sunrise'
Elderberry 'Sutherland Gold'
Endive 'Bianca Riccia'
Hops 'Brewers Gold'
Lettuce 'Black-Seeded Simpson', 'Australian Yellow', 'Winter Marvel'
Mustard 'Tokyo Bekana'

I'm always experimenting with flower and edible combinations in my garden. The best often include chard. I start a package of 'Rainbow' chard seeds in spring; then I pair the yellow-stemmed ones with bright marigolds, red varieties with bright red verbena, and pink chard, shown here, with 'Pink Wave' petunias.

Persimmon (spring foliage)
Purslane 'Golden'
Rosemary 'Golden Rain'
Sage (pineapple) 'Golden Delicious'
Thyme (lime)

EDIBLES WITH PURPLE TO RED FOLIAGE
Amaranth 'Hopi Red Dye'
Banana 'Red Jamaica'
Basil 'Purple Ruffles', 'Red Rubin'
Beet 'Bull's Blood'
Brussels sprouts 'Red Rubin'
Cabbage 'Mammoth Red Rock', 'Red Drumbeat', 'Red Express'
Chard 'Rhubarb', 'Ruby'
Elderberry 'Guincho Purple', 'Thundercloud'

Fennel 'Bronze'
Hyacinth bean (varieties with purple-veined leaves)
Jamaica
Kale 'Redbor', 'Red Russian'
Lettuce (many red varieties)
Malabar spinach 'Red Malabar'
Mustard 'Red Giant', 'Osaka Purple'
Okra 'Little Lucy', 'Red Burgundy'
Orach 'Double Purple'
Pac choi 'Red Choi'
Pepper 'Black Pearl', 'Bolivian Rainbow', 'Filus Blue'
Perilla 'Purple Perilla'
Plum 'All Red'
Rhubarb 'Cherry Red', 'Chipman's Canada Red', 'Crimson Red'
Sage 'Purpurascens'

EDIBLES WITH SILVER, BLUE-GREEN, OR GRAY-GREEN FOLIAGE
Artichoke
Borage
Cabbage
Cardoon
Catmint
Cauliflower
Chives
Collards
Eggplant
Kale 'Dwarf Blue Curled', 'Lacinato'
Lavender
Marjoram
Olive
Oregano
Papaloquelite
Pea
Pineapple guava
Rosemary
Sage
Scented geranium 'Peppermint'
Sea berry
Sea kale
Thyme (silver)

EDIBLES WITH VARIEGATED FOLIAGE
Alpine strawberry 'Variegata'
Basil 'Pesto Perpetuo'
Horseradish 'Variegata'
Kiwi (arctic beauty)

Lemon 'Variegated Pink Eureka'
Mint (pineapple) 'Variegata'
Nasturtium 'Alaska', 'Jewel of Africa'
Pepper 'Fish Pepper', 'Jigsaw', 'Largo Purple'
Sage 'Icterina', 'Tricolor'
Scented geranium 'Gray Lady Plymouth', 'Peacock'
Society garlic 'Silver Lace'
Thyme (creeping lemon)

Fragrant Edibles

Fragrance adds an extra dimension to any garden. A plant can produce fragrance from its flowers, fruit, or leaves. Stroll through a garden and smell the sweet fragrance of a ripe strawberry or the clean resinous scent of a pine tree to brighten your day; and for many of us, a brush by a tomato plant brings back summer memories with a long-gone relative. The following edible plants offer a range of fragrances:

PLANT	FRAGRANT PART
Almond	*Flowers*
Apple	*Flowers*
Artichoke	*Flowers*
Basil	*Leaves*
Blueberry	*Flowers*
Chamomile	*Leaves*
Citrus	*Flowers*
Crabapple	*Flowers*
Kiwi	*Flowers*
Lavender	*Flowers, leaves*
Loquat	*Flowers*
Mint	*Flowers, leaves*
Natal plum	*Flowers*
Pine nut	*Leaves*
Plum	*Flowers*
Rose	*Flowers*
Rosemary	*Flowers, leaves*
Sage	*Leaves*
Strawberry	*Fruit*
Sweet bay	*Leaves*
Tomato	*Leaves*

Water Plants

In general, water plants like wet feet. Some can live in marshy conditions. Others must have their roots submerged at all times; their leaves float on or rise above the water. Use water plants in ponds, along streams, in marshes, or even in large containers with little or no drainage. See the "Cranberry," "Ginger," "Lingonberry," and "Lotus" entries in the Encyclopedia and the other plants in Appendix A for growing information. Choose from the following edible water plants:

Cattail
Cranberry
Galangal
Lotus
Marsh mallow
Rice (cultivated and wild)
Taro
Vietnamese coriander
Wasabi
Water chestnut
Watercress

Asian-Style Garden Edibles

Today designers and gardeners are borrowing some of the traditional elements from Asian-style gardens when creating a relaxing oasis, meditation garden, or personal

If you think you need a pond or stream to grow edible water plants, think again. Some, such as watercress and the water chestnut shown here, thrive in a solid container with rich potting soil as long as they have daily watering. My water chestnuts are on an automatic drip system so they get a daily "top up" to keep the soil soppy wet.

In an area as small as 3 by 3 feet you can grow enough edible flowers for the most adventurous cook. Here you see yellow violas, Johnny-jump-ups, orange nasturtiums, yellow calendulas, purple chives, and white butterfly-like arugula flowers. Their color and flavor add drama to salads.

sanctuary. In choosing Asian plants, people don't generally think of edibles, yet many such perennial plants are traditionally included in these naturalistic gardens. In addition, I included a few Southeast Asian tropical specialties that impart their characteristic flavors to the curries and stir-fries of southern Asia. Select from among these plants to give an Asian touch to a permanent landscape:

Asian chives	*Loquat*
Bamboo	*Lotus*
Cherry	*Mitsuba*
Galangal	*Persimmon*
Ginger	*Plum*
Jujube	*Tea*
Lemongrass	*Wasabi*
Lime leaf	*Water chestnut*

Edible Flowers

Many plants have dual-purpose flowers: they're gorgeous in the garden and flavorful in the kitchen. Note that although some of the flowers listed below are those of vegetables and herbs, not all vegetable flowers are edible; tomato flowers, for example, are toxic. Not all herbs have culinary uses; some are medicinal and others are simply lovely to look at.

Caution: Always take care to identify the flowers properly before you eat them. Never eat flowers from a plant on which toxic chemicals have been applied. And never eat flowers directly from a nursery, as it is likely that they have been sprayed with toxic pesticides.

For more information on how to grow and use these flowers, see Appendix A and consult my book *The Edible Flower Garden* and Cathy Wilkinson Barash's *Edible*

Flowers: From Garden to Palate. The following list includes the tastiest and most versatile edible flowers:

ANNUALS

Anise hyssop	*Pansy*
Arugula	*Pea*
Borage	*Runner bean*
Broccoli	*Safflower*
Calendula	*Shungiku*
Johnny-jump-up	*Squash*
Mustard	*Viola*
Nasturtium	

PERENNIALS

Apple	*Pinks*
Beebalm	*Redbud*
Chives	*Rose*
Citrus	*Rosemary*
Daylily	*Sage*
Elderberry	*Scented geranium*
Lavender	*Thyme*
Lemon verbena	*Tulip*
Lilac	*Violet*
Pineapple guava	

Although the visual appeal of an artistically landscaped yard usually receives the greatest emphasis, a good design should appeal to all the senses. The fragrance of strawberries ripening in the sun, or a tomato plant as you brush past it, hints at the flavors to come. The sweetness of a ripe, juicy peach, a crunchy walnut, or a tangy lime gratifies your sense of taste. Everyone appreciates sun-warmed grapes in the hand and the texture of rough hickory bark. And auditory delights can include the splash of a fountain and the songs of birds nesting in the trees.

The total effect of a landscape is more than just the sum of its parts. Not all the factors are entirely under your control—but this is as it should be. A quail scurrying down a path or a flock of cedar waxwings eating berries that are rightfully yours can bring as much pleasure as carefully selected plants. The acrobatic antics of squirrels occasionally enchant you, even though the little monsters might decimate your butternut crop. These are some of the unplanned pleasures that a good landscape design invites and enhances.

For further inspiration, peruse a number of wonderful books on the subject, including Lee Reich's *Landscaping with Fruit* and Fred Hagy's *Landscaping with Fruits and Vegetables.*

A Gallery of Design Ideas

It's one thing to talk about design in the abstract and another to see how it all unfolds. The following edible landscapes cover various styles, situations, and regions to help show how different gardeners and designers use the many principles and elements of design.

Mexican Talavera pottery chickens create a themed mini–herb garden near my front door. Yellow violas and thyme are on the upper level; variegated sage, lemon thyme, and lemon basil sit left to right on the lower level. Using the same style of pottery and limiting the colors to yellow and blue—dynamic opposites—result in a very tight design. Added interest comes from my 'Black Satin' blackberry vine, a three-season show-off: a mass of pinkish blossoms in late spring through early summer, colorful berries in summer, and yellow foliage in fall.

Opposite: Can you find 11 edibles in this picture? Hint: Most are in containers. In the foreground, left to right, are watercress in bloom, fine-leaved 'Delfino' cilantro, and tasty tulips. Upright curly mint rises behind the tulips. Leaf lettuces adjoin the path; 'Tuscan Blue' rosemary (ideal for aromatic barbecue skewers) stands tall behind. Find chives and creeping thyme nestled in the gravel and a nasturtium wandering near the back steps. A 'Satsuma' Japanese plum tree flowers above an evergreen pineapple guava, which screens my neighbor's house.

This Harrisburg, Oregon, edible landscape with raised beds was designed by the owner's daughter with her mother's comfort in mind. Under the wooden trellis at the rear is a lovely outdoor sitting room, furnished with a small table and chairs and a comfy armchair, that provides a fabulous view of the garden. As we age, more of us should consider installing raised beds; they are much easier on backs and knees, so we can continue to get pleasure from gardening.

I spotted this spectacular view into Jeff and Ellen Bolch's Savannah, Georgia, backyard through a gate. The drama arises from 'Red Giant' Japanese mustard flanking a classic bronze cherub fountain; the plant's size and shape are in perfect proportion to the fountain. The architecture and the fountain's style clearly called for a formal garden, as was designed by John McEllen. Viewed through the gate, the fountain and mustard make a perfect triangle; the balanced symmetry reinforces the formal style.

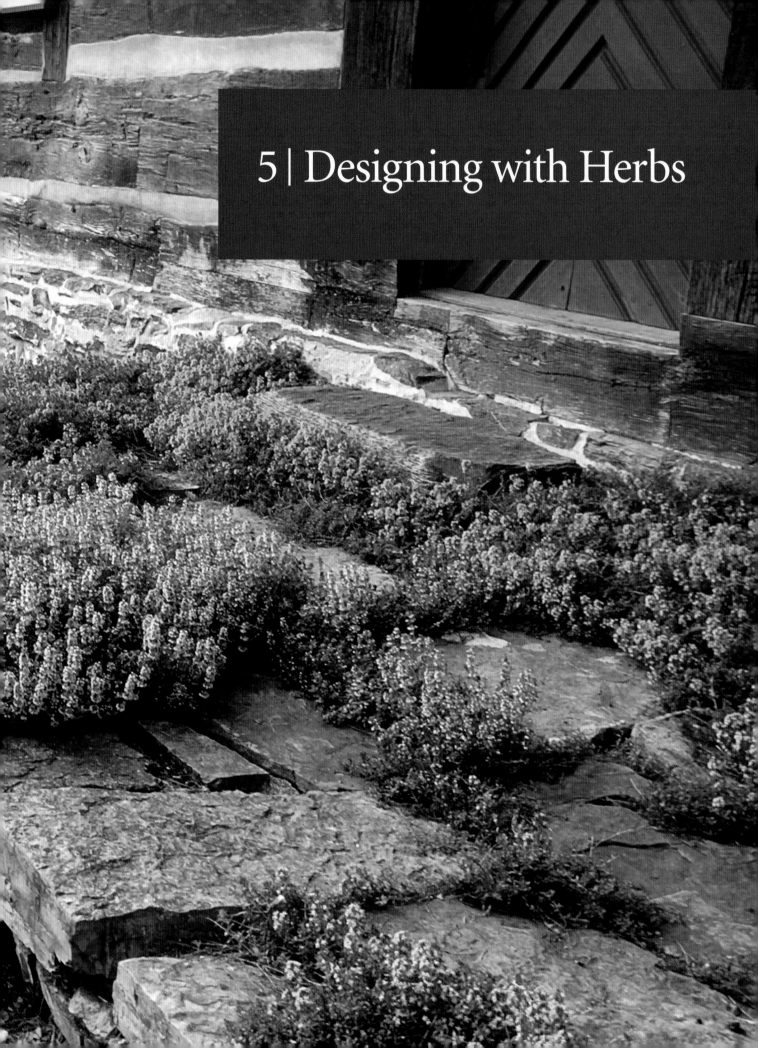

5 | Designing with Herbs

Although I grew up with plenty of fresh garden vegetables, I was herb deprived. Like many Americans in the mid-twentieth century, my mother cooked with little seasoning. The only herb she used was dried sage from a tin to flavor turkey stuffing. I have my dear husband, Robert, to thank for giving me Julia Child's *Mastering the Art of French Cooking*, which introduced me to cooking with herbs early in our marriage. When we moved from Massachusetts to California a few years later, I had ample space to grow herbs for my kitchen.

Today I couldn't cook without a garden full of herbs. Of course, on my quest to explore edible landscaping, I've grown many gardens that featured only herbs, including an entire border of variegated herbs and an herbal entry garden bordering my front steps. My spice garden was a delightful variation (herbs are generally leaves or flowers, while spices are seeds or bark) that showcased dill, anise, coriander, fennel, and a patch of unusual mustards for seeds—brown, white, and black.

As a designer, I weave culinary herbs throughout a landscape. Chives and parsley create enchanting edgings around flower beds; a carpet of sweet woodruff sets off a hedge of espaliered apples; and for drama, I add a sculptured sweet bay or rosemary topiary. And I look to herbs for interesting foliage or a dash of color in a container or flower border.

Before we go further, let me define "herb" more fully. In the broadest sense, an herb is a "useful" plant whose leaves, blossoms, or stems are used as an ingredient in cooking, dyes, cosmetics, medicine, or a combination of these applications. Because the term is so broad, the focus in this book is on culinary herbs, while edible flowers and some spices are also included.

This chapter delves into how to design an herb garden as well as how to incorporate herbs into other parts of your landscape. You'll find information and photos of herbs throughout this book. Herbs are major players in Chapter 4 in the lists of landscape uses for edibles, especially in the entries for ground covers, flower borders, and gold, silver, and red foliage plants. Chapter 8 and Appendix C cover growing plants in containers, and the Encyclopedia provides detailed growing and harvesting information for the most popular herbs: basil, chives, mint, oregano, parsley, rosemary, sage, sweet bay, and thyme. Finally, Appendix A includes basic information on dozens of less common herbs, including many ethnic favorites.

Throughout this chapter—and the book—I mention spectacular or unusual culinary herbs, such as mioga ginger, angelica, variegated basils, and hundreds of other fabulous plants that are seldom available in local nurseries. These can be found online through herb specialists like Nichols Garden Nursery, Richters Herbs, Thyme Garden Herb Company, and Well-Sweep Farms.

Practical Considerations

We are in an herbal culinary renaissance fueled in part by the Internet, where you can find recipes for every herb noted here. And if I haven't convinced you to grow these herbs for pleasure, then grow them purely for your health; most herbs are high in antioxidants. The health of your garden benefits, too, because when culinary herbs bloom they attract legions of beneficial insects.

Herbs are so easy to grow and incorporate into a garden plan that I think of them as edible plants with training

Preceding pages: Lee Stoltzfus designed this entry garden in Pennsylvania's Amish country, softening the stonework with thymes and a licorice plant. *Above*: The Cloister Garden at Festival Hill in Round Top, Texas, invites visitors to explore the world of culinary herbs.

wheels. If you simply provide lots of sun, good drainage, and occasional harvesting, herbs such as chives, fennel, oregano, sage, savory, and thyme will thrive.

Learn from Others: Visit Herb Gardens

If you're new to herbs, it's helpful to familiarize yourself with the broad range of herbs, and one of the best ways is to visit public herb gardens. You'd be surprised to find how many cities have them—often planted by a local chapter of an herb society. In Washington, D.C., take in the National Herb Garden at the U.S. National Arboretum. In New York City, visit The Cloisters with its wonderful medieval herb garden. If you're in the Midwest, take a gander at the magnificent formal herb gardens at the Minnesota Landscape Arboretum near Minneapolis and the Missouri Botanical Garden in St. Louis; and visit Powell Gardens in Kansas City, Missouri, to see the "longest living wall in North America"—a rock wall filled with culinary herbs and drought-resistant flowers. And in California, you'll find many unusual culinary herbs at a number of the wineries in the Napa Valley and at the Huntington Botanical Gardens in San Marino. Fine historic restorations include Old Sturbridge Village in Massachusetts and Colonial Williamsburg in Virginia.

Closer to home, check out local public herb gardens; they may offer classes (identification or cooking classes). Consider volunteering; you can learn a lot and make new horticultural friends—plants and people.

The more herb gardens you visit, the more you'll be exposed to culinary herbs from around the world. Before long, you'll be able to identify them like a pro. Most herb gardens allow folks to gently rub a leaf between their fingers to get the scent.

Caution: Do *not* taste the herbs at any public garden; the plants would soon disappear if everyone took even a leaf or two. Plus, not all herbs are safe to eat. Some are medicinal in controlled dosages and can be lethal when too much is consumed. For instance, foxglove, often found in herb gardens, is the source of the heart drug digitalis, and the plant is toxic if ingested.

Herb Garden Basics

Culinary herbs include perennials, which are permanent parts of a garden; biennials, which are a varied lot and, depending on the climate, generally live for only two or so seasons; and annuals, which live only one season. These categories can be broken down further to indicate how much cold an herb can take. Most annual herbs tol-

---

The Essence of Flavor

Numerous essential oils give herbs their varied flavors as well as some of their medicinal properties. Although you may find the same essential oil in a diversity of herbs, the amount of that oil and its combination with other oils vary from one herb to another. It's an oversimplification to assign a specific herb's flavor to any single oil, because the same oils show up in a number of herbs. For example, the essential oil carvone is a primary flavoring in caraway, yet you find the same oil—in a different amount and combined with other essential oils—in caraway thyme. Geraniol, which gives a citrus flavor to lemon thyme, is also a component of lemon balm. The anise-flavored oil estragole is in both French tarragon and anise hyssop.

Cooks use their knowledge of herb flavors to substitute one herb for another. Therefore, if you don't have lemon thyme for a salad, you can add a few sprigs of lemon balm. Or if the recipe for Vietnamese salad rolls calls for Vietnamese coriander, you can use cilantro or culantro instead. Although the flavors aren't identical, they are similar enough to be satisfactory alternatives.

When looking for a particular flavor, choose from among the following herbs:

- Anise flavor—'Anise' basil, anise hyssop, chervil, fennel, French tarragon, Mexican tarragon
- Celery flavor—lovage, mitsuba
- Cilantro flavor—culantro, papaloquelite, Vietnamese coriander
- Lemon flavor—lemon balm, lemongrass, lemon thyme, lemon verbena, 'Mrs. Burns Lemon' basil
- Mint flavor—costmary, peppermint, spearmint
- Oregano flavor—Cuban oregano, Mexican oregano, Sicilian oregano, sweet marjoram

Delve further into the fascinating world of essential oils in *The Big Book of Herbs* by Arthur O. Tucker and Thomas DeBaggio.

---

erate very little frost; some, like basil and nasturtium, tolerate none. Half-hardy annuals, including chervil and cilantro, survive temperatures in the high 20s. Hardy perennials tolerate winter temperatures that dip well below 0°F; some, like chives and sage, can withstand cold down to −30°F. Yet others, such as rosemary and lavender, are called half-hardy perennials, as temperatures below 15°F will kill them. And tender perennials like lemongrass and pineapple sage tolerate little or no frost.

A cold climate need not be an obstacle, however, because you can move plants onto a sun porch in fall or treat them as annuals and replant them in spring. See "Overwintering Tender Plants Indoors" in Appendix C for more information. Cooperative Extension websites

Herbs for Every Zone

I asked three passionate gardener-cooks from different climates to name their 10 favorite herbs that grow well in their own gardens and to tell how they use them in their kitchens.

Ellen Ecker Ogden, Vermont Culinary Capers, Manchester, Vermont

Ellen is a longtime food gardener, cooking teacher, and author. She co-founded The Cook's Garden seed company more than two decades ago; her latest cookbook is *From the Cook's Garden*.

Ellen gardens in Zone 4. Her frost-free growing period is from June 6 to September 1. Not thwarted by a short season, she grows nearly 20 different herbs—perennials and annuals—in a 10-by-10-foot herb garden. Not all the perennials come back reliably, but she considers that a good excuse for trying new ones. Ellen is especially excited about 'Lady' lavender, which blooms its first year, as a formal border plant.

ELLEN'S TOP 10 HERBS

- Basil 'Fino Verde'—small-leaved plant is quite ornamental and the flavor is always sweet, never bitter, and fantastic for pesto.
- French tarragon—rich flavor blends in well for a béarnaise sauce on chicken or fish.
- Garlic chives—garlicky flavor is a must-have to blend with dill and basil for herb butter; freeze well and give fresh herb flavor.
- Italian parsley—mix into pesto to add nutrient value (antioxidants and vitamin K) and flavor.
- Lemon balm—great in fruit desserts, even a simple summer berry salad.
- Lovage—adds terrific flavor to tomato consommé and gazpacho.
- Rosemary—combine with thyme, garlic, and olive oil for a standard meat and poultry marinade that kicks up the flavor.
- Sage—the crucial herb for seasoning poultry; chop leaves and mix into a cheddar cheese omelet.
- Summer savory—enhances mild-flavored vegetables; especially good on buttered summer squash.
- Thyme—chop leaves and mix into egg salad; cream into butter to top steamed vegetables.

Jim Long, Long Creek Herbs, Blue Eye, Missouri

Jim grows about 300 different herbs that reflect his culinary travel adventures. He teaches about cooking with herbs and has written 27 books as well as numerous herb columns for periodicals.

Jim can grow many herbs in his Zone 7 garden; the tropicals thrive in the warm, humid summers (he overwinters tender perennials like lemongrass and lemon verbena indoors). Mediterranean herbs prefer drier conditions, so he provides good drainage for lavender, rosemary, and sage to prevent root rot.

JIM'S TOP 10 HERBS

- Basil ('Greek Columnar', 'Green Pepper', 'Lime', 'Magical Michael', and 'Thai')—blend 'Greek Columnar' with blackberry juice for a delectable sorbet. For a fabulous basil salad, combine different basils with halved cherry tomatoes and balsamic vinegar.
- Lavender—'Hidcote' and 'Munstead' make lovely lavender cookies (sugar cookies with pulverized fresh or dried flowers).
- Lemongrass—good in cake icing; makes a tasty tea.
- Lemon verbena—best as a tea herb; for freshest flavor blend crushed leaves, ice, and cold water rather than boiling water.
- Marjoram—"dirty cheese" is a crowd-pleasing hors d'oeuvre: mix equal parts chopped chives, parsley, and marjoram with farmer's cheese and olive oil.
- Mexican tarragon—use instead of French tarragon (doesn't grow well in his climate); makes a stimulant tea.
- Oregano 'Sicilian'—this cross between marjoram and oregano has the best flavor for pizza and spaghetti sauces.
- Rosemary—use cut branches as skewers for grilled chicken.
- Sage 'Berggarten'—has big leaves that are flavorful dipped in tempura batter and fried.
- Vietnamese coriander—use like cilantro in salsa or soup; harvest often so flavor remains delicate.

Deborah Madison, Santa Fe, New Mexico

In the 1980s, Deborah and her staff at Greens Restaurant in San Francisco elevated vegetarian cooking from good-for-you to elegant and compelling. Her book *Vegetarian Cooking for Everyone* is one of my favorites.

Deborah grows herbs in a Zone 5 desert garden. It's a fierce climate—very dry and windy—so the fresh herbs that do make it are precious. Spring produces the most succulent herbs, which she tosses into salads and soups to add layers of flavors. If midsummer heat and wind toughen and brown the herbs, she replants. Perennial herbs like rosemary don't always survive winter.

DEBORAH'S TOP 10 HERBS

- Anise hyssop—enjoy the scent in the garden; makes a lovely tea.
- Chervil—delicate flavor in salads; wonderful with asparagus.
- French tarragon—great in spring with eggs, savory custards, and salads; plant dies back by midsummer.
- Lovage—a must-have herb; the celery flavor complements potatoes, salads, and soups (especially tomato); hollow stem is a great straw in a bloody Mary.
- Rosemary—pound into a paste with juniper berries, garlic, sage, peppercorns, and parsley and place under poultry skin before baking.
- Rose-scented geranium—great with blackberries and other rose family fruits, including poached peaches.
- Sage—in spring the almost minty flavor goes well with peas and asparagus; later in the year it enhances winter squash.
- Salad burnet—great cucumber-flavored garnish with rose petals and Hendrick's gin for a cooling summer beverage.
- Sorrel—in salads and omelets, and on salmon; in spring soups, especially mushroom; make puree to freeze and use in sauces.
- Sweet marjoram—has high floral notes; use often instead of basil; excellent with tomatoes, chicken, and zucchini dishes.

and local nursery personnel can help you select herbs best suited to your climate.

Although herbs are among the easiest plants to grow, poor cultivation makes them straggly and unappealing. Consider the exposure in your yard. Only chervil, chives, cilantro, daylily, mint, nasturtium, parsley, salad burnet, sweet woodruff, viola, and wasabi are shade tolerant; most herbs need full sun. Yet, in the hottest-summer areas, most culinary herbs benefit from afternoon shade; in cool-summer climates, heat-lovers like basil and lemongrass do best when planted near a warm south-facing wall with protection from the wind. As a rule, pests and diseases seldom bother culinary herbs. Even deer, the nemesis of many gardeners, leave the majority of herbs alone.

It is easy and economical to grow most herbs from seed; as with vegetables, the variety of culinary herbs as seeds is much greater than as container-grown plants. However, French tarragon, lemongrass, ginger, scented geranium, sweet bay, and some sages can only be grown from cuttings, divisions, or—in the case of ginger—rhizomes. You can buy most common culinary herbs as small plants at local nurseries from spring through early summer.

A rule of thumb: fertilize annual herbs with all-purpose organic fertilizer when you plant and again in midseason, after a large harvest, and if leaves turn pale. Feed herbs in containers every 3 to 4 weeks. Perennial herbs need little fertilizer unless they are growing in very sandy soil or in containers.

Once herbs are established and are putting out new growth, lightly harvest by cutting off the end of a stem—a few leaves at a time. As the plants grow and flourish, the easiest way to keep herbs healthy, vigorous, and neat looking is to harvest them often. With continual harvests, perennial herbs, such as lavender, oregano, rosemary, sage, and thyme, need only a spring pruning to renew woody growth and remove winter damage. Without it, the centers splay and the plants become rangy. Prune herbaceous herbs—anise, cilantro, dill, fennel, and parsley—only to remove yellowing leaves and to shape the plant. Keep harvesting basil and mint as they grow, and they will stay lush, compact, and tender. Refer to the individual entries in the Encyclopedia for detailed information.

For information on soil preparation, seed starting, planting, and maintenance, see Appendix C. For more details on growing herbs, see *Landscaping with Herbs* by Jim Wilson and *Growing Herbs: From Seed, Cutting & Root* by Thomas DeBaggio. And consider joining the

Fresh garden herbs add panache to many other ingredients. From left to right are roasted peppers with garlic; mozzarella balls marinated in olive oil with chopped thyme and basil; dried tomatoes in olive oil with oregano, thyme, and rosemary; and chopped basil layered with Parmesan cheese to preserve it.

Herb Society of America to learn from the many members and their years of experience.

Tips for Beginners

While herbs are notoriously easy to grow, still some pointers help because a few missteps can damage even the toughest plants. Overwatering, underwatering, excessive shade, poor drainage, and careless harvesting can stunt growth or even kill plants. Also, some simple strategies like locating herbs close to the kitchen allow you to become more familiar with the plants while encouraging you to use them more.

- Herbs are low maintenance, not *no* maintenance.
- Site the herb bed where it receives full sun (at least 6 hours, including midday sun).
- Make sure the soil drains well; most culinary herbs die in soggy soil.
- Start small; a great way to begin is with one plant each of oregano, sage, and thyme; two chive plants; and three or four basil plants.
- Annual herbs often are sold in 2-inch containers with four to eight herbs growing together; separate young plants and transplant them singly; otherwise they will crowd each other out and grow poorly.

Starting Small: A Double-Barrel Herb Garden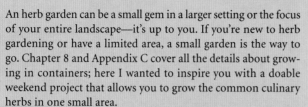

An herb garden can be a small gem in a larger setting or the focus of your entire landscape—it's up to you. If you're new to herb gardening or have a limited area, a small garden is the way to go. Chapter 8 and Appendix C cover all the details about growing in containers; here I wanted to inspire you with a doable weekend project that allows you to grow the common culinary herbs in one small area.

A few years back, I saw a barrel-on-barrel herb tower in a magazine—a brilliant concept featuring a smaller wooden barrel sitting atop a larger one. The two barrels give more surface area for the herbs to spill from and a lot more soil to hold nutrients and water, and root room for all the extra herbs. It is such a great way to grow plenty of herbs in a small space; you don't even have to lean over to plant or harvest. Whether you live on country acreage, on a suburban lot, or in a condominium, this weekend project can provide you with enough fresh herbs to bring your cooking to a whole new level—all within reach of your kitchen. A word of caution: this is much too heavy to put on a deck, balcony, porch, or roof.

To avoid soil compaction and subsequent bad drainage, I set filler material—a mass of 1-inch-diameter and wider twigs (or use pieces of Styrofoam or upside-down 1-gallon plastic nursery containers) in the bottom quarter of the barrel. And to prevent the top barrel from tilting or compacting the soil in the bottom barrel, I placed a couple of 2 by 4s, each 2 feet long, on the soil in the bottom barrel to distribute the weight of the top barrel and keep it level.

I chose chives, thyme, and creeping winter savory for the top barrel. You can use them or your favorite small herbs like dwarf basil, German chamomile, curly parsley, or chervil. In the bottom barrel I planted larger herbs—oregano, French tarragon, 'Thai' and sweet basils, sage, and lemon thyme—to cascade out the front. Italian parsley, rosemary, any basil, and lavender are also great choices.

Depending on where you live, you can find wooden wine or whiskey barrels at most nurseries and home improvement stores (see "Rosalind Creasy's Edible Patio Garden" in Chapter 8). Or you could use a very large terra-cotta or recycled plastic container on the bottom and a smaller matching container on top. If you are going to use drip irrigation as I did (it is the most efficient way to water), you'll need to connect your line to a nearby water source.

MATERIALS

Drill with ½-in. drill bit

Large barrel, 42 in. wide, 24 in. tall

Small barrel, 30 in. wide, 17 in. tall

Filler material

Soilless potting mix, 3 to 4 bags, each 2 cu. ft.

All-purpose organic fertilizer

Homemade compost, worm castings, compost tea, or other source of microbes

2 boards (common framing lumber, not pressure treated), 2 by 4s, each 2 ft. long

Herb plants

½-in. solid distribution tubing, cut to length as needed

¼-in. solid distribution tubing, cut to length as needed

¼-in. tubing with laser cuts or in-line emitters spaced every 6 in., 20 to 30 ft.

½-in. end cap

1 bag of ¼-in. connector barbs, tees, and goof plugs

Punch

12 or so irrigation stakes (look like giant hairpins)

Organic compost for mulch

- Perennial Mediterranean herbs (fennel, lavender, oregano, rosemary, sage, sweet marjoram, and thyme) are quite drought tolerant and require little supplemental water in rainy climates.
- Annual herbs and tropical perennials need an inch of water a week—from rain or irrigation.
- Many culinary herbs have a range of colors, flavors, and landscaping uses. Seek out herbs like red or cinnamon basil, lemon or silver thyme, and upright or creeping rosemary.
- Get familiar with herbs by focusing on a few at a time and experimenting with them in different dishes.

Armed with these basics, you are well on your way to a lifetime of herbal enjoyment—in both the garden and the kitchen.

Design Aesthetics

A marvelous sense of serenity arises when you relax with a cup of tea in a well-designed herb garden. Most of the plants are relatively low growing (less than 36 inches tall) with a mounded shape, giving an uninterrupted view of the entire garden. Your eye is washed with soft foliage tones of grays and greens. The slightest breeze wafts the scent of something sweet or spicy. Some of that serenity may come from history itself. Our ancestors lived and cooked with these or similar herbs for countless generations. By creating your own herb garden, you become part of that continuum—the ongoing but ancient connection between people and plants.

Herbs have a venerable garden history. Unlike vegetables and fruits, home gardeners rarely grow herbs in long, straight rows for high production, so you are free

INSTALLATION

1. To ensure good drainage, drill eight ½-in. holes, evenly spaced, in bottom of both barrels. Set large barrel in place and add filler material to bottom quarter of barrel.

2. Fill barrel to within 1 in. of rim with soilless potting mix. Add fertilizer (following package directions) and compost, worm castings, or other bacterially active material; incorporate into top few inches of mix. Add more mix if necessary.

3. Center and set 2 by 4s on top of soil and level them. Place small barrel on 2 by 4s; level it and fill barrel following step 2.

4. Plant herbs in both barrels.

5. Connect ½-in. solid distribution tubing to closest water source; run it to barrels.

6. Insert ¼-in. solid distribution tubing into ½-in. solid distribution tubing using connector barb; then run ¼-in. solid distribution tubing up back and to first barrel.

7. Measure two lengths of ¼-in. emitter tubing, equal to twice inside circumference of each barrel. Insert ¼-in. tee into ¼-in. solid distribution tubing. On one side of tee, connect emitter tubing and run it up to top barrel; loop it twice around base of plants. Connect another length of emitter tubing on other side of tee and loop it twice around base of plants in bottom barrel. Secure all tubing with irrigation stakes.

8. Run irrigation system and flush out any debris in line; plug ends of emitter tubing with goof plugs.

9. Apply few inches of mulch over soil and work it around plants. Gently wet entire surface of soil using spray nozzle on garden hose. Repeat watering at least three times to make sure soil is completely soaked. Keep soil moist but not soggy

I grow must-have herbs that do well in most of the country. A smaller barrel (with chives, winter savory, and thyme) nests atop an outsized whiskey barrel with 'Thai' and sweet basils, oregano, lemon thyme, French tarragon, and sage.

for next few weeks until herbs are established and start to put out new growth. Once plants are growing well, use drip irrigation system.

Once this garden is established, you'll see that you get a real bang for your buck. As your tastes expand, you can experiment with new annual herbs each year (or seasonally), while the hardy perennial herbs are the mainstays of this garden and will live for many years in most climates.

to visualize them interplanted in flower borders and growing in containers. And, of course, we've all seen herb gardens, sometimes planted in swaths but more often in classic geometric patterns. When designing an herb garden, follow the same landscaping aesthetics of unity, line, scale, color, and formal and informal styles common to all good designs.

Unity and Line

Many culinary herbs, including oregano, French tarragon, thyme, marjoram, and lavender, unify an area because of their similar shape, size, foliage color, and texture. Yet they also tend to spill and spread and look like they need gathering up. Consequently, designers have traditionally used tight lines when designing herb gardens—crisp brick or stone paths and/or low-growing hedges or rows of curly parsley or chives, often in geometric patterns.

Scale

When designing an herb garden, consider the setting and scale of the space. Because herbs are usually small, a few plants clustered in a bed by themselves will appear insignificant in front of a large house. Instead, make 4- to 5-foot-wide beds on either side of the front walkway or along the driveway. You can also create a planting area around a patio or install large, raised planters and fill them with culinary and ornamental herbs. As a bonus, when herbs are grown near a patio, their scents waft to folks enjoying the outdoor space. Other ideas: plant herbs along a garage wall or use diminutive varieties in a corner of a rock garden.

Color

Herbs are calming influences in a garden. They are mostly about foliage—in soothing hues of green and gray. Often their blooms are pale, dainty blossoms of pink, lavender, blue, white, or yellow. Yet the flowers—as well as plants with more brightly colored foliage—can add an exclamation point to an otherwise subdued palette. Highlight a sea of gently mounding plants with chives' bright lavender flower spikes or white garlic chive blossoms; add contrasting color with pools of deep maroon 'Purple Ruffles' basil and bronze fennel. Include edible and non-edible flowers in the garden for more color; for edibles, think bright yellow calendula, 'Tangerine Gem' marigold, and 'Scarlet Gleam' nasturtium, and for non-edibles, consider hot pink portulaca, 'Purple Wave' petunia, and heliotrope. To provide a broader range of foliage color and form, gardeners often add non-edible herbs, such as gray or green santolina, green or golden feverfew, germander, calamint, and hyssop as well as some of the ornamental-only sages and thymes.

Fragrance

What culinary herbs may lack in color or size, they make up for in fragrance. Simply brushing against the plant on a warm summer day releases the volatile essential oils, perfuming the air. Some plants, like low-growing mints and thymes, are effective between stepping-stones, while others are best enjoyed close up—think window boxes and raised beds. Scents range from rose to citrus, pine to spice, sweet floral to savory. The fresh aroma of mint, the sparkle of lemon verbena and lemon thyme, and the perfume of rose and lavender are irresistible. As if the fragrances themselves are not enticing enough, they are a preview of the marvelous flavors with which herbs will imbue your cooking.

Formal and Informal Designs

Formal herb gardens include symmetrical beds in geometric shapes—primarily circles and squares—low clipped hedges, masonry or mowed-grass paths, classic statuary and ornamentation, and topiary. Frequent pruning and deadheading are necessary to keep the herbs tidy and maintain a clean, crisp look. See "Geometric Herb Gardens" later in this chapter for three plans to get you started with classic formal designs.

If you prefer a more casual style, consider an informal herb garden or border, which, in contrast to a formal garden, is designed with flowing lines, blowsy plants that touch each other and can overflow the garden, stepping-stones, or gravel paths that wind through the beds, and has the relaxed feel of a cottage garden. An advantage is that an informal garden does not require as much maintenance as a formal one.

Either style can work in a garden of any size. Imagine a formal geometric design of diminutive herbs in a big container; using larger plants, the same design can fill a suburban front yard—with space for topiary or espaliered fruit trees. The same holds true for an informal garden. A big container chock full of parsley, sage, basil, rosemary, chives, and thyme—must-haves for many cooks—makes a lovely scene outside the kitchen door, perfect for easy picking. In fact, this year I converted my strawberry barrel into an herb barrel with these very same herbs plus dill and cilantro. And an informal border of herbs is picture perfect in front of a picket fence. An herb garden, whether formal or informal, is limited only by your imagination.

Incorporating Herbs into a Landscape Design

Many culinary herbs have an esteemed history in classic landscape designs that continues to the present day. Following are some general guidelines for using both annual and perennial herbs in a landscape:

- Plant shorter herbs and flowers at the front of the border and taller herbs in the back.
- Make harvesting herbs and flowers more convenient by including a few stepping-stones among the plants to provide access to the middle of the bed.
- Use neutral herbs—those with small gray-green leaves and a shrubby habit, such as oregano, thyme, winter savory, sage, and French tarragon—as background plants for showier ones.
- Utilize herbs with unusual colors and forms (chives with their grasslike foliage, tall fountain-shaped fennel, and fancy-leaved sages and basils) as accent plants or focal points in a border.
- Try combinations of herbs and flowers, like red basils with white dwarf zinnias or golden and purple sages with yellow and lavender million bells.
- Use gray-foliaged herbs as peacemakers between more powerfully colored flowers.
- Grow lots of herbs in containers so you can spot them around the garden and move them to change the look of the garden in minutes.

Gudi Riter's 9-by-9-foot herb garden lies in the middle of a brick patio. The clipped boxwood hedge, geometric shape, birdbath, and four miniature red roses give it a formal air. A fabulous cook who helps me test recipes, Gudi grew up in Germany and can't imagine cooking without fresh herbs. This little garden contains most of her favorite perennial herbs—oregano, chives, lemon and French thymes, savory, and sage—as well as parsley grown as a biennial. Annual herbs such as basil and cilantro fill it out.

Experiment with your herb plantings to find the most pleasing combinations for both the garden and the kitchen.

Annuals

Annual culinary herbs work best in an annual flower border or in containers where you can see them up close and harvest them—near the kitchen. Or plant them in a tightly structured bed surrounded with boxwood or germander, or grow them adjacent to a geometric brick or stone path. Combine short-lived summer herbs (basil, perilla, borage, German chamomile, summer savory, and dill) with annual flowers like strawflower, cosmos, zinnia, and petunia. Pair cool-season annual herbs like chervil and cilantro with viola and nasturtium—all of which have edible flowers.

Perennials

As a landscape designer, I consider most perennial herbs to be versatile, small, and neutral enough to "dress up" or "dress down," so I include them in almost any decor or color scheme. I incorporate them in formal and naturalistic gardens, add them to flower and vegetable borders, and interplant them among low-growing evergreens. When herbs have slightly disparate shapes, heights, and foliage colors, tie them together visually in the time-honored fashion by surrounding them with geometrically shaped low hedges.

A few perennial herbs grow fairly large, so designers often give them specific status in prescribed garden formulas. Take culinary varieties of roses, for example. Designers group compact varieties in formal geometric beds and surround them with low hedges of herbs (lavender is ideal in appropriate climates), while they train sprawling types over arbors or plant them toward the back of large, sweeping informal shrub borders. For centuries, compact types of thyme have been grown between stepping-stones. Rosemary, lavender, thyme, and some sages lend themselves to shearing, allowing you to fashion them into small hedges that surround herb gardens. And you can train them into topiaries. Fragrant lavenders are

Rosalind Creasy's Magic Circle Herb Garden ✍

The odyssey of my Magic Circle Herb Garden began when I decided I wanted a dramatic focal point for my front yard—one that I could view from any angle. A bold geometric design would provide year-round interest and be the perfect framework for an ever-changing display of annual and perennial culinary herbs and flowers. The inspiration came from a magazine photo of a small garden with rectangular granite slabs laid out in a circular pattern, interplanted with flowering ground covers and with a gazing globe at the center.

The garden my crew and I created was on a much larger scale; in fact, it filled nearly half of my front yard and took 4 days to complete. I sited the circle to border my front walk—already planted with salvias, roses, and society garlic—and a

slender, deep-blue trellis adorned with hops and perennial morning glories. I designed a slightly raised circular bed with a birdbath as the central focal point. Instead of granite slabs, I chose 3-foot-long, tapered, 2-by-12 redwood planks—which I was lucky enough to find as free scrap at my local lumberyard—for the spokes of the wheel. Other options are to purchase 2 by 12s and cut them to length or to use lawn or paving stones instead.

We planted hardy perennial herbs, including licorice, lovage, French tarragon, sage, chives, and pinks, in the border around the outside edge of the circle and interplanted them with tender perennials—rose- and lemon-scented geraniums along with sweet marjoram. I'm an enthusiastic advocate of

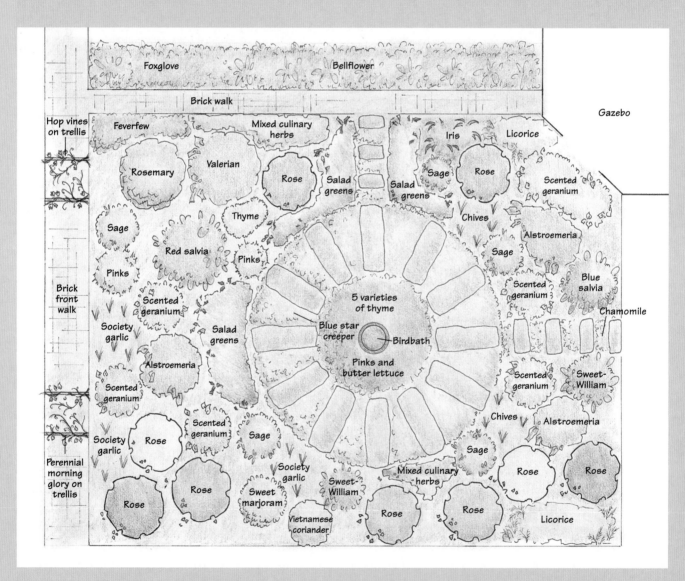

The Magic Circle Herb Garden is a variation of the classical circular herb garden with rays emanating from the round garden at center. Here, I used a birdbath as the focal point.

I filled my garden with thyme, chives, sage, pinks, rosemary, lavender, and roses, but couldn't resist giving it a backdrop of stately but poisonous foxgloves. This view from the street was captured the second spring when the garden had filled in and was in its full glory. Dog walkers, joggers, cyclists, and even the occasional driver stopped to get a better look.

mixed plantings and always enhance herb gardens with vegetables and flowers. On the trellises bordering the front walk we added currant tomatoes and runner beans and surrounded the circle with a colorful medley of geraniums, zinnias, cosmos, salvias, and heirloom plume celosias. Probably because it was so serene and almost mystical, a neighbor named it the Magic Circle.

I had planned to take out the garden after the second summer and replace it with another demonstration garden, but it was hard to part with. So I did a variation—a spring garden filled with dewy fresh salad greens.

Of all the gardens I've ever created, the herb circle is my favorite—and my neighbors', too. In fact, the day we finally took it out to make way for another project, one of the guys from down the street stopped to exclaim, "No! You just can't take this one out; it'll break my heart."

Summer plantings include numerous basils. In this section, the upright 'Mrs. Burns Lemon' and the darker green, young plants of sweet basil are interplanted with purple verbena and cupflower. White-flowering 'Aztec Dwarf Runner' beans cover the fence.

For decades, designers overlooked herbs when planning flower gardens. This arresting flower border shows some of what they've missed. Jeff Dawson, former manager of the Kendall-Jackson winery garden, created this in-your-face herb and flower border, comprising purple and lemon basils, dwarf gold zinnias, and purple amaranths.

especially nice growing along paved paths. Versatile plants, lavenders can also be woven into traditional knot gardens or interspersed with shrub plantings. In mild-winter areas, consider sweet bay as hedging (clipped or unclipped), prune it into elaborate topiaries, or grow it in large urns.

For optimal growth, combine perennial herbs in a flower garden with other perennial plants that have similar cultural requirements, such as easy-to-grow coneflowers, gaillardia, daylily, yarrow, goldenrod, coreopsis, and compact varieties of joe-pye weed. Ferny-foliaged fennel and dill provide a great backdrop for substantial flowers like dahlia, black-eyed Susan, and large geraniums.

Specialty Herb Gardens

Herbs are extremely versatile in the garden, yet when most folks think of a culinary herb garden, they picture the classic geometric herb garden described below. For me an herb garden has a much broader scope; it can be a garden of edible flowers, spices, exotic herbs, and much more.

For example, diminutive herbs, such as creeping thyme, 'Fino Verde' and 'Spicy Globe' basil, Roman chamomile, and chives, are perfect for a mini–herb garden. Imagine fashioning a dainty rosemary topiary as the centerpiece in

a dish garden (a miniature garden in a shallow container) with a selection of the aforementioned plants.

Tropical-style gardens continue to be popular, and herbs fit right in. Some of the tallest, namely lovage and angelica, easily grow to 6 feet and are at home with large-leaved plants like bananas and cannas. Enhance the tropical feel of a temperate herb corner with perilla (red and green) and 'Lettuce-Leaved' basil. If you live in a warm climate, grow authentic tropical herbs—ginger, lemongrass, and Cuban oregano.

Consider an ethnic herb garden. If you love Mexican cuisine, grow Mexican oregano, papaloquelite, culantro, and cilantro. An herbes de Provence garden would comprise lavender, sweet marjoram, summer savory, French thyme, rosemary, oregano, fennel, and sweet bay.

Some herbs, like basil and thyme, come in so many different varieties that a single-species garden can generate a lot of visual—as well as culinary—appeal. A basil garden might include 'Aussie Sweetie', 'Spicy Globe', 'Mrs. Burns Lemon', 'Thai', and deep purple 'Red Rubin'.

Or think about an herb garden with variegated leaves like green and white 'Pesto Perpetuo' basil; yellow and green 'Icterina' sage; purple, green, and white 'Tricolor' sage; green and white variegated 'Silver Lace' society garlic; and yellow and green lemon thyme.

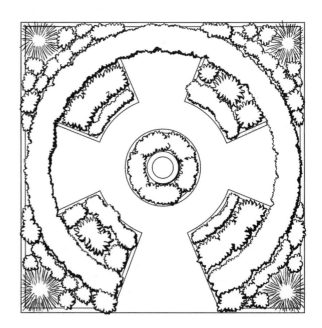

This beautiful design has a central focal point set off by the circular path and surrounding square. Traditionally, the inner circle is planted with a dramatic plant. As an alternative, you can pave the center and create a platform for a container or fountain. Create this open garden in a lawn or patio area; to highlight it, enclose it with a hedge or fence.

Geometric Herb Gardens

The time-honored geometric herb garden has a long history dating back to medieval monasteries. The three most common designs, illustrated here, are based on a circle, a triangle, and a square. Replicate one of these a dozen or more times over a half-acre and you can create a garden comparable to the famous French Jardins de Villandry. Other patterns include the spokes of a wheel, a checkerboard, and elaborate designs like those in a hand-sewn quilt. For a broad look at the many ways herb gardens were tailored to fit different eras and tastes, peruse books on the history of garden design and old herbals.

You can create any of the three 20-by-20-foot geometric gardens shown here in a weekend. Choose herbs with unusual forms, such as chives, dill, or fennel, for the middle of the beds, and select herbs with a uniform shape, such as thyme and curly parsley, or ones that can be easily sheared, like rosemary, winter savory, and dwarf lavenders, as edging plants.

Installation is simple: First, mark off a 20-by-20-foot area using stakes and string. Remove any existing sod, gravel, or ground cover. If the soil is poorly drained, make 12-inch-high raised beds. Select one of the designs shown and trace it on the ground using stakes and string (or lime or flour). Dig out the pathways. Amend the soil in the beds

with compost or other organic matter. Install the path material—brick, stone, or lawn. Finally, plant the beds with your chosen herbs. Your geometric herb garden will fill in during the first summer, and with a few trimmings each year, will give many seasons of pleasure.

Edible Flower Gardens

For me, the value of edible flowers, beyond their beauty, is their range of flavors. In my book, even when a flower is safe to eat, it's not worth including if it doesn't taste good. Of course, safety is of utmost importance since some flowers are poisonous. And while all culinary herb flowers are edible, vegetable flowers often are not. For example, eggplant, tomato, and potato blooms are poisonous.

To learn which flowers are edible, check out the only two books on the subject that I trust: Cathy Wilkinson Barash's *Edible Flowers: From Garden to Palate* and my book *The Edible Flower Garden*. Cathy's thorough research of the subject has resulted in her vetting nearly 100 flowers, most of which she has grown herself. She has been indulging her passion in edible flowers since childhood and is the first to caution, "Don't eat it unless you can positively identify a flower as safe and edible."

And to see a creative, small-space edible flower garden, I found no better place to visit than the edible flower

A variation on equilateral triangular beds that together form a square, this garden design appears more difficult to create than it really is. Paths cut diagonally across the garden, forming four triangular beds. Create a square path at the center of the design by squaring off the innermost points of each triangle. Create this garden in a lawn or patio area.

This simple yet elegant garden is a variation on the traditional four-square garden; the central paths bisect at right angles, creating four squares. For this rendition, remove the innermost corner of each square to form the space for a path and small square at the very center. A hedge or fence around the perimeter provides privacy and strengthens the design.

maven herself at her Cold Spring Harbor, New York, home (Zone 7). Over the course of several visits, her pie wedge–shaped garden was filled with dozens of different plants, varying from season to season and some from year to year. Stepping-stones bisect the garden, leading from the patio to a compost pile that is well concealed by a flavorful 'Gertrude Jekyll' rose. For several years, a large cedar arbor, variously covered with scarlet runner beans, hyacinth beans, and a climbing rose, led you down the path.

Although Cathy's favorite edible flower, pineapple guava, is not hardy, she had a small tree growing in a large tub that she moved into her sunroom in fall. Its showy, tropical-flavored blossoms adorn the plant in early spring when little is blooming outdoors. Her enthusiasm for creating recipes is boundless; the only limits are the seasonality of the flowers. From violet-infused chocolate cake topped with candied violets and tulip tuna salad in early spring, to summer's southwestern-style fried squash blossoms and anise hyssop–mushroom pizza, to autumn's pineapple sage corn fritters, Cathy's edible flower creations are mouthwatering. When flowers are plentiful, she chops edible blossoms, blends them into butter or cream cheese, and freezes the mixtures to use for baking and for dips during the off-season.

Herb Combos

Certain combinations of herbs and flowers seem meant for each other. The following are just a few compatible groupings to get you started:

- A border of gray sage, oregano, and sweet marjoram interplanted with pink geraniums, fronted by a border of 'Homestead Purple' verbena
- A sprightly combination of citrus-flavored herbs in a large urn: fountain-shaped lemongrass at the center flanked by lemon and lime basils—all surrounded with variegated lemon thyme and 'Orange Gem' marigold
- An appealing border for humans and hummingbirds filled with pineapple sage and red beebalm interplanted with flowering red salvias
- A Thai cuisine lover's fantasy mixture: Thai chilies, 'Thai' basil, and mint for curries and wraps interplanted with tropical-looking dwarf cannas in bright colors
- A tea garden overflowing with German chamomile, jamaica, anise hyssop, and lemon verbena; in a mild climate, a planting of tea at the back of the border
- A smoky dark backdrop of bronze fennel, red basil, and red perilla for sparkling white 'Sonata' cosmos

See the "Edible Flowers" section in Chapter 4 for a listing of landscape-worthy plants. You probably have some edible flowers like daylilies in your garden already but may not have considered them for eating. For an unexpected burst of color and flavor, plant broccoli at the back of the flower border. Once you've had your fill of broccoli, let the green florets open to yellow blossoms and mix them into a salad or stir-fry. When zucchini or other squash is going gangbusters, practice "family planning" by harvesting the flowers.

Plant edible flowers in annual or perennial borders, or tuck them into corners of the vegetable garden to help attract beneficial insects. Picture a flower garden that boasts the tastiest varieties of rose, with a front border of thyme, chives, and dwarf nasturtium. Incorporate anise hyssop, sage, lavender, and dill in another area. Add a backdrop of pineapple sage, fennel, lovage, and Japanese red mustard. All have great edible flowers and visual pizzazz.

Exotic Herb Gardens

While most folks are aware of common herbs like parsley, rosemary, and sage, once they start growing herbs they soon learn about dozens more. I'm always learning, too. Wanting to feature some exotic herbs in this book, I turned to Rose Marie Nichols McGee to design and create an herb garden that would showcase both exotic culinary species and some of the latest varieties of common herbs. Rose Marie grew up at her parents' renowned herb nursery, Nichols Garden Nursery, so you could say that she knows herbs from the ground up. I met her when I still had much to learn about herbs, and she was a generous teacher.

Rose Marie chose a sunny area adjacent to a large shed behind her house in Corvallis, Oregon. In late spring, her son, David, and her husband, Keane, helped remove a weedy 22-by-22-foot area of sod and incorporate some compost. Rose Marie wanted a focal point in front of the shed, so they rolled in cedar stumps from a downed tree and gathered up a bunch of containers and set them atop the stumps. In these, she planted an 'Improved Meyer' lemon, lime leaf, 'Arbequina' compact olive tree, lemongrass, chili peppers, and a columnar apple in the very center. She placed some 'Icterina' sage and roses in the beds and planted different creeping thymes between the paving stones. She finished filling the beds with some of her favorite herbs—borage, garden sorrel, 'Sicilian' oregano, willow-leaf sweet bay, winter savory, mioga ginger, garlic chives, society garlic, anise hyssop, lemon verbena, and a collection of her

This little garden in Corvallis, Oregon, is full of surprises and could qualify as a gourmet cook's fantasy herb garden. Specifically grown for this book to illustrate how little space it takes to grow a huge range of so-called exotic herbs, it lies behind the home of Nichols Garden Nursery owners Rose Marie and Keane McGee. Over the years, Rose Marie has developed hundreds of exotic recipes for her books and website from the many edibles in her gardens.

favorite basils, including 'Green Pepper', 'Greek Columnar', and 'Blue Mountain'.

When I visited the garden, I asked Rose Marie to name a few choice ways to cook with the more unusual species. In autumn, when basil has faded, she sprinkles tarragon leaves generously on a salad. 'Sicilian' oregano is essential for the Greek food her family adores. She uses lime leaf and lemongrass for Thai soups and curries. Mexican oregano, combined with cumin and garlic, makes black beans come alive. Curry leaf, with an aroma reminiscent of curry powder and a distinct citrus and pepper flavor, is traditional in southern Indian cuisine.

Rose Marie likes to fry the leaves in a little butter or oil and crumble them before adding them to a dish. Both she and her husband enjoy "experimental cooking"— exploring new uses for the many exotic herbs she grows.

For more information on exotic herbs and their culinary largesse, read Carole Saville's *Exotic Herbs*.

Herbs range from common plants such as chives and parsley to exotic edibles such as galangal and pineapple guava flowers. The beauty of herbs is that there is always room in an edible landscape to add more as your palate becomes more sophisticated and your tastes change.

A Gallery of Design Ideas

Herbs bring visual grace to any garden and enliven the kitchen, as well. Include them wherever you can tuck them in or, better yet, devote large areas to these incredible plants. For inspiration, see what gardeners from around the country have done with herbs.

Marcie and Daniel Hawthorne's hilltop herb garden in San Luis Obispo, California, enjoys a nearly frost-free coastal climate and exemplifies many design principles. Three levels give dimension; a grape arbor and native oaks form a roof over the garden; stones and succulents (and limiting flower color to shades of pink) unify the design; and steps lead the eye to a pond and distant hills. Daniel built the retaining walls and pond with native stone from the property. Marcie, an adventurous cook and artist, grows standard herbs and lemongrass, 'Thai' basil, pineapple sage, ginger, and water chestnuts.

Meadowbrook Farm, a distinctive estate garden outside Philadelphia, was designed by the late J. Liddon Pennock Jr., a floral designer and horticulturist. The herb garden follows a traditional four-square formula with geometric beds around a square within a square. The classic style of the columns and containers and the clipped formal shapes of the main plants add to the formality. Among the herbs are garlic chives, sweet bay trimmed as topiary, a ferny planting of dill, and creeping thyme as ground cover.

I designed this hillside garden with herbs among perennials (iris and penstemon) and orchard trees (apricots, plums, and apples). I limited the flower colors to purple and yellow and curved the path to go along the crest of the hill. Two does made their home on this property. Fortunately, deer shun most culinary herbs, though these devoured many of the other so-called deerproof plants we added. Years later, they still avoid the rosemary, oregano, lavender, chives, thyme, and garlic chives planted along the walk.

Herbs are wonderful in borders, such as this dramatic row of lavenders, but they also work well tucked here and there to break up the stark look of a large patio. Mother and son Sandra and Andrew Hogan tore up the parking area on their Greenwich, Connecticut, property to create this herb garden with bluestone paths. The many shades of gray herbs partner beautifully with the house color.

6 | Designing with Vegetables

My first garden memories are of helping my father plant corn and lima beans in his vegetable garden at our Needham, Massachusetts, home when I was five. After planting, we eagerly anticipated the first signs of life emerging from the soil. Each morning Dad and I headed out to the garden. The exhilaration we felt when we discovered the first few shoots was palpable.

Our yard was pretty standard for its time. The fenced-in backyard vegetable garden lay in a sunny area to the left of the garage—bordered on one side by a wide path leading back to the house. Fruit trees guarded both sides of the walkway. My dad cared for the vegetable garden and fruit trees and mowed the lawns. He planted vegetables in orderly rows and tied up the tomatoes with old nylon stockings. In fall he stocked the root cellar with potatoes, beets, and carrots and checked every few days for spoilage.

As a child, I was vaguely aware of an overall garden rhythm. In autumn Dad cleaned up vegetable debris, spread fallen leaves on some beds, and planted others with annual rye. In spring he spread manure, turned it all under, and we started planting again. His soil was rich and light; the vegetables we harvested in summer and fall were healthy and bountiful.

Years later when I started my own vegetable garden, I forgot this process and just dug some holes in a corner of my new yard, which was heavy clay, and planted a few tomatoes; they hardly grew at all. In desperation, I took a few leaves to the nursery. Fortunately, Al, an experienced nurseryman, took me under his wing. As he was talking about my lack of soil preparation, I began to recall my father's garden—the smell of the manure and mulches, and the feel of the soft, fluffy soil. Al said that vegetables are hard-working plants that need the sun's energy and lots of organic matter in the soil to produce. From then on, I took his words to heart.

Today, my front-yard vegetable garden is completely integrated into a lively edible landscape. Visitors can pick luscious cherry tomatoes as they walk up my front steps and stroll along the pathway to my front door; they also pass boxwood, roses, and coreopsis. The beds are filled with red basil, dramatic zucchini plants, and pimento and chili peppers. Yet with all that edible bounty, passersby see only a great garden. My vegetables have leapt the backyard fence!

Only 20 years ago it would have been unimaginable to include vegetables in a book on landscaping. Since the early 1900s, conventional Western landscape designers have pretty much limited designs to hardscaping, exotic woody plants (trees and shrubs), a few hardy perennials, and large lawns. I propose that vegetables not only belong in a home garden but are a vital part of our new sustainable model, a world in which every person takes responsibility for *some* of his or her own food.

This chapter helps get you started in that new direction. It covers not only vegetable garden planning and basics, but also the aesthetics of designing with vegetables, making the most of these edibles' ornamental attributes. The gallery of design ideas at the end of the chapter is sure to provide inspiration, no matter where you live and garden.

Practical Considerations

Where do you start if you want to grow only a few vegetables? Most folks head to the nursery and buy several tomato plants and a packet of zucchini seeds; some ask for garden advice. Then they go home and start planting. If they select a garden space that has good soil and gets full sun, water the plants throughout the growing season, and pull a few weeds, they will have vegetables to harvest. Of course, they may encounter a few pest problems. Some are universal, such as flea beetles, while others are more regional. Eastern and midwestern gardeners might find a lethal squash borer or two on their zucchini, for example; southerners risk losing their eggplants to nematodes. Yet, by and large, every gardener will pick enough flavorful, soul-satisfying vegetables to get hooked and will want to grow more.

With a little guidance, they—and you—can grow even better, more productive, and beautiful vegetables next season. Here's how.

Planning

Over the years, I have come up with a list of questions that I ask all my edible-landscaping clients; I'm sharing them—along with some of my suggestions—with you.

Preceding pages: Designer Linda Vater's potager in Oklahoma City is edged with clipped boxwoods and filled with peppers, tomatoes, and basil.

Grow what you like to eat. At harvest time experiment by combining ingredients—raw in salads, roasted, or grilled. One afternoon I picked a mouthwatering mix of 'Persian' cucumbers, 'Golden Dawn' and 'Raven' zucchini, 'Green Ruffles' basil, 'Blushing Beauty' peppers, and 'Sungold', 'Celebrity', and 'Early Girl' tomatoes.

◆ *Where do I put the garden?*
Site the garden in a place that gets at least 6 hours of sun, well away from trees with their shade and greedy roots. Locate it near a source of water, as seedlings require daily watering. Consider the cook; he or she is happiest when a garden is close enough to dash out for tomatoes or just-ripe melons. Open your mind to all the possibilities: you could remove a strip of front lawn, commandeer an unused parking area, or add some planters or barrels to the patio.

◆ *How big should the garden be?*
A vegetable garden can be any size. A small garden—200 square feet (20 by 10 feet)—is ample for four tomato, six pepper, six broccoli, a few dozen bush bean, and two zucchini plants plus an interplanting of greens and a few herbs. If you also want a bean tepee, cucumbers, more tomatoes, chilies, chard, and basil, you're looking at a 500-square-foot garden. To include corn, trellises of pickling cucumbers and melons, and enough winter squash for a family of four, 1,000 square feet is optimal. Installing a 200- to 500-square-foot garden is a doable weekend project. A 1,000-square-foot garden obviously requires more time.

◆ *How do I want to access the beds?*
Limit the width of garden beds to 5 feet; any wider and it's hard to weed or harvest. Place stepping-stones in the beds to prevent soil compaction. Surround the beds with paths at least 2 feet wide to provide room for walking and a wheelbarrow. Mulch the paths with organic matter such as wood chips or straw. In wet climates, line the paths with gravel or stone to keep your feet dry.

◆ *How much time and effort do I want to put into the garden?*
A few tomatoes and peppers and a zucchini require little time. A dozen tomato plants and a few

tepees of pole beans take more time and effort since the tomatoes and beans need staking and tying. In addition, the harvest is generous; unless you share it, you'll have to freeze, dry, or can it. The Encyclopedia evaluates the time and effort needed for each vegetable.

♦ *What do I want to grow?*
Make a list of the vegetables that would make a difference in your cooking. It's hard to find mâche and red carrots in most local markets; perhaps they will be among your choices. If you remember the fun of harvesting potatoes with your grandmother, you may want to share that joy with a child. Maybe you've always fancied those big heirloom tomatoes in rainbow colors. Think past the limitations of the grocery store. For example, the lowly zucchini is multidimensional when you grow it yourself. The flowers are perfection in frittatas, and baby zucchini are delicious sautéed whole; or let the zucchini grow larger to stuff and bake. And the different colors—dark to light green, yellow, and striped—add another dimension to your garden.

♦ *What grows well in my climate?*
Northern and high-altitude areas generally have short, cool summers. Vegetables that require a long growing season, such as Mexican chilies and some heirloom tomatoes as well as heat-loving okra and watermelon, are not suitable in such climates. Instead, seek out short-season varieties that tolerate cool conditions. In some parts of the Deep South, summers are so hot that autumn and winter are better suited for "summer" vegetables. Many southern gardeners plant tomatoes in early spring, harvest a quick crop before it gets hot, and plant another crop in early fall. Look for seed companies in Sources and Resources that carry varieties for short and cool seasons.

♦ *Are deer, raccoons, and/or rabbits likely to be garden pests?*
If you prepare a feast of vegetables, they will come. A fence at least 8 feet tall works best for deer; a

Warm-Season vs. Cool-Season Vegetables

When I first moved from Boston (Zone 5) to Northern California (Zone 9), I wasn't sure when to plant my vegetables. In my new climate, local newspapers made much ado about fall being a great time to plant some vegetables, but which ones? After years of muddling through, I had a "eureka moment" when I heard a Cooperative Extension agent say that the edible part of a vegetable indicates whether it's a warm- or cool-season plant. To sum it up:

Leafy vegetables, such as this pac choi, kale, lettuce, mustard, and chard from my 100-square-foot garden, grow best in cool weather.

♦ You eat the *seeds* or *fruit* of a *warm-season vegetable*, which grows best when temperatures are between 70 and 100°F. (Botanically speaking, vegetables like tomatoes and squash are fruit.) For example, since you eat the seeds of corn and beans, and the fruit of eggplants and cucumbers, plant these vegetables in spring so they have a long warm summer to grow. Most warm-season vegetables cannot tolerate any frost.

♦ You eat the *roots*, *tubers*, *bulbs*, *flower buds*, or *leaves* of a *cool-season vegetable*, which grows best between 50 and 70°F. Since you eat the roots of radishes and carrots, the flower buds of broccoli and artichokes, and the leaves of spinach, arugula, lettuce, and chard, they are all cool-season vegetables. Plant in early spring or early fall (in winter in mild climates). Although some cool-season vegetables, such as beet, cabbage, and carrot, tolerate hotter weather, they flourish in cool weather. Many of these plants— radish, spinach, and arugula, for example— not only grow poorly in hot weather, but they also become tough and inedible. Most cool-season vegetables tolerate mild frosts.

Of course, there are exceptions to any rule. Although you eat the tubers of sweet potatoes, they need hot weather—and even though you eat the seeds of peas, they prefer it cool. And why is winter squash called winter squash even though it wants heat? Because its hard skin makes it a good keeper—lasting through much of the winter—while its thin-skinned cousin, summer squash, does not store more than a week or so.

2-foot-tall electric fence keeps raccoons away; and a 2-foot-tall fence of rabbit wire controls rabbits. See Appendix D for more detailed information.

◆ *Where will the compost pile be?*
Since the compost pile is the engine that runs the garden, most people prefer to site it near the vegetable garden so they don't have to haul debris or compost any distance. Make sure there is a nearby water source for dampening the pile as needed.

After you've reviewed and answered these questions, you'll have a realistic objective for your garden. Then you're ready to get down to basics.

Vegetable Garden Basics

You'll find plenty of information between the covers of this book to get you well on your way to growing a vegetable garden. See Chapter 2 for all the dirt on soil and analyzing your property and Appendix C for general how-to information on everything from preparing the soil and sowing seeds to harvesting. Contact your local Cooperative Extension Service for climate-specific information on vegetables you want to grow and recommendations of the best varieties for your area.

Tips for Beginners

If you haven't grown vegetables before, I encourage you to consult one of the classic books on vegetables, especially *The Vegetable Gardener's Bible* by Edward C. Smith, *Burpee: The Complete Vegetable & Herb Gardener* by Karan Davis Cutler, *Lasagna Gardening* by Patricia Lanza, and *How to Grow More Vegetables* by John Jeavons. In addition, follow these tips for a prize-winning vegetable garden:

◆ Make sure your garden has rich, organic, well-drained, fluffy soil with a pH between 6.0 and 7.0; it's critical for growing healthy vegetables.
◆ Position plants so tall ones like corn and staked cherry tomatoes are in the northernmost part of the plot, where they won't shade shorter vegetables.
◆ Interplant long-lived tomatoes, peppers, and other such plants with fast-growing plants like spinach, lettuce, and radishes; harvest them before the larger plants fill in.
◆ Provide support for sprawling plants, including most tomatoes, cucumbers, pole beans, and peas,

to save space, prevent diseases, and make vegetables more accessible for harvesting.
◆ Allow ample room between plants so they can grow to their full size without rubbing elbows with their neighbors. Good air circulation prevents many diseases.
◆ Determine the first and last frost dates for your area and plan your vegetable garden accordingly. Planting recommendations on seed packets, in plant catalogs, and in garden books are based on those dates.

Many longtime gardeners, myself included, learned by trial and error. Following these tips will save you from many failures and encourage bountiful harvests.

Design Aesthetics

Feel the warmth of the sun on your back as you plant tomato seedlings in spring, smell the vines as you tie them up, hear bees buzz as they pollinate the flowers, and finally taste the first warm, sun-ripened cherry tomato. Each of these events is a rich aesthetic—and sensual—experience, yet traditional backyard vegetable gardens, with their haphazard look, generally lack a visual aesthetic. So, for ages, homeowners thought that they couldn't grow vegetables as a featured element in their landscape design and certainly not include them in the front yard; they had to relegate these edibles to "the back 40" since they would be unsightly. Fortunately, over the past 20 years, we've loosed the vegetable garden from its homely roots, transforming it into a new art form. The New American Vegetable Garden is now a legitimate ornamental style.

Let me start with a common concern. Whenever I give presentations on edible landscaping, there is usually some apprehensive gardener in the audience who asks what a front-yard vegetable garden looks like in winter. My response is always the same, no matter where I'm giving the presentation: "If you've given the area a comfortable sense of scale, created interesting lines, and added a third dimension, you already have the solution to the problem."

In winter, my father's garden just looked like a bunch of snow-covered lumps, which was the winter rye. Not as ugly as a totally barren garden or a large expanse of brown lawn for that matter, but nothing to write home about. By contrast, my mother's garden (although it was mostly flowers, it easily could have been vegetables) was dynamic in winter. A white picket fence separated her garden from Dad's, and a hedge bordered two sides. Its focal point was

Sherry and Jerry Cash's Oklahoma City garden (designed by Roger Runge of Garden Design Associates) bowled me over. A far cry from parallel rows in the "back 40," this raised garden surrounded by native stone with stone squares arranged on diagonal lines has both high style and function. The squares beautifully suppress weeds and keep the soil cool in summer and warm it in spring. Here, summer vegetables had been harvested, leaving chives and the last of the summer basil. Many types of kale fill the bed.

a large white trellised bench. A long grape arbor entry, a large linden tree, and a lengthy flower bed completed the scene. The composition gave it pizzazz in all seasons and from any viewpoint—even from my second-story bedroom, and especially when it snowed. That same area could have been planted primarily in edibles and it would have had the same winter appeal. It's not just the plants; it's the design of the garden that gives it style.

Once you've answered the questions in the "Planning" section earlier in this chapter, you're ready to incorporate some of the design principles and elements covered in Chapter 4 to create a beautiful vegetable garden, one snazzy enough for the front yard.

Line

Traditionally, the American vegetable garden has been rectangular or square and planted in straight rows. Look at it from either end and all you see are straight lines that draw your eye out of the area—like an endless highway. Viewed from the side, you look across the rows and see a solid mat of plants with no lines.

When I visited the Findhorn Foundation Center in Scotland 30 years ago, I had an epiphany. Their garden had long rows of similar plantings—celery, bush beans, peppers, parsley, leeks, and runner beans. They planted the shorter vegetables at the front of the garden, with each row successively taller. *But,* unlike in a typical vegetable garden, the rows curved from left to right. There I was, standing in the middle of a giant arc that seemed to wrap around me. It gave a sense of place that no straight-line planting could ever achieve.

You can take this concept of curved beds and make it more suitable for a home garden by adding a path down the middle, putting a bench at the center, and planting some flowers along the edges, creating a veritable retreat—a feast for your eyes and your kitchen. Or, as

Starting Small: A Tomato Box

If you're new to vegetable gardening or don't have a lot of time to garden, it's best to start small and then get more ambitious down the road when you have more experience. Growing six to eight tomato plants in a raised wooden box is a great and almost foolproof way to start.

The benefits of growing tomatoes (or other plants) in this kind of box are many:

- No weeding: the plants shade the soil, preventing germination.

- Versatility: you can grow most vegetables and herbs and some fruits, such as strawberries; you could even grow pumpkins and let them trail out onto the grass for a season.

- The soil in the raised box drains quickly so roots don't rot.

- Tomatoes get off to a fast start; the soil heats up earlier in spring.

- Mole and gopher problems are easily solved; staple ¼-inch hardware cloth to the bottom of the box before adding soil.

- If you wrap the box in rabbit wire or hardware cloth so it extends a foot above the rim, you can ward off rabbits.

- Ideal for older gardeners or those with bad backs: no bending is required for tying up plants or harvesting fruit.

Your tomato box should last for many years and provide hundreds of pounds of luscious tomatoes.

MATERIALS
4 pine boards (common framing lumber, not pressure treated), 2 by 12s, each 12 ft. long; cut into 9-ft. lengths (sides) and 3-ft. lengths (ends)

Screwdriver

Wood screws

Level

Hammer

Galvanized nails

Garden soil

Organic compost

Soilless potting mix

All-purpose organic fertilizer

David Mill of Pottstown, Pennsylvania, created this tomato box. His simple design: long, narrow boxes made of sturdy lumber that eliminate the need for midway supports and corner posts. "It transformed my harvest from fair to fabulous," says David, "with no early blight."

8 tomato plants

8 stakes or tomato cages, 6 ft. tall

INSTALLATION

1. Screw boards together to make two rectangular boxes.

2. Choose area that gets full sun; set one box on ground and level it.

3. Place other box on top of first box and toenail boxes together with galvanized nails.

4. Fill boxes with mixture of good garden soil, compost, potting soil, and all-purpose organic fertilizer (following package directions).

5. Plant eight tomatoes in box, evenly spaced. Stake each plant or surround it with large tomato cage.

Water and watch the tomatoes grow. A friend in Pennsylvania built this tomato box and grew three tomato plants—a cherry, 'Celebrity', and 'Early Girl'—with a whopping yield: 471 cherry, 166 'Celebrity', and 112 'Early Girl' tomatoes, for a total of 67½ pounds in one season.

---

shown in the photo of Sherry and Jerry Cash's Oklahoma garden, stone squares in a decorative pattern give the area personality. One technique I've used to give interesting lines to a vegetable garden is to paint wooden trellises in a bright color and install them upright to support vines or lay them down horizontally in the beds and interplant them with greens and herbs (see the photo in the "Wheat" entry in the Encyclopedia).

Another way to vary the lines in a vegetable garden is to use the time-honored geometric shapes of traditional herb gardens. See "Geometric Herb Gardens" in Chapter 5 for inspiration. Also look to historical European vegetable garden styles, including French potagers, medieval cloister gardens, and English cottage gardens, for more ideas.

Scale

For decades, while driving through different regions of North America, I've been struck by the sight of all the small garden beds—plunked in the middle of large lawns or in front of two-story houses—that seem to have no relevance to their surroundings. Often the scale is completely off, as if the tiny beds were an afterthought. Extensive lawns and substantial houses need large garden beds to balance the landscape.

When you create planting beds, whether they are edible or not, make them sizeable, and do it proudly and with the exuberance necessary to create a true sense of place. Reserve small beds for around the patio, along pathways, or as borders. Try designing a number of small beds that together form a large, pleasing geometric shape. Any garden bed needs to be in proportion to the buildings and space around it.

Formal and Informal Designs

Formal vegetable gardens have a long history in European potagers and parterres. In such gardens, the design goal is to give a feeling of balance and restraint by arranging the plants in a repeating pattern, such as six cabbages on either side of a border or lettuces in a geometric pattern. You'll find flowers in formal vegetable gardens, but they are generally limited to domesticated, highly bred species, such as tulips, roses, geraniums, and dahlias. Espaliered fruit trees and clipped blueberries, currants, or other shrubs add traditional appeal.

By contrast, informal vegetable gardens are more relaxed and have fewer restrictions. Paths may be curved or straight, beds vary in size and shape, plants differ in height,

Katrina Blades designed her Birmingham, Alabama, potager in the classic style. The beds edged with neat clipped boxwood hedges are filled with red beets, chard, and lettuces. The white wall and the focal-point urn, along with the hedges, are the formal components of this elegant garden.

and the number of species is far greater. This feeling of bounty—rarely static—evolves from year to year and develops a personality all its own. The gardener goes from being the designer in charge to an editor who often thins out plants that are overabundant. After a few years, many plants gain volunteer status, come up on their own, and are allowed (or encouraged) to reseed. This bounteous style delights garden visitors of the human kind and is amazingly alive with wildlife. Birds feed from plants that have gone to seed, butterflies have a much wider selection of flowers from which to sip, bees and dragonflies flit about, and pest-devouring toads have places to hide.

I welcome volunteer plants. I like the whimsy they add and the fact that they are time- and money-savers since I don't need to replant them year after year. Self-seeding old-fashioned ornamentals—kiss-me-over-the-garden-gate, tall cosmos, species zinnias, plumed celosia, alyssum, and many others—are right at home in my gardens, too. After you've been gardening in one place for a number of years as I have, theoretically you could just lightly rake the beds, water them, and see what happens. My guess is you'd have an exuberant, bountiful garden.

Color

Once the bones of the vegetable garden are in place, it's time to think about adding color. For eons, vegetable gardens have been green—all green. There seemed to be an unwritten law, "There shall be no color in the vegetable garden." Twenty-five years ago, I found out how deep-seated that mindset was when I designed and planted a vegetable garden for a client and, as always, included flowers in the design. At their garden party, friends oohed and aahed over the great tomatoes and rich "beany" string beans, but most of the conversation centered on the flowers. I overheard guests saying, "Can you believe it? She put flowers in the vegetable garden?" Thank goodness that issue is behind us; today most people enthusiastically welcome such intermingling.

The list of flowers you can add to vegetable gardens is almost endless. At Disney World's Epcot Center, I saw giant red amaranths and rows of yellow and orange marigolds surrounding a bed of golden and orange chard. The Kitchen Garden at Denver Botanic Gardens has featured a pumpkin patch backed by sunflowers in diverse colors. The colorful flowers are a relief from basic green, but their most important effect is subtler: attracting— and feeding with their nectar and pollen—the beneficial insects that control pests. (See the "Attracting Beneficial

Garden writer Linda Askey's Birmingham garden (designed by Charlie Thigpen of The Gardener's Gallery) is informal and capricious. It's an environmentally smart garden, making use of recycled concrete. Just outside the garden, a hedge of basil is seen on the left and taro on the right behind a large sugar pan. Within the garden are a multitude of plants, including okra, tomatoes, summer squash, and a large fig tree.

Insects" sidebar in Appendix D for information on beneficial insects and the flowers that attract them.) Always include a few flowers in a vegetable garden.

Once free of any green restraints, you can begin to look at vegetables in a painterly way. Use your imagination—the sky's the limit. Start by selecting colorful vegetable varieties; you'll discover a wide range of plants and colors. For example, if you're partial to burgundy and purple, there are dozens of vegetable varieties with burgundy foliage, like chili peppers, cabbages, and beets; and, of course, the fruits of purple peppers and eggplants. Some of the flowers that precede the vegetables are showy, too, like the large clusters of scarlet runner bean blossoms and the huge yellow squash flowers that peek out from under the dramatic leaves. For detailed lists of showy edible varieties, see Chapter 4.

You can use other techniques to bring in even more color. Perhaps the simplest is to paint garden objects; just choose your favorite hues. A single vibrantly colored gate, picket fence, or wall invites visitors into a vegetable garden, proudly declaring, "I am a significant visual space." Vivid containers enhance the garden, too. Most nurseries showcase an array of gorgeously colored glazed containers in a wide range of sizes (bring them inside in fall so frost won't damage the finish). Add zest to your vegetable garden with painted bamboo stakes and colorful cushions for your garden chairs. Take advantage of garage sales to find recycled ceramic tiles, old retro metal motel chairs, and cobalt blue bottles to enliven the garden. The point is that a vegetable garden is no different from any other ornamental garden when it comes to adding color.

I designed a "Greens Garden" up my front walk to show off the many foliage colors and textures of various greens. I edged the bed with chartreuse feverfew on one side and parsley on the other. Numerous fancy mustards, purple baby pac choi, and lettuces, such as red 'Forellenschuss' and deep green 'Reine de Glace', fill the bed, mixing and contrasting their many different colors.

Taste

Most of this section has covered visual aesthetics, yet the main reason we grow edibles is to enjoy great flavor: sugar-sweet carrots, spicy and smoky hot peppers, and tomatoes with a deep rich flavor. When you choose vegetable varieties, you want the best, but not all varieties are created equal. The greatest virtue of a particular variety may be its disease resistance or productivity. While that's all well and good, you also want—and deserve—fantastic flavor. Here are some ways to discover what suits your taste—before you plant:

- Visit farmers markets. If you like a specific farmer's long frying pepper, for instance, ask for the variety name and where it was grown—farmed locally outdoors or in a greenhouse.
- Attend vegetable tastings at county and state fairs and Slow Food events.

- Share information with other gardeners and find out which varieties they like.
- Ask at local nurseries; some offer less common organic or heirloom starts. (At big home improvements stores, you most often find varieties selected for most of the country—not premium ones for your area.)
- Start some vegetables from seed, as this offers you the best selection of really good varieties. Growing edibles from seed isn't a big challenge. Think about it; most of us wouldn't be here if our ancestors hadn't been able to start their own seeds!
- Try a variety more than once before you write it off since a particular season may have been unfavorable for that variety. (For example, a lot of rain waters down the flavor of tomatoes and melons, whereas a cool summer makes them less sweet; hot weather makes snap peas tough and lettuces bitter).

◆ Above all, trust your own tastes and preferences. It doesn't matter that a chef likes the meaty flavor of 'Buttercup' squash if you prefer the more subtle 'Cornell's Bush Delicata'. Choose the varieties you and your family like.

Follow these suggestions to ensure a flavorful harvest instead of suffering through ho-hum tomatoes or tasteless melons.

Incorporating Vegetables into a Landscape Design

Historically, mainstream designers, who design primarily for industrial and estate gardens, seldom considered incorporating perennial vegetables such as asparagus, artichoke, cardoon, horseradish, Jerusalem artichoke, and rhubarb—by far the most popular attractive perennial vegetables, though there are also less common ones like chayote and oca—despite the fact that all would add visual interest to any garden. Today that is changing.

Those same designers seldom considered annual flowers—much less vegetables, most of which are annuals—as true landscaping plants, and short of adding a bed or two of these blooms, didn't factor annuals of any kind into a garden scheme. Yet the under-recognized and undervalued importance of all annuals is their impermanence and wide emotional appeal. Add them as splashes of color—accents you can change whenever you want. The ritual of planting annuals is one of the best ways I stay connected to my garden and its soil.

Perennials

Since perennial edibles require a permanent space in the garden, you should start with them.

Asparagus is the most popular, and because it has unique cultural needs, it is usually grown in its own bed. If you've seen asparagus only in the supermarket, you might not have a clue about how it grows. In spring, the asparagus stalks rise up out of the ground. Cut individual spears off at ground level as you need them for about 6 weeks. At that point, allow emerging stalks to grow up and leaf out, renewing the plant for next year's harvest. The 4-foot-tall, fernlike plants remain attractive for the rest of the growing season. In autumn, the fronds turn a rich yellow, adding an unexpected dash of seasonal color. During one of my visits to Longwood Gardens in Pennsylvania, I photographed a 3-foot-deep bed of asparagus beautifully screening the compost area from the vegetable garden. Tall yellow marigolds grew in front of the asparagus; the flowers stood out brilliantly against the dense green background.

The large silvery foliage of artichoke and cardoon is magnificent in a landscape. Both plants make dramatic statements in any perennial border. In Zones 7 to 9, where artichoke is hardy, the leaves tend to die back to the ground in midsummer. My favorite way to mask that empty space is to plant tall cosmos in early summer; after the harvest, when the leaves start to die back and you cut them down, the cosmos is already a foot or so tall. Once there is no competition for light, the cosmos shoots up to its full height within a few weeks. In several months, when new artichoke leaves emerge and begin to grow, it's time to tear out the cosmos. Often yellow finches help themselves to the cosmos seeds, encouraging the plants to reseed themselves.

Although rhubarb's harvest season may be short, its bold presence persists until frost. It is a traditional kitchen garden plant; no doubt your grandmother grew it near her back porch. In arid climates, where rhubarb gets spider mites that disfigure the foliage, it is probably best planted in the "back 40," but healthy bright red stems and dramatic large leaves are striking on either side of a path or in mid-border. Plant it where you can sit with a cup of tea and watch the late afternoon sunlight transform the red stems into stained glass. Show it off in a border with daylilies running alongside the

Self-Sowing Edibles

Find out which of these vegetables self-seed in your climate. Depending on your preferences, some are blessings while others may be nuisances. Some drop their seeds in place; others spring from your compost. Encouraging the self-sowers you enjoy saves time and energy. After a few years, you'll recognize the leaves of your favorite seedlings so you don't accidentally pull them up. The following are the most common self-seeding edibles:

Arugula	Miner's lettuce
Beans	Mustard
Beebalm	Orach
Chili peppers	Shungiku
Lettuce	Tomatillos
Mâche	Tomatoes (heirloom and cherry types in particular)

Dean Riddle's Vegetable Garden ✎

While I was leafing through a kitchen gardening book, photos of landscape designer Dean Riddle's garden in New York's Catskill Mountains (Zone 5) grabbed my attention. So many of the components resonated with me: the use of materials like the stone-bordered raised beds and twig fence, the obvious health of the plants, the efficient use of space, and the good cultural practices, like growing many different species and including flowers to attract beneficial insects. It's a simple design, striking a nice balance between formal and informal. The rustic shed and inclusion of cottage garden plants like cleome, tall cosmos, sunflowers, and nicotiana counter-balance the classic geometric four-square design and the repetition of more restrained plants like germander and Gem series marigolds. Raised beds provide a shadow line, that is, a pleasing line around the beds; a French blue chair acts as a focal point, holding your eye in the garden.

Fortunately, the photographer, my friend Dency Kane, has been shooting Dean's garden for a number of years. Viewing her other images allowed me to see the garden in its iterations over time. In the photos, a central focal point looked like a raised bed surrounded by a wattle fence. Imagine my surprise when Dean told me it was a tire planter. He explained

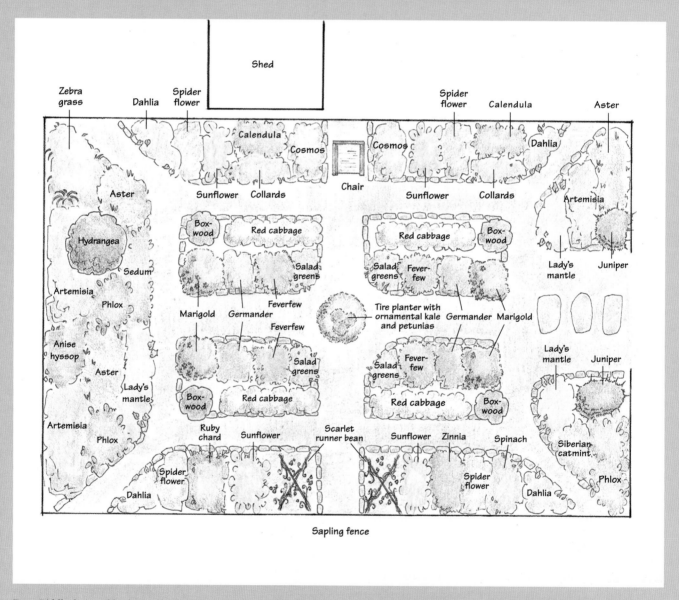

Dean Riddle designed his bountiful vegetable garden using the classic four-square concept, which is not only eye-pleasing but also functional. The raised beds are built of stone and a tire planter is in the middle of the garden. The beds are filled with countless vegetables and flowers.

Dean doesn't plan every square inch of his garden; he edits emerging seedlings, leaving red orach, nasturtiums, and others. He sweeps the paths every few weeks and scrapes young "weeds" growing out of place. Cabbage, ornamental kale, herbs, and greens are among the edibles here.

that he had never dreamed of using the truck tire that had been there when he moved onto the property, but when he laid out the garden, it seemed like exactly the right thing. Indeed it is!

The Catskills are a cool-summer area; the garden is in a valley where the cool air sinks. Dean has learned what he can grow (cherry tomatoes, lettuces, nasturtiums, beets, arugula, short-season bell peppers, and cole crops) and what he cannot (basil and big tomatoes). A favorite dish from the garden is warm lentil salad with roasted red peppers and feta cheese, topped with arugula flower buds, which add a nutty, peppery flavor and tender crunch—and a challenge for his guests to identify.

While Dean's garden is very specific to its site, rising from the hollow toward the mountains beyond, it is such a versatile and thoughtful design that gardeners all over North America can easily embrace the four-square concept and make it their own.

In early spring, the "bones" of Dean's vegetable garden are clearly visible. The raised rock beds drain well and warm up early in spring. Dean fashioned the twig fence from saplings. Hardware cloth—nailed to the bottom rails of the fence and buried a few inches below ground—keep rabbits at bay.

garage or combine rhubarb with ruby chard, red landscape roses, or red geraniums in a patio bed.

Horseradish and Jerusalem artichoke are in a category by themselves as they are invasive. Keep both within bounds by planting them in bottomless trash cans so the roots are contained and will not spread. Horseradish has slightly undulating basal leaves that grow to 36 inches long; a dramatic variegated horseradish with green and white leaves is smaller and easier to keep in bounds, though it often reverts to green. When not eaten by flea beetles, horseradish adds substance when growing alongside smaller-leaved plants like black-eyed Susan and purple coneflower. Jerusalem artichoke, with its small, sunflower-like blossoms, grows 8 to 10 feet tall, so set it at the back of a border and provide support or else it will flop. It is a splendid companion for large grasses, canna, and joe-pye weed. A bonus: Jerusalem artichoke is a magnet for beneficial insects and birds.

Two substantial rhubarb plants flank the entrance to David White and Robert Jakob's Long Island, New York, garden. Their large, dramatic leaves are in bold contrast to the small leaves of the boxwood and blueberries close by. When afternoon sun hits the red stems, the effect is like stained glass against the wood trellises.

Annuals

To me, annual vegetables are like garden eye candy, from the brightly colored stems of 'Rainbow' chard to 'Australian Yellow' lettuce and variegated 'Fish Pepper' chili pepper. All are spectacular additions to the decorative garden.

Whimsy, a bit of surprise, and delight—annual vegetables can add joy to any ordinary ornamental landscape. When visiting Denver Botanic Gardens, I was tickled to see big orange pumpkins hanging down from a large white arbor. As I stood there taking photographs, I turned and saw children pointing with glee at the pumpkins growing in such a delightful way.

One recent spring, I grew a bed of tulips underplanted with a mesclun salad mix. It was such a success that I now underplant fall bulbs with all sorts of salad greens. I've also grown edible table arrangements—low containers filled with herbs or greens to put on the table instead of a flower arrangement. My favorite was Bibb lettuces planted in a geometric design in a shallow square terra-cotta container; it was a showstopper. On another occasion I planted purple baby pac choi with white violas in the corners of the same square for another eye-catching centerpiece. Needless to say, the container lived outside and was only brought to grace the table for special guests.

Specialty Vegetable Gardens

In 1984 I took out our front lawn and started using the area as my trial garden. Since then, with the help of a succession of gardeners, I've changed my front garden and planted all sorts of new edibles twice a year—that adds up to nearly 50 trial gardens. Having read Barbara Damrosch's book *Theme Gardening*, first published in 1982, I thought it seemed like a fascinating way to organize a garden space. I found that, given the thousands of vegetables and herbs I could grow every season, making each one a specialty garden with a theme helped limit my choices each season. For instance, in 1992—the 500th anniversary of Columbus's landing in the New World—I planted a garden full of indigenous plants, including the "three sisters" (beans, corn, and squash, a trio of companionable plants that Native Americans traditionally grew together), tomatoes, chili peppers, sunflowers, and amaranths.

I've grown scores of children's gardens; you'll see photos in this and other chapters. Over the years, I must have planted and cooked produce from at least a dozen

In his Decorah, Iowa, garden, photographer David Cavagnaro was aiming for a tropical foliage theme with decorative cannas and coleus. He enhanced it with textural and bold-leaved annuals: savoy cabbage, collards, and a small grouping of frilly, chartreuse-hued kale. Borage, with its edible blue flowers, seems to dance about in the foreground. The gently curved lines of his vegetable plantings are much more exciting than the straight lines in the adjoining farmer's field.

distinct specialty salad gardens—some in containers, many combined with edible flowers. I've grown an Italian wild greens garden, a salsa garden, and a rainbow garden that featured everything from blue potatoes and rainbow-colored chard to red carrots and purple artichokes. As it turns out, it was great fun to choose different subjects and to do all the research; these specialty gardens have been a great tool to help limit my choices and to learn more with every vegetable garden I grew.

The following are a few of the almost limitless types of specialty or theme gardens to get you thinking about what type of vegetable garden you want to grow.

Ethnic Gardens

Until the 1970s, the American palate and cooking repertoire were fairly narrow; the preferences that dominated and limited our cuisine were for soft foods—salty or sweet—nothing bitter, and heaven forbid, nothing spicy or too chewy. Salads were formulaic, certainly no fruit, baby greens, and balsamic vinegar in view. Most vegetables were boiled or sautéed; potatoes were baked or boiled, rarely roasted, much less with olive oil and rosemary.

Yet change has come; we're slowly expanding our palate. From Mexican cuisine, we're learning about chilies and toasting vegetables to intensify flavors, and spicy salsa has now overtaken ketchup as the most popular condiment in America. European salads are multidimensional with their peppery arugula, bitter radicchio, and sour sorrel. From China we're gaining an appreciation of stir-fried, slightly crisp vegetables—even greens.

As an edible gardener, you have the opportunity to explore ethnic cuisines not available to even the most sophisticated chefs unless they have gardens; growing vegetables gives you the widest possible choices. One

Rick Bayless, chef-owner of Frontera Grill and Topolobampo in Chicago, grows a wide range of Mexican specialty plants in his home garden, including many varieties of chilies, tomatoes, amaranths, herbs, and greens.

packet of seeds costs less than a pound of most specialty food and provides flavorsome fare for multiple seasons. To get started growing ethnic vegetable gardens, see the descriptions for the seed companies listed in Sources and Resources.

Grain Gardens

It's hard to convey the feeling, but the hair stood up on the back of my neck as I prepared to harvest my first crop of wheat. My friends and I—hedge shears in hand— stood in front of these primordial golden stalks, cut the heads off, and then tossed them onto an old sheet. Why, I asked myself, had I never done this before? Probably because I thought I needed a section of prairie and a McCormick reaper to make wheat growing worthwhile.

That was nearly 25 years ago, when I was searching for an uncommon edible to expand the American gardener's image of an edible garden, especially the vegetable garden. As it turns out, there is no set definition of a vegetable, so I decided to stretch the concept as far as I could. As I looked through the Bountiful Gardens catalog, I noticed all the different grain seeds and was inspired. What a fun project it would be to grow my own wheat and then grind it to bake bread! I called John Jeavons (co-owner of Bountiful) to ask if it would be worthwhile to grow a small patch of wheat. He was equally enthusiatic, telling me that in about 100 square feet I could grow enough to make 20 loaves of bread. And that's how my adventure with grains started.

In the ensuing decades, I have grown hull-less oats and flax seed and gloried in a score of wheat harvests. Our harvesting method is a melange of John's recommendations and my neighbors' and my experiences over the years. Traditionally, our 4th of July begins early in the morning, when neighbors, friends, and family come here to join in the wheat harvest. Adults and children alike head into the garden, cut off the wheat heads, and nowadays toss the heads into a garden cart so they are easier to carry to the driveway, where we empty them onto an old sheet (a hard surface like a driveway is essential). Then we cover our harvest with another sheet and take turns doing the "tennis shoe twist"—stomping until the wheat berries separate from the husks. We take off the top sheet, remove any large pieces of straw or debris (for the compost), then gather up the bottom sheet and pour wheat berries back into the cart. I've found that an electric leaf blower is just dandy for gently blowing away the chaff. We grind up enough wheat berries to make two loaves of bread, which the children ceremoniously offer to the neighbors at the annual block party later in the day.

Wheat is one of the easiest edible crops to grow. It needs little fertilizing and has few pests and diseases. Try growing other grains, too—barley, oats, rye, and even rice (no, you don't need a paddy). Refer to the "Wheat" entry in the Encyclopedia for detailed information on growing wheat and Appendix A for information on other basic grains.

Heirloom Gardens

While there is no official definition, an heirloom vegetable is considered to be any open-pollinated variety (not a hybrid) that has been in cultivation for at least

Veggie and Flower Combos

I use my patio garden as a stage to audition different edible plants—do they grow well in containers and are they beautiful enough for an edible landscape? The star of the show this season was 'Scarlet Bees', a dwarf scarlet runner bean. Behind the 'Blue Wave' petunia are chilies and a container of edamame. Thyme, basil, and strawberries thrive in the foreground.

Over the years I've tried many combinations of annual edibles and non-edibles; here are some of my favorites:

- A geometric design of orange tulips underplanted with mesclun salad mix, bordered with parsley or frilly lettuces
- Red or orange cherry tomatoes growing over an arbor interplanted with blue or purple morning glories or black-eyed Susan vine
- A walkway bordered with intense, red-leaved 'Bull's Blood' beets mixed with white alyssum
- Cucumbers climbing up a green trellis forming a backdrop for a big splash of coral gladiolus
- Gold zucchini interplanted with large yellow dahlias bordered by red-orange species zinnias
- A bed of fernlike carrots surrounded by dwarf nasturtiums
- Pimento or red cherry peppers planted among red coleus or in front of the silvery green culinary sage edged with a row of dwarf red salvia

- A path bordered by dwarf red runner beans backed with giant red and white striped peppermint zinnias
- A large brick planter filled with upright burgundy-leaved cannas, underplanted with dark green sweet potato foliage intermingling with the bright leaves of ornamental sweet potato vine—both cascading down the face of the container
- A grouping of collards and bush winter squashes surrounded by large pink cosmos that serve as a backdrop and planted in front with vibrant purple verbena
- A windowbox filled with with a combination of purple kale, chartreuse mustards, and dwarf pink stock
- A large curved flower border planted with dahlias, echinaceas, and vivid zinnias and framed on each end with a ten-foot-long planting of ferny asparagus

For many more edible and ornamental annual combinations, consult the individual vegetable entries in the Encyclopedia and Appendix A.

They say it takes a village, and that's what it takes--friends, family, and especially neighbors--to harvest my wheat. In November we sow the wheat, and come the 4th of July everyone helps harvest, thresh, and grind it and make the first two loaves of bread. The children then ceremoniously present the loaves at our evening block party, and we break bread together.

50 years. Since the middle of the twentieth century, seed companies have offered mostly hybrid vegetable varieties, which meant that gardeners could not save the seeds, as they don't grow true to type. Consequently, thousands of open-pollinated varieties, many beloved by generations of home gardeners, were lost. This was not just a problem in the United States. According to the United Nations Food and Agriculture Organization, in the past century three-quarters of biodiversity in crops has been lost. Fortunately, in the 1970s, many gardeners became aware of this loss of genetic diversity, started saving their old varieties, and are now dedicated to preserving many of them.

Over the years I've attended conferences at Seed Savers Exchange, visited heirloom trial gardens and home hobby gardens filled with old-time varieties, and met many fascinating people. Amy Goldman, author of three books on heirloom vegetables (*The Heirloom Tomato, Melons for the Passionate Grower,* and *The Compleat Squash*), gardens in New York's Hudson River Valley. Amy grows hundreds of heirlooms both to preserve their DNA and document their individual characteristics. I may never forgive her for serving me a luscious heirloom melon at its peak of ripeness—wrapped in a cloud of perfumed fragrance, seductively smooth as it wrapped around my tongue, honey sweet, and downright sensual—bedecked with a scoop of homemade

vanilla ice cream. Since then, every time I've had a slice of melon I compare it with that perfect melon. Unless you grow melons yourself, you are limited to commercial varieties—sorry substitutes for the real thing. Store-bought melons have a cardboard texture, a light sweetness, and only a hint of melon flavor. I have grown melons on numerous occasions—mostly modern varieties—but only a few California summers were warm enough to produce a great melon, and none had the depth of flavor that Amy's had.

Many books on vegetables include melons, despite the fact that we eat them like fruit—as a dessert. Technically speaking, however, both squash and tomatoes fall under the botanic appellation of fruit (as do melons). Here are some of Amy's favorite heirloom tomatoes (all her favorites are indeterminate except as noted), squash, and melons:

- ‘Burpee's Globe’ tomato—a perfect pink globe, honey sweet; introduced by Burpee in 1935.
- ‘German Pink’ tomato—a luscious, meaty, pink beefsteak tomato; historic as it was one of two varieties given to Kent and Diane Whealy, which inspired them to found Seed Savers Exchange; brought from Bavaria by Diane's great-grandfather, Michael Ott, in 1883.
- ‘Green Giant’ tomato—large green beefsteak; sweet, juicy; potato-leaved type.
- ‘Marina di Chioggia’ winter squash—amazingly warty green squash; long enjoyed in Italy for its delicious flavor; born to be gnocchi and ravioli.
- ‘Petit Gris de Rennes’ French cantaloupe—dates back nearly 400 years; small, green and brown speckled; intensely sweet orange flesh and a melting texture.
- ‘Red Brandywine’ tomato—Amy's research unequivocally confirms that the original ‘Brandywine’, as introduced by Johnson and Stokes in 1889, was red and had standard tomato leaves; she describes it as one of the best-tasting tomatoes.
- ‘San Marzano’ tomato—Italian red plum, determinate, great taste in the right climate; Amy's research shows that this tomato revolutionized the tomato-canning industry in the 1920s.
- ‘Winter Luxury Pie’ pumpkin—introduced in 1893; small elegant pumpkin with fine lacy markings; makes the smoothest, most velvety pumpkin pie ever.

A large section of Amy Goldman's garden is devoted to growing heirloom squash and melons so that she can gather information for her many books and save the seeds of rare varieties that are in danger of becoming extinct. Seen here, with Amy, are a few of her favorites, including 'Yokohama', 'Red Warty Thing', and 'Cocozelle' squash, as well as 'Jenny Lind' and 'Early Frame Prescott' melons.

There are many variations on heirloom gardening. Some gardeners, like Amy, specialize; she's partial to tomatoes, squash, and melons. Others choose species across the board and grow a few old squash varieties among their heirloom tomatoes and spruce up the plot with heirloom flowers like hollyhocks, kiss-me-over-the-garden-gate, and love-lies-bleeding. Still other heirloom gardeners enjoy recreating a garden their grandparents grew or growing old-time oddities like top-setting and knob onions, huge 'Cow Horn' okra, and purple orach.

Valuable books for seed savers are *Heirloom Vegetable Gardening* by William Woys Weaver and *Seed to Seed* by Suzanne Ashworth, which is filled with seed-saving techniques for individual species. Visit heirloom vegetable websites and choose heirlooms that catch your fancy. Help keep these precious gene pools alive. Seed Savers Exchange in Decorah, Iowa, has the most comprehensive information on heirlooms; go to www.seedsavers.org.

Children's Gardens

When I speak about children's gardens, my presentations are full of fun projects—with the underlying message I learned years ago from Alice Skelsey and Gloria Huckaby's book *Growing Up Green*: "Gardening is caught—not taught." An elderly woman came up to me in tears after I finished my talk at the Garden Symposium at Colonial Williamsburg. "You answered why my grandchildren don't want to garden with me," she said. "I wanted them to learn to garden, so first I made them weed an area, they planted it, and I guess I nagged them to keep it up. So now they won't join me in the garden."

I hadn't realized how lucky I was when I started gardening with my dad. We had the joy of watching seedlings emerge, and together we searched for cutworms that ate some of the young plants. Every time I found one, he cheered. I was the hero in our garden story. When I was five years old he deeded me my own vegetable garden—a

Old Westbury Gardens on Long Island, New York, featured a children's garden with rainbow-colored vegetables that kids love: purple string beans, chard in many colors, red lettuces, and a toy box full of cherry tomatoes in all hues. Extra produce went to a local soup kitchen as part of Plant a Row for the Hungry, a program sponsored by the Garden Writers Association.

little plot adjacent to his big garden—with no rules. The only thing I ever harvested from that little plot was a deep love of gardening and the outdoors.

When I first moved my edible garden to the front yard in 1984, I didn't invite any of the neighborhood children in. I was afraid they would damage plants or pick flowers and vegetables. At the end of the third summer, I figured that since we were going to pull out the whole garden and put in a new one for winter, why not let some of the kids pull carrots that were ready to harvest and pick flowers. And pick them they did—for over an hour. They arranged the hundreds of flowers on the lawn next door, took the loot home, and put flower arrangements all over their houses. They christened it "The Flower Fling," and my life was never the same! Bless their hearts, they taught me to take the brakes off and enjoy the garden with all my might.

The kids were such a joy that I invited them more often. First we developed some basic ground rules:

Don't come over without an invitation. Always ask your parent's permission. And there are people places and plant places—the paths are for people and the beds are for plants. Soon I was photographing them planting peas, pulling carrots, and harvesting strawberries. Once I planned for the kids to plant sunflowers, but they decided that a "let's use Ros's hand lens and go look for spiders" session would be much more fun. Fortunately, I had learned not to have an agenda set in stone.

In the past 20 years I've grown lots of theme gardens for "my kids," including an Alice in Wonderland garden with a teahouse and bean and cherry tomato maze. I've grown plots of wheat and peanuts for them to plant and harvest, made pumpkin patches, and grown rows of strawberries for them to enjoy without asking. I've come full circle, and I see the time I spend with the kids in my garden as a priceless gift. Now my grandson Alex, who visits from time to time, has helped harvest wheat and plant a corn patch.

Enjoy your garden with children and pass the gift on. Here are a few ways to get started:

- Grow sprouts on your kitchen counter. Children have a short attention span, and many sprouts are ready to eat in less than a week. Go online for a quick introduction to sprouting.
- Plant a wine barrel with seed potatoes; layer the top foot or so with straw to make it easy to harvest the spuds.
- A bean tepee is always a winner. In addition to the fun of picking beans, kids have a great summer playhouse. Plant the beans on the outside of the poles or the plants will likely get walked on; line the floor with lots of straw to keep it from getting "icky."
- Grow pumpkins. When they are fully grown but not yet ripe (the skin still fairly soft), let the children write their initials on the side of their pumpkin with a ballpoint pen. As the pumpkins ripen, the letters become brown and hard, standing out against the orange skin. Children can have their own personalized Halloween pumpkin.
- Get a large hand lens and go hunting in the garden for creepy crawlies.
- Put in a small chicken coop; nothing delights children more than feeding chickens and gathering eggs. My neighborhood kids do it enthusiastically, day after day. And the chickens cheerfully recycle the sunburned tomatoes and spent bean vines, which eventually end up fertilizing the beds.
- Plant an arbor with several colors of cherry tomatoes. Let children pick and eat the fruits to their heart's content.

As you can see, there are endless variations on a garden full of vegetables. For more information and inspiration for designing with vegetables, seek out *The Ornamental Vegetable Garden* by Diana Anthony, *Beautiful American Vegetable Gardens* by Mary Tonetti Dorra, and *Creative Vegetable Gardening* by Joy Larkcom.

A Gallery of Design Ideas

Gardeners all across the country are embracing vegetables in their landscapes. These creative designs highlighting vegetables are certain to inspire you, whether your gardening space is large or small.

When I began working with Marva and John Warnock in Los Altos, California, 10 years ago, Marva envisioned a large vegetable and flower garden. Since all the topsoil had been removed and the ground compacted for building a large house, by necessity my design called for raised beds. My vision was a living circle of productive gardens. Marva decided a dramatic gazebo was in order; later additions were an arbor and a brick patio. Now, fruit trees line a far fence and beds overflow with beans, tomatoes, squash, herbs, and countless flowers.

Opposite: There's always room to tuck in a few edibles—even on the steps. I created this mini–edible garden using various lettuces, 'Early Girl' tomato, pimento pepper, basil, and sage. I added a splash of color with vibrant containers and salvaged fence posts that I painted and topped with yellow caps.

What a difference a yellow chair makes at North Hill, Wayne Winterrowd and Joe Eck's Vermont garden. The setting is perfection, with the tapestry of amazingly healthy lettuces; neat rows of alpine strawberries, onions, and broccoli; and clever pea tepees. But it's the terra-cotta forcing pots used for blanching chicory frisée and the simple yellow chair that give the garden its extra charm.

Opposite: A tepee makes an artful, space-saving support for large vines like pole and runner beans or passion fruit. We painted the bamboo poles blue before setting up the tepee, so it was a colorful focal point before the runner bean seeds germinated. By August, the beans were producing well. In early fall, we allowed the pods to mature and dry, then used the beans for winter soups.

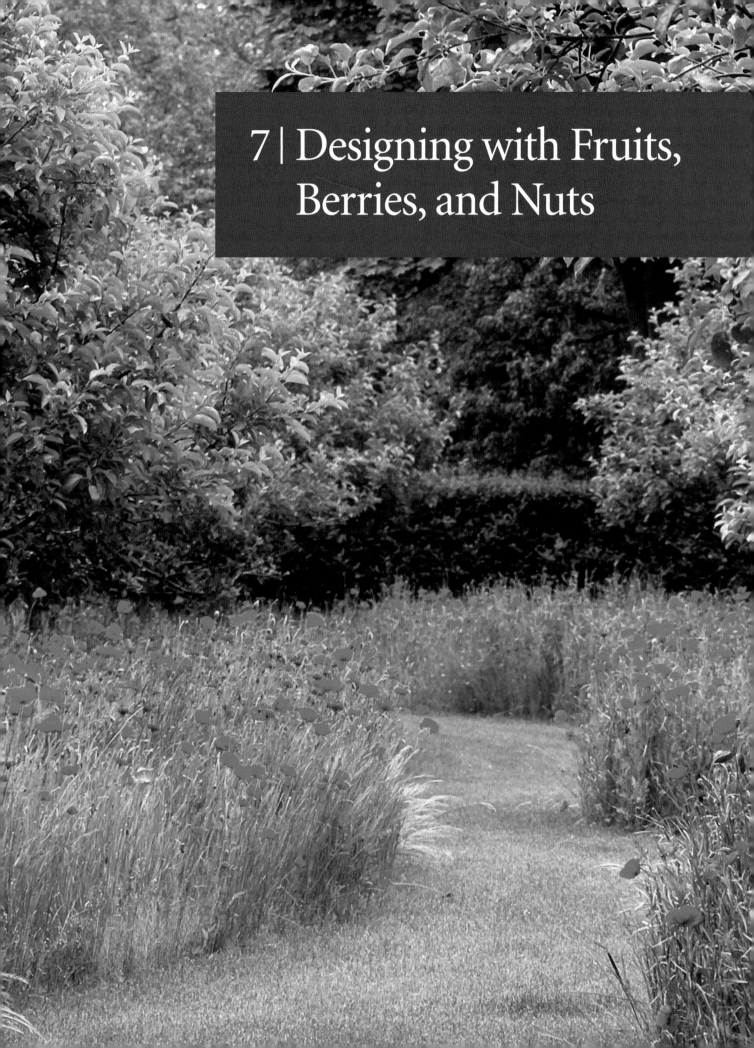

7 | Designing with Fruits, Berries, and Nuts

I usually start the day with a bowl of oatmeal topped by a handful of seasonal fruit. Sounds a bit routine, doesn't it? But, oh, what a routine! In fact, breakfast is my daily celebration of the seasons in my garden. In January I savor the last of the persimmons and Asian pears that I harvested and stored in the refrigerator. When they're gone, I switch to home-canned applesauce as well as my dried figs and blueberries, which keep me happy until late April. That's when I resume my garden harvest ritual: I take my bowl out to the front yard garden in search of what's ripe.

Luscious strawberries start off the fresh fruit season with a blast of flavor, even though the neighborhood children may beat me to the earliest ones. Soon enough, along come my favorite—ripe blueberries. They are so unlike the jumbo store-bought varieties that taste and feel as if they're filled with cotton batting; mine are complex, slightly tart, and very sweet—absolutely heavenly. Then the harvest crescendo builds. Late June brings juicy 'Satsuma' plums, the first of the blackberries, and more blueberries and strawberries. Late July and my first crop of figs is ripe for the plucking, and a luscious early melon is ready to pick—an elegant sufficiency in anyone's book. In late summer the 'Pink Pearl' apple tree starts to bear its intensely flavored fruit, the blackberries and blueberries are putting on a whole new push, and the strawberries keep coming. September brings more figs, apples (it's time to make applesauce), and a few berries here and there. October heralds the first of the pineapple guavas, persimmons, and Asian pears; they will see me to the New Year, when the cycle begins anew. I may not have an orchard, but this edible landscape is my piece of Eden.

I haven't always grown a seasonal feast of fruits. When I moved into this house in the Santa Clara Valley in 1968, there were only apricots on the property—three full-size 'Blenheim' trees, part of a once-thriving orchard. For more than a decade, I cared for them in their declining years, their demise no doubt hastened by the lawn a previous owner had installed.

Long before the Santa Clara Valley was transformed into Silicon Valley, tourists came in droves each spring to ooh and aah over the clouds of blossoms—as far as the eye could see. 'Comice' pears, 'Bing' cherries, 'Santa Rosa' plums, 'Nonpareil' almonds, and 'Blenheim' apricots—they set the gold standard for fruit and nuts worldwide. I learned a lot from those trees and from the old orchardists in the area, too. Like many fruits, apricot trees require yearly pruning to produce new fruiting buds and renew themselves. A farmer turned arborist taught me how to prune. I took classes to learn how to manage the diseases without toxic sprays (apricots get brown rot, exacerbated by lawn sprinklers raising the humidity; so if you don't spray fungicide, the tree drops lots of rotting fruit on the lawn). Full-size trees produce huge numbers of apricots in a short time. I learned from neighbors, who also had old fruit trees, how to make apricot nectar. And because there was so much fruit in the valley, a few of the old processing sheds were still operating; I learned from those folks how to prepare a 6-foot-long tray of my "cots," which they dried for me, and to use them to make apricot brandy.

My apricot trees are long gone—and so are my neighbors' orchard trees, the old-timers who took care of them, and the drying sheds. But I'm grateful for all I learned from them. And most of all, being immersed in such luscious bounty instilled in me the deep conviction that growing food utilizes our soil for a much higher purpose than growing lawn grass and azaleas.

Practical Considerations

Whether it's strawberries in hanging baskets, a fig tree in a large container, blueberries along with azaleas as foundation plants, a handsome nut tree to provide summer shade and a bounty of nuts, a few espaliered fruit trees, or a mini-orchard or -vineyard, fruits, berries, and nuts deserve space in every garden.

These plants range in size from perennial alpine strawberries no more than 6 inches tall to kiwi and grape vines that can beautifully cover an arbor to majestic nut trees that can grow more than 50 feet tall. Zone envy need not come into play. You can always grow a less hardy plant, such as a pineapple guava or citrus, in a large container and move it outdoors for summer and indoors for winter. The care and time needed to cultivate a successful harvest vary tremendously, too. There are so many plants from which to choose, no doubt

Preceding pages: Spreading apple trees in Susan and Alan Patricof's East Hampton, New York, landscape thrive among the pollen-rich poppies and bachelor's buttons.

A single fruit tree like this 'Jonagold' apple makes a statement in front of any home. It starts in spring with fragrant pink blossoms, then bears a bounty of delicious red fruits, and ends its growing season with glowing fall foliage. How many ornamental landscape plants are so rewarding?

you'll find the right ones that meet your expectations and suit your growing conditions.

Planning

I love to see a great-looking new petunia in the nursery and on a whim bring it home and plant it. But I'd never consider doing that with a fruit or nut tree—or even a vine. These plants need thoughtful consideration. Is it the best variety? Do I have room? And when does it fruit—in the middle of my annual summer camping trip?

A good way to get started is to ask yourself the same questions I ask my clients:

- *Where is the best place to grow my fruits, berries, and nuts?*
  An area in full sun with fast-draining soil produces the sweetest fruits. Grow soft fruits, such as nectarines and cherries, away from where people walk or sit. Provide protection from wind, which can tear off heavily laden branches.

- *What size trees should I choose?*
  Fruit trees range from 5 to 40 feet tall; many nut trees grow to 100 feet. Most gardeners choose dwarf and compact varieties and prune them to keep them short and manageable.

- *How many trees do I need to get fruits or nuts?*
  It depends on the variety. Self-pollinizing (aka self-fruitful) trees and shrubs don't need another similar plant growing nearby in order to produce a crop. Some require another plant of the same variety as a pollinizer; others, like 'Bing' cherries, need a different named variety, in this case 'Black Tartarian'. Refer to individual Encyclopedia entries for specifics.

- *Realistically, how much time and effort do I have to care for the plants and to harvest them?*
  Fruits like blueberries stay on the bush for weeks, but blackberries are demanding, requiring daily picking. A peach tree needs lots of effort, too: prune hard every year, spray for disease prevention, and eat or process the whole crop within a

When planning a garden, don't forget critter control. The focal point in this English garden is a formal fruit cage filled with blueberries, gooseberries, and currants underplanted with strawberries. Black wire mesh on the sides and top keeps out critters such as deer, rodents, and birds, yet the mesh is large enough to let bees in to pollinate the flowers.

few weeks. In contrast, a pomegranate or American persimmon requires less effort—minimal pruning and a harvest over many weeks.

- *What do I want to grow?*
  Try fruits and nuts at local farmers markets. Attend tastings offered by chefs and your local Cooperative Extension Service. If friends or neighbors grow fruit or nuts, try theirs; other folks can give you a realistic idea of how much effort is needed and what grows well in your area.
- *How will I protect the plants from critters?*
  See Appendix D for specific information on critter control. Generally, fences, traps, or bird netting could be in order, especially for nuts and berries. Or screen in the fruit to create a cage.

Because fruits, nuts, and berries take a few years to get established and produce, it makes sense to do your homework ahead of time.

Climate

If you're growing an annual melon, you only need to consider one growing season. However, when it comes to perennials and woody plants, a number of climatic factors affect your fruit, berry, and nut selection. To help you, individual entries in the Encyclopedia include basic climate information. The following are the most important factors to consider:

Cold hardiness. Some plants are extremely hardy. 'McIntosh' apple, for instance, can survive –40°F; Japanese persimmon is less hardy and will die at –10°F; and tropical plants like banana perish at 28°F. While the plant itself might survive low winter temperatures, some fruits and nuts, such as apricots, almonds, and filberts, bloom early, so their flowers are killed by late spring frosts. If Mother Nature complies and you don't get a late frost, you may get fruit every 4 or 5 years, and for some folks that's enough.

Chill factor. This has to do with how warm the winter is. Most deciduous fruit trees need to accrue a measurable number of hours with temperatures between 33 and 45°F to thrive; this differs from species to species and variety to variety. For the best flavor and healthiest fruit, choose a variety that is tried and true in your climate.

Humidity. This is a serious issue in some areas. For example, apples and pecans are prone to scab, while grapes can be destroyed by anthracnose in very wet weather. High humidity inhibits pollination in olives so they don't set fruit. If you live in a rainy, humid climate, choose fruits acclimated to wet conditions. When possible, select disease-resistant varieties.

Summer heat. Figs, peaches, and oranges need heat to develop their sugars, yet most blackberry varieties wither in dry heat. Hot, humid summers often mean more diseases; in areas with hot, arid summers, pollen can dry out and some fruits sunburn. For information on how heat affects plant choices, consult *Heat Zone Gardening* by H. Marc Cathey.

Fruit and Nut Tree Tips for Beginners

Getting to know the basics about fruit and nut trees will help you avoid many common pitfalls. Following are some tips to start you off if you are new to growing these trees.

- Be aware that most fruit and nut trees do not bear fruit until they are 3 to 5 years old—some even older.
- For the best harvest, plant in full sun and well-drained soil.
- The single biggest mistake new fruit gardeners make is not to prune and train young fruit trees. It is *critical* to prune a tree the first few years to establish a strong branching structure and, unless you want a 30-foot tree, to keep it small.
- Once the tree is fruiting, prune yearly to control size and encourage new fruiting wood.

- Thin out immature fruits for sweet, large fruits and to prevent some pests and diseases.
- When selecting grafted fruit trees, find out about both the scion (the fruiting wood above the graft or bud union) and the rootstock that are the best performers for your area. In cold-winter climates, make sure both are hardy; in mild-winter areas, low chill can be a factor. When possible, look for varieties resistant to your region's pests and diseases.
- Unless heavily pruned, most fruit and nut trees grow too tall for a home garden. For apples, choose dwarfing rootstocks; however, for most other fruits, a dwarfing rootstock still produces a large tree. Consistent and timely pruning keeps trees at a manageable height.

Keeping these tips in mind will help ensure beautiful and productive fruit and nut trees.

The Basics of Growing Fruits, Berries, and Nuts

With the exception of bananas, melons, peanuts, pineapples, and strawberries—all of which are herbaceous—the fruits, berries, and nuts covered in detail in this book are woody perennials. Since they are going to live more than a decade or two, it behooves us to do our homework so they will thrive.

Information abounds on growing fruits and nuts. The following books are among the most helpful sources: *All About Growing Fruits, Berries, and Nuts* from Ortho Books; *The Backyard Orchardist* and *The Backyard Berry Book,* both by Stella Otto; and, for western gardeners, *The Home Orchard: Growing Your Own Deciduous Fruit and Nut Trees* from the University of California.

Be aware that many websites have information for commercial growers rather than home gardeners. Offering a lot of help for home gardeners are Cooperative Extension Services—especially Cornell University (www.gardening.cornell.edu), Purdue University (www.hort.purdue.edu/ext), Texas A & M University (aggie-horticulture.tamu.edu/extension/fruit), and the University of California at Davis (homeorchard.ucdavis.edu).

Check out organizations dedicated to growing fruits and nuts in a home garden: California Rare Fruit Growers (www.crfg.org), Midwest Fruit Explorers (www.midfex.org), Home Orchard Society (www.homeorchardsociety.org), North American Fruit Explorers (www.nafex.org), and the venerable Northern Nut Growers Association (www.nutgrowing.org).

Fruit and nut tree nurseries with especially helpful websites include Raintree Nursery (www.raintreenursery.com) and Dave Wilson Nursery (www.davewilson.com). The Edible Landscaping forum (www.ediblelandscaping.com/planttalk) is a place where home gardeners can talk to each other about edible gardening.

Details on fruit, berry, and nut growing follow. For specific plants, refer to their individual entries in the Encyclopedia.

Tree Size

I wish I had known, when I planted a 'Satsuma' plum tree nearly 20 years ago, what I know now. It's only 14 feet tall and I thought I was keeping it small. After all, full-size plums grow to 25 feet. But my "small, semi-dwarf"

All About Flavor

What looks like a strawberry, sometimes smells like a strawberry, but doesn't taste like a strawberry? What I call a modern "Frankenstein" berry. As an elder of the tribe, I feel obligated to shout from the highest rooftop, "You are being gypped! And to a certain extent, you have sold your soul." What you're missing is what you would have enjoyed before plant scientists started breeding for size and shipability: real, fully ripe, just-picked strawberries with a flavor that is the sweet essence of summer. And ripe plums and peaches, with juices that drip down your chin when you bite into them and a taste that is perfumed ecstasy.

Unfortunately, a whole generation has grown up with cardboard strawberries, peaches, plums, and apples; the flavors and textures of the real fruits are all but lost in our collective memories. We asked for the impossible: big, perfect, cheap fruits. We wanted them out of season—peaches in the cold of November and apples in June—and farmers tried to give them to us. But how can these fruits be great when farmers pick them half-ripe, and the breeder selects for varieties that are half cellulose or mature in the cool of fall—all so they can be jounced in a truck for 1,500 miles, kept for 10 days wrapped in plastic, and made available to us anytime we want them, completely out of season? Not to mention the tons of fruit air-freighted from halfway around the world.

I selected most of the recommended fruit, berry, and nut varieties in this book for their taste. To learn more about some spectacular historic varieties, go to the Slow Food website www.slowfoodusa.org for its Ark of Taste; visit local farmers markets and ask for samples—taste and savor. We gardeners and consumers brought back heirloom tomatoes from near extinction, causing a resurgence to the point that they are now mainstream. We can accomplish the same for fruits and again have the succulent flavors enjoyed for generations. How do we do this? Grow some of your own fruits, frequent farmers markets, and buy only what's in season (read grocery labels for country of origin). We will prevail.

Fruits, Berries, and Nuts for Every Zone

Consider your climate before you choose your fruits, berries, and nuts. For gardeners in the West, visit Dave Wilson Nursery's website, www.davewilson.com, where Ed Laivo offers detailed information on choices for home gardeners. I consulted two fruit experts, Lee Reich and Mark Rieger, and asked them to provide information for northern and southern climates.

Lee Reich, New Paltz, New York

Lee Reich, a self-ascribed "fruit nut," is the author of several books I recommend, including *Uncommon Fruits for Every Garden* and *Landscaping with Fruit.* As he says, "Fruit is both my vocation and avocation." Although Lee now resides in New York's Hudson River Valley (Zone 5), his fruit- and nut-growing experience includes Wisconsin and Delaware. In choosing his favorites, Lee's criteria are "ideal edible landscape plants that are low maintenance, don't need spraying, look pretty as long as possible, and taste really good." A non-cook, his choices are based on fruits he can eat out of hand. Blueberries are his hands-down favorites.

LEE'S FAVORITES FOR THE NORTH AND MIDWEST

- Alpine strawberry—Stays in place and makes a nice edging or potted plant; "love white-fruited ones since birds don't eat them."
- Blueberry—"Did my doctorate on blueberries. My plants never failed in 17 years." All taste good. Highbush is great as a landscape shrub or hedge, lowbush as a ground cover.
- Chestnut—"One of the prettiest trees I grow." Blight-resistant Asian hybrids have good flavor: 'Colossal' (glossy green foliage turns rich yellow brown in autumn), 'Eaton River', and 'Bisalta #3'.
- Cornelian cherry—One of the first trees to bloom in spring, when branches are smothered in small yellow blossoms; nice bark, good shape, easy to grow, pest resistant.

People and wildlife savor the cherrylike fruits of a number of shrubs, including Nanking cherry. Sometimes called Manchu cherry, this easily grown and very hardy member of the plum family bursts with festive white flowers in spring, followed by scarlet fruit in summer and sunny yellow foliage in autumn.

- Filbert—Lovely vase shape; attractive catkins hang on into winter. New blight-resistant and blight-immune varieties from Oregon State University: 'Lewis', 'Clark', and 'Santiam'.
- Hardy and arctic beauty kiwi—Year-round interest: bark in winter, arctic beauty variegated foliage gorgeous throughout the growing season. Grape-size fruits have a smooth, edible skin—no peeling necessary. Other non-variegated varieties have tasty fruit and are pretty.
- Medlar—Attractive small tree with gorgeous flowers and nice foliage. "There's no other plant I can pick and eat fruit from in midwinter as I ski by."
- Nanking cherry—Fast-growing bush covered with blossoms in spring and fruit in summer ("plenty for me and the birds"); taste between sweet and sour cherry. A driveway hedge makes easy picking. Plants bear very quickly.
- Pawpaw—Beautiful all season: great pyramidal shape, large leaves look very tropical but not flashy, lovely fall color. Fruit tastes like crème brûlée when topped with cassis.
- Persimmon—Attractive foliage all summer, handsome bark, and "bright orange fruits are gorgeous clinging to bare branches in autumn." Secret to good American persimmon: grow a named variety; don't plant a seedling. 'Szukis' is very cold hardy.
- Red currant—Easy to grow, takes some shade (requires shade in warm areas), tolerates neglect. Beautiful fruits dangle from stems like jewels. Easiest plant to espalier.
- Serviceberry—Especially 'Saskatoon' (*Amelanchier alnifolia*); sweet and juicy like cherries with a hint of almond. Beautiful year round with early flowers, nice shape, gorgeous fruits, handsome bark, stunning fall color in some varieties. Often planted as an ornamental, the tasty fruit foolishly overlooked.

Although these plants are suited for the North and Midwest, they will grow in most areas of the country except in the Deep South and desert areas.

Mark Rieger, Gainesville, Florida

Mark Rieger, professor of horticulture at the University of Florida in Gainesville (Zone 9), has taught and been involved in fruit crop research since 1982. His *Introduction to Fruit Crops* is an excellent text and general reference on the subject, and his website www.uga.edu/fruit/ has a wealth of information on fruits. Mark says, "I eat fruit for breakfast every day."

MARK'S FAVORITES FOR THE SOUTH

- Asian persimmon—Among the most attractive fruit crops you can find: beautiful dark green leaves and large bright red-orange fruit. Very hardy. Even the so-called "non-astringent" cultivars like 'Fuyu' can pucker your mouth if fruit is picked too early; "best left until the leaves fall off in late autumn and the trees have a 'Charlie Brown Christmas tree' appearance—no leaves but covered with large, beautifully colored fruit."
- Avocado—'Mexicola' produces small fruits of good quality year after year. Best in Zone 9 and south. Comes back into fruiting as soon as 2 years after being killed back.

Figs are hardy to Zone 8, which covers much of the Southeast and the Gulf Coast, but they freeze to the ground when temperatures get much below 10°F. In borderline areas, train the flexible branches in a linear espalier on a south-facing wall, where extra heat helps keep the tree warm. The same technique works in cool coastal gardens where extra heat in summer sweetens the fruits.

- Blueberry—Rabbiteye and southern highbush are easy to grow and reliable producers in the South. "Documented to make you smarter and healthier (really!)." Plant three or more varieties to stretch the picking season from June through mid-August.

- Fig—One of the mainstays of edible landscaping in the Deep South, this delicious fruit is a reliable producer and an attractive specimen. 'Brown Turkey' and 'Celeste' are best.

- Hardy citrus—Several species and complex hybrids of citrus grow in areas where freezes occur annually; many do well in large containers farther north (bring them inside on coldest winter nights). Tip: buy plants propagated from cuttings (not grafted); they come back true to type if frozen to the ground. Some of the best: 'Meyer' lemon—Produces bouquets of fragrant flowers each spring; generally bears well in a container. Kumquat—Small, beautiful, evergreen trees with little, bright orange fruit for several months. Hardy to at least 20°F; grows in courtyards north to Charleston. Edible peel is sweeter than the tart pulp. 'Changsha' mandarin—easily survives temperatures down to the mid-teens; grows along the Gulf Coast and throughout the Georgia–South Carolina coastal plain region. 'Owari' satsuma—One of the best-quality hardy citrus; flavor on a par with commercial Japanese mandarins; hardiness similar to that of 'Changsha'.

- Loquat—Beautiful small to mid-size ornamental throughout the Southeast. However, since it flowers in November, fruits ripen only in mild-winter areas (Zone 9 and south). Earliest fruiting plant of the season (ripe fruit in March) in northern Florida. Small, yellow-orange, tart, and juicy fruits are well worth the effort.

- Muscadine grape—Another Old South tradition; practically bulletproof from Zone 7b south. Strong-growing vines need support and spur pruning annually to keep from becoming a tangled mass. Cultivars of bronze, red, and black fruits; most are excellent and sweet. Skin is thicker than on other grapes and is often discarded before popping the pulp in your mouth. "Some of the best juice I've ever had."

- Pineapple guava—Attractive shrub grown as an ornamental throughout the South. Handsome bark, "large, showy flowers with edible petals will amaze your friends with their tropical flavor," smallish green fruits—a real delicacy. Best for fruit: 'Coolidge' and 'Choiceana'; interplant them for good pollination.

- Red mulberry—Amazingly adaptive tree grows from the Mid-Atlantic to Miami; reliable and early fruit for the landscape; strong growers need plenty of room. Keep away from cars and patios, as ripe fruits fall and leave purple stains. Birds will love you for planting them, but add to the staining problem.

- Thornless blackberry—Does very well throughout the Southeast; can be invasive, producing large, flavorful fruit in abundance. 'Navaho' and 'Arapaho' are common cultivars.

Note that blueberry also appears on Mark's list. What a versatile fruit!

Climacteric vs. Non-Climacteric Fruits

Fully ripe fruits are prone to bruising, so commercial farmers harvest them before they reach their peak—often green. At home, you can pick each piece of fruit at its pinnacle of ripeness, right off the plant. But what happens when you need to harvest them early because you're going on vacation or an early frost is predicted?

Climacteric fruits continue to ripen after harvest: apple, apricot, avocado, banana, fig, guava, kiwi, mango, melon, nectarine, peach, pear, persimmon, pineapple guava, plum, quince, and the fruit we consider a vegetable—tomato.

Non-climacteric fruits don't ripen any further once they're picked: blackberry, blueberry, cherry, citrus, grape, olive, pineapple, pomegranate, raspberry, and strawberry.

I purchased these picture-perfect apples and pears at a Pennsylvania Amish market. Both types of fruit are climacteric, meaning they ripen further after harvest. In fact, you need to harvest European pears under-ripe and allow them to ripen for a few weeks to have a smooth texture; otherwise, they are usually gritty.

tree is so tall that we need an 8-foot ladder and a long-handled tool to prune the tree and harvest the fruit; even then, much fruit dangles temptingly just out of reach and eventually falls to the ground with a splat. Fortunately, the birds don't go after my plums because it would be really hard to cover the tree with netting.

Fruit tree sizes—standard, semi-dwarf, and dwarf—are determined only to an extent by the rootstock. Remember, a dwarf is relative to the size of the standard tree—a semi-dwarf of a 45-foot tree may grow 30 feet tall (nearly three stories high). If you want to grow a large apple tree and let migrating birds enjoy the fruits that are beyond your reach or make cider from the windfalls, by all means do so. For most gardeners, a tree less than 8 feet tall is more realistic.

The harvest from most dwarf or semi-dwarf trees is plentiful but not overwhelming. You get ample fruit for preserving, but not in such quantity that you need to spend much time canning, freezing, or drying—as you would with the yield from a standard-size tree. Furthermore, small trees are easier to spray, prune, and harvest than standard trees, and they generally bear fruit 2 or 3 years earlier. Even better, their size makes them feasible for even the smallest yards. Consistent pruning is what keeps fruit trees within bounds.

Grafting: Rootstocks and Scions

Most fruit and nut trees are two different plants grafted together. The bottom part is a named rootstock, such as 'M7'. According to Ed Laivo of Dave Wilson Nursery, one of the nation's largest wholesale fruit tree growers, the important issues in choosing a rootstock (which may be the same or a different plant) are "the things you don't know you need to know." Ed contends that it's soil adaptation, disease resistance, and precocity (how young the tree will bear) that are the main issues, more so than size control. Fruit breeders put much research into finding the best rootstock for a particular fruit. When choosing a tree, it is as important to find the best rootstock for your area as it is to choose the named variety.

Growers graft the rootstock to the scion (shoot of the desired plant cultivar chosen for its fruit, nuts, or other qualities), such as a 'Golden Delicious' apple. The resulting plant is always given the scion's name. For example, only the top, or scion, portion of a 'Seckel' pear is the 'Seckel' variety; the rootstock is a different pear cultivar, such as 'OHxF333'. The resulting grafted plant is a semi-dwarf tree called 'Seckel'. In some cases, the rootstock is a totally different plant, as when pear scions are grafted onto quince rootstocks.

Grafted trees aren't the only way to go. Some breeders and growers believe that a fruit tree grown from the seed of a superior parent is healthier and withstands the elements better than a grafted tree. Oikos Tree Crops and St. Lawrence Nurseries offer seedling fruit and nut trees.

Thinning

Fruit trees have a tendency to produce more fruits than they can properly ripen. Most types of fruit trees naturally thin some of their immature fruit in what is called "June drop," but they seldom drop enough. For the best harvest, thin young fruits when they are about an inch across, leaving 6 to 8 inches between fruits. Thinning increases the size of the remaining fruits, boosts air circulation, cuts down on diseases, evens out the harvest so one year is not heavy and the next very light, prevents limbs from breaking under the load, and keeps the tree vigorous. Do not add the fruits you remove from the tree to your compost pile, as they may be wormy.

Pruning

Prune plants to shape them for aesthetic reasons and to control size, repair damage, promote good air circulation, provide light to the interior of the plant, and inhibit or promote fruit production in some species. Pruning is a somewhat intuitive process; you have to jump in and be assertive, not timid. An unpruned plant is worse off than an overly pruned one—especially a fruit tree. In fact, you are better off replacing a fruit tree more than 3 or 4 years old that has been left unpruned with one that you keep pruned from the get-go. So much emphasis has been placed on dwarfing rootstocks, but a good pruner can control the size of most trees better than most rootstocks. For basic pruning information, see Appendix C and the individual fruit entries in the Encyclopedia.

Espalier

In the mid-seventeenth century, Father Legendre of Hanonville, France, developed espalier—a training technique that forces plants to grow flat, as if one-dimensional. Generations of gardeners have found espalier to be an elegant and efficient way to fit most fruit trees, numerous fruiting vines, and some shrubs into a small yard. While many grow espaliers against a wall or fence, you also can utilize them as freestanding screens or hedges. An informal espalier can be as simple as training a fruit tree to grow flat by not letting any limb grow outward. Photos of espaliered fruits can be found throughout this book.

The fastest way to have beautiful espaliered fruits is to purchase a pre-trained tree. Some local nurseries carry a selection and will demonstrate how to prune and maintain the espalier. Other sources include Henry Leuthardt Nursery in New York, which specializes in apples and pears, and Apple Art Espalier in California, which carries espaliered apples, figs, pears, persimmons, pineapple guavas, plums, and pomegranates.

If you cannot find the plants you want pre-trained, purchase young untrained ones and prune them yourself. You can espalier most standard, semi-dwarf, and dwarf fruits.

An espaliered tree requires a minimum of three prunings annually. How you prune depends on the shape you want as well as the type of tree. Proper training is an exciting challenge. Loquats or figs, for example, can be trained to a two-story espalier, but they require major pruning effort—with a tall ladder. Consult pruning books recommended in the Bibliography, and seek the advice of local nursery people and your County Extension Service on how to prune each species.

Supports

While espaliers give the impression of one dimension, edibles trained over an arbor, trellis, or pergola are standouts in three dimensions, lending their own

On a visit to Kew Gardens in London, I saw this gooseberry trained as a fan espalier with a planting of alpine strawberries at its base. I also saw a gooseberry grown as a standard—pruned to a central trunk with the branched top spilling out to form a small weeping tree, as is sometimes done with tea roses today.

Fruits for Espalier

The most popular fruits are commonly espaliered in the following styles:

Apple (dwarf or semi dwarf)—espalier easily to many forms: candelabrum, double cordon, Belgian fence, hedges, and palmetto.

Apricot—prune to hedges and fan shapes; requires heavy pruning.

Cherry—prune to a cordon.

Citrus—calamondin, lemon, kumquat, and limequat are easiest to espalier; prune to six- or eight-armed cordon; needs supports, requires constant pruning.

Currant and gooseberry—use as fan espaliers against cool walls.

Fig—large espalier with natural form or low, horizontal-armed, formal shape; well suited to hot south walls that protect the plant from cold and warm it with summer sun.

Grape—train to a four-armed Kniffen system along wires; south walls are good because the sun can sweeten the fruits.

Loquat—very large; espalier as a two-story plant; fairly slow growing in vertical cordon or informal shape.

Peach and nectarine—fruits form on new wood only; require vigorous pruning to produce new fruiting branches and to maintain espalier form; best shapes are hedge and fan.

Pear—takes well to candelabrum, double cordon, Belgian fence, hedges, or palmetto.

Persimmon—Asian persimmon is best for a large, informal espalier.

Pineapple guava—marvelous, large, informal espalier; shows off dramatic shaggy bark.

Pomegranate—best in informal shapes or six- or eight-armed cordon; needs constant pruning.

A pomegranate is pruned in a four-armed horizontal form, or cordon.

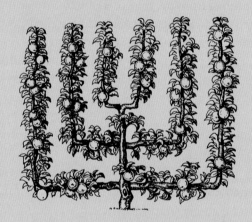

An apple is trained to a six-armed palmette verrier.

The Belgian fence pattern, which requires at least four trees, is most often used with apples and pears.

Most fruit trees, like this persimmon, can be trained in informal shapes.

In the no-man's-land between my driveway and my neighbor's, I mixed fruits, berries, and nuts among ornamentals. On the bottom tier, from front to back, are boxwood, peanuts, and sulfur cosmos; on the second tier, 'Sunshine Blue' blueberries underplanted with 'Tristar' strawberries; on the third tier, dwarf 'Pink Pearl' apple underplanted with 'Eleanor Roosevelt' iris; and on the top level, 'Misty' and 'Berkeley' blueberries sheltered by 'Fuyu' persimmon and 'Improved Meyer' lemon.

special charm to a garden. Their greatest virtue is to narrow the viewer's focus and frame a view. Vines— grapes, hops, and kiwis (both tender and hardy types)—and roses are obvious choices for training on an arbor, but also consider citrus, apples, pears, and persimmons.

Design Aesthetics

It's interesting to me how many people say that they envy me my house in the middle of an edible garden. No doubt that is partly because I can walk outside and pop ripe fruit right into my mouth for months at a time. While many gardeners enjoy lovely yards, I believe fruiting plants add certain aesthetics—a missing dimension—that no other plants can.

Here's my theory: First, your eyes spot a ripe fruit by its bright color and sensual shape. I am convinced that this harkens back to our primal selves, the ancient hunter-gatherers, who I imagine took great pleasure in discovering a ripe fruit. As your nose takes in the sweet aroma, anticipation builds. Joy is on its way. Once you bite into the fruit, its sweet juices flood your senses; now you are living fully in the moment. My flower gardens and landscape designs bring a lot of joy to visitors, but only when they are invited to sample some of the fruits do I see people really light up; the smiles come instantly. Whether it's a delivery woman sneaking a blueberry or two from my driveway planting (you think I don't see you?) or the three-year-old from across the street hunting for and biting into a luscious ripe strawberry, these are the joys my fruits bring into my life. And this extra dimension can easily be part of yours.

Trees, shrubs, and vines are the building blocks of the home landscape. In most American yards for the better part of the twentieth century that meant non-fruiting (or if they did fruit, they were not edible for humans) exotic ornamentals, such as Norway spruce and English ivy;

Starting Small: A Strawberry Barrel

At my local nursery, I saw a unique wine barrel planter with two levels of holes around the sides and many different herbs spilling out of it—like an old-fashioned, clay strawberry jar. I thought it was a very clever way to grow a lot of plants in a small space, and I was visualizing strawberries dangling out the holes, gleefully out of reach of most slugs, pillbugs, and mold.

I wanted something eye-catching, so my crew and I painted the barrel blue before drilling 18 holes (two rows of 9). I chose day-neutral 'Tristar' strawberries because they bear for many

I painted the wine barrel a lovely shade of blue to enhance the silvery hoops and show off the ripe berries. This photo shows the barrel through step 4, including adding a second layer of enriched potting mix and fertilizer.

months and send out fewer runners than many other varieties. To facilitate watering, we installed a mini–watering system using drip tubing—connected to the irrigation system with my other large planters.

We planted the barrel in May, fertilized it monthly with hydrolyzed fish, and by late August we had the first of our strawberries. The next year, the barrel produced pints of berries from May through September. The following spring, we dug up the old mother plants, replanted all the holes with the runners, and, starting in May, the plants produced through September. Not only does the showy blue barrel get a lot of admiring comments, but I haven't seen a critter on a berry yet!

MATERIALS

Drill with ½-in. and 2-in. drill bits

Large wine barrel, 42 in. wide, 24 in. tall

½-in. solid distribution tubing, cut to length as needed

¼-in. tubing with laser cuts or in-line emitters spaced every 6 in., approx. 30 ft.

½-in. end cap

1 bag of ¼-in. connector barbs, tees, and goof plugs

Soilless potting mix, 3 bags, each 2 cu. ft.

All-purpose organic fertilizer

Homemade compost, worm castings, compost tea, or other source of microbes

24 day-neutral strawberry plants

12 or so irrigation stakes (look like giant hairpins)

Organic compost for mulch

---

favorites from China like hydrangeas, tea roses, and wisteria; and, of course, Kentucky bluegrass (native to Africa). People rarely included fruit and nut trees, not even adding a stunning blueberry bush to a shrub border or foundation planting alongside the pervasive azaleas and junipers. Fortunately, all that is changing, as the many examples in this chapter demonstrate.

Of course, the fruits themselves are often the great show-offs—deep blue grapes, lipstick-red strawberries, brilliant orange persimmons, and apples in hues from deep buttery yellow to dark burgundy—to name but a few. Yet there are also show-off nuts like the purple-leaf filbert with nut clusters in burgundy-fringed cases. When it comes to color, also consider foliage—tricolor (pink, green, and cream) variegated arctic beauty kiwi, purple-leaved elderberry, and the wonderful hues that so many leaves turn in autumn, from vibrant to subtle yellows and burgundies.

Incorporating Fruits, Berries, and Nuts into a Landscape Design

As you will see, fruits, berries, and nuts run the gamut of plant types—trees, shrubs, vines, herbaceous perennials, and annuals—and you can choose varieties suitable for any climate as you think about incorporating them into your home landscape.

Trees

Trees hold a special place in all our minds. In fact, when I drive by or revisit a client's garden, I can remember every tree I selected and where it came from. There is something spiritual—almost mystical—about trees; 20 years after planting a 5-foot-tall whip, I can go back and find an amazing living entity now 20 feet tall. Trees provide shade and clean the air; large, mature ones give a sense of place and a roof for the garden. They provide

INSTALLATION

1. Drill seven ½-in. drainage holes, evenly spaced, in bottom of barrel. Then drill nine 2-in. holes 9 in. up from base of barrel, spaced 9 in. apart. Drill another row of nine holes 9 in. up from first row, staggered between holes in lower row.

2. Connect ½-in. solid distribution tubing to closest water source and run it to barrel. Measure length of emitter tubing long enough to go around inside of barrel at least six times; connect it to solid distribution tubing. Thread unattached end of emitter line through one of lower holes, and bring it up out of barrel (get it out of way for time being).

3. Add soilless potting mix up to lower level of planting holes. Following package directions, sprinkle one-third of recommended amount of fertilizer along with compost, worm castings, or other bacterially active material, and mix it in.

4. Set one strawberry plant in each hole; to avoid air pockets, press plant in place and gently pack mix around it. Lay ring of emitter tubing around plant roots and secure it with irrigation stakes.

5. Repeat steps 3 and 4, setting plants in higher row of holes. Bring emitter tubing up through soil and circle it around roots.

6. Fill barrel—to within 1 in. of top—with potting mix, add fertilizer and compost or other material, and mix together. Plant remaining strawberries 6 in. apart and firm into place.

7. Bring emitter tubing up, loop it around inner edge of barrel, and weave it among plants and toward middle of barrel. Turn on irrigation system; flush out any debris in line. Once line runs clear, plug end of emitter tubing with goof plug.

'Tristar' strawberries, a day-neutral variety that bears fruit for up to 5 months, spill out of the barrel just begging to be picked. When my neighbor's toddler spies the ripe berries and picks up their sweet scent, she heads straight for the barrel.

8. Mulch with few inches of compost; work it around plants. Use gentle spray nozzle to softly wet soil; repeat at least three times to completely saturate entire barrel. For next few weeks—until plants start to put out new growth—keep soil lightly moist but not soggy. Once plants are growing well, use new irrigation system.

This weekend project will provide enough fruit to top your cereal all summer long.

---

shelter for wildlife, and if we are lucky, some share their fruits and nuts with us.

By its very stature, a single tree has the power to be a tone-setting, front yard focal point—from any indoor or outdoor vantage point. Plant trees in clusters or in artful rows, such as for an allée, and they become the foundation of your landscape design. On a large property, site pecans or almonds along both sides of a long drive; when mature, they will create a marvelous overarching tunnel. Instead of edging the property with trees, plant a "V" with a focal point (an arbor, gazebo, fountain, or weeping plum) at the end. Utilize trees to divide the space into outdoor "rooms"—for privacy, entertaining, and play.

Most homeowners start their wish list with the most familiar, such as pears, apples, and walnuts, but there are dozens of others to consider. If you'd like a pear tree, instead of a European type, consider Asian pears. How about a hedge comprising an early-ripening apple or two, a late variety, and one that stores well for winter? And instead of a walnut, consider a butternut or filbert.

Landscape Options

When I design a landscape from scratch or a major renovation, I select the trees first since they are the most substantial plants. For instance, with just two or three fruit trees I can create a screen to block an unwanted view, such as a neighbor's garage. The trees will be covered with flowers in spring, followed by handsome green leaves and most probably bright fruit in summer, and a show of color in autumn. I could use these trees as a cornerstone for a children's fantasy play area, replete with swing and playhouse. To set off this space, I might surround it with lightweight trellising, such as bamboo or black-painted concrete reinforcing wire (using steel T-posts for support), with an attractive entryway (arched,

A venerable 'Bosc' pear tree in Darryla Green's Oregon side yard produces outstanding fruit. It also anchors a raised flower and herb bed that provides blooms for the house and herbs for the kitchen.

Home Orchards

For the second half of the twentieth century, most commercial fruit or nut orchards were planted in long parallel rows with what orchardists call a "clean floor"—bare soil—so tractors, spraying and pruning rigs, and harvest trucks could drive up and down the rows to eliminate weeds and pests, trim the trees, and haul in the harvest. In addition, humongous irrigation pipes were often situated parallel to the rows to distribute water evenly. These practices dictated straight rows and did away with wildflowers, clovers, grasses, and other cover crops that nurture beneficial insects, build soil by adding nitrogen and organic matter, discourage erosion, and provide a more sustainable system. In the early twenty-first century, a combination of events—rising petroleum prices (which in turn raised prices of chemical sprays and fertilizers) and consumers demanding more organics—led orchardists away from "clean floor" cultivation and back to the more sustainable practices of old.

Today's home fruit growers can adopt a sustainable model by clustering plants that need similar care. Instead of long, boring rows, there are dozens of imaginative ways to plant using sound design principles so that fruit or nut trees become an exciting part of the landscape. For example, create a strong line by planting a neat row of different fruit trees across the back of the yard or along the driveway. To establish more of a sense of place, front the row with a low hedge, say, dwarf boxwood or rosemary, to define the area better. Or surround the trees with a rustic fence covered with shrub roses for color, and underplant with wildflowers to attract beneficial insects. Picture dwarf fruit trees in raised planters on the perimeter of a patio with gravel walks between them; it is a charming outdoor "room," with the trees providing some privacy.

Creating an orchard meadow isn't simply a matter of throwing grass or wildflower seeds all around the trees. It takes management, including at least yearly mowing, leaving a cleared area unplanted and un-mulched around the base of the tree to help deter voles, sowing the right seeds for your area and to renew the soil, providing critter control, and avoiding and controlling invasive weeds. Good resources include *Meadows* by Christopher Lloyd and the University of Connecticut's web pages on meadows (ladybug.uconn.edu/wildflowermeadows.htm); consult Rodale's website (www.rodaleinstitute.org/) to learn more about cover crops and no-till methods.

Permaculture advocates offer yet another option. They create orchards that are more like a natural wood-

perhaps) planted with cherry tomatoes and/or mini-pumpkins. I would mulch the area under the trees heavily (5 to 6 inches), using pine needles or shredded leaves to provide a soft landing for tree climbers, protect the shallow roots, maintain soil moisture, and prevent the area from becoming muddy.

Trees are so versatile. Encircling an area with trees can create a space for people to meditate or entertain. Many fruit trees are suppler than you realize; some can be trained like vines. Beyond two-dimensional espalier, consider training two figs up and over what would ordinarily be a grape arbor. I have long fantasized about having an arbor over my front walk trained with Asian persimmons, perhaps with a climbing rose at the very front. Just imagine the color in fall.

land and cluster fruit or nut trees and underplant them with nitrogen-fixing shrubs to help feed the trees. In a woodland orchard, however, it's all-important to provide adequate air circulation within and among trees to avoid diseases; always select disease-resistant varieties.

See Chapter 8 to learn how to grow a mini-orchard in a small space.

Shrubs

The shortest woody fruiting plants are subshrubs, including cranberry, lingonberry, and lowbush blueberry varieties barely a foot high. These cold-loving, ground-hugging plants grow best under acidic, almost boggy conditions. Petite bell-like white or pink blossoms and colorful berries (red or blue) make them showy ground covers and stellar plants in containers.

Currant and gooseberry are a bit taller—3 to 6 feet—as are the shorter highbush blueberry varieties that range from 2 to 8 feet. Use these wonderful freestanding "woodies" in large, sweeping shrub borders by themselves or combined with native or locally adapted flowering shrubs and perennials such as edible alpine strawberry and daylily as well as non-edibles like holly, viburnum, and bleeding heart. A 3- to 4-inch-deep layer of mulch out to the drip line gives a neat and tidy appearance. Install fairly large stepping-stones among the shrubs and ground covers to give access for pruning and harvesting without compacting the soil.

As productive and showy as grape, kiwi, and subshrubs are, large shrubs are the workhorses of the home landscape. Growing from 10 to 20 feet tall, cornelian cherry, elderberry, Nanking cherry, pomegranate, rabbiteye blue-

A split-rail fence planted with roses surrounds this side yard orchard. Plum, apple, and pear trees underplanted with California poppies create the perfect landscape (designed by Matt Walker) for this dramatic house.

David Cavagnaro's Fruit Garden

David Cavagnaro, an extraordinary man, is an acclaimed photographer, writer, and conservationist. He was the first garden manager at Seed Savers Exchange and has been a good friend for well over 20 years. Living and gardening in northeastern Iowa (Zone 3), David "experiences frost 11 months of the year." Nonetheless, he takes edible landscaping to a new level while going back to the traditional skills of grafting, seed saving, and preserving food. He overlays all this production with an extraordinary level of aesthetics from garden to table.

Even before building his current home and extensive gardens in 1991, David set his goals: sustainability and self-sufficiency. He never drew a design on paper; his strategy was to work with the topography. He was lucky to have "a sensitive bulldozer guy, who buried the original weed-filled topsoil as he scraped and leveled the surface, and covered everything deeply with good soil." The garden closest to the house was originally a rose and flower garden, but over the years more fruits, vegetables, and edible flowers replaced plants that were strictly ornamental.

Instead of fencing the area, David positioned grape and raspberry trellises as well as hedges "as a labyrinthine barrier around the garden to deter deer." In addition to the gardens by the house, he has an extensive fence-enclosed vegetable garden in which he grows numerous heirlooms for eating (fresh and preserved) and seed saving.

David is a firm believer in using recycled materials. He found wire and old barn wood from which he fashioned fences and trellises. His grapes come from cuttings from neighbors' plants. In addition, Elmer Swenson (a hybridizer

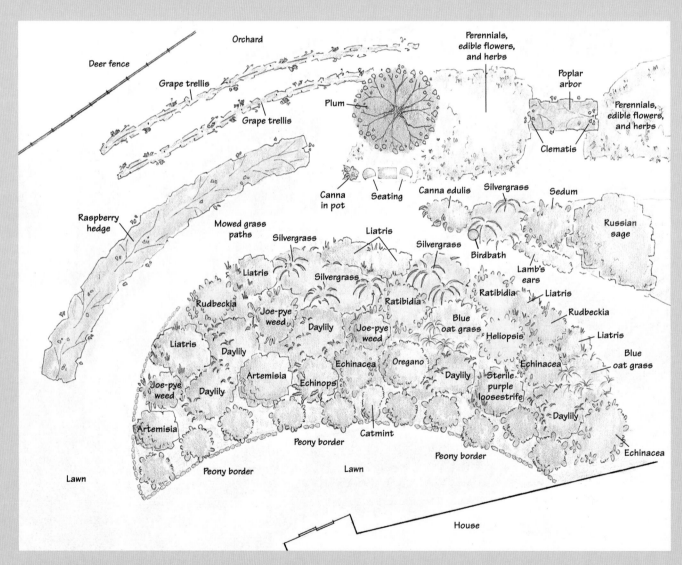

David's garden has evolved over the years, starting with roses planted in bare earth. With its abundant fruits, it has become an elegant edible landscape that contributes to David's self-sufficiency.

David filled the foreground bed with perennials, edible flowers, ornamental grasses, and prairie natives. He surrounded it with a feast of fruits—a raspberry trellis and grapes trained on wires partially screen the orchard, nearly hidden in a swirl of morning mist. A 'Tokah' plum shades a seating area with two chairs and a small table.

known for his cold-climate varieties) shared many plants, including table and wine grapes. "I grafted fruit trees on apple rootstock I grew from seed, and dug up suckers from plum trees on my previous farm."

Every time I visit David's garden, I'm struck by its beauty and its bounty. The view from his living room porch reveals a lovely perennial garden encircled by fruiting vines and trees. It is truly amazing what David harvests and produces each year just from the various fruits he grows: 25 gallons of apple juice and 35 gallons of grape juice as well as currant and raspberry juice; "raisins" from grapes and currants; applesauce (with many variations combining apples with raspberries, currants, and pears); canned plums; and a freezer full of strawberries, currants, cherries, and raspberries. He is also a great cook and is famous for his edible mandalas—works of art that he arranges on a platter in 15 minutes from his own fruit, vegetables, and edible flowers.

When David and Joanie Cavagnaro purchased their property, it was overgrown farmland. Following the topography, David and a skillful bulldozer operator sculpted the soil to create the setting for a future landscape. Here, Joanie plants roses in the bare terrain.

berry, sea berry, and native fruits, such as beach plum and serviceberry, are deciduous. Fairly easy to maintain once established, these multistemmed plants are primarily vase shaped, requiring only an annual pruning to remove dead-wood, renew the plant, maintain a pleasing shape, and keep them tidy. Such productive beauties can screen a neighbor's camper or garage and delineate property boundaries. Interplant them with lilac and non-edible weigela and evergreens; make a hedgerow for native and migratory birds by planting enough for humans and critters, or line the driveway and create a welcoming colorful entry. Try your hand at training them as small trees. However you treat them, large shrubs will provide an abundance of treats for you and local wildlife.

Brambleberries

Brambleberries fall into three categories—erect shrubby types, semi-erect types, and trailing types that can spread to 10 feet. Attach the stems of all but the stiffest vertical varieties to wires, or train the plants along trellises or fences to prevent them from flopping and becoming a thicket. Note, however, that many brambles sucker, requiring a root barrier and/or vigilant pruning to keep them in bounds. For ease of harvest, prune upright types to 5 to 6 feet tall. Either weave the trailing types through double rows of wires or train them on the tops of fences and trellises.

For too long, raspberries and blackberries have been underutilized in home landscapes. When kept controlled and tidy, they add a wow factor to any patio planting. I have a magnificent thornless 'Black Satin' blackberry that spreads 6 feet in either direction atop my wall; I often ask dinner guests to help themselves to a perfect berry or two to drop into their champagne. Practical as security barriers, the thorny types are equally chic. Train rows of brambles on wires to surround and frame a large perennial flower and herb garden or to screen a dog run or utility area.

My 'Black Satin' blackberry bears pink flowers starting in late spring, then fruits from early July to late August, weaving its berries among the blooms of my exuberant 'Polka' climbing rose. The blackberry is beautiful, but the intensely flavored berries add a dimension to my front patio far beyond any mere ornamental vine. One year the harvest from this one plant measured nearly 30 pints.

Vines

Woody vines add their own unique twist to a landscape. The most versatile are grape and kiwi.

Kiwi plants are long, robust vines that need the strong support of a permanent trellis or arbor. Female vines can spread from 10 to 20 feet. Keep the male vine (necessary for pollinizing) smaller by pruning it back after it flowers. Cover a patio or breezeway with the large, dramatic female vines. It's heavenly to look up at the flowers and fruits hanging down—easy picking, too. Since you harvest the fruit before it is ripe, fruit drop is not an issue.

Grapevines are more versatile in the landscape than kiwi vines. A woody grapevine can grow 20 feet to cover a huge arbor, yet a talented pruner can train the grape as a compact, 6-foot-tall, stand-alone, weeping tree. Train grapevines on wires in either a single or double cordon (arms) to serve as a screen or decorative fence substitute. An ever-growing number of homeowners are discovering that they can train parallel rows of grapes in the cordon manner for a small vineyard—a delightful way to landscape a part of the yard. Traditionally, winery planners grow roses at the ends of grape rows for decoration and as mildew indicators. Since the roses develop mildew more readily than grapes, the savvy vineyard master gives the grapes a preventive sulfur spray at the first sign of disease on the roses. Lavender traditionally frames a vineyard. Plant poppies and other wildflowers between rows to attract beneficial insects and add a whimsical touch.

A friend in Pennsylvania trained her grapes to run up the balustrade of an outdoor staircase; it made for easy picking despite the height. In his small-space garden in Des Moines, Iowa, another friend trained grapes up 8-foot-tall posts topped with pipes fashioned like the ribs of an umbrella; they were spectacular with bunches of grapes dripping down.

Herbaceous Plants

Herbaceous plants—annual or perennial—have fleshy (not woody) aboveground parts. Some very popular herbaceous fruits and nuts—namely, melons, peanuts, and strawberries—grow in most parts of the country. (The more exotic herbaceous fruits are covered in the "Tropical and Other Tender Edibles" section, below.)

Melons and peanuts, started from seeds in spring after all threat of frost is over, generate their summer or fall harvest and then die. To crop well, they need warm

Grapevines are extremely versatile. Even in a relatively small space, you can create a mini-vineyard like this one in front of Tra Vigne restaurant in St. Helena, California. Underplanting the grapevines with wildflowers makes the scene more bucolic and encourages beneficial insects that provide pest control.

temperatures. As a rule, melons are long, vining plants with rich green, heart-shaped leaves. Train them to grow on a decorative trellis or to cascade over a retaining wall or the sides of a large planter. Consider compact bush varieties when you want a super-productive flower border; alternate them with bush squash and a colorful mix of zinnias. Bush varieties are also perfect for large containers.

The peanut's growth habit (it develops a peg—a shootlike structure—from the pollinated flower that enters the soil where the peanut will grow) is ideal for close-up observation, fascinating to the child in all of us. This annual, perky, green-leaved legume is beautiful in the front of flower borders. My favorite combo is peanuts with dwarf yellow and orange cosmos. Like other legumes, the peanut fixes nitrogen in the soil; it makes a superb annual ground cover between newly planted trees or shrubs. And there is the bonus of neighborhood kids whooping with delight as everyone helps harvest the peanuts. Later they can help clean, shell, roast, and finally eat the nuts.

Nothing is quite so eye-catching as a strawberry plant or two with dangling red fruits in hanging baskets, large containers, or raised planters. With their deep green leaves and small white or pink flowers, strawberries are quite fetching. One caveat: once mature, most varieties put out foot-long runners, making them a bit

Alpine strawberries are fruits with the flavor volume turned up. Gardeners at the Robert Mondavi Winery in Napa Valley, California, use them as a ground cover in a large bed. The fruity aroma entices visitors into the area, while the lush green leaves create a frilly carpet.

more challenging as a neat and tidy ground cover. That said, if you remove the runners, you can use the plants to line a flower border or as a mass planting in front of shrubs; provide stepping-stones between the plants for their care and harvest.

Alpine strawberries may be lesser known, but they are more versatile than garden strawberries landscaping-wise. With no runners, alpines remain neat looking when planted near a lawn or a walkway. Smaller, more intensely flavored fruits last longer on the plants than garden strawberries. Both flowers and fruits sit above light green foliage in a truly ornamental fashion. And because they tolerate light shade, they are perfect lining a woodland walk combined with other shade plants like impatiens and small hostas.

Desert Plants

What's a desert dweller to do? Desert growing is filled with the challenges of caliche soils, finding water-saving irrigation techniques, and too much hot sunlight—yet great sweet fruits are still possible. Select from among the many drought-tolerant plants native to arid climates, such as carob, date, fig, jujube, olive, pineapple guava, pine nut, pistachio, pomegranate, and prickly pear. Also consider some temperate fruits, such as apricot, peach, plum, and strawberry, especially if you provide afternoon shade during the hottest part of the year.

Contact your local Cooperative Extension Service for specific plants. *Desert Gardening* by George Brookbank covers many cultural techniques to ensure a generous harvest. *The Sunset Western Garden Book* includes many specific varieties, and the numerous Sunset landscaping books feature ideas for desert garden design.

Tropical and Other Tender Edibles

If you live in a tropical climate, where frosts seldom occur and the weather is warm and humid, there are dozens of tropical fruits to include in your landscape. Highly productive papaya, banana, and plantain grow from 10 to 20 feet tall. Cluster these iconic plants in large beds near patios and pools to appreciate their sculptural leaves rustling in the breeze, softening the edges of the day. Drape the fleshy vines of the epiphytic dragon fruit over a trellis, and position it so that its enticingly fragrant nighttime blooms fill a lanai. Combine them with edible ginger and lemongrass to enhance your kitchen repertoire. In Florida, think of large shrubs like the native sea grape and strawberry guava and vines such as passion vine and monstera with its huge leaves.

The tropics produce dozens of large edible trees, from litchi to mango, macadamia to allspice. Give them lots of space and keep the fruits clear of paved surfaces. And remember to place them so they can shade your hot south wall and save on air-conditioning costs.

Tropicals are native to humid climates, but some—for instance, pistachio and tamarind—succeed in drier mild-winter climates, such as Southern California southward into Mexico. Some tender plants like olive and pineapple guava, though not tropical, flourish still a little farther north.

Even if you live in a temperate zone, you can grow some of the more compact tender plants in containers and move them indoors in autumn: natal plum, coffee, chocolate, dwarf banana, tree tomato, cherry of the Rio Grande, miracle fruit, and Chilean guava, to name a few. You might even consider growing a pineapple or two. What an exotic and fanciful plant it is—a spiky bromeliad with a large, yellow, fragrant fruit perched like a top hat on the plant, with its own set of spiky leaves. See Appendix C for information on growing edibles in containers and how to provide cold-weather protection. For information on growing edibles indoors, see *Greenhouse Gardener's Companion: Growing Food & Flowers in Your Greenhouse or Sunspace* by Shane Smith.

I saw miniature pineapples at a home improvement store and couldn't resist their charms. These bromeliads are at home in a container, creating a fruity surprise on a patio. To my delight, they tasted good, too.

An edible garden wouldn't be the same without at least a few of the wide range of fruits, berries, and nuts available to home gardeners. It doesn't matter where you live or how large or small your gardening space, you're sure to find varieties that you enjoy and that will flourish in your climate.

A Gallery of Design Ideas

With the great range of fruits, berries, and nuts from which to choose, there are innumerable ways to create an edible landscape that features them. You can draw inspiration from what these gardeners have done.

This Eugene, Oregon, landscape is the epitome of simplicity and elegance. Homeowners Rebecca Sams and Buell Steelman, who are landscape designers, have the perfect living advertisement for their company, Mosaic Garden Design and Construction, right in their backyard. Their goal was a creative, functional, and sustainable space. The four-tree peach orchard forms the cornerstones for the stacked stone sphere that Buell designed and built. The gravel makes for easy fall cleanup and lets rainwater percolate down to the tree roots.

Architect David Dodson created a mini-orchard behind his office in Corvallis, Oregon. Apples, peaches, and plums line up in a tidy, curving sweep of lawn along the path that leads to the office. A work break affords time for David to make a quick check for pest problems or to judge when a fruit is ready for harvest.

Instead of a routine grouping of shrubs or a freestanding fruit tree in front of their Southampton, New York, cottage, William Sofield and Dennis Anderson designed the garden with three espaliered apple trees that march across the yard, bearing flowers in spring, fruit in late summer, and golden leaves in fall. All that style, and the espaliers screen the house windows from headlights, too.

Citrus has long been associated with formal gardens. At the Van Vleck House and Gardens in Montclair, New Jersey, the repeated use of trellises, citrus in containers, and similar beds of lettuces and other salad greens gives a supremely formal feel to this edible landscape. The gardens, designed by June Bonasera, are intended to preserve the spirit and beauty that originally surrounded this late-nineteenth-century house. The cold winters would soon kill off the citrus if the gardeners didn't bring them indoors before the first hard frost.

8 | Designing for Small Spaces

Although some folks may consider my total edible garden space (about 2,000 square feet) large, I have no thousand-foot beds for sizeable patches of corn, rows of fruit trees, or a big pecan tree—much less room to let my chickens run. Practically speaking, I grow food in a number of small spaces. Containers hold forth with berries, veggies, and herbs on a front yard brick patio. Lining the front walkway are several rectangular beds; both plants and design change from season to season. The area separating my driveway from my neighbor's is a major fruit-producing spot. For many years, the backyard has been home to two productive spaces that I call the "Pomegranate Patio" and the raised-bed "Plum Garden." Within the confines of these small front and backyard gardens, I produce hundreds of pounds of fresh vegetables and fruits each year.

"Small space" means different things to different people. Maybe you have a minimal garden area and would love to grow pumpkins for your grandchildren. Or you want to enjoy specialty herbs or the paprika peppers your grandmother used in her cooking, but you live in a condominium and have just a small balcony or patio. Perhaps you're fascinated by the many different types of apples but have a typical suburban plot. Or like many of us you want to reduce your grocery bills by growing some of your own food. In this chapter I'll show you ways to do all this and more in small garden areas. I'll talk about techniques to maximize your space, including growing edibles in containers, choosing compact varieties, and going vertical. And you'll learn how productive a 100-square-foot area can be. You'll find detailed information about soil, composting, planting, and container gardening basics in Appendix C.

Practical Considerations

The biggest concern when planning a small garden is how to make every inch count. How do you fit in your wish list of vegetables and herbs, as well as some berries or other fruits, and make your garden look lovely enough to enjoy viewing through the living room window? Let's begin by looking at the practicalities of dealing with limited garden space.

Preceding pages: Redwood brown and deep green unify my edible patio garden, lush with strawberries, tomatoes, cucumbers, herbs, and more.

Small-Garden Basics

Small yards present different challenges than large ones. Sometimes you need to get creative to find enough full sun for your tomatoes. Or maybe you think you don't have room for a large fruit tree and its pollinizer, or ample space for a compost bin. Almost anything is possible in small gardens; you just need to plan carefully and sometimes think out of the box. For a time-honored way to organize and grow in small spaces, see Mel Bartholomew's book *All New Square Foot Gardening*.

One of the first challenges in a small space can be sunlight—or lack thereof. Small gardens, particularly city gardens—unless on the tallest rooftop—receive less sun than larger gardens because surrounding buildings and trees cast shadows on them. A small yard might receive full sun in the winter and be in complete shade in the summer, or the opposite might be true. In planning a garden for a courtyard, patio, or deck of an apartment, study your sun patterns carefully (see the "Garden Shadows" sidebar in Chapter 2). You may find that containers on rolling casters are a simple solution, allowing you to move your edibles to take advantage of changing sun patterns.

If you're concerned about your ability to grow fruit productively in a limited area, rest assured that you can grow and harvest plenty. Espaliered fruit trees and deciduous vines, such as grapes, flourish when trellised against a south-facing wall. And they benefit the environment while reducing air conditioning and heating bills; their leaves shade the wall in summer, while bare limbs let the sun's warming rays shine through in winter. Vining vegetables, including cucumbers, beans, and tomatoes, can work the same magic. For the ultimate in small-space fruit growing, read about what Gene Yale has done in his suburban Chicago garden later in this chapter.

When a gardening book recommends composting, people with small gardens usually sigh and say, "Nice, but…" Even small properties often have an out-of-the-way corner or space under a tree that is perfect for a small prefab recycled-plastic composter. Or put one of the tumbler-type bins near the back door and camouflage it with plants. Ellen Spector Platt, who gardens on the roof of an 18-story apartment building in New York City, recommends, "Alternate layers of kitchen waste with a layer of fine soil and a nitrogen source like garden

The handsome trellis and fencing in Edwin and Verna Streeter's Michigan lakefront garden serve dual purposes. They discourage deer and rabbits as well as provide support for butternut squash, cucumbers, pole beans, pumpkins, and lots of tomatoes. The garden comprises rectangular raised beds along the sides and five square beds down the center—chockablock with zucchini, beets, peppers, onions, cabbage, broccoli, and herbs.

foliage and cottonseed meal, and you're in business." For some gardeners, a worm bin under the sink or in the garage is the most space-saving method.

And it's especially important to remember that high yields start with good rich organic soil. No matter what size the garden is, adding ample amounts of compost or manure and organic matter to your soil provides lots of humus and eliminates the need for chemical fertilizers and pesticides that inhibit microbes. Advocates of raised-bed gardening say raised beds are more productive because the soil drains well and warms up faster in spring.

Another tip for getting the most out of your small growing area is to practice interplanting. Basically, this means utilizing as much garden space as possible. In spring, consider sowing seeds for radishes, arugula, baby greens, and beets in the empty space between slow-maturing tomatoes, peppers, and cucumbers. They're in and out of the garden within 21 to 40 days—so quickly that they don't impinge on the main crop. In late summer, remove your spent bush bean and early cucumber plants and intercrop with transplants of kale, cilantro, heat-tolerant lettuces, mustard, pac choi, and green onions because they grow quickly and tolerate light frosts.

Finally, think "up." Grow vining plants vertically on supports, espalier fruit trees, utilize window boxes, and stack small planters on top of larger planters as shown in "Starting Small: A Double-Barrel Herb Garden" in Chapter 5. As you look through the photographs in the book, you will see how often intensive gardening techniques are used.

Edible Plants for Small Spaces

The most obvious way to maximize your harvest in a small space is to select naturally small edibles, such as blueberry bushes, instead of huge walnut trees. Choose super-productive varieties for the greatest yield per square foot. Or opt for a large edible you can control, like most grape varieties and even a 'Black Satin' blackberry. Although sizeable (its canes can reach 10 feet in length), this berry is easy to keep to three or four canes, trained along the top of a wall or fence. Unlike many of its kin, it doesn't sucker readily, so there is no intimidating thicket to fight off. And it's thornless, so it doesn't slash you when you work in close quarters or walk nearby.

Hybridizers and nursery growers are aware of a large new market—people who want to grow edible plants in small yards or in containers—and have responded by developing many compact vegetables and dwarf fruit trees. Quite a few are even more beautiful than their full-size cousins. Instead of 6-foot-tall gawky okra plants, look for diminutive 18-inch-high okras with red foliage. Forget those sprawling 12-foot-long watermelon or winter squash vines; grow small icebox watermelons and 'Cornell's Bush Delicata' winter squash on compact vines. Some seed companies devote sections of their catalogs to these smaller edibles; www.ContainerSeeds.com specializes in them.

See Appendix B for a list of recommended edible plants for small gardens.

High-Yield Tips for Beginners

In addition to the practices and plants suggested above, you can apply techniques used by experienced gardeners to make their efforts more productive. To get the most food from a small garden area:

- ◆ Plant mesclun salad and stir-fry green mixes; they produce a lot in a short time.
- ◆ Choose plants that produce over a long period of time, such as eggplants, chili peppers, chard, and kale, which yield a large total harvest for the space they take.
- ◆ Grow indeterminate tomato varieties, which produce more fruit over a longer period than determinate varieties.
- ◆ Plant pole beans, peas, and vining cucumbers, which are more productive than bush types, as they grow vertically and for a longer season.
- ◆ Choose day-neutral strawberries, which bear from early summer through fall, outproducing spring-bearing types.
- ◆ Include plants that are in and out of the garden quickly—for example, radishes, lettuce, arugula, and green onions—among your other edibles.

For more information on maximizing your harvest, consult *How to Grow More Vegetables* by John Jeavons. Johnny's Selected Seeds provides a detailed list of quick-growing plants through the seasons on their website.

Today, countless compact edibles are available; look for ones with names that include "mini," "bush," "compact," "dwarf," or "Nana." Here, bush beans grow on a small bamboo tepee so they take up less space and are easier to pick. Many determinate, bush-type tomatoes like this 'Window Box Roma' provide heavy yields.

Design Aesthetics

Just as choosing the right clothes can make a petite person look taller or a heavy person look more svelte, time-honored techniques can be used to create the illusion of

A small corner of my yard provides flowers for the house as well as tomatoes, chili peppers, and cilantro for a great pot of chili. A red bench, containers, and flowers catch the eye, while the fine-textured ground covers of thyme, Irish moss, and creeping mint give the illusion that this is a spacious garden area.

spaciousness in a small garden. A number of the design principles discussed in Chapter 4 are also helpful, especially line, scale, balance, and unity.

Creating the Illusion of Space

One of my favorite design techniques for creating an illusion of space is to incorporate a path, planting bed, small lawn, or deck at an angle across a client's yard. This leads the eye along a diagonal line, as opposed to a short direct line to a close-in fence. Another is to place a mirror on a garden wall to reflect a view of another part of the garden. Additionally, a garden with different levels holds your attention. I also like to use a collection of containers or a series of planter boxes to add complexity. Visual stop-and-go makes you overlook the smallness of any space.

Many designers use a technique borrowed from Asian landscapes. When there is lots of interest in a small area, the eye stops to savor one visual treat after another; for example, a ripening peach, the gnarled limbs of a grapevine on an arbor, a planter box laden with cherry tomatoes, or a small pond filled with water lilies and water chestnuts. As the eye rests on each different element, you get a feeling of spaciousness. A window into a small garden—a moon gate or a square cut in a fence—adds a sense of hidden space. Or it can provide an opening to view a special feature in another part of the garden.

Fine-textured plants increase the perceived size of a yard. Since objects in the distance—whether in a painting or a landscape—always seem smaller than those in the foreground, psychologically you associate small

Starting Small: A 100-Square-Foot Garden

In spring 2008 I decided to grow a demonstration plot to document how much food could be grown in a very small space. I chose a 5-by-20-foot patch—100 square feet—an area that is small enough for most people to set aside for food production and doesn't take much time or effort. As it was in the front yard, of course my new little garden had to look attractive.

To make it simple, I chose only vegetable varieties that were available at my local nursery as transplants and, in my experience, were either super-productive or expensive to buy as produce at the market (variety names are noted in the "Plants" list). The only vegetable grown from seed was zucchini—sowing seeds is more economical and zucchini germinates quickly. Against my better judgment, I didn't thin each hill of zucchini to one seedling but left two. If I had it to do over again, I'd make one hill with one yellow and one green zucchini and use the other hill for two bush cucumber plants. After decades of gardening I'm probably a bit blasé, but even I was amazed that it all grew so quickly—within a few weeks we were picking as many outer lettuce leaves as we needed.

It's an easy weekend project that anyone can do. The most important thing is to choose an area that gets at least 6 hours of full sun a day. It's a small enough space that you can create it out of one end of your lawn and not even miss that section of grass.

To see how much food I could produce in 100 square feet, I put in 2 tomato, 6 bell pepper, and 4 basil plants; started 2 green and 2 yellow zucchini plants from seed; and filled in with 18 lettuce plants. In just over a month, I harvested enough lettuce for 232 individual salads.

MATERIALS

Twine and stakes

Spade

Bags of compost, 4 cu. ft. total (or a few wheelbarrows of homemade compost)

All-purpose organic fertilizer

8 sturdy 8-ft. stakes

6 sturdy 4-ft. stakes

Mallet or hammer

Trowel

Drip irrigation (optional)

Newspaper

Organic compost for mulch

PLANTS

2 tomato plants—'Better Boy' and 'Early Girl' (or 'Big Beef', 'Cherokee Purple', or any indeterminate cherry tomato)

6 bell pepper plants—2 'California Wonder', 2 'Golden Bell', 1 'Orange Bell', and 1 'Blushing Beauty' (for hot pepper lovers: 'Hungarian Hot Wax Banana', 'Jalapeno')

Zucchini seeds—green 'Raven' and yellow 'Golden Dawn' (or substitute 'Salad Bush' or 'Spacemaster' bush cucumber for one hill of zucchini)

4 basil plants

18 lettuce plants—6 'Crisp Mint' and 6 'Winter Density' romaine, and 6 'Sylvestra' butterhead (or try other lettuces, such as 'Speckled Trout', 'Marvel of Four Seasons', or 'Red Sails')

12 dwarf marigold plants

INSTALLATION

1. Find spot with well-drained soil with at least 6 hours of full sun a day. Using twine and stakes, measure off 5-by-20-foot area. Remove any weeds; if area is lawn, dig up sod and use it to patch any spotty areas.

2. Use spade to dig area to depth of at least 8 to 12 in. Break up any clods and remove rocks and perennial weed roots. Mix compost and organic fertilizer (add according to package directions) evenly into soil in entire plot.

3. If possible (depending on site orientation), site tall plants on north side so they won't shade shorter ones.

items with distance. Thus, small-leaved plants, including most herbs, blueberries, asparagus, and alpine strawberries, convey a feeling of expanse, whereas plants with large, broad leaves, such as rhubarb, banana, chard, and zucchini, stop and fill the eye.

Creating a little mystery goes a long way in distracting the observer from space limitations. Visitors will wonder what lies behind an espaliered apple or around a woven screen, not giving much thought to the size of the space. My neighbor created a meditation walk between a large hedge and her back fence with decorative stepping-stones and a lovely statue along the walk. Visitors are enticed to enter by a hint of the entrance from the patio.

I kept meticulous records each time I harvested. From April to September, this little organic garden produced 77½ pounds of tomatoes, 15½ pounds of ripe bell peppers, 14⅓ pounds of lettuce, 2½ pounds of basil, and a whopping 126 pounds of zucchini! I saved nearly $700 in fresh vegetables that spring and summer.

4. Use four 8-ft. stakes for each tomato; pound stakes 2 ft. into ground, 18 in. apart, to form 18-by-18-in. "cage." Dig planting hole at center of each cage; plant a tomato in each hole. Wrap twine around stakes for support.

5. Use one 4-ft. stake for each pepper plant; allow at least 18 in. between plants; pound stakes 18 in. into ground. Plant each pepper about 4 in. in front of stake.

6. Sow three zucchini seeds of two different varieties in two separate hills spaced about 5 ft. apart. Or seed one hill with zucchini and the other with cucumbers. Once seedlings are up and growing, thin to two most vigorous plants per hill.

7. Plant basils a few feet in front of tomatoes, allowing 10 in. between plants.

8. Plant lettuces where there is room between transplants; they will be out of garden by time zucchini, peppers, and tomatoes fill in.

9. Stagger marigold plants along front of bed.

10. Deeply water all plants and seeded areas. Install drip irrigation, if applicable.

11. To prevent most weeds, lay six to eight sheets of wet newspaper between plants to cover any bare soil. Top with 3 to 4 in. of remaining organic compost as mulch.

Going Vertical

Vertical gardening is just plain practical—and pretty, as well. By growing upward, plants do not take up valuable ground—potential growing space—for anything but their roots and branches. Vertically grown plants are generally healthier than those sprawling on the ground because with increased air circulation and more leaves exposed to sunlight, the fruits do not rot. Desert gardeners, on the other hand, soon learn that vertical plants are more prone to drying winds; if they face south, the fruits and leaves can sunburn. Under these harsh conditions, give vertical plantings shelter from the wind and afternoon shade.

Both vines and climbers will grow up. Vines have ways of pulling themselves off the ground and onto sup-

Many fruits grow well in containers—strawberries and blueberries in particular. Strawberry fruits can hang down over the sides, thus avoiding slugs and rot diseases. Blueberries need very acidic soil to thrive. If your soil is neutral or alkaline, plant blueberries in a large container with acidic potting soil.

hog wire—are all easily mastered do-it-yourself projects. Or you can purchase trellising materials. The commercial options are vast and include swirly metal stakes of many colors, red tomato ladders, black wrought iron arches, powder-coated steel trellises with decorative finials, and wood pyramidal tuteurs—plain or painted. Look to repurpose old fencing and even tall antique bed headboards to support edible plants. Good sources for trellises are urban salvage yards, local nurseries, Gardener's Supply Company, and SimplyArbors.com.

Growing Fruits Beautifully in Small Spaces

Over the centuries, home gardeners have employed many ways to get maximum fruit harvests out of a small area. They grow dwarf trees, use decorative pruning techniques like espalier, and take advantage of other garden structures to grow plants vertically—think grape arbors.

For more unusual methods, do a little research and call on your creativity. A grapevine can be grown as a small weeping tree, a time-honored Italian training technique. Fig arbors are also common in Italy. Pears have been trained attractively along short fences at Colonial Williamsburg, and the Heartland Harvest Garden at Powell Gardens near Kansas City, Missouri, has numerous examples of espaliered fruit trees.

Most gardener-cooks prefer to have a manageable number of fruits throughout the growing season rather than a few huge harvests. With good planning, you should be able to enjoy your fruit season from spring through fall. Here are a few suggestions for growing fruits in small spaces:

ports; think pea, squash, and grape tendrils or the twisting stems of Malabar spinach and hops. Climbers like tomatoes and roses may want to grow up, but physically they cannot unless secured onto a support. Although some make good ground covers when given the space, vines reach for the sky and make superlative wall covers, area dividers, and shade providers. Vines are versatile—they soften stark architectural lines, add privacy, and extend limited garden space. Most of all, they move the focal point up, adding to the diversity of the garden.

For eons, gardeners have found countless ways to support edible plants. Bean tepees for children to hide in, English-style pea brush (as supports made from spring prunings are called), inexpensive bamboo trellising from renewable bamboo groves, and extra-sturdy wooden posts supporting 4-inch hardware cloth sometimes called

- Grow four or more different blueberry varieties for a 2-month-long harvest.
- Share adjoining side yards with your neighbors and plant fruit trees.
- Choose compact varieties of standard fruit trees, such as 'Weeping Santa Rosa' plum and 'North Star' sour cherry; both are compact and self-fertile.
- Practice summer pruning, which keeps your trees small.
- Espalier trees to fit into a shallow space.
- Train trees as standards or look for columnar varieties like 'Colonnade' apple.
- Visit www.davewilson.com for fruit tree options, techniques for keeping trees small, and for help in selecting varieties for your climate and space limitations.

Some popular fairly large trees, such as peaches, plums, cherries, apricots, and pears, need another tree as a pollinizer. Yet you may have only enough room for one tree. Solve this problem and extend the harvest by planting two varieties—early and midseason—in a slightly enlarged planting hole. Needless to say, this works best for dwarf varieties or trees kept small with summer pruning. Some nurseries offer fruit trees with the pollinizer grafted right onto the main tree. Especially in urban situations, it's important to attract pollinating insects, so include lots of plants with small flowers, such as culinary herbs, in your garden.

Growing Edibles in Containers

I'm addicted to growing edibles in containers. Nowadays, I have 20 or more containers going at any one time. I didn't always have so many. Years ago my only container successes were spider plants and philodendrons grown in my office. My problem was watering. I'd do fine for a while, but eventually life got too hectic or I'd be on the road and the kid next door would forget to water. All it takes is a day or two of hot weather and the poor plants either become diseased or die.

People who have no open soil nonetheless manage to garden—in containers—on balconies, tiny patios, even the edges of carports, wherever the sun reaches. And gardeners with plenty of space increase their close-in enjoyment by keeping some potted herbs on the kitchen steps, placing showy containers up the front walkway, and decorating their outdoor living space. Others with yards that are mostly shaded roll containers around on the patio to catch available rays. And there are gardeners with very small gardens, urban dwellers, and greenhouse gardeners who rely solely on growing edibles in containers.

As a landscape designer, I find that interesting containers add sparkle to an otherwise dull corner of any garden, large or small, and nicely fill in seasonal empty spaces within a small yard. Containers add dimension to a flat garden, They can function as a focal point—either a large container by itself or a cluster of interesting containers—and add color to a monochromatic planting. They also bring plants up close so you can readily enjoy the fragrance of otherwise low-growing plants like mint or sweet violets.

All in all, containers are a delight to use in just about any landscape design. In fact, you can fill a small garden space and produce lots of food in a stylish manner using only containers.

For more ideas on container gardening, see *The Bountiful Container* by Rose Marie Nichols McGee and Maggie Stuckey and *Incredible Vegetables from Self-Watering Containers* by Edward C. Smith.

Solving Small-Space Challenges

If you think you have no room for a garden, look for a space that is underutilized for its original purpose. A carport can be used to support a fruiting vine, containers can be installed on a flat roof to grow edibles, even a children's sandbox can be converted to a fruit tree planter. Maybe a seldom-used driveway takes up a lot of the yard or your property is on a steep slope; other homeowners with small yards have turned these spaces into productive gardens and you can, too.

A few edible water plants can be grown in containers if the soil is kept very moist. Here, watercress blooms in a dramatic blue container—with no drainage holes—sitting in a saucer. A Shrubbler emitter automatically adds water daily so that the plant never dries out. Grow water chestnuts and wasabi the same way.

Rosalind Creasy's Edible Patio Garden

Over the last 25 years my containers have run the gamut from modern metal cylinders, coir hanging baskets, and shallow square terra-cotta containers to self-watering plastic pots. If I had to choose only one style, I'd select wine barrels. You'll understand why as you read on.

I live in a cool-summer area; most years I struggle to get really sweet tomatoes and melons. The warmest part of my garden is near the driveway, but I grew tomatoes and eggplants in the soil a few too many times and ended up with parasitic root knot nematodes. After trying to deal with these pests to no avail, I decided to outfox them by bricking over

the devils and making a patio. I designed a wall on three sides of the area to make it a paradise for growing all my heat lovers—watermelons, tomatoes, peppers, basil, and a fig—in containers. Having struggled with growing edibles in small containers, I knew I didn't want to repeat that frustration. Yet I had success growing a few plants in barrels, so I put in a demonstration barrel garden to show off their potential to other gardeners.

It turns out that there are all sorts of barrels, not just the half wine barrels I'd seen in nurseries and home improvement stores. On a trip to Napa Valley I saw stacked wine barrels of

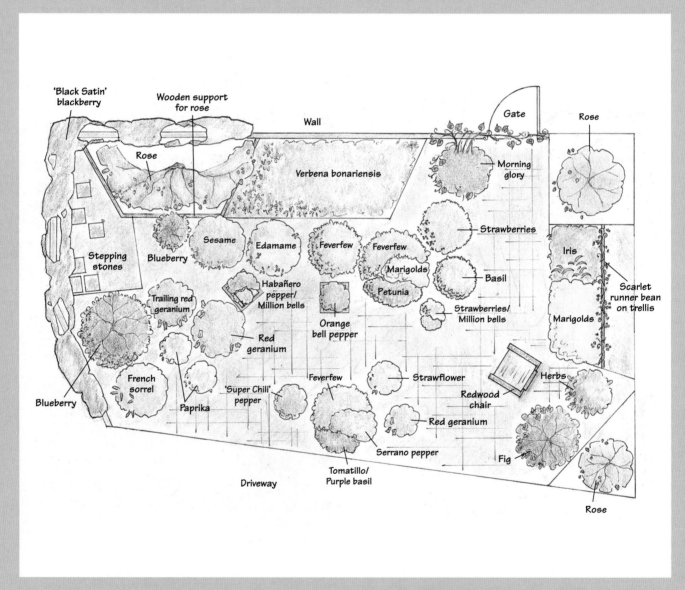

I designed my front yard patio as a sunny, warm space to grow heat-loving vegetables and fruits as well as to trial edibles in containers. A few permanent beds contain a blackberry vine, a large climbing rose, flowers, and a big trellis for annual vines. There are nine permanent wine barrels; in addition, every year I change out decorative containers of varied sizes, shapes, and colors.

One recent summer my patio was ablaze in reds, yellows, and blues, including the wall. Among the mix of plants were blueberries, French sorrel, edamame, and plenty of peppers, including paprika, yellow and red bells, variegated 'Fish Pepper', and super chilies. Every year I plant some edibles that I've never grown or tasted before.

all sizes in front of The Wine Barrel Store. They had huge used whiskey barrels and reworked wine barrels in various shapes and sizes, so I had an assortment delivered to my house. I also searched online and found lots of used barrels—Jack Daniels whiskey barrels, Japanese sake barrels, and large red plastic pickle barrels, to name just a few.

Take my advice when filling large containers. After a few failed attempts using heavy potting mixes, I consulted soil and container experts, who told me to put a lot of twigs in the bottom third of the containers and add more perlite to the mix. Since then, I've had no problems with soil rotting in large containers. In a few years, I'll have to remove the soil and replace the decayed twigs.

As you can see from the photos, the area takes on very different looks when I paint the wall or gate, add a trellis or two, and move around the furniture. In the two iterations shown, you get a sense of the range of plants I have grown in different seasons.

The following autumn I painted the wall purple and found some fun new pots. The shallow square terra-cotta container was ideal for planting Bibb lettuces in a geometric pattern. Other pots contain colorful ornamental cabbages, 'Graffiti' cauliflower, mesclun mix, carrots, golden celery, and lettuce.

Darcy Daniels decided the unused driveway alongside her Portland, Oregon, house was a great place for an edible garden. Removing the concrete driveway strip was the first step.

Repurposing a Driveway

Some properties have a long driveway that ends in a garage used as storage space for everything but the car. It's only logical to transform some of that unused driveway space into an edible landscape. Before starting any work, check with local authorities to find out whether removing a driveway is allowed in your municipality.

Darcy Daniels, a landscape designer in Portland, Oregon, moved into her 1920s house in 1999. She found that she barely used her concrete runner driveway. Since the city encourages residents to use their lots to the fullest, Darcy was inspired "to make unconventional use of the driveway, create a structural garden that would look good in all four seasons, and grow edibles vertically, beautifully, and organically."

She had the concrete ripped out and created a garden about 9 feet wide and 45 feet long; she kept enough of the driveway for one car to park outside the garden gate at the street end. Darcy lined the sides of the 18-inch-high timber beds with thick poly liner (the type used to control bamboo) and filled them with a mix of soil, compost, and grit; she used compacted gravel for the 3½-foot-wide path.

Darcy planted the first garden in spring 2006. She succeeded in growing up—turban and 'Tromboncino' squash, tomatoes, and purple pole beans made use of the wire support. Three columnar 'Golden Sentinel' apples stand tall and narrow along the length of the bed. The garden produced an abundance of edibles—parsley, cilantro, sage, strawberries, garlic, hot peppers, lettuces in a variety of leaf shapes and colors, several green and purple-leaved basils, chard, spinach, zucchini ("because it is a bush, it has a small footprint"), eggplant, broccoli, and raspberries. To see more of Darcy's garden go to www.bloomtowngardendesign.com.

Managing a Small Hillside

Small hillside gardens can be both dramatically beautiful and productive, but they also pose numerous challenges. Sloping ground is hard to plant, weed, and water; disturbed soil easily erodes and slides; and rain and irrigation water must be carefully channeled away from structures. *Note:* For all but the most gradual slopes, it is mandatory to bring in a structural engineer or licensed contractor to help design walls and drainage systems.

In the spring of 2003, Cheryl and Alan Rinzler hired me to create an edible landscape on the small hillside site of a garden that was mostly destroyed in the Oakland Hills firestorm of 1991. The area was overgrown with weedy vines and countless waist-high weeds. A big cleanup revealed six wonderful levels. Twin dwarf pear trees on the lowest level were ideal where they were. The second level had a great old stone and mortar retaining wall (with what looked like a built-in planting box jutting out a third of the way up) that kept most of the hill in place; the upper walls were stacked stones with room for plantings between the stones. The "bones" of the garden were in place.

Cheryl enjoys cooking, and a narrow planting bed on the bottom level provides ample room for all the basic culinary herbs close to the kitchen. The second level is wide enough for sizeable vegetable beds for tomatoes, squash, and peppers. On the third level, I chose carpet roses and strawberries to cascade over the wall. The fourth level became a narrow patio with containers of citrus and room for chairs. An old plum tree shades the back beds on the left, so little was planted

Darcy Daniels' driveway is reborn as a garden. Raised beds provide a generous harvest and trellises form a screen between neighboring houses. The zigzag path draws the eye in. Stained glass panels and Keith Yurdana's custom embellishments of an iron grid topped with blown glass and stone offer the visual stop-and-go a small space needs to pique interest.

there. On the sunny right side I added numerous fruits: a bed for blackberries; a grape arbor, fig tree, and pears going up the terraces; and a lime tree pruned as a hedge on the far right.

In the case of this garden, the semi-destruction of the firestorm rendered a nice hillside garden into a highly productive, beautiful space that the family enjoys viewing from the house and patio.

Specialty Small-Space Gardens

Even in a small yard, you can have a specialty edible garden. Perhaps you're crazy about Chinese or Thai food. A few large containers of cilantro, chilies, garlic, and the many stir-fry greens take up little space on a patio or in a raised bed. If heirloom apples are your passion, grow

a mini-orchard. Apple trees easily can be kept to the size of most shrubs and restricted to 4 or 5 feet across. Use your creativity; you can do much more with a small space than you think.

Mini-Orchards

While orchards bring to mind a large area, you can grow many pounds of fruit and many different varieties in a small yard by putting in a mini-orchard. Growing fruit intensively, however, requires specialized knowledge. Fortunately, there are associations of fruit specialists, such as the Home Orchard Society and the North American Fruit Explorers, whose members can help get you started. I have relied on these organizations for years. In fact, at a California Rare Fruit Growers meeting, I learned of a member in Southern California (Zone 10)

Cheryl and Alan Rinzler's hillside garden has been brought back to life and filled with edibles. From the easy-to-reach herbs on the lowest level and ample vegetable beds on the second level to the less-visited, low-maintenance fruits including fig, lime, and pear trees growing on the higher levels, this garden offers beauty and a variety of food for the kitchen.

who converted her small front yard lawn into an Eden of fruit and nut trees. She took the flat, uninspiring area with its straight front walk and created swirled brick paths to either side before putting in her trees, which she underplanted with succulents, herbs, and edible flowers. She now harvests macadamia nuts, many types of citrus, cherimoya, longans, sapote, bananas, avocado, and 10 varieties of guava.

Another hobby gardener passionate about fruit is Gene Yale. A member of the Midwest Fruit Explorers, he has a most remarkable mini-orchard in his small backyard in suburban Chicago. Not content with a mere collection of trees, Gene planned and planted an eye-pleasing, geometric pleasure garden. Each tree is in its own defined bed; grass paths tie all the beds together. In this creative design Gene grows 93 different apple vari-

eties in his small backyard. Some are modern varieties, others antiques. More than 50 trees—the smallest—are grafted on 'M27' or 'P22' rootstock, grow 3 to 4 feet tall, and produce about two dozen apples per tree. His "larger" trees, which grow about 6 feet tall and bear about 50 apples each, are grafted on 'M111' with a 'M27' interstem. For photos and detailed information on Gene's garden, visit www.midfex.org/yale/intro.html.

Water Gardens

Today we think of water plants in terms of fancy ponds and the latest gorgeous water lily; yet throughout history, people have grown water plants for food, especially in Asia, where tillable land is scarce. A quick Internet search reveals information on growing many of these plants, as well as a host of recipes. There are familiar edible plants like watercress and water chestnut; plants native to North America like wild rice and cattail; as well as plants from Asia such as wasabi and taro—all of which you can grow in a pot. Like lotus, most of these plants are highly ornamental; the only reason home gardeners have not grown them to eat is that they have not been in our radar as edibles.

A small preformed plastic pond kit available from a water garden supply house is all you need to grow a few lotus plants and a good supply of water chestnuts. As long as you have a sunny place, the pond can go anywhere except—because of its weight—on a deck. To make the plastic pond a thing of beauty, sink it into the ground and camouflage the edges with creeping plants. You will need a submersible pump to keep the water moving to provide enough oxygen for fish and plants, and a grounded outdoor electric outlet in which to plug the plug—or look into a solar-generated pump.

Water lily pads, which are actually floating leaves, keep oxygen in the water and maintain stable water temperature. You need one medium to large water lily for every 9 square feet of surface area in your pond. Pot up your edible water plants in plastic containers, nearly filled with good, heavy soil enriched with a water plant fertilizer. After planting, top off each container with gravel or sand to keep the soil from washing out. Place the containers at their proper levels in the water (consult directions that come with the plants). Raise the containers as needed using flat rocks or bricks.

For more information on other edible water plants, see Appendices A and B, and for valuable how-to information, check out *Sunset Water Gardens*. Water gardening suppliers carry everything you need, are knowledgeable, and are usually willing to instruct beginners. Also contact Lilypons Water Gardens and Van Ness Water Gardens nurseries.

Growing edibles in tight quarters is not only possible, it's an opportunity to create a small gem of a landscape. Even in very limited space you can have an aesthetically satisfying garden that supplies you with many pounds of produce year after year.

A Gallery of Design Ideas

There is a long-standing misconception that edible gardening entails big vegetable gardens and long rows of fruit trees. You can grow all sorts of edibles in ways you'd never think possible in small spaces. Look at what gardeners from different parts of the country have created in their limited garden areas.

One year I created a garden in my front yard featuring dusty miller, a favorite plant of mine. To draw visitors into the space, I lined the path, which ends at a magnificent cherry tomato arch, with these silvery plants. I used pink and purple flowers to further enliven the area. Front to back, the beds mirror each other with potted eggplants and lots of edibles in the ground, including peppers, zucchini, roses, and more.

Angular raised beds, wrought iron fences, and brick paths give a formal feel to David Clem's front yard design in Des Moines, Iowa. In July, cabbages, collards, and kohlrabi flourish in the raised beds. In the background are a dwarf crabapple tree, a genetic dwarf peach tree, and a soon-to-be-harvested bed of potatoes.

Handsome stone retaining walls help make the most of a small garden space. They absorb extra heat needed for growing squash and hold the soil as they terrace the slope in this Pacific Northwest garden. In such a rainy climate, the kohlrabi and lettuces need good drainage, which the raised beds provide.

I first started my edible landscape in a raised bed right off the street, in a parking strip. Over the years this bed has evolved. Here you can find, left to right, sage, society garlic, nepitella, peppers of all sorts, purple basil, thyme, yellow roses, and a potted calamondin. Behind the fence, lima beans form a privacy screen. Cherry tomatoes are trained up and over the entry arbor on the right. Most visitors cannot resist popping one or two candy-sweet tomatoes into their mouths as they come up the front walk.

An Encyclopedia
of Edibles

Euell Gibbons went into the wilds to discover edible plants; I went into my well-stocked pantry to discover which foods I might want to grow. My pantry may include more exotic edibles than most, owing to my lifelong interest in cooking and my inability to resist the siren call of seed catalogues. Still, with few exceptions, the foods discussed here could be called "domesticated," as they have a long history in the cuisine of many cultures.

This encyclopedia describes, in detail, plants that provide delicious food and beautify the home landscape. Few reference books emphasize the beauty inherent in edible plants or direct you to varieties especially suitable for a landscape. This book does. But how to limit the selections? My first criterion, of course, is whether the plant fits well into a landscape situation. For example, while I've trialed corn, radishes, and wasabi in my landscape, they are a design challenge. Corn can look pretty agricultural in rows (yet can make a wonderful maze); radishes grow for only about 6 weeks and then leave a vacant spot; and wasabi is really, really fussy, so unless conditions are perfect, it usually looks scruffy. These plants, and many like them, are included in Appendix A, which follows this encyclopedia. If space were not a consideration, I would devote a full entry to every one of the plants in that list.

Beyond their landscaping suitability, the edibles in this encyclopedia include the obvious must-haves, such as blueberries, strawberries, and tomatoes, which most people love to eat and can grow. To those I added many of the edibles I've fallen in love with in my own landscape, including the dwarf 'Pink Pearl' apple, 'Black Satin' blackberries, and frilly red and green basils. My clients have delighted in the many pear, plum, citrus, and fig trees we planted, giving those plants a big vote of confidence. The many gardeners I have met over the years have also unwittingly helped me choose entries. People were so enthusiastic about the peach- and orange-colored chards, purple cauliflower, and yellow zucchini grown by the crew at Disney World for the rainbow vegetable seminar I presented there. The greatest accolades came for a display I built for the San Francisco Flower and Garden Show, showing the vast selection of lettuces growing in geometric patterns. And the gorgeous paprika peppers and cherry-size hardy kiwifruits I pass around at Master Gardener seminars never cease to garner acclaim.

The selections also come from my awareness that growing your own food not only graces a landscape but can save substantial amounts of money. So I included easy-to-grow staples like tomatoes and cucumbers.

A Typical Encyclopedia Entry

Each entry contains the common name, botanic name, relative effort necessary to grow the plant, hardiness zones (if perennial), thumbnail sketch, uses in the kitchen and the landscape, and information on growing and purchasing.

Entry Title

Plants are listed alphabetically by the most often used common name. Sometimes the heading is for a multiple entry, such as "Apple and Crabapple" or "Peach and Nectarine," for closely related plants. For individual entries, the botanic (Latin) name follows the entry title so there is no question as to a plant's identity. The botanic name always includes the genus, sometimes followed by "spp.," indicating that there is more than one desirable species. In that case, the various species (and sometimes subspecies, abbreviated "ssp.") are generally listed in "Varieties."

Botanic names are constantly evolving and are not always agreed upon. Dayna Lane, my longtime editorial assistant, who most recently worked at the U.S. Botanic Garden in Washington, D.C., helped assemble the most up-to-date Latin names. The primary resources for determining the names were three websites: GRIN Taxonomy for Plants (USDA, Agricultural Research Service, Germplasm Resources Information Network), www.ars-grin.gov/cgi-bin/npgs/html/tax_search.pl; IPNI (International Plant Names Index), www.ipni.org; PLANTS Database (USDA National Research Conservation Service), plants.usda.gov/; and two books: *Index of Garden Plants: The New Royal Horticultural Society Dictionary*, by Mark Griffiths (the online version of the index is found at rhs.org.uk/rhsplantfinder/plantfinder.asp), and *Zander: Handwörterbuch der Pflanzennamen*, 16, by W. Erhardt et al.

Preceding pages: 'Black Satin' blackberries cascade over a patio wall.

These selections of herbs and vegetables from Renee's Garden are as beautiful harvested as they were growing in the garden. Shown, clockwise from top left, are basil, eggplants, chard, muskmelon, peppers—round and narrow—and cherry tomatoes.

Effort Scale

My experience with students and clients has shown that newcomers to edible gardening tend to get carried away, not realizing that the degree of effort it takes to grow and use edibles varies widely. With that in mind, I designed the Effort Scale to eliminate unpleasant surprises; it shows at a glance what each plant requires in time and skill.

The Effort Scale is a simple 1 to 5 ranking of how easy/difficult it is to obtain, grow, harvest, use, and preserve a plant and its edible portion. A NO. 1 ranking indicates minimal effort, while a NO. 5 indicates both high maintenance and considerable effort. *Note:* The Effort Scale is approximate, meant to serve only as a guide. Households and climates vary.

Zones

The zone numbers listed for perennials, shrubs, and trees correspond to numbers on the USDA Plant Hardiness Zone Map on the next page. Many factors influencing the microclimate of your particular property—such as the direction the garden faces, winds, and topography—can affect hardiness by a zone in either direction. Because annuals grow for one season and die, hardiness is not a factor, so they are listed as "Not Applicable," as are biennials and perennials that are grown as annuals.

Thumbnail Sketch

Each entry begins with a brief overview of the pertinent landscaping features and possibilities of each plant. This is particularly useful when deciding what to grow.

How to Use

In the Kitchen

This is where we all have the most fun, planning ahead for cooking with the incredible edibles we grow. This section is chock-full of my favorite ways to prepare these foods and, in some cases, some new culinary avenues to

USDA Plant Hardiness Zone Map

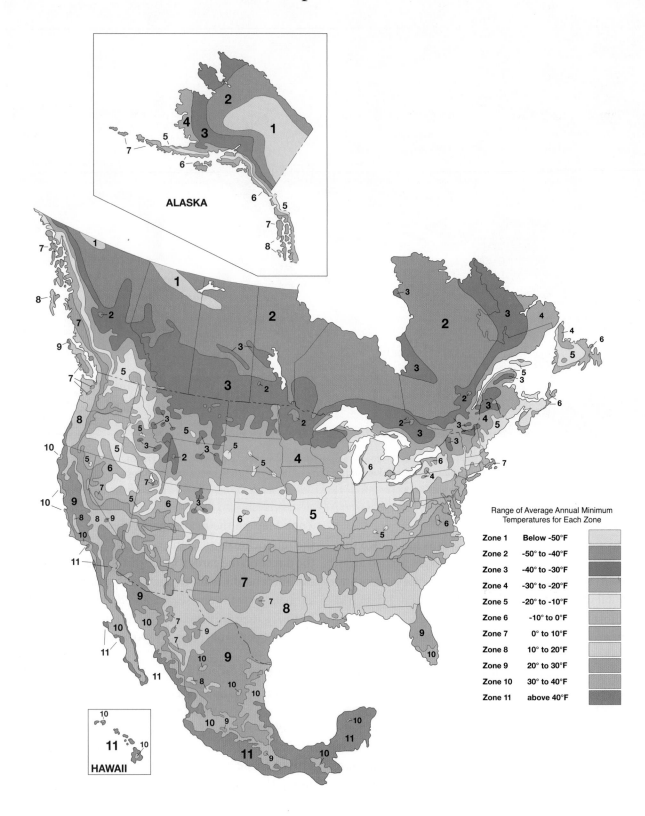

Range of Average Annual Minimum
Temperatures for Each Zone

Zone 1	Below -50°F	
Zone 2	-50° to -40°F	
Zone 3	-40° to -30°F	
Zone 4	-30° to -20°F	
Zone 5	-20° to -10°F	
Zone 6	-10° to 0°F	
Zone 7	0° to 10°F	
Zone 8	10° to 20°F	
Zone 9	20° to 30°F	
Zone 10	30° to 40°F	
Zone 11	above 40°F	

ALASKA

HAWAII

This is the most up-to-date plant hardiness zone map published by the USDA at the time this book went to press, with figures from 1990. The USDA is working on an updated version to reflect our warming climate, and it will be released when the data are complete. For an interactive version of the current map, go to www.usna.usda.gov/Hardzone/ushzmap.html.

explore. Garden food is the most healthful cuisine we can consume, so I highlight the nutritional benefits. If a fruit or vegetable can be preserved, the preservation method is discussed here.

In the Landscape

This section includes a brief description of the particular plant and suggestions for its use in the landscape. *Note:* In many cases, I suggest ways of combining plants, including inedible species. If a plant is not included in Appendix A, consider it inedible.

How to Grow

The basics for successfully growing the individual plant are described here. This information supplements the material about planting and maintenance in Appendix C. For plants requiring more than the basics, including woody shrubs and trees, I use headings to cover climate, exposure and soil, fertilizing, watering, pruning, pests and diseases, and harvesting. For some easy-to-grow annuals, I provide the basics without headings.

Climate

For each plant I provide specific information on weather limitations (for example, heat, cold, and humidity), as well as information on where it grows best. Many fruiting plants require a certain number of hours of winter chilling—temperatures below 45°F but above 33°F—in order to produce well. You'll see the requisite number of chill hours listed for many fruit tree varieties, for example.

Exposure and Soil

Most edible plants require full sun. Some thrive in partial shade, especially in areas with hot summers; a few prefer full shade. (See Chapter 2 for information on the hours of daily sunlight needed by plants that thrive in full sun, partial sun, and full shade.) Special soil, pH, and drainage needs are noted in this section. As a rule, annual vegetables need much more organic matter and soil preparation than do fruit and nut trees or perennials.

Planting

This section is included only in cases where the information differs from that in Appendix C.

Fertilizing

The fertilizing requirements of individual plants are described briefly. For heavy feeders, specific timing and

Melons have a luxuriant look growing in the garden. In a day or two, when this 'Charentais' melon is ripe, the flavor will be divine. Harvesting at just the right time is crucial because peak ripeness is fleeting.

product recommendations are provided. I generally suggest rich, organic soil and compost as mulch.

Watering

The watering needs of the specific plant are noted here. These are more critical in arid and hot parts of the country, but during a drought the information is relevant anywhere.

Pruning

This section covers specifics for pruning the particular plant (including diagrams where necessary) that go beyond the information in Appendix C.

Pests and Diseases

Specific pests and diseases affecting the plant are described. I cover treatments for the most common pests and diseases in Appendix D; in this section I note only plant-specific treatments.

Harvesting

This section discusses how to determine ripeness, as well as when and how to harvest—if details are necessary. When possible, I include estimated yields for mature standard-size trees or shrubs.

For crops grown from seed and then transplanted, check the seed packet for a rough idea of when to harvest. The number of days to harvest listed on the packet is generally from transplanting into the garden. Warm weather speeds up the timing; cold weather slows it down.

How to Purchase

Fellow gardeners may sometimes give you seeds or divisions of edible plants; more often you will find edibles as seeds, in containers, or as bare-root plants at nurseries. Whenever possible, buy plants locally, as nearby nurseries know what grows best in your area. Fruit trees are bred and grafted onto rootstocks that are appropriate for certain soil types, weather, and disease resistance. Late winter into spring (also early fall) is when nurseries offer the greatest variety of edible plants, including vegetable seeds, onion seedlings, and tender evergreens for mild-winter regions.

When you go looking for edibles, beware of non-fruiting varieties like peach trees that don't bear edible peaches, or flowering almond trees that don't produce almonds. There are *flowering* plums, crabapples, cherries, quinces, pomegranates, pears, currants, and gooseberries—all handsome flowers, but no fruit. As my father used to say, "Big noise at the head of the stairs, but no one comes down." Thus, when you shop for edibles, stress the words "edible" and "fruiting."

It is still uncommon for local nurseries to carry a large selection of edible plants other than the standard tomato and herb transplants, vegetable seeds, and fruit trees, so I recommend the best sources for particular plants. The source names are abbreviated from their full names listed in the Sources and Resources section in the back of this book.

Pollinizers

A *pollinizer* is the plant that donates the pollen, while a *pollinator* is the agent (such as bee, moth, bat, or hummingbird) that transfers the pollen. A *pollinated plant* receives the pollen. A plant that pollinizes itself is self-fertile, self-fruitful, or self-pollinizing. When a pollinizer is necessary, it's best to plant it at the same time as the plant that will receive the pollen. When the fruit is not used—when leaves, stalks, or roots are the edible parts—pollination is not a concern.

Rootstocks

Choosing the rootstock is just as important as choosing a specific variety of tree for its superior fruit or nuts. The rootstock determines size, disease resistance, cold tolerance, the age at which the tree first bears fruit, and soil adaptation. Look for rootstocks suited to your area.

Varieties

Selecting plants for aesthetic qualities took some doing, since edible species often come in many varieties, some more decorative than others—showier blossoms, more attractive foliage, or more interesting forms. I chose the varieties based on my experience and that of many others in the landscaping business, always favoring those I judged to be the tastiest, most disease resistant, and readily available. The varieties range from ancient heirlooms to the latest hybrids, from those that grow well in Maine to those that flourish in Oregon to ones that succeed in San Diego. And I've noted the special characteristics of each.

Almond

Prunus dulcis

Effort Scale

NO. 2
Vulnerable to mites, squirrels, and birds
Harvesting standard-size tree is time consuming

Zones

5 to 9

Thumbnail Sketch

Deciduous tree
Standard, 20 to 30 ft. tall; dwarf varieties, 8 to 10 ft. tall
Propagate by grafting or budding
Needs full sun
Leaves are bright green, narrow, to 3 in. long
Blooms in very early spring
Flowers are profuse, white or light pink
Nuts are edible; harvest in summer
Use as street tree, accent plant, interest plant, screen, or patio tree;
    dwarf varieties as large shrubs or in containers

How to Use

In the Kitchen

Almonds are versatile nuts, delicious for eating out of hand—raw or
roasted. In parts of the Middle East salted almonds are street food.
Add roasted almonds—slivered or chopped—to salads, vegetables,
and meats. Cutting-edge chefs love the velvety richness that green
(unripe) almonds add to their culinary creations; I find their mild
almond/anise flavor delicious in salads and savory dishes. In a variety
of forms, almonds impart flavor and texture to candies and pastries.
Amandine is haute cuisine.

In the Landscape

This deciduous tree spreads its branches, displaying clusters of delicate white blossoms in spring, making it an excellent accent or interest plant. 'Garden Prince', a natural genetic dwarf, covers itself with
light pink flowers as showy as any ornamental spring-flowering tree.
With their narrow, bright green leaves, almond trees do not form
a solid mass; consequently, they provide ideal shade for drought-
tolerant perennials and shrubs. Set back from paved surfaces, almonds
make lovely small shade or patio trees; plant them to line an oak
woodland walk. Dwarf varieties are striking in very large containers
or planted at the back of a shrub border.

How to Grow

Climate

Almond trees grow well in only a few climates. They need between
250 and 500 chill hours and are generally limited to the drier sections
of the West Coast. Although hardy to 10°F, they bloom early—in February and March—and are easily nipped by a frost. Nuts fail to form
properly if summers are too cool or the humidity is high.

Looking at this tree with its handsome narrow leaves, you might mistake
the cluster of almonds for small unripe peaches. Like its close relative
peach, almond is in the genus *Prunus*. Remove the fuzzy husk to reveal
the recognizable almond shell.

Exposure and Soil

Almond trees need full sun. They tolerate a variety of soils if well
drained.

Fertilizing

Mulch annually with compost.

Watering

Trees are drought resistant once established. In rainy climates, almonds
need no extra watering. In arid regions, give them an occasional deep
watering.

Pruning

Prune young trees to an open center. Almonds bear on spurs that are
productive for about 5 years. Once the trees are established, prune out
any deadwood and encourage new spurs by removing 20 percent of
the old wood each winter.

Pests and Diseases

Almonds are susceptible to a number of the problems that affect
peaches, but not as often or as seriously. Spider mites can be a major
pest in hot dry weather, but squirrels and birds are the most problematic. In some neighborhoods, squirrels make quick work of the
crop and litter the ground with hulls. Avoid the mess by tightly netting the trees while the nuts ripen or underplant with a ground cover
to hide the debris. You can do as growers in parts of the Middle East
do to foil critters: harvest the nuts when they have grown to full size
but are green, or unripe, and jellylike inside, usually in midspring.

Harvesting

Almonds have both a fleshy outer hull and an inner shell, which contains the kernel. In late summer to early fall (once the hulls have split open and the shells are partially dry), pick the nuts from the tree. Spread them out in a single layer and dry them in their hulls for a day. Remove the hulls by hand; dry the unshelled nuts in the sun for another week. Store in a cool, dry place.

A mature, standard-size tree yields about 20 to 25 pounds of nuts annually.

How to Purchase

Local nurseries carry bare-root and container-grown plants in season. Order bare-root plants from Bay Laurel, Raintree, Rolling River, or Trees of Antiquity.

Pollinizers

Most standard-size almond trees need cross-pollinization; some of the new shorter varieties are self-fertile and perfect for home gardens. If there isn't ample room to plant two full-size trees separately, plant more than one variety in the same hole, choose a self-fertile variety, or use a dwarf variety as the pollinizer.

Rootstocks

The most common rootstocks for almonds on the West Coast are peach seedlings. 'Lovell' offers some resistance to wet conditions. 'Marianna 26-24', a plum rootstock, has some resistance to oak root fungus. 'Nemaguard' or 'Nemared' offers resistance to root-knot nematodes.

Varieties

'All-in-One'—sweet nut; very large, showy, white flowers; self-fertile; semi-dwarf; quite hardy but needs hot summer to ripen, Zones 6 to 9; pollinizes 'Nonpareil'.

'Garden Prince'—medium-size, sweet nut; showy, pink flowers; self-fertile; genetic dwarf to 8 ft.; low chill.

'Hall's Hardy'—hard-shelled, slightly bitter nut with only fair flavor; pink flowers; blooms late; partially self-fertile; hardy; pollinizer for 'Mission'.

'Mission' ('Texas')—small nut, satisfactory flavor; white flowers; good for cold-winter areas; needs 'Nonpareil' or 'Hall's Hardy' as a pollinizer.

'Ne Plus Ultra'—large, high-quality nut; white flowers; pollinizer for 'Nonpareil'.

'Nonpareil'—best nut available; widely grown; white flowers; pollinizer for 'Ne Plus Ultra'.

Alpine strawberry

See Strawberry

American custard apple

See Pawpaw

Apple and Crabapple

Malus spp.

Effort Scale

NO. 4
Pests and diseases can be major problems, particularly in wet-summer areas
Fertilizing and mulching necessary
Picking up fruits necessary
Harvesting standard-size tree is time consuming

NO. 3 for disease-resistant varieties, in dry climates, and for trees kept small

Zones

3 to 9, depending on variety

Thumbnail Sketch

Deciduous trees
Standard varieties, 20 to 30 ft. tall; semi-dwarf varieties, 12 to 18 ft. tall; dwarf varieties, 5 to 12 ft. tall
Propagate by grafting or budding or from cuttings
Need full sun
Leaves are soft green, 2 to 3 in. long; new growth is woolly
Bloom in spring
Flowers are white or pink
Fruits are edible; harvest in summer or fall
Use as interest trees, patio trees, small shade trees, espaliers, large shrubs, hedges, or screens; dwarf and columnar varieties in large containers

How to Use

In the Kitchen

Apples are among our true blessings; lip-smacking, crunchy delights to eat out of hand as the famed snack that "keeps the doctor away." Summer apples generally do not store well; wrap old-time keeper apples individually in newspaper, pack in barrels, and store in a cool place. Applesauce, when canned or frozen, provides a touch of freshness in winter. Baked apples with walnuts and cranberries are sublime treats, dried apples are popular with tots, apple butters make delicious spreads, and, of course, apple pie is the great American dish. Try your hand at vinegar, chutney, apple leather, and apple jelly.

Until Prohibition, homemade hard cider was a common beverage. Nowadays, gardeners are brightening at the prospect of making their own cider, both sweet and hard, as nurseries reintroduce old cider apple varieties. You, too, can have a go at this complex-flavored libation; check out *Cider: Making, Using & Enjoying Sweet & Hard Cider* by Annie Proulx and Lew Nichols.

Although some folks enjoy tangy crabapples, these little fruits are more popular in beautiful jelly. Cider makers add crabapples to sweet dessert apples to give the cider a tannic snap. Pickle the fruit whole for an attractive garnish for a holiday platter. Note: Not all crabapples produce edible fruits; some are too tannic.

In the Landscape

Not only are apple trees productive, but their fragrant blossoms dazzle; profuse pink buds burst into white or pink flowers up to 1½ inches wide. Most apple leaves are a soft medium green, with gray fuzz on the undersides. Apple trees come in more sizes than any other fruit tree. Standard trees grow to 30 feet, whereas some dwarf and semi-dwarf varieties can be kept to 5 feet. Taller forms function as shade trees or screens; smaller forms are ideal in decorative containers, as espaliers, and as fruitful hedges. Narrow, non-branching, columnar varieties reach 10 feet, perfect for enclosing an herb garden without overwhelming it. *Note:* Do not plant apple trees near windows or painted walls, as control of most of their pests and diseases requires sprays, which can stain.

Crabapples are even showier. In spring their blossoms are rosier, and at harvest time their fruits are more colorful. While full-size crabapple trees are usually shorter than apple trees, they make excellent shade trees.

Both apples and crabapples form stately yet informal lines along a driveway. They are superb interest plants with their consistent beauty—if diseases are kept under control.

How to Grow

One of the best sources on growing organic apples is *The Apple Grower* by Michael Phillips, covering it all—from planting to making cider—in detail.

Climate

Apples and crabapples are the hardiest of the popular fruits; a few survive down to –40°F, but most are not that stouthearted. Varieties of both grow in all but Zones 10 and 11. In Zones 8 and 9, choose low-chill varieties.

Exposure and Soil

To grow the sweetest fruit and prevent diseases, plant apples and crabapples in full sun. They grow best in well-drained garden loam supplemented with organic mulch.

Fertilizing

Renew soil nutrients annually by applying 3 to 4 inches of compost and/or aged manure in spring. Avoid overfeeding; trees kept on the lean side have fewer pest and disease problems and less winter injury. However, if the leaves are pale and the tree has put on only a few inches of new growth in summer, apply a nitrogen source, such as blood meal or fish meal, the following spring and water it in.

Watering

In climates with regular summer rain, well-established trees do not need watering. In dry-summer areas, deep watering is essential at least every few weeks.

Pruning

Whether full-size or dwarf, young apple and crabapple trees should be trained to a central or modified central leader system. Prune 2-year-old trees to have four or five scaffold limbs, starting 2 to 3 feet above the ground (depending on how short you want to keep the tree), distributed around the compass points at least 6 inches apart vertically.

Both apples and crabapples bear primarily on long-lived fruiting spurs. Once established, prune annually when the trees are dormant; cut out weak growth, dead, or crossing branches. To discourage dis-

Set off by lawn, an apple tree serves as a focal point in David Cavagnaro's Decorah, Iowa (Zone 4), edible landscape. Red beebalm and yellow daylilies—both edible flowers—are the stars of the perennial bed in the foreground.

eases, keep the canopy open so air and sunlight can better penetrate the center. Cut back drooping branches on older trees to prevent shading of lower foliage and fruit.

There are several ways to prune; since some options depend on the variety and climate, ask for specific information on how to prune your tree when you choose it. Summer pruning is an effective way to control tree size. A good time to do this is a few weeks after blossom drop when you thin the fruit, and again a month later.

Pests and Diseases

Apples and crabapples are prone to many pests and diseases. In fact, it is a real challenge to grow them organically east of the Mississippi. Among the most serious problems are codling moth, plum curculio, San Jose scale, fireblight, and powdery mildew, all of which are covered in Appendix D. I'll deal with the others here.

Apple maggot flies are small black flies with dark banding on the wings; larvae tunnel in developing fruits in eastern and northern gardens. The Ladd Apple Maggot Fly Trap and Lure captures many, as does scrupulously cleaning up dropped fruits.

Woolly apple aphids are reddish with a waxy coating. Unlike most aphids, they primarily attack the roots and other woody parts of the tree, causing galls and burs. When aboveground, control with light-

What a spectacular show of color apple blossoms put on in spring—from white through pale pink to deep pink. When checking out varieties to grow, consider flower color as well as which apples best serve as pollinizers for other apple trees.

weight oil. However, once underground, they stunt the tree's growth. If they are problematic, look for apples grafted onto 'M111' or 'M106' rootstock.

Apple scab, a common fungal disease of apples and crabapples, causes scabby, deformed fruit, brown leaves, and partial defoliation. Cedar apple rust is another fungus that affects these trees, causing orange spots on the leaves. It spends part of its life on alternate hosts—red cedars or junipers. Both fungi are most prevalent in cool, wet weather. The numerous varieties of apples that resist apple scab, cedar apple rust, powdery mildew, and, to some extent, fireblight should be the first choice where these are potential problems. To control existing fungal diseases, prune your trees for good air circulation and meticulously clean up all leaves and fruit from the ground in fall. For cedar apple rust, apply sulfur spray at bud break and then weekly for about 8 weeks. The spray schedule for apple scab is much more complex and climate specific; consult your Cooperative Extension Service for details.

Harvesting

Apples generally ripen gradually over a few weeks and require several pickings. As the fruits begin to fully color, pick a few from different parts of the tree and taste them. The object is to harvest them when the sugars are fully developed and before the apples get the slightest bit mushy. Lift the apple up toward the branch and twist slightly; if the fruit breaks off easily, it is usually ripe. Also examine the seeds; when fully ripe they are dark brown to black. The so-called winter apples ripen in storage; pick them slightly under-ripe, and ripen them slowly in a dark, cool place.

Over time, you'll learn at which stage each apple variety tastes best to you. When I had a 'Golden Delicious' apple tree, I harvested the apples light green, when they were much snappier and more flavorful than store-bought yellow ones, and my 'Pink Pearl' apples are just right when light yellow. Monitor the maturity of your apples because the quality of ripe fruits left on the tree declines quickly. *Note:* I remember my father telling me that when apples (and other fruit) drop from the tree, they are ripe and need to be picked. My first season growing apples, I found the fruits that dropped first were not ripe—merely wormy. After that, I learned to taste the apples on the tree as they began to color.

A mature standard apple tree yields about 400 pounds of apples; a semi-dwarf, 160 to 200 pounds; and a dwarf, 50 to 60 pounds. It takes 50 to 60 pounds of apples to make 2 to 3 gallons of cider.

How to Purchase

Purchase trees bare root or in containers from local nurseries, or bare root from Ames' Orchard, Bay Laurel, Burnt Ridge, C & O, Cummins, Johnson, Miller, Nature Hills, or Willis. Fedco and St. Lawrence offer huge selections of very hardy apples. Southmeadow and Trees of Antiquity have antique varieties. Apple Art and Henry Leuthardt specialize in espaliers, and Edible Landscaping offers several espaliered apples.

Pollinizers

Most apples need a pollinizer; most crabapples are self-fertile. Make sure your chosen apple varieties can pollinize each other; some are incompatible, while others are sterile.

Rootstocks

Full-size apple trees are large, to 30 feet tall, and the harvest is enormous—far more than the average family wants to deal with. And, of course, you need a ladder and other accouterments to prune, spray, and pick large trees. The practice of dwarfing fruit trees has been going on for a long time. In the early 1900s, two English research stations (in Malling and Merton) sorted, identified, and classified apple rootstocks. The Malling-Merton (M or MM) number has a specific meaning; for example, 'M9' produces an apple tree that grows 6 to 9 feet tall, and 'M7' a semi-dwarf that grows 12 to 15 feet tall. The M or MM number is still part of the name of many of these small apple trees. (There is no correlation between M number and tree height.)

Research in the ensuing years has added to the rootstock choices. Some are more drought tolerant; others resist woolly apple aphid. A recent one, 'Bud 9', is great for growing in containers and in cold climates. Besides the advantages mentioned above, trees on dwarfing rootstocks usually bear fruit a few years earlier and their size makes them feasible for even the smallest yards. For the most complete and up-to-date information on the many rootstocks available, go to www.davewilson.com/roots.html.

Apple rootstocks are much more effective than rootstocks for other major fruits in controlling tree size. Dwarfing rootstocks keep apple trees small, allowing them to grow as large shrubs. However, there are some disadvantages to dwarf trees: They are reputed to be shorter lived than standard trees. Also, many of the rootstocks in common use have shallow root systems, and sometimes the graft is fragile, making the staking of a newly planted dwarf tree essential.

In addition to dwarfing rootstocks, there are rootstocks for medium- and full-size apple trees. Before making your choice, gather as much information as possible and consult your local Cooperative Extension Service.

Varieties

There is a feast of apples out there to discover and grow. Visit local orchards and farmers markets to try local varieties, or order tasting selections from Applesource.

For fresh eating, choose dessert apples such as 'Cox's Orange Pippin', 'Fuji', 'Golden Delicious', 'Gravenstein', and 'Gala'.

For baking and pies, most folks prefer varieties that have a distinct, tart apple flavor and retain their shape when cooked, like 'Granny Smith' and 'Northern Spy'.

For applesauce and cider, flavor and not texture is king. Two great sauce apples are 'Gravenstein' and 'Pink Pearl'. For cider, most experts prefer a blend of apples including some sweet and medium-sweet varieties—plus a few crabapples for bite—for best flavor.

Apple trees are amazingly adaptable and versatile; there are varieties suitable for severe or warm winters, ones that fruit early or late, old-time and modern varieties, and others resistant to diseases.

Organizations interested in preserving hundreds of old-time apples include North American Fruit Explorers, Seed Savers Exchange, and Home Orchard Society. In Massachusetts, the Worcester County Horticultural Society and Old Sturbridge Village maintain historical apple orchards and are eager to have you learn of their place in American history.

APPLE

These apples have superior fruits. For eastern gardeners, many are extremely disease resistant. Unless otherwise noted, the varieties described here need a pollinizer and are hardy from Zones 4 to 8.

'Anna'—early; light green; crisp and sweet; outstanding fresh or cooked; self-fruitful; for parts of Southern California and the southern seaboard, 200 chill hours, Zones 6 to 9.

'Cox's Orange Pippin'—antique; midseason; striped red and yellow; England's famous dessert apple, juicy, aromatic; self-fruitful; needs cool conditions for best flavor; 800 chill hours.

'Enterprise'—late; large, red fruit; crisp, spicy flavor; good storage apple; immune to scab, resists cedar apple rust and fireblight, some susceptibility to powdery mildew; 750 chill hours, Zones 5 to 7.

'Fuji'—midseason; cylindrical dessert fruit with yellowish green skin; crisp, excellent fruity flavor; superior storage apple; highly susceptible to fireblight; self-fruitful, good pollinizer; needs warm fall for good flavor, 350 to 450 chill hours, Zones 6 to 9.

'Gala'—early; red dessert fruit; great sweet flavor; some resistance to cedar apple rust and powdery mildew, highly susceptible to fireblight and apple scab; use 'Golden Delicious' as pollinizer; 500 chill hours.

'Golden Delicious'—antique; midseason; yellow fruit; sprightly flavor, great fresh or cooked; mostly self-fruitful, pollinizer for 'Gala' and 'Red Delicious'; susceptible to cedar apple rust, some resistance to scab; adaptable, 600 to 700 chill hours.

'Golden Sentinel'—midseason; columnar tree; very large, golden yellow fruit, sweet and juicy; productive; needs pollinizer; disease resistant; 800 chill hours, Zones 4 to 9.

'Granny Smith'—antique; late; green, tart, all-purpose apple; self-fruitful, good pollinizer; excellent in areas with long summers, 400 to 500 chill hours.

'Gravenstein'—antique; early; striped yellow, green, and red; great for applesauce and baking; vigorous; pollinize with 'Empire', 'Fuji', or 'Gala'; widely grown, 700 chill hours, Zones 4 to 9.

'Honeycrisp'—late; red over green; crisp, sweet, delicious; great fresh, very good keeper; best for cold climates, 800 chill hours.

'Liberty'—early; red fruit, sweet, great flavor fresh or cooked; resists cedar apple rust, apple scab, fireblight, and powdery mildew; self-fruitful; 800 chill hours, Zones 4 to 7.

'McIntosh'—antique; early; red and green dessert fruit; snappy flavor and tender flesh in cold climates; stores poorly; susceptible to scab; improved offspring now available; partly self-fruitful, pollinize with 'Red Delicious' or 'Gala'; 900 chill hours, Zones 3 to 7.

'Northern Spy' ('Northern Pie Apple')—antique; late; tart red fruit, good for pies, good keeper; slow to bear; susceptible to scab, resists fireblight; pollinize with 'Golden Delicious'; favorite on East Coast in cold areas, 1,000 chill hours, Zones 4 to 7.

'Pink Pearl'—early; large, green to yellow apple with pink blush; pink flesh; tart, great for applesauce and pies, good keeper; bright pink flowers; 600 chill hours, Zones 3 to 9.

'Scarlet Sentinel'—midseason; most dwarfing columnar apple tree; large, greenish yellow fruit with red blush; abundant, closely spaced fruit; sweet flavor; disease resistant; 800 hours, Zones 4 to 7.

Cut into a 'Pink Pearl' apple to reveal its inner beauty. I slice these apples, delicious eaten out of hand, to make a show-stopping tart. Pick 'Pink Pearl' when the translucent yellow skin hints at the pink flesh underneath.

'Williams Pride'—antique; early; red striped fruit; rich, spicy flavor; long-lasting blooms; resists apple scab, fireblight, powdery mildew, and cedar apple rust.

CRABAPPLE
'Dolgo'—tart, red, ½ to 1 in.; delicious for jewel-toned jelly; heavy bearer; beautiful white flowers; disease resistant; self-fruitful; good pollinizer for apples; extremely hardy, 500 chill hours, Zones 3 to 9.
'Geneva'—native Canadian crabapple; 2½ in., dark red skin, tart red flesh; resists scab; Zones 4 to 8.

Apricot

Apricot (standard apricot), *Prunus armeniaca*
Japanese apricot (ume, Japanese plum), *P. mume*
Manchurian apricot, *P. mandschurica* (*P. a. var. mandschurica*)

Effort Scale

Apricot (standard)
NO. 3
Mulching necessary
Susceptible to numerous diseases and pests
Soft fruit ripens all at once
Medium to large harvest; uncertain in cold-winter areas
Pruning necessary

Japanese apricot
NO. 2
Mulching necessary
Somewhat susceptible to a few diseases and pests
Soft fruit ripens all at once and needs preserving
Medium-size harvest
Some pruning recommended

Manchurian apricot
NO. 1
Mulching necessary
Late spring frosts can eliminate summer harvest
Birds and critters get much of the harvest

Zones

4 to 9, depending on variety

Thumbnail Sketch

Deciduous tree
10 to 25 ft. tall
Propagate by grafting or budding or from cuttings or seeds
Needs full sun
Leaves are rich green, oval, 2 to 3 in. long; new growth is often bronzy
Blooms in early spring
Flowers are white, pink, or red, 1 in. across, often showy
Fruits are edible; harvest in summer; seeds edible in a few varieties, toxic in others

Use as interest tree, small shade tree, espalier, screen, hedge, or container plant

How to Use

In the Kitchen
Stone fruits—members of the genus *Prunus*—are among the most important fruit trees in the Northern Hemisphere. Here, I'm focusing on the most apricot-like fruits—those with the rich orange to yellow flesh typical of the standard apricot. Interspecific hybrids (crosses between apricots and plums, called apriums or pluots) are in the "Plum" entry.

Apricots are 1½- to 2-inch, peachlike fruits native to China. Less fuzzy than peaches, they have their own glorious yellow-orange color, often tinged with red. Commercially, apricots grow in only a few parts of the country and do not ship well, so many folks have never had the pleasure of a tree-ripened apricot. The aristocratic apricot is elegant however you serve it: a few perfectly ripe halves topped with a dollop of crème fraiche, dried and sprinkled over a green salad, chopped in granola, or brandied and layered in an English trifle. Can halved apricots in syrup; make jams, preserves, fruit leather, and glazes; or puree the fruits and make heavenly apricot nectar. Apricots truly are a gold mine in the pantry. The possibilities with this summer jewel are endless.

The Japanese apricot, often called ume or Japanese plum, is renowned in Japan and China. The small, sour fruits are not usually eaten raw. Instead, cooks make *umeboshi* by flavoring dried salted ume with red perilla (*shiso*) and serve it with rice. Macrobiotic staples, such as salad dressings and brown rice entrees, rely on a paste made from salted ume; in Japan, it is a favorite in sushi. Preserve ume in sugar or use it to make vinegar or a sweet liqueur.

As the majority of plants of the small-fruited Manchurian apricot are seedlings—not grafted varieties—they are a flavor gamble. The quality ranges from that of a standard apricot to very sour fruits great for jam, or insipid and best left for the birds.

In the Landscape
Apricots are spreading, deciduous trees to 25 feet. Their popcorn-white blossoms, while sparse, contrast sharply with their almost black bark, making them exceptional interest plants. In spring the emerging young leaves are bronzy, maturing to deep green and turning brilliant yellow in autumn for a colorful finale.

Apricots are useful as small shade trees, but not over paving because of fruit drop. As hedges, you can keep apricots to a height of 7 feet with summer pruning.

In cold climates the hardy, pink-flowered Manchurian apricot grows from 15 to 20 feet tall and is a handsome, large deciduous shrub or small tree. In fall its yellow or orange foliage brightens the landscape. Plant a row as an informal screen, windbreak, or hedgerow—the plants will become a wildlife shelter.

How to Grow

Climate
Most standard apricots are as hardy as peaches, but they bloom early, so the flower buds are often killed by a late spring frost. In humid climates, apricots are prone to many of the same diseases that infect peaches. The optimum climates for apricots are the drier regions in Zones 7 to 9. All apricots have some chilling requirement, most over 600 hours, but there are a few low-chill varieties.

That said, apricots are such a delectable treat that in colder climates folks grow numerous trees that seldom fruit, and if they do, it is a cause for celebration. Later-blooming varieties are now available and are worth a try in Zone 6. In colder climates, look for varieties grafted onto Manchurian apricot rootstock. Other possibilities are the hardier Manchurian apricots, which withstand Zone 4 winters.

Japanese apricots have been grown successfully as far north as Philadelphia and St. Louis, although late frost may still pose a threat.

Exposure and Soil

Apricots fruit best in full sun and rich, very well-drained soil.

Planting

In cold-winter climates, plant apricots where they will be in the shade of a wall or structure through the last frost date in spring—to keep them from blooming too early. After that, they require full sun. See "Garden Shadows" in Chapter 2 for a method to predict where winter shade will be. Mulch heavily to keep the ground cold late into spring, and paint the trunk with whitewash to reflect light and heat.

Fertilizing

Mulch with compost in spring and fall. When growing apricot trees in cold climates, keep in mind that a healthy, lean tree is better able to withstand the cold. Give mature trees some nitrogen fertilizer before they break dormancy in spring.

Watering

In dry-summer areas, occasional deep watering is necessary. Don't overwater trees in heavy soils.

Pruning

Standard apricots bear on fruiting spurs that live for 3 or 4 years. Prune annually to force new growth. Train to a vase shape and follow the same procedure as with peaches, but prune less radically. Summer pruning is used to limit height. Thin the fruit to 2 inches apart for small-fruited varieties and to 4 inches for large ones.

Japanese apricots need far less pruning to produce fruits but can tolerate heavy pruning. Prune Manchurian apricots for shape and to thin the fruit. Do not disturb the roots; if you do, suckers will grow.

Pests and Diseases

Standard apricot trees are susceptible to brown rot and bacterial leaf spot. Good fall sanitation is a must. Destroy all old fruit and leaves, where disease organisms overwinter. To prevent bark cankers and cut down on borer problems, every few years paint the trunk from 3 inches belowground to the first branch scaffold with light-colored latex paint diluted with an equal amount of water. If your soil is nematode infested, grow apricots on Manchurian rootstocks. **Caution:** Never use sulfur sprays on apricot trees or you will burn the blossoms and foliage.

Japanese and Manchurian apricots have few disease and pest problems, although brown rot is prevalent in damp weather.

Harvesting

I speak from experience when I warn folks not to leave town during the short harvest season or they will return to find 50 pounds of fruit rotting on the ground. Most apricots ripen in early to midsummer. The fruits are ready to pick when slightly soft and fully colored; apricots do not ripen further once they are harvested. Choose fairly firm fruits for canning and fully ripe ones for eating fresh and drying. Mature standard apricot trees yield 150 to 200 pounds annually.

A low-chill apricot thrives in a Southern California garden. I usually discourage planting soft fruit over pavement, but here secure footing for a ladder and the raised back porch allow for easy daily harvesting as the fruits ripen.

How to Purchase

Purchase bare-root plants in late winter or container-grown plants through summer at local nurseries in favorable climates. Sources for standard apricots include Bay Laurel, One Green World, Raintree, Rolling River, Stark Bro's, Trees of Antiquity, and Willis. Edible Landscaping and Raintree carry Japanese apricots; Gurney's and St. Lawrence offer Manchurian apricots.

Pollinizers

All apricots bear heaviest with cross-pollinization. Most standard apricots are somewhat self-fruitful, although some varieties in cold climates need a pollinizer. Manchurian apricots can pollinize many of the cold-hardiest varieties.

Varieties

Flavor differs less among apricot varieties than is the case with most other fruits. The major differences lie in hardiness, bloom time, winter-chill requirements, and disease resistance. Choose the best variety for your climate. The Japanese have numerous varieties of ume apricots; but the few varieties generally available in North America are sold only by flower color.

'Blenheim' apricot, sometimes called 'Royal' or 'Royal Blenheim', may be small in size but it is superbly packed with flavor. It is rich, succulent, and intensely sweet—sublime. Many consider it the standard by which other apricots are judged.

APRICOT

All the varieties described here are freestone and self-fruitful.

'Autumn Glow' ('Autumn Glo')—late; tops in many taste tests; for mild-winter areas, 800 chill hours, Zones 5 to 8.

'Blenheim' ('Royal')—early; considered the gold standard for flavor and texture; early bloom; grown in California, 500 chill hours, Zones 5 to 9.

'Goldcot'—midseason; juicy, flavorful fruit; use fresh, freeze, or can; developed in Michigan, 800 chill hours, Zones 4 to 7.

'Gold Kist'—early; excellent-quality fruit; productive; good for mild areas, 300 chill hours, Zones 7 to 9.

'Harcot'—early; excellent fruit; sweet, rich, juicy; disease resistant; upright form; frost-hardy late blooms ideal for northern areas, developed in Canada, 700 chill hours, Zones 4 to 8.

'Harglow'—late; sweet, firm, flavorful fruit; compact tree; resistant to canker and brown rot; good for northern areas, 800 chill hours, Zones 5 to 8.

'Moorpark'—midseason; aromatic, juicy, great rich flavor; good fresh and for canning; well suited to the West Coast, marginal in the Southeast, 600 chill hours, Zones 5 to 8.

'Puget Gold'—late; large and flavorful; semi-dwarf to 15 ft.; developed in Washington to set fruit in frosty weather, 600 chill hours, Zones 5 to 9.

MANCHURIAN APRICOT

For good fruit production plant more than one variety. Unless otherwise noted, these varieties have white springtime flowers and are hardy in Zones 4 to 8.

'Moongold'—early; 2 in.; one of the hardiest, most versatile apricots; semi-dwarf; use 'Sungold' as pollinizer.

'Scout'—antique; midseason; 1½ in., excellent for cooking; Canadian introduction, Zones 3 to 7.

'Sungold'—antique; late; 1 in.; good for eating fresh or in preserves; covered with bright pink blossoms in spring; use 'Moongold' as pollinizer.

Artichoke and Cardoon

Cynara spp.

Effort Scale

NO. 3
Spent fronds and flower stalks need removing
Need dividing every 3 or 4 years
Artichoke requires regular watering
Mulching and fertilizing needed
Occasional pests
Winter protection required in many areas

Zones

Artichoke, 8 to 9
Cardoon, 6 to 11

Thumbnail Sketch

Artichoke
Herbaceous perennial sometimes grown as annual
3 to 5 ft. tall
Propagate from divisions or seeds
Needs full sun; afternoon shade in hot climates
Leaves are gray-green fronds, 4 ft. long
Blooming time varies
Flowers are lavender thistles, 4 to 6 in. across
Flower buds are edible; harvest season variable
Use in herbaceous border, as interest plant, or in large container

Cardoon
Herbaceous perennial sometimes grown as annual
3 to 7 ft. tall
Propagate from divisions or seeds
Needs full sun or partial shade
Leaves are gray-green, deeply lobed, 4 ft. long; some varieties have tiny spines
Blooming time varies
Flowers are lavender thistles, 2 to 3 in. across
Stems and root are edible; harvest in midsummer
Use in herbaceous border or as interest plant

How to Use

In the Kitchen

The artichoke is a giant thistle whose flower buds, when cooked, are deliciously—and expensively, for those who must buy them—edible. The bud is served whole as a vegetable or, with the "choke" inside removed, as an edible serving dish for seafood and chicken. To eat a whole artichoke, pull off the outside leaves and use your teeth to scrape the flesh from the base of the leaf. Tender young hearts of artichokes are used as an hors d'oeuvre, in salads, on pizza, or in a savory bread pudding. To preserve artichokes, freeze or pickle the hearts, or pickle whole small artichokes (less than 3 inches in diameter).

Cardoon is a close relative, but instead of the flower buds, the fleshy leaf bases are enjoyed. The flavor is somewhat similar to an artichoke's but stronger and more buttery, with overtones of bitterness reminiscent of radicchio. Cut the inner stalks and heart into suitable pieces. Remove the jagged outside of the leaves and any large strings (as with celery). Slowly simmer the pieces 20 to 40 minutes, or until tender. Steam or bake sections of leafstalk and serve with béchamel sauce or anchovy butter. Cardoon is not generally preserved.

There are a number of biologically active chemicals in the leaves of artichokes and cardoons, in particular cynarin, which gives them their pleasantly bitter taste. Traditional herbalists, and now modern scientists, have found these chemicals improve liver function, stimulate the secretion of digestive juices, and lower cholesterol.

In the Landscape

Both artichoke and cardoon leaves—huge, silvery gray, and deeply lobed—are quite different from anything else, making them dramatic accent plants in any border. Under average conditions they grow to at least 4 feet and spread as wide. Six to eight artichoke plants or four cardoon plants should be ample for a family of four. When not picked for eating, both develop massive blue-purple thistlelike blossoms that are extremely showy both fresh and dried, and the favorites of bumblebees and other beneficial insects.

Artichoke and cardoon can be used as mini-shrubs, in containers, or as accent plants to line a walk or driveway, and both tolerate seaside conditions. In areas with warm, arid summers, artichoke tends to die back in the summer. Try interplanting it with tall pink and white cosmos, which will grow up and hide the thinning foliage. Under most conditions, the cosmos will reseed itself after providing cut flowers all summer. Cardoon generally holds its leaves throughout midsummer.

How to Grow

Climate

Artichoke and cardoon plants produce best in climates with cool, moist summers. In cold winters protect them with an overturned basket filled with leaves placed over the roots. In the coldest-winter areas, bring the roots inside; keep them moist and cool. Under desert conditions artichoke buds and cardoon stalks become tough. Cardoon plants tolerate much harsher conditions than artichokes; given protection they survive to 0°F but can grow as far south as northern Florida and San Diego. (In fact, they grow so well there they become noxious weeds.) To control their spread, remove seed heads before the thistlelike seeds blow away. *Note:* Do not grow cardoon near wild areas.

Exposure and Soil

Artichoke needs full sun in cool-summer areas; in hotter climes it requires afternoon shade. Cardoon is more versatile and can grow in full sun or partial shade. Grow both in rich, well-drained soil enriched with lots of organic matter.

Planting

Start artichoke and cardoon from offshoots or seeds. Plant these large thistles at least 4 feet apart in mild climates, 2 feet apart in harsh-winter areas. Provide deep mulch and keep the plants moist but not saturated until they are established. When growing artichokes and cardoons as perennials, dig them up and divide them every 3 or 4 years to prevent overcrowding.

Fertilizing

For artichokes, add extra nitrogen halfway through the growing season and after harvest. For succulent cardoon leaves, fertilize in spring.

Watering

Water artichokes regularly throughout the growing season. Cardoon is quite drought tolerant, but the stalks will be pithy if drought stressed.

Pests and Diseases

Aphids, slugs, and snails can damage young plants. Rabbits and deer leave both of them alone. Botrytis, a fungal disease, is serious but not

Cardoon is a showstopper in my garden for most of the year. Here, early in the season it is handsome and relatively low growing. Both the red Mexican salvia and red fencing are good foils for the silvery gray leaves.

common. It forms gray mold on leaves in warm, muggy summers. Since there is no known cure, destroy affected plants.

Harvesting

Harvest young artichoke buds when they are still tight, before they start to open. The younger the bud, the tenderer it is, and the more of it is edible.

Historically, cardoons are blanched a month before harvest, usually in spring. The leaves are tied near the top and the leaf bases wrapped in 2 feet of burlap or newspaper to exclude the light. This process makes the leaf bases less bitter.

To harvest cardoon, remove the prickly outside leaves and discard them. Cut off the remaining whitened inner leaves as with a celery bunch.

How to Purchase

Artichoke and cardoon offshoots are available at some local nurseries and from online sources. For a greater choice of varieties, grow plants from seeds available from Nichols, Baker Creek, and Cook's.

Varieties

ARTICHOKE (GLOBE ARTICHOKE), *CYNARA SCOLYMUS* (*C. CARDUNCULUS SCOLYMUS* **GROUP**)

The most commonly grown artichoke is 'Green Globe'. 'Imperial Star' is extra vigorous and productive; each artichoke can produce up to eight buds from transplants in 90 days; great for northern gardens. 'Violetto' has purple buds. (In Italy, cooks shave raw young buds into thin slices and sprinkle with lemon juice, olive oil, and

Large, gray-green, coarsely textured leaves add drama to any garden. Harvest flower buds before they begin to open; steam and serve simply with aioli or melted butter. In addition to three big buds, note one developing lower on the plant.

Parmesan cheese, and serve as an appetizer.) The buds turn green when cooked.

CARDOON, *C. CARDUNCULUS* (*C. CARDUNCULUS* **CARDOON GROUP**)

Although cardoon is not often sold by variety name, named varieties are worth seeking out as they have beefier, tenderer stalks. Look for 'Gigante', 'Gobbo di Nizzia', and 'Tenderheart'.

Asparagus
Asparagus officinalis

Effort Scale
NO. 3
Initial soil preparation can be heavy work
Vulnerable to some pests
Weeding and mulching necessary

Zones
2 to 8; arid Zone 9

Thumbnail Sketch

Herbaceous perennial
3 to 5 ft. tall
Propagate from seeds or rooted crowns
Needs full sun
Leaves are tiny and fernlike
Blooms in summer
Flowers are white to green, insignificant
Female plant has red berries
Young shoots are edible; harvest in spring
Use as background for herbaceous border, as screen, or to line a walk

How to Use

In the Kitchen

Despite their high price, those first spring bunches of asparagus in the market are irresistible to asparagus lovers. Imagine the money-saving delights you could have every spring with a bed of your own—a bed that will continue to feed you for decades. Fresh-harvested asparagus spears have a sweetness similar to peas, and their season is equally fleeting. Most aficionados favor the simple approach to cooking asparagus: steam the stalks until just tender and serve with a touch of butter, or roast or grill the stalks with olive oil and rosemary. If you have a yen for an elegant approach, try asparagus and ribbons of Fontina cheese in an omelet, or prepare asparagus tips with goat cheese over fresh pasta. Freeze asparagus to enjoy it out of season.

In the Landscape

Asparagus is a very long-lived herbaceous perennial that dies back to the ground in fall; the edible spears break through the soil in spring. The shoots that are not cut for eating develop into airy, ferny foliage 3 to 5 feet high, which are elegant lining a walkway or growing along a split-rail fence, as a billowy background in a flower bed, or hiding a compost pile. The colorful bonus is the transformation of the green foliage to yellow in autumn. Plant a border of native perennials like tall prairie coreopsis, echinacea, and Mexican hats in front of your asparagus patch, or try a bed of annuals such as red salvia, orange nasturtiums, or bush squash in front for a contrast of color and form.

How to Grow

Climate

Asparagus grows in most areas of the Northern Hemisphere except the very coldest sections and the Deep South, where warm, humid winters foster diseases and prevent the plant from going dormant and renewing itself.

Exposure and Soil

Asparagus needs a deep, rich organic soil with good drainage. Bad drainage will kill the plants. Asparagus needs full sun.

Planting

Start asparagus from seeds or year-old rooted crowns (the base of the plant); crowns bear a year earlier. The average family needs about 30 to 40 plants of the old-time varieties or 20 to 25 mature all-male hybrids.

Because asparagus lives in the same place for many years, it pays to prepare the soil well. In a vegetable garden, for the productive all-male varieties, plant two rows 10 feet long and 4 to 6 feet apart. You'll need double the row length for other varieties. Spade generous amounts of aged chicken manure and compost into the top 2 feet of soil. Then dig two trenches 6 to 8 inches deep and 12 inches wide. Place the crowns in the bottom—about 12 inches apart—with their roots well spread out. Cover with 3 to 4 inches of soil. As the shoots grow, gradually add soil—1 to 2 inches at a time—until the trench is filled, taking care not to cover the shoots completely. This process also helps control weeds in the new bed. Once the trench is filled to ground level, mulch with 3 to 4 inches of straw, leaves, or compost.

The trench dimensions are for a standard vegetable bed. If you are lining a walk or planting behind a flower border, the depth and width of the trench are the same, but you can vary the length of the trenches to suit your design.

Fertilizing

Maintain a 4- to 6-inch-deep layer of organic mulch to provide nutrients and to help control weeds. Supplement with a light dressing of aged chicken manure or fish fertilizer in the spring—more if the plants are pale or spindly.

Watering

Asparagus requires moderate amounts of water only during the growing season. In rainy climates, supplemental watering is usually not needed, except in a drought. In arid climates, water deeply once a week.

Pruning

In mild climates, to help control pests cut down plants when they turn brown; in cold climates the dead growth helps hold snow to insulate the roots. Remove all branches and debris in spring before the new spears appear.

Pests and Diseases

The asparagus beetle, which is black and red, is the most serious pest. Fall cleanup helps remove breeding adults and eggs. After the first two

Perennial asparagus is paired with annual nasturtiums at the Pounder Heritage Vegetable Garden at Cornell Plantations in Ithaca, New York. The nasturtiums' lighter green, round leaves and orange edible flowers contrast with the ferny asparagus.

springs, keep all spears cut for a few weeks during harvest. Covering the bed with floating row covers during harvest time can help. If the beetles take over, spray pyrethrum two or three times, at weekly intervals. Some gardeners report fewer beetles on all-male plants.

Asparagus rust, fusarium crown rot, and root rot are serious problems on older varieties, but all-male cultivars are quite resistant. To prevent fusarium, purchase only certified fungus-free roots and be sure to provide great drainage. Cercospora leaf spot can be a problem in hot, humid areas. Good hygiene helps control all diseases. Gophers can devastate asparagus plantings. If you have a problem with gophers, line the trench to 2 inches above soil level with hardware cloth before you plant.

Harvesting

To harvest, cut the spears an inch below soil level, taking care to avoid the roots; cut spears before the tips start to open. The second year—when the spears are larger than a pencil—harvest them for 2 weeks. In subsequent years, harvest until the spears begin to thin to less than ½ inch in diameter, usually 4 to 6 weeks into the harvest season. Harvest every 3 days if the weather is cool, or daily if it is hot.

The first mouthwatering stalks of asparagus emerging from the earth are sure signs of spring. Cut the stalks just below ground level with a sharp knife. Harvest for 6 weeks; then uncut shoots will develop into fernlike leaves.

How to Purchase

Buy bare-root crowns in early spring at local nurseries or from Gurney's, D. Landreth, Johnny's, or Nourse. Choose hardy varieties for the North and heat-tolerant varieties for the South.

Varieties

'Jersey Giant'—hybrid, all-male; great for cold climates; fusarium and rust resistant.

'Jersey King'—hybrid, all-male; widely adapted; heat and fusarium tolerant; rust resistant.

'Jersey Knight'—hybrid, all-male; heat tolerant; fusarium and rust resistant.

'Purple Passion'—open pollinated; widely adapted; extra sweet and tender purple spears; add vinegar or lemon juice to the cooking water to retain some purple color.

'UC 157'—hybrid; heat tolerant; commercial variety in California and Washington; not reliably hardy.

'Viking'—open pollinated; hardy; from Canada; rust tolerant.

Aubergine

See Eggplant

Avocado

Persea americana

Effort Scale

NO. 2 in California
Watering and fertilizing needed

NO. 3 in Florida and Hawaii
Watering and fertilizing needed
Susceptible to disease and some pest problems
Large, long harvest of fruit is time consuming

Zones

9 to 11

Thumbnail Sketch

Evergreen tree
Standard, 20 to 40 ft. tall or more; dwarf varieties, to 12 ft. tall
Propagate by grafting or budding
Needs full sun
Leaves are dark green, 4 to 8 in. long; new growth is bronzy
Bloom time depends on variety
Flowers are insignificant
Fruits are edible; leaves of some varieties are edible; harvest season varies
Use as shade tree or screen; dwarf varieties as large shrubs or in containers

How to Use

In the Kitchen

Avocados are 3 to 6 inches long and pear shaped. For those who love them, their buttery, yellow-green flesh is one of the world's most toothsome pleasures. Enjoy avocados raw, combined in salads with tomatoes and sweet onions, and as a garnish in Mexican recipes. Mashed (think guacamole), they are a must-have at any party; halved, they transform into decadent edible bowls for seafood salads.

Clinical studies show that the monounsaturated oils in avocados help lower LDL (bad) cholesterol. The oil content varies considerably with the avocado type and variety. Guatemalan and hybrid crosses are the common avocados. Some of the Mexican varieties grown only in home gardens and not sold in groceries in the United States have the high oil content that some of us lust after. The fruits and leaves of these varieties have an aromatic anise flavor; in Mexico, folks dry, grind, and add the leaves to marinades for barbecued meats.

In the Landscape

Growing to 40 feet or more, with an equally wide spread, this evergreen gives marvelous shade. However, for ease of harvesting, keep the tree shorter. Where it grows well, an avocado is a beautiful specimen. The flowers are not important, nor do the green or black fruits offer ornamental accents. The tree is the thing, with big, lush, green leaves that are bronzy in new growth. Leaf drop is constant, so the tree is a nuisance over a patio or path, though the fruit does not drop readily. Grow dwarf varieties in tubs or plant them as large accent shrubs or a small screen.

How to Grow

For much more detailed information on growing avocados consult the California Rare Fruit Growers (www.crfg.org).

Climate

Guatemalan avocado varieties are hardy to about 30°F; some of the Mexican varieties are hardy to the low 20s. In all cases, significant frosts damage flowers and small fruits; protect the trees from wind. Most avocados are limited to the warmer areas of California, Florida, and Hawaii; a few Mexican varieties survive the warmer areas of the Gulf Coast. In borderline climates, cover containerized dwarf and young trees or bring them inside.

Exposure and Soil

Avocados thrive in full sun and deep, rich, very well-drained soil. Roots rot where the water table is high. Avocados are intolerant of salt in the soil or in irrigation water.

Fertilizing

In most soils, avocados need a few light applications of organic all-purpose fertilizer supplemented with chelated iron every spring and early summer. In Florida, fertilize avocados as you would citrus. Mulch avocados thickly with avocado leaves or compost, as they are very shallow rooted.

Watering

Keep the soil moist but not wet; never let water sit around the base of the plant. When avocados are grown in containers, salts build up in the soil. To avoid salt burn, flush the container once a month by flooding it three or four times within an hour.

Pruning

To control size and shape, pinch out new growth. Protect exposed branches from sunburn by painting the bark with light-colored latex paint diluted with an equal amount of water.

Pests and Diseases

The major pests of avocados are squirrels and rats, which can strip the tree. To protect the crop remove lower branches and use tin trunk wraps. In Florida, scale is a pest. In Southern California, persea mites cause small, yellow and black dead spots on the leaves, which eventually drop. Consult your local Cooperative Extension Service to determine which predatory mite will control the pest mite.

Diseases include cercospora fruit spot, avocado scab, and anthracnose. Give the trees three or four sprayings with neutral copper; check with your Cooperative Extension Service about the proper timing. All growers struggle with *Phytophthora cinnamomi* root rot when soils are soggy; adding gypsum (up to 25 pounds a year, a bit at a time) along with 6 to 12 inches of organic mulch can thwart the fungus.

Treat chlorosis with chelated iron. Salt burn manifests itself as stunted growth and/or brown leaf edges. Treat it by giving the surrounding soil a deep watering at every third or fourth irrigation. Avoid manures and commercial fertilizers.

Harvesting

Harvest avocados when they are mature but still hard. Cut the fruits off the branch—do not pull—and ripen at room temperature until they give slightly to pressure. Rock-hard fruits can take 2 weeks to ripen. A healthy 10-year-old tree produces 100 to 150 pounds of fruit in California, 50 to 100 pounds in Florida and Hawaii.

It is normal for avocados, particularly the Guatemalan group, to bear heavily one year but poorly or not at all the next.

How to Purchase

Purchase avocados at local nurseries. Check out Garden of Delights and Tams; Wayside offers a dwarf variety; Pine Island carries Florida varieties.

Pollinizers

Avocado flowers are classified as one of two types—A or B. For the best fruit set, grow both an A and a B. If space is limited, graft a branch of one type onto the other.

Varieties

Three main groups of avocados are grown in the United States: Mexican, Guatemalan, and numerous hybrids. In parts of South America, the West Indian avocado (*Persea americana* var. *americana*) is also grown. Limited to South Florida, this group is the least hardy, but it has a low oil content preferred by some cultures and dieters.

MEXICAN, P. A. VAR. *DRYMIFOLIA*

'Bacon'—good-quality green fruit; flower type A; upright tree bears in winter; hardy to 24°F, for California.

'Don Gillogly'—soft, black-skinned fruit with rich flavor; flower type A; bears in late summer; dwarf tree to 10 ft., good for containers; grows in all climates.

'Mexicola'—small, black, thin-skinned fruit with rich anise/nutty flavor, very high oil content of 20 percent; flower type A, self-fruitful in California; bears in fall; tall tree; rootstock for other varieties,

Avocado trees are without doubt among the handsomest evergreens. The fruit varies by type from green and smooth skinned to black with pebbly skin. No matter the variety, avocados are delicious fruits easily grown in warm climates.

rarely available in nurseries; hardy to 18°F (tree defoliates), for California and northern Florida.

'Gwen'—excellent fruit similar to 'Hass', 18 percent oil content; flower type A; bears spring into fall; dwarf tree to 12 ft.; good in containers and greenhouse; hardy to 28°F.

'Hass'—black, pebbly skin; excellent fruit, 19 percent oil content; flower type A; bears in July; open spreading tree; hardy to 26°F, grown in California.

'Whitsell'—green skin; flower type B; excellent quality; bears midwinter to fall.

HYBRID

'Choquette'—large, green fruit with excellent flavor; flower type A; spreading tree bears late fall; resistant to anthracnose; hardy to about 26°F, Florida favorite.

'Fuerte'—green skin; flower type B; good quality; bears late fall to spring; hardy to 27°F.

'Murashige'—large, green fruit with excellent flavor, 20 percent oil content; flower type B; bears spring to summer; medium-size upright tree; for Hawaii.

Bamboo

Bambusa spp.
Phyllostachys spp.

Effort Scale

NO. 2 in mild climates
Easy to grow

NO. 3 in cold climates
Winter protection necessary

Preparing shoots for eating is time consuming

Zones

7 to 11 (a few are hardier)

Thumbnail Sketch

Perennial evergreen grass
Edible types, 8 to 60 ft. tall
Propagate from divisions
Needs full sun; afternoon shade in hot climates
Leaves are bright green, 2 to 3 in. long
Woody, ridged canes are very decorative
Flowers bloom infrequently and are insignificant
Shoots are edible; harvest in spring or summer
Use as hedge, container plant, interest plant, screen, or windbreak

How to Use

In the Kitchen

Asians consume lots of young bamboo shoots, which are high in minerals, fiber, and antioxidants, and very low in calories. The familiar canned product cannot pretend to compare with succulent fresh bamboo shoots, whose flavor is reminiscent of crisp, sweet, young corn. Sauté with ginger, garlic, and soy sauce and serve as a side dish, or add shoots to stir-fried dishes, curries, and soups. Use bamboo shoots like any boiled vegetable; you can substitute fresh in any recipe calling for canned shoots.

Most shoots are bitter unless parboiled for 15 to 20 minutes or until tender. Change the water after the first 10 minutes, and drain shoots when they are done. Then peel off the outer sheaths of developing leaves to expose the white fleshy shoot, and remove any woody base. Cut small-diameter shoots into thin rings; discard the nodes (the hard, solid sections). Cut large-diameter shoots into thin slices lengthwise. Cook immediately. Raw shoots deteriorate very quickly, so use them within a day or two.

The easiest way to preserve bamboo shoots is to parboil them and then freeze them in plastic bags. The frozen shoots remain crisp.

In the Landscape

Bamboo is one of the most useful and beloved plants in Asia. A clump, windbreak, hedge, or screen of bamboo gives an Asian feel to any garden. Planted in containers, these plants accent an informal pool or an entryway. The woody, ringed canes are graceful, highlighted by the narrow green leaves. A poised row of bamboo makes a delightful and very effective screen that comes alive in a breeze.

When planting bamboo it is critical to remember that there are two kinds: running and clumping. Running bamboo does run; it can come up in your neighbor's asphalt driveway 10 feet away. Before planting running bamboo, install an underground barrier. In the coldest climates the growth is not as invasive; in Hawaii running bamboo can become a noxious weed. The clumping type stays confined, sending up only basal stems. Stands of bamboo are useful in controlling bank and hillside erosion.

Bamboo is a valuable building material in Asia, a renewable resource that grows fast and efficiently. With bamboo in your yard, you have an almost inexhaustible source of stakes and fencing materials. For how-tos and inspiration look through Carol Stangler's book *The Craft & Art of Bamboo*.

How to Grow

For an in-depth look at growing bamboo, consult *The Gardener's Guide to Growing Temperate Bamboos* by Michael Bell and *Bamboo for Gardens* by Ted Jordan Meredith. Visit the American Bamboo Society website: www.americanbamboo.org.

Climate

Most edible bamboos are either tender or semi-hardy; only a few are hardy below 0°F. To protect new shoots in winter, mulch well.

Exposure and Soil

In most areas bamboo grows best in full sun; in the hottest-summer regions give it some afternoon shade. In the coldest climates plant bamboo against a protected south wall. All species prefer well-drained loam high in organic matter.

Planting

When planting running bamboo, install a rhizome barrier to control its growth. Many growers rely on 36-inch-wide, 30 to 60 mil plastic sheeting available from major bamboo nurseries. Place it along a 33-inch-deep trench so it rises at least 3 inches above soil level. Another option is to pour a 4-inch-wide concrete header 3 feet deep, or plant in large, bottomless, underground metal containers, like old garbage cans.

Fertilizing

The first year, feed with a balanced fertilizer. Thereafter, dropped leaves and an occasional application of nitrogen provide sufficient nutrients to maintain moderate growth. For more vigorous plants and numerous shoots, fertilize more heavily.

Watering

Most bamboos are somewhat drought tolerant, but they produce the most succulent shoots when well watered. Do not let them dry out the first year. Bamboo litter, while valuable mulch, can prevent water from penetrating the root area, so watch for pooling water.

Pruning

For beauty, trim the lower leaves to expose the canes. Thin out 3-year-old canes.

Pests and Diseases

Bamboo has few damaging pests or diseases in North America. However, an introduced bamboo mite has spread to many parts of the South and West; once established, it is hard to control. Sometimes a leaf spot fungus or rust appears in warm, humid climates. Occasionally aphids or cottony bamboo scale can be a problem, especially in spring.

Harvesting

To harvest, cut the shoots of the large-diameter species before or just as they emerge from the ground in early spring. Before cutting, carefully expose the shoots by clearing away the soil around them, making sure not to disturb other shoots. Allow the slenderer species—1 to 2 inches in diameter—to grow to a foot tall before harvesting. For any kind of bamboo, do not harvest all the shoots; the plants need to renew themselves. New shoots of clumping bamboos usually appear in summer or fall, while running bamboos generally send up their shoots in spring.

How to Purchase

Local nurseries carry many types of bamboo. Other sources include Forestfarm, Raintree, and Tripple Brook. Bamboo Giant, Bamboo Sourcery, and Lewis Bamboo specialize in bamboo plants; they also carry an array of bamboo products.

Varieties

Most species of bamboo are edible, but many are not palatable. These are best for eating:

Giant timber (*Bambusa oldhamii*)—15 to 55 ft. tall, 4-in. stems; clumping; bitter flavor; some drought tolerance, Zones 9 to 11.

Moso (*Phyllostachys edulis* [*P. pubescens*])—20 to 70 ft. tall, 8-in. stems; running; bitter flavor, must be cooked; prefers heat and humidity, Zones 7 to 11.

Nude sheath (*P. nuda*)—30 to 35 ft. tall, 1½-in. stems; running; tasty shoots; dark green leaves; among the hardiest edible bamboos, to −10°F, Zones 5 to 11.

Sweetshoot (*P. dulcis*)—20 to 30 ft. tall, 1½-in. stems; running, produces many shoots; considered one of the sweetest; Zones 7 to 11.

Timber (*P. bambusoides*)—15 to 50 ft. tall, 6-in. stems; running; quite bitter, needs much boiling; excellent for fences; Zones 7 to 11.

Bamboo is a renewable resource for landscape design—edible, ornamental, and utilitarian. At the Hakone Estate and Gardens in Saratoga, California, bamboo is in its full splendor. Here, edible timber bamboo thrives behind a bamboo fence.

Yellow groove (*P. aureosulcata*)—12 to 25 ft. tall, 1½-in. stems; running; sweet, can be eaten raw; yellow grooves on olive green stems; Zones 6 to 11.

Banana and Plantain

Musa spp.

Effort Scale

NO. 3
Constant fertilizing necessary
Mulching and watering needed
Large crop ripens over a short time
Winter protection needed in most areas

Zones

10 and 11

Thumbnail Sketch

Herbaceous perennials
6 to 25 ft. tall
Propagate from rhizomes or suckers
Need full sun for most, partial shade for some
Leaves are dramatic, 5 to 9 ft. long
Flowers are large, podlike, green or red, interesting

Bananas fruiting in a Florida landscape are a spectacular sight. The female flowers at the tips of the embryonic bananas are fertilized by male flowers (not seen) as the colorful covering unfurls. There's always plenty of fruit to share.

Fruits are edible; flowers are edible; harvest season varies
Use as interest plant, near a pool, on a patio, or in atriums; dwarf varieties in containers or warm greenhouse

How to Use

In the Kitchen

The commercial banana we know and love is long, narrow, and sweet. Marvelous food for traveling and snacks, it is easy to peel and eat. Additionally, it is healthful without being high in calories and so is popular in smoothies. However, such delicacies as banana cream pie and flaming bananas cancel out any low-calorie advantage. Freeze banana pulp or make banana bread and freeze. Dry sliced bananas into "chips." Freeze whole bananas dipped in chocolate.

Plantain, a close relative of banana though less sweet, is enjoyed in most tropical climates. When green, it is firm and starchy. Use it somewhat like a potato: serve boiled or fried as a side dish, or dice and add to soups and stews. When yellow to black ripe it is sweeter; enjoy it in desserts—for instance, sauté with butter, sugar, and rum, and serve over ice cream.

Cut either banana or plantain leaves in squares to wrap around fish, spicy rice mixtures, or tamale dough before steaming or grilling. The natural wrapping imparts a perfumed flavor to the food inside.

In the Landscape

Banana and plantain plants grow tall—6 to 25 feet—but stay narrow. Their tremendous leaves, which can reach 9 feet long and 2 feet wide, lend a bold accent to a yard. They give a tropical appearance to courtyards and sunny atriums and are attractive near pools. The leaves make soothing noises as they rub together in a gentle breeze. Grow dwarf bananas in containers or in a warm greenhouse.

How to Grow

Climate

Banana plants are tender. They freeze at 28°F; most varieties need 18 months of frostless, very warm weather to produce fruit. Plantains are slightly hardier. Both grow well in South Florida and Hawaii, and with mixed results in Southern California. Cover plants to protect from frost. In borderline climates, plant against a hot south-facing wall or grow one of the many dwarf varieties in a container and bring it inside for winter.

Exposure and Soil

Most banana and plantain varieties need full sun and protection from strong winds, which can tatter the foliage and knock down fruit-laden stalks. Both plants need slightly acidic, rich, well-drained garden loam, and deep organic mulch.

Planting

Bananas and plantains need a long, warm growing season to become established before winter. Plant them in March or April. Dig a 3-by-2-foot hole for each rhizome; space dwarf varieties 10 feet apart and large plants 15 feet apart. Amend the soil with copious amounts of compost. If you are getting your start from a neighbor's plant, select a rooted sucker with a strong stem; let it dry out for a day before planting.

Fertilizing

Bananas and plantains are extremely heavy feeders: fertilize monthly throughout the growing season with an all-purpose organic fertilizer and keep them well mulched.

Watering

The large leaves permit evaporation of great quantities of water. Water heavily. In hot or windy weather, water daily. Do not let the plants dry out.

Pruning

Banana plants sucker profusely and must be cut back regularly. Allow only one stalk to grow the first year; thereafter limit the plant to three or four stalks. Prune off all other suckers. Fruiting occurs only once on each stalk and the fruit is borne in large, heavy bunches. After bearing, a stalk dies and should be cut down. Keep others growing to replace it. It usually takes 12 to 18 months for a stalk to start flowering. After the fruits set, remove spent male flowers from the end of the bunch to lessen the weight on the stalk. *Note:* Sap, which was once used to make ink, stains clothing.

Pests and Diseases

Bananas and plantains have very few pests and diseases, except for nematodes in some parts of the country. Snails can disfigure new growth; rodents eat ripe fruits if they are not harvested when green. A fungus, Panama disease, is sometimes a problem in Florida; avoid it by planting a fungus-resistant variety.

Harvesting

Cut down the entire fruit stalk when the bottom handlike cluster is fully formed and the fruit is still green. Bananas ripen in succession from the top down. Hang the bunch for 2 weeks to develop full flavor. You get a large harvest all at once, so some form of preservation is needed.

How to Purchase

Buy container-grown bananas from local nurseries in banana-growing climates or order from JD Andersen, Pine Island, or Stokes Tropicals.

Varieties

Avoid the many "ornamental" banana plants, which—while lovely—produce no edible fruit.

BANANA

'Apple'—great flavor, short fat bananas; to 18 ft. tall.

'Dwarf Cavendish'—large clusters of sweet fruit; fairly hardy; resists Panama disease; produces mature fruits in a year; most readily available dwarf variety, to 6 ft. tall.

'Goldfinger'—excellent, sweet fruit in large bunches; resists nematodes; to 13 ft. tall.

'Ice Cream'—melting, sweet flesh; blue-green leaves; susceptible to Panama disease; to 20 ft. tall.

'Lacatan'—good, sweet fruit; resistant to Panama disease; to 18 ft. tall.

'Lady Finger'—delicate, small, 5-in. fruit with excellent, sweet flavor; to 20 ft. tall.

'Rajapuri'—small, sweet fruit; some wind and cold tolerance; dwarf to 8 ft. tall.

'Red Jamaica'—maroon fruit with orange flesh and good flavor; very striking plant to 20 ft. tall; reddish bronzy green leaves; very tender. 'Dwarf Red Jamaica' to 7 ft. tall.

PLANTAIN

'Orinoco'—usually the only variety available; almost triangular, 10-in. fruit; burgundy veins and trunk; cold hardier than most; susceptible to Panama disease; to 20 ft. tall; dwarf available.

Basil

Ocimum spp.

Effort Scale

NO. 2
Must be planted annually
Watering and fertilizing usually needed
Pinching and harvesting are time consuming

Zones

Not applicable

Thumbnail Sketch

Annual or tender perennial herb
12 to 36 in. tall
Propagate from seeds or cuttings

Needs full sun; tolerates partial shade
Leaves are bright green, purple, or variegated, 1 to 3 in. long
Blooms in summer
Flowers are white or pink, small; attract bees
Leaves and flowers are edible; use for seasoning; harvest in summer; seeds are flavorful
Use in flower bed, herb garden, flower or foliage border, or container

How to Use

In the Kitchen

Where do I start? Basil is the quintessential must-have herb in so many cultures; its range of culinary uses could fill several books. I love the flavor the fresh aromatic leaves bring to soups, salads, stews, and pasta, to name a few dishes. In Thailand, basil is essential in curries, and the seeds are used in sweet drinks; in Vietnam, it's a must for salad wraps. Add basil to green salads; use it in marinades and dressings; chop and incorporate it into soft cheese or butter; and substitute the larger basil leaves for lettuce in sandwiches. For many people, basil is best known as the base for pesto and *insalata caprese* (a classic Italian dish: basil leaves with sliced tomatoes and fresh mozzarella cheese drizzled with olive oil). When I want a homemade pizza, I spread pesto—instead of tomato sauce—on the dough, add roasted red and yellow peppers and Monterey Jack cheese, and bake—a truly colorful, tasty, and healthy garden pizza.

When dried, basil loses most of its flavor. Try other methods to preserve basil for out-of-season use. Make pesto and freeze it for up to 6 months (leave out the cheese and garlic; add them before serving). Chop basil, freeze it in ice cube trays, and store the cubes in freezer bags. Or layer chopped basil with Parmesan cheese in an airtight container and refrigerate (keeps for up to 2 months).

In the Landscape

The exact origins of the common warm-season basils, which grow to 24 inches tall, are not clear but are probably southern Asia and

Plant basils to create a patchwork quilt of color and leaf shapes. Here, holy basil, 'Green Ruffles', 'Red Rubin', and 'Mrs. Burns Lemon' offset the shock of color from Thai peppers at the National Herb Garden in the U.S. National Arboretum.

northern Africa. The less common tender perennial basils grow to 36 inches tall and are native to South America. The common variety (known as basil or sweet basil) bears 2- to 3-inch-long, glossy, bright green leaves. With so many basil varieties, it's easy to find the perfect one for almost any landscape; keep at least one pot of basil near the kitchen.

All basils add a fresh touch of color to the grays in a culinary herb garden, and their heady scent on a warm day perfumes the air. Visually basil adds sparkle to a mixed flower bed. For practicality, the small-leaved bush varieties—both green and purple—present a semi-formal edge and bring order to a vegetable border. Planted among carrots, basil adds solidity; planted among lettuces, it conveys another shade of green. Green basils combine well with other annuals like dwarf marigolds, red gomphrena, and salvias. Purple-leaved varieties—great additions to most flower borders—set off annual vinca, alyssum, and dwarf zinnias.

The upright perennial basils grow larger than the standard varieties. Although they seldom flower in North America, their green, purple, or variegated foliage makes them delightful in the middle of a flower border. All basils thrive in containers.

How to Grow

Basil succeeds in all but the coolest climates. Grow it in well-drained, fairly rich soil in full sun, and water regularly.

Planting

Start seeds indoors 6 weeks before your last frost date. Plant the seeds ½ inch deep and 2 inches apart; keep them in a warm place (75°F or more). Water gently; the slippery seeds wash away easily. The seeds should germinate within 14 days. Transplant 3-inch (or taller) seedlings outdoors when the weather is reliably warm; space them at least a foot apart. Water well, and mulch.

Feed at least twice during the season with an organic all-purpose fertilizer (more often for containers) to keep the leaves large and succulent. Pinch back young plants to keep them bushy. Remove flower spikes as they appear for best leaf production and flavor.

Pests and Diseases

Basil has few pest problems except for occasional fusarium wilt, which can be avoided by choosing disease-resistant varieties such as 'Nufar'.

Harvesting

Snip off stems with at least five or six leaves as needed for use as a fresh herb. For a large harvest, shear plants midseason and then feed; or wait until the end of the season and pull out the plants and remove the leaves. The best use of a large harvest is pesto.

How to Purchase

Local nurseries carry basil seeds and small plants in spring. Sweet basil is widely available. Try some of the dozens of distinctive cultivars, some of which are listed below. Often the same plant has more than one name; I included also-known-as names, or aka's, when possible.

Varieties

Local nurseries sometimes carry specialty basils. Seed sources include Johnny's, Park, and Renee's; and sources of both plants and seeds include Mulberry Creek (plants online only), Nichols, Richters,

Thyme Garden, and Well-Sweep. The basils listed below are *Ocimum basilicum*, unless otherwise noted.

'Anise'—purplish leaves; pink flowers; distinctive licorice flavor.

'Aussie Sweetie' (*O. × citriodorum*)—same as 'Greek Columnar' and 'Lesbos'; tender perennial; soft green leaves; does not flower at northern latitudes; complex spicy flavor; distinctive upright habit; a red variety is available.

Bush basil (*O. b.* 'Minimum', aka *O. minimum*)—6 to 12 in. tall; tiny leaves; white flowers; great in containers and used as an edging; spicy fragrance; a classic for pesto; similar types include 'Dwarf', 'Fino Verde', 'Pistou', 'Window Box Mini', and 'Spicy Globe'.

'Cinnamon'—narrow green leaves with red veins; cinnamon flavor; same as 'Mexican' or 'Mexican Spice'.

'Green Pepper' (*O. selloi*)—tender perennial native to South America; large, emerald green leaves; reddish flowers; distinctive green bell pepper flavor and scent.

Indian basil—a green basil to 3 ft. tall, spikes of lavender flowers; in India the almost flavorless seeds are added to a mixture of milk and rose water for texture and to boost health; same as 'Subja'.

'Lettuce-leaved'—broad, green leaves to 4 in. long; great in sandwiches and salads; similar to 'Salad Leaf'.

'Lime' (*O. × citriodorum*)—to 12 in. tall; light green leaves; spicy lime flavor.

'Magical Michael'—compact, green basil with uniform growth; purple flowers; classic basil flavor.

'Mrs. Burns Lemon'—strong grower; narrow green leaves to 1½ in. long; an improved lemon basil; great lemon flavor.

'Nufar'—one of the few hybrid basils; green leaves; good flavor; resistant to fusarium wilt.

'Pesto Perpetuo' (*O. × citriodorum*)—upright growth; striking green and white variegated foliage; mellow basil flavor; Zones 9 to 11.

'Purple Bush'—small, purple-green leaves; dwarf bushy plant great for containers and edging; strong flavor similar to 'Minimum Purpurascens Well Sweep'.

'Purple Ruffles'—large, deep purple, ruffled leaves; pink flowers; one of the best red basils.

'Red Rubin'—deep purple leaves; pink flowers; flavorful (not great for pesto as it turns brown); tints white wine vinegar a rich pink; improved red basil.

'Siam Queen'—compact plant; small, green leaves; deep purple flower buds and shoots; anise flavor.

Sweet basil—green leaves; the most commonly offered basil; varies tremendously in quality and flavor depending on the seed source.

'Sweet Dani'—vigorous plant; green leaves; delightful lemon flavor; same as 'Sweet Dani Lemon Basil'.

'Thai'—rangy plant; purple-tinged foliage; strong, aniselike aroma.

Bay laurel

See Sweet Bay

Beach plum

See Plum

Bean

Fava bean, *Vicia faba*
Lima bean, *Phaseolus lunatus* (*P. limensis*)
Runner bean, *P. coccineus*
Snap bean, bush and pole, *P. vulgaris*

Effort Scale

NO. 3
Must be planted annually
Watering and light fertilizing needed
Vulnerable to some pests and diseases
Harvesting is time consuming

Zones

Not applicable

Thumbnail Sketch

Annual or perennial grown as annual
Vines, 6 to 15 ft. long; bushes, to 36 in. tall
Propagate from seeds
Needs full sun
Flowers in summer
Flowers are white, lavender, purple, or red
Seeds and pods are edible, flowers in some species are edible; harvest in summer
Use bush types in flower beds, raised beds, or planter boxes; vining types on arbors, trellises, or fences

How to Use

In the Kitchen

For me, green snap beans—cooked until just tender with a little salt, pepper, a dab of butter, and a grating of ginger for zing—are one of life's gustatory experiences. Dress up beans with almonds or cheese sauce. The dramatic purple beans turn green when they are cooked (add vinegar to cooking water to preserve some color); children call them magic beans. Freeze, can, or pickle snap beans to enjoy out of season.

Young runner bean pods are delicious in a pureed soup; sprinkle the colorful edible flowers atop the soup for color and crunch; the dry beans add wonderful flavor to minestrone. Lima beans are home cooking at its best, whether fresh or dried in a succotash, especially with bacon and cream.

To preserve shelled immature beans, blanch 2 minutes and freeze. Store all mature dried beans in airtight containers, freeze for 1 or 2 days to kill any weevil eggs; move to a cool, dry place. Fava beans, also called broad beans, are a cool-season treat similar to lima beans; great with olive oil and garlic. **Caution:** Some people are allergic to fava beans, so if you are eating them for the first time, try just a bite or two.

In the Landscape

Whether bush or pole, beans are grown as annuals. Gardeners usually relegate them to the vegetable garden, but well-grown plants have attractive leaves and handsome, long, green, yellow, or purple pods.

The Idea Garden at Longwood Gardens in Kennett Square, Pennsylvania, shows off the versatility of beans. Bush beans form a blanket of green bordered by yellow marigolds, while pole beans climb skyward, defining the space.

The beans with small, white or lavender flowers are restful and appealing in the garden. Use a sea of lush green bush beans to set off showy flowers like dwarf sunflowers, salvias, or petunias. The showier beans add a distinctive style, even whimsy. Purple-podded beans with regal names like 'Purple Queen' and 'Royal Burgundy'—with their deep purple flowers, foliage, and beans—give a rich look. I combine them with dwarf pink and purple dahlias that have burgundy foliage.

For a fanciful touch, create an arched passageway of pole beans and morning glories between the lawn and children's play area; or make a bean tepee with purple and yellow string beans. Brilliant red scarlet runner bean flowers, large snowy 'White Dutch Runner' blossoms, and vivid 'Purple Tepee' blooms—all are decorative on a trellis, arbor, or fence. Build a large planter box, add a trellis, cover it with runner beans, and voilà—privacy from your neighbor's patio. Plant them to cover a humble chain-link fence, and enjoy a bonus—ever-present hummingbirds and bumblebees darting among the runner bean flowers.

Fava beans are stiff, upright plants, suitable for the back of a flower border or in a vegetable garden. Most varieties have white flowers with a black blotch; a burgundy-flowered variety is worth seeking out.

There are many more wonderful types of beans to use in your garden, including hyacinth beans (*Lablab purpureus*), yard-long beans (*Vigna unguiculata*), and soybeans (*Glycine max*), all of which are included in Appendix A.

How to Grow

Beans grow in summer in most areas of the country. In very hot-summer climates with mild winters, grow bush beans in the spring

In addition to being beautiful in the garden and tasty in the kitchen, the many varieties of beans—including fresh and dried, pole and bush, string and yard long, and green, purple, and yellow varieties—make a stunning still life.

and again in the fall. Although runner beans yield few beans when temperatures are in the high 80s, they glory in cool northern summer gardens.

Fava beans grow as 6-foot-tall, upright, herbaceous annuals and have little tolerance for hot weather; they tolerate numerous frosts but not weather in the low teens. They need at least 90 days of cool weather to produce a good crop.

Exposure and Soil

All bean plants need full sun and loose, very well-drained garden loam with plenty of added humus.

Planting

If you have not planted beans in the bed before or are growing them in a container, purchase "bean inoculant" (Rhizobia bacteria, which help plants to fix nitrogen), and follow package directions. Plant snap beans only after the soil is really warm; temperature is critical, as cold, wet seeds rot. Plant seeds 1 inch deep, 2 inches apart. Water, and cover the planting with floating row covers or bird netting. Thin bean seedlings to 4 inches apart. When they reach 6 inches tall, mulch with 3 inches of compost and train the tall vining types to a trellis. Pole beans produce for a few months, bush beans a month or so. For a continued harvest, make two plantings of bush beans a few weeks apart. Production slows in very hot weather, so try to get your plants producing before the dog days of summer. Sow fava bean seeds in spring at the same time as peas.

Fertilizing

Beans seldom need extra fertilizer, but if they are pale and spindly apply hydrolyzed fish.

Watering

Water infrequently but deeply—at the base of the plants to prevent diseases.

Pests and Diseases

Beans have their share of pests and diseases—beetles that chew foliage and, in humid climates, diseases that disfigure leaves—all of which cut down on production and quality, and make the plants look scraggly. Practice these techniques for best harvest: rotate beans with other plants, keep the bed free of weeds, and in humid climates do not crowd plants.

The lineup of pests includes Japanese, Mexican bean, cucumber, and flea beetles; aphids; and slugs, to name a few. Mexican bean beetles have small, beige larvae, and the adults look like tiny copper-colored ladybugs with 16 black spots. They congregate under the leaves and skeletonize them. To control Mexican bean beetles, cover the plants with row covers or purchase *Pediobius foveolatus* (tiny beneficial wasps) for release when larvae are present.

Rust is a bean disease that appears as brown pustules on the underside of the leaf. Prevalent on pole and lima beans, it thrives in high humidity and where warm days are followed by cool nights. A spray of sulfur every 10 days helps eradicate rust. Anthracnose, alternaria, halo blight, and curly top are other diseases; choose resistant bean varieties.

The only pests that affect fava beans are black aphids, which wash off with a strong spray from a garden hose.

Harvesting

To prolong the harvest of snap types, keep the immature pods picked; when too many pods mature, the plants stop producing. If you want runner beans as snap beans, pick them very young. If you let them grow bigger, use them to make a delicious pureed runner bean soup and strain out the strings and fiber. Allow the runner bean pods to mature to brown, and then shell them and dry the beans.

Harvest young fava bean pods just as they start to fill out, and you can eat them raw or cooked without removing the inner skin. Harvest mature fava beans when the pods are plump and the shelled beans about the size of large limas. If skins are tough, remove them.

To prevent spreading diseases, do not harvest or handle bean foliage when it is wet.

How to Purchase

Local nurseries often carry a limited variety of seeds; find extensive choices at Baker Creek, Bountiful Gardens, Johnny's, Nichols, Park, Renee's, Seeds of Change, Seed Savers, and Territorial.

Varieties

For all bean varieties, check the seed packet for days to maturity.

SNAP BEANS

Pole varieties climb 10 to 15 ft. tall; bush varieties grow about 2 ft. tall on their own, but will reach a foot or so higher if trained on a mini-tepee.

'Blue Lake'—pole; one of the tastiest and most productive snap beans.
'Dragon's Tongue'—classic heirloom; bush; yellow wax bean with purple markings.
'Kentucky Wonder'—heirloom; pole; one of the best snap beans.
'Musica'—pole; long, meaty beans; flat pods to 9 in.; popular in southern Europe.
'Purple Queen'—bush; purple pods, flowers, stems, and leaf veins; mosaic resistant.
'Purple Tepee'—pole; purple pods, flowers, stems, and leaf veins.
'Ramdor'—pole; French filet type; yellow pods; heavy bearing.

'Rocdor'—bush; productive yellow snap bean; great for the North.

'Roma II'—bush; green Italian Romano type; great flavor; resistant to rust.

'Royal Burgundy'—bush; purple podded; great for the North.

'Tenderpod'—compact bush; stringless snap; early; widely adapted.

RUNNER BEANS

All have green pods; unless stated otherwise they have maroon seeds with black markings. Pole varieties grow 10 to 15 ft. tall.

'Aztec Dwarf Runner'—bush, to 36 in. tall; ancient variety; white flowers, white beans.

'Dwarf Bees'—bush, to 24 in. tall; use in large containers; red flowers; same as 'Scarlet Bees'.

'Hestia'—bush, to 24 in. tall; use in containers and front of border; red and white flowers.

'Painted Lady'—heirloom from early 1800s; pole; late-season, excellent beans; striking plant with red and white flowers.

'Scarlet Runner'—heirloom from 1700s; pole; red flowers.

'Sunset Runner'—pole; produces early; distinctive flavor; salmon pink flowers.

'White Dutch Runner'—pole; great flavor; white flowers, white beans.

LIMA BEANS

Pole limas climb 8 to 10 ft. tall.

'Christmas'—pole; maroon and green when fresh, dries to maroon and white; large beans, excellent quality; tolerates hot-summer climates well.

'King of the Garden'—pole; green when fresh, dries to white; large beans, excellent quality.

FAVA BEANS

'Negreta'—early crop when planted in spring; Italian variety; dry beans are purple.

'Windsor'—large beans, white when dried; plant spring or fall; classic English variety.

Blackberry

See Brambleberry

Blueberry

Vaccinium spp.

Effort Scale

NO. 2 in acid soil
Constant mulching necessary
Must be kept moist
Susceptible to some diseases
Vulnerable to a few pests, including birds

NO. 3 in neutral soil
The same issues as for acid soil plus maintaining soil acidity

Zones

3 to 10, depending on variety

Thumbnail Sketch

Deciduous shrub
12 in. to 18 ft. tall, depending on variety
Propagate from cuttings or seeds
Needs full sun or partial shade
Leaves dark green in summer, some yellow or scarlet in fall; 2 to 3 in. long
Blooms in spring
Flowers are pink to white, small, bell-like, in clusters
Fruits are edible; harvest in spring or summer, depending on the variety
Use as hedge, screen, interest plant, or ground cover; in shrub border, pine woodland, or container

How to Use

In the Kitchen

Blueberries are soft, blue fruits jam-packed with nutrients. In fact, according to the USDA, it takes five servings of fruits and vegetables like peas, carrots, apples, squash, and broccoli to equal the antioxidant power of ½ cup of blueberries. At our house, half of the fruits

Northern highbush blueberries are handsome landscape plants. The lovely sweet woodruff ground cover is a good companion as it also thrives in some shade and acid soil.

don't make it into the kitchen. Luckily, we manage not to snack on all of them as we harvest or we'd miss some wonderful treats. Blueberry-topped cereal or pancakes with blueberry syrup turn breakfast into a banquet; yogurt smoothies with blueberries are a staple. Blueberry muffins right out of the oven are irresistible, dried blueberries are great in trail mix, and blueberry pie or cobbler (especially à la mode) is food for the gods.

To freeze: Wash and pat dry berries, place them in a single layer on a cookie sheet, and freeze. Once frozen, pour berries into freezer bags and freeze. Defrost berries to use in muffins and smoothies, or make them into jams and syrups.

To dry: Choose firm berries. Wash and pat dry, then spread on a plastic screen. Place in a warm, dry place out of direct sun. Stir occasionally. Berries should be dry in 4 or 5 days unless the weather is damp. Dry berries rattle when stirred and exude no moisture when squeezed. To reconstitute dried berries, cover with water and refrigerate for several hours. Use in any recipe that calls for canned berries.

In the Landscape

If you have room for only a few edibles, blueberries should be among your top choices. There are blueberries suitable for most parts of the country: highbush (northern and southern varieties), half-high, lowbush, rabbiteye, and some hybrid crosses. Blueberries are primarily deciduous shrubs with dark green or blue-green leaves that put on a great fall flourish, turning red or yellow. Clusters of pinkish white flowers appear from spring to summer, depending on the variety.

Blueberries ripen over time, and when ripe hang on the shrub a couple of weeks. After they turn dark blue, a whitish coating indicates they're ready to pick. Blueberries are well worth growing—organic berries at the store average 5 cents apiece.

Berries turn from green to red to the grayish blue fruit we love. Some varieties have red or yellow twigs that contrast beautifully with snow. All in all, blueberries put on a year-round show far superior to that of the ubiquitous burning bush.

Because they differ in size and shape, these plants have varying landscape uses. Standard highbush blueberries grow 6 to 12 feet tall, are somewhat vase shaped with an open growth habit, and are equally valuable in a mixed shrub border, as a hedge, or as a boundary planting. Southern highbush crosses are a varied lot; some, like 'Sunshine Blue,' are small and nearly evergreen in warm-winter areas. The half-highs range from 2 to 4 feet tall and are great for shrub borders, including foundation plantings, combined with other acid lovers like azaleas and rhododendrons, and are stunning in containers. Lowbush blueberries are shorter still and spread by layering, forming a mat of greenery suitable for a woodland edge, a ground cover in wild gardens, or lining a woodland walk. Rabbiteye plants, which can grow to 18 feet tall, make excellent hedges and screens. All blueberries are good container subjects because their appearance varies continually.

How to Grow

Climate

Blueberries are native to North America. Northern highbush and lowbush are suitable for northern climates. They prefer cool, moist growing conditions, need 1,000 or more chill hours, and grow well in Zones 3 to selected parts of Zone 10. Rabbiteye blueberries are adapted to the southeastern United States. They are less hardy and more tolerant of warm weather than the other two species, and need less winter chill to produce good fruit. Southern highbush blueberries are crosses between the highbush and native southern species; they are less hardy than the northern types and are usually low chill; a few varieties are highly adaptable.

Exposure and Soil

Highbush, half-high, and rabbiteye blueberries produce better in full sun or partial shade; they definitely need afternoon shade in hot-summer areas. Lowbush plants take full sun to dappled shade. Grow blueberries in very acidic (pH 4.5 to 5.5), light or sandy, well-drained soil. If azaleas and mountain laurel grow well for you, blueberries will, too. If your soil is neutral or only slightly alkaline, mix in large amounts of acidic organic matter and granulated sulfur, following package directions; then apply acidic mulch (pine needles or composted oak leaves) to maintain the high acidity. Be vigilant; surrounding alkaline soil or dryness in arid climates can affect the pH. Rabbiteye and some southern highbush plants tolerate less acidic soil.

Planting

Blueberries have a shallow, matlike root system devoid of the root hairs found on most plants; their roots seldom penetrate compacted soils. Dig a wide (not deep) planting hole in very fast-draining soil. Do *not* add fertilizer to the planting hole. If in doubt about good drainage, plant on a mound or raised bed. Plant tall varieties 6 feet apart, shorter ones 2 to 3 feet apart. For very alkaline soils, grow blueberries in almost pure peat moss in large containers. Soak the peat moss before planting and do not let it dry out; it is tricky to re-wet. Add a 4-inch layer of organic mulch to keep the roots moist and cut down on weeds. When weeding or working in the soil, take care not to disturb the shallow roots.

Fertilizing

Blueberries have fibrous woody roots that burn readily and are more susceptible to botrytis fungus if there is too much nitrogen in the soil. In northern gardens, withhold any nitrogen fertilizer the first year. Every spring apply generous amounts of compost or pine needles and a nitrogen source like alfalfa or soy meal. Highbush plants and some vigorous modern varieties should put on about 12 inches of new growth a year. In soils with a high pH, chelated iron and magnesium may be needed to alleviate chlorosis. Test your soil.

Watering

Keep northern blueberries slightly moist at all times; rabbiteyes require less water. The rule of thumb for most types is at least 1 inch of water a week. For all blueberries, a deep mulch helps to retain moisture. In arid climates, instead of using drip emitters, install mini-sprayers to keep the surrounding air and soil moist and to maintain proper acidity.

Pruning

Do not prune blueberries the first few years except to remove broken or weak branches. Fruit is produced primarily on smooth, colorful new wood; old, non-productive wood is gray with rough bark. In subsequent years, in Zones 3 and 4, lightly prune highbush plants; thin out some of the oldest branches, and spindly, weak growth. In Zones 5 to 7, prune highbush and rabbiteyes in late winter; remove some older, woody branches to thin out the center, and remove any weak growth. In Zones 8 to 10, prune highbush varieties after fruiting. For larger berries, cut back the tips of the canes so only four or five large fruit buds remain on each twig. Prune lowbush berries almost to ground level every few years; because pruned bushes won't fruit the next year, prune only half the bed at a time.

The illustration at top right shows a highbush blueberry before pruning and after proper pruning.

Pests and Diseases

The major problem is nutritional; when soil acidity is not maintained consistently, nutrients are unavailable to the plant and it becomes chlorotic.

Birds are the worst pests. Use reflective strips or netting before the fruit starts to ripen. A "blueberry cage" (a homemade protective structure with screening that keeps birds out and lets bees in) is the ultimate solution. Fence to protect against rabbits. To prevent winter vole damage, keep mulch away from the base of the plants. The blueberry fruit fly, cranberry fruitworm, and plum curculio can be problems in the East; the larvae burrow into the berries. Handpick adults and shrunken berries. Shallow cultivation uncovers pupating fruit fly larvae in the soil. The cranberry fruitworm encases berries in a web; control with *Bt* if populations are large. Summer-weight horticultural oil sprays control scale.

Mummy berry causes berries to rot in moist weather. Plant resistant varieties; remove and destroy rotten berries. In southern gardens, stem canker can be a problem; remove diseased tissue and plant resistant varieties.

Harvesting

Blueberries ripen from early spring to early fall; the exact timing depends on the variety and climate. To ripen completely, blueberries need to stay on the plant for a week after they turn blue and develop their grayish cast. They do not ripen more once harvested. Berries are ripe when they are sweet and easily fall off. A "tickling" motion

A mature blueberry bush often has many old, weak, or crossing branches. Prune by removing about one-quarter of the oldest and weakest growth. If the fruits were small, prune off some of the top growth.

works the best, with a small colander held under the clusters to catch the falling berries. Most mature plants yield 5 to 6 pints of fruit annually.

How to Purchase

Local nurseries carry bare-root and container-grown plants. Bay Laurel, Burnt Ridge, Gurney's, Indiana Berry, Johnson, One Green World, and Raintree offer many varieties. Waters carries three prized varieties. Ison's and Willis have rabbiteye blueberries. Hartmann's and Fall Creek offer the greatest selection of all types.

Pollinizers

While a few varieties are self-fruitful, most need at least one other variety to produce a prolific crop of larger berries. The chief pollinators are native bees.

Varieties

To extend your harvest, choose cultivars that ripen at different times. For information on varieties for your area, contact your local Cooperative Extension Service.

NORTHERN HIGHBUSH, *VACCINIUM CORYMBOSUM*

Northern highbush varieties are the primary commercial berry. Unless otherwise noted, all are hardy in Zones 4 to 7 and need more than 1,000 chill hours.

'Berkeley'—midseason; large berries, excellent flavor; tall, spreading plant; great fall color, yellow branches in winter; some mildew resistance; for the Northwest and Northeast, Zones 5 to 7.

'Bluecrop'—midseason; medium-size fruit, excellent flavor; erect, tall, sparse foliage, scarlet fall color; tolerates hot weather, hardier and more drought resistant than most; 800 chill hours.

'Bluejay'—blooms, ripens early to midseason; good-quality, large fruit; yellow to orange fall color; resistant to mummy berry.

'Blueray'—midseason; large, aromatic, flavorful berries; spreading plant, bright yellow branches in winter; for New England, West Coast, and hot-summer climates, 800 chill hours.

'Chandler'—mid- to late season; very large, flavorful berries; large leaves, medium-tall shrub, fall color in mild-winter areas.

'Duke'—blooms late, ripens early; mild, sweet flavor, medium-size berries; self-fertile; to 6 ft. tall; yellow to orange fall color; resists mummy berry.

'Earliblue'—earliest; large berries; tall, upright growth; large leaves, red fall color; some mildew resistance; good for Northwest, Michigan, and Northeast, Zones 5 to 7.

'Northland'—early; medium-size fruit, good flavor; to 4 ft. tall, spreading; yellow to orange fall color; hardy to –30°F, Zones 3 to 7.

'Patriot'—early; large berries with flavor that is both sweet and acidic; upright growth to 6 ft. tall.

HALF-HIGH, *V. CORYMBOSUM* × *V. ANGUSTIFOLIUM*

These hardy, compact plants (Zones 3 to 7) survive the coldest winters with protective snow cover. These varieties bear in midseason.

'Northcountry'—medium-size fruit, sweet, wild berry flavor; compact, 24 in. tall, 4 ft. wide, heavily branched; red twigs, scarlet fall leaf color; one of the best.

'Northsky'—small berries, sweet; to 18 in. tall; glossy foliage, dark red in fall.

LOWBUSH, *V. ANGUSTIFOLIUM*

Lowbush blueberries grow wild in much of Maine, Canada's Atlantic provinces, and Alaska and are often unnamed seedlings. Unless otherwise noted, plants are hardy in Zones 3 to 7. A few varieties are offered in catalogs.

'Brunswick'—pea-size berries; great flavor; 8 to 12 in. tall, 5 ft. wide.

'Burgundy'—pea-size berries; intense flavor; to 12 in. tall, 36 in. wide; bronze new growth in spring, red fall foliage.

'Top Hat'—cross between a compact highbush and a lowbush; large, excellent fruit; late; to 24 in. tall; bright red fall foliage; great for containers; less fussy about soil; Zones 5 to 8.

SOUTHERN HIGHBUSH, INTERSPECIFIC CROSSES OF *V. CORYMBOSUM*, *V. VIRGATUM*, AND *V. DARROWII*

Except as noted, these varieties are hardy in Zones 7 to 10 and are self-fertile, though they bear more heavily with a pollinizer.

'Jubilee'—early; outstanding berries; productive; upright to 8 ft.; 500 to 700 chill hours, Zones 5 to 9.

'Misty'—very early; large berries, excellent flavor; heavy producer; to 5 ft. tall, semi-evergreen; pink flowers; popular in the West, Zones 5 to 7.

'O'Neal'—early; large fruit, sweet, mild flavor; to 6 ft. tall; red stems; 200 to 400 chill hours, Zones 5 to 9.

'Sharpblue'—early; large berries, intense flavor; blue-green leaves, semi-evergreen in mild climates; pink flowers, blooms year round in mildest areas; 300 to 500 chill hours, Zones 7 to 10.

'Sunshine Blue'—long ripening period begins midseason; medium-size berries, mild flavor; dwarf plant to 36 in. tall, semi-evergreen; pH tolerant; frost hardy, 150 chill hours, Zones 5 to 10.

RABBITEYE, *V. VIRGATUM* (*V. ASHEI*)

Rabbiteye blueberries are large and typically very light blue; they have more pronounced seeds and thicker skins than northern varieties. The plants have a low chill requirement and ripen poorly in cool climates; some varieties bear into October. They are grown in Zones 7 to 9 unless otherwise noted. Plant 10 ft. to 12 ft. apart.

'Climax'—early; medium-size, dark blue berries, good flavor; hold well on the plant; to 10 ft. tall, upright spreading form; great fall color.

'Premier'—early; large, firm fruit, good flavor; handsome shrub, spectacular fall foliage; grown into northern Florida.

'Southland'—late; medium-size berries; compact bush; good pollinizer for 'Tifblue'.

'Tifblue'—late; excellent berries; upright growth to 16 ft. tall; great fall color; for cooler parts of Southeast.

'Woodard'—early; large, high-quality fruit; moderately vigorous bush; more spreading and shorter than other rabbiteyes; popular in South, including Texas, Zones 6 to 9.

Brambleberry

(blackberry and raspberry)
Rubus spp.

Effort Scale

NO. 3
Heavy pruning necessary
Mulching necessary
Vulnerable to diseases and some pests, including birds
Most types need some vine training
Harvesting is time consuming
Winter protection needed in coldest areas

Zones

Raspberry, 3 to 10
Blackberry, 5 to 9

Thumbnail Sketch

Deciduous bushy or tall vining plants with biennial canes
5 to 25 ft. tall, depending on species and variety
Propagate from cuttings or suckers or by tip layering
Need full sun; tolerate some shade
Leaves are compound, dark green above, white underneath; stems usually prickly
Flowers are white or pink, 1 in. across
Fruits are edible, red, black, yellow, white, or purple; harvest in summer and fall
Use as barrier, hedges, wildlife shelterbelt; trailing types on trellises and arbors

How to Use

In the Kitchen

Few folks nowadays have tasted homegrown, just-picked raspberries, and when they do it is a revelation. Agriculture has selected for firm fruit that endures shipping and has a long shelf life; the succulent old varieties never make it to the market. Yes, they take some care to grow, but are they worth it? You bet!

Brambleberries are highly nutritious treats. In fact, blackberries rank among the highest in anthocyanins, the cancer-fighting antioxidants. Red or black raspberries heaped on cereal, crushed and spooned over ice cream, or dripped over peach Melba—what elegant fare! Just as superb are sun-warmed blackberries straight off the vine or in homemade yogurt, or in a tangy syrup served with sparkling water. And what would autumn be without raspberry vinaigrette over baby greens and sliced pears? Aficionados can never get enough berries, so grow a hedge of them—enough for jam, pie, and your cereal bowl. Freeze, can, or dry brambleberries; make them into syrup, wine, vinegar, or jam.

In the Landscape

Life has few guarantees, but no dogs and children will push their way through a thorny brambleberry hedge. Thornless varieties do exist, but even they are pretty impenetrable.

Brambleberries come in different forms—erect shrubby, semi-erect (sometimes called semi-trailing), and trailing types. The erect varieties are great as hedges or along fencerows. While some are best trellised, many are freestanding. To use brambleberries in a landscape successfully, keep them properly pruned and trained. Laxity creates a nightmare of rampant vines.

How to Grow

The two major types of brambleberries are raspberries and blackberries. The raspberry-type fruits come off the vine without the core, while the blackberry types come off core and all. Confusingly, both types of berries can be either red or black.

Red raspberries are the hardiest, growing on upright canes or semi-erect vines. There are summer-bearing red raspberries and ever-bearing varieties, which bear in summer and fall. They fruit on "primo" canes (first-year growth) in summer or fall and bear another crop the next spring on "flora" canes (second-year growth).

Blackberries can be upright or trailing. Some trailing blackberries, such as boysenberry, grow only in Zones 8 and 9. However, most are hardier, growing in Zones 5 to 9. Upright blackberries are generally limited to the Midwest and East.

Climate

Some varieties of red raspberries are able to survive in milder sections of Zone 3. Most black raspberries are hardy only to Zone 5. Neither does well in the hottest-summer areas; only a few varieties grow south of the Mason-Dixon Line or in the arid Southwest. Blackberries have a wider range, with a selection for all but the coldest-winter areas, the deepest South, and desert areas.

To provide winter protection in the coldest areas, mulch canes in fall with 12 inches of straw. If critters are a problem, or where canes are long, trench the soil and bury canes in 3 to 4 inches of soil, uncovering them as soon as possible in spring. In southern gardens with wide winter temperature swings, brambleberries can break dormancy prematurely during a warm spell; a freeze following the warm weather will destroy the fruiting canes. To avoid this, try fall-bearing types that fruit the first year, and mow them down in winter.

As a rule, hot weather is damaging: flavor suffers, the fruits do not separate from the stem well, and the fruits sunburn.

Exposure and Soil

Brambleberries need full sun; in hot climates provide light afternoon shade and encourage good leaf cover by keeping the plants well watered and fertilized. All prefer very well-drained, slightly acidic soil with lots of organic matter. Shallow rooted, the plants are susceptible to root rot in soggy soil.

Planting

Good drainage is key; plant in raised beds if necessary. Prepare the planting bed with generous amounts of aged manure. Spacing varies widely depending on the brambleberry, from 2 feet apart for some red raspberries to 12 feet apart for vigorous trailing types; directions usually come with the plants. Some varieties are stiff and upright or

Blackberries are red before ripening to black. Harvest when you can easily pluck off the berries, core and all. My thornless 'Black Satin' yields up to 20 pounds of berries a season—enough for several neighborhood ice cream socials.

can be pruned short enough to stand by themselves. Many, however, are better trained. Grow these between parallel wires or on some other form of support.

Planting depth for brambleberries varies from 1 to 2 inches lower than the nursery soil line (dark line on the cane). When planting brambleberries, cut off the top growth above the four or five primary buds or shoots coming up from the crown to assure a strong root system. In warm regions plant in fall, elsewhere in spring.

Fertilizing

Too much fertilizer produces lush growth and few berries. Feed sparingly with well-rotted manure in spring; mulch with compost or leaves to renew the soil and reduce weeds.

Watering

Keep the soil fairly moist but not soggy. Provide 1 to 2 inches of water a week, depending on the climate. Do not let brambleberries dry out, as they seldom recover.

Pruning

Prune all brambleberries annually for productivity and to keep them from becoming a dense thicket. Brambleberries bear fruit on biennial canes; any cane that bore fruit dies back to the crown. Raspberries sucker profusely into paths, and many of the large blackberries root at the tips of branches far from the mother plant.

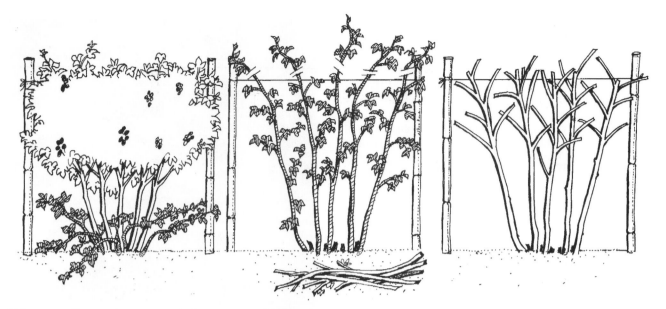

This sequence illustrates how to prune single-crop raspberries, black raspberries, and upright blackberries. *Left:* Tie 2-year-old bearing canes to the wire. New shoots will emerge from the ground, as shown. *Center:* Once the second-year canes have finished fruiting, cut them to the ground. Select the five or six most robust new canes and tie them to the wire. *Right:* In spring tip-prune the new 2-year-old canes.

Prune single-crop raspberries, black raspberries, and upright blackberries following the series of illustrations above. They show the bush with its 2-year-old fruit-bearing canes tied to the wire. Next year's fruiting canes (identified by the striping) sprawl on the ground below. After the harvest, cut the 2-year-old canes to the ground. Select six of the healthiest new canes and tie them to the wire. Encourage new lateral growth along the wire: cut the six canes to within a few inches of the wire; lop off the remaining canes at ground level. In winter, prune canes back to 5 feet high and cut lateral branches back to about 18 inches long. Remove all suckers that arise away from the crown as they appear.

Pruning is slightly different for everbearing red raspberries as the canes bear twice—in summer or fall and again in spring. After the fall crop, remove the tops of the canes that bore fruit. The lower part of the canes will have lateral branches that bear in spring. Remove these canes completely after spring fruiting.

Trailing blackberries grow rampantly and need support. Train on wires, or on a trellis or post (see illustrations on the next page). Like raspberries, they bear on biennial canes. Train them like single-crop raspberries. After the summer harvest, cut down old canes. Select five or six vigorous canes from those growing along the ground and cut them to 4 feet long. Train them along the wires or tie them to the trellis or post, and remove all other canes.

Pests and Diseases

Birds can be a problem. One solution is to plant mulberries or elderberries to lure them away; netting is another. Rabbits, gophers, and voles can damage vines.

Wilting foliage indicates borers may have invaded the canes. Cut the cane off below the damage; if there are no borers, look for disease symptoms described below. In northern gardens, raspberry fruitworm larvae and adults eat fruits and leaves. Remove and destroy infested fruits; in autumn, carefully cultivate around plants to bring up hibernating larvae; spray blossoms with pyrethrum the next spring. For an infestation, treat the soil with beneficial nematodes in spring.

Diseases are the most serious obstacle in growing brambleberries. To avoid most problems, buy certified virus-free plants, control aphids (they can spread viruses), and destroy any wild blackberries within a few hundred feet. Anthracnose is a problem in warm, rainy weather; the symptoms are oval, purple-brown spots with white centers on the canes, and leaves with small, yellow spots. To control, purchase resistant varieties, spray with lime sulfur just as the leaves emerge in spring *and* at blossom time, keep irrigation water off the plants, avoid too much nitrogen, thin the canes for good air circulation, and destroy all affected canes after harvesting.

Watch for viruses, which appear as mottled, deformed-looking growth, most commonly on black raspberries. Verticillium wilt is a serious problem with red raspberries. Blackberries are the most prone to diseases, especially orange rust, which shows up as red-orange spores on the leaf undersides. Viruses, verticillium wilt, and orange rust have no cure. Remove and destroy the plant as soon as you diagnose the problem.

Harvesting

Harvest brambleberries when they are fully colored and dead ripe; as a rule, the riper the berry, the sweeter it is. Some varieties deteriorate quickly, so check them daily. When it comes to picking, there are two types of brambleberries. Some, such as red raspberries, just drop off with the gentlest touch when they are ripe, leaving the core behind. Others retain their solid core and more pressure is needed—grasp lightly at the top where the berry is the firmest and gently twist; a ripe berry will come off easily, leaving the stalk behind. You'll know when you apply too much force in either case, as the berry will squish in your fingers. Handle berries gently because they bruise easily. Large, trailing plants yield about 2 pints of berries per foot of row, and erect, shrubby types about 1 pint per foot of row.

How to Purchase

Purchase brambleberries bare root in early spring or in containers through late spring. Combine early-, mid-, and late-season varieties

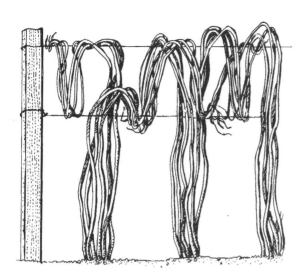

Weave trailing brambleberries along a two-wire trellis.

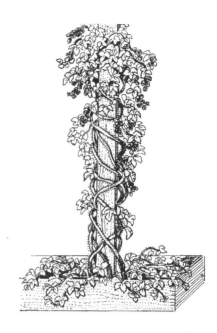

Train long, trailing types of brambleberries on a post.

to extend the season. Local nurseries usually carry varieties adapted to the area; home improvement stores may not. Other sources include Bay Laurel, Burnt Ridge, Cox, Cummins, Edible Landscaping, Ison's, Miller, Jersey Asparagus, Johnson, One Green World, Raintree, and St. Lawrence. Hartmann's, Indiana Berry, and Nourse carry a large selection.

Pollinizers

Most brambleberries are self-fertile.

Varieties

Note: Yellow raspberries tend to be more disease prone than red varieties and have a milder flavor; black raspberries are also more disease and sunburn prone than red raspberries, and have drier, seedier fruits.

BLACKBERRY, *RUBUS* SPP. AND HYBRIDS

All grow in Zones 5 to 9 unless otherwise noted.

'Apache'—huge berries; great flavor; ripens July; erect, thornless; very productive; resists orange rust and anthracnose; 300 chill hours.

'Black Satin'—large, flavorful berries; ripens July into August; semi-erect to 10 ft., thornless, few suckers; resists anthracnose and leaf spot; good for small spaces; needs heat for good flavor.

'Boysen' and 'Thornless Boysenberry'—large, wine red fruit; sweet-tart, aromatic; long season begins July; long trailing canes; great honey plant; best in South and West.

'Kiowa'—very large berries; firm and flavorful; ripens August, long harvest; erect, thorny; resists rust, tolerates anthracnose; low chill.

'Logan Thornless'—large, lavender red berries; tart, great for pies; ripens June; trailing; drought resistant; resists mosaic virus; needs winter cold; for the West, Zones 5 to 8.

'Marion'—large berries, ripens red to black; superior flavor in cool Northwest; ripens July; cross of 'Boysen' with wild blackberry; trailing, thorny; Zones 7 to 9.

'Navaho'—firm fruit; sweet; ripens July; erect, thornless; heat tolerant, grows from Michigan to northern Florida.

'Olallie' (olallieberry)—shiny black berries; famous for their intensely sweet and complex flavor; old-time variety; ripens July; trailing; productive; good even near the Pacific Ocean, great for California, Zones 7 to 9.

'Prime-Jan'—flavorful berries; ripens in late summer on first-year erect canes and early summer the next year if not cut down, or mow down yearly to simplify pruning; thorny; does poorly in hot-summer areas, Zones 7 to 9.

'Triple Crown'—large berries; great flavor; ripens August; thornless, semi-erect canes need support; good for East and West Coasts, Zones 5 to 8.

BLACK RASPBERRY (BLACK CAP), *R. OCCIDENTALIS*

'Bristol'—good flavor; late; resists powdery mildew, susceptible to anthracnose; widely planted in the East as far south as North Carolina, Zones 5 to 8.

'Jewel'—excellent, large berries; early, long season; anthracnose resistant; Zones 4 to 8.

RED RASPBERRY (INCLUDING YELLOW AND PURPLE), *R. IDAEUS*

'Anne'—large, firm, yellow berries with acceptable flavor; fall bearing; fruits high on plant; Zones 4 to 8.

'Autumn Bliss'—large, firm, red berries; great flavor; everbearing, disease resistant; give afternoon shade in hot, arid climates; Zones 3 to 10.

'Bababerry'—red fruit; fine flavor; everbearing; low chill, stands heat well; for Florida, Texas, and Southern California, Zones 6 to 9.

'Boyne'—deep red berries; medium sweet, aromatic; midsummer; short plant; Zones 4 to 8.

'Canby'—red berries; excellent flavor; early summer; nearly thornless; resists mosaic, good from Northeast to the West Coast, Zones 5 to 8.

'Caroline'—large, red berries; flavorful; early fruiting, everbearing, starts early in the season; resists gray mold; tolerates southern conditions, Zones 4 to 9.

'Fall Gold'—large, golden yellow fruit; soft, sweet; everbearing; tall canes can be mowed down in fall; virus prone; Zones 4 to 8.

'Heritage'—good-quality, red berries; everbearing; suckers prolifically, can be mowed every spring; some success in South, Zones 3 to 10.

'Kiwi Gold'—large, yellow fruit; excellent flavor; fall bearing, thorny; Zones 4 to 8.

'Royalty'—large, purple fruit; intense flavor; midsummer; tall; thorny, non-suckering canes; resists raspberry aphid and raspberry fruit worms; Zones 4 to 8.

'Tulameen'—large, red fruit, great flavor; late summer; not for heavy soils; Zones 5 to 8.

Broccoli and Cauliflower

Brassica spp.

Effort Scale

NO. 3
Must be planted annually
Need rich, organic soil
Constant moisture and fertilizing needed
Susceptible to many pests and diseases

Zones

Not applicable

Thumbnail Sketch

Annuals and biennials grown as annuals
8 to 36 in. tall
Propagate from seeds

This Denver garden exemplifies the design principles of color, texture, form, and line. Creating a living collage are, from front to back, red-veined beets, ruffled 'Marvel of Four Seasons' lettuce, blue-green broccoli, and flowering green-leaved bush beans.

Need full sun; partial shade in hot climates
Some heads (flower buds) are ornamental—green, blue-green, purple, white, or orange
Bloom in warm weather
Flowers are yellow
Flower buds, flowers, stems, and young leaves are edible; harvest varies with climate
Use in herbaceous border, vegetable garden, flower bed, raised bed, or container

How to Use

In the Kitchen

Both broccoli and cauliflower are terrific raw in crudités platters; include some colorful varieties to enliven the plate. Raw or lightly steamed, they are welcome additions to salads. Enjoy them simply lightly steamed with a little olive oil or butter. Toss them into stir-fries, and make gratins or cream soups. To maintain the color of purple broccoli or 'Graffiti' cauliflower, cook with a dash of vinegar or wine. When winter chill sets in, make a hearty casserole of lightly steamed white cauliflower and sautéed leeks; top with grated Cheddar cheese and breadcrumbs.

Broccoli raab (or rapini) is wonderful in spring; it's like a tonic—very healthy and slightly bitter. Prepare it in the traditional manner; lightly steam, sauté in olive oil with garlic, and serve over pasta. Sprouting broccoli is mild flavored and delicious raw in salads or stir-fried.

Like other cabbage family members, broccoli and cauliflower are nutrition giants.

In the Landscape

There are heading and sprouting broccolis, including green and purple, plus the chartreuse, sculptured 'Romanesco'. Include broccoli in a decorative setting, as it stays in the garden for months. One year I created a mixed border along my front walk with endive in the front, red tulips mid-border, and broccoli and Japanese red mustard in the back. Grow cauliflower in containers to best enjoy it at its short-lived peak.

How to Grow

Broccoli and cauliflower tend to be more vigorous and have fewer problems than their cousin cabbage. They are cool-season vegetables that bolt and go to seed in hot weather. Grow them in full sun (partial shade in warm climates) in rich, well-drained soil.

Planting

Before planting, prepare the soil by working copious amounts of compost and manure into the top 6 inches. In spring, start broccoli seeds indoors 6 weeks before the frost date; start cauliflower a little earlier. Sow in late summer for fall harvests. Plant seeds ½ inch deep. Or buy transplants and place in the garden about 2 weeks before the last average frost date. Space plants 18 inches apart, more for Romanesco varieties. Set transplants a few inches deeper than they were in their containers. Apply a deep mulch to keep the soil cool and prevent weeds.

Blanch (protect from sunscald) heirloom white cauliflower heads by tying the leaves over the heads. The leaves of modern varieties grow over the heads.

Apply hydrolyzed fish or an all-purpose organic fertilizer at planting and again a month later. Keep plants watered; they do not tolerate drying out.

Pests and Diseases

Pests and Diseases
Northern gardeners have to deal with cabbage root flies. Prevent the larvae from entering the soil with a 12-by-12-inch square of black plastic. Cut a 6-inch slit in the center and slip it down around the plant to ground level. Protect new plantings from cutworms with cardboard collars. Cover with floating row covers to keep off flea beetles, cabbage loopers, and cabbageworms until plants are a good size.

Clubroot is a serious fungal disease that affects members of the cabbage family. Rotate members of this family in a 3- or 4-year rotation with other vegetable families to discourage the fungus.

Harvesting
Cut off the main broccoli head when the buds begin to swell. I let the plants remain in the garden as most varieties produce delicious, small heads as side shoots along the main stem. Harvest shoots and leaves of both broccoli raab and sprouting broccoli. Cut as much as you need at a time; they all resprout.

Harvest cauliflower when heads are full but before the curds begin to separate. Some gardeners also leave cauliflower in the garden to produce small side shoots.

How to Purchase

Most local nurseries carry seeds and a limited selection of transplants. Companies specializing in cool-season vegetables have the greatest selection: Johnny's, Stokes Seeds, Nichols, Harris, and Territorial. Seeds of Change and Baker Creek offer heirloom varieties.

Varieties

BROCCOLI, *BRASSICA OLERACEA* VAR. *ITALICA*
'Calabrese'—Italian heirloom; flavorful; tight, dark green heads to 8 in.; produces many side shoots; 60 to 90 days.
'Di Cicco'—heirloom; compact; 4 in., blue-green; produces many small shoots; 50 to 70 days.
'Packman'—hybrid; early; good for fall planting; large, dark green heads; many shoots; 50 to 55 days.
'Romanesco'—Italian heirloom; good for cool northern areas and as fall crop in warm regions; eye-catching with spiraling, chartreuse head; more like a cauliflower; 85 to 90 days.

BROCCOLI RAAB (RAPINI, CIME DI RAPA), *B. RAPA* VAR. *RAPA* (*B. R.* VAR. *RUVO*)
This fast-growing, quintessential, lightly bitter Italian green has spiked leaves surrounding green buds.
'Early Fall Rapini'—lots of flower buds and large leaves; great broccoli flavor; to 16 in. tall; 45 days.
'Spring Raab'—Italian heirloom; slow to bolt; late; overwinter in mild climates; 45 days.

CAULIFLOWER, *B. OLERACEA* VAR. *BOTRYTIS*
'All Year Round'—white head, self-blanching; great flavor; can do successive sowings; 70 to 80 days.
'Cheddar'—yellow-orange head; delicious raw or cooked; easy to grow; 80 to 100 days.
'Early Snowball'—heirloom; needs blanching; solid, crisp white head; 60 to 85 days.
'Graffiti'—eye-catching purple head; large plant; 80 days.
'Panther'—lime green head; best for fall harvest; easier to grow than most varieties; 75 days.
'Snow Crown'—pure white head, self-blanching; fast growing, best for fall crop; 53 days.

CHINESE BROCCOLI (CHINESE KALE, GAI LON), *B. O.* VAR. *ALBOGLABRA*
Cooks treat this easy-to-grow plant like a sprouting broccoli or broccoli raab.
'Blue Star'—crisp, tender; blue-green stalks and flower heads; 45 days, spring; 55 to 60 days, fall-winter.
'Green Delight'—similar to 'Blue Star'; slightly smaller; grows well in mild to warm areas; harvest variable.
'Green Lance'—disease resistant; 50 days.

SPROUTING BROCCOLI (CAVOLO BROCCOLI), *B. O.* VAR. *ITALICA*
Instead of sending out a central head, this versatile green produces small buds and leaves.
'Purple Sprouting'—heirloom; to 30 in. tall; very hardy; plant in fall to overwinter; produces an abundance of loose foot-long heads in spring; harvest variable.
'Spigariello' ('Minestra Nero')—heirloom; to 36 in. tall; many small buds; tasty leaves; 45 days.

Broccoli raab

See Broccoli and Cauliflower

Butternut

See Walnut

Cabbage

Brassica oleracea var. *capitata*

Effort Scale

NO. 3
Must be planted annually
Needs rich, organic soil
Constant moisture and fertilizing needed
Susceptible to many pests and diseases

Zones

Not applicable

Thumbnail Sketch

Biennial grown as annual
6 to 18 in. tall
Propagate from seeds
Needs full sun; light shade in hot climates
Leaves are ornamental—curled, ruffled, green, blue-green, red, purple, or blue
Flowers are yellow, usually not seen

Leaves are edible; harvest varies with climate
Use in herbaceous border, vegetable garden, flower bed, raised bed, or container

How to Use

In the Kitchen

Think cabbage in the kitchen and what comes to mind—coleslaw, sauerkraut, or maybe corned beef and cabbage? Many cultures have classic recipes that feature cabbage: Italian minestrone soup, English bubble and squeak, Irish *culcallon*, French braised red cabbage, and eastern European stuffed cabbage. *Tip:* To keep the color in cooked red cabbage, add an acid like red wine or vinegar; otherwise the anthocyanins fade to an unappetizing gray-red.

Chinese cabbage is tenderer with good crunch and a milder flavor. I make a fabulous Asian coleslaw by combining Chinese cabbage with cilantro, ginger, peanuts, and a touch of cayenne, tossed with a rice wine vinegar–peanut oil vinaigrette. In Asia cabbage is a winter mainstay: pickled in Japan and Korea as kimchee, and dried in China for use in soups. Use the many types of Chinese cabbage fresh in stir-fries, soups, salads, and sandwiches.

Surprise—flowering cabbage leaves are edible, too. Use young leaves in a salad, line a large salad bowl with the fancy greens, or make a gorgeous edible mandala. They tend to be more fibrous than their kale cousins.

The pointed heads of 'Winnigstadt' cabbage prevented this beautiful heirloom from becoming a commercial success; it doesn't ship well. Visitors seeing it at Old Sturbridge Village in Massachusetts are inspired to raise it from seed.

As a rule, spring and Chinese cabbages are tenderer and tastier than late and storage types. Cabbage is an excellent source of vitamin C, fiber, and glutamine (an amino acid with anti-inflammatory properties).

In the Landscape

There are red- and green-leaved cabbages and crinkly savoy types. And there are Chinese types that are tall and cylindrical or open and round. Use cabbages in containers, annual flower borders, and modern geometric plantings. Red cabbages are perfect with frilly green mustards or marching through a bed of purple pansies.

Puckery savoy cabbages and flowering cabbages, which resemble giant peonies, are spectacular in raised beds, flower borders along a lawn, and in modern linear plantings. The fringed or crinkled cabbage foliage comes in shades of pink, purple, blue, or marbled cream. Combine them in large containers with purple-flowering bush peas and lacy fennel for a kaleidoscope of colors and textures. The mini-cabbages are ideal for geometric patterns in square containers; the pointed, cone-shaped 'Arrowhead' is a real attention grabber.

How to Grow

Most cabbages weigh 2 to 4 pounds, storage cabbages 4 to 8 pounds. For small families and fresh eating, grow mini-cabbages.

Climate

Cabbages are cool-season vegetables. With so many varieties from which to choose, there are some for every landscape. In warm-weather areas, grow them as fall and winter crops.

Exposure and Soil

These fast-growing, short-lived plants thrive in full sun but prefer afternoon shade in hot weather. They require fast-draining, slightly alkaline soil.

Planting

Start seeds in early spring for a late spring crop and in midsummer for a fall crop. Start seeds indoors for a jump on the season. Transplant seedlings a few inches deeper than they were in their containers and 12 inches apart. Apply a deep mulch to keep the soil cool and prevent weeds.

Fertilizing

Apply hydrolyzed fish or an all-purpose organic fertilizer at planting and again a month later.

Watering

Keep cabbages evenly moist; do not let the soil dry out completely. But do not overwater, which can be the catalyst for fungal diseases.

Pests and Diseases

Keep in mind that when you grow cabbages in an out-of-the-way vegetable garden, pest control is not as important as when the cabbages are the stars of your garden design; after all, any tattered leaves are removed in the kitchen. But left unchecked, in most climates caterpillars, slugs, and snails can give cabbages a ratty and tired appearance, making the design come up short.

Cabbages are vulnerable to aphids, caterpillars, flea beetles, slugs, and the notorious white European cabbageworm, whose larvae create huge holes in the leaves. Cabbage root fly is a pest in northern gardens. Keep larvae from entering the soil by slipping a 12-by-12-inch square of black plastic (with a 6-inch slit in the center) over the plant and laying it flat at ground level. Protect new plantings from cutworms with cardboard collars. Cover with floating row covers to keep off flea beetles, cabbage loopers, and cabbageworms until plants are a good size.

Clubroot is a serious fungal disease. Rotate cabbage family members in a 3- or 4-year rotation with other vegetable families to discourage the fungus.

Harvesting

Harvest heading types before the head splits and the flower stalk starts to emerge. Cut individual leaves from the outside of leaf cabbages as soon as they have at least eight leaves; never remove all the leaves.

How to Purchase

Most local nurseries carry seeds and a limited selection of transplants. Companies specializing in cool-season vegetables offer the greatest selection: Johnny's, Stokes Seeds, Nichols, Harris, and Territorial. Kitazawa, Evergreen, and New Dimension specialize in Asian varieties. Seeds of Change, Baker Creek, and Seed Savers offer many heirloom varieties.

Varieties

CABBAGE

Cabbages are designated early, midseason, or late. Spring-planted early cabbages reach maturity before the heat of summer; midseason and late cabbages mature before fall frost. Late cabbages are often the large storage cabbages, available in supermarkets.

'Alcosa'—midseason; mini–savoy cabbage; round, dense, wrinkled head; deep blue-green leaves; sweet flavor improves in cold weather.

'All Seasons'—early to midseason; heat resistant; flavorful, good header.

'Arrowhead'—early; mini-cabbage; pointed cone shape; thin, sweet, tender leaves.

'Early Jersey Wakefield'—heirloom; early; one of the best tasting; conical green head.

'Gonzales'—early; mini-cabbage; light green leaves; slightly spicy; excellent for containers, small spaces, geometric designs.

'Mammoth Red Rock'—heirloom; early; large, round, red head; good flavor.

'Red Drumhead'—heirloom; late; deep purple, flavorful; handles heat well; holds up to cold, wet weather; slightly flattened head.

'Red Express'—early; compact, round, red head; good flavor.

'Samantha'—hybrid; midseason; small, pointed-head savoy; dark green, crinkled leaves; great flavor.

'Super Red 80'—hybrid; early; mini–red cabbage; plant closely for single-serving cabbages; tender, crisp; lightly peppery.

'Winnigstadt' ('Early Winnigstadt')—heirloom; early; dark bluish green, wavy leaves; rich flavor; hard, pointed heads to 9 in. tall and 7 in. diameter; excellent keeper.

CHINESE CABBAGE (NAPA CABBAGE), *BRASSICA RAPA* VAR. *PEKINENSIS*

There are three types of Chinese cabbage: barrel shaped, cylindrical (Michihili), and loose-leaf (the least commonly grown).

'Bilko'—hybrid; barrel shaped; mild, sweet flavor; slow to bolt; resistant to club root and fusarium yellows.

'Blues'—hybrid; barrel shaped; blue-green leaves; slow to bolt; 3 to 4 lb.

In downtown Anchorage, Alaska, cabbages (interplanted with edible pansies) wow passersby with their sculptural form, which echo the edging stones. Anchorage's cool summers with nearly endless daylight produce ideal growing conditions.

'Jade Pagoda'—hybrid; cylindrical; most popular Michihili; medium green leaves with white ribs; slow to bolt; to 6 lb.

'Mini Kisaku'—mini-cylindrical; early maturing; interior of head is yellow; very crisp; to 2 lb.

'Tenderheart'—hybrid; mini–barrel shaped; early maturing; slow to bolt; medium green leaves; one-meal size; 2 lb.

'Wong Bok'—cylindrical; tender; sow in early summer; to 10 in. tall.

Calamondin

See Citrus

Cantaloupe

See Melon

Cardoon

See Artichoke and Cardoon

Cauliflower

See Broccoli and Cauliflower

Chard

(Swiss chard, silverbeet)

Beta vulgaris ssp. *vulgaris* (*B. vulgaris* ssp. *cicla*, *B. vulgaris* var. *flavescens*)

Effort Scale

NO. 2
Must be planted annually
Watering, mulching, and fertilizing needed
Weeding and pest control sometimes necessary

Zones

Not applicable

Thumbnail Sketch

Biennial grown as annual
18 to 24 in.
Propagate from seeds
Needs full sun; partial shade in hot, dry climates
Leaves are deep or bright green, or deep red; stems can be white, red, yellow, orange, purple, or pink
Flowers are not usually seen
Leaves are edible; harvest season varies
Use in flower border, raised bed, or container

How to Use

In the Kitchen

This show-off beet cousin is a must-have in my fall, winter, and spring gardens. In fact, chard is so productive and its uses in the

Heirloom 'Rainbow' chard, also known as 'Five Color Silverbeet', is attention grabbing, especially when planted so the morning or late afternoon sun shines through the colored ribs like it would through stained glass. Harvest outer leaves as needed to reveal new stems.

kitchen so versatile, it's comparable to zucchini in summer. I seed thickly; soon 2- to 3-inch seedlings are ready to use as baby greens in mixed green salads—sometimes with crisp pancetta or roasted beets. As the remaining plants mature, there are more options. Slice chard leaves to use in minestrone soup and frittatas; sauté them in olive oil and garlic for a quick side dish; mix cooked leaves with pasta sauce for a nutrition boost. Use chard in most recipes that call for spinach.

Chard's wide, substantive, and sometimes colorful stems take longer to cook than the leaves. I sauté white or yellow stems by themselves and add seasonings, or stuff them with ground meat and cover with marinara sauce and bake. The very colorful stems bleed and fade when cooked; so to take advantage of the color, I cut the raw stems into matchsticks and sprinkle them over a salad or mince them into a confetti to toss on appetizers, salads, or cooked greens. When I have a large harvest, I blanch and freeze the leaves.

Like many greens, chard is a nutritional powerhouse with vitamins A, C, E, and K, magnesium, manganese, potassium, and more. Lots of fiber, too.

In the Landscape

Chard grows upright and straight. Its strong supporting midribs, while sometimes white, come in colors as vivid as cherry red; deep, golden, or bright yellow; orange; and pink; its deep green leaves are usually slightly ruffled. The colorful 'Rainbow' chard, often called 'Five Color Silverbeet,' is handsome enough to be planted in a flower border. Chard colors and forms make designing fun.

Try 'Ruby' chard with strawberries in a flower border around the patio. Imagine tall orange chard, with its upstanding, bright orange stalks abutting a bed of low escarole rosettes or growing in a container with dwarf orange and yellow nasturtiums. And for a children's fantasy, plant a rainbow garden with yellow, orange, red, and green chards, and purple mustards; choose flowers of each color to accompany the greens.

Plant chard where you can take in the spectacle of the early morning or late afternoon sun shining through the stalks like organic stained glass; an edible landscape can be a garden sanctuary, too.

How to Grow

Climate

Chard is a cool-season crop that loves cool, mild conditions; it tolerates summer heat with humidity and afternoon shade. Chard survives light frosts.

Exposure and Soil

This fast-growing plant does best in full sun but needs afternoon shade in hot, dry weather. Before planting, add a few inches of organic matter, and work it into the top 6 inches of soil.

Planting

Start seeds indoors or sow directly in the garden in spring or fall. Broadcast the seeds, cover lightly with fluffy soil, and tamp in place. Cover the bed to keep birds away and prevent cats from digging. Keep the bed lightly moist until the seeds sprout. Once seedlings emerge, mulch the area with an inch of organic matter; keep it weeded. Water regularly.

Fertilizing

For best flavor and tenderness, chard needs to grow quickly and unchecked; apply hydrolyzed fish or all-purpose organic fertilizer at planting and again 6 weeks later, and if you are harvesting it often, again in a month or so. In frosty areas, do not fertilize when the soil temperature is below 40°F.

Pests and Diseases

Chard is generally quite pest and disease free. However, aphids, snails, and slugs are occasional problems, and birds devour young seedlings when given a chance. Rabbits feast on chard whenever possible. In some areas, leaf miners, the larvae of a fly, tunnel through the leaves, creating small or sometimes even large disfiguring dead sections. They are most active in warm summer weather. Remove dead leaves as you see them to cut down on the population.

Harvesting

Harvest the entire plant when very young. Personally, I prefer to pick or cut off a few outer leaves at a time as I need them; the benefit is that the plant will keep producing new leaves from the crown. In many areas, a spring planting lasts into late fall if outer leaves are harvested as needed. Fall-planted chard produces beautifully until spring in mild-winter climates. Put the harvested leaves in plastic bags and refrigerate immediately; they will keep for several days. Before using, wash well in at least three changes of water to eliminate any critters and remove grit.

How to Purchase

Local nurseries carry chard seeds; some offer young transplants. For the greatest variety, order from Bountiful Gardens, D. Landreth, Seed Savers, Seeds of Change, Johnny's, Park, Nichols, Renee's, Territorial, or Cook's.

Varieties

'Barese'—pale green stems and veins; thick, dark green leaves.
'Bright Lights'—All-America Selection (1998); many stem colors, including gold, orange, pink, purple, red, and white in varying intensities—pastel, too; lightly savoyed bronze or green leaves; milder flavor than most chards.
'Bright Yellow'—young plants are all yellow; as they mature stems and veins remain yellow and leaves turn green.
'Fordhook Giant'—heirloom, 1934; broad, white stalks and veins; tolerant of light frost.
'French Swiss'—large, thick, white stalks; tender, green leaves.
'Golden Sunrise'—thick, golden stalks; deep green savoyed leaves.
'Rainbow' ('Five Color Silverbeet')—a mix of brilliantly colored stems in pink, yellow, orange, red, and white; gorgeous green leaves.
'Rhubarb'—heirloom, 1857; deep crimson stalks and veins; dark green, wrinkled leaves.
'Ruby' ('Ruby Red')—crimson stalks; heavily wrinkled, green leaves; may bolt if exposed to frost.

Cherry

Prunus spp.

Effort Scale

NO. 3
Vulnerable to some pests, particularly birds, and diseases
Harvesting is time consuming

Cherries, wonderful cherries! There are many varieties, and some, like these 'Montmorency' sour cherries, are great for pies and jam; others are sweet treats for consuming fresh.

Zones

4 to 10, depending on variety

Thumbnail Sketch

Deciduous tree
Sweet cherry, standard, 20 to 40 ft. tall; dwarf varieties, 8 to 15 ft. tall
Sour cherry, standard, to 20 ft. tall; dwarf varieties, 8 to 12 ft. tall
Propagate by grafting or budding
Needs full sun
Leaves are deep green, serrated, 2 to 6 in. long
Blooms in early spring
Flowers are white, in large clusters, showy
Fruits are edible; red, black, or yellow; harvest in summer
Use as shade tree, interest plant, large screen, or container plant

How to Use

In the Kitchen

Cherries, glorious cherries! If you have ever lived near a cherry tree, you know the pleasure of picking and eating your fill, and beyond. The luscious globes of the sweet cherry tree—can them, use them in jams and in chilled cherry soup, include them in cobblers and clafouti, and, of course, flame them in cherries jubilee. Sweet cherry jam is a rich delight; sour cherry jam has more tang and cherry flavor. Freeze or can sweet cherries to use in cherries jubilee.

Sour cherries are eaten raw, too, but their main use is in that great American favorite, cherry pie. Seldom available in the market, sour cherries have an intense cherry flavor and intriguing tartness. Many people prefer the complex flavors of sour cherry jam to that of sweet cherry jam. Sour cherries are also great canned, frozen, dried, or as wine. Substitute dried cherries for raisins in most recipes calling for raisins.

An inexpensive cherry pitter makes preparing cherries easier; this tool is available in cookware stores and mail-order nurseries offering cherry trees.

Cherry trees are a visual treat through four seasons. Spring brings clouds of white flowers, followed in summer by bright red cherries that contrast handsomely with green leaves. Foliage turns yellow in fall, and in winter shiny streaked bark stands out.

In the Landscape

Sweet and sour cherries are among the most beautiful deciduous trees. Even without their fruit, they are handsome additions to a yard. In winter, the dark reddish brown or silvery bark lends texture; in spring, both types of cherry trees burst forth with masses of showy white flowers. Later, the colorful fruits themselves are decorations among the rich green, serrated leaves.

Sweet cherry trees grow very large. Sour cherry trees, though large, are the smaller of the two, growing to 20 feet. Both look fine along a driveway, make an excellent specimen tree that can be admired up close, and are useful as a medium-high screen. Semi-dwarf trees grow 8 to about 15 feet tall; use them as informal hedges or screens and as stylish accent plants.

For information on small bush cherries (including Nanking cherry and western sand cherry) and the cherry/plum crosses, see the "Plum" entry.

How to Grow

Climate

Sweet cherry trees have a somewhat limited range. While fairly hardy, most varieties bloom early; thus a late frost can kill the flowers. And most have little tolerance for very hot weather. They require some winter chill (from 500 to 1,000 hours, depending on the variety). Dry climates are ideal; rain on ripe cherries causes the sugary fruits to absorb water and split; high humidity creates the conditions that are ideal for many cherry diseases. The Great Lakes area and the West Coast are best for growing cherries successfully.

Because they are hardier, bloom later, and can tolerate more heat, sour cherries have a much broader range. They grow along the Atlantic coast and in the Midwest, the colder sections of the West Coast, and mountainous areas of the Southeast; they require at least 1,000 hours of chill.

Exposure and Soil

Cherries need full sun and prefer light, well-drained, sandy soil; they falter and die in heavy, wet soils. Check drainage before planting. If conditions are less than ideal, mound the soil a foot or so before you plant and choose 'Mazzard' or one of the 'Gisela' rootstocks.

Fertilizing

A 6-inch-deep layer of compost mulch and a small amount of manure every spring usually provide ample nutrition for cherries. If the foliage is pale and the tree is putting on only a few inches of new growth a year, apply a small amount of nitrogen fertilizer. Too much nitrogen increases the tree's susceptibility to diseases and freeze damage.

Watering

Cherry trees have a shallow root system; keep the soil fairly moist but never soggy. Sour cherry trees tolerate more drought. Trees grafted to 'Gisela' rootstocks are shallow rooted and need more frequent watering than trees on standard rootstocks.

Pruning

Train young sweet cherry trees to a modified central leader and sour cherries to an open center. Prune 2-year-old trees to have four or five scaffold limbs starting 3 feet above the ground, distributed around the compass points, spaced at least 1 foot apart vertically. Untrained cherries form weak, narrow crotches prone to splitting. Avoid this by bending the main branches 30 to 60 degrees away from the trunk; tie them down, or brace away from the trunk with pieces of wood grooved at each end.

Sweet cherries bear fruit on long-lived fruiting spurs and on new wood. Annual pruning (summer pruning is best) is critical to keep the trees at a manageable height—less than 8 feet tall. Sweet cherry trees tend to develop bare branches with fruits on the end. To get the branches to fill out and force side branching, pinch the tips of these shoots.

Sour cherries need annual pruning to encourage new wood as the fruiting spurs produce for only a few years. They also require height control for ease of harvest. In addition, thin the branches to improve air circulation.

Pests and Diseases

The species name for sweet cherries is *avium*, which loosely translates as "for the birds." Birds are the biggest problem; cover the tree with netting to provide protection. In some areas, cherry fruit fly maggots ruin the fruit. Once the fruit matures, it drops and the maggots burrow into the ground. To prevent next year's infestation, lay a tarp under the tree once the fruit forms, and pick up worm-filled fruits and destroy them. This also prevents the larvae from entering the soil to pupate. Other pest problems include tent caterpillars, aphids, and the plum curculio.

During very wet years, brown rot and cracking fruit ruin the harvest. In moist climates, cherry leaf spot overwinters on dead leaves; control the fungus by pruning for good air circulation and doing a thorough fall cleanup. Bacterial canker (characterized by dead branches and shoots with bronzy exudates) is a problem in some areas. Avoid winter pruning, which can spread the disease; plant resistant varieties; and apply copper spray in fall and again in winter to control the bacteria.

There are a number of reasons why your tree may not have cherries: many varieties do not bear until their fifth year, you might have an ornamental variety, a late frost may have destroyed the flowers, or very rainy weather kept away bees or other pollinators.

Harvesting

Harvest cherries a few days after they color up and when they come off easily with just a gentle tug. Mature large cherry trees produce 50 to 100 pounds of fruit annually; trees kept small yield far less.

How to Purchase

Buy sweet cherry trees bare root in late winter or in containers through summer from local nurseries, or order bare root in late winter from Adams County, Bay Laurel, Burnt Ridge, C & O, Cummins, Edible Landscaping, Johnson, Miller, Nature Hills, One Green World, Raintree, Rolling River, Stark Bro's, or Trees of Antiquity. Fedco and St. Lawrence carry hardy cherry varieties.

Pollinizers

Most sweet cherries need a pollinizer. Be sure to choose the right varieties; many are incompatible. If you don't have room for two trees, plant a self-fertile variety or two varieties that pollinize each other in one planting hole. Sour cherries are self-fruitful.

Rootstocks

Specific cherry varieties are grafted onto named rootstocks. Following are some of the major rootstocks and their characteristics.

'Colt'—produces a tree approximately 70 percent smaller than the standard 'Mazzard'; some resistance to bacterial canker and crown gall; hardy to −10°F.

'Gisela 5' ('Giessen 148-2')—produces a tree 50 percent smaller than 'Mazzard'; some tolerance of heavy soil; not drought tolerant; may sucker; tolerates −20°F.

'GM61/1'—dwarfing, produces a tree 8 to 12 ft. tall; frost resistant; few suckers; tolerates fairly heavy soils.

'Mahaleb'—produces a tree a bit shorter than the standard 'Mazzard'; needs deep, well-drained soils; early cropping; very cold hardy.

'Mazzard'—most common commercial rootstock, produces a tree 20 to 30 ft. tall; fibrous root system; tolerates wet, heavy soils.

Varieties

There are scores of cherry varieties. Consult local nurseries and your Cooperative Extension Service to determine which varieties growing on which rootstocks are best for your area.

SOUR CHERRY, *PRUNUS CERASUS*

All produce red-skinned fruit and, unless otherwise noted, are hardy in Zones 4 to 9.

'English Morello'—antique; red juice; late; 700 chill hours.

'Meteor'—antique; clear juice; self-fruitful; natural dwarf; 800 chill hours.

'Montmorency'—clear juice; self-fruitful; popular; large, spreading tree; 700 chill hours, Zones 4 to 7.

'North Star'—small fruit, red juice; compact, 8 to 10 ft. tall, attractive; bears at an early age; resists brown rot and cherry leaf spot; good in rainy, humid climates; very hardy, 800 chill hours.

SWEET CHERRY, *P. AVIUM*

All require 700 chill hours unless otherwise noted.

'Bing'—soft, dark red fruit, fine flavor; prone to cracking; midseason; needs a pollinizer, usually 'Black Tartarian'; spreading tree and heavy bearer; Zones 5 to 8.

'Black Tartarian'—excellent black cherries; one of the earliest; can be pollinized by most sweet cherries; tree very erect; Zones 5 to 7.

'Craig's Crimson'—firm, sweet, deep red fruit, excellent flavor; midseason; self-fruitful; genetic semi-dwarf, with dwarfing rootstock can be kept to 8 ft. tall; a winner in southern gardens, 800 chill hours, Zones 5 to 10.

'Emperor Francis'—red cherries; late; good for the North; tolerant of soil types, good disease resistance; use 'Rainier' as pollinizer; Zones 5 to 7.

'Lapins' ('Self-Fertile Bing')—large, dark red, heart-shaped cherries, great flavor; midseason; resists cracking and bacterial canker; self-fertile, good pollinizer; 800 chill hours, Zones 5 to 9.

'Rainier'—firm fruit, yellow blushed red, excellent flavor; midseason; spreading tree; 'Bing' good pollinizer; best in drier spring climates, Zones 5 to 9.

'Royal Anne' ('Napoleon')—French antique; yellow blushed red, great flavor; midseason; prone to cracking, best for canning; large, spreading tree; Zones 5 to 8.

'Stella' ('Compact Stella')—dark, large, firm, heart-shaped fruit, fair flavor; midseason; self-fertile, good pollinizer for other varieties; 500 to 600 chill hours, Zones 5 to 9.

'Sweetheart'—sweet, bright red, crunchy, flavorful; late; resists cracking and bacterial canker; self-fruitful; tree is upright; productive. Zones 5 to 9.

Chestnut

Castanea spp.

Effort Scale

NO. 2
Raking of husks, nuts, and leaves is often needed
Occasional pest problems
Harvesting large crop is time consuming

Zones

5 to 9

Thumbnail Sketch

Deciduous tree
30 to 70 ft. tall, 20- to 40-ft. spread
Propagate by grafting or from seeds
Needs full sun
Leaves are deep green, coarsely toothed, 3 to 7 in. long
Blooms in early summer
Flowers are small and white, on large catkins, showy

Chinese chestnuts are spectacular flowering trees in spring—and they bear delicious nuts in fall. Here, the homeowner planted one to screen the neighbor's house. A bonus is the dramatic beauty the tree adds to the otherwise drab side yard.

Nuts are edible; harvest in early fall
Use as shade tree, screen, or large interest tree

How to Use

In the Kitchen

Roasted chestnuts are a cold-winter treat. City people associate them with street vendors, picturesquely warming their hands over the hot coals on which they roast their wares; others imagine a holiday scene with "chestnuts roasting on an open fire."

Chestnuts are among the sweetest nuts. They are delightful on their own when pureed and presented as a bed for roast game, and when lending richness to braised red cabbage, roasted onions and carrots, and stuffing for roast turkey.

Their high water content means that chestnuts must be cured before eating or storing. The curing process evaporates moisture, converts starches to sugars, and makes the nuts easier to peel. Curing is easy; set the nuts out at room temperature for 3 to 7 days or until they give slightly when squeezed between your thumb and forefinger. Because of their moisture content, chestnuts have a short shelf life at room temperature. Store in the refrigerator for up to a month; freeze for up to a year.

Cook chestnuts before eating. Be forewarned: like popcorn, chestnuts explode when heated, so before roasting, cut an "X" in each nut with a sharp knife. Place the nuts in a shallow pan and roast at 375°F for 15 to 25 minutes. Peel off the outer shell and inner skin while still warm and eat as is or use the nuts in numerous recipes.

In the Landscape

Our memories of chestnuts are associated with the native American chestnut, *Castanea dentata*, tragically decimated by blight in the early 1900s, and the European chestnut, *C. sativa*, fondly remembered by our immigrant ancestors. Sadly, nowadays neither chestnut will grow to nut-bearing size east of the Rockies because of the blight. Happily, however, Chinese and Japanese chestnuts (*C. mollisima and C. crenata*), which are relatively blight resistant, are available. Today you can find healthy hybrids between Asian and second-generation American chestnuts, and promising research to reintroduce the American chestnut is under way.

Chestnuts are magnificent spreading trees that lend stature to a spacious yard. They are what trees are all about—stateliness and permanence—inspiring the thought "Now, there's a real tree!" A chestnut tree can shade a hot south side of a house, making a dramatic statement with its long, sweeping branches. In the East, chestnuts grow well on lawns—unlike most fruit and nut trees. Chestnuts shed their catkins in summer and their husks and leaves in fall; the debris is easily managed when the trees are surrounded by a lawn that can be raked, or along country lanes where the debris becomes forest duff. And, wherever these trees grow, their sturdy trunks provide firm support for the most ambitious of tree houses.

How to Grow

For much more detailed information on growing and obtaining chestnuts, visit the website for the Northern Nut Growers Association at www.nutgrowing.org and the American Chestnut Foundation at www.acf.org.

Climate

With a tolerance to low temperatures from −15 to −25°F, chestnut trees have the added advantage of blooming in early summer, which means their flowers escape damage from late frosts. However, these trees grow poorly in hot, humid climates.

Exposure and Soil

Chestnut trees require full sun and slightly acidic, sandy, well-drained soil. They succumb to crown rot in heavy clay soils. Apply a few inches of compost and top-dress with well-aged manure every spring to provide ample nutrition.

Watering

In areas with rainy summers, supplemental watering is usually unnecessary. In arid-summer areas, water deeply every few weeks.

Pruning

Prune a chestnut tree as you would a pecan tree. To avoid disease problems, prune in early summer.

Pests and Diseases

Chinese and Japanese chestnuts are reasonably resistant to the blight fungus *Endothia parasitica*, which destroys American and European chestnuts. Chestnut weevil larvae may feast on the nutmeats. Weevil-affected nuts might still be edible if you destroy the insects before storing the nuts; kill them in the egg stage by soaking the nuts in 122°F water for 45 minutes. Dry and store.

Harvesting

Grafted chestnuts occasionally bear as early as their second year, but most trees take 5 to 7 years to produce. Nuts are ripe when they fall and the husks, or burs, open. Once you notice a few on the ground, shake the tree and pick up the nuts or simply gather them from under the tree every few days. Once the husks are open, you want to beat the squirrels to them. Nuts left too long on the ground quickly deteriorate. A mature tree yields 50 to 75 pounds of nuts annually.

How to Purchase

Buy chestnuts bare root or in containers from Burnt Ridge, Nolin River, Oikos, Rhora's, or Willis.

Pollinizers

Chestnut trees need cross-pollination, so plant more than one variety. If space is limited, plant the two trees in one hole to form a multistemmed tree.

Varieties

'Basalta #3'—large, flavorful nuts; good pollinizer; blight resistant.

'Colossal'—large, sweet nuts, easy to peel; Asian-European hybrid; spreading habit; some blight resistance; needs 'Nevada' as a pollinizer.

'Crane'—good flavor and keeping qualities; for southern and middle chestnut-growing areas.

'Eaton River'—large, sweet nuts; productive; ornamental tree.

'Nevada'—tasty nuts; productive; ripens a few weeks after 'Colossal'; 400 low-chill hours, good for mild-winter areas.

'Qing'—sweet nuts, easy to peel; Chinese variety; resists chestnut blight; keeps well.

'Sleeping Giant'—large, sweet nuts, peel easily; blight resistant; spreading form; cross between Chinese, American, and Japanese varieties.

Chinese leeks

See Chives

Chives

Chives, *Allium* spp.
Society garlic, *Tulbaghia violacea*

Effort Scale

NO. 1
Very easy to grow
Dead foliage and flowers must be trimmed off after blooming
Aphids an occasional problem

Zones

3 to 10; grow tender chive species and society garlic as annuals in Zones 3 to 6

Thumbnail Sketch

Garden chives (Allium schoenoprasum)
Perennial herb
12 to 24 in. tall
Propagate from seeds or divisions
Needs full sun
Leaves are blue-green, tubular, grasslike, to 9 in. tall
Blooms in late spring
Flowers are lavender to purple, clustered in cloverlike heads

Leaves and flowers are edible; use as seasoning; harvest all growing season

Use in flower bed, rock garden, or herb garden; as edging or in container

Garlic chives (Chinese chives), A. tuberosum
Perennial herb 16 to 20 in. tall
Propagate from seeds or divisions
Needs full sun
Leaves are grayish green, flat, and grasslike, to 12 in. tall
Blooms in spring and summer
Flowers are white or mauve, flat-headed umbels, 1½ to 2 in. across, fragrant
Leaves and flowers are edible; use as seasoning; harvest all growing season
Use in flower bed, rock garden, herb garden, or container

Chinese leeks (Chinese leek flower, fragrant-flower garlic), A. ramosum
Perennial herb to 30 in. tall
Propagate from seeds or divisions
Needs full sun or partial shade
Leaves are blue-green, flat, and grasslike, to 24 in. tall
Blooms in late spring and late summer
Flowers are white, flat-headed clusters, 1½ in. across
Leaves, flower buds, and flowers are edible; use as seasoning; harvest all growing season
Use in flower bed, rock garden, herb garden, or container

Society garlic (Tulbaghia violacea)
Perennial herb to 24 in. tall
Propagate from seeds or divisions
Needs full sun or partial shade

Creating a pretty pink picture are 'Angel Face' rose, chives, and scented geranium. All have edible flowers; the flavors, respectively, are sweet perfume, onion-garlicky, and lemon. The chartreuse hues of 'Icterina' sage and Bibb lettuce add color contrast.

Leaves are blue-green or variegated white and green, flat and grasslike, to 18 in. tall

Blooms from spring through fall

Flowers are lavender, flat-headed sprays, 1½ in. across

Leaves and flowers are edible; use as seasoning; harvest all growing season

Use in flower bed, rock garden, or herb garden; as edging or in container

How to Use

In the Kitchen

These herbs all have an aromatic onion or garlic flavor. Use them to flavor and garnish salads and cream sauces. Sprinkle common chives on a soup or stew to add a fresh fillip, and work them into cream cheese and serve with smoked salmon on toast. Flowers of all chives and society garlic are edible; harvest when they first open. For cooking, break into individual florets as the flavor is intense. Sprinkle over vichyssoise for a flavorful accent.

In China, they garden-blanch Chinese leek flower stems and buds by covering them until tender and white; stir-fry or prepare as you would asparagus. To preserve chives, freeze harvested leaves or bring a growing plant of garden chives indoors for a few months of use in early winter.

In the Landscape

All these grasslike herbaceous perennials are delightful in herb gardens, rock and flower gardens, and containers. The plants of the common garden chives and society garlic are attractive enough to be used as edgings.

Garden chives have bright, blue-green tubular leaves with lavender cloverlike blossoms in late spring. Garlic chives have grayish, grassy leaves and flat clusters of starlike, white or mauve flowers in late summer. Garlic chives can get weedy if the flower heads go to seed. Chinese leeks, a similar but much better choice, have similar but larger white flowers, bloom in spring as well as late summer, and reseed sparingly.

Society garlic is a real star in the landscape, giving color to perennial borders and herb gardens from late spring through fall in mild-winter areas. Compact 'Silver Lace' is striking with green and white variegated leaves.

All chives and society garlic combine well with frothy pink alyssum or blue ageratum, variegated sage, and thyme.

How to Grow

Garden chives, garlic chives, and Chinese leeks are successful in all parts of the United States. Society garlic is a semi-hardy perennial grown in Zones 7 to 9. All prefer full sun, fairly rich soil, and even moisture. Remove old flower heads and dead leaves from all species. Divide plants every 2 or 3 years.

Harvest chives as needed, cutting off the leaves with scissors; the flowers are best just as they open; they get papery if they fully open and the seeds start to ripen.

How to Purchase

Nurseries carry garden chive seeds and plants in spring. Or get some from a friend who is dividing plants. Two varieties of interest are 'Grolau', a common chive with pink flowers that is well suited to indoor growing, and 'Profusion', a variety that produces sterile lavender flowers, especially good for edible flowers. You can find garlic chives at specialty herb nurseries. Look for Chinese leek seeds from companies specializing in Asian vegetables and herbs. Retail nurseries carry society garlic plants (in 4-inch and 1-gallon pots) and seeds, or you can order small plants online or from catalogs.

For information on other members of the Allium family, including onions, leeks, and garlic, see Appendix A.

Cime di rapa

See Broccoli and Cauliflower

Citrus

(calamondin, grapefruit, kumquat, lemon, lime, lime leaf, limequat, mandarin orange, pomelo, sour orange, sweet orange, tangelo)
Citrus spp.

Effort Scale

NO. 2

Fertilizer and mineral supplements usually needed

Deep watering required, particularly in arid climates

Susceptible to some pests and diseases, particularly in humid climates

Cold protection needed in borderline climates

Mulching necessary

Some pruning needed

Zones

8 to 11

Thumbnail Sketch

Evergreen shrubs or trees

4 to 25 ft. tall, depending on type

Propagate by grafting or budding

Needs full sun or light shade; afternoon shade in hottest climates

Leaves are bright green, 2 to 7 in. long

Bloom time depends on type

Flowers are small, white, fragrant but not showy

Fruits are edible; harvest season varies with type; fruits showy; flowers of most species are edible; leaves of lemons and lime leaf used as seasoning

Use as interest tree or shrub, screen, formal or informal hedge, foundation plant, or espalier; on arbor or in container

How to Use

In the Kitchen

For breakfast, squeeze lime juice on melon and spread lemon marmalade on toast. Add thinly sliced lemon to your morning tea. Blood oranges, sliced and arranged with thin onion rings, make a luncheon side salad. Broil half a grapefruit with a little sherry for dessert for your evening meal. Such might be your citrus scenario for one day.

It's well known that citrus fruits are very high in vitamin C and potassium. What's not known is that, as a rule, the darker and more colorful the fruit, the more nutrition in the juice. For example, ruby red grapefruit has more antioxidants and nearly 50 times more beta-carotene than white varieties.

Citrus types, common and exotic, lend a high note to everyday food. Salted preserved lemons perfume a baked chicken. Small kumquats and limequats, their sweet rind and sour pulp pickled, are taste sensations as a garnish for meats. Mandarin oranges are enjoyable just as they come from the tree. Canned, they make a delectable addition to a Chinese-style almond float. Pomelos, one of the parents of the grapefruit, resemble their offspring but are larger. Eat them raw and savor them in sections as you do grapefruit, but peel off the heavy membrane. Cut fresh young lemon leaves thinly and add to soups or fresh cheese in the Italian manner. Lime leaf is a key ingredient in many rich Thai curries.

Thanks to Americans' growing interest in new foods, there is a huge variety of unusual citrus to explore. For instance, you might eat 'Cara Cara' pink navel orange fresh or try your hand at making English-style, bitter marmalade with the famous 'Seville' sour orange. And there are fabulous Mediterranean lemons, including 'Genoa' from Italy and 'Limonero Fino' from Spain, that chefs are now excited about. Or how about the juice from the tart red 'Rangpur' lime from India for your iced tea? Add thin slices of the unique aromatic rind of 'Yuzu' citron, long favored in Japan, to soups and simmered dishes. Variegated calamondin, 'Australian Finger Limes', 'Buddha's Hand' citron, 'Marrakech Limetta': no longer your mother's standard oranges and lemons, citrus is moving onward and upward.

Most varieties of citrus remain good to eat when left hanging on the tree. All citrus fruits make good marmalade. Candy the rinds of all types; can mandarins and kumquats. Citrus juices are easily frozen. For a refreshing drink out of season, pour the juice of lemons or limes into ice cube trays; when the juice is frozen, transfer the cubes to zip-top freezer bags. To drink, drop cubes in a glass, and add water and sugar to taste.

In the Landscape

Citrus plants are stellar additions to any yard in a suitable climate. They fit in with any design and, with fruit prices rising apace, your efforts are soon repaid. You can trim these evergreens—with their bright green, very dense foliage—as rounded shrubs or trees. The fragrance of numerous small, white citrus flowers is heady; and their orange and yellow fruits are decorative in the winter when few plants have any color at all.

Breeders have created a citrus for every niche, large or small. Most citrus trees come in standard and dwarf forms. The taller plants can shade a hot south wall or screen a view, but smaller trees are more manageable for care and harvest.

Most citrus trees are terrific for lining a driveway or as single specimens—formal or informal depending on how you prune them. Take advantage of their sweet perfume; plant a dwarf citrus near the front entry to welcome guests. Train these versatile plants as espaliers on walls and fences or over an arbor. (In desert areas avoid hot west walls.) Or utilize them as hedges and screens. Incorporate large shrub types in a border, and smaller varieties, such as Key lime and lime leaf, in foundation plantings. Thorny citrus make excellent barrier plants. And, of course, all dwarf citrus are good in containers.

As versatile as citrus plants are, they grow poorly in a lawn. The trees need deep watering and are prone to root and crown rot from frequent, shallow lawn watering. Since lawns and citrus are both heavy feeders, they compete for soil nutrients.

At the Allied Arts Guild in Menlo Park, California, orange tulips are harbingers of spring. The brilliant color of their edible flowers echoes that of the fruit in these well-pruned, shiny-leaved orange trees. Clipped boxwoods add to the formality of the space.

How to Grow
Climate

Most citrus are native to mild regions of Southeast Asia and are only marginally hardy. The best climate for citrus is determined by two factors: the amount of possible frost and the amount of heat available. For example, San Francisco is frost free enough for most citrus to grow and develop fruit, but it does not have enough heat to sweeten oranges and grapefruit, although limes and lemons do well. In any case, citrus are limited to those parts of the country where the temperature does not fall below 20°F—the mild-winter areas of Arizona, California, Florida, Hawaii, and Texas, and the warmest areas of the Gulf Coast.

To help you decide which citrus, if any, are appropriate for your climate:

Can take some frost (most to least hardy)—kumquat, calamondin, 'Meyer' lemon, mandarin orange, sweet orange, tangelo, pomelo, grapefruit, and standard lemon.

Require long periods of high heat—most sweet oranges, pomelo, mandarin orange, tangelo, and most grapefruits.

Require moderate amount of heat—lemon, calamondin, lime, kumquat, lime leaf, and 'Oroblanco' grapefruit.

Exposure and Soil

Except in the hottest climates, citrus prefer full sun but tolerate some shade. In desert areas, afternoon shade is recommended. Lemon, kumquat, and mandarin orange are shade tolerant—but only with ample heat. Legginess indicates too little sun. In cool climates, plant citrus against a south-facing wall or near a patio that will reflect heat from the pavement; provide protection from cooling winds.

All citrus grow best in well-drained loam. They tolerate soil pH from 6 to 7.5 and respond well to organic matter added to the soil before planting. Mulch annually with compost; be sure to keep it at least 6 inches from the trunk.

Variegated plants are outstanding in any garden, especially for their nighttime magic as the white portions of the leaves seem to float in the air. 'Variegated Pink Eureka' lemon has pink-fleshed fruit; its skin ripens to yellow with white stripes.

Planting

Citrus are grafted fruit trees. When choosing a variety, it helps to know both the fruit type and the rootstock. Rootstocks determine dwarfing, resistance to root rots and/or nematodes, or adaptation to drought or salty soils. When possible, buy your citrus nearby as local purveyors have probably done your rootstock homework for you. Your Cooperative Extension Service can also provide information.

Plant anytime in frost-free climates. Elsewhere plant citrus in early spring to give them time to adapt before winter sets in. Young plants are susceptible to sunburn; wrap the trunk with trunk wrap or paint with a mixture of equal parts water and light-colored latex paint. Keep trees deeply watered but not soggy.

To learn more about citrus in detail, consult *Citrus: Complete Guide to Selecting & Growing More Than 100 Varieties for California, Arizona, Texas, the Gulf Coast & Florida* by Lance Walheim. Also, visit the websites of Four Winds Growers; the Cooperative Extension Services of the University of California at Davis, Texas A&M University, and the University of Florida; and California Rare Fruit Growers.

Fertilizing

Citrus need high amounts of nitrogen and sufficient amounts of the trace minerals iron, zinc, manganese, and magnesium. In sandy soils and in rainy climates, nitrogen readily leaches from the soil and needs replacing. In alkaline soils, trace minerals may be chemically unavailable; apply them on a regular basis. Supplement a fertilizer regime by mulching with 3 or 4 inches of compost after the soil warms up in spring. To increase cold tolerance in frosty areas, do not prune or apply nitrogen after midsummer.

Nutrient deficiencies are common when growing citrus. Pale leaves indicate nitrogen deficiency (or bad drainage or cold damage); yellowing between the veins usually indicates iron, zinc, and/or magnesium deficiency. Applying a foliar feed with kelp when leaves are half developed in spring quickly corrects deficiencies.

Watering

Citrus need moist but not soggy soil; drip irrigation is ideal. If plants dry out, the fruit will drop. After trees are established, water deeply every 2 to 3 weeks in dry-summer areas, more often in light soil, heat, or windy conditions. Container plants always need regular watering.

Pruning

Citrus have thin bark susceptible to sunburn. Do not remove lower branches that shade the trunk; if the trunk is exposed, paint it as described in the "Planting" section. Prune to shape and to remove dead or crossing branches and suckers. Pinch back new growth regularly to control shape and size, and help spindly growth fill in.

Pests and Diseases

Consult your Cooperative Extension Service to learn about diseases in your area. Fungi are prevalent in humid areas. The most common reasons citrus do poorly are that they are planted in a lawn or have been given poor drainage or too much water.

Some pests—aphids, scale, mealybugs, and spider mites, in particular—can be a nuisance. To control these pests, try a water spray first; if that is not effective, use a light oil spray formulated for evergreens. The Asian citrus psyllid—which can cause citrus greening, a bacterial disease fatal to citrus—is an increasing problem; check with your local Cooperative Extension Service for control. Ants are a common culprit as they "farm" the sucking insects and protect them from predators.

Harvesting

Most citrus fruits can hang on the tree for many weeks after they ripen. If you are in doubt about ripeness, use clippers to harvest a few and test them.

How to Purchase

Buy citrus locally to find plants selected for your climate and grafted onto rootstocks adapted to local conditions. To control pest and disease problems, gardeners in citrus-growing states are not allowed to order plants from other citrus-growing states. Major citrus nurseries: in Florida, Brite Leaf; in California, Four Winds Growers (largest selection); in Arizona, Greenfield; and in Georgia, Willis. Acorn Springs and Logee's carry a few citrus.

Pollinizers

Most citrus are self-fruitful.

Varieties

CALAMONDIN, × *CITROFORTUNELLA MICROCARPA*

Very small, round, sour fruit is borne throughout the year on a handsome, upright plant. Standard and variegated varieties are available, good for indoor growing. Calamondin is among the hardiest of citrus.

GRAPEFRUIT, *CITRUS PARADISI*

Large, yellow-skinned fruit are sweet if given enough heat; tree or large shrub.

'Marsh'—seedless, white fleshed; 12 to 18 months to ripen; handsome tree with large leaves; good in desert heat, the West, Hawaii, and Florida.

'Oroblanco'—cross between a pomelo and a grapefruit; large with sweet, white flesh, no seeds, thick rind; vigorous; produces sweet fruit under cooler than ideal conditions.

'Ruby Red' ('Redblush')—red fleshed only in very warm climates, white in cooler regions; good in all citrus climates.

KUMQUAT (NAGAMI), *FORTUNELLA* SPP.

The small fruits have very sweet rind and sour flesh; they can be eaten in one bite or made into marmalade. Full-size plants grows 6 to 15 ft. tall, dwarfs to 4 ft. tall. Very ornamental because the fruits hang on for a long time, kumquats do well in containers and indoors.

Meiwa (*F. crassifolia*)—adapted to all citrus regions, popular in Florida.

Nagami (*F. margarita*)—popular in the West and Florida.

LEMON, *CITRUS LIMON*

Yellow fruits decorate an oval-shaped tree to 20 ft. tall; a dwarfing rootstock produces a smaller plant. Standard lemons do poorly in Florida; try 'Improved Meyer' or a lime instead.

'Eureka'—standard lemon; bears year round; attractive shrub, new growth purplish; grown in the West.

'Improved Meyer' (*C. × meyeri*)—lemon-orange cross; strong, aromatic flavor; bears year round; to 10 ft. tall, grows in the West, Hawaii, Florida, and indoors; hardiest lemon.

'Lisbon'—full-size, handsome, thorny tree; more tolerant of heat and cold than 'Eureka'; bears year round; grown in Arizona and California.

'Variegated Pink Eureka' ('Pink Lemonade')—yellow peel with white striping, pink flesh; bears year round; leaves green and white; fussy, often grown indoors.

LIME, *CITRUS* SPP.

A mature lime tree is dense, rounded, and 15 to 20 ft. tall; dwarf limes are available. Some lime varieties are quite thorny.

'Bearss' (*C. × latifolia*)—a Tahiti lime selection; seedless; bears in winter; use green or yellow (ripe); thorny; grows in most citrus regions.

Key lime (West Indian lime, Mexican lime, [*C. aurantiifolia*])—small, juicy, green to yellow (ripe); produces year round; very tender; grown in South Florida and Southern California; good indoors; seedling lime.

LIME LEAF (MAKRUT, KAFFIR LIME), *C. HYSTRIX*

Not a true lime, this plant is grown for its leaves, which perfume curries and soups of Southeast Asia. While it is commonly called kaffir lime, I avoid this name because it is a racial slur in southern Africa. Very frost sensitive, the small shrub has unusual hourglass-shaped leaves, bronze new growth, and bumpy, sour edible fruits. It is good for containers and indoor culture.

LIMEQUAT, × *CITROFORTUNELLA FLORIDANA*

A cross between lime and kumquat, a limequat is shrubby, quite angular, and open. A dwarf form is available. Fruits hang on limequats a long time.

'Eustis'—quite tender; grown in the West.

'Lakeland'—a little hardier than a lime; available in Florida.

MANDARIN ORANGE (SATSUMA, TANGERINE), *CITRUS RETICULATA*

Mandarins are beautiful, upright-branching, small trees; dwarf varieties are available. There are many cultivars in addition to the ones listed here. Look for new seedless types such as 'Tango' and 'Gold Nugget'.

Clementine—group of mandarins including 'Clemenules', 'Esbal', 'Fina', and 'Marisol'; variable bearing season; drooping, small trees; need less heat than most mandarins.

'Dancy'—peels easily, seedy; bears December to April; upright tree; needs lots of heat for sweet fruit; grows in Florida and the desert West.

'Owari' (satsuma)—small tree, quite spreading; seedless fruit ripens very early, in late fall; doesn't hold well on tree; good for northern Florida, Gulf Coast, and the West.

POMELO (POMMELO, SHADDOCK), *C. MAXIMA*

This grapefruit relative produces very large, typically yellow-fleshed fruit that needs less heat than grapefruit. Ripens anywhere from early winter in warmest-summer areas to early spring in coolest areas. Peel individual sections because of the heavy membrane.

'Chandler'—the variety commonly available in most citrus areas; pink flesh.

SOUR ORANGE, *C. AURANTIUM*

The highly ornamental tree produces large, waxy, perfumed flowers followed by clusters of deep red-orange fruits that remain on the tree for a year. The very tart fruits are excellent for marmalade. Group trees for a hedge, screen, or windbreak.

'Bouquet des Fleurs' ('Bouquet')—dark green foliage; exceptionally large, fragrant flowers; 8 to 10 ft. tall.

'Seville'—used as street tree in Southern California and Arizona; good specimen plant; seedy fruit of Spanish marmalade fame; 20 to 30 ft. tall.

SWEET ORANGE, *C. SINENSIS*

These large, round, formal-looking trees have dense, dark green foliage; they are very large shrubs on dwarfing rootstocks.

'Hamlin'—juicy, nearly seedless; bears October to February; popular in Arizona, South Texas, and Florida; fairly hardy.

'Moro'—blood orange; dark red pulp, excellent, rich flavor; slow to bear; January to May fruiting; grows in most citrus areas, but may not develop dark color in Southeast.

'Pineapple'—juice orange; some seeds; popular in Florida, South Texas, and Arizona.

'Valencia'—common juice orange; upright tree; summer bearing, long harvest period; not recommended for Arizona or Gulf Coast, popular in California and Florida.

'Washington Navel'—seedless; winter and spring fruiting; common variety in the West including Hawaii but not in the desert; in Florida and Texas, look for other navels. Other navel varieties include pink 'Cara Cara'.

TANGELO-MANDARIN HYBRIDS, *C. × TANGELO*

All varieties are crosses and produce better with a pollinizer.

'Fairchild'—sweet, juicy; bears in winter; mandarin-tangelo cross; good in the desert.

'Minneola'—bright orange, great mandarin flavor, few seeds; January to May bearing; mandarin-grapefruit cross; grows in Florida and the West.

'Orlando'—medium size, flattened, peels easily; bears a month earlier than 'Minneola'; mandarin-grapefruit cross; grows in Florida and West.

'Temple'—deep reddish orange, strong flavor; January to April bearing; orange-mandarin cross; popular Florida variety.

Crabapple

See Apple and Crabapple

Cranberry and Lingonberry

Vaccinium spp.

Effort Scale

NO. 2
Keeping plants sufficiently moist takes attention
Weeding usually needed
Harvesting is time consuming
Heavy mulching often needed for winter protection

Zones

Cranberry, 3 to 7
Lingonberry, 2 to 7

Thumbnail Sketch

Cranberry, evergreen shrub or vine; lingonberry, evergreen shrub
Low-growing mat 2 to 18 in. tall; to 36 in. wide
Propagate from cuttings or by layering
Need full sun; partial shade in hot-summer climates
Leaves are elliptical, deep or medium green, ½ in. long
Cranberries bloom in spring, lingonberries in May and midsummer
Flowers are pink, small, in clusters, resemble lily-of-the-valley

Lingonberry is one of the most underutilized ornamental as well as edible ground covers. A member of the heath family (like blueberries), it bears dainty bell-like flowers in spring that turn into tart red berries in summer. In autumn, some leaves turn red.

Fruits are red, edible; harvest cranberry in fall, lingonberry in midsummer and fall
Use as ground cover in boggy areas, among stepping-stones, in rock garden, or in containers

How to Use

In the Kitchen

Cranberries are the small, red berries that are the main ingredient in the sweet-tart, glistening, deep crimson jelly and sauce that traditionally accompany the Thanksgiving turkey feast. Their tartness adds a balancing note to an otherwise overfull groaning board. Originally cranberries were smaller and tarter, but modern breeding has selected for large berries with lots of pulp for the juice industry.

They add color and zing to any meal as relish, juice, sherbet, or an addition to a salad mold. Toss dried cranberries into a green salad along with toasted pecans. Dried cranberries and cranberry leather are delicious, lightweight, take-along foods for campers and a good snack food for kids and adults, too. High in vitamin C and full of antioxidants, cranberries have a well-documented ability to prevent urinary tract infections (by acidifying urine), which makes them a nutritional plus in any form. Foxberries are a close relative, and where they are native, they are used in the same manner as cranberries.

Lingonberries are also related to cranberries but are smaller and a bit tarter. They, too, are packed with vitamin C and antioxidants. In Scandinavia and northern Europe, folks adore lingonberries in tangy pancake syrups and luscious sauces for wild game.

When fresh, all three types of berries keep well in the refrigerator for a few weeks. You can make delicious, jewel-toned jellies and syrups. The berries are easy to freeze—no blanching necessary; just put them into zip-top freezer bags or dry them and add them to cereals and breads, or make fruit leather.

In the Landscape

Cranberries, foxberries, and lingonberries are diminutive evergreen vines related to blueberries. If you have just the right conditions— that is, a cold climate and a patch of very acid, moist, but well-drained soil—they could be the perfect solution to what would otherwise be a landscaping conundrum.

These compact, formal-looking vines make a lovely ground cover, especially under other acid lovers like blueberries, mountain laurels, and rhododendrons. The plants have small, bright green leaves, clusters of pink, bell-shaped flowers, and bright red berries. Plant them in rows to line a woodland walk; nestle the dwarf varieties among stepping-stones. Most grow well in containers and are graceful spilling over the sides of a planter box.

How to Grow

If you grow lowbush blueberries (a close relative) successfully, you can grow cranberries, foxberries, and lingonberries. For more information on growing cranberries, visit www.cranberrycreations.com.

Climate

Cranberries and foxberries grow wild from Alaska through Canada to New Jersey. Lingonberries are native to northern Europe, northern Asia, and North America from Alaska to Eastern Canada, Greenland, and the northern United States.

Farmers grow cranberries commercially in Maine, Massachusetts, New Jersey, Michigan, Wisconsin, Minnesota, Oregon, Washington, and parts of Canada—areas with fairly cold winters.

Exposure and Soil

The plants thrive in full sun, though they need afternoon shade in hot-summer areas. Very acid soil (pH 3.2 to 4.5) and constant moisture are key requirements.

Planting

Prepare the soil as you would for blueberries. Plant the vines of all three types 2 feet apart in either early spring or early fall. Once plants are established, apply a few inches of pine needles or leaf mulch. In subsequent years, add more mulch until you maintain a level 6 inches deep. For all the types, if your winters drop below 10°F with little snow cover, mulch the plants heavily to protect next year's fruiting wood.

Fertilizing

If the leaves are rich green and growing well, no supplemental fertilizer is needed. If they are light green and spindly, apply an organic source of nitrogen such as blood meal in early spring; don't apply it after mid-June as it will stimulate new growth susceptible to winterkill.

Watering

Keep the plants moist but not soggy. Watering during a drought or in dry climates is essential. Commercial flooding of cranberry bogs is done primarily for mechanical harvesting. The fields don't stay flooded.

Pruning

To renew a well-established bed, prune back upright stems.

Pests and Diseases

In the home garden these plants have few pests or diseases, but weeds can ruin a planting. Remove any weeds before planting, and keep the plants well mulched and well weeded. The cranberry fruitworm, which envelops the berries in a web, is a problem in some areas and not others. Control a serious infestation with *Bt*.

Harvesting

Cranberries bloom only in spring and the fruit is harvested in fall. The native foxberry blooms once in May and fruits in midsummer. European lingonberry also blooms once in May and fruits in midsummer, but then it blooms again in midsummer and sets out a second crop of fruit in fall. These various plants do not fruit until they are 2 or 3 years old.

How to Purchase

A few local nurseries carry cranberry and lingonberry plants in 4-inch or 1-gallon pots. Order plants from Edible Landscaping, Miller, One Green World, or Raintree (offers a handy lingonberry harvesting rake). For foxberries, contact native plant nurseries in cranberry-growing areas.

Varieties

CRANBERRY, *VACCINIUM MACROCARPON*

Modern hybrids are quite similar. If you want smaller and tarter berries, try heirloom varieties; if you live in Massachusetts, you may be able to find the old-timers 'Howes' and 'Early Black'.
'Ben Lear'—early-ripening wild clone from Wisconsin.
'Hamilton'—dwarf to only 2 in. tall.
'Pilgrim'—hardy to –30°F.

'Stevens'—large berries.
'Thunderlake'—described as a "no bog" cranberry, meaning it's tolerant of normal garden conditions.

FOXBERRY (COWBERRY, MOUNTAIN CRANBERRY), *V. VITIS-IDAEA* SSP. *MINUS*

Sometimes available in local nurseries that carry native plants, foxberries are similar to cranberries but are darker red, smaller, and tarter.

EUROPEAN LINGONBERRY, *V. VITIS-IDAEA*

'Red Pearl'—from Holland, vigorous, to 16 in. tall.
'Sanna'—to about 10 in. tall; large fruit.
'Sussi'—Swedish introduction; short, creeping plant to 8 in. tall; small fruit.

Cucumber

Cucumis sativus

Effort Scale

NO. 3
Must be planted annually
Vulnerable to some pests
Regular watering and some weeding necessary
Vining types must be trained
Fertilizing and mulching needed

Zones

Not applicable

Thumbnail Sketch

Annual
Bush types, 24 to 36 in. tall; vining types, to 6 ft. long
Propagate from seeds
Needs full sun
Leaves are light to dark green, depending on variety
Flowers are bright yellow, 1 to 2 in. across
Fruits are edible; harvest in summer and early fall
Use in herbaceous border, raised bed, or container; vining types on fences and trellises

How to Use

In the Kitchen

Cool as a cucumber is not an empty phrase. Crispy slicing cucumbers with a creamy dressing are cooling, as is cold cucumber soup with dill. Thin-skinned Persian types are perfect simply sliced, chilled, drizzled with a little lemon juice, and sprinkled with salt for a light summer appetizer. In India raita, a condiment of grated cucumbers in yogurt, tempers the heat of a hot curry, and in Mexico cucumber, limes, and sugar are combined and pureed for a cooling *agua*. And, of course, there are the old-fashioned icebox bread-and-butter pickles; clearly we think of cucumbers when things get hot.

To preserve cucumbers, make pickles (venture beyond sweet and dill to spicy and herbal) or relish.

Cucumbers are extremely productive vines that can produce upward of 30 pounds of fruit in the growing season. Plant in a raised bed for good drainage. For better circulation train the vines to grow on a twig trellis.

In the Landscape

Most cucumbers have fairly rough, ivylike leaves. Some leaves, such as 'Armenian', are 3 inches across and light green; many others, both vining and bush types, are 4 to 5 inches wide and dark green. Cucumber flowers are yellow, small, and cup shaped. While they occasionally peek out from under the leaves, neither the flowers nor the green fruits are especially showy; the cucumber's primary virtue is its uniform blanket of green. I trellis the vining types to use as a backdrop for a row of spectacular red gladiolas or showy red and white 'Peppermint Stick' zinnias. I created crawl-through bamboo trellises to allow my long Japanese varieties to hang straight, and to provide a tunnel for the neighborhood children to explore.

Bush-type cucumbers are useful in flower beds near a patio or front walk; plant petunias or verbena to dress them up. They do well in large containers on balconies, porches, or patios. The compact varieties are short enough that you can plant tall varieties of cosmos and marigolds behind them to peek glowingly over the cucumbers.

How to Grow

Like most members of the Cucurbitaceae family (think squash and melons), cucumbers are warm-season annuals. These fast-growing, short-lived plants thrive in full sun, but they tolerate shade in hot climates.

Planting

In short-summer areas, start seeds in late spring, but do not set out your transplants until the soil has warmed and all danger of frost has passed. Or start cucumbers outside in warm, rich, organic soil supplemented with aged manure or an all-purpose organic fertilizer. Traditional gardeners plant in hills (mounds a few feet across); they sow three or four cucumber seeds in each hill and thin to two seedlings per hill. At planting time, give the vining varieties some sort of support, whether a decorative trellis, stake, or fence, to keep the vines off the ground. Plant bush varieties singly in containers and flower borders.

Plant seeds at the depth recommended on the seed packet and water in well. Protect seedlings with an overturned berry basket or bird netting until they are a few inches tall. Once the seedlings are up, thin to 6 inches apart. Keep the area weeded. Tie up vining varieties as they grow.

Cucumber plants need moist but not soggy soil. If the plants dry out, the fruits get bitter. Apply hydrolyzed fish or an all-purpose organic supplemental fertilizer about 6 weeks after planting.

Pests and Diseases

Young cucumber plants are susceptible to cutworms and slugs. If adult striped and spotted cucumber beetles have been problems in the past, grow cucumbers under row covers until they are large enough to withstand the onslaught. Remove the covers when blossoms appear so bees can pollinate the flowers. Once the plants are a few inches high, put down a ½-inch layer of wet newspapers and cover with an inch of organic mulch to keep the plants from drying out, suppress most weeds, and limit cucumber beetles' access to the roots to lay their eggs.

Mildew can be a problem, particularly late in the season. Other diseases that affect cucumbers are mosaic virus and bacterial wilt, both of which can kill cucumber plants in the Northeast, and anthracnose in the Southeast. The symptoms of mosaic virus are mottled and shriveled leaves; bacterial wilt causes the plants to sicken and die; anthracnose shows up as brown patches on the leaves and moldy fruit. Pull up affected plants and destroy them, as no cure is known for these conditions. Plant resistant varieties, control insects that spread the diseases, and rotate crops every 2 or 3 years.

Harvesting

Pick cucumbers when they are immature. If you let them get large and ripen (turn yellow), the vine stops producing flowers and, in turn, cucumbers. Dwarf bush cucumbers yield 4 to 6 fruits per plant, larger vining types 10 to 30 per plant. I harvested 41 cucumbers (of varying sizes) from one 'Slicemaster' plant I grew in a wine barrel.

How to Purchase

Most local nurseries carry seeds and a very limited selection of transplants. Find many more varieties from Johnny's, Park, Pine Tree, Stokes Seeds, Renee's, Nichols, Harris, and Territorial. Kitazawa carries many Asian varieties. Seeds of Change, Baker Creek, and Seed Savers offer heirlooms. Southern Exposure has heat- and disease-resistant varieties.

Varieties

STANDARD VINING

These are similar to the cucumbers sold at the market.

'Marketmore 76'—long, green, American-type slicer; productive; good disease resistance.

'Orient Express'—hybrid; reliable; vigorous; crisp; no bitterness.

'Slicemaster'—hybrid; early, productive; 8-in. dark green fruit; grow in large container.

'Sweet Success'—hybrid; 12-in.-long, dark green fruit; thin skin; no bitterness.

BUSH
Compact vines grow like a bushy plant 24 to 36 in. tall and wide.
'Bush Pickle'—hybrid; light green, 5-in. fruit; great for containers.
'Fanfare'—hybrid; dark green, 8-in. fruit; tolerant of most cucumber diseases.
'Spacemaster'—dark green fruit to 8 in. long.

ASIAN
Quite long with thin skin and mild flavor, these cucumbers are rarely bitter.
'Suyo Long'—Chinese variety; to 15 in. long; green, ribbed, and warty; burpless, almost seedless; no bitterness.
'Tasty Jade'—hybrid; Japanese variety; slender, to 12 in. long; parthenocarpic (produces fruit without being pollinized); resists mildew.

PICKLING
Shorter than standard cucumbers, pickling types produce a large crop over a short period of time.
'Diamant'—hybrid; dark green, smooth; disease resistant; delicious eaten fresh.
'Endeavor'—curved and knobby; crispy, good fresh; disease resistant; long harvest.

SPECIALTY
These cucumbers are a varied lot with unusual-looking fruits.
'Armenian'—light green, ridged fruit; easy to digest if picked before seeds mature.
'Lemon'—heirloom; small, round, yellow fruit; pick young for best flavor.
'Striped Armenian' ('Striped Serpent')—long, S-shaped, green fruit with lighter stripes.

Currant and Gooseberry

Ribes spp.

Effort Scale

NO. 3
Some pruning necessary
Mulching needed
Control of occasional pests and diseases necessary
Harvesting is time consuming

Zones

3 to 8

Thumbnail Sketch

Deciduous shrubs
3 to 6 ft. tall
Propagate from cuttings or by layering
Need full sun; some shade in hot-summer areas
Leaves are medium green, small to 3 in., palmate, decorative
Bloom in spring
Flowers are small, green to pink, not showy
Fruit is edible; harvest in summer
Use as foundation plants, interest plants, or informal hedges or in containers; some varieties for cascading over retaining walls or espaliering

How to Use

In the Kitchen
The vermillion color of red currant jelly seems right out of a cathedral window, and the flavor (to keep the imagery consistent) is heavenly. Use red currants in sauces and sherbets, or make a unique spiced garnish (with cloves, vinegar, and sugar). White currants are sweeter than red—lightly tart and juicy—and delightful eaten fresh. Clove currants are black and have a slightly resinous overtone, which adds interest to sauces for meats, or a spicy fruit salsa. Black currants, highly prized in northern Europe, have three times the antioxidants of blueberries and three times the vitamin C of oranges. Use them to make wine or juice. Their strong acidic flavor perks up other fruit juices and smoothies; reduce the juice as a glaze for roast duck. The famous French liqueur cassis is made from black currants.

Some small, green, pink, or purple-red gooseberries are extremely tart, tasting somewhat like juicy rhubarb, while some European vari-

Red currants are such pretty shrubs with their small, maplelike leaves. They are more tolerant of shade than other fruits and berries. With the sun shining through the fruits, the berries look like rubies and garnets hanging from the stems.

eties are sweet enough to eat fresh. Gooseberry lovers rave about gooseberry pie à la mode and gooseberry fool (a traditional Scottish dessert). Other favorites are jams, jellies, and spiced gooseberries.

Use currants and gooseberries to make jams, jellies, juices, sauces, and wine. Preserve by canning, freezing, or pickling.

In the Landscape

Currants and gooseberries are often grown as multistemmed shrubs. Red and white currants are thornless, growing 3 to 4 feet tall and wide. Black currants are thornless and more vigorous, reaching 5 feet tall and wide. Clove currants grow to 6 feet high and wide. They strut their stuff in spring: bright yellow, red-tinged flowers spice the air with the perfume of vanilla and clove. Currants grow in long clusters (strigs) that can be quite showy, while gooseberries form singly or in small bunches. Incorporate currants in a mixed shrub border or form an informal, low hedge.

Most gooseberries are thorny and create great barriers. Their modest size (3 to 5 feet tall and wide) makes them ideal foundation plantings or an understory for spreading trees. Those with a weeping shape cascade nicely over a retaining wall. When pruned to a tree form, they become striking specimen plants lining a walk, or espaliered along a cool wall. Both currants and gooseberries grow well in large containers.

How to Grow

Climate

Currants and gooseberries are extremely hardy and have high chilling requirements. They prefer cool, humid summers and suffer when temperatures get into the mid-80s. Clove currants, native from Texas to Minnesota, can take whatever weather comes their way.

Exposure and Soil

In hot climates, site currants and gooseberries under high-branching trees with filtered sun or where they will receive morning sun. In cooler areas, they thrive in full sun. The plants prefer well-drained, slightly acid, good garden loam; they tolerate sandy soil if they are heavily mulched and get consistent watering.

When planting in a row, space red and white currants and gooseberries 4 feet apart, and black currants 5 feet apart.

Fertilizing

Renew the soil with a deep mulch every spring. Apply an all-purpose organic fertilizer yearly to provide nitrogen and potassium. Too much nitrogen stimulates succulent growth that is susceptible to mildew.

Watering

Currants and gooseberries are shallow rooted; if they dry out, they recover slowly and are more prone to mildew. Keep the soil moist initially; once the plants are established, provide about an inch of water a week.

Pruning

Prune all currants and gooseberries in winter to remove dead and weak branches and stimulate new fruiting wood.

Black currants bear most heavily on 1-year-old stems; train them as multistemmed bushes. If your new plants are dormant, trim them back to one bud per stem, and allow them to develop during the first summer. That winter, remove any weak growth; the remaining healthy stems will fruit the next summer. The following winter, cut all 2-year-old wood (that fruited in summer) down to the ground,

allowing six strong stems of 1-year-old wood to fruit the next summer. Continue to prune mature black currants this same way every year. Clove currants fruit on 1-year and older wood. They need pruning only to maintain shape and to remove dead or damaged wood.

Red and white currants and gooseberries bear fruit on new wood and on the spurs of 1- and 2-year-old wood. The age is easy to tell; older stems peel, and they get darker and thicker. These plants may be a hobbyist's dream come true; train them in decorative styles, including a fan espalier or three-level cordons on wires, or graft them onto other *Ribes* to transform them into small trees. For the less adventuresome, train them like black currants, with a balance between 1-, 2-, and 3-year-old stems.

Pests and Diseases

Currants (especially black currants) and gooseberries are hosts to white pine blister rust, which is fatal to pine trees, but the currants and gooseberries remain unscathed. The plants are banned in a number of counties that protect white pines because the fungus must live on both them and the pine trees to complete its life cycle. Although there are many rust-resistant varieties of currants and gooseberries, check with your local Cooperative Extension Service to be sure they are allowed in your area before you order plants. For resistance to diseases, pests, deer, cold, and drought, look no farther than clove currants.

Powdery mildew was once a most serious disease, especially on European gooseberries; now there are many resistant gooseberry varieties. Another fungal disease, anthracnose, discolors leaves, producing dark spots. Sulfur is a treatment for anthracnose, but avoid using it on gooseberries as it damages some varieties.

Occasional pests are aphids, mites, and scale. Currant fruit fly and gooseberry fruitworm larvae burrow in the fruits; control with *Bt*.

Harvesting

Harvest under-ripe fruit for the best jams, jellies, and juices. Fully ripe berries are sweeter and best for eating out of hand. To remove currants from a strig, use a table fork and gently run the tines down the cluster.

Currants yield 2 to 3 quarts of fruit per plant annually, gooseberries 3 to 4 quarts.

How to Purchase

Local nurseries carry bare-root currants and gooseberries in spring and container-grown plants throughout the growing season. Order bare-root plants from Burnt Ridge, Edible Landscaping, Hartmann's, Raintree, Indiana Berry, Nourse, and St. Lawrence.

Pollinizers

Currants (except for black currants) and all gooseberries are self-fruitful.

Varieties

Choose varieties that produce good edible fruits. Avoid native varieties that produce inferior fruits and ornamental varieties grown only for their flowers. Check with your local Cooperative Extension Service to be sure the plants are allowed in your area before you order.

BLACK CURRANT, *RIBES NIGRUM*

Plant more than one variety, as black currants need a pollinizer.
'Ben Sarek'—large fruit; compact bush to 36 in. tall; high yielding; good frost tolerance.

'Consort' (*R.* 'Kerry' × *R. ussuriense*)—assertive flavor preferred by many Europeans; highest in antioxidants; used for jelly; immune to rust.

'Titania'—large berries; excellent mild flavor; long season of ripening; vigorous, upright growth habit to 6 ft.; resistant to mildew and rust.

CLOVE CURRANT, *R. ODORATUM*

Look for species rather than named varieties.

RED CURRANT AND WHITE CURRANT, *R. RUBRUM* (*R. VULGARE, R. SATIVUM*)

'Blanka'—large, white fruit, flavorful; reliable, heavy yields; spreading growth habit; attractive green and red foliage.

'Jhonkheer Van Tets'—large, dark red fruit; superior flavor; untidy habit, grow as a cordon; mildew and aphid resistant; susceptible to late frosts, poor heat tolerance.

'Pink Champagne'—pink fruit; good flavor; upright growth, vigorous; no leaf diseases.

'Red Lake'—red berries; popular variety; resists rust and oak root fungus.

'White Imperial'—white berries; low acid, fairly sweet; compact, spreading, not erect; resistant to mildew and rust.

EUROPEAN GOOSEBERRY, *R. UVA-CRISPA* UNLESS OTHERWISE NOTED

'Hinnonmaki Yellow'—yellow-green fruit; great flavor reminiscent of apricot; bears midseason; spreading habit.

'Invicta'—large, high-quality, green fruit; spreading, thorny, large, vigorous, needs consistent pruning; resists mildew; Zones 4 to 9.

'Poorman' (American gooseberry, *R. hirtellum*)—red berries; high quality; ripens late; vigorous, productive; very hardy; resists mildew.

'Tixia'—large, bright red fruit; upright growth; few thorns.

'Welcome'—pink to red berries; makes red jam; almost thornless; somewhat resistant to anthracnose.

Eggplant

(aubergine)
Solanum melongena

Effort Scale

NO. 2
Must be planted annually
Some pest and disease problems
Watering and fertilizing necessary

Zones

Not applicable

Thumbnail Sketch

Herbaceous perennial grown as annual
24 to 36 in. tall
Propagate from seeds
Needs full sun and warm conditions
Leaves are grayish green and velvety, 4 to 5 in. long
Blooms in summer

Eggplants—both plants and fruits—are striking in and out of the garden. The fruit comes in a range of sizes and colors, including narrow Japanese, magenta and white heirloom 'Listada de Gandia', deep purple 'Dusky', and small white eggs.

Flowers are purple with yellow stamens, 1 to 2 in. across; some varieties showy
Fruits are purple, lavender, green, red, or white: edible; harvest in summer; most varieties showy
Use in flower bed, vegetable garden, herb garden, raised bed, or container

How to Use

In the Kitchen

Ratatouille, moussaka, parmigiana—the names of eggplant dishes reveal this versatile plant's Mediterranean origin. Grilled eggplant is one of my favorites; combine it with tomatoes in a vegetarian focaccia sandwich, or layer it in lasagna.

Except when prepared as a luxury item, such as pickled baby eggplant, use this vegetable fresh. Of course, you can always make extra parmigiana and freeze it for up to 3 months.

In the Landscape

Any one of the physical attributes of eggplant would make it a lovely plant; together they make eggplant one of the most beautiful vegetables for any landscape. The large, downy leaves with their purplish cast lend themselves to seductive adjectives like velvety and dusky, and the fruits to silky, smooth, and curvaceous. Add the spectacular fruit colors, which include dark purple to near black, white to lavender, green to red and orange—and some are even striped. Finish off with the gracefully drooping purple blossoms with contrasting bright yellow stamens for more eye-catching interest.

All eggplant fruits are decorative—the most common varieties with their large, dark purple, oval fruits and the smaller, slenderer Japanese type—gorgeous in a border or in an ornamental container combined with purple million bells spilling out the side. For a serene perennial border, choose tall bronze fennel and lavender *Verbena bonariensis* for the background; feature the large, gray leaves of cardoon and artichoke, the pink flowers of echinacea, and a collection of Japanese eggplant mid-border; and for the front, plant pink-flowering chives and thyme. Now that's an edible landscape!

How to Grow

Eggplant is a tender herbaceous perennial that is usually grown as an annual in North America. While many of eggplant's climate requirements are similar to those of tomato, its relative, it has less tolerance for cool weather and frost. Do not plant seedlings in the ground until at least 3 weeks after your last frost date and nighttime temperatures are at least 55°F. Start eggplant seedlings inside about 2 months before transplanting. Sow seeds ¼ inch deep and an inch apart in a flat with commercial seed-starting mix. Keep the seedbed moist and in a very warm room.

Eggplant grows best in full sun, in well-drained garden loam amended with compost and fertilized with blood meal or fish meal. Six plants are enough for the average family. Set plants 2 feet apart, mulch with a few inches of compost, and stake the large-fruited varieties. When the plants start to flower, apply a balanced organic fertilizer. Eggplant needs moderate watering; never let it dry out.

Pests and Diseases

Flea beetles, spider mites, and whiteflies can be a nuisance; mildew will develop in very humid climates. Where flea beetles are severe, they disfigure and stunt the plants. Eggplant is very susceptible to fusarium wilt; rotate the plantings to where no eggplants, tomatoes, peppers, or potatoes have grown for 3 years. If you have consistent problems with flea beetles or fusarium wilt, try growing eggplant in large containers instead of in the ground.

Harvesting

The fruit is ready to pick when it is fully colored, but before it begins to lose its sheen and before the seeds inside turn brown. To help prevent fruits from deteriorating, cut rather than pull them from the plant. Plants will produce more when you harvest regularly. On average, a plant yields six to eight large fruits; small-fruited varieties yield more.

How to Purchase

Local nurseries offer a limited selection of eggplant seeds and transplants. For the greatest selection, go to Renee's, Johnny's, Nichols, and Tomato Growers; for heirlooms, check out Seeds of Change, Baker Creek, and Seed Savers. Choose short-season varieties that mature in 65 days or less for northern climates; select Italian varieties for warm-summer areas.

Varieties

'Dusky'—deep purple, pear-shaped fruit to 5 in.; popular; productive; great for containers; early, 56 days.
'Fairy Tale'—hybrid; striking 4-in., narrow fruit striped maroon and white; dwarf, great for containers; 55 days.
'Ichiban'—Japanese type; deep purple, slender fruit to 8 in.; excellent quality; 61 days.
'Listada de Gandia'—Italian heirloom; large, 6- to 8-in., elongated fruit, striking magenta and white stripes; late, 90 days.
'Neon'—hybrid; bright magenta, 4- to 6-in., elongated fruit; productive; 65 days.
'Orient Express'—hybrid; deep purple, elongated fruit to 8 in.; early, 58 days.
'Rosa Bianca'—Italian heirloom; dramatic, large, globe-shaped, lavender to white fruit; 80 days.

Elderberry (elder)

Sambucus spp.

Effort Scale

NO. 2
Suckers must be removed on most varieties
Pruning necessary
Harvesting and processing are time consuming

Zones

3 to 9, depending on species

Thumbnail Sketch

Deciduous shrub or tree
6 to 30 ft. tall
Propagate from seeds, cuttings, or suckers
Needs full sun; most tolerate partial shade
Leaves are divided into leaflets, medium green or purplish black, 6 to 12 in. long
Blooms in June or July
Flowers are small, white, or pink, in clusters 6 to 10 in. across, fragrant
Fruits and flowers are edible; harvest in summer and fall
Use as informal hedgerow, screen, accent plant; in shrub border or wildlife garden

How to Use

In the Kitchen

Elderberries—small, blue or purplish black fruits—are an excellent source of vitamin C and antioxidants. Enjoy them cooked in pies and jellies or fermented into champagne or wine. Add dried berries when you make muffins. Mix the flowers into pancake batter to sweeten a Sunday breakfast. Or brew them into an aromatic tea.

Caution: Do *not* eat any elderberry fruit or flowers raw. Red elderberry fruit is *not* edible even when cooked and can cause digestive problems. The stems, leaves, bark, branches, and roots of *all* elderberries contain toxic alkaloids; remove them before using the flowers or berries.

Elderberries grow in large clusters. Always separate the berries from the tiny stems before cooking. One technique is to hold the clusters over a large pan and use a fork to dislodge the berries. Another is to briefly freeze the clusters on cookie sheets; before they defrost, "tickle" the clusters and the berries will fall off. You can freeze, can, or dry elderberries as well as make them into jam, jellies, or wine.

In the Landscape

A number of elderberry species grow in North America; some are native, and others were introduced from Europe. Native elderberries can be vigorous—sprawling to 30 feet or more. They provide food for birds in wild gardens and, if their fruit is tasty, for the homeowner, too. Using European and American stock, breeders developed a number of varieties that are less unruly and make handsome additions to the yard, including the very showy 'Black Beauty' and 'Guincho Purple', both with striking pink flowers and purple foliage. All of these selections are hardy, deciduous shrubs, 6 to 10 feet tall, easily pruned to clumping, somewhat fountain-shaped shrubs.

Elderberries have magnificent clusters of white or pink flowers, decorative berries, and long compound leaves. This combination of features makes them useful in landscapes, with—or instead of—weigela, lilacs, or other large deciduous shrubs. Elderberries are excellent informal hedges and screens, lovely in shrub borders and wildlife gardens and as the focal point of a large perennial planting.

How to Grow

Climate
Elderberries are extremely hardy. Wild varieties grow from Florida north to Nova Scotia and as far west as California. That said, the most notable fruiting varieties are seldom grown except in cold-winter climates.

Exposure and Soil
The plants are most productive growing in moist, fertile soil in full sun, but will tolerate partial shade. They can grow in wet conditions only with very good drainage.

Fertilizing
Apply a 6-inch-deep layer of mulch in spring to provide nutrients and control weeds.

Watering
For elderberries, 1 inch of water a week is sufficient.

Pruning
Once the bushes are 3 years old, prune every spring to control growth and renew fruiting wood. Cut out any deadwood, weak branches, and all shoots over 3 years old; prune the remaining younger shoots back by half. Elderberries tend to sucker and spread; keep them within limits by removing suckers that extend more than 2 feet from the crown whenever they appear. For elders growing in the lawn, use a mower to trim off succulent suckers. If a plant gets totally out of bounds; cut it down to the ground to renew it.

Pests and Diseases
Birds find elderberries irresistible and can plunder the bushes overnight. Pick berries as soon as they are ripe. The best solution is to net the shrubs, which is easier when they're pruned 6 feet or shorter.

Harvesting
Ripe berries are deeply colored and slightly soft; pick them before they start to shrivel.

How to Purchase

Local nurseries offer bare-root or container-grown elderberries. Order from Edible Landscaping, Forestfarm, Miller, One Green World, or Raintree.

Pollinizers
Most varieties require a pollinizer. For good fruit set, plant more than one variety.

Varieties
AMERICAN ELDERBERRY, *SAMBUCUS CANADENSIS*
The native American sweet elder has the largest and most flavorful fruit. The following cultivars are compact, growing only 6 to 10 feet tall. They are best adapted to cold-winter regions in Zones 3 to 8. Grow two plants to ensure pollination.

Thyme Garden Herb Company in Alsea, Oregon, has marvelous display gardens. In early summer, elderberries are at their height of splendor; the fragrant umbels of off-white edible flowers attract beneficial insects. Caution: Do not eat the flowers raw.

'Adams'—popular; large, juicy berries; ripens early September.
'Johns'—large, purple-black berries; ripens mid-August.
'Nova'—somewhat self-fruitful; sweet, heavy bearer; ripens in mid-August.
'York'—vigorous bush; large berries; ripens in September; yellow fall foliage; plant with 'Nova' as a pollinizer.

BLUE ELDERBERRY, *S. CERULEA* (*S. MEXICANA*)
Best suited to the West Coast, Zones 5 to 9, this very tall, sprawling, self-fertile species is best used as a screen or on a large property. There are no named varieties.

EUROPEAN ELDERBERRY, *S. NIGRA*
While less hardy (Zones 5 to 7) and less flavorful than American elderberry, the European species is more vigorous, growing 10 to 20 ft. tall, and includes some striking varieties. The following elders are very attractive and not as vigorous. When choosing for fruit, avoid varieties bred only for their decorative foliage. Plants are generally self-fertile.
'Allesso'—popular in Europe; dark green foliage, large flower clusters; handsome plant 4 to 5 ft. tall.
'Black Beauty'—bears good fruit in fall when pollinized by another European elder; spectacular purple-black foliage; lemon-scented, pink blossoms; grows 5 to 6 ft. tall.
'Guincho Purple'—good fruit; deep purple foliage; pink flowers; striking plant to 15 ft. tall.
'Sutherland Gold'—finely cut leaves emerge coppery red in spring and become golden yellow by summer; juicy, deep purple fruits contrast beautifully; grow in partial shade to maintain foliage color; adds a graceful look while lighting up any dim part of the landscape; 5 to 8 ft. tall.
'Thundercloud'—deep red to purple foliage; abundance of reddish pink flower clusters in spring, followed by tasty, bluish black berries in fall; upright shrub to 10 ft. tall.

Feijoa

See Pineapple guava

Fig

Ficus carica

Effort Scale

NO. 2
Raking of spoiled fruits and dead leaves necessary
Sizeable harvest
Pest and disease control needed in some climates

Zones

8 to 11

Thumbnail Sketch

Deciduous tree
Standard, 15 to 30 ft. tall; dwarf varieties, to 10 ft. tall
Propagate by grafting or air layering or from cuttings
Needs full sun
Leaves are large, medium green, deeply lobed, palmate, 4 to 9 in. long
Usually "blooms" in summer
Flowers are insignificant
Fruits are edible; harvest in summer and fall
Use as shade tree, interest tree, espalier, large shrub, screen, or container plant

The lawn growing beneath this fig tree makes it a cinch to rake up the fallen fruit. However, the tree's size overpowers the house and ensures only the birds and squirrels can feast on the fruit up high.

How to Use

In the Kitchen

A ripe, plump, soft fig—black, brown, or green—is a real old-fashioned sweetmeat. Figs are familiar yet exotic. Fig Newtons were standard lunch-box desserts for many of us, and dehydrated figs are favorite dried fruits. And then there are fresh figs—heavenly simply eaten out of hand and so sublime poached in white wine syrup and served with pecans over ice cream. Or combine them with another Mediterranean favorite—olives—in a green salad, or stuff them with whipped Stilton cheese as a light yet hearty appetizer. Dry figs or can them. Southerners traditionally put them up in brandy. Plain or fancy, figs figure into a lot of great food.

Just for the record: the "fruits" of the fig are not true fruits but actually fleshy receptacles for the tiny flowers that grow inside.

In the Landscape

A fig tree is a beauty the year round. Its smooth gray bark, reminiscent of an elephant's hide, is dramatic against a sodden winter sky. In spring and summer, the bark contrasts sharply with the tree's rich green, deeply lobed leaves. In some climates, the leaves turn bright yellow in autumn. The trunk can become gnarled with age.

Although figs can grow to 30 feet, you can easily keep them pruned to 10 feet. As large trees, figs offer dense shade. As small trees or shrubs—in or out of a container—they make superb accent plants. The eye-catching bark and leaves lend themselves well to espalier.

A fig's softness makes fruit drop a nuisance if the tree is planted too near a patio or deck, but the close-up beauty of the plant and the aroma of the fruit make them worthwhile.

How to Grow

Climate

A mature fig tree is semi-hardy (to 5 to 10°F).

Exposure and Soil

Figs require full sun; the more heat they receive, the sweeter the fruits. They thrive in very well-drained, average to poor soil. Add lime where the soil is acid; in parts of Texas with highly alkaline soil, acidify the soil to prevent root rots.

Planting

In borderline cold areas or where summers are cool, provide figs with extra heat by planting them near a south- or west-facing wall; heat-absorbing pavement nearby also helps. The harvest from container-grown plants is limited but still worth the effort. In Zone 8 (where the plants often freeze back to the ground) and much of the Southeast, figs grow best as large shrubs. Most figs need only about 100 hours of winter chill.

Fertilizing

Figs are shallow rooted; mulch to save water and discourage weeds. Use organic mulches for the nutrients. Too much nitrogen promotes leaf formation rather than fruit production. Apply nitrogen fertilizers only if the tree is producing less than 12 inches of new growth a year.

Watering

Water young figs weekly—more in very hot weather. Mature figs are drought tolerant, but in arid climates, deep watering every 2 weeks optimizes fruit quality and production. In the Southeast, sandy soils, nematode problems, and drought make supplemental watering necessary.

Pruning

In most areas, train figs to a single-trunk, open-vase shape, with three or four main limbs that begin to branch out about 3 to 4 feet up the trunk. In cold-winter areas, train figs as large shrubs. Allow young trees to sucker until they have five or six more basal branches. If they are killed in a freeze, cut them back and allow new suckers to develop.

The type of fig—one crop a year or two—dictates the manner of pruning. In the two-crop types, such as 'Black Mission' and 'Conadria', the early crop of figs (called breba) is borne on the ends of the previous year's growth, usually in early summer. These figs are good for cold climates and cool-summer areas as the fruits are produced early in the summer and not lost to fall frosts. When pruning, do not cut off much end growth or you risk losing that year's harvest.

Fig trees require only light pruning to produce fruit. Prune out winter damage or broken limbs at any time. Once the tree is established, prune to control size and growth, right after summer fruiting. For fall-maturing varieties, prune half the branches in summer, the rest after fruiting.

Pests and Diseases

Figs are susceptible to very few pests and diseases. In humid southern areas, fig rust makes rusty spots on the leaves and can cause defoliation. Spray with neutral copper when the leaves reach full size and again a month later. Where nematodes might be a problem, plant in nematode-free soil and keep trees well watered, or grow them in containers.

In some parts of the South, tiny insects can enter the "eye" at the bottom of the fruit, introduce diseases, and "sour" it. To prevent damage, plant varieties with closed eyes, such as 'Celeste', 'Conadria', and 'Texas Everbearing'. In gopher country, plant trees in wire baskets to avoid gnawed roots. Squirrels, rats, and birds glory in a fig harvest. To save some of the crop, wrap bird netting around the whole tree if it is young, or around a few large branches when mature.

Harvesting

Fully ripe fruits are fairly soft and droop at the neck; figs do not ripen once harvested. If the stem exudes white sap, it is not ripe enough. In humid climates, use a food dehydrator when drying figs. A mature tree yields 25 to 35 pounds of fruit per year.

How to Purchase

Local nurseries carry bare-root figs in early spring and container-grown trees all summer. Order from Bay Laurel, Edible Landscaping, One Green World, Trees of Antiquity, and Willis. Tripple Brook carries the especially tough 'Hardy Chicago'.

Pollinizers

Figs for the home garden are self-fruitful.

Varieties

A number of factors will influence your choice: climate, disease resistance, a breba crop (varieties producing an early crop in addition to the main crop later in the season are noted below), tree size, and flavor. Most figs are great fresh and dried.

Some figs have European and American names; others have different monikers in various parts of the country. This list gives the widely accepted name followed by alternate names.

A harvest of figs is great fresh or dried. Super sweet, figs are nutritious and very sensual. My favorite ways to prepare them are halved and topped with blue cheese or wrapped with bacon (secured with a toothpick) and quickly grilled.

'Alma'—greenish yellow fruit, light breba crop; closed eye; needs a long, warm summer; hardy, small tree; best for Texas and the Gulf Coast.

'Black Jack'—long, purplish fruit with red flesh, sweet and juicy; ripens in summer; semi-dwarf, good for containers; ideal for California gardens.

'Black Mission' ('Mission')—black fruit, rich flavor, prolific breba crop; large tree; resistant to oak root fungus; popular in California.

'Celeste' ('Blue Celeste', 'Honey Fig', 'Violette')—bronze-colored fruit with tight eye; light breba crop; hardiest of common figs; seldom pruned as it reduces crop; popular in Southeast.

'Conadria'—white fruit, excellent flavor; resistant to decay; light breba crop; small eye makes it good for the Southeast; large tree best in hot climates.

'Hardy Chicago' ('Bensonhurst Purple')—sweet, purplish brown fruit in late summer; hardiest fig, can die back to the ground in winter, resprout in spring, and fruit prolifically; grows well in a container.

'King' ('Desert King')—deep green, sweet; good breba crop, little fall crop; do not prune heavily; great for cool coastal gardens.

'Striped Tiger' ('Panachee')—unusual green and white striped fruit; fine flavor, sweet, good fresh; ripens late; not hardy, best in Northern California.

'Texas Everbearing' ('Dwarf Everbearing', 'Brown Turkey')—dark brown fruit, sweet, best used fresh; moderately closed eye; light breba crop; prune to force new growth; good in containers; quite hardy, good for cooler areas of the Southeast.

'Violette de Bordeaux' ('Negronne')—'Black Mission' type for cooler climates; rich flavor; breba crop; small tree, good for containers; very hardy.

Filbert

(hazelnut)
Corylus spp.

Effort Scale

NO. 3
Vulnerable to some diseases and pests, including birds and squirrels
Moderate amount of pruning needed
Mulching beneficial
Some raking required
Harvest must be processed

Zones

4 to 9

Thumbnail Sketch

Deciduous tree or shrub
Standard, 15 to 25 ft. tall; Turkish, to 75 ft. tall

Filberts are popular in the Northwest; in the Midwest, folks call them hazelnuts. Whatever name they're known by, these striking fringelike coverings that range in color from green to burgundy appear on the immature nut clusters of some varieties in summer.

Propagate by layering
Needs full sun; afternoon shade in warm climates
Leaves are dark green or purple, woolly underneath, 4 in. long
Blooms in winter or very early spring
Female flowers are inconspicuous; male flowers are showy catkins
Nuts are edible; harvest in early fall
Use as large shrub, hedge, screen, small multistemmed tree, or interest tree

How to Use

In the Kitchen

Filberts are tasty, round, hazel-colored nuts. In Italy, they are used in nougat and are famous in gelato, often combined with chocolate. Oh, how we love Nutella. Throughout Europe, where hazelnuts are the original praline nuts, they are celebrated in chocolates of all descriptions. The nuts are a delectable and nutritious snack when roasted and salted, and they make marvelous poultry stuffing. Toss them in a green salad for crunch or add them to vegetable and rice dishes. Whip up memorable desserts: filbert pie, filbert meringues, and fudge and brownies with filberts added. How decadent can you get?

Store filberts in high humidity with temperatures in the 50°F range; they quickly become rancid at room temperature. The foolproof way to preserve filberts is to shell and freeze them. To toast, place shelled nuts in a shallow pan and bake in a 350°F oven until fragrant—about 15 minutes; watch them because they burn easily. Remove the skins by rubbing a rough towel vigorously over the nuts while they are still warm.

In the Landscape

Filberts have large, dramatic leaves that clearly stand out from each other. Most European varieties are multistemmed—lovely trained to sculptural shapes. Pyramidal Turkish filbert makes a great screen when given ample room to spread. The fringed, frilly green coverings on the nuts—occasionally pink edged, burgundy, or cream—grow in clusters of three to seven and add another level of ornamentation to this already beautiful tree. In winter, attractive male catkins decorate the bare branches.

Grow filberts as decorative screens or accent plants. Most types sucker profusely, making them admirable choices for informal hedges or screens. In England, they are popular in hedgerows, as they provide shelter and food for wildlife.

How to Grow

Climate

Although European filberts are quite hardy, their late-winter flowering exposes the delicate blossoms to frosts. Winterkill generally happens around 15°F, limiting nut production and consequently the filbert's distribution.

Filberts grow best in the inland areas of the Northwest. All filberts do poorly in arid areas and in high summer heat. Success in growing European filberts in the East has been mixed; try locating them in a cold, northern exposure to prevent a warm winter day from inducing premature bloom. Or grow the hardier Turkish tree hazel.

Exposure and Soil

Filberts need full sun in cool coastal climates and afternoon shade in warmer ones. They do best in deep, well-drained garden loam. Mulch with 3 to 4 inches of organic matter.

Planting

Plant filberts 15 feet apart; for a hedge, space plants 5 feet apart.

Fertilizing

Organic mulches generally provide ample nutrition. If the leaves become small or pale, or the shoots are growing less than 6 inches a year, apply nitrogen in moderate amounts. In cold-winter areas, too much nitrogen produces growth susceptible to winterkill.

Watering

Filberts need occasional deep watering in arid-summer areas. In the Northwest, mature trees seldom need watering.

Pruning

For a tree form, prune the young plant to a single trunk with four to six main branches and train to an open center; for a multistemmed shrub, prune to three main trunks. Filberts bear on the previous year's wood, so thin lightly—at the end of the blooming season—to encourage new growth. For a single-trunk tree, remove suckers three or four times a year.

Pests and Diseases

Aphids, mites, and budworms may be a problem; control with dormant oil in winter and early spring. Common pests include jays, crows, and squirrels.

The most serious problem is Eastern filbert blight—a fatal fungal bark disease on the East Coast and in commercial plantings in the West. Spray with oil and copper at bud break and again a month later for some protection, or select resistant varieties.

Harvesting

Filberts normally bear nuts in alternate years. A mature filbert yields up to 20 pounds of nuts during a bearing year. The nut is ripe when you can push it around within the husk and loosen it—even though it may still be slightly green. If you can, gather nuts before they fall and the birds and squirrels discover them. Some varieties shell more easily than others; remove the green husk and inner shell of the nut.

How to Purchase

Buy bare-root filberts in spring or container-grown plants in summer from local nurseries. Order from Edible Landscaping, One Green World, Rhora's (which carries uncommon varieties), or Willis. Raintree offers a huge selection.

Pollinizers

A filbert needs a pollinizer. Choose varieties carefully, as not all filbert varieties pollinize all others; compatible cultivars must bloom at similar times.

Varieties

Be careful when choosing filbert varieties, since some are only ornamental and bear few or inferior nuts.

AMERICAN FILBERT, *CORYLUS AMERICANA*
To 8 ft. tall and producing showy catkins in spring followed by small nuts, American filbert is most successful in Zones 5 to 8.

CHINESE FILBERT, *C. CHINENSIS*
This filbert is an ornamental, low-maintenance shrub to 6 ft. high. It bears small nuts in cream-colored, decorative clusters.

EUROPEAN FILBERT, *C. AVELLANA*
'Barcelona'—most popular filbert; commercial variety; large, excellent quality; 'Halls Giant' is pollinizer; some resistance to blight and mites; needs moderate chilling.
'Clark'—good nut production; no problems with Eastern blight or filbert mites.
'Epsilon'—medium to small nuts; excellent pollinizer for other filberts; very resistant to filbert blight.
'Lewis'—large nuts; bears early; pollinizes 'Epsilon'; resists filbert blight.
'Halls Giant'—grows to 15 ft.; large nuts; great pollinizer for 'Barcelona' and other varieties; medium blight resistance.
'Santiam'—semi-dwarf; productive; blight resistant.

PURPLE LEAF FILBERT, *C. MAXIMA 'PURPUREA'*
This shrubby filbert to 10 ft. tall bears showy catkins in spring and purple leaves that hold their color until midsummer. Its nut clusters are in burgundy-fringed cases. Pollinize with American filbert. Purple leaf filbert is disease resistant and adapted to Zones 4 to 8.

TURKISH TREE HAZEL (TURKISH FILBERT), *C. COLURNA*
A large, graceful, non-suckering tree with a pyramidal form to 75 ft. tall, Turkish tree hazel produces small, pointed nuts with good flavor. This species, which resists filbert blight, is widely adapted to Zones 4 to 7.

Foxberry

See Cranberry and Lingonberry

Fraises des bois

See Strawberry

Gai lon

See Broccoli and Cauliflower

Galangal

See Ginger

Garlic chives

See Chives

In Florida and Hawaii, ginger can get 4 to 5 feet tall and 6 to 8 feet wide. Yet the spreading rhizome takes well to container culture, making it feasible for northern gardeners to grow the pungent spice in a barrel.

Ginger

Ginger, *Zingiber officinale*
Mioga ginger, *Z. mioga*
Galangal, *Alpinia galanga*

Effort Scale

NO. 2
Frequent fertilizing needed
Constant watering necessary
Winter protection necessary in most areas

Zones

7 to 11

Thumbnail Sketch

Herbaceous perennial with tuberous rhizomes
3 to 4 ft. tall
Propagate from division of rhizomes
Needs partial or full shade
Leaves are light green, straplike, 6 to 12 in. long
Blooms in spring
Flowers are yellow-green touched with purple, insignificant, seldom seen
Rhizomes and shoots are edible: harvest in fall; mioga flower buds are edible
Requires many months of temperatures above 55°F to mature the rhizomes
Use in shade border, raised bed, or container, or as houseplant

How to Use

In the Kitchen

Fleshy ginger rhizomes (called "roots" in the food world), with their hot and pungent bite, are a traditional Asian flavoring. Ginger is in the same family as turmeric, cardamom, and galangal, all of which prefer tropical conditions and have strong, distinctive flavors. Grate fresh, peeled ginger rhizomes into vegetable dishes and marinades, slice into stir-fry dishes, and use in just about any recipe that calls for soy sauce and garlic. Crystallized ginger root is a delicious addition to Asian coleslaw and zucchini bread. Puree young, tender ginger shoots and leaves to add zing to sauces and soups.

Use mioga ginger buds and young shoots in tempura. The edible flower buds appear at ground level; enjoy them raw, and pickle the shoots for a garnish.

Finely sliced galangal root is a common ingredient in Thai cuisine, where it is used in traditional curries, rice and seafood dishes, and its famous coconut soup.

Store whole rhizomes in a warm, dry place for 1 to 2 months; for longer storage, peel and puree the rhizomes, and store in vinegar or freeze. Pickle sliced ginger and galangal or freeze. Candy ginger in sugar syrup.

In the Landscape

The stems of ginger and its relatives can grow to 4 feet. Their narrow, bright green leaves give these species an airier appearance than the strictly ornamental gingers. Plant them with begonias and cannas. If you don't harvest the plants regularly in frost-free areas, they grow quite large. When grown indoors, they stay much smaller and are a nice foil for larger-leaved houseplants.

How to Grow

Climate

These tender, deciduous perennials are tropical plants needing long, warm, humid summers to develop sizeable rhizomes. While they are especially well adapted to Florida, the Gulf States, and Hawaii, they are definitely worth growing in other climates.

Exposure and Soil

They prefer a warm, shady spot with rich, moist, fast-draining soil; they will rot in cold, wet soil.

Planting

In Florida and similar warm, humid regions, plant ginger in early spring and harvest it 7 to 9 months later. In cold-winter areas, start ginger indoors in spring and move it outside when the temperature is above 70°F. Plant the rhizomes in 5-gallon containers—large enough for good rhizome development and small enough to move indoors so the rhizomes can mature in fall. Use a light potting mix containing peat moss, loam, sand, and compost.

Three plants are sufficient for most families. When planting outdoors, prepare a 2-by-3-foot bed by digging to a depth of 12 inches, mixing in 4 to 5 inches of well-rotted manure and compost, and gently firming the soil. Make an indentation and firmly place 2-inch-long pieces of rhizome on top of the soil, 12 inches apart. Do not cover with soil or the rhizomes will rot. Lightly cover with a few inches of organic mulch. Keep the soil evenly moist and fertilize every month with hydrolyzed fish. In dry climates, occasionally sprinkle the foliage with water.

Harvesting

Under most conditions, ginger is ready to harvest after 5 months, but for a bigger harvest, wait a few months. Ginger rhizomes stop growing and go dormant when the temperature dips below 55°F for a few weeks. At this point, either harvest the rhizomes as they are or bring the entire plant indoors and keep it in a warm, well-lit room until the rhizomes fully mature. Carefully harvest the rhizomes to avoid nicking them. When harvesting, save a small rhizome or two to replant, thus maintaining your own source of this delightful spice.

How to Purchase

Buy fresh ginger and galangal roots at produce stands or in Asian markets in spring. If possible, choose rhizomes that show good growth buds (like "eyes" on a potato). Look closely; some markets break off the shoots to keep the rhizomes from sprouting. Cut the rhizomes into 2-inch pieces and let them dry for a few days before planting. If you are unable to find them locally, some Asian seed companies and Stokes Tropicals carry them. Asian nurseries in Hawaii and Florida carry mioga ginger.

Gooseberry

See Currant and Gooseberry

Grape

Vitis spp.

Effort Scale

NO. 3
Susceptible to some pests and diseases
Extensive yearly pruning needed
Harvesting and preserving are time consuming

Zones

4 to 10

Thumbnail Sketch

Deciduous, climbing woody vine
Can reach 50 to 100 ft.; usually kept at 12 to 20 ft.
Propagate by grafting or budding, from seeds or cuttings, or by layering

Needs full sun
Leaves are medium or bluish green, palmately lobed, 4 to 8 in. across
Blooms in spring
Flowers grow in clusters, insignificant
Fruits and leaves are edible; harvest fruits in early fall, leaves in summer
Use on pergola, fence, arbor, or patio cover; train as a weeping tree

How to Use

In the Kitchen

Grapes, wonderful grapes! These fruits are luscious and juicy when fresh. A platter piled high with different kinds of grapes makes a lovely centerpiece and an elegant dessert along with cheese. Some grapes, such as 'Concord', though eaten fresh are mainly used to make jelly. Grape juice is a nutritious choice—and more complex when made from wine grapes; and, of course, wine grapes have a story all their own. The latter are not necessarily palatable fresh, but where wine is concerned, the proof of the vintage is in the drinking, not the eating.

Grapes are traditionally grown on arbors and, with the many varieties to choose from, thrive in a wide range of climates. This rustic arbor is the entry to the Children's Garden at Old Westbury Gardens on Long Island, New York.

Blue table grapes make excellent pie; white grapes add texture and flavor to chicken or meat salads; any grape suitable for eating out of hand belongs in a fruit cup. Can grapes whole or as juice. Freeze seedless grapes whole or dry to make raisins. Preserve grapes as jelly, jam, and conserves. Or pickle them and make them into vinegar. The most famous way of preserving grapes, of course, is to make them into wine. Choose varieties carefully for wine.

The fruit of the vine is not the grape's only gift. Dolmas, brined grape leaves stuffed with a meat mixture, are a Middle Eastern delicacy. The best varieties for tasty leaves, according to grape guru Lon Rombough, include all vinifera grapes and 'Aurora', 'Baco Noir', 'Beauty Seedless', 'Flame Seedless', 'Perlette', and 'Valiant'.

In the Landscape

Grapes are gnarled, woody, climbing vines with peeling bark. Dramatic lobed leaves are medium blue-green. Most turn yellow in fall; some turn red.

You can train grapevines to climb on or cling to many different structures. They are beautiful on pergolas; the grapes themselves are eye-catching hanging down through the lattice of a patio arbor. To espalier grapes against a wall, string wires along the wall to support the vine. Espalier treatment on a south-facing wall is advantageous in cool-summer areas; the wall absorbs extra heat that sweetens the grapes. Train grapes as small weeping trees as a focal point near a patio. Or line a walk or arrange them geometrically on the edge of an herb garden to supply an enthusiastic winemaker.

A mini-vineyard is another option for the home landscape. Line a dozen or so vines up a drive and surround them with a hedge of lavender to form a small vineyard; make a larger planting in a rect-

angle of vines on wires and surrounded by shrub roses; or design an archway of vines across your driveway. It will give drama and help the vines to soak up extra heat. You don't have to visit Tuscany to sit under an arbor and smell the ripening grapes, to reach up and pluck a few ripe ones, or to just lean back and enjoy a glass of homemade wine—that's fine living in your own yard.

How to Grow

Four major classes of grapes grow in the United States: American, European, muscadine, and hybrids of the previous three. They differ in taste, use, climate adaptability, pruning requirements, and disease susceptibility.

American grapes (aka fox grapes), native to the Northeast, grow in bunches, have skins that easily slip off, and are generally eaten fresh or made into jelly, juice, and occasionally wine.

European grapes have tight skins and a typically winey flavor and consist of three types: wine, dessert, and raisin.

Muscadine grapes, best characterized by 'Scuppernong', are native to the Southeast. They grow in loose clusters, have a slight musky flavor, and are eaten fresh or made into jelly and occasionally a fruity wine.

Hybrids combine characteristics of American, European, and muscadine grapes.

For more information on growing grapes refer to Lon Rombough's *Grape Grower: A Guide to Organic Viticulture*; for info on creating a mini-winery, Jeff Cox's *From Vines to Wines: The Complete Guide to Growing Grapes and Making Your Own Wine*. A web search on "wine making" reveals dozens of wine-making suppliers and how-to sites. But the definitive source of information is the University of California at Davis's website, wineserver.ucdavis.edu.

Climate

You can grow some type of grape in all but the high desert and coldest parts of the Midwest. All grapes are heat lovers, growing strong and producing sweet fruits in the sun. Without heat, grapes are sour and the vines are disease prone. The American 'Concord' type is hardiest and is the principal grape grown east of the Rocky Mountains and north of Delaware. European grapes are less hardy, usually tolerating cold only to 5°F and requiring many hours of heat to produce good grapes. Although grown in milder sections of the East and Midwest, they are best suited to California, Arizona, and Oregon. In the Southeast, muscadine grapes thrive. They take heat and humidity, are fairly tender, and are seldom grown north of Delaware. Many hybrids have been developed for specific areas of the country. Consult your Cooperative Extension Service for information about climate adaptability of the variety you are interested in. It is important to choose varieties suitable for your area.

Exposure and Soil

All grapes require full sun. In the coldest areas, plant against south-facing walls and provide extra shelter during the chilliest nights. Grapes need deep, well-drained soil. They are not as fussy as most fruits about fertility but will fruit better on fertile soil.

Fertilizing

Apply compost in spring; if the vines have been pale in the past, apply manure or some other form of nitrogen. Too much nitrogen at season's end produces few grapes and lush foliage susceptible to winter cold. In cold areas, do not apply nitrogen after midsummer.

It may never occur to you to grow wine grapes if you're not planning to make wine, but there's good reason to do it. Wine grapes make scrumptious jelly and grape juice that are high in antioxidants. My Zinfandel jelly is fabulous!

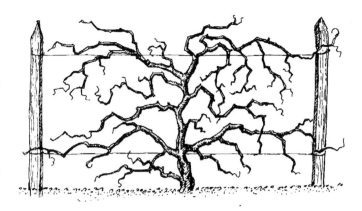

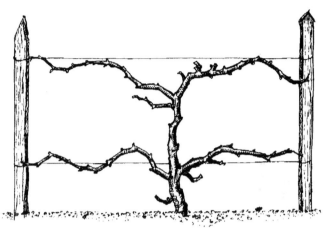

The four-arm Kniffen system works well for training American grapes and most wine grapes on wires. Above: Before pruning, the vine has a lot of extra wood. Below: After pruning, only the four "arms," each with 8 to 12 buds, remain.

Watering

In arid climates, encourage grapevines to grow deep roots with occasional deep watering that penetrates the soil to 3 feet. Apply water to the base of the plants, since grapes in arid climates develop fungus problems if watered from above. Grapes grown on sandy soils in the Southeast respond well to drip irrigation. In cold-winter areas, stop watering after August to allow the vines to harden off for winter.

Pruning

All grapes require heavy pruning to maintain the vine at a manageable size (an unpruned vine can stretch 100 feet); to encourage continuous growth of new wood and fruiting buds (grapes bear fruit on the current year's growth); to remove unproductive old canes (excess growth from the preceding season); and to favor 1-year-old wood that will be ready to take over the next year (the best fruiting wood is produced from the buds of the preceding year's wood).

Train grapevines to have a strong basic scaffold (trunk) with branches only in the renewal area; prune all these branches yearly. The renewal area can be 7 to 8 feet high up on an arbor, spread out on four arms, or trained along a fence.

Different types of grapes require different types of pruning. American grapes do not bear fruit on buds near the main stem; leave longer canes than you would for other types. Leave at least 10 to 12 buds on each cane. European wine grapes bear too heavily for that many buds; cut back to two or three buds—a spur. Prune off most of the previous year's growth; leave only these few spurs near the main trunk.

Muscadine grapes bear on spurs that produce for 3 or 4 years. Prune severely to keep vigorous canes from crowding each other out and for aesthetics. Train them on a single wire 5 feet off the ground or on arbors; cut back annually to three-bud spurs.

Arrange grapes to be trained against a fence or on parallel wires in the four-arm Kniffen system. In this system, train four canes—two in each direction (see illustration). Use a sturdy support as grapevines are heavy and long lived. This training system is most commonly used for spur- and cane-pruned grapes.

Pests and Diseases

Japanese beetles are sometimes a problem, birds raid vines in some areas, deer munch the fruit and leaves, grape berry moth larvae can chew their way through grapes, and grape leafrollers deform the leaves.

Fungal diseases are the limiting factor when growing grapes, especially in humid climates—mildew (powdery white fungus on leaves and fruit), anthracnose (blotches of brown spots on leaves and fruits), and black rot (turns fruit black and rotten). Select varieties of American, muscadine, or hybrid grapes, as they resist diseases better than classic European-type grapes. Good pruning provides good air circulation. Choose the right grape for a particular climate and avoid susceptible varieties. Avoid grapes that require an aggressive fungicide program. In wet weather even these measures do not seem to help. In arid climates, to avoid overspray, do not plant grapes near lawns.

Pierce's disease is a serious grape problem in the Southeast; there is no cure. In affected areas, plant muscadine grapes or an immune European grape ('Blue Lake', 'Lake Emerald', 'Morris', or 'Stover').

Harvesting

Cut bunches of grapes when they are fully colored and sweet. Ripe grapes come off easily in your hand, and their seeds are brown. Grapes do not ripen further after picking.

How to Purchase

Buy bare root in late winter or in containers throughout the year. Table grapes, both American and European, are often available in local nurseries as well as at Rolling River and Stark Bro's. Find table and wine grapes at Adams County, Burnt Ridge, Edible Landscaping, Ison's, Johnson, One Green World, Raintree, and Trees of Antiquity. Look to Cummins, Miller, and St. Lawrence for hardy varieties. Ison's, Johnson, and Willis carry large selections of muscadines for southern gardens. Bay Laurel and Rolling River have a wide choice of wine grapes.

Pollinizers

Except for muscadines, most grapes are self-fruitful. Muscadines come in two types—perfect flowered (self-fruitful), and female only, which needs a pollinizer. The perfect-flower types pollinize themselves as well as other varieties that are female only. Check carefully when you order to make sure you have a suitable pollinizer.

Varieties

Hundreds of grape varieties exist. I chose the following for disease resistance, availability, and quality of fruit. For the coldest areas, look for grapes developed by Elmer Swensen (table grapes: 'Swensen Red', 'Petit Pearl'; wine grapes: 'La Crosse', 'St. Pepin', 'St. Croix').

AMERICAN GRAPE (FOX GRAPE), *VITIS LABRUSCA*

These varieties are best adapted to the East, Midwest, and Northwest.

'Beta'—blue grape; heavy producer; disease resistant; good for coldest climates.

'Concord'—the standard to which other American grapes are compared; excellent blue, slip-skin grape; good for jelly and juices; tolerates cool summers; 'Concord Seedless' also available.

'Fredonia'—one of the best black grapes; hardy vine; early ripening.

'Himrod'—American hybrid; best white seedless for the East; very hardy.

'New York Muscat'—reddish black dessert grape; vine not very vigorous.

'Niagara'—old variety; white table grape; vigorous; heavy bearer; moderately hardy.

EUROPEAN GRAPE, *V. VINIFERA*

These grapes are generally limited to wine-growing areas of California, Washington, and Oregon.

'Cabernet Sauvignon'—red wine grape for cool summers; needs a long growing season.

'White Riesling'—white wine grape; for cool areas, one of the hardiest; produces good wine in Geneva, New York.

'Zinfandel'—red wine grape; makes good jelly; for mild winters and cool summers.

European table grapes are for warmer parts of the East and West. They are generally spur pruned.

'Black Monukka'—reddish black, seedless; one of the hardiest European grapes.

'Olivette Blanche' ('Lady Finger')—deep green grape; prune to cane.

MUSCADINE GRAPE, *V. ROTUNDIFOLIA*

Muscadine grapes are for the Southeast. All are excellent eaten fresh or made into jelly or wine. Perfect-flower varieties do not need a pollinizer.

'Carlos'—gold with a pink blush; vigorous; quite hardy; disease resistant; perfect.

'Fry'—very large, bronze grape; high yield; particularly good in Florida; female needs a pollinizer (use 'Southland').

'Scuppernong'—*the* muscadine, used as a benchmark; bronze fruit with distinctive flavor and aroma; oldest American grape variety; many imitations exist, be sure to get the real one; female needs a pollinizer.

'Southland'—black grape; for southeastern Gulf Coast, Florida; perfect.

HYBRIDS

The following American-European hybrids are wine grapes suitable for colder regions.

'Baco Noir'—dark red grape, small, in clusters; productive; wine needs long aging.

'Foch Grape'—red grape; early ripening; widely adapted; favorite of organic growers.

'Missouri Riesling'—American white grape; produces semi-dry wine similar to European Riesling; most mildew-resistant wine grape.

Grapefruit

See Citrus

Hazelnut

See Filbert

Heartnut

See Walnut

Hican

See Pecan and Hickory

Hickory

See Pecan and Hickory

Honeydew

See Melon

Hops

Humulus lupulus

Effort Scale

NO. 2
Needs training
Large amounts of water required
Diseases a problem in some climates
Must be cut to the ground annually to control rampant growth

Zones

3 to 11

Thumbnail Sketch

Deciduous, herbaceous perennial vine
Twines 15 to 25 ft.
Propagate from seeds or cuttings
Needs full sun
Leaves are light green, lobed, 3 to 5 in. long
Blooms in summer

Flowers are decorative; small, papery, green cones

Female flowers are edible, use as seasoning, harvest in fall; shoots are edible, harvest in spring

Use on trellis, arbor, or fence; as accent or interest plant; or in large container

How to Use

In the Kitchen

If you plan on making beer, a single female plant will provide all the hops (female flowers) you need for brewing. The conelike blooms are covered with yellow glands that contain the prized aromatic bitters called lupulin. The use of hops in beer has overshadowed the fact that the tender, spring shoots are edible; treat them like asparagus. Early American colonists steamed hop shoots—a favorite dish in Belgium and France, known as *jets de houblon.*

Hop shoots resemble thin, branched asparagus; you need a lot for a meal. To prepare, snap off the top 6 inches of the shoot, cook, and serve as you would asparagus. When boiling hop shoots, add lemon juice to prevent discoloration.

Home brewing adds a new twist to your edible landscape. Grow your own hops and herbs to create a signature ale to enliven any party. Dry hops in a shady warm area or in a food dehydrator until papery. Quality deteriorates quickly; freeze in heavy-duty zip-top plastic bags or sealable glass jars and use within 6 months. Hop vines yield ½ to 2 pounds of dried flowers per plant. Grow your own barley for even more control over your libation's flavor. An indispensable book is *The Homebrewer's Garden* by Joe and Dennis Fisher.

In the Landscape

This fast-growing herbaceous perennial vine can attain 25 feet in a season. With its large, light green, hairy, maplelike leaves, it is a handsome, quick cover trained on an arbor, trellis, or fence. The conelike flowers of late summer have a refreshing pine aroma and quake like the seed spikes of rattlesnake grass in the slightest breeze.

Given support posts, the vine transforms into a small weeping tree, perfect in a large container or planter box, or as a small specimen in the yard. Train the vine to wind around twine strung vertically across the front of a porch to provide shade in summer. Hop vines pair well with moonflowers, blue morning glories, and scarlet runner beans.

How to Grow

Hops grow just about anywhere except in desert areas. The vine requires full sun and humus-rich, well-drained soil. Work compost and a balanced organic fertilizer into the planting hole; plant bare-root divisions 1 inch deep, bud side up. Space plants 6 feet apart. Provide plenty of water after they sprout in spring. Hops grow vertically and rampantly so they need a strong support. The shoots wind clockwise and cling with hooked hairs; to train the plant to spread horizontally, hand-guide the stem tips. Hop vines rarely bloom the first year, and they die back to the ground every autumn.

Pests and Diseases

Downy mildew can be a problem in rainy-spring areas; powdery mildew is primarily a problem in the Northeast; and mites can build up in hot, dry climates. To prevent mildews, plant resistant varieties, carefully strip the leaves off the bottom 3 or 4 feet of the vine to improve air circulation, and, in the fall, clean up all litter and dispose of it.

Look closely at the overlapping flower bracts of hops; they resemble a miniature pinecone. It is actually the pollen (which is not visible because it is between the bracts) that provides the flavor so revered in beer making.

Harvesting

Harvest new shoots in spring; thin them out as soon as they appear or you'll have a tangle of vines. Leave the four to six most vigorous shoots to grow on. Fertilize in early summer. Pick hops mid-August to September, depending on variety and weather. At maturity, hops develop a drier, papery feel and lighten in color. Clip off the clusters. In fall, cut the vines back to ground level; mulch well to protect from winter freezing.

How to Purchase

Purchase bare-root divisions of female plants in early spring from Nichols, One Green World, Raintree, or Thyme Garden. If they arrive too early for planting, keep them moist and refrigerated. Some states prohibit importing hop plants, but not seeds. In that case, locate an herb nursery in your state, or order seeds; cultivars may not come true from seed and you'll get male and female plants.

Varieties

There are two types of cultivars: bittering (adds bitter flavors to beer) and aroma (imparts smell and taste to beer; best for eating). Catalogs often include alpha percentages; higher numbers indicate more bittering compounds. Beer flavors vary with the cultivars used. When choosing varieties for your garden, select for taste and the intended use you prefer.

'Brewers Gold'—heirloom, ancestor of most high-alpha hops used around the world; golden green foliage; heavy producer; alpha 8 to 10 percent.

'Cascade'—popular all-purpose strain in many American light lagers; somewhat resistant to downy mildew; alpha 5 to 7 percent.

'Kent Golding'—aroma type, traditional English hops for ales and lagers; delicate flavor; alpha range from 4.5 to 6.5 percent.

'Mt. Hood'—aroma type; mild flavor for Bavarian-style lagers; alpha 4 to 5 percent.

'Nugget'—bittering type for ales and stouts; resistant to downy mildew; vigorous; alpha 12 percent.

'Willamette'—aroma-type hybrid for English-style ales; spicy aroma; resistant to downy mildew; alpha 3.5 to 6 percent.

Japanese plum

See Apricot

Kaffir lime

See Citrus

Kaki

See Persimmon

Kale

Brassica oleracea var. *viridis* (*B. o.* var. *acephala*, *B. o.* Acephala Group)

Effort Scale

NO. 2
Must be planted annually
Needs rich, organic soil
Constant moisture and occasional fertilizing needed

Zones

Not applicable

Ruffled blue-green leaves of 'Dwarf Blue Curled' kale form the centerpiece of a vignette from my front yard garden. Surrounding it are lemongrass, blue-green leeks, brilliant-hued monkey flower, pallidosum daisy, and ferny fennel.

Thumbnail Sketch

Annual or biennial grown as annual
8 to 36 in. tall
Propagate from seeds
Needs full sun; light shade in hot climates
Leaves are ornamental—curled, ruffled, green, blue-green, red, purple, or blue
Blooms in warm weather
Flowers are yellow, usually not seen
Leaves and flowers are edible; harvest varies with climate
Use in herbaceous border, vegetable garden, flower bed, raised bed, or container

How to Use

In the Kitchen

When young, kale leaves are delicious raw in salad. I like to add them to coleslaw for flavor, texture, and especially color. Stir-fries are a great medium for kale—whole young leaves, chopped older ones. If you are cooking a red variety, maintain leaf color by sautéing with apples or a little vinegar. Take advantage of late fall and winter pickings and make some warm, homey soups. Kale is great in Tuscan bean soup, and it's traditional in Portuguese *caldo verde* (soup with kale, potatoes, and chourico). As the plant starts to flower, cut the stalks, steam lightly, and then sauté in oil with garlic; serve over pasta. Sprinkle flowers in salads or on a cheese platter. Kale has high concentrations of phytonutrients, especially carotenoids, lutein, and zeaxanthin. It's high in vitamins A and C as well as fiber.

Like flowering cabbage, flowering kale is edible. The leaves are much tenderer than those of flowering cabbage, and with all the different forms from frilly to cutleaf, they add diversity to salads and edible mandalas. Gussy up a plain plate of vegetables by placing colorful kale leaves around the edges; mix colors for a more dazzling display.

In the Landscape

Kale is among the loveliest greens, with leaves that are incredibly varied—from frilly and crinkled to smooth and velvety in many shades of green plus red, chartreuse, deepest gray-green (nearly black), and bicolored. Flowering kale is a show-off cousin that looks like a giant bouquet nested on the ground. Shorter kales, including the flowering type, make good edgings and work well in the front of a border. The delicate-looking Russian kales are at home in a border of lettuces and annual flowers. Taller varieties (choose from among a multitude of textures and colors) are ideal in the middle of a border with cardoon behind purple tulips and yellow calendulas in spring, and among chili peppers and chrysanthemums in fall. A grouping of a kale variety, such as deeply colored 'Lacinato', makes a stunning accent. All kales are well suited for containers. When kale goes to flower, sprays of small, pale yellow blooms rise a foot or more above the leaves.

How to Grow

Like other members of the cabbage family, kale is a cool-season vegetable—but unlike broccoli, cauliflower, and cabbage, it is quite pest and disease free. It thrives in full sun, although in warm climates it benefits from some afternoon shade. Provide well-drained, organic, fertile soil.

Planting

Plant standard kale seedlings 12 inches apart, and tall varieties 18 inches apart. Stake the plants when they are about a foot tall to prevent them from falling over in the wind or under snow. Loosely tie the plants to stakes. Mulch with a few inches of compost. When spring planted, most varieties keep producing, looking stately and beautiful well into the heat of summer. When fall planted, kale keeps going through winter unless it gets too wet. It can survive under a blanket of snow. Tender, succulent greens need to grow quickly and unchecked; apply hydrolyzed fish or an all-purpose organic fertilizer at planting and again a month later. Keep plants well watered.

Harvesting

Pick young leaves as soon as the plant is large enough to withstand harvesting. Harvest outer leaves as needed and the plant keeps producing new inner leaves. Flavor improves and becomes sweeter after a frost.

How to Purchase

Local nurseries offer some seeds and young plants in spring and fall. Many carry mature flowering kale plants; I use them only for show unless I know they were grown organically. Companies specializing in cool-season vegetables offer the greatest selection: Nichols, Johnny's, Pinetree, and Territorial. Renee's, Stokes Seeds, and Burpee also have kales. Baker Creek, Bountiful Gardens, Seeds of Change, and Seed Savers carry heirloom varieties.

Varieties

'Dwarf Blue Curled' ('Dwarf Blue Scotch')—very frilled, blue-green leaves; 12 to 15 in. tall.

'Lacinato' ('Tuscan', 'Dinosaur', 'Black Kale')—18th-century Italian heirloom; straplike, savoyed leaves vary from grayish to dark green; 18 to 36 in. tall.

'Nagoya White'—flowering kale; ruffled, white-centered kale with greenish purple outer leaves; to 8 in. tall. Also 'Nagoya Red' and 'Nagoya Rose'.

'Redbor'—spectacular deep red-purple leaves; color deepens and leaves get curlier with cold weather; 24 to 36 in. tall.

'Red Russian' ('Ragged Jack')—Russian heirloom; blue-green, slightly frilled and cut leaves with purple veining; to about 24 in. tall; hardy to –10°F. Also 'White Russian'.

'Red Ursa'—very frilled blue-green leaves with purple veining; heat tolerant, very bolt resistant; 24 to 30 in. tall.

'Winterbor'—resembles curly parsley with thick, blue-green leaves; 18 to 24 in. tall.

Key lime

See Citrus

King nut

See Pecan and Hickory

Kiwi

(kiwifruit, Chinese gooseberry)
Actinidia spp.

Effort Scale

NO. 2
Pruning and tying required
Fertilizing necessary
Watering necessary in arid climates
Large but manageable harvest

Zones

Arctic beauty kiwi, 3 to 9
Fuzzy kiwi, 7 to 9
Hardy kiwi, 4 to 9

Thumbnail Sketch

Deciduous, perennial woody vine
Twines 20 to 30 ft. (arctic beauty, 10 to 15 ft.)
Propagate by grafting or budding or from cuttings
Needs full sun; afternoon shade in hot climates
Arctic beauty leaves are pink, green, and cream, 3 to 5 in. long; fuzzy kiwi leaves are green, 6 to 8 in. long, new growth bronzy; hardy kiwi leaves are deep green, 3 to 5 in. long, veins and new growth sometimes reddish
Blooms in spring
Flowers are cream colored, 1 to 1½ in. across; only fuzzy kiwi is showy
Fruits are edible; fuzzy kiwi, brown, 3 in. long, fuzzy, harvest in fall; hardy and arctic beauty, green skinned, about 1 in. long, in clusters, harvest varies from late summer to fall
Use on trellis, arbor, pergola, or fence

How to Use
In the Kitchen

The familiar commercial kiwis are brown, egg-shaped, fuzzy, unappealing-looking objects. However, one taste of the bright green flesh beneath the rough exterior quickly alters that opinion. The flavor is sharp but sweet, with overtones of strawberry, melon, and pineapple.

Peel and eat these vitamin C–packed fruits out of hand or add them to fruit compotes or salads. The round slices are glimmering garnishes for desserts; in Australia, they are often the icing on the cake, so to speak, of Pavlova (the national dessert, a meringuelike cake). An enzyme in kiwi juice, similar to an enzyme in papaya, acts as a tenderizing marinade for meats.

Hardy and arctic beauty kiwis are a different experience altogether and gaining wide appeal. Native from China to Siberia, the fruits are much smaller—about an inch long—grow in clusters, and are smooth skinned. Pop them into your mouth like grapes. Sweeter than their commercial cousins, they have an intense flavor and aroma. With no peeling necessary, they are perfect for school lunchboxes; mix them halved into fruit or chicken salad.

Refrigerate slightly under-ripe, putting firm kiwis of all types in sealed bags for up to 3 months. Bring out a few at a time to ripen.

A strong formal arbor supports this tender kiwi vine. Both the down-facing cream-colored flowers and the brownish green fruit seem to play hide-and-seek among the leaves. The homeowners keep the kiwi pruned to maintain the formality of the space.

Kiwis that are picked when ripe store for only a few weeks and soften quickly. All types of kiwis make bright and zesty jams and juices.

In the Landscape

All kiwis are strong, twining, fast-growing, deciduous vines that need a firm and sturdy support. If properly attached, they are extremely useful for covering arbors, pergolas, and strong fences. All elements of the plants contribute to their overall effect.

Arctic beauty kiwis are beautiful, more controlled vines. Some folks grow a male solely for its outstanding red, green, and white variegated foliage (note, however, that the foliage does not fully color up in young plants). Why not add a female for the succulent fruit, too?

A warm bronzy fluff covers fuzzy kiwi's new growth; the round leaves are dark green on top with a lighter underside; and the light brown branches are gnarly. Cream-colored flowers open in May, followed by clusters of brown fruit.

Hardy kiwi has smaller flowers that are usually hidden under the leaves. Some varieties have showy new red growth and stems, and a few even have colorful red fruits peeking out from the foliage.

When properly harvested, all kiwi fruits are firm and do not attract birds. The vines have no soft fruit to drop on a patio or sidewalk.

How to Grow

A little reality check: it takes time until kiwi vines start bearing fruit—about 2 years for arctic beauty kiwi and 3 or 4 years for fuzzy and hardy kiwis.

Climate

Fuzzy kiwi has the most limited range—the warmer parts of Zone 7 to Zone 9. It needs approximately 230 days without frost and, depending on the variety, has a chilling requirement of up to 800 hours. Commercially this kiwi grows in the cooler areas of California and in the Northwest.

Hardy and arctic beauty kiwis have a wider climate range; some even thrive in Zone 3. However, while very hardy when dormant, the vines burst into flower as soon as the weather warms, so the crop can be lost to a late frost; in some cases the vines die. To avoid this, plant them where they get little winter sun (a north-facing slope or wall, or in the shade of a tall building); avoid frost pockets.

No kiwis adapt to desert climates or Zones 10 and 11. They require huge amounts of water and so are prone to drying out. All kiwis do poorly in very windy areas, as the vines are brittle and break.

Exposure and Soil

Kiwi grows best in full sun but tolerates some shade. In the hottest areas, it requires afternoon shade. Arctic beauty is particularly sensitive to bright sunlight in hot climates as the variegated foliage burns easily. Kiwi grows best in slightly acidic good garden loam; without excellent drainage, the plants easily succumb to root rot.

Planting

Before planting, have a substantial support system in place. You can grow kiwis on a strong wooden trellis with support wires similar to ones used for grapes, or create a wire support system against a wall. If you intend to keep kiwis in tight control, plant them along a sturdy metal fence at least 6 feet tall. Or grow them vertically up and over a pergola or patio arbor where you have easy access to the fruits hanging down from above. Use at least 6-by-6-inch lumber to support the heavy weight of the fruit-laden vines. Arctic beauty kiwi does not get as large and can grow happily on an ordinary garden trellis. Plant fuzzy and hardy kiwi plants at least 15 feet apart, and arctic beauty kiwi plants 10 feet apart.

Fertilizing

Most experts recommend withholding fertilizer when planting kiwi vines. Once established, they need nitrogen and potassium, which you can provide with an application of organic mulch in early spring and 5 pounds of aged manure per vine in late winter and again after fruit set. If the vines turn pale, give them more nitrogen the next season.

In Zones 3 to 5, don't fertilize after June. After the first hard frost, apply 3 to 4 inches of organic mulch and cover the lower vines with tree wrap. Remove the wrap in spring before the buds emerge.

Watering

In fairly rainy climates, kiwi vines grow well without supplemental water; in arid climates, water regularly during the growing season. Do not let the soil dry out.

Pruning

Here is the simplest way to train a kiwi vine: In the first season, the plant usually produces at least one strong shoot; gently tie it up—straight up toward the top of the support and do not let it twine. Remove any shoots that come up from the crown. Once the main shoot reaches the top of the support, pinch it to stop its vertical growth, and gently secure it. Let two laterals grow from the top. Once it goes dormant, cut off any side shoots that have grown from the main stem. Pruning while the plant is dormant cuts down on excessive "bleeding."

In the second growing season, choose two new shoots that emerge from the top of the main vine and train them to fan out horizontally over the pergola or wires. These shoots ("cordons") form the framework from which the lateral fruiting arms ("laterals") will branch.

Gently tie the cordons and laterals to the support. In the second winter, trim each lateral back to 12 to 18 buds.

From the third season on, a kiwi vine requires serious pruning to stimulate new fruiting wood and prevent the vine from becoming a tangled mess. Once the vine is 3 years old, start winter pruning by removing water sprouts, weak growth, and excessively curly shoots, but retain the fruiting spurs that grow on the shoots off the cordons. To stimulate new fruiting spurs, shorten last year's new growth on the cordons to 2 or 3 feet. Repeat this each year until the cordons fill out the structure. (If the cordons stop growing, cut them back quite a bit to stimulate new growth.)

Once you have a mature fruiting vine, winter pruning entails thinning out the fruiting laterals to 6 inches apart and cutting the remaining laterals back to about 18 inches to keep the heavy fruit clusters near the structure. From spring into early summer, prune every few weeks to control the size of the vines, remove tall vertical shoots and any curlicue vines that wind around neighbors, and keep vines off the ground.

Male vines are more vigorous than females and if not pruned heavily tend to overtake them. After flowering, cut most of the vigorous vines way back, but leave some of last year's wood with some spurs to produce flowers next spring. In hot climates, do not prune heavily in the summer or the vines will sunburn.

For more information on pruning kiwis, consult *The Pruning Book* by Lee Reich.

Pests and Diseases

Kiwi vines seldom have pest problems, although cats may find the bark attractive as a scratching post; if so, protect the lower 3 feet or so with chicken wire or hardware cloth. In some areas, deer, gophers, rabbits, and voles can be a problem. Root knot nematodes are a problem in some southern soils; use beneficial nematodes to control them.

The major disease problem is root rot in poorly drained soil. Kiwi vines have very fleshy roots that rot easily if water sits on them for only a few hours. If you have any doubts about your drainage, plant in raised beds.

Harvesting

Most kiwi varieties ripen from October through November; arctic beauty ripens in August. Pick kiwis just before they are fully ripe and start to soften. However, if you harvest them too soon, they have a tart taste and shrivel. Harvest when still fairly firm, refrigerate in airtight bags for months, and bring them out as needed to ripen. When kiwis are fully ripe, like peaches they give slightly to a little pressure of your fingers. Experiment by picking and ripening a few to become familiar with the best time to harvest. Arctic beauty kiwi produces 10 to 15 pounds of fruit per vine; fuzzy and hardy kiwis can yield more than 100 pounds per vine.

How to Purchase

Buy kiwis in containers from local nurseries. For the widest range of kiwi varieties, contact these companies: Bay Laurel, Edible Landscaping, Hartmann's, One Green World, Raintree, and Tripple Brook.

Pollinizers

Most female kiwi plants require a male to pollinize them; depending on the species and variety, one male can service up to eight females. 'Issai' is one of the few self-fruitful kiwis, though it bears more heavily when cross-pollinized.

Varieties

ARCTIC BEAUTY KIWI, *ACTINIDIA KOLOMIKTA*
'Frost'—large, bright green fruit; very sweet, high in Vitamin C; very productive; ripens early to mid-August; Zones 3 to 7.
'Male Kolomikta' ('Male')—pollinizes all female arctic beauty varieties; sometimes sold as 'Ornamental'.
'September Sun'—1-in. green, grapelike fruit, in clusters in late August; leaves have some variegation; compact; widely adapted but must have chill.

FUZZY KIWI, *A. DELICIOSA*
'Elmwood'—very large, fuzzy, brown fruit; large flowers; use 'Matua' as pollinizer; more adapted to fluctuating temperatures, good for East Coast.
'Hayward'—fuzzy, brown fruit, very large; needs male pollinizer, common commercial variety; needs 800 chill hours.
'Matua'—pollinizer for 'Elmwood', 'Hayward', and 'Saanichton'.
'Saanichton'—similar to 'Hayward' but hardy to about 5°F; needs 'Matua' as pollinizer.
'Tomuri Male'—pollinizer for 'Vincent'; low chill, adapted to Southern California.
'Vincent'—tasty, medium-size fruit; adapted to Southern California, needs 100 chill hours; pollinize with 'Tomuri Male'.

HARDY KIWI, *A. ARGUTA*
'Ananasnaja' ('Anna')—uniquely fruity tasting; small, smooth fruit; very productive; showy red stems; best in Zones 5 to 7.
'Dumbarton Oaks'—green, slightly ribbed fruit; vines bear in September; good for short-season areas, Zones 5 to 7.
'Issai'—small, grapelike, smooth, green fruit, sweet; self-fruitful; for Zones 5 to 8.
'Ken's Red' (*A. arguta* var. *purpurea* × *A. melanandra*)—cherry-size fruit; sweet flesh and skin are reddish purple; low chill, good for the Gulf region, Zones 6 to 9.
'Male'—pollinizes all female hardy kiwis.
'Meyer's Cordifolia' (*A. arguta* var. *cordifolia*)—round, green fruit; great flavor; for southern areas, Zones 5 to 9.

Unlike the familiar fuzzy kiwi sold in grocery stores, hardy kiwi withstands colder temperatures. Shown here growing at Edible Landscaping in Afton, Virginia, the plant is hardy to Zone 5. Eat the cherry-sized fruit, skin and all.

Kumquat

See Citrus

Lemon

See Citrus

Lettuce

Lactuca sativa

Effort Scale

NO. 2
Succession plantings needed
Watering, mulching, and fertilizing needed
Some weeding and pest control necessary

Zones

Not applicable

Thumbnail Sketch

Annual
6 to 12 in. tall
Propagate from seeds
Needs full sun; tolerates partial shade
Leaves include many shades of chartreuse, green, bronze, red, and bicolors

My Magic Circle Herb Garden was transformed into a greens trial garden. I harvested individual leaves until we couldn't keep up, and then filled boxes to bring to the local food bank—a welcome change from their daily iceberg lettuce.

Flowers are not usually seen
Leaves are edible; harvest most in cool part of the year
Use in flower border, raised bed, hanging basket, or container

How to Use

In the Kitchen

There are dozens of greens used in salads worldwide, but lettuce is by far the most popular, be it leaf lettuce, butter, Romaine, or crisp-heads like iceberg. Lettuce is the keystone of salads of all sorts, but what would a BLT be without the L? And in France, braised butter lettuces are a traditional side dish for roast chicken. However, it is in salads that these greens truly stand out. Imagine velvety butter lettuce with pears, walnuts, and raspberries; crisp Romaine in a Chinese chicken salad; or red-leaf lettuce combined with spicy arugula, bitter escarole, and crisp pancetta. All challenge the old notion that a salad is a large wedge of iceberg lettuce doused with thick Thousand Island dressing.

Lettuce is not the most nourishing green, but as a rule, the darker the green or red, the greater the nutrition. According to the National Institutes of Health ratings of the antioxidant value of foods (Oxygen Radical Absorbance Capacity), highly colored red-leaf lettuce measures 2,380 ORAC units, and butter lettuce 1,423 units, but pale iceberg lettuce only 438. For more about ORAC values, visit www.oracvalues.com.

In the Landscape

Since they are in the garden for such a short time, salad greens are not considered major players in the landscape, yet the many lettuces provide a most impressive palette of textures, forms, and colors. Lettuces are a study in green—the chartreuse of 'Black Seeded Simpson', the sparkling bright green of butter lettuce, and the deeper green of many Romaines. Of course, there are the many shades of bronze and red—speckled and burnished, too. And then there are all those leaf shapes and textures—from cut and frothy to curly and ruffled through oak leaf and 'Deer Tongue' to savoyed and smooth. Sizes vary, too, from diminutive 4-inch 'Tom Thumb' to 14-inch 'Oscard Oak Leaf'.

It is possible to create a picture by combining curly green 'Slow-bolt', the reds of the crisp-headed 'Silva', and the smooth-leaved 'Bibb' lettuce. The possibilities are limitless for creating your own patterns—geometric chevrons and squares, or wavy free-form lines of bronzes and greens. All lettuces are at home in containers—together or mixed with arugula and chard or annual flowers like calendulas and violas, both of which are edible. And in a mixed flower bed, the various lettuces are effective in combination with violas, nasturtiums, fibrous begonias, and alpine strawberries, or underplanted among your tulips.

How to Grow

Lettuces are in their glory in the cool, fairly damp weather of spring and fall. These fast-growing, short-lived plants grow best in full sun, and they tolerate afternoon shade in hot weather. Start them from seeds in spring or fall; direct-sow in place, or start them indoors and move them out into the garden. As warm weather approaches, select more heat-tolerant varieties such as 'Deer Tongue', 'Reine de Glace', and 'Marvel of Four Seasons'.

Planting

Before planting, add a few inches of organic matter and an all-purpose fertilizer, and work them into the top 6 inches of soil. Broadcast the seeds, cover lightly with fluffy soil, and tamp in place. Cover the bed with netting or floating row covers to keep birds away and prevent cats from digging. Keep the bed lightly moist until the seeds sprout and throughout the growing season. Once seedlings emerge, thin plants to 6 inches apart or more, mulch the area with an inch of organic matter, and keep it weeded. For best flavor and tenderness, these greens need to grow quickly and unchecked; apply hydrolyzed fish or all-purpose organic fertilizer at planting and again 6 weeks later.

While it is customary to harvest individual heads of lettuce, the leaves can be continuously cut off; new leaves will grow. Lettuce is well suited for baby greens, either by itself or mixed with other greens such as arugula, mustard, and cresses. To grow a small patch, rake the area smooth, broadcast the seeds as you would a grass mix, mulch lightly, water, and cover the area. Keep the bed moist but not soggy. Once the seedlings are a few inches tall, cut across the bed with kitchen scissors, making sure to cut ½ inch above the crowns of the plants. Fertilize and within a few weeks a second crop will be ready to harvest. This method is called the cut-and-come-again salad garden.

Pests and Diseases
Lettuces are vulnerable to few pests or diseases, though aphids, armyworms, and slugs are occasional problems; rabbits and birds can devour young seedlings.

Harvesting
In my experience, 18 plants provide enough lettuce for a family of four for about a month. Harvest the plants in their entirety or pick a few outer leaves at a time. Put in plastic bags, refrigerate immediately, and use within a few days. Before eating, wash well in at least three changes of water to eliminate critters and grit. Transplant seedlings into empty spaces left by harvested plants.

How to Purchase

Seeds for dozens of varieties of lettuces are readily available and easy to sow; nurseries offer seedlings. Mail-order companies with numerous varieties include Johnny's, Nichols, Cook's, Renee's, Stokes Seeds, Harris, Ed Hume, Seed Savers, and Territorial.

Varieties
BUTTERHEAD (BIBB)
Butterhead cultivars have smooth, bright green leaves and grow in a low rosette.
'Buttercrunch'—crisper butterhead; somewhat heat tolerant; 55 days.
'Deer Tongue' ('Matchless')—heirloom; compact green head; slow to bolt; 46 days.
'Marvel of Four Seasons' ('Four Seasons', 'Merveille des Quatre Saisons')—French heirloom; tender red and green leaves, dark red in cold weather; tolerates heat; hardy; 45 to 55 days.
'Tom Thumb'—heirloom; miniature, grows to size of tennis ball; medium green leaves; tender; perfect for single serving; 52 days.
'Winter Marvel'—pale green head; hardy; plant in fall for spring harvest.

CRISPHEAD (ICEBERG)
Very crunchy, mild-flavored crisphead produces a dense, rounded head that looks like a green cabbage.
'Great Lakes'—classic, dense green head; 88 days.
'Red Iceberg'—beautiful red and green foliage; large head; slow to bolt; 50 days.
'Reine de Glace'—handsome, dark green, pointed leaves; slow to bolt; 62 days.

Spring arrives in style with lettuces among vibrant pink tulips. Intersperse seeds or transplants in fall bulb plantings. Protect lettuce from hard frosts for a longer harvest, and then replant in early spring. Experiment with what works in your climate.

LOOSELEAF (CUTTING)
Tender, thin, and mild-flavored leaves in red, chartreuse, shades of green, and bicolors.
'Australian Yellow'—heirloom; bright chartreuse leaves; slow to bolt; 50 days.
'Black-Seeded Simpson'—heirloom; bright green; delicate flavor; 45 days.
'Lollo Rosso'—magenta and green leaves; small and frilly; great for baby lettuce; 55 days.
'Slowbolt'—heirloom; one of the best for heat tolerance; light green, frilly leaves; 50 days.

ROMAINE (COS)
More upright than most lettuces, Romaine has sturdy, crunchy leaves with a firm rib down the center.
'Crisp Mint'—thick, crunchy leaves; mint green color; 55 days.
'Forellenschuss' ('Speckled Trout')—Austrian heirloom; red speckled leaves; tolerates summer heat; 55 days.
'Parris Island'—heirloom; crunchy and crisp; resists bolting; 66 days.

Lime
See Citrus

Lime leaf
See Citrus

Limequat

See Citrus

Lingonberry

See Cranberry and Lingonberry

Lotus

(sacred lotus, Chinese lotus)
Nelumbo nucifera

Effort Scale

NO. 3
Rhizomes usually available by mail order only
Controlling algae necessary
Winter protection and storage required in most zones

Nothing is quite as spectacular as a lotus in full bloom—from its dramatic leaves to its majestically iconic flower. In Ton Stam's backyard water garden in Des Moines, Iowa (Zone 5), this plant comes back bigger every year.

Zones

5 to 11

Thumbnail Sketch

Herbaceous perennial
3 to 5 ft. tall
Propagate from seeds, more often from rhizomes
Needs full sun
Leaves are silvery blue-green, 18 to 24 in. across, on long stems
Blooms in summer
Flowers are white, pink, or rose; single or double; showy; 8 to 12 in. across
Leaves are edible, harvest in spring; seeds and rhizomes are edible, harvest in late summer to fall; flowers are edible in summer
Use in pond, pool, or large water container

How to Use

In the Kitchen

The lotus plant is a gem; all parts are edible. The enlarged rhizomes (often referred to as roots, tubers, or tuberous roots) may be familiar from Asian dishes; sliced, they reveal a decorative pattern of holes. Harvest the rhizomes in late summer to fall (before the water freezes in cold regions) and store in water until you're ready to prepare them. Their flavor is aromatic and they remain crisp when cooked. Thinly sliced, lotus "root" dresses up a tempura plate; chop and add it to chicken soup and stir-fries. Float the flower petals on a clear soup. Use tender, young lotus leaves raw as part of a green salad or lightly cooked as a hot vegetable. The mature leaves make an aromatic wrapper in which to steam fish. Use mature leaves *only* if you have several plants; removing too many leaves at a time harms the plant. The seeds inside those fascinating 3-inch pods are edible, too—dried, roasted, or pickled in the Japanese manner.

The flowers are usable as soon as they develop. Allow the seeds to dry before eating them. Peel off the bitter skin and discard the green seed bud at one end. If you don't use the harvested rhizomes right away, can, freeze, or dry them.

In the Landscape

The sacred lotus is a large perennial for a water garden, where it is guaranteed to be a standout among other blooming plants. The 2-foot-wide, silvery blue-green leaves rise well above the water. The many-petaled, fragrant flowers, which can measure 8 to 12 inches across and come in white and various shades of pink, rise above the leaves. The buds take about 3 days to open fully; as soon as they are open, the seedpod begins to form. This show of abundance is yours for a lifetime as long as you do not eat all the rhizomes or let them freeze.

How to Grow

Lotus needs full sun and prefers fairly heavy, rich soil. Lotus rhizomes are oval and are joined together at narrowed sections. Break the connections to make separate plants. In mid- to late spring, plant one rhizome in a round, 25-gallon water-plant container (lotuses grow in a circle and will die if they run into an obstacle) so that the growing tips point straight upward and are about ¼ inch above the soil. Place the container in the water garden, adjusting so that the water level is between 6 and 10 inches above the container rim. Add water periodically to maintain the correct level.

Fertilize monthly during the growing season with special water-garden fertilizer. Protect lotus rhizomes from freezing. In the coldest-winter areas, lift them from the container and store them in damp sand in a cool place. *Hint:* If fish overwinter successfully in your water garden, so will lotus.

How to Purchase

Rhizomes are available at water-garden supply houses and a few nurseries from April to June. Look for lotus "roots" at a local Asian grocery; they may sprout when put in water.

Mandarin orange

See Citrus

Maple

(sugar maple)
Acer saccharum

Effort Scale

NO. 3
Some raking required
Making syrup is time consuming

Zones

4 to 8

Thumbnail Sketch

Deciduous tree
50 to 75 ft. tall
Propagate by budding or from seeds
Needs full sun
Leaves are medium green, palmate, 4 to 6 in. across; turn yellow, red, or orange in autumn
Flowers are insignificant
Sap is edible; harvest in late winter to early spring
Use as street tree, shade tree, or lawn tree; in woodland garden

How to Use

In the Kitchen

Warm maple syrup is the most delicious topping for pancakes and waffles. Children (adults, too) delight in making letter-shaped candies by pouring hot syrup in the snow. Maple syrup and maple sugar are handy in the kitchen for puddings, pies, frostings, and a sinfully delicious topping for ice cream. All these confections are sweet, sweet, sweet. In fact, a recipe for maple-walnut tart (*Tarte au Sirop d'Érable*) ends with the suggestion, "If the sweetness of the tart is overpowering,

World renowned for its deliciously sweet sap, sugar maple puts on a spectacular show of fall color. To be sure of colorful leaves, buy a named variety. Use this maple to line a rural lane or as a screen along your property line.

accompany each serving with a wedge of lemon." For all its sugariness, maple syrup, unlike many sweeteners, contains numerous minerals, amino acids, and vitamins.

In the Landscape

The New England and Midwest countryside in fall would be anemic without sugar maples in blazing red, orange, and clear yellow. What glory these trees give to autumn! In addition to this spectacle, they provide shade for hammocks and porches on hot, sultry August days.

Instead of planting a half-acre of lawn to mow, consider a grove of maples and a woodland path edged with blueberries, wild strawberries, and wildflowers—an exciting composition requiring much less work. Use maples as screens to block a view or to shade a hot south wall. They are beautiful street trees for suburban areas.

How to Grow

Maple trees grow in most of the Northeast and Midwest, from New England west to Oklahoma, in Eastern Canada, as far south as northern Alabama, and parts of the Northwest and Northern California. But although the tree has a wide growing range, sap production is good only where a wide differential occurs between the day and night temperatures during late winter to early spring. In mild-winter areas, tapping the trees for sap is unrewarding.

Maple trees are not fussy about soil as long as it is well drained. However, the largest amount of and highest-quality syrup is produced on rich, humusy, loam soil. Sugar maples do not cotton to hot, dry conditions or warm winters. In arid climates, they require occasional deep watering.

A number of pests and diseases bother this tree, but they usually don't kill it. Natural predators generally keep these problems in balance. Maples generally do not do well under city conditions, as air pollution and salty streets weaken them. In fact, acid rain in New England is threatening the maple syrup industry.

Harvesting

Tapping maple trees for sap is a great family activity from February through April, depending on the climate and weather. All you need for a pint of maple syrup are a few large sugar maple trees. Elaborate equipment is not necessary for tapping trees. Gather some clean, 1-gallon milk jugs (or make buckets out of shortening cans) and metal hooks to hang them. Order inexpensive metal spiles (the hollow tubes used as spigots).

Go out on a warm, bright day that follows a cold, freezing one—the kind of weather that makes the sap "run" (the tree sends nutrient-rich sap up from the roots into the branches). Look for sugar maples at least 12 inches in diameter at your shoulder. Drill an upward-slanting hole just large enough for the spile to fit 1 inch deep into the living tissue just under the bark. Trees 15 to 24 inches in diameter can take up to three holes; those larger than 24 inches can take four.

Hang the bucket on the spile, and cover the bucket. To hang a milk jug, cut a hole near the cap threads and hang the jug so the spile is inside it. Put the cap on the jug to keep dirt out. Check the buckets every few hours to see how they are filling. A good-size tree can produce 2 or more gallons of sap a day.

Pour all the sap from the buckets or jugs into clean, large plastic or metal containers. Gather a large amount of firewood, some cinder blocks or large rocks, and a large metal washtub. The sugar content of maple sap averages 2 to 3 percent of the whole, which boils down in 10 to 20 hours on an open fire to evaporate the excess liquid. Don't attempt this inside, as steam will deposit sugar on the ceiling. Place the washtub on cinder blocks and start a fire under it. Pour all the sap into the tub and boil until it is 7 degrees higher than the boiling point of water. A candy thermometer will register 219°F at sea level; the boiling point for the sap decreases 1 degree for every 550 feet above sea level. Skim off any scum as it forms.

Once the boiling syrup is concentrated, run it through a felt filter to remove debris and niter (sugary granules); pour the finished syrup into sterilized jars and tighten the lids. Turn the jars upside-down immediately to sterilize the caps, or run the jars through a water bath canner until they reach 180°F. Sealed syrup keeps indefinitely in a cool dark place. Refrigerate after opening.

A number of sources offer supplies for the amateur syrup maker. The Yankee Grocery (www.yankeegrocery.com) and Atkinson Maple Syrup Supplies (www.atkinsonmaple.com) offer inexpensive metal spigots for tapping the trees, hooks for holding the containers, and how-to booklets that cover many of the specifics for large-scale syrup making. For a great look at the history of sugaring, visit the American Maple Museum (lcida.org/maplemuseum.html) in Croghan, New York, near the Canadian border.

How to Purchase

Local nurseries offer sugar maple trees, usually in a range of sizes.

Varieties

'Bonfire'—fast growing, to 50 ft.; more tolerant of adverse conditions than most; orange and red fall color.
'Commemoration'—smaller form to 50 ft.; orange fall color.
'Fall Fiesta' ('Bailsta')—vigorous, to 75 ft.; yellow, orange, and red fall color.
'Green Mountain'—to 75 ft.; red and yellow fall color; does better under adverse city conditions and is more drought tolerant than other varieties.

OTHER SYRUP TREES

The following maples also give good syrup, though not up to the standards of the sugar maple:
Big-leaf maple (*Acer macrophyllum*)
Big-tooth maple (*A. saccharum* ssp. *grandidentatum*)
Black maple (*A. s.* ssp. *nigrum*)
Red maple (*A. rubrum*)
Rocky Mountain maple (*A. glabrum*)

Birches also produce sap that you can boil down for syrup. Sweet birch (aka black birch, *Betula lenta*) sap flows copiously, usually in April. Collect it the same way as maple sap; it has a lower concentration of sugar, necessitating a longer boiling time. You can make birch beer—a potent brew—from the sap, too. Look for sweet birch trees at local nurseries and garden centers.

Marjoram

See Oregano and Marjoram

Melon

(cantaloupe/muskmelon, honeydew, and watermelon)
Cantaloupe/muskmelon, honeydew, *Cucumis melo*
Watermelon, *Citrullus lanatus* var. *lanatus*

Effort Scale

NO. 3
Must be planted annually
Vulnerable to some pests
Regular watering and some weeding necessary
Needs fertilizing and mulching
Some training of vining types needed

Zones

Not applicable

Thumbnail Sketch

Annual
Bush types, 24 to 36 in. wide and tall; vining types, to 6 ft. long

Propagate from seeds

Needs full sun

Leaves are light to dark green, depending on variety

Flowers are yellow, 1 to 2 in. across

Fruits are edible; harvest in summer and early fall

Use in herbaceous border, raised bed, or container; vining types on fences and trellises

How to Use

In the Kitchen

Classifying the different types of melons is a bit complicated. Botanists divide what most of us call cantaloupes into numerous categories. For our purposes, I've simplified it to cantaloupe/muskmelon types with skins that are usually netted and fragrant, and smooth, thin-skinned honeydew/Crenshaw types that are not fragrant. Watermelons are another category of melon; they come in many shapes, sizes, and colors and can be seeded or seedless.

'Ambrosia' was the first melon I ever grew, and what a revelation! Luscious, honey-sweet flesh that nearly melted in my mouth. Few Americans today have experienced such a melon. For decades modern breeders developed serviceable, solid-flesh commercial-type melons, which though sweet and perfect for shipping, have little flavor and succulence.

Cantaloupe-type melons are superb to eat fresh—perhaps with a squirt of lime or a scoop of vanilla ice cream. Wrap slices of them in prosciutto for an appetizer. Sprinkle cubes of watermelon with chili powder or blend them with mint for a quick and easy cold soup. In Mexico I fell in love with that country's famous *aguas*—all types of melons blended with water, shaved ice, and lime. Of course the resorts kick it up a bit, using the wide variety of melons as a base for margaritas.

Melons do not preserve well—except for watermelon rind. Make this traditional southern condiment by peeling and cutting the thick rind of some of the old varieties into chunks, and pickling them in vinegar with sugar, cinnamon, and cloves. I often serve it as an accompaniment to curried dishes in lieu of chutney.

If you are a lover of melons, you must read Amy Goldman's *Melons for the Passionate Grower,* in which she describes dozens of heirloom melons in detail, along with complete growing instructions and recipes.

In the Landscape

Cantaloupe-type melons bear medium green, ivy-shaped leaves, about 4 or 5 inches across. Watermelons have heavily lobed, silver to dark green leaves. All melons have small, yellow flowers that are not especially showy. The fruits range from 3-inch, cream or light orange spheres to mammoth, 2-foot-long, black watermelons with yellow spots. The most decorative are the orange and brown tiger-striped heirloom "pocket" melons.

The vining types are great spilling out of a large container and combined with ornamentals with bronze or burgundy foliage. With melon vines you need to use your imagination. Do you have a slope perfect for showing off your melons? Interplant them with 'Purple Wave' and 'Pink Wave' petunias for a big splash. How about an old leaky wheelbarrow that you can paint a bright color? Plant a few melons in it and roll it to a hot corner of concrete—maybe near the kitchen porch.

Bush-type melons are useful in flower beds near a lawn; add color with drifts of cockscombs in a host of pinks and yellows. They also do well in large containers on balconies, porches, or patios.

How to Grow

Melons are all about heat. They thrive in full sun, and in cool-summer areas you need to provide as much heat as you can. In vegetable gardens you can lay black plastic on the soil to absorb the sun's rays, but in a decorative landscape that is hard to make work. Instead, I grow melons in large containers because elevated soil warms easily. For good measure, I place the containers on my brick patio to absorb even more heat. Other gardeners grow them in raised boxes or let the vines cascade over a low stone wall that gives off heat at night.

Planting

In short-summer areas, start seeds indoors a few weeks before your last frost date, but do not set out your transplants until the soil and the weather are reliably warm. Or start your melons outdoors after all threat of frost has passed and the weather is warm. Plant in rich, sandy, organic soil supplemented with aged manure or an all-purpose organic fertilizer. Traditional gardeners plant in hills (mounded areas a few feet across), sowing three or four seeds per hill and then thinning to two plants.

Plant the seeds an inch deep and water in well. Protect the seedlings with an overturned berry basket until they are a few inches tall.

Many of the old-time melons are sweeter and more succulent than commercial varieties. Three outstandingly flavorful heirloom melons are, from left to right, 'Hopi' cantaloupe, 'Old Bidwell' muskmelon, and 'Turkey' honeydew.

Once the seedlings are up, thin to 6 inches apart. Keep the area weeded and tie up the vining varieties as they grow. Melons need moist but not soggy soil. Apply hydrolyzed fish or an all-purpose organic supplemental fertilizer about 6 weeks after planting.

Melon vines are usually allowed to sprawl along the ground, but that limits their landscape use; they tend to climb on and over their neighbors. Trellis small-fruited melons, especially pocket melons, but larger-fruited melons are more challenging, requiring a sling (netting or soft cloth) to secure the heavy fruit to a sturdy support.

Pests and Diseases
Melons are susceptible to most of the same pests and diseases as cucumbers, their relatives in the Cucurbitaceae family.

Harvesting
How do you know when to harvest a homegrown melon at its peak of perfection? It takes practice and attention. In fact, some markets in France have specialists to help customers judge melon ripeness. For cantaloupes, look for color changes and a sweet fragrance; some varieties get a little softer; most will "slip" (pull off the stem with little effort). The tendril and leaf next to the melon begin to brown. For honeydew/Crenshaw types, the rind turns from green to yellowish, it changes from a smooth waxy look to a duller finish, and the bottom of the melon starts to soften slightly. Watermelons usually develop a spot on the bottom that changes from white to cream. And to quote Mark Twain, on thumping watermelons with your knuckles, "A ripe melon says 'punk' when thumped, a green one says 'pink' or 'pank.'"

How to Purchase

First select a variety suitable for your climate. You can grow most melons in regions with sultry, hot summers, but in short- or cool-summer areas, select early short-season melons. Beyond that, there are hybrid melons, open-pollinated melons, and vines of varying lengths.

Most local nurseries carry seeds and a very limited selection of transplants. Seek out many more melon varieties from Park, Stokes Seeds, John Scheepers, Gurney's, Renee's, Nichols, and Johnny's, and heirlooms from Seeds of Change, Baker Creek, and Seed Savers. Southern Exposure offers a large selection of heirlooms as well as heat- and disease-resistant varieties.

Varieties
CANTALOUPE/MUSKMELON, *CUCUMIS MELO* VAR. *RETICULATUS*
Americans call fragrant melons with orange flesh and a netted rind cantaloupes, but most are actually muskmelons.

'Ambrosia'—hybrid; the gold standard for flavor; salmon-colored, soft, melting, extremely fragrant flesh; 1-day window of peak ripeness for picking; resistant to powdery mildew; 5 lb.; 86 days.

'Jenny Lind'—heirloom; small, turban-shaped, 1½-lb. fragrant melon with green flesh, sweet; suitable for trellising without extra support for the fruit; 75 days.

'Minnesota Midget'—heirloom; early; 4-in. fruit weighs 12 oz. to 1½ lb., sweet; compact vine to 36 in. long; resists fusarium wilt; 65 days.

HONEYDEW/CRENSHAW, *C. M.* VAR. *INODORUS*
These melons are generally green skinned with green flesh (some have orange flesh).

'Crane' ('Eel River')—heirloom; teardrop shape; fragrant orange flesh; harvest when green specks on skin turn orange; 4 to 7 lb.; 80 days.

'Super Dew'—hybrid; pale green skin, green flesh; 6 lb.; 80 days.

SPECIALTY MELONS
'Charentais' (*C. m.* var. *cantalupensis*)—French heirloom, a classic; very sweet and fragrant; green to yellow rind and orange flesh; 1-day window of peak ripeness for picking; heavy producer; 3½ lb.; 90 days.

'Kincho'—hybrid; highly prized in Asia; thin golden skin, crisp white flesh, small seed cavity; crisp and juicy, eat out of hand like an apple; mildew tolerant; 3- to 4-in. fruits; 50 days.

WATERMELON, *CITRULLUS LANATUS* VAR. *LANATUS*
Watermelons range in size from 4 to 30 lb. and usually have red flesh and black seeds.

'Moon and Stars'—heirloom; black rind with a sprinkling of stars and a single round moon; produces sweet fruit under fairly cool conditions; up to 30 lb.; 95 to 105 days.

'New Orchid'—hybrid; striped, deep green rind; orange flesh with sherbetlike flavor; "icebox" size to 7 lb.; 80 days.

'Sugar Baby'—hybrid; black rind, red flesh; to 8 lb.; 76 days.

'Yellow Doll'—hybrid; early; semi-compact vine; green rind, yellow flesh; 5 to 8 lb.; 65 days.

Mint
Mentha spp.

Effort Scale

NO. 2
Vulnerable to some pests and diseases
Pruning needed to keep trim and bushy

Zones

3 to 10 for most species

Thumbnail Sketch

Perennial herb
6 in. to 36 in. tall
Propagate from seeds, cuttings, or divisions
Needs full sun or partial shade
Leaves vary from deep green or variegated to light green, 1 to 2 in. long
Blooms in summer
Flowers are lavender, purple, or white, tiny, in spikes
Leaves and flowers are edible; use as flavorings; harvest season varies
Use as ground cover or in herb garden, rock garden, or container

How to Use
In the Kitchen
I experienced the cultural significance of mint tea decades ago while wandering the ancient spice market in the Old Cairo Bazaar. Every owner beckoned me into his humble shop and offered a boiling hot

cup of very sweet mint tea. They combined a concentrated tea and sugar mixture with boiling water, which they ceremoniously poured into a cup from a height of at least 3 feet—simultaneously cooling and adding life to the tea. Once officially welcomed, I sipped the tea and enjoyed the presentation of their wares. Such tea ceremonies slow the frantic pace of daily life and give people a chance to connect.

Over the years, I developed my own mint tea ceremony using a Bauhaus-inspired clear glass teapot. I invite guests—usually my grandchildren or neighborhood children—into the backyard to pick fresh mint leaves. After I put the kettle on to boil, we wash the mint and stuff the leaves into the strainer basket of the teapot, and then I pour the boiling water over the leaves to the brim. As part of the ritual, we take a few moments to smell the clean fragrances and watch the swirls of green mint oil as they form spiraling vortices. We steep the tea for 5 minutes and retire to the living room to drink mint tea and discuss our day.

Mint is more versatile than just as a beverage base for mint juleps and mojitos. Chop peppermint for a fresh flavor in salads or add it to melted butter to season boiled new potatoes and baby carrots. Spearmint jelly is *de rigueur* with roast lamb. Mint is a fresh-tasting addition to ice cream, candies, and whipped cream. Spearmint is often used in Asian and Middle Eastern dishes.

In the Landscape

These clean-smelling plants deserve a place in the garden just so you can pick a sprig to enjoy its pungency. Most mints have one common flaw: their underground stems spread—invasively—and must be controlled in containers or by a deep header. (I'm sure that someone at our first house is still mowing mint in the lawn as I did because 40 years ago I planted spearmint nearby.)

Common mints have crinkly leaves and can grow as high as 36 inches; leaf color varies with type. Use the tall, upright Curly mint with dark green leaves combined with other vigorous and colorful perennials such as the yellow-flowering hypericum 'Sunny Boulevard' and the pink-flowering *Centranthus ruber*. Together they will thrive, even in the most neglected part of your garden. All mints combine beautifully with impatiens and begonias. Green and white 'Variegata' peppermint is spectacular cascading out of a tall container.

How to Grow

Standard mints are hardy to Zone 3. They grow best in rich, moist soil and prefer light shade but will grow almost anywhere with ample water. Grow them in pots to control their spread, and repot once a year. Cut the old root ball in half, replant in fresh potting soil, and add fertilizer. Share the other half with a friend or dispose of it. Prune mints often to keep them bushy.

Pests and Diseases

Mints are attractive to whiteflies. Control them by cutting the foliage back almost to the crown and spraying with insecticidal soap. If the plant continues to be infested, move it to an exposed part of the garden with good air circulation. Rust is another problem, especially if the planting is crowded. Destroy the diseased plant and choose a more open exposure for a new plant.

Harvesting

Pick the stems and leaves anytime you want them in the kitchen. For drying, harvest leaves during a rainless spell; they do not dry easily when moist. Dry like oregano.

Mints can be thugs in the garden as their square stems root readily when they touch soil. Control them by growing them in containers. Here, grapefruit mint, at left, and spearmint in a terra cotta container complement a firecracker plant.

How to Purchase

For best quality and superior selection, buy mint plants, not seeds, at local nurseries or from Nichols, Richters, Thyme Garden, or Well-Sweep.

Varieties

There are so many mints, including citrus types—both lemon and lime—and fruity ones, too. These are the most popular:

Curly mint (*Mentha spicata*)—very upright with dark green, curled leaves; spearmint flavor.

'Ginger'—dark green, gold-flecked leaves; ginger flavor with mint overtone.

Orange bergamot mint (*M. × piperita* var. *citrata*)—purple-edged leaves; citrusy mint flavor.

Peppermint (*M. × piperita*)—dark green leaves; distinctive flavor; stomach soother; used in candies. 'Variegata' is green and white.

Pineapple mint (*M. suaveolens* 'Variegata')—light green leaves with variegations; tastes like pineapple with mint overtone.

Spearmint (*M. spicata*)—dark green leaves; distinct flavor.

'Vietnamese Mint' (*M. × gracilis*)—popular in Southeast Asia for its sweet spearmint flavor.

Mioga ginger

See Ginger

Mizuna

See Mustard

Mulberry trees bear prolifically. The fruit ripens over time, white berries gradually turning red and finally purple. Fruit drop makes the area underneath slippery. Birds flock to the trees, but there is usually enough fruit for them and humans.

Mulberry

Morus spp.

Effort Scale

NO. 2
Vulnerable to some diseases and pests, including birds
Harvesting is time consuming

Zones

4 to 11

Thumbnail Sketch

Deciduous tree
8 to 50 ft. tall, depending on variety
Propagate by budding or from seeds or cuttings
Needs full sun
Leaves are light to medium green, heart shaped, 6 to 10 in. across
Blooms in spring or summer
Flowers are insignificant
Fruits are black, white, or red; edible; harvest in spring and summer
Use as background plant, screen, or wildlife shelterbelt; weeping varieties as interest plants

How to Use

In the Kitchen

Mulberries look like elongated brambleberries in red, black, purple, or white. Sweet and juicy, they are a concentrated source of vitamin C and minerals; dark ones are packed with antioxidants. Depending on the variety, mulberries can be quite seedy, and the flavor varies. The best are delicious and relatively seedless; poorer-quality berries are best described as insipid. I often eat the fruits right off the tree (purple-stained lips are a giveaway); once they get as far the kitchen, they make delicious jams, jellies, syrups, and wine. Add mulberries to an apple pie or an English trifle for a delightful change of pace and color.

Dry mulberries outdoors by setting them in a warm, dry place, out of the sun, in a single layer on a screen for 4 or 5 days, or dry them indoors in a dehydrator. To freeze, lay the fruits on a cookie sheet and place it in the freezer. When the mulberries are frozen, put them in freezer bags. Or mix 1 cup of sugar with 5 cups of fruit, put the mixture in a container that seals well, and freeze.

In the Landscape

Mulberry is a deciduous tree that can attain a height of 15 to 50 feet, though it can easily be kept much smaller. With age, it develops a spreading crown. Mulberry leaves are almost tropical looking. Some cultivars are especially showy and are ideal as accent plants: 'Black Beauty' develops a beautiful, somewhat pendulous form; 'Contorta' has a gnarled trunk and twisted branches; and 'Pendula' is spectacular with its gracefully arching branches that hang down. I have fond memories from childhood of making berry "pies" and rolling corn silk cigarettes with friends under my grandmother's weeping mulberry. 'Contorta' and 'Pendula' seldom grow taller than 8 feet—perfect for lining a walkway or growing in very large decorative containers.

Use the standard, more readily available mulberry to screen a yard from the roadway, create a grouping to shelter wildlife, or provide a good background for a shrub border. Plant several close together to make a dense screen or hedge. Mulberry grows well in a lawn and as a shade tree, but at fruiting time, it is hazardous to sit underneath one. Fruit drop makes the tree undesirable near patios and sidewalks for the mess and the stains produced by the dark-colored fruits.

Some gardeners plant this tree as a foil for birds, which will eat the mulberries and ignore the more desirable cherries.

Note: When buying a mulberry tree for fruit, make sure you do not get the more common fruitless varieties.

How to Grow

The three species of mulberries covered here are black (*Morus nigra*), red (*M. rubra*), and white (*M. alba*). The names refer not to the color of the fruits but to the color of their buds.

Climate

There are major differences in climate preferences among species. Black mulberry, native to western Asia, is hardy to 0 to −10°F. It grows as far north as Virginia in the East and Seattle in the West. Red mulberry is native to North America from Massachusetts to the Gulf Coast, and white mulberry is native to China. Some of the red and white mulberry cultivars are very hardy (to −20°F), while others are far less so (hardy only to 25°F); read the descriptions carefully when choosing a tree.

Exposure and Soil

Mulberry trees need full sun and prefer deep garden loam; they do poorly in shallow chalky or gravelly soils.

Fertilizing

Mulberries need only an annual application of organic mulch.

Watering

The trees are somewhat drought tolerant once established, but they drop their fruit if moisture is lacking.

Pruning

Prune only to shape, control size, and remove deadwood during the dormant season to lessen bleeding. Mulberries fruit on spurs on old wood as well as new wood. Never prune branches more than 1½ inches in diameter, as the wounds bleed profusely and may never heal.

Pests and Diseases

Birds are the chief pests, but there are usually enough berries for you and the birds to share. Bacterial canker may a problem. Remove by cutting into the diseased branch at least a foot below the cankerous tissue; between cuts sterilize the pruning instrument with a 10 percent bleach solution.

Harvesting

Mulberries are ripe when they are slightly soft. Red and white mulberries are ready to harvest in late spring. Most of the black varieties ripen in late spring through summer. Gather berries as they fall. The easiest way to harvest mulberries is to spread an old, clean sheet under the tree when most of the fruit is ripe and gently shake the tree. Picked red, when they are not quite ripe, mulberries are tart, excellent for jellies and pies. *Note:* Use latex gloves to protect your hands from staining.

How to Purchase

Mulberry trees are available bare root or in containers from local nurseries and these sources: Bay Laurel, Burnt Ridge, One Green World, and Raintree.

Pollinizers

Mulberries are self-fruitful.

Varieties

BLACK MULBERRY, *MORUS NIGRA*

'King James'—large, dark red fruit; grows to 30 ft. tall; Zones 8 to 10.

RED MULBERRY, *M. RUBRA*

'Geraldi Dwarf'—large, black fruit; compact growth to 6 ft. tall; Zones 5 to 8.

WHITE MULBERRY, *M. ALBA*

'Beautiful Day'—white, sweet fruit, good dried or eaten fresh; to 30 ft. tall; Zones 6 to 8.

'Pakistan'—unusual red to black fruit, to 4 in. long, sweet and fairly firm; long ripening period; spreading tree does well in dry and southern climates, Zones 7 to 10.

'Pendula' ('Weeping')—small, black, tasty fruit in early summer; weeping form, 6 to 8 ft. tall, needs support; Zones 4 to 9.

HYBRID CROSS, *M. ALBA* × *M. RUBRA*

'Illinois Everbearing'—large, sweet fruit; bears from June through early fall; full-size tree to 35 ft. tall, can be kept much smaller; Zones 4 to 9.

Muskmelon

See Melon

Mustard

(Indian mustard, mustard greens)
Brassica spp.

Effort Scale

NO. 2
Must be planted annually
Needs rich, organic soil
Constant moisture and occasional fertilizing needed

Zones

Not applicable

Thumbnail Sketch

Annual
12 to 36 in. tall
Propagate from seeds
Needs full sun; light shade in hot climates
Leaves are ornamental; curled, ruffled; green, chartreuse, purple, or bronze
Blooms in spring, summer, or fall, depending on variety
Flowers are yellow
Leaves, flowers, and seeds are edible; harvest varies with climate
Use in herbaceous border, vegetable garden, flower bed, raised bed, or container

How to Use

In the Kitchen

Cooks and gardeners grow mustards for either their piquant leaves or seeds for making condiment mustard. As a rule, the younger the leaf, the less the bite. All mustards add dense nutrition when included in a salad or added to a soup. In the South mustards are staples as a "mess o' greens," cooked up with ham for Sunday dinner. In addition to the common mustards, we grow a host of mustards from Asia, including mizunas and giant red mustards, which are indispensable in Asian cuisine in basic stir-fries, soups, and dumplings. My favorite ways to use crunchy, wasabi-tasting mustard leaves is to top a ham sandwich with a leaf or two and to chop the leaves and toss them into chicken salad.

Make condiment mustard by allowing plants to form seedpods and harvesting the seeds when the pods turn yellow; process them in a blender with white wine vinegar, black pepper, salt—and water if needed.

In the Landscape

The most spectacular greens are giant-leaved Japanese red mustard and mizuna. Japanese mustard leaves are bronze on top and chartreuse below. Mizuna, which is among the mildest mustards, produces finely serrated leaves (both green and deep red types) in a foot-tall rosette, creating a delicate contrast in a container or salad bed. Both are showy additions to a flower border. Red mustard is spectacular in formal beds with chartreuse lettuce, white tulips, and frilly green kale. Curly chartreuse mustard looks a bit like leaf lettuce and can be included in a salad grouping interplanted with edible flowers.

In just 3 weeks this unidentified mizuna with lacy burgundy red foliage produced baby greens, which were great in salads. Chartreuse mustards including 'Tokyo Behana' are also featured in this bed, with red baby pac choi in the foreground.

In my Zone 9 garden, I've had great success sprinkling Japanese mustard seeds around spring-flowering bulbs like tulips and daffodils when I plant the bulbs in early winter. In cold-winter areas, sow the seeds as the bulbs come up in the spring. The mustards eliminate any "soldiers in a row" look that bulb plantings might have. And not only can you keep the harvest going for a month or more, but the plants continue to grow as the bulb flowers fade, hiding the ripening bulb foliage.

Grow many different kinds of mustards and experiment with their shapes and colors in the garden and with the dozens of ways to serve them.

How to Grow

Mustards are easily grown and have few pests and diseases. Most mustards are cool-season (spring or fall) crops that grow best in full sun in rich, well-drained, loamy soil. All grow best in cool weather; sow seeds in early spring or late summer. In mild climates, they make lovely winter greens. Some mustards tolerate some summer heat. Without sufficient water, they become too spicy.

Plant mustard seeds ¼ inch deep and 2 inches apart. If growing plants to maturity, thin mustard and mizuna to 12 inches apart,

18 inches for giant mustards. Sow all mustards in spring or fall by broadcasting seeds over good soil and raking them in.

In addition to full-size plants, consider growing baby mustards (especially red ones) in the cut-and-come-again method. You can have a bed of only mustard varieties or combine them with lettuces and arugula as they all grow at about the same rate. Plant seeds in containers for a quick crop of salad greens or a spicy mixture of stir-fry greens.

Protect the seedlings from birds and mulch well with an organic mulch. Keep the bed weeded and water regularly or the leaves might become too hot to eat.

To harvest mustard, begin by cutting a few young outer leaves of each plant as soon as it has at least eight leaves. Continue picking outer leaves until they are too hot or tough for your taste.

For seed mustard, harvest the seed heads before they mature and split.

How to Purchase

A limited selection of mustard plants and seeds can be obtained from local nurseries. For a much larger selection consult these seed companies: Seeds of Change, John Scheepers, Southern Exposure, Nichols, Stokes Seeds, and Harris. They carry some leaf mustards, primarily American types. For the largest selection see Kitazawa, which has dozens of varieties, as does Gourmet Seed. Richter's carries seeds for condiment mustards.

Varieties

MUSTARD, *BRASSICA JUNCEA*

'Florida Broadleaf'—semi-upright plant; oval to round, serrated, medium green leaves; 50 days.

'Green Wave'—spicy with horseradish bite; upright, large, ruffle-edged, green leaves; 50 days.

'Osaka Purple'—spicy tang; deep purple leaves in cold weather; to 30 in. tall; 70 days.

'Purple Wave'—hot and spicy; lightly frilled, green-edged purple leaves; robust; 55 days.

'Red Giant' (*B. j.* var. *rugosa*)—leaves deep purple-red in cold weather, savoyed; slow to bolt; hardy; 45 days.

'Savanna'—early; tender; smooth, dark green leaves; multiple harvests; 35 days.

'Southern Giant Curled'—large upright plant; frilled, dark green, very curly leaves; 48 days.

'Tendergreen' (*B. rapa* var. *periviridis*)—mild and tender for cooking a "mess o' greens" in spring; flowering shoots good in salads; 45 days.

'Tokyo Bekana'—mild tasting; chartreuse leaves; heat and cold tolerant; 20 days to baby greens, 45 days to maturity.

CONDIMENT MUSTARD

Condiment mustards are easy to grow, reach 36 inches tall, and produce spikes of bright yellow flowers. Plant in spring and stake plants. Harvest seedpods before they shatter.

Brown mustard (*B. juncea*)—stronger mustard, for European-style mustards.

White mustard (*B. hirta*)—for a milder condiment mustard.

MIZUNA, *B. RAPA* VAR. *JAPONICA*

Upright stalks are topped by deeply serrated leaves, from light green through deep red.

'Golden-Streaked Mizuna'—heavily serrated, lime green leaves; 25 days to baby greens, 45 days to maturity.

'Mizuna'—green leaves, white stems; vigorous; slow to bolt; cold tolerant; 50 days.
'Ruby Streak'—green with dark red, finely cut foliage; 20 days to baby greens, 45 days to maturity.

Nasturtium

Tropaeolum spp.

Effort Scale

NO. 2
Must be planted annually in most climates
Fairly frequent watering needed in arid climates

Zones

Not applicable

Thumbnail Sketch

Self-sowing annual
Dwarf varieties, to 12 in.; vine, to 10 ft.
Propagate from seeds
Needs full sun; partial shade in hot climates
Leaves are round, green or blue-green, occasionally variegated, 2 to 3 in. across
Blooms in spring, summer, and fall
Flowers are red, mahogany, yellow, orange, rose, or cream colored, 2 to 3 in. across
Flowers, flower buds, leaves, and seedpods are edible; harvest all season
Use in flower bed, herb garden, or container; vining types on trellises, over retaining walls, or in hanging baskets

How to Use

In the Kitchen

All parts of the nasturtium are edible, adding pizzazz to any savory dish. Pickle the flower buds or young seedpods as a substitute for capers. Tender, young leaves add a peppery zing to salads. The blossoms are the most recognized edible flowers—seen as garnishes in restaurants everywhere. Stuff the flowers with herbed cream cheese or add them to a pasta, green, or meat salad to brighten the flavor. The numerous cultivars may look different, but their flavors are very similar.

In the Landscape

In Zones 9 to 11, these charming plants seem perennial as they reseed and bloom in the same space year after year. Their large, lily pad–shaped, bright green leaves form a bold backdrop for the brilliant flowers, which can be red, orange, apricot, yellow, mahogany, rose, or cream colored and have a lightly spicy fragrance. Some nasturtiums have double flowers.

Use dwarf plants (*Tropaeolum minus*) that grow to 12 inches tall in herb gardens and flower borders. Have fun choosing and intermixing the many cultivars. Interplant them with lettuce, carrots, spinach, chard, or alpine strawberries. The vining kinds (*T. majus*), which can trail to 10 feet, are lovely in containers or hanging baskets, flowing over a rock wall, interplanted with vining peas or cucum-

bers, or climbing up a fence or a post. However you use them, nasturtiums are always bright spots that lift the spirit.

Note: Nasturtiums can be invasive in mild coastal areas. Don't plant them near wild areas.

How to Grow

Nasturtiums grow so easily that most gardens should have some. They thrive in any well-drained, lightly moist but not soggy soil in full sun, although in hot climates they do best in partial shade. Rarely do they need feeding; in fact, if you apply too much nitrogen, they stop blooming and just grow leaves. Nasturtiums cannot tolerate frost. In milder climates, they self-sow. They are generous in their blooming habits, so you can have bouquets over a long period.

If black aphids are a problem, aim the garden hose at the pests; if they persist, spray the entire plant with insecticidal soap, or pull it out and destroy it.

How to Purchase

Nasturtium seeds are available in mixed or separate colors on most nursery and garden center seed racks and from Renee's, Nichols, Baker, Burpee, Abundant Life, and Ed Hume.

Varieties

'Alaska'—dwarf; green and white foliage; mixed colors; blooms held above foliage.
'Empress of India'—heirloom; dwarf; deep red-orange flowers; blue-green leaves.
'Glorious Gleam'—blooms in shades of orange and yellow; vining form 24 to 36 in. long.
'Jewel of Africa'—cream-striped foliage; rich blossom colors (yellow, cream, red, and peachy pink); vining form 4 to 5 ft. long.
'Strawberries and Cream'—dwarf; cream and red flowers.
Whirlybird series—dwarf; upturned semi-double flowers with no spur in which critters can hide; mix of seven bright colors; blooms held above foliage.

A tableau of nasturtiums illustrates the range of flower and leaf colors and sizes. 'Alaska' has variegated leaves, Whirlybird series spurless flowers, and 'Empress of India' bluish green leaves. All have a delightfully spicy-sweet flavor.

Nectarine

See Peach and Nectarine

Olive

Olea europaea

Effort Scale

NO. 3
Very easy to grow
Some pruning needed
Pests are a problem in some areas
Harvesting and preserving are very time consuming

Zones

9 to 11

Thumbnail Sketch

Evergreen tree or shrub
25 to 30 ft. tall
Propagate by grafting or budding or from cuttings
Needs full sun
Leaves are gray-green with whitish undersides, narrow, 1 to 3 in. long
Blooms in spring
Flowers are fragrant but insignificant
Fruits are edible if processed: harvest in fall or winter
Use as a multistemmed tree, interest plant, screen, or large shrub; to line a driveway or near an herb garden

Green olives turn black when they are fully ripe, though even ripe olives from the tree are surprisingly bitter and require processing. Olive oil is generally pressed from ripe black olives. Some olives are picked green for brining and pickling.

How to Use

In the Kitchen

Salade Niçoise, pot roast Provençale, Greek and Spanish olives—the recipes alone indicate that the Mediterranean area is olive country. The fruits of the olive tree are versatile and add great richness: green olives for martinis and black ones for Mexican tacos. Green or black, they are a favorite garnish for pizza, sandwiches, and salad plates. The flavorful and healthful oil improves salads and adds a distinctive flavor to browned meats and poultry as well as roasted vegetables.

Olive oil is tasty and very versatile in the kitchen as it has a higher smoke point than some other oils. Admittedly, making olive oil and curing olives can be a bit of a job, but the fun of making your own superior product—and the savings for folks who use a lot of oil—can make the effort worthwhile. **Caution:** The standard method for removing olives' bitterness is to soak them in caustic lye. Improperly canned olives pose a risk of botulism. Take care when processing your olives.

To preserve, pickle, or make oil, obtain brochures on oils from the University of California Cooperative Extension Service or visit www.oliveoilsource.com for information on preserving olives in many forms, links to sources of trees, home olive oil presses, books, and many recipes.

In the Landscape

Olive trees are extremely beautiful; in fact, they are among the loveliest of the edible ornamentals. Their gnarled trunks, graceful branching structures, and soft gray-green foliage give them the appearance of living sculptures. These trees are often cursed as a nuisance because the dropped olives are exceedingly messy, but they are so beautiful that people put up with the inconvenience. Olive trees are particularly effective in a Mediterranean-style landscape; their sculptural qualities show to their best advantage against light stucco walls. Olive trees make wonderful evergreen screens, are dramatic lining a country road, and make a stunning focal point for an herb garden.

Avoid planting olive trees near patios, sidewalks, lawns, or where cars are parked. Their oil, although tasty in salads, is slippery and stains hard surfaces. The ideal location is one in which the tree is surrounded by drought-tolerant ground covers (Mediterranean culinary herbs like rosemary and thyme), gravel, or organic mulch.

How to Grow

Climate

To fruit well, olives need high heat, some winter chill, and no late frosts that can kill the blossoms. Olive trees are hardy to 15°F. The fruits, which ripen late in fall, need a very long summer to mature and are injured by temperatures below 27°F.

High humidity inhibits pollination, which—for fruit production—limits these magnificent trees to Northern California and the warmer parts of the Southwest.

Exposure and Soil

Olive trees need full sun. They adapt to a wide variety of soils but are most attractive and grow best on deep, well-drained, neutral soils.

Fertilizing

On garden soils, olives produce plenty of fruit without being fed. Mulch is beneficial.

Watering

Even though olive trees are extremely drought tolerant, in arid climates water them deeply at least twice a year—in spring when the tree is flowering, and in fall before the harvest season. Monthly watering is even better.

Pruning

When an olive tree is young, you have two choices: prune all suckers leaving one main trunk, or select three to five suckers to train into a multistemmed tree. Stake the suckers for the first few years to keep them at the angle you prefer. Prune olive trees annually to shape them; keep them short enough to harvest the fruit and to thin the tree to accent its graceful nature. If you want very large olives, thin the fruits. Olive trees tend to fruit in alternate years unless you prune moderately and thin the fruits.

Pests and Diseases

For years, olives were unaffected by most pests and diseases. Occasional problems included scale and a disease that produces galls (a swelling of plant tissue) on the twigs or branches. Control the galls by cutting them out; be sure to sterilize your tools between cuts. Recently, the olive fruit fly larvae (a pest introduced into California) has been a problem as the flies produce many generations a year. For best control, clean up all fruit from the ground and remove any fruit still on the tree when winter arrives. An option is to use spinosad in combination with olive fruit fly traps to monitor the population. For the latest information, visit the University of California at Davis website www.ipm.ucdavis.edu/PMG. Do not plant an olive where verticillium wilt is a problem, since the tree is quite susceptible.

Harvesting

The average mature olive tree produces 30 to 40 pounds of olives annually, enough for the average olive oil–loving family. If you plan to use them whole, handpick to avoid bruising the fruit, but if you plan to make oil, use a bamboo pole to knock the olives off the tree onto a tarp. Pick olives green for curing, and green or black for olive oil. For the highest-quality oil, use green olives even though they yield less oil than fully ripe black ones. Olives must be processed in some manner (such as brining or pickling) to remove the bitterness before they are edible.

How to Purchase

In appropriate climates, you might find container-grown olive trees at local nurseries. Or order from Acorn Springs, Raintree, or Willis. Often landscape contractors can obtain large olive trees that were dug up from an orchard to make room for development; these transplant very well.

Pollinizers

Some varieties are self-fruitful and others need a pollinizer, as noted below.

Varieties

Make sure you choose a fruiting variety; many "fruitless" varieties produce only a few, poor-quality olives. The following varieties yield great olives.

'Arbequina'—Spanish olive, early ripening, for curing and oil; self-fruitful; verticillium resistant; compact variety.

'Leccino'—Tuscan origins, early bearing, for oil and semi-ripe black olives; needs 'Maurino' as a pollinizer.

'Manzanillo'—commercial olive, large fruits, excellent for oil and preserving; ripens several weeks earlier than 'Mission'; low growth habit; needs 'Arbequina' as a pollinizer.

'Maurino'—Tuscan origins, early ripening, for oil; somewhat disease resistant, tolerates cool conditions; pendulous habit; pollinates most varieties, semi-self-fruitful.

'Mission'—"American" olive (found at California missions), medium-size fruits, good flavor, high oil content, for oil and preserving; freestone; quite cold tolerant; readily available; self-fruitful.

Orange

See Citrus

Oregano and Marjoram

Origanum spp.

Effort Scale

NO. 1
Oregano is very easy to grow; marjoram easy.

Zones

Oregano, 5 to 9
Marjoram, 7 to 9

Thumbnail Sketch

Perennial herbs grown as annuals in cold climates
24 to 30 in. tall
Propagate from seeds, cuttings, or divisions
Need full sun
Leaves are dull gray-green, small
Bloom in summer
Flowers are white or lavender, small, in spikes or knots
Leaves are edible; use as seasoning; harvest year round
Use in herb garden, drought-tolerant border, hanging basket, or container; let sprawl over rock wall

How to Use

In the Kitchen

Oregano's aromatic, slightly spicy leaves jauntily season pizza, spaghetti sauce, soups, stews, and salads. Marjoram, often called sweet marjoram, is a bit milder and sweeter than oregano; you can use it in recipes that call for oregano, but it won't pack the same punch. Try it in omelets and marinades or where you want subtle undertones. A pinch of marjoram perks up many vegetables and adds interest to fish and meats.

Unlike with many other herbs, the flavor of both plants holds true in dried leaves. To dry, hang bunches upside down in a well-ventilated, warm, dry place. Once the leaves are brittle-dry, strip the stems, and put the leaves in sealed jars or heavy-duty zip-top plastic bags. They store for up to a year in a cool, dark space.

Use upright oregano as a vertical element in a perennial or herb border or among compact shrubs. Cut it back by half several times a year to keep it from getting woody. 'Cambridge Blue' lobelia is a superb color foil.

What gives oregano and marjoram their distinctive aroma and flavor is the essential oil carvacrol. There are numerous other oregano-like plants containing this oil that South American cooks favor. Mexican oregano (*Lippia graveolens*), a tender perennial, is the most common. Use it in Mexican dishes or as a substitute for Italian oregano, although the flavor is slightly different. Cuban oregano (*Plectranthus amboinicus*) has a more pungent oregano flavor.

In the Landscape

Oregano is an herbaceous perennial that grows to heights of 24 to 30 inches. Although it is inclined to be rangy, its gray-green leaves and pale pink flowers make it an intriguing addition to a flower border. Cut back tall oreganos to keep them bushy or use the plant's ranginess to advantage, letting it spill over a rock wall. Combine oregano with the pink and lavender hues of alyssum, society garlic, ivy geraniums, and marjoram.

Marjoram bears knots of white or light lavender flower buds; hence the name knotted marjoram. More compact than oregano, it consorts well with chives, dittany of Crete, lavender, and 'Silver Mound' artemisia. Every herb garden needs oregano and marjoram.

How to Grow

Oregano and marjoram are simple to grow from seeds, cuttings, or divisions. They need well-drained, medium-rich soil; plenty of sun; and only moderate supplemental water. In cold-winter climates where they aren't hardy, bring the plants indoors to a sun porch or sunny windowsill. Or treat them as annuals; if they don't come back in spring (they can surprise you and withstand a mild winter beyond their hardiness zones), start new plants. Keep oregano and marjoram pruned back so they don't become woody.

Harvesting

Harvest fresh oregano and marjoram anytime during the growing season. Cut the stems and pull off the leaves. However, if you are planning to dry the leaves, harvest before the plant begins to flower to ensure a rich flavor.

How to Purchase

Oregano and marjoram are promiscuous and readily interbreed, making it difficult at times to purchase a superior culinary plant, much less seeds. In fact, the nursery trade offers plants of dozens of lovely ornamental oreganos and marjorams with unusual foliage and flowers, yet many are not suitable for cooking. Before buying any plant, taste a leaf to be sure it pleases your palate. Specialty herb nurseries often featuring exceptional culinary oreganos include Richters, Nichols, Goodwin Creek, Mulberry Creek, and Thyme Garden.

Varieties

OREGANO, *ORIGANUM VULGARE*
'Greek' (*O. v.* ssp. *hirtum*)—dark green leaves; grows to 18 in. tall.
'Sicilian'—cross between oregano and marjoram; white flowers; refined flavor.
'Verona'—bushy ground cover; grows to 8 in. tall.

MARJORAM (SWEET MARJORAM), *O. MAJORANA*
'Variegata'—especially showy; white and yellow variegated leaves; prostrate habit; a bit weak on flavor.

Parsley

Petroselinum spp.

Effort Scale

NO. 2
Must be planted annually
Must be kept fairly moist

Zones

Not applicable

Thumbnail Sketch

Biennial herb usually grown as annual
6 to 24 in. tall, depending on variety
Propagate from seeds
Needs sun or light shade; partial shade in hot climates
Leaves are curly or flat, dark green
Flowers (in second season) greenish yellow, in umbels, not usually seen
Leaves are edible; use as seasoning; harvest year round; dig Hamburg roots in winter
Use as edging or in herb garden, flower border, raised bed, or container

How to Use

In the Kitchen

For decades, curly parsley was the ubiquitous green garnish (looks pretty, but don't eat it) in restaurants and homes across the country;

fortunately, times have changed. Many chefs select Italian, or flat-leaf, parsley for cooking because it has a stronger, sweeter flavor than curly parsley. Both types of parsley have aromatic leaves; pick them fresh to use as a garnish and as a seasoning in salad dressings, soups, stews, and sauces. Because parsley is rich in vitamins A and B and iron and contains oodles of antioxidants, adding ½ cup of chopped leaves to pizzas and soups is a great way to "sneak" in some nutrition.

Hamburg parsley has edible, strong-tasting leaves and a thick root with a nutty celery flavor that is delicious grated raw into salads or cooked and added to cream and vegetable soups, mashed potatoes, or stews.

In the Landscape

Gardeners generally grow these herbaceous biennials as annuals. Curly parsley is a small, frilly-leaved herb with a formal look. Its dark green stems with segmented leaves are 6 to 8 inches long. This type of parsley neatly edges an herb garden or flower bed—think red or deep pink geraniums. Interplant it with shorter flowering annuals like bedding begonias or dwarf marigolds and zinnias.

Both Italian and Hamburg parsley, with their fairly flat, cut leaves, grow to 24 inches tall and fit well in the middle of a flower border. Combine them with dwarf cosmos; the pink tones of the Sonata series or hot reds and oranges in the Bright Light series make great partners. A superb edible combination for light shade comprises all three parsleys with white violas, a color mix of dwarf nasturtiums, and alpine strawberries.

How to Grow

Climate

Parsley is easy to grow and thrives in all areas of the country.

Exposure and Soil

Parsley prefers full sun in mild areas and partial shade in hot climates; it tolerates more shade than most herbs. Growing the plants in rich, well-drained, yet fairly moist soil will reward you with colanders full of fresh, flavorful leaves.

Planting

Before planting, soak the seeds overnight or up to 24 hours to encourage sprouting; otherwise they can take up to a month to sprout. Once growing, the plant keeps going until fall.

Parsley tolerates light frost and overwinters in Zones 9 and 10. In cold-winter areas, some folks pot parsley up and bring it indoors in late fall; others just let it die. I'll let you in on a lazy gardener's secret. In fall, leave parsley alone, mark the spot in case it dies back to the roots, and come spring, it will likely sprout new leaves.

Pests and Diseases

Anise swallowtail butterflies lay their eggs on parsley foliage. When they hatch, the harlequin-bedecked caterpillars add a lively dimension to my garden as they munch the leaves (dill and fennel greens, too)—to the fascination of the neighborhood kids. I plant enough for humans and butterflies.

Harvesting

Begin harvesting parsley leaves—a few outer stems at a time—when the plant has four or five healthy stalks. Gently cut the stem away from the base of the plant. Once it has become a green bouquet, harvest as needed to use fresh. Some cooks swear that the leaves have a better texture and more flavor if you harvest before the plant starts

to flower. Greenish flowers are not showy; pick them as they form to keep the plant from going to seed. The ideal way to preserve parsley is to chop and freeze it in zip-top freezer bags. Although you can dry it like oregano, it loses a lot of its flavor.

Dig Hamburg parsley root, also called turnip-rooted parsley, in late fall and store as you would carrots—in the crisper drawer of the refrigerator—for a month or so.

How to Purchase

Purchase small plants or seeds at local nurseries in spring, or seeds from Territorial, Nichols, Johnny's, Richters, Seeds of Change, Baker Creek, or Renee's.

Varieties

CURLY PARSLEY, *PETROSELINUM CRISPUM*
'Favorit'—tightly curled leaves; uniform, very dark green color; 13 in. tall.
'Forest Green'—compact plant; long stems; dark green, double-curved leaves.
'Moss Curled'—standard curled variety used as a garnish in restaurants.

HAMBURG PARSLEY (TURNIP-ROOTED PARSLEY), *P. C. VAR. TUBEROSUM*
'Arat' (*P. c. var. radicosum*)—forms long, straight, white roots to 11 in.; nutty flavor with carrot and celery overtones; harvest a few leaves for outstanding flavor.

ITALIAN PARSLEY (FLAT-LEAF PARSLEY), *P. C. VAR. NEAPOLITANUM*
'Giant Italian' ('Giant of Italy')—heirloom; very flavorful; produces large stalks; plant is 24 to 36 in. tall.
'Single' ('Plain')—heirloom; great flavor.
'Survivor'—vigorous and healthy; disease and freeze resistant.
'Titan'—Small, dark green leaves; sweet flavor.

Plant curly parsley for a neat border—alone or with a short annual like dainty, edible Johnny-jump-up. Rich green, fringed leaves add a formal look to an otherwise informal design. Parsley grows back quickly, so harvest whenever you need it.

Pawpaw

(American custard apple)
Asimina triloba

Effort Scale

NO. 3
Finding good varieties is difficult
Establishing plant is sometimes hard
Hand pollination necessary for a generous harvest
Pruning and removing suckers usually needed
Fertilizing and mulching necessary

Zones

4 to 9

Thumbnail Sketch

Deciduous shrub or tree
20 to 25 ft. tall

One of the few native American fruit trees, the pawpaw makes a dramatic accent plant at the Chicago Botanic Garden, with its distinctive pyramidal shape and large leaves. It is easily cultivated and produces an abundance of fruit.

Propagate by grafting, from seeds, or by layering
Needs full sun or light shade
Leaves are oblong, light green, large, 8 to 12 in. long
Blooms in spring
Flowers are maroon, cup shaped, 1 to 2 in. across
Fruits are edible; harvest in fall
Use shrub form as accent, screen, or hedge; tree form as interest plant
    or small specimen

How to Use

In the Kitchen

The pawpaw is the American relative of Peru's cherimoya. The custardlike, yellow-orange flesh of the pawpaw tastes like a luscious cross between a banana and a pineapple. Enjoy the fruits fresh; the simplest way is to cut them in half, remove the seeds, and spoon out the sweet flesh. Do not eat the seeds or peel. Have fun with the fruits in the kitchen; use them in custard pies, plum-type puddings, breads, cookies, muffins, and preserves—even pawpaw ice cream.

Pawpaw fruits are very perishable—eat, cook, dry, or freeze them within 3 days. Dried or frozen pawpaw flesh is an excellent addition to breads and muffins. To freeze pawpaw, wash, peel, and seed the fruits. Pack the pulp in rigid plastic containers and keep in the freezer for up to 6 months. When thawed, the fruit is very soft; eat it promptly.

Note: Some pawpaws have white flesh, but they are not very good for eating. Look for varieties with darker-fleshed fruits.

In the Landscape

The pawpaw is native to the United States from Texas north to Michigan and south to northern Florida. It is a slow-growing, deciduous, multistemmed shrub or small tree that grows to 25 feet. The gracefully drooping, light green, foot-long leaves make the plant practical as a screen or informal hedge. When trained as a pyramid-shaped tree, the pawpaw contrasts well with similarly shaped evergreens. It grows well in a lawn and is dramatic enough to be an accent plant. The maroon flowers and the 5-inch fruits, which turn from green to brown, are not showy but add interest to the tree.

How to Grow

Even though pawpaw is indigenous, it can be difficult to establish, and plants seem to vary in their need for cross-pollinization.

Climate

Pawpaw is generally hardy to −30°F. It requires some winter chilling and hot summers to produce well; the plant is outstanding in the Midwest.

Exposure and Soil

Although pawpaw needs full sun to fruit well, dappled shade is best for the first few years as the plant becomes established. Pawpaw prefers well-drained, slightly acidic, rich garden loam.

Planting

Pawpaw can be temperamental about being transplanted. Some research indicates that filling the planting hole with a mixture of equal parts of soil and vermiculite helps; others suggest that pawpaw needs a symbiotic soil fungus to grow properly, and that soil from around the base of another pawpaw should be added to the planting hole. Whichever method you choose, handle the plant with care.

Cut the main trunk back to a foot above the graft line at the time of transplanting. Keep young trees well watered the first year. Make sure that the area at least 2 feet out from the trunk of young trees is weed free.

Fertilizing

When a pawpaw is not planted in rich bottomland, it appreciates an annual application of organic mulch and moderate fertilizing. If your soil is low in potassium, add it annually.

Watering

Pawpaw grows best in areas that get at least 30 inches of rain a year; it needs weekly irrigation in arid climates.

Pruning

The plant naturally suckers and forms thickets if not controlled. To keep the grafted named variety, or to grow as a tree, remove all suckers as they appear. If planting a grouping, allow suckers to come up only where you want them, and remove all others. A pawpaw suckers less as it ages.

Pests and Diseases

Pawpaw has very few pests and diseases. The leaves and twigs do not attract deer and rabbits, although many critters enjoy the fruits. The foliage is a preferred food of the zebra swallowtail butterfly—another good reason to grow pawpaw.

Harvesting

The fruits are ready to be picked when they are fully colored, are slightly soft like a peach, and have a pleasant fragrance.

How to Purchase

The plant is available in containers as named seedlings or grafted named varieties from some local nurseries and from Burnt Ridge, Edible Landscaping, and Raintree. Nolin River and Peterson Pawpaws carry many different cultivars.

Note: Pawpaw does not ship well, resulting in relatively little scientific and commercial attention. There are, however, many pawpaw devotees; for more information on this unusual native fruit, visit www.pawpaw.kysu.edu.

Pollinizers

To ensure pollination, plant at least two different varieties no more than 30 feet apart. Even though hand pollination greatly enhances fruit production, it is not always necessary. Flies are the pollinators, not bees.

Varieties

Some grafted named varieties have been produced, but most of the available plants are selected named seedlings from natives.

'Davis'—4 oz.; excellent flavor; large seeds.

'NC-1'—12 oz.; excellent flavor; few seeds.

'Overleese'—12 oz.; excellent flavor; oval with a few large seeds.

'Shenandoah'—12 oz.; sweet, succulent; a few large seeds; productive.

'Sunflower'—8 oz.; good flavor; few seeds; ripens slightly later than other varieties; partially self-pollinizing.

'Taylor'—4 oz.; mild flavor; fruit grows in clusters.

'Taytoo'—10 oz.; light yellow flesh, early ripening; excellent flavor; productive.

This bicolor chartreuse and maroon snow pea is one of the new varieties Dr. Calvin Lamborn, who bred the 'Sugar Snap' pea, is now working on. I've been lucky to trial a few, including this showstopper and some purple-podded snap peas.

Pea

Pisum sativum

Effort Scale

NO. 3
Must be planted annually
Mulching and training needed
Pests and diseases occasionally a problem
Harvesting is time consuming

Zones

Not applicable

Thumbnail Sketch

Herbaceous annual vine
Climbs by tendrils 2 to 8 ft. tall
Propagate from seeds
Needs full sun; afternoon shade in hot weather
Leaves are blue-green, oval, 1 to 2 in. long
Blooms in spring or winter

At North Hills in Vermont, Joe Eck and Wayne Winterrowd grow vegetables in style. Semi-formal supports are made from tied branches of red-twigged dogwood; peas grow inside and outside the forms. Vining peas are in the background.

Flowers are legume type, white, pink, or lavender
Seeds, pods, tendrils, and flowers are edible; harvest in season
Use in herbaceous border, raised bed, or large container; vining types on trellises or over retaining walls

How to Use

In the Kitchen

"How luscious lies the pea within the pod," wrote Emily Dickinson. Today, fresh-shelled peas are as rare as real pearls. There are five categories of peas: edible-podded snow pea types; thicker, crunchy-podded snap peas; standard shelling peas (including French-style petits pois); starchy soup peas; and varieties bred for leaves and tendrils that are eaten stir-fried or used as a garnish.

With fond thoughts of my grandmother—when I was little and helped her shell peas, she let me pop most of mine into my mouth—I eat half my pea harvest before I get into the house. Peas and ham in a cream sauce over fettuccine, shepherd's pie with mashed potatoes and garden peas, petits pois with mint and butter—such elegant peasant food. Dried peas are starchier than fresh and make fabulous soups and a delicious hummus.

The sweet, crunchy, succulent pods of snow and snap peas dress up a raw vegetable platter. And Dr. Calvin Lamborn, who developed the 'Sugar Snap' pea, is working on purple and yellow snow peas, so soon you'll have a rainbow of crudités. The pods are also tasty when steamed briefly or tossed into a stir-fry. Today, chefs lust after home gardeners' pea shoots and flowers to use in salads. In China, pea shoots, sometimes called tendrils, have been used for centuries as a vegetable; cook them as you would spinach or stir-fry them with ginger. The youngest tendrils are crisp and sweet—great for garden munching or garnishing.

Blanch snap peas, snow peas, or shelled peas for 2 minutes and freeze. Dry soup peas and store in airtight containers.

Caution: Do not confuse or combine edible peas with sweet peas; ornamental sweet peas are poisonous.

In the Landscape

Pea plants range from 8-foot-long climbing vines to 2- to 4-foot-high bushes. Most have small, delicate, bluish green leaves and white, legume-type flowers; all produce tendrils. Except for the nearly leafless varieties that cling to each other with lots of tendrils, peas need a support system, be it a trellis or an open fence. Grow both short and tall varieties along the back of an annual flower bed of stock and snapdragons, or plant the bushy ones around a small bamboo teepee in a large patio container and let your guests pick their own hors d'oeuvres.

Some edible varieties are especially decorative, including varieties with lavender purple flowers that bloom in beautiful clusters; semi-leafless varieties that show off their clusters of white flowers and pods above tight compact plants resembling a clipped hedge; and new, fancy-leaved varieties that look like frilly little bushes.

How to Grow

Climate

Peas thrive in climates with a long, cool spring. Young plants tolerate light frosts, but temperatures below 28°F kill mature plants. In hot weather, plants are mildew prone and bear poorly. Fall crops are possible if planted 60 days before the first expected frost. In mild-winter areas, peas grow from fall through spring. In areas with a short spring, plant seeds 30 days before the last frost date.

Exposure and Soil

Peas grow best in full sun, though they prefer afternoon shade in hot weather. Give them very well-drained soil.

Planting

If you have not planted peas in the bed before or are growing them in a container, purchase pea inoculant (*Rhizobia* bacteria that help plants to fix nitrogen), and follow package directions. Plant pea seeds directly in the garden, about 1 inch deep, and 2 inches apart. If your season is very short or you have trouble germinating peas, start them inside on damp paper towels until they sprout. Carefully plant the delicate seedlings 1 inch deep, tamp down, and water in place. Peas need little nitrogen, but they require extra potassium and phosphorus at planting time. Cover the bed with floating row covers or bird netting to protect the seedlings; remove when plants are 12 inches tall. If slugs are not a serious problem, apply an organic mulch at this time to cut down on weeds and watering.

Trellis tall varieties; all varieties benefit from support, for disease control and ease of harvesting. Use short posts with biodegradable netting or string; or for a rustic look, stick pea brush (twiggy tree prunings) in the soil for peas to cling to (pull both twigs and peas at the end of the season and compost them).

Pests and Diseases

Pests include the pea weevil, aphids, and thrips. For control, rotate your crops, clean up debris, and spray plants with pyrethrins, if needed. To prevent powdery mildew, fusarium wilt, and pea enation mosaic virus, which plagues peas in the Northwest, choose resistant varieties and clean up all debris after the season.

Harvesting

Peas are ready for harvest about 3 weeks after blossoms set. You can expect 2 to 3 pounds from a 15-foot row over a 1-week period. The harvest season lasts from 2 to 6 weeks depending on the variety and weather. Tall vining peas bear the longest.

How to Purchase

Pea seeds are readily available at local nurseries and from Baker Creek, Bountiful Gardens, Burpee, Fedco, Johnny's, Nichols, Pine Tree, Renee's, Seeds of Change, Seed Savers, Southern Exposure, and Territorial.

Varieties

While all pea shoots are edible, 'Usui' (sometimes called 'Snow Pea Shoots') was bred for its exceptionally tender shoots, and Dr. Lamborn is developing a frilly-leaf pea that is great for cooking, as well.

SHELLING PEA, *PISUM SATIVUM*

'Alderman' ('Tall Telephone')—heirloom; 6 ft. tall, vining; prolific; resists fusarium; 75 days.
'Garden Sweet'—holds its sweetness long after harvest; 4 ft. tall; 75 days.
'Maestro'—very sweet; 24 in. tall; disease resistant; 60 days.
'Survivor'—nearly leafless, produces masses of intertwining tendrils; needs no support, 24 in. tall; good disease resistance; 70 days.
'Thomas Laxton'—heirloom; sweet; 6 ft. tall, vining; prolific; resists fusarium; 75 days.
'Wando'—heirloom; withstands both heat and cold better than most varieties; 30 in. tall; 70 days.

SNAP PEA, *P. S. VAR. MACROCARPON* (CROSS BETWEEN SHELLING AND SNOW PEAS)

'Sugar Ann'—crisp, great flavor; 24 to 30 in. tall; early, 60 days.
'Sugar Snap'—the original and still the best snap pea in my book, though breeders have let the seed quality deteriorate and the pods are no longer consistently fat and succulent; 7 ft. tall; 65 days.
'Sugar Sprint'—stringless; 24 to 30 in. tall; powdery mildew resistant, enation virus tolerant; early, 62 days.
'Sugar Star'—stringless; 24 to 30 in. tall; mildew resistant, enation virus resistant; very early, 55 days.

SNOW PEA, *P. S. VAR. MACROCARPON*

'Dwarf Grey Sugar'—reddish purple flowers; can be tough; 28 in. tall; 57 days.
'Oregon Sugar Pod II'—24 to 30 in. tall; enation virus resistant; 60 days.
'Snow Wind'—nearly leafless; produces an abundance of peas; powdery mildew resistant; 70 days.

SOUP PEA, *P. SATIVUM*

'Blue Pod Capucijners'—heirloom; deep purple flowers and pods; pick when young and flat to use like snow peas; 5 to 6 ft. tall; 80 to 85 days.
'Blue Pod Desirée'—purple flowers and pods; 18 to 24 in. tall; 80 to 85 days.

Peach and Nectarine

Prunus persica

Effort Scale

NO. 5
Vulnerable to many diseases and pests
Heavy pruning necessary
Mulching necessary
Large yield must be harvested quickly
Cleanup of fruit is mandatory

Zones

5 to 9, depending on variety

Thumbnail Sketch

Deciduous trees
15 to 20 ft. tall
Propagate by budding or from cuttings
Need full sun
Leaves are narrow, 3 to 6 in. long
Bloom in spring
Flowers are pink, showy in some varieties
Fruits are edible; harvest in summer
Use as interest trees, espaliers, screens, or container plants

How to Use

In the Kitchen

Fresh peaches and nectarines are lasciviously juicy and sweet. The yellow-fleshed ones are rich and tangy; the white-fleshed varieties are amazingly sweet and even more aromatic. Both bring a real taste of summer to our menus. When cooked or canned, both fruits change in flavor but are as delicious and adaptable. Peach upside-

Fuzzy-skinned peaches with a rosy blush epitomize the succulence of summer. Just imagine the sweet juice dripping down your chin as you take a bite. Try your hand at homemade peach ice cream or add slices to fresh or frozen yogurt.

down cake mixes the flavor of peaches with brown sugar, and peach jam on hot corn bread is a classic. Peaches and nectarines can be canned, spiced, pickled, dried, brandied, and made into jams, jellies, fruit leather, chutney, nectar, and brandy. The fruits can also be frozen. Whether served as a salad, a simple dessert consisting of a perfect specimen, or sliced as a topping for ice cream, peaches and nectarines with their luscious, not-too-sweet, not-too-acid flavors are among summer's small ecstasies.

In the Landscape

If you choose a variety of peach or nectarine with showy flowers and good form and maintain it with care, the tree will serve as an interest plant and can be substituted for a small flowering tree in the landscape, such as a redbud or an ornamental peach. It can be used as a small tree near a patio or driveway if planted back far enough to prevent fruit from dropping on the pavement. Planting it near the street is tempting fate—and passers-by, who might help themselves.

While peaches are traditionally trained to a simple tree form, they can also be grown in a hedge-type planting, or you can plant a number of varieties in the same hole. And when we think hedgerow we often think straight borders, but consider planting the trees in a large circle, so children have a delicious, secret space inside of about 10 feet across. Combining many varieties of peaches and nectarines has the advantage of a smaller harvest of different types over an entire season—say, an early, yellow-fleshed peach and a late-season, red-fleshed peach, plus a midseason, yellow-fleshed nectarine and a late, white-fleshed nectarine.

Note: Do not plant peach or nectarine trees near windows or in front of a brick or painted wall, as the trees may need to be sprayed with oily substances.

How to Grow

Climate

Probably no fruit tree elicits more wishful thinking than a peach. But no matter what you wish, neither peaches nor nectarines survive very cold winters—period. Some very hardy peach varieties, such as 'Reliance', widen the range somewhat, but none are successful much below −15°F. Peaches and nectarines do poorly in areas with very warm winters, too, since they have a chilling requirement, and the varieties available for such weather are second-rate.

Exposure and Soil

It is extremely important that peaches and nectarines receive full sun and be given good drainage in heavy soils. They grow best in well-drained sandy loam or in raised beds.

Fertilizing

Feed peaches and nectarines with moderate amounts of nitrogen in the spring, and keep the trees mulched with compost during the growing season. The symptoms of nitrogen deficiency are lack of vigor and a yellowish or light green leaf color. If these symptoms appear, apply more nitrogen fertilizer in early summer. If you live in a cold-winter area, it is critical to apply the nitrogen by July 1.

Pruning

Train young trees to an open vase shape. Peach and nectarine trees need heavy pruning to produce good fruit in most climates. If you're in one of the coldest peach climates, consult your local Cooperative Extension Service for pruning information. Dormant-prune in early spring just as growth is starting so that pruning wounds heal quickly

and thus are less apt to become diseased. Peaches and nectarines bear on 1-year-old wood only; therefore new wood must be continually produced to permit fruiting in the following year. To prune, thin out a number of branches, particularly in the middle of the tree, to allow sunlight to enter and good air circulation to occur. Prune heavily, removing one-third to one-half of the new growth, which is generally reddish. Remove any weak growth or crossing branches. Further summer pruning is usually recommended to let sunlight color the fruits and help control tree size, especially if intended as a hedge.

The crops that peaches and nectarines set are usually too heavy, and the fruits must be thinned when they are an inch across. Leave 6 to 8 inches between early peaches and nectarines, 4 to 5 inches between late-ripening fruits, and somewhere between the two for midseason varieties. If you do not thin, the fruits will be small and the branches may break from the weight.

Pests and Diseases

Peaches and nectarines are a real challenge for growers trying to maintain their landscapes with a minimum of chemicals. To prevent many problems, choose resistant varieties and plant in a sunny spot with good air circulation. Keep the trees well mulched and pruned to prevent still more afflictions.

Peach leaf curl is the most serious and widespread problem and is most likely to occur in cool, wet weather. The foliage develops bumpy, red, swollen areas and eventually shrivels and drops, and the fruit is misshapen. A Bordeaux mixture or lime sulfur should be applied in late fall and again just before flower buds start to swell in spring to give good control. Spraying is useless once the disease manifests in spring.

Brown rot is a common problem on shoots and on fruits just before they ripen, and powdery mildew is a serious problem in damp climates. Peach tree borers—blue-black moths with an orange band—are deadly. One or two can kill a young tree by girdling the trunk. Check around the crown every few weeks for "sawdusty" holes. San Jose scale and plum curculio are sometimes problems, too.

Harvesting

The fruits ripen over 2 or 3 weeks. Plan to be at home for the harvest, since ripe fruits won't wait. Peaches and nectarines are at their sublime best when they are completely ripe. Before you pick any fruit, make sure it is fully colored and has no green left near the stem, comes off the tree easily in your hand, and gives slightly to the touch.

Homegrown peaches and nectarines bruise very easily; handle them like eggs. Expect to harvest 100 to 150 pounds yearly from a mature, full-size tree.

How to Purchase

Peaches are available bare root from local and mail-order nurseries in early spring, and in containers throughout the growing season. Nurseries with a particularly large selection include Bay Laurel, Adams County, Ison's, Mid City, C & O, Trees of Antiquity, Johnson, Miller, and Stark Bro's.

Pollinizers

Most peaches and nectarines are self-fruitful.

Rootstocks

Specific peach and nectarine varieties are grafted onto named rootstocks. 'Citation' rootstock produces an 8- to 14-foot tree that is hardy, tolerates wet soils, and resists root knot nematodes. 'Lovell' produces a taller tree to about 20 feet and is hardy, but it is susceptible to crown gall and to nematodes in sandy soils. 'Nemaguard' produces a large tree to 25 feet and is not very hardy. Although resistant to root knot nematodes, it is susceptible to many diseases; in poorly drained soil, plant a tree with a 'Nemaguard' rootstock on a mound.

Varieties

Most of the varieties of peaches and nectarines listed have showy flowers; some are resistant to diseases. Peach and nectarine flavors range from sweet to intensely acidic to bland; the texture can be firm or soft, stringy or fine grained. As a rule, the white-fleshed varieties are sweeter and have less acidity. Some of those listed here are classics, and others are new varieties with more disease resistance.

Peaches and nectarines come either with a loose pit—freestone—or clingstone, with the pit attached to the flesh. A freestone is easier to work with in the kitchen.

Unless otherwise noted, the varieties described here are freestone and are hardy from Zones 6 to 9.

PEACH, *PRUNUS PERSICA* VAR. *PERSICA*

'Arctic Supreme'—midseason; clingstone, red skin over white flesh, very sweet; 700 chill hours, Zones 4 to 8.

'Babcock'—antique; early; small, white fleshed, aromatic, low acid; overripens quickly; showy blossoms; low chill.

'Belle of Georgia' ('Georgia Belle')—antique; midseason; white-fleshed, melting fruit, traditional for ice cream; moderate chill, Zones 5 to 8.

'Frost'—mid- to late season; excellent yellow, Elberta-type eating peach; showy blossoms; resistant to peach leaf curl; moderate chill, Zones 7 to 9.

'Indian Free'—antique; midseason; red-tinged yellow flesh, tart, mealy when overripe; needs a pollinizer; showy blossoms; some resistance to peach leaf curl; moderate chill, Zones 5 to 9.

'J. H. Hale'—antique; late midseason; classic yellow fleshed, sweet, fine grained; won't sweeten in cool summers; needs a pollinizer; moderate chill.

'La Feliciana'—early midseason; yellow flesh, sweet; bred at LSU for southern gardens, low to moderate chill, Zones 8 to the cooler parts of 9.

'Loring'—midseason; large, yellow fleshed, firm textured; taste-test winner; late blooming; requires heavy pruning; moderate chill.

'Madison'—midseason; golden yellow, outstanding flavor; very tolerant of frost during blooming; high chill.

'Monroe'—late; fine textured, yellow; showy pink flowers; disease tolerant; high chill, Zones 5 to 9.

'Red Baron'—midseason; rich, firm, yellow fleshed; showy, double, red flowers; low chill.

'Redhaven'—early with long ripening season; yellow fleshed, has a bit of a tang, great for freezing and canning; moderate chill, Zones 5 to 9.

'Reliance'—early; large, yellow fleshed; showy flowers; not the tastiest peach, but one of the hardiest; moderate chill, Zones 4 to 8.

'Saturn' ('Peentau')—antique; mid- to late season; donut shaped, white flesh, thin red skin, very sweet; dark pink flowers; productive; low chill, Zones 5 to 9. 'Galaxy' is similar new variety with larger, sweet, donut-shaped fruit.

'Suncrest'—mid- to late season; large, yellow, firm, melting, very juicy; classic eating peach immortalized by David Mas Masumoto's book *Epitaph for a Peach*; showy blossoms; moderate chill.

Do you dare to sit and eat a peach? The tree has a beautiful round shape and should be kept small for easy harvests. The fruit is preceded by pretty pink blossoms in spring; choose the showiest varieties for your climate.

NECTARINE, *P. P.* VAR. *NUCIPERSICA*

'Cavalier'—late; yellow; showy flowers; highly resistant to brown rot; moderate chill.

'Harko'—mid- to late season; yellow semi-freestone, sweet, great flavor; showy flowers; tolerates brown rot; moderate chill, Zones 5 to 8.

'Honey Kist'—early; yellow flesh, acidic and sweet; high chill.

'Independence'—early; yellow, rich flavor; showy flowers; takes warm winters; moderate chill.

'Red Chief'—late; white flesh; showy flowers; highly resistant to brown rot.

'Zee Glow'—late; yellow flesh, red skin, classic sweet and acid flavor; showy pink flowers; moderate chill.

Pear

Pyrus spp.

Effort Scale

NO. 3
Vulnerable to numerous pests and diseases
Harvesting large crop is time consuming
Some varieties need to ripen in cold storage before eating

Zones

4 to 9

Thumbnail Sketch

Deciduous tree
Standard, 30 to 40 ft. tall; semi-dwarf, 8 to 20 ft. tall; any tree can be kept under 6 ft. with proper pruning
Propagate by grafting or budding

People can get snookered by pears—not knowing when they're ripe or if a variety needs refrigerator ripening. 'Seckel' pears are versatile and among the easiest to grow—and harvest. Simply pick them and enjoy their intense flavor immediately or store them.

Needs full sun

Leaves are deep green, 1 to 2½ in. long; most varieties turn yellow in fall

Blooms in spring

Flowers are white; grow in clusters, showy, 1 to 1½ in. across

Fruits are edible; harvest in summer or fall

Use as interest tree, small street tree, espalier, patio tree, or container plant; when kept short by summer pruning, good for informal hedge and large shrub border

How to Use

In the Kitchen

An American pear grower I met described his first memorable pear experience thusly: "I was in France, and my father-in-law-to-be brought one perfectly ripe pear on a plate to the table and proceeded to peel it with his knife—never touching it with his fingers. Once it was peeled, he cut off slices and offered them to the three of us to savor, one magnificent piece at a time. That luscious and fragrant piece of fruit became a celebration. I decided then and there that when I returned to America I wanted to become a pear farmer and share that experience with the world." Unfortunately, given modern agriculture, a perfectly ripened pear is a delight not too many Americans have experienced.

Served with Camembert or Brie, an exquisitely ripe European pear is a dessert course acceptable in even the haughtiest cuisines. Asian pears proffer a completely different experience. Smaller and crisper (and sometimes slightly gritty), they are aromatic, sweet, and juicy. All pears are a welcome addition to a green or fruit salad. 'Bosc' and 'Seckel' pears are superlative fanned out atop a tart; they hold their shape when poached or roasted and served with tasty sauces flavored with liqueurs, raspberries, or cranberries.

To preserve pears for out-of-season delights, dry or can them; or make into jam, butter, pickles, chutney, nectar, or brandy. 'Seckel' pears pickled with cinnamon and sugar are fabulous. Some old varieties (perry pears) are traditionally used to make a hard cider known as perry.

In the Landscape

The shape of most pear trees is strongly vertical, almost like that of a candelabrum. Glossy leaves follow the big spring show of white flower clusters. An advantage of pears is that the fruit is produced on long-lived spurs, so the showy blooms do not have to be pruned off. Asian pears are vigorous trees with slightly larger leaves that often turn red in autumn. The applelike fruits are usually round.

Full-size pear trees are excellent shade trees and do better than most fruit trees in a lawn. While never ideal, you can grow pears in lawns, though in the East and Midwest only; crown rot is a major problem in arid-summer areas. Since you pick most varieties before the pears drop, fruit drop over patios and walks is a non-issue. Use any size pear tree to line a driveway, plant near a patio, or as an entrance accent or small street tree. When kept under 8 feet tall, pears make a handsome hedge or a dramatic espalier.

Note: Do not plant pear trees near windows in case the trees need to be sprayed.

How to Grow

Pears can take from 4 to 6 years to produce their first crop and are well worth the wait.

Climate

Pear trees are hardy and bloom fairly early. They are fussier about climate than apples, so select the variety carefully if you live in an area with late frosts or where winters are warm. Pears need winter chill; the amount depends on the variety. Most pears flourish in cool-summer areas.

Exposure and Soil

Pears grow best in full sun in good garden loam. While they prefer good drainage, they tolerate heavy soil and poor drainage better than other popular fruits. This is not true of pears grafted onto quince rootstock, however.

Fertilizing

Avoid a large amount of nitrogen, which encourages succulent new growth susceptible to fireblight and fall freezing. Too much growth usually indicates too much nitrogen. Pears respond well to 4 or more inches of organic mulch renewed annually. To avoid rodent problems, keep the mulch well away from the trunk or wrap the trunk with plastic rodent guards.

Watering

Pear trees require moderate amounts of water. Where summers are arid, deep watering once a month is usually sufficient. In rainy-summer areas, supplemental watering is usually unnecessary for mature trees. Mulch to retain soil moisture.

Pruning

Train young trees to three or four main branches and a modified central leader form. Pears bear fruit on long-lived fruiting spurs and need little heavy regular pruning except to shape, remove dead or weak growth, control size, and maintain good air circulation. With established trees, thin about 10 percent of the branches and fruiting spurs annually. The easiest way to keep the trees a manageable size is to train them to top out at around 6 feet and maintain that size with both winter and summer pruning. Thin fruit of both species to cut down on diseases and to increase the size of the fruits.

Pests and Diseases

Pears are beset with some of the same pests and diseases as apples— namely European codling moth, San Jose scale, scab, and fireblight. To control scale, follow the dormant spray recommendations for fruit trees in Appendix D. Pear scab is primarily a problem in coastal and northern gardens with high humidity and cool weather; control the disease by planting resistant varieties.

Pears are less affected than apples by the diseases that strike both—except for fireblight. This bacterium can be fatal to some commonly grown pear varieties. In spring after petal fall, look for branches that suddenly turn brown or black and curl up at the end; immediately remove and destroy them, and avoid too much nitrogen fertilizer. The best control for fireblight is to choose resistant varieties; there are many.

Another possible pest, pear psylla, overwinters as adults in debris and under the bark. To control the pest, remove all debris in fall and spray dormant oil when buds start to swell in spring. If psylla appear in the canopy later, use neem or soap sprays, or apply summer-weight oil.

Rabbits and voles take a toll on young pear trees in winter. Wrap the trunks with tree wrap or fine wire mesh to protect them; remove snow from around the trunk so critters do not have a place to hide. Deer graze pear trees; protect with fencing or apply deer repellents continually.

Harvesting

Harvest European pears before they fully ripen and give only slightly to thumb pressure. If you have ever eaten a grainy, sawdusty pear that had a brown center, it was probably picked ripe. Instead, pick the pears just as they start to color, are still firm, and are at the point when a small upward tug separates the stem from the branch. Fruits picked too early shrivel or have little flavor. To prolong the season, store summer types in the refrigerator and bring out a few at a time to ripen.

To cure winter pears like 'Comice', store them—ideally in a large box of sand—at as close to 32°F as possible for 3 to 4 weeks with high humidity before taking any out to ripen at room temperature; do not let them freeze. Most winter pears store for 4 months, though most tend to deteriorate slowly in quality after the third month.

Like apples, Asian pears ripen fully on the tree and do not ripen further once harvested. They are quite firm, and even when fully ripe, give only slightly when pressed. Mature, full-size pear trees produce between 150 and 250 pounds annually.

How to Purchase

European pears are readily available bare root or in containers at local nurseries and mail-order sources. Good sources for pears include Adams County, Bay Laurel, Cummins, Mid City, One Green World, Peaceful Valley, Raintree, Stark Bro's, and Trees of Antiquity. Henry Leuthardt offers espaliered pears; One Green World and Raintree carry antique perry pear varieties.

Pollinizers

Nearly all varieties need pollinizers. Most varieties cross-pollinize; notable exceptions are 'Seckel' and 'Bartlett', which will not reliably pollinize each other, and 'Magness', which does not pollinize any other variety. Some Asian varieties do not cross-pollinize readily with European pears.

Rootstocks

Pears grafted onto quince to produce small trees are prone to winter injury, susceptible to fireblight, need staking, and are not suitable for alkaline soils. *Pyrus communis* rootstocks are hardy, produce trees from semi-dwarf to full size, and tolerate acid and alkaline soils. Trees on *P. betulifolia* rootstock resist soilborne pests and diseases, do best in acid soils, are marginally hardy, and produce vigorous trees. Most Asian pears are grafted onto *P. betulifolia*. Because *P. calleryana* rootstock is not hardy, it is best for warm-winter areas. It is tolerant of acid soils and resists oak root fungus, fireblight, and crown rot. 'OHxF333', a semi-dwarf rootstock, produces a 20-foot tree (50 to 70 percent smaller than standard) that tolerates a broad range of soils and resists fireblight. Some Asian pears are sold on this rootstock.

Varieties

Take care to choose varieties that are hardy in your climate. Unless otherwise noted, the pear varieties described here are hardy in Zones 5 to 9 and require 800 chill hours. If you garden in a mild climate, select lower-chill varieties. Other considerations are which flavors entice you; whether you prefer succulence or substance, tangy or sweet flesh; and if you have room to refrigerate a large harvest. For

A striking pear espalier in British Columbia, Canada, lends high style to a plain wall, with the bonus of luscious fruits. Start a meal by serving fresh sliced pears on butter lettuce with blue cheese and end with a pear tart— truly elegant fare.

more information on growing pears, antique varieties, and cooking with pears, consult *The Great Book of Pears* by Barbara Flores.

EUROPEAN PEAR, *PYRUS COMMUNIS*

Some of the most popular European pears have stood the flavor test of time. They are sublime—akin to a royal treat—although they ship poorly and many are susceptible to fireblight. To learn what all the fuss is about, search online for organizations offering antique pear tastings. Fedco, Southmeadow, and Trees of Antiquities carry many old varieties. St. Lawrence has a large selection of very hardy European pear varieties.

'Bartlett' ('Williams')—antique 1700s; early; popular, juicy; does not store well; good pollinizer of other pears; self-fertile in arid West, pollinize with 'Bosc', 'D'Anjou', or 'Winter Nelis' elsewhere; susceptible to fireblight; tolerates high heat, 800 chill hours, Zones 4 to 8. 'Harvest Queen' is similar, resists fireblight.

'Blake's Pride'—midseason; blend of acid and sugar, rich aromatic taste; pollinize with 'Bosc', 'D'Anjou', or 'Harrow Delight'; fireblight resistant.

'Bosc'—antique 1807; late; large, russeted brown pear; top flavor, melting flesh, great for eating fresh or cooking; stores well; needs another pear for pollinization; 700 chill hours, Zones 4 to 8.

'Comice'—antique 1849; late; greenish color; the gold standard for eating pears, rich and buttery; stores well, needs post-harvest refrigeration to develop flavor; semi-dwarf; self-fruitful in West; susceptible to fireblight; well suited to the Northwest, 600 chill hours, Zones 4 to 9.

'Flemish Beauty'—antique 1830; aromatic, large fruit with fine flavor; ripen off the tree; bears young; susceptible to fireblight; Zones 4 to 9.

'Harrow Delight'—early; fine flesh, outstanding flavor; productive; pollinize with other pears; very fireblight resistant, russet resistant; Zones 5 to 8.

'Kieffer'—Asian pear hybrid; late; large, gritty fruit great for canning but not eating fresh; self-fruitful; fireblight resistant; for mild southern and coldest climates, 350 chill hours.

'Magness'—midseason; similar to 'Comice'; needs a pollinizer; fireblight resistant; good for Northeast, Zones 4 to 7.

'Moonglow'—midseason; fair dessert quality, good for canning, stores well; resists fireblight and leaf spot; large tree; 700 chill hours.

'Seckel'—antique 1790; late; small, 2-in., brown fruit, connoisseur's choice for canning and pickling; stores well; not as exacting about when to pick; resists fireblight; tough, small tree, good pollinizer; 700 chill hours, Zones 5 to 8.

'Warren'—late; 'Comice'-like fruit; stores well; similar characteristics but resists fireblight; pyramidal shape; needs a pollinizer; 500 chill hours.

ASIAN PEAR (PEAR APPLE, NASHI), *P. PYRIFOLIA*

These crisp pears do well in all pear climates except the very coldest, generally needing less chill than European pears. Except as noted, all produce round fruit. They are available from Adams County, Bay Laurel, Burnt Ridge, Edible Landscaping, Mid-City, One Green World, and Peaceful Valley.

'Hosui'—early; rich, sweet, great Asian variety; stores for 2 months; susceptible to fireblight and bacterial canker; pollinize with 'Shinko' or 'Bartlett'; 450 chill hours, Zones 5 to 9.

'Kosui'—early; russeted fruit, great flavor; ripens in a short season; susceptible to diseases in rainy Northwest; needs a pollinizer; 900 to 1,000 chill hours, Zones 6 to 9.

'Shinko'—late; sweet brown fruit, crisp, refreshing flavor; stores well; 450 chill hours.

'Shinseiki'—early; juicy fruit, keeps well on tree 4 to 6 weeks; self-fruitful; large tree, very susceptible to fireblight; 450 chill hours.

'Tsu Li'—early; juicy, crisp, pear shaped; use 'Ya Li' as pollinizer; vigorous tree; 300 chill hours, Zones 4 to 9.

'Ya Li'—early; slow to bear; large, juicy, aromatic, sweet, pear shaped; resists fireblight; red fall foliage; use 'Tsu Li' as pollinizer; 300 chill hours, Zones 6 to 9.

Pecan and Hickory

Carya spp.

Effort Scale

NO. 3
Susceptible to many pests and diseases
Fertilizing necessary
Raking usually necessary
Harvesting a large crop is time consuming
Hickory nuts are hard to open

Zones

Pecan, 5 to 9
Hickory, 4 to 9

Thumbnail Sketch

Deciduous trees
75 to 100 ft. tall
Propagate by grafting or budding or from seeds
Need full sun
Leaves are compound, medium green
Bloom in late spring or early summer
Flowers are not showy
Trees slow to bear, nuts are edible; harvest in fall
Use as shade trees, street trees, or screens in large yards

How to Use

In the Kitchen

When you have a pecan tree, you are a rich person. The nuts, which might as well be flecked with gold in the marketplace, are so versatile that having them in your cupboard ensures fabulous eating. Braise pecans in soy sauce for a great hot snack; glaze them with brown sugar and sprinkle over a salad. What would the holidays be like without pecan pie? While pecans are fairly high in fat, the fat is mostly polyunsaturated; and ten pecan halves contain only 65 calories as well as a host of proteins, vitamins, and minerals.

Rich, white hickory nuts have a sweet, distinctive flavor and are considered by some to be among the finest nuts in the world, prized for eating fresh as well as in pies, cakes, breads, and cookies. The nuts are hard to shell but well worth the effort. To make the job easier, purchase a hard-shell nutcracker.

Store unshelled pecan and hickory nuts in a mesh bag in a dry place with good air circulation for months. For the best quality, shell nuts after harvesting, put in sealed containers, and freeze. The quality will hold for up to a year. As a culinary bonus, you can smoke meat over a fire of hickory prunings for a down-home flavor.

In the Landscape

I grouped pecans and hickories together as they are in the same genus, *Carya*. Hican is a cross between the two. Both pecans and hickories are native to North America. Like most nut trees, they are large, stately, and long lived. Their cut leaves and graceful branching patterns provide good shade along with the tree's edible bonus. Shade from a few pecans or hickories planted in a large backyard can lower the temperature 5 to 10 degrees on a hot, sultry day. 'Cheyenne' pecan is a compact variety more suitable for small yards.

Line a driveway, block a view, or shade a hot south wall with hickories or pecans. Hickories have unique shaggy bark that is striking when viewed up close. Both pecans and hickories turn a lovely shade of yellow in fall before dropping lots of leaves that require raking in manicured yards.

How to Grow

Climate

Pecans grow from the East Coast west to Iowa and Texas, from Illinois south and into Mexico, and in warm inland parts of California. Southern varieties need 270 to 290 warm growing days, northern varieties 170 to 190 warm days. At present, no pecan varieties reliably produce nuts in the Northeast or Northwest. Pecans are more prone to diseases in humid conditions.

Shagbark hickory's native range extends from southern Quebec south to northern Florida and Mexico, and from the East Coast west to Minnesota. The natural range of shellbark hickory is from southern Ontario south into Louisiana and west to Oklahoma. Under humid conditions, hickories are more prone to diseases.

Exposure and Soil

Provide full sun and ordinary garden soil pH. Pecan and shellbark hickory, native to the river bottoms of the Midwest and South, need deep, well-drained, rich, alluvial soil. Attempts to establish either on shallow soils less than 3 feet deep with poor drainage are rarely successful. Shagbark hickory, indigenous to uplands and river bottoms, can adapt to drier conditions, but it will grow slower and produce fewer nuts.

Planting

These trees have massive root systems. Plant them at least 40 feet apart and at least 20 feet from foundations, driveways, and power lines. Pecan and hickory trees are difficult to establish if their long taproots have been injured. After removing the tree from the container, if possible check the roots for damage before planting. To plant: Dig a hole deep enough to accommodate the entire length of the taproot. Gently place the root in the hole without bending it; carefully place the soil around the root and tamp in place. Water the tree well and keep it mulched. Stake if necessary.

Fertilizing

Pecans require more care than hickories. Orchardists recommend fertilizing new pecan trees once in June with a high-nitrogen organic fertilizer; some supplement with seaweed sprays, as well. For the next 3 years, make three small applications of nitrogen fertilizer—in April, May, and June; water in well. Mature pecan trees over 4 years old

The shapes and textures of nut cousins are fascinating. On the left are smooth-shelled pecans; in the center are hicans, showing how the different crosses of pecans and hickories can produce unique nuts; and prickly hickories appear on the right.

respond well to nitrogen fertilizer. A rule of thumb is, if the growth is less than 6 inches, apply more nitrogen fertilizer; if it is more than 20 inches, apply less the next season. Avoid nitrogen fertilizer after June, to prevent freeze damage the next winter. If the trees are in a lawn, it is hard to keep them well fertilized. Apply nitrogen fertilizer on the lawn and water it in deeply; better yet, use a root feeder. Give pecans an annual spring application of 2 or 3 inches of organic mulch.

Pecans suffer from zinc deficiency in some soils, indicated by chlorotic leaves and "rosettes" (small, flat whorls of leaves). Where these symptoms appear, foliar-spray a special-formula fertilizer containing zinc two or three times in spring.

Grow hickories more like wild native trees; once established, they need no fertilizer unless they show signs of nutrient deficiencies.

Watering

In sandy soils or in hot climates, provide supplemental watering, though shagbark hickories are more drought tolerant than pecans. All young nut trees require at least 1 inch of water a week, more in hot weather. Mature pecan trees need deep watering every few weeks from April through husk-split in September. In moist climates, mature hickories generally need no supplemental watering.

The root area of mature nut trees is at least twice the diameter of the canopy; irrigate to cover the entire area. Trees growing in a lawn require extra-deep watering.

Pruning

Train to a strong central leader with wide-crotched branches (where they meet the main trunk) at an angle of no less than 45 degrees. Prune new trees to establish a strong branching structure. Do not allow major branches to come off the main trunk opposite each other. Once the tree is shaped and established, it will not need regular pruning to produce nuts. Annual shaping and removal of dead growth is sufficient. Hickory prunings will keep you supplied with wood for your barbecue.

Large pecan trees are almost as iconic in the South as live oaks dripping with Spanish moss. Steamboating down the Mississippi River, I saw hundreds of stately, tall specimens with lots of nuts—enough that critters cannot steal them all.

Pests and Diseases

A number of pests and diseases may attack pecans and hickories, depending on location. The most likely pests are weevils, scale, shuckworm, webworm, and aphids. The most common problem is protecting the harvest from critters. To beat them, collect nuts off the ground as soon as they fall. As the trees age, they are so productive that sharing the nuts is seldom problematic; in fact, it helps local wildlife.

The most serious and common disease of pecans is scab, a fungus that attacks the leaves and nuts. Dormant spraying helps control scab as well as some other pests and diseases of pecan. In humid areas, unless you choose varieties resistant to scab, the average pecan tree needs to be sprayed many times during the year to produce high-quality nuts.

Harvesting

Pecan trees do not bear nuts until they are 5 to 7 years old, hickories sometimes 10; it depends on the health of the plant and the variety. Pecans, and especially hickories, tend to bear nuts in alternate years. While this is normal, it is exacerbated by a diseased or weakened condition.

A 10-year-old pecan tree bears around 10 pounds of nuts annually, and a mature tree about 100 pounds. Hickory trees produce a much smaller and variable harvest. Before storing the nuts, spread them in a thin layer on screens in a warm area out of the sun for about 2 weeks.

How to Purchase

Pecan and hickory trees live for hundreds of years, so resist bargain trees. Instead, in late winter or early spring buy bare-root trees from local nurseries or from Nolin River, Oikos, Rhora's, or St. Lawrence.

Pollinizers

A few varieties, such as 'Colby' pecan, bear a fair crop when planted singly, but most pecan and hickory cultivars need a pollinizer. If there are other pecans or hickory trees growing nearby, none is needed, as these nut trees are wind pollinated. Most hickory trees cross-pollinize readily; on the other hand, pecan pollination is complex. Varieties shed their pollen at different times, so it is critical to select compatible cultivars. When purchasing trees, have the nursery help you. Plant at least two varieties within 200 feet of each other.

Varieties

Nut trees are generally offered as named varieties, although seedling trees have their advocates. Seedlings are generally considered a bit hardier, but nut quality is not guaranteed. If you have room, plant a few named varieties and a few seedlings.

Choose a pecan variety suitable for your part of the country. In the list below, hardy pecan varieties for short growing seasons are designated as Northern, those resistant to some major fungal diseases prevalent in humid areas as Southeastern, and those that tolerate alkaline soils as Western.

Pecans are judged by cracking quality—how easily the shell cracks—and whether the nut comes out in one piece. "Papershell" refers to nuts that crack easily.

When choosing a hickory, you'll do best with a cultivar from your climate zone.

PECAN, *CARYA ILLINOINENSIS*
Northern Pecan
'Colby'—nuts have good flavor but poor cracking quality; from Illinois; very hardy.
'Giles'—high-quality nuts; best for the southern part of northern zone.
'Kanza'—large nuts mature early; pollinizes 'Major'; disease and cold resistant.
'Major'—best flavor, good-size nuts, good cracking quality; pollinizes 'Kanza'; one of the best for the North.
Southeastern Pecan
'Caddo'—small, high-quality nuts; early ripening; excellent tree for small yards, attractive foliage; good scab resistance.
'Choctaw'—high-quality nuts; must have best soil and care; scab resistant; beautiful tree.
'Desirable'—high-quality nuts; limited scab resistance; not good for West Texas.
'Nacono'—high-quality nuts; new from USDA; strong-growing tree; scab resistant.
'Pawnee'—good-quality nuts; early ripening; resists aphids but not fungal diseases; especially good for northern Texas.
Western Pecan
'Cheyenne'—excellent cracking quality; small tree, best one for small yards; also grows in Southeast, but susceptible to aphids there.
'Western-Schley' ('Western')—most commonly grown; susceptible to scab; vigorous tree for Arizona, California, New Mexico, and West Texas.

HICKORY

Shagbark Hickory, *C. ovata*

'Abundance'—thin-shelled nut with good cracking quality; from Pennsylvania.

'Silvis'—thin-shelled nut; productive; from Ohio.

'Weschcke'—nuts crack well; bears at an early age; from Iowa.

'Wurth'—large, thin-shelled nut; good scab resistance; from Kentucky.

Shellbark Hickory (king nut), *C. laciniosa*

'Fayette'—large, thin-shelled nut; from Pennsylvania.

'Keystone'—best-cracking shellbark; annual bearing; from Pennsylvania.

'Lindauer'—good-cracking nut; weevil resistant, healthy foliage; from Illinois.

'Nook'—large nut with thick shell; squirrel proof and weevil resistant; from Illinois.

HICAN, *C. ILLINOINENSIS* × *C. OVATA* (OR *C. ILLINOINENSIS* × *C. LACINIOSA*)

A natural cross between pecan and either hickory, hican looks and grows like its cousins. While not as commonly cultivated, this handsome tree is worth seeking out for its nuts, which are much larger than those of either parent. They are easier to shell than hickory nuts, with a flavor considered a blend of both pecan and hickory.

a whole dish. Capsaicin, responsible for the heat, releases endorphins (those feel-good brain chemicals), so it feels like good pain.

Peppers have found their way into the cuisines of many countries. Chiles rellenos from Mexico are sublime, and salsas, made from peppers of all degrees of heat, are indispensable. Italians poach cherry peppers in wine and stuff them with cheese for antipasti. Hungarians dry deeply flavorful paprika peppers to make sumptuous chicken paprikash served in sour cream gravy. Around the globe, hot peppers are key in curries, kimchee, stir-fries, and chili. Peppers are a good source of vitamin C. Green (immature) peppers may be vitamin rich, but allow them to ripen to red, yellow, or orange, and vitamin C doubles, vitamin E quadruples, and beta-carotene increases eightfold.

Chop sweet bell peppers and freeze in plastic bags; once thawed, they will lose their crunch. Roast large sweet or hot peppers, peel, and freeze in zippered bags. To preserve thin-walled chili peppers, hang them up to dry in a warm, dry place, or put them in a dehydrator. Smoked and dried jalapeños are called chipotles. Many peppers are scrumptious pickled.

In the Landscape

These herbaceous perennials from south of the border are handsome, dark green plants with upright growth. With a plenitude of 2- to 4-inch-long, somewhat glossy leaves, the plants appear very lush. Some chili peppers bear purple or variegated green, white, and purple

Pepper

Capsicum spp.

Effort Scale

NO. 2
Must be planted annually in most climates
Some watering, fertilizing, and weeding necessary

Zones

10 to 11; grow as annual elsewhere

Thumbnail Sketch

Herbaceous perennial usually grown as annual
18 in. to 4 ft. tall
Propagate from seeds
Needs full sun; tolerates some shade in hot climates
Leaves are green or purple, 2 to 4 in. long
Blooms in summer
Flowers are white or purple, insignificant
Fruits are edible; harvest in summer
Use in flower border, raised bed, herb garden, or container

How to Use

In the Kitchen

The fruits of the pepper plant—whether green or red bells or hot peppers—are popular in stews, casseroles, and marinades. Use them as a vegetable in dishes like steak smothered with peppers and onions or roasted red pepper soup, or as a seasoning. Fiery, small peppers pack a wallop; sometimes just one—fresh, dried, or pickled—spices

'Habañero' pepper with its orange lantern-shaped fruits is perfect growing in a terra-cotta square pot. This extremely hot pepper is disease and heat resistant in most parts of the country. Use it in flower borders, herb gardens, or hanging baskets.

leaves. All types of peppers produce insignificant flowers in white or purple. The fruits come in all sizes, shapes, and colors; some varieties festoon the plant with upright peppers of yellow, orange, purple, and/or red—all at one time.

While a few varieties of peppers are awkward looking, most are decorative among dwarf zinnias, red verbena, annual vinca, fancy-leaf geraniums, and portulaca. Some compact, small-fruited peppers are designated and sold as ornamental; in fact, they are so beautiful some gardeners think they are not edible. All are hot, some blazingly so; some are tastier than others, so try one, you may like it. Be aware, however, that as ornamentals they have likely been sprayed with chemicals at the nursery or in production. Compact pepper varieties make a dazzling edging for an herb garden or flower bed and are indispensable for seasonal color in containers. Plant cultivars with purple foliage among green and white variegated herbs and magenta coleus for a nine on the wow-factor scale. For an even splashier display, combine gaillardia and 'Thai Hot' peppers, a striking combo in old-fashioned clay pots—the colors are perfection together.

How to Grow
Climate
A warm-weather crop, peppers usually do not set fruit unless the temperature is 65 to 80°F. Most varieties need a long growing season—80 to 120 days; start plants indoors in northern gardens.

Exposure and Soil
Peppers prefer full sun except in arid, hot climates, where large-fruited varieties benefit from afternoon shade to protect against sunburn (or cover fruits with shade cloth). Grow peppers in fairly rich soil.

The name of this bell pepper, 'Blushing Beauty', may be a bit misleading. It starts out a lovely ivory, then blushes pink, and finally turns brilliant red—more than a blush in my book. For best flavor, wait for ripe red.

Planting
Start seedlings indoors 6 to 8 weeks before your last frost date. Plant 18 to 24 inches apart, depending on the variety. If tiny plants are starting to produce flower buds, pinch them off for 3 weeks to force energy into making leaves and roots. Keep the soil moist but not soggy. Mulch with 2 inches of organic matter; stake large varieties.

Fertilizing
Feed peppers before the plants start to bloom and in midseason. Keep in mind that sweet peppers need more nitrogen than chili peppers and more than tomatoes.

Watering
Give peppers a deep watering weekly.

Pests and Diseases
Although subject to most of the same pests and diseases as tomatoes, peppers are more resistant. Be sure to clean up debris and rotate plantings (see the "Tomato" entry for more details).

Harvesting
Pick sweet peppers in the green to red stage. Allow hot peppers to ripen completely; the exceptions are poblanos and jalapeños, which are best picked green. You cannot dry unripe peppers; they rot. Sweet peppers produce 1 to 2 pounds per plant.

How to Purchase

Seeds and transplants are available at local nurseries and the companies listed in the "Tomato" entry. Pepper specialists include Cross Country, Pepper Gal, and Tomato Growers. Check out Johnny's for cool- and short-summer varieties; Park for showy and compact varieties; Seed Savers and Seeds of Change for heirloom and open-pollinated varieties; and Native Seeds and Redwood City for native and southwestern varieties.

Varieties
SWEET PEPPERS
The following are particularly showy sweet peppers.

'Blushing Beauty'—hybrid; large, beautiful bells; ivory, pink, and red peppers simultaneously on the same plant; 18 in. tall; resists numerous diseases; 75 days.

Cherry—hybrid, early, and spicy varieties; red, small, round; great for stuffing and pickles; 30 in. tall; lovely in the garden; 90 days.

'Golden Bell'—large, yellow, sweet; prolific; 24 in. tall; 80 days.

'Gypsy'—hybrid; wedge shaped, yellow, thin walled, medium size; close to Hungarian sweet types; 24 in. tall; produces under cool conditions; 70 days.

'Pimento'—red, heart shaped, delicious, thick walled, medium size; 24 in. tall; 90 days. 'Pimento Super' and ribbed 'Super Red Pimento' are heavy producers.

'Valencia'—blocky orange bell, large, very sweet, thick walls; vigorous; 24 in. tall, good foliage cover; resists tobacco mosaic virus; 68 days.

STANDARD HOT PEPPERS
Hot peppers come in a kaleidoscope of colors, and habits varying from tall and willowy to compact and spreading. The following are spectacular in both the garden and the kitchen.

'Bolivian Rainbow'—small, very hot, colorful, red and yellow fruit; purple foliage; tall plant, upright to 36 in., showy; 80 days; 'Largo Purple' and 'Filius Blue' are similar.

'Fish Pepper'—unusual hot, 2-in., green and white fruit ripening to red and white striped; prized in cooking; leaves variegated green and white, too; striking plant; 75 days.

'Habañero'—orange, lantern-shaped, fiery chili with fruity taste; lush-looking plant, peppers peek through; many variations, some not hot; late bearing, to 140 days.

'Hungarian Hot Wax Banana'—yellow, 3-in.-long, mild peppers, very showy, turn from yellow to orange to red, hang down; many variations, all showy; 80 days.

'Jalapeño'—narrow, 3 in., red, thick walled; traditional medium-hot pepper for eating fresh. Ornamental variations: 'Jaloro', red, orange, yellow, and green fruits, 70 days; 'Purple Jalapeno', purple fruits, 90 days.

'Tabasco'—small, pointed, red, yellow, and orange hot pepper; tall plant to 36 in.; 120 days.

'Thai Hot'—elongated, small peppers held upright; clear hot flavor; 90 days to mature.

ORNAMENTAL PEPPERS

In the 1970s a new class of peppers was introduced, designated as "ornamental" because they are so flashy. Hundreds of small fruits ripen to a dazzling array of colors, most held proudly above the foliage; some have purple foliage. Quick to show off, some ripen in less than 70 days. Vigorous plants scoff at hot and cool conditions; the fruit rarely sunburns. Compact (8 to 12 inches tall), they branch low to the ground—ideal for landscaping.

The parents of these cultivars are native chiltipins (tiny bird peppers), Thai peppers, and cayennes—all venerated, very hot peppers. These show-offs are edible. Most are very hot (use like their ancestors), but some are acrid, so try a bit in salsa to see if you like their flavor.

'Black Hungarian'—shiny, 2-in., black fruit ripens to red; green foliage, purple flowers; 75 days.

'Black Pearl'—bronze to black foliage; round, purple fruit ripens to red; 90 days.

'Pretty in Purple'—lots of 1-in. purple fruit; hot; purple-green foliage; 60 days.

'Super Chili'—green to orange to red, 2½-in., narrow, hot fruit; 75 days; 'Prairie Fire' and 'Riot' are similar, 55 days.

'Sweet Pickle'—red, orange, yellow, and purple; long, chunky, upright peppers; 65 days.

Peppermint

See Mint

Persimmon

Diospyros spp.

Effort Scale

NO. 2
Occasional pruning necessary to shape
Sucker growth must be removed from American persimmon
Large harvest

In autumn the fruits on persimmon trees add brilliant color to the landscape, even on the dreariest of days. The fruits will persist on the tree long after the leaves drop.

Zones

American persimmon, 4 to 10
Asian persimmon, 6 to 10

Thumbnail Sketch

American persimmon
Deciduous tree or shrub
20 to 40 ft. tall
Propagate by grafting or budding or from seeds or cuttings
Prefers full sun; tolerates some shade
Leaves are dark green, shiny, oval, 6 in. long
Blooms in spring
Flowers are greenish yellow, 1½ to 2 in. across, not showy
Fruits are edible; harvest in fall
Use as interest plant, shade tree, large shrub, or screen

Asian persimmon
Deciduous tree
10 to 25 ft. tall
Propagate by grafting or budding or from cuttings
Needs full sun

'Hachiya' persimmons in a basket are pretty enough to decorate a holiday table. This most elegant of edible ornamentals is extremely disease resistant and is widely grown in western gardens in Zones 7 to 10. It's my favorite in smoothies.

Leaves are heart shaped, glossy; chartreuse in spring, dark green in summer, red-orange in autumn, 5 to 7 in. across
Blooms in late spring
Flowers are yellowish white, not showy, 1½ to 2 in. across
Fruits are edible; harvest in autumn; leaves edible
Use as interest plant, screen, shade tree, or espalier; some varieties as patio tree

How to Use
In the Kitchen
Folks living in the East, where American persimmon is native, relish the fruit, yet little has been done to domesticate the tree. On the other hand, Asian persimmon has been in cultivation for thousands of years; there are hundreds of varieties. You could call this tree the "apple" of Asia.

Both American and Asian persimmons have beautiful orange fruits you can eat raw. Most varieties are good only when dead ripe and very soft; otherwise they have a puckery quality. Taste an astringent, under-ripe persimmon just once in your life and you'll never forget it. By contrast, a fully ripe persimmon is velvety and sweet. There are a few superb varieties that are delicious when firm ripe like an apple. Persimmon leaves are high in vitamin C; in Asia, they dry the leaves and steep them in hot (not boiling) water to make tea.

Use both types of persimmons in desserts. A fabulous pudding, similar to English plum pudding, is a Thanksgiving tradition at our house. Enjoy persimmons in cookies and breads. A firm 'Fuyu' persimmon is sensational cut in sections and wrapped with prosciutto, chopped and sprinkled over oatmeal and yogurt, or added to a green salad with feta cheese and pecans. Try freezing a seedless persimmon. Eaten out of its skin, it's like sherbet. Or peel it and add to yogurt or silken tofu and honey for a great smoothie.

Dry or freeze persimmons. Use the pulp as a substitute for applesauce in recipes. The Japanese peel and dry persimmons by a time-consuming technique called *hoshi-gaki,* which makes them pliable, soft, and sugary. To learn about this process and/or order some of these treats, visit www.penrynorchardspecialties.com.

To freeze, put the pulp of the persimmons in containers. Force out the air by placing plastic wrap directly onto the pulp. Though it tends to darken with time, the frozen fruit lasts for about 6 months.

In the Landscape
The trees that bear these glorious fruits are deciduous. Both species are slow growing and may reach 30 feet, but you can keep them smaller with pruning. The bark has a fascinating checkered pattern. In summer, the big leaves become shiny and dark green; in autumn, most turn bright yellow-orange or red. As if that were not enough, those orange, decorative fruits add their own beauty. When the leaves drop off, the fruits stay on the bare tree, resembling orange Christmas tree ornaments. Heart-shaped Asian fruits grow up to 5 inches long. American persimmons bear smaller (to 2 inches), rounder fruits, which nestle in the foliage.

The unique bark, handsome foliage, and colorful fruits combine to make any persimmon tree one of the finest edible ornamentals. Persimmons are stunning accent plants, small shade trees, and fine espaliers; their fall foliage color is breathtaking. When planting near a walkway, choose only firm Asian varieties that do not drop soft fruit.

How to Grow
Climate
American persimmon is hardier than the Asian species, growing as far north as Rhode Island and across to the Great Lakes. Asian persimmon is hardy to about 0°F; it flourishes on the West Coast, and in the East it is limited to areas below the Ohio River and warmer parts of Zone 7. It grows poorly in high desert heat.

Exposure and Soil
Both species prefer good garden loam but will succeed in less than optimum conditions. They require good drainage and will grow where oak root fungus is a problem. Mulch new trees with several inches of organic mulch and keep well watered through the first three summers. In cool-summer areas, persimmon trees are slow to break dormancy; new trees might not leaf out until early summer! If leaves are delayed, whitewash the trunk to prevent sunburn.

Fertilizing
An annual 4-inch application of mulch, preferably compost, is all the trees need. Avoid large amounts of nitrogen around young trees as it causes the fruit to drop.

Watering
Once well established, the trees need very little watering in rainy climates. In arid climates, deep watering once every few weeks is generally enough in hot inland areas, every 6 weeks along the coast. Persimmons can tolerate drought but will produce fewer fruits.

Pruning
Train young trees to a modified central leader with three to five main limbs. Prune mature trees to remove dead or crossing branches, to get rid of weak growth, for shape, and to shorten branches to prevent them from breaking under too heavy a fruit load. Remove suckers from American persimmon. It is common for persimmon trees to drop many immature fruits in summer. They tend to alternate bear—a heavy crop one year, a light one the next. To mitigate the problem, thin the fruits in heavy-bearing years.

Pests and Diseases

In dry-summer areas, persimmons have very few pests and diseases. If rodents are a problem, wrap the trunk with commercial tree wrap. In the East, if flat-headed borers appear, remove them by hand. In the Southeast, anthracnose and other diseases sometimes bother the trees.

Harvesting

Persimmon trees can be slow to bear, sometimes taking 6 years for the first crop. Other reasons for no fruit include too much nitrogen fertilizer or water, a hot dry spell when the tree bloomed, or the lack of pollination. The fruit of all American persimmons and some Asian varieties are not edible until dead ripe and soft like a tomato. To foil birds and squirrels, pick fruits when firm and fully colored and let them ripen indoors. Use clippers to harvest the fruits; take care not to bruise the skin. To ripen astringent persimmons quickly, freeze overnight; once thawed, they are ripe. Large-fruited Asian varieties can produce 50 to 75 pounds of fruit a year, while 'Fuyu' and American persimmons produce 25 to 30 pounds.

How to Purchase

Purchase persimmons bare root in spring or in containers in summer from local nurseries. In cold-winter areas purchase trees grafted to hardy American persimmon rootstock. Order either type of persimmon from Edible Landscaping, One Green World, or Raintree. Nolin River carries American persimmons; Bay Laurel and Willis stock Asian persimmons.

Pollinizers

Persimmons have complicated sex lives. Wild American persimmons are dioecious (trees produce either male or female flowers; you need one of each to produce fruit) and the fruits have seeds. American persimmons cannot pollinize Asian varieties and vice versa. Now it gets a bit more complicated. Asian varieties can have male, female, and/or perfect (both sexes) flowers on the same tree. Further, some Asian varieties like 'Hachiya' can produce fruits (seedless) without being pollinized (called parthenocarpic). 'Fuyu' and 'Jiro' both produce male and female flowers on the same tree. While some American persimmons are sold as self-fertile, most produce much better with a pollinizer. In the East, some Asian persimmons require a pollinizer; plant either 'Fuyu' or 'Gailey'.

Varieties

AMERICAN PERSIMMON, *DIOSPYROS VIRGINIANA*

American persimmons are often available as seedlings, but for consistent fruit quality and fewer seeds, choose a grafted variety.

'Early Golden'—very good flavor; often self-fertile.

'John Rick'—excellent flavor, superior variety.

'Meader'—almost seedless, excellent flavor; bears at an early age; self-fertile; red and yellow fall foliage; developed in New Hampshire.

'Ruby'—large fruit; ripens over long period; self-fertile; leaves resist spotting; handsome tree.

'Szukis'—medium to large, non-astringent fruit; self-fertile, good pollinizer; Zones 4 to 9.

ASIAN PERSIMMON (KAKI), *D. KAKI*

'Fuyu' ('Fuyu-Gaki')—tomato shaped, non-astringent, can eat when firm, usually seedless; one of the best; small tree; fine fall color; needs a pollinizer in the East (use 'Gailey').

'Gailey'—red fruit, astringent when seedless; grown as pollinizer for other varieties; available locally in the East.

'Hachiya'—large, astringent fruit, usually seedless, great for drying; heavy bearer; not good for some parts of the East, widely available in the West.

'Jiro'—tomato shaped, non-astringent, similar to 'Fuyu'; self-fertile; very cold hardy.

'Saijo'—elongated, yellow, astringent; self-fertile; small tree; hardy to Zone 6.

'Sheng'—tomato shaped, non-astringent; self-fertile; to 10 ft.

Pineapple guava (feijoa)

Acca sellowiana (*Feijoa sellowiana*)

Effort Scale

NO. 1
Easy to grow
Fruit drop needs some attention

Zones

8 to 11

Thumbnail Sketch

Evergreen shrub or small tree
10 to 18 ft. tall
Propagate from cuttings, by grafting, or from seeds
Needs full sun; partial shade in warm climates
Leaves are oblong, deep green above, light gray-green below, 2 to 3 in. long
Blooms in spring or summer
Flowers have pink fleshy petals, dark red stamens; 1½ in. across, showy

Pineapple guava is nothing if not prolific—in fall the plant is covered with fruit. Scoop the pulp, with a somewhat resinous sweet flavor, out of the peel. The best indication of the fruit's ripeness is when it starts to drop.

Fruits and flower petals are edible; harvest flowers in spring, fruit in fall

Use as screen, formal or informal hedge, espalier, patio tree, multi-stemmed tree, accent, container plant, or houseplant

How to Use

In the Kitchen

Pineapple guava, sometimes called feijoa, is a gray-green, oblong fruit native to the mountains of South America. Its slightly gritty flesh is tangy, resinous, and sweet, especially when the fruit is allowed to ripen fully (it falls off the tree when ripe). Pineapple guava is a powerhouse of fiber, lycopene, vitamin C, and potassium. Serve it simply—cut it in half like a miniature melon and use a small spoon to scoop out the flesh. Peel and slice the fruit for an exotic addition to a fruit salad or serve with cheese. It makes a delicate-flavored jelly the color of palest gold. Preserve the pulp by freezing or making fruit leather, jelly, or jam.

Pineapple guava flower petals are succulent, as sweet as honey, and have a slight perfume. Remove the petals from the flowers and sprinkle over a salad, add to a fruit salsa, or decorate a dessert.

In the Landscape

Pineapple guava is an overachieving ornamental. As a small multi-stemmed tree it is handsome growing near a patio. The bark is mottled in interesting patterns and the leaves are ever changing—deep green one minute and then silver another. In early summer, the profusion of flowers adds deep red to this color display. Pineapple guava is in the Myrtaceae family; as with others in that family its blossoms give the appearance of little brushes. The 2- to 3-inch-long egg-shaped fruits are light green.

Grown as a shrub, pineapple guava is as useful as it is beautiful—serving as a windbreak, screening a poor view, accenting a yard, giv-

Green leaves with a gray underside, drought tolerance, and few pests make pineapple guava a winner. Showy spring blooms with bright red stamens and pink petals are a bonus—they're among the tastiest and most substantive edible flowers.

ing privacy, and providing protection for songbirds. When trained as a clipped hedge, the flowers and fruits are limited to the inside branches, resulting in a smaller crop of each. Versatile pineapple guava can grow in containers and raised beds and along walkways and is lovely espaliered. In northern climates, grow it in a container and move it indoors to a sunroom when the weather cools. This is truly a multifaceted edible ornamental.

How to Grow

Climate

Pineapple guava is hardy to about 10°F, which limits its growth to the Pacific Coast, Deep South, and warmer parts of the Southwest. In Zone 7, plant against a warm, south-facing wall and give winter protection; plants can survive defoliation. Cool-summer areas produce the tastiest fruits. Pineapple guava requires some winter chill and will not set fruit in the desert or South Florida; in the cooler parts of Hawaii it grows so well it can become a weed.

Exposure and Soil

This plant prefers full sun in cool climates, partial shade in warm-summer areas. It is adaptable to most soils but needs good drainage.

Fertilizing

Unless planted in barren soils, pineapple guava is a light feeder. A modest application of organic fertilizer in the spring and an organic mulch provide sufficient nutrition.

Watering

Although pineapple guava is fairly drought tolerant, the fruit quality improves with regular watering. In well-drained soil, it tolerates quite a bit of water; in fact, it can grow adjacent to a lawn.

Pruning

Remove any suckers that sprout from below the root graft. Pineapple guava can take any amount of shearing, but severe pruning reduces fruit production. Prune lightly to shape and control height yearly—in late spring or after harvest.

Pests and Diseases

Few serious pests or diseases affect pineapple guava; squirrels and birds occasionally eat the blossoms and fruit. Dispose of any decaying fruit from under trees.

Harvesting

The fruits are rarely ripe until they fall from the tree.

How to Purchase

You can grow pineapple guava from seed, but cuttings and grafted varieties produce the best fruits. Local nurseries in areas where they are adapted carry plants, as does One Green World.

Pollinizers

Some varieties require a pollinizer; most commonly grown varieties produce a modest amount of fruit when grown alone. For a large harvest, plant two varieties.

Varieties

The majority of pineapple guava plants sold in nurseries are seedlings that have variable fruit and are not self-fertile. Select two plants to assure cross-pollinization and for a better chance at superior fruit. A few varieties are offered by specialty nurseries, such as One Green World, and a handful of local nurseries in mild-winter areas. Look for the dwarf 'Nikita' and the full-size old-timers 'Coolidge' and 'Pineapple Gem'; all three varieties are self-fertile and have proven fruit quality.

Plantain

See Banana and Plantain

Plum

Prunus spp.

Effort Scale

NO. 3
Large plum trees vulnerable to pests and diseases, especially in the East; bush plums less susceptible
Some pruning necessary
Fertilizing and mulching necessary
Large harvest needs immediate attention

Zones

European plums, 4 to 9
Japanese plums and interspecific hybrids, 6 to 9
Other plums, 3 to 9

Thumbnail Sketch

Deciduous tree or shrub
Standard, 15 ft. tall; dwarf and bush varieties, 6 to 20 ft. tall
Propagate by budding or from cuttings; bush types from suckers
Needs full sun
Leaves are medium green above (some varieties wine red), slightly woolly below, narrow, 2 to 4 in. long
Blooms in spring
Flowers are white or pink, to 1 in. across, abundant, showy
Fruits are edible; harvest in summer
Use as interest tree or screen; dwarf varieties as hedges and shrub borders or container plants; bush types in wildlife shelterbelt or containers; beach plum for seaside plantings

How to Use

In the Kitchen

Plums are the most varied of the stone fruits. From luscious, large domesticated beauties to succulent, sweet or tart native plums, they have a valued place in the kitchen. Plums covered here are European, Japanese, the crosses between plums and apricots called interspecific hybrids, as well as the many small-fruited native, introduced, and hybrid bush and cherry plums. Most types are marvelous fresh or canned and in cobblers, fruit leather, sauces, jams, jellies, and sweet and tangy southern libations called "shrubs."

Plums are a varied lot: large and juicy Japanese types; European plums with dense, intensely sweet flesh; and flavorful cherry plums. All are sweet treats and versatile in the kitchen. Here, plums tempt visitors at France's famous Château de Villandry.

European plums include the very sweet Italian and French prune plums that are ideal for drying. Transformed into prunes, they are equally delicious eaten out of hand, stewed with spices, made into a filling for Danish pastry, or used in stuffing for roast pork. The famous Green Gage and Mirabelle plums are fabulous eaten fresh off the tree and sublime arranged on a French tart.

The Japanese varieties and the plum-apricot crosses are all excellent for eating out of hand, layering in a cobbler, or making jam. Cook them into rich and salty Asian plum sauces, sharp sauces for grilled meats, or sweet ones to serve over ice cream.

The many other small plums are similar in taste to plums or sometimes cherries. The red, yellow, or purplish black fruits are small (1 to 2 inches). Full of vitamin C, some are too tart to eat fresh and therefore are used canned and in jams, jellies, sauces, and pies.

You can freeze or can all plums, or make them into sauces, jams, or wine. Prune plums are best for drying. Commercially, they are dipped in a lye solution to make the skin porous, but if you use a home dehydrator, a few pricks of the skin on each fruit usually does the job.

In the Landscape

Plums range from polite small to medium-size trees with graceful vase or round shapes to bushy native plums that form large thickets along country roads. In early spring, thousands of white blooms cover plums (a few types have pink flowers). The leaves are usually green, but a few cultivars have wine red foliage; some turn yellow or red in fall.

A 'Satsuma' plum is the anchor and focal point of my backyard "Plum Garden." In front is an herb garden with dozens of plants in pots and even growing between stepping-stones. The plums make a jam that friends describe as sinful.

Standard trees are lovely along a driveway; keep them far enough away from pavement so fruit drop isn't a problem. Plums are fine accents in any yard and are at home in a mini-orchard underplanted with native wildflowers and clovers that attract beneficial insects. Pendulous 'Weeping Santa Rosa' is outstanding, whether espaliered or allowed to grow naturally. Like most fruit trees, plums rarely thrive in a lawn.

Bush-type plums make beautiful hedgerows as they are among the earliest flowering shrubs. Use them as flowering accents and free-standing shrubs; some require continual pruning to remove suckers. Plums are a delight near a patio, as long as they're not so close that fruit drops on it.

Beach plums are great medium to large shrubs or trees and informal flowering hedges. These plants become even more attractive as their dark, shiny bark gnarls with age. In a seaside planting, wind-blown plants take on picturesque forms. Some are quite thorny and are excellent barrier hedges.

How to Grow

Grow standard plums as single specimen trees or in an informal hedge-type planting comprising three or four different varieties that bear at different times, or plant a few varieties in the same planting hole. Combining many varieties of plums has the advantage of a smaller harvest of different varieties over time.

Climate

The many plums need different climatic conditions. Let's start with the coldest areas—Zones 3 to 5—where the hardiest plants are cherrylike plums. The native western sand cherry is a star performer in northern climates like Wyoming, Minnesota, Colorado, and into Manitoba. They need heavy winter chilling and do poorly in mild-winter areas. Beach plums are native to coastal Maine to Virginia. They're not as cold hardy as other bush plums but grow fruitfully in mild parts of the Midwest and New England.

Damson and European plums are the next hardiest group; some grow in Zone 4, with most in Zones 5 to 9. They grow primarily from maritime Canada south to Georgia and west to the Rockies and along the West Coast. Plums bloom earlier than apples, so crops occasionally are lost to a late frost (avoid this by planting plums on the side of a hill so that cold air sinks away).

Most Japanese types are best in Zones 6 to 9, and because they are prone to many diseases, especially bacterial leaf spot in hot, humid weather, they are grown primarily from southern New England south to the mountains of Georgia through the Southwest and up the West Coast to British Columbia.

Plums do poorly in Zones 10 and 11 because they need some winter chilling. In the warmest parts of Zone 9, order low-chill varieties.

Exposure and Soil

Plums need full sun and soil high in organic matter, with a pH between 6 and 8. European and Damson plums grow best on clay or heavy loam; Japanese types do better on lighter soils with good drainage. Bush plums thrive on a wide variety of soils and tolerate fairly poor drainage, though they do not prefer it. Beach plums grow in poor soil but need good drainage.

Fertilizing

The domesticated plum trees benefit from a deep organic mulch yearly to replenish soil nutrients. If your plum is not growing vigorously or if the leaves get pale, supplement with nitrogen. Supplemental nitrogen is seldom needed for bush plums.

Watering

In arid regions, plums need deep watering every 1 or 2 weeks, depending on the temperature. If the tree has been dry for quite a while and fruits have begun to form, delay watering until after harvest or the fruits split. Bush plums seldom need extra watering.

Pruning

Train both European and Japanese varieties to an open center. When mature, European plum trees need annual light thinning and shaping to control height; they bear only on long-lived spurs. When mature, Japanese varieties require fairly heavy annual pruning; they bear on both long-lived spurs and 1-year-old wood, and tend to bear too heavily if branches are not thinned and some shortened. Japanese types set too much fruit; thin in June. You can grow both types of plums in a small area if you prune in summer to control size and shape.

American native plums and most bush and cherry plums bear fruit along the entire length of their branches and can take some shearing. Tailored bushes still bear fruit, but the yield is much smaller than on untrimmed plants. For the first few years, all bush plums bear fruit without regular pruning but look better with some shaping.

Renew mature bushes by cutting back a few older branches to the ground. Prune all by August.

Train beach plums and taller bush plums as small trees with constant pruning to maintain shape. Their natural form is a shrub; they sucker readily unless kept pruned.

Pests and Diseases

Plums are not as plagued by pests and diseases as cherries and peaches. That said, black knot, which looks like wads of black gum on the branches, is a common and serious disease east of the Rockies. Plant resistant varieties and control by removing and destroying infected branches. Control bacterial canker, fairly common in humid climates, by removing all diseased and dead branches. Plum curculio can be problematic in some gardens in the East. In most areas of the country, scale, mites, aphids, and brown rot are occasional problems, as are birds and squirrels.

Bush plums have few pests and diseases, though birds sometimes beat you to the goods. Plum curculio and brown rot are occasional problems.

Harvesting

European plums and cherry plums do not ripen after harvest, so pick them when they are fully colored and give slightly to the touch. Harvest Japanese plums and plum-apricot crosses just before they are fully ripe and ripen them indoors. Mature standard-size trees produce 50 to 100 pounds of plums; dwarf varieties produce 25 to 50 pounds.

How to Purchase

Purchase plants bare root in early spring or in containers throughout the year from local nurseries. Adams County, Bay Laurel, C & O, Cummins, Edible Landscaping, Johnson, One Green World, Raintree, Stark Bro's, and Trees of Antiquity all carry a number of varieties. Fedco, Southmeadow, and St. Lawrence carry a large selection of very hardy plums. Plants of the Southwest carries seeds of the native western sand cherry.

Pollinizers

Some plums are self-fruitful, but all bear more heavily with a pollinizer. With a few exceptions, European plums pollinize European plums, and Japanese plums pollinize Japanese plums. When hardy plum hybrids are grown in northern climates, pollination is sometimes a problem; seedlings of hardy American plums pollinize them quite well.

Rootstocks

Specific plum varieties are grafted onto named rootstocks. Consult local nurseries and your Cooperative Extension Service for the rootstocks best for your area.

'Citation'—produces a semi-dwarf about 12 ft. tall; hardy to Zone 4; resists root knot nematodes.

'Lovell'—produces a large tree to 20 ft.; susceptible to crown gall and nematodes in sandy soils.

'Marianna 2624'—produces a semi-dwarf 10 to 15 ft. tall; tolerates fairly heavy soils; resists root knot nematodes, some resistance to oak root fungus.

'Myrobalan'—produces a tree about 15 ft. tall, mostly for European varieties; good anchorage for windy areas; tolerates wet soils; susceptible to oak root fungus and root knot nematodes.

'Nemaguard'—produces a large tree to 25 ft.; sensitive to bad drainage; resists root knot nematodes; susceptible to many diseases.

Varieties

There are scores of plum varieties. For simplicity's sake, I've divided them into four groups: European, Japanese, interspecific hybrids, and other plums. As with rootstocks, consult local nurseries and your Cooperative Extension Service for plums best suited to your area.

EUROPEAN PLUM, *PRUNUS DOMESTICA* SSP. *DOMESTICA*

Damson—European wild plums with small, blue fruit; variable fruiting times and flavors; for cooking; resists bacterial leaf spot and black knot; self-fertile; widely adaptable, 400 chill hours. Improved varieties: 'Blue Damson', 'French Damson', and 'Shropshire'.

'French Improved Prune'—midseason; small, deep purple, very sweet; freestone; good for drying and freezing; large tree; self-fertile; 800 chill hours.

Green Gage ('Reine Claude')—antique; midseason; greenish yellow, exquisite flavor, good fresh or cooked; small tree; resists bacterial leaf spot; self-fertile; widely adapted, 500 chill hours, Zones 5 to 9. Modern variations are 'Bavay's Green Gage' and 'Golden Gage'.

'Italian Prune'—late; purple skin, freestone, rich flavor, sweet; use fresh, dry, or can; vigorous, self-fertile; 800 chill hours.

Mirabelle—European wild plum selections, famous in France; variable fruiting times and flavors; freestone; sweet, eat fresh or make brandy; spreading tree; needs a pollinizer; Zones 5 to 8.

'Stanley'—late; dark blue prune plum; juicy, sweet, meaty; good fresh, cooked, made into preserves or plum pudding; freestone; resists black knot; semi-dwarf to 12 ft.; self-fertile, good pollinizer popular in East, South, and Midwest; 800 chill hours, Zones 5 to 8.

JAPANESE PLUM, *P. SALICINA*

'Au Roadside'—early; large plum, magenta skin, high-quality red flesh; use fresh or cooked; some resistance to brown rot, good resistance to most other plum diseases; self-fertile; 700 chill hours.

'Burgundy'—long harvest; one of the best-flavored plums for fresh eating, deep red flesh; self-fertile, great pollinizer; 250 to 400 chill hours.

'Delight'—mid- to late season; cross between Japanese and cherry plum; tangy, flavorful, good fresh or cooked; clingstone; very productive; pollinize with 'Sprite'; 400 chill hours.

'Emerald Beauty'—late; fruit holds on tree; tasty, crisp, sweet, green flesh; good fresh or cooked; freestone; pollinize with 'Flavor King Pluot' or 'Late Santa Rosa'; 800 chill hours.

'Hollywood'—late; red skin and flesh; use fresh or for jelly; unique leaves are green above, red below; flowers white to pink; needs 'All Red' or 'Stanley' as pollinizer; Zones 5 to 9.

'Ozark Premier'—late; red, tasty, for eating fresh and cooking; resists brown rot, canker, and bacterial spot; partially self-fertile, popular in South; 800 chill hours.

'Santa Rosa'—early; crimson, high-quality fruit for eating fresh and cooking; upright growth; resists black knot, prone to diseases in Deep South; self-fertile; widely grown, great in West; 300 chill hours.

'Satsuma'—antique; midseason; wine red; one of most luscious for eating fresh, great jelly; fruit cracks in wet weather; needs 'Santa Rosa' as pollinizer; 300 chill hours.

'Sprite'—mid- to late season; cross between Japanese and cherry plum; sweet, flavorful, good eaten fresh or cooked; freestone; pollinize with 'Delight'; 400 chill hours.

'Weeping Santa Rosa'—early; similar to 'Santa Rosa'; 8 to 10 ft. tall, weeping habit; stake for the first 2 years; self-fertile; 400 chill hours.

INTERSPECIFIC HYBRIDS

Fruit tree breeder Floyd Zaiger introduced new stone fruits designated as interspecific hybrids. Pluots, the most popular, are smooth-skinned fruits that are a cross between a plum (75 percent) and an apricot (25 percent) and have a sweet, sprightly flavor.

'Dapple Dandy Pluot'—late; among the tastiest; maroonish skin with white and red flesh; freestone; use 'Burgundy', 'Flavor Supreme Pluot' or 'Santa Rosa' as pollinizer; 500 chill hours.

'Flavor Supreme Pluot'—early; sweet, rich flavor with no tartness; purple skin, red flesh; freestone; pollinize with any Japanese plum; 500 to 600 chill hours.

OTHER PLUMS

'All Red' (purple-leaf plum), *P. cerasifera*—early; tasty red flesh; 1-in., round, deep red fruit; deep red leaves, fragrant white flowers; to 12 ft. tall; disease resistant; self-fertile but produces better crop if pollinized, use 'Hollywood'; Zones 5 to 9.

American plum (sloe or wild plum), *P. Americana*—native; early; red, 1-in. fruit, great for preserves and jellies; white flowers; great yellow or red fall color; to 15 ft. tall; usually sold as seedling trees or seeds; used in wildlife shelterbelts; great pollinizer for hybrid plums; Zones 3 to 8.

Beach plum, *P. maritima*—native; mid- to late season; red-purple fruit, makes most delicious jelly; to 10 ft. high and wide, can be trained as small tree; can be thorny, tolerates seaside conditions; resistant to brown rot; needs a pollinizer; for East Coast, Zones 4 to 8. Varieties include 'Jersey' and 'Premier'.

Chickasaw plum (sand plum), *P. angustifolia*—native; early to mid-season; ½-in., red to yellow, tart fruit best in preserves and jellies; white flowers, yellow fall foliage; multistemmed, large shrub to 25 ft. high and wide; drought tolerant; grows in thickets from southern New England to northern Florida and through much of West; Zones 4 to 9.

Nanking cherry (Manchu cherry), *P. tomentosum*—scarlet fruit, tart; good for eating fresh, cooked, or made into wine; fragrant white flowers in spring; reddish brown bark; dense shrub good for foundation planting, hedge, or border; to 10 ft. tall, 15 ft. wide; plant two or more for cross-pollination; Zones 3 to 7.

Western sand cherry, *P. besseyi*—native plum; sweet, cherry-sized, dark red fruit good fresh or dried; shrub 3 to 8 ft. tall; showy white flowers; crimson fall color; Zones 3 to 6.

Pomegranate

Punica granatum

Effort Scale

NO. 1
Very easy to grow
Pruning needed to shape
Occasional watering necessary
Fruit processing requires work but is not necessary

Zones

7 to 10

Thumbnail Sketch

Deciduous shrub or small tree
10 to 20 ft. tall

Propagate from seeds or cuttings
Needs full sun
Leaves are bright green, yellow in fall, 2 to 3 in. long; new growth is bronzy
Blooms in spring or summer
Flowers are bright red-orange, light salmon, or white; 1½ to 2 in. across; showy
Fruits are edible; harvest in late summer into fall
Use as multistemmed tree, patio tree, large shrub, screen, interest plant, hedge, barrier, espalier, or container plant

How to Use

In the Kitchen

The big, round, red pomegranate fruits swell to bursting with seeds covered in a vermillion gel. This tangy-sweet seed covering (aril) gives pomegranates their special quality. In Mexico, cooks decorate salads and desserts with these luscious rubies. The popularity of the pomegranate, native from Iran to India, has led to many creative recipes, especially for the juice. Flavorful and packed with antioxidants, the juice can be extracted to use in drinks (especially lemonade and teas) and sorbets, to marinate meat and poultry, to make into jelly, and as the base for grenadine syrup. The simplest and least messy way to eat a homegrown pomegranate (harvested while the skin is still pliable) is to freeze overnight and then defrost it, massage the fruit with your thumbs, roll it a bit to crush the arils inside, cut a hole, insert a straw, and suck out the tangy nectar. As the poet Hildegarde Flanner once said, "Do not be ashamed of the ecstasy. It does not last."

There are other ways to prepare the fruit. Cut a small section off the top and bottom and score the sides in six places, cutting just through the rind. Core the blossom end and pull the fruit apart revealing the ruby arils to eat as is. For juice, place halves cut side down in a citrus squeezer and squeeze. Pomegranate juice stains and tends to splatter, leaving the kitchen looking like the set of a bad "slasher" movie. To remain unscathed while processing a lot of pomegranates, submerge the fruits in water as you work with them. When you separate the seeds from the pulp underwater, the seeds sink to the bottom of the container, and the waxy fiber and skin float to the top.

To extract the juice, place seeds in a blender, 2 cups at a time, and puree for a minute. Pour the juicy pulp into a cheesecloth bag and allow it to drip through. For more about pomegranates, visit www.pomwonderful.com.

In the Landscape

This deciduous woody plant is striking when pruned into a large, fountain-shaped shrub or a small, somewhat pendulous tree—providing beauty over a long period. Its new growth is bronzy; the long, narrow leaves are a bright green and, in most climates, turn yellow in fall. The showy, fluted, orange-red flowers are produced in clusters. Some fruits remain on the tree after the leaves drop, decorating the bare branches. Knowledgeable gardeners leave a few fruits to burst open, entreating hungry birds.

The pomegranate is one of the most ornamental and versatile of the edible plants. Create a striking combo by pairing it with nandina in a shrub border or against a wall, or grow it as a small interest tree, shrub, hedge, screen, or espalier. Informal pomegranate hedges with their occasional thorns create both an impenetrable barrier against intruders and a refuge for nesting birds. Trim occasionally to keep the plant from looking scruffy.

How to Grow

Climate

Pomegranate prefers hot summers and low humidity, so it does poorly in places like the coastal Northwest and South Florida. Its tolerance for very high temperatures makes it a good desert plant, but it has been grown successfully as far north as Washington, D.C. While a few varieties are hardy to 10°F, these have poor flavor. In the cooler zones, place pomegranate against a hot south- or west-facing wall and provide winter protection.

Exposure and Soil

Pomegranate needs full sun and prefers very well-drained, good garden loam with a pH between 5.5 and 7. However, it tolerates a somewhat higher pH, and sodium in limited amounts. The plant is resistant to oak root fungus.

Fertilizing

Apply an organic nitrogen fertilizer in late winter (in sandy soils, fertilize again in spring). Too much nitrogen delays fruit maturity and inhibits total fruit production. Add organic mulch in spring. In soils with a high pH and high amounts of calcium and phosphorus, plants can suffer from zinc deficiency, which causes chlorotic leaves and stunted growth. In the spring, apply a few extra inches of compost and spray the foliage a few times with chelated zinc.

Watering

Pomegranate is drought resistant, but for superior fruits, water as you would citrus. Do not water after a long dry spell if fruits have formed or they will split. Instead, water deeply after harvesting the fruit.

Pruning

Pomegranate fruits most heavily on 2- to 5-year-old wood, but it produces whether it is pruned heavily or not at all. Train a young pomegranate as a bush or a single- or multistemmed tree. To train as a shrub: The first year, select five or six of the strongest suckers (branches emerging from the base) to form the main branches, and remove the rest. In subsequent springs, leave the original trunks and remove any extra suckers. Cut out crossing or drooping branches and any deadwood. To renew the plant and keep it trim, thin out some of the many branches every few years.

To train to a single-trunk tree form, the first year cut all growth to the ground except one strong, straight sucker; this becomes the trunk. To create a multistemmed tree, leave three strong suckers to become trunks. To maintain the tree form, remove all basal suckers except the chosen trunk or trunks every spring. As the years go by there will be fewer suckers. Keep the canopy size to about 6 feet or you will need to prop the branches up to prevent them from breaking. Remove any deadwood and all crossing and drooping branches. Every year, thin and shape for a compact, neat appearance.

Pests and Diseases

Pomegranate has only a few pests and diseases. Scale, thrips, and mites are occasional but not serious problems. Oil sprays smother scale and thrips; sulfur controls mites. A fungus that causes the leaves to drop and the fruit to split can be a problem in the humid South. Copper sprays are helpful. In California, a fruit heart-rot fungus is sometimes a problem if it rains during flowering. The best control for all fungal problems is to remove mummified fruits from the tree and rake up old leaves and fallen fruits in fall and destroy them (do not compost).

On the opposite side of my backyard from the "Plum Garden" is my "Pomegranate Patio," which showcases a 'Utah Sweet' pomegranate. It sports red flowers in summer and yellow leaves in fall, but unlike typical pomegranates, the fruit's skin is pink.

Sometimes a pomegranate does not bear fruit, or the fruits are small and very dry. The most common reason is that you have an ornamental-only variety. Other causes are plant stress, freeze damage, too much nitrogen, or humidity.

Harvesting

Pick blemish-free pomegranates when they are just ripe and colored; they store for months in a cool, dry place. However, test a few fruits for flavor before you harvest many as they do not ripen further after harvest.

How to Purchase

Bare-root or container-grown plants are available in late winter from local nurseries. Mail-order sources include Acorn Springs, Bay Laurel, Edible Landscaping, One Green World, Raintree, and Willis. Durio has the largest selection.

Pollinizers

Pomegranates are self-fruitful.

Varieties

As noted previously, many pomegranates flower beautifully but do not set fruit; be sure to get a fruiting type. Numerous edible varieties have been developed, with fruit in many sizes, shapes, and skin colors—yellow, orange, white, red, or purple—and tart or super-sweet selections. As interest in this fruit's powerful health benefits grows, more varieties will be introduced. Consult the website for the California Rare Fruit Growers to keep up-to-date.

'Eversweet'—has no hard seeds; ripens a month sooner, is hardier, and does better in cool weather than 'Wonderful'.

'Granada'—large, red fruit; quite hardy.

'Nana'—dwarf pomegranate, to 4 ft. tall; very small fruits with little edible flesh.

'Spanish Ruby'—red fruit; available primarily in Florida.

'Utah Sweet'—especially sweet, pink fruit; pliable skin.

'Wonderful'—most frequently grown for its large, deep red fruit and rich wine flavor; the common commercial variety.

Pomelo

See Citrus

Potato, sweet

See Sweet potato

Pumpkin

See Squash

Quince

Quince (European quince, common quince)
Cydonia oblonga
Flowering quince (ornamental quince), *Chaenomeles* spp.

Effort Scale

Quince
NO. 3
Vulnerable to some pests and diseases
Mulching helpful
Fruits must be processed

Flowering quince
NO. 1
Some pruning required
Few pests and diseases
Small harvest

Zones

Quince, 3 to 9
Flowering quince, 5 to 9

Thumbnail Sketch

Quince
Deciduous tree or large shrub
15 to 20 ft. tall
Propagate by budding or from cuttings
Needs full sun
Leaves are oblong, deep green, yellow in fall, woolly underneath, 4 in. long
Blooms in spring
Flowers are white or pale pink, 2 in. across, showy
Fruits are edible; harvest in fall
Use as interest tree or shrub, patio tree, screen, espalier, hedge, or container plant

Flowering quince
Deciduous shrub
4 to 6 ft. tall
Propagate from cuttings
Prefers full sun; tolerates partial shade
Leaves are oblong, glossy green, 1½ to 3 in. long
Blooms in late winter
Flowers are white, coral, pink, red, or bicolors 2 in. across, showy
Fruits are edible; harvest in late summer or fall
Use as interest shrub in bloom, in hedgerow for wildlife, or in container

How to Use

In the Kitchen
Most of the yellow, orange, or green, oblong fruits of quince are too hard and astringent to eat raw, yet they are complex and aromatic, with an applelike flavor when cooked (and they keep their shape). Combine with apples for sauce or pie. Bake the fruit like apples, or spice and use to make chutney. Cooked and spiced quince can also be canned. Quince is very high in pectin and can be made into a thick fruit paste and rolled in sugar. In Greece, quince is a kitchen staple, frequently substituted for apple, often served with meats. Quince is best known for the quintessential, exquisitely flavored, golden jelly.

Flowering quince has a long culinary history in eastern Europe and Russia, where the tangy, lemon-flavored fruits are a major source of vitamin C; some call it the "lemon of the north." Most varieties are best cooked, made into syrups that can be added to tea, served in cooling drinks, or used as the base for a delicious amber jelly. Some folks grind up the fruit with equal parts of sugar and refrigerate for up to 2 months; use a teaspoon or two in your morning tea for a healthful treat.

In the Landscape
The gnarled and twisted form that quince develops with age brings an interesting shape to the landscape, whether the tree is used as an accent near a patio or as a container plant. Delicate pinkish flowers sit above the foliage in spring and in fall; colorful fruits add visual interest. Quince is a good espalier subject. Line a garden walk with quinces grown as trees or shrubs. As shrubs, they can also be used as a solid screen or hedge.

When using flowering quince in a landscape, I am struck with the irony of it all. The common quince tree, which is truly lovely, is not considered part of the landscape gardening repertoire, yet the flowering quince, a rather ratty-looking plant when in leaf, is considered standard design material. I use flowering quinces as part of a hedgerow for wildlife along with elderberries and old roses, or in a mass planting of flowering shrubs. They are spectacular in bloom; sprays of their colorful buds and flowers brought indoors look impressive, even when displayed by the most casual flower arranger.

How to Grow
Climate
Quince will grow in much of the United States, except for the warmest, most humid areas, where fireblight is more problematic. It is subject to severe winter injury at −15°F. Flowering late in spring, it is not harmed by frost.

Flowering quince is hardy to −20°F and does poorly in hot, humid summers.

Exposure and Soil
Quince requires full sun. Unlike most fruits, it tolerates somewhat poor drainage but prefers well-drained, fairly heavy loam. It does not fruit well in very heavy or very light soils.

Flowering quince tolerates some shade and adapts to many conditions, but it becomes chlorotic in highly alkaline soils (high pH).

Fertilizing
An annual application of compost mulch is generally all the fertilizer that is necessary. Avoid using any high-nitrogen fertilizer on quince as it encourages succulent new growth that is particularly susceptible to fireblight.

Watering
Quinces are somewhat drought tolerant but bear more reliably with good soil moisture.

Pruning
Quince is a shrub that can readily be trained as a tree. Remove suckers as they appear. Prune in winter to maintain; the plant can take heavy pruning as it fruits on the tips of current growth. In areas where fireblight is severe, keep pruning to a minimum, as it encourages susceptible succulent new growth.

When growing flowering quince solely as an ornamental, prune heavily after flowering. For fruit production, do not prune after blooming and instead allow the fruits to develop. In late winter, before blooming begins, renew the plant by thinning about a quarter of the good-size branches. Bring the cut branches indoors, set them in water, and they will bloom.

Pests and Diseases
Quince is susceptible to many of the same problems as apple trees, but it is less affected. Codling moth is the most common pest. Curculios, scale, and borers are sometimes problems. Fireblight is the most common disease. Pests and diseases seldom bother flowering quince.

Harvesting
Most quince varieties ripen in fall. Pick the fruits when they have turned color and are fragrant. Handle carefully; the skin bruises easily even though the fruit is hard.

At the Genesee Country Village & Museum near Rochester, New York, a handsome quince tree takes center. Hostas provide a reliable and colorful ground cover. An apple relative, quince is often cooked with apples into a sauce.

How to Purchase
Quinces are available from local nurseries bare root in late winter to early spring and in containers throughout fall. Or order from Bay Laurel, Edible Landscaping, One Green World, or Raintree. Flowering quinces selected for their fruits are available from One Green World.

Pollinizers
All quinces are self-fertile.

Varieties
QUINCE

'Kaunching'—huge, grapefruit-size, sweet fruit, eat fresh; from Russia, where it is served with vegetables and meats, and used for desserts.

'Orange'—large, round fruit; orange-yellow flesh; matures late August, good for cool-summer areas.

'Smyrna'—oblong, yellow fruits, strong fragrance; stores well; vigorous tree.

FLOWERING QUINCE

'Tanechka'—red-orange flowers; medium-size fruit; spreading small shrub.

'Toyo-Nishiki'—red, white, and pink flowers; big fruit, makes delicious syrup; upright shrub.

'Victory'—scarlet flowers; large fruit.

Rapini

See Broccoli and Cauliflower

Raspberry

See Brambleberry

Rhubarb

(garden rhubarb, pie plant)
Rheum rhabarbarum

Effort Scale

NO. 1
Mulching necessary
Regular watering necessary in arid climates

Zones

2 to 8

At the Denver Botanic Garden's Potager Garden, the bee skep (old-fashioned bee hive) is the focal point for a charming pondside planting. Included are white- and red-stemmed rhubarbs, oregano, red amaranth, and thyme.

Thumbnail Sketch

Herbaceous perennial, grown as annual in high desert
3 to 5 ft. tall
Propagate from seeds or divisions
Needs full sun; partial shade in desert
Leaves are large, deep green, wavy, 1½ ft. wide; stems are red or green
Blooms in summer
Flowers are cream, greenish, or reddish, in tall spikes
Stalks are edible; harvest in spring
Use as interest plant or foundation plant; in herbaceous border, flower bed, or container

How to Use

In the Kitchen

In many parts of the country, rhubarb is the first "fruit" of spring, although its edible stalks classify it as a vegetable. Cook the thick, fleshy leafstalks of this striking plant in traditional rhubarb pie, sauces, and stew; my favorite is strawberry-rhubarb pie—sweeter than straight rhubarb. You can even make rhubarb wine. Preserve rhubarb as jam or wine. Freeze or can stewed rhubarb.

Caution: Rhubarb leaves are deadly poisonous if eaten.

In the Landscape

A rhubarb plant is an investment in the future—a long-lived addition to the yard. An herbaceous perennial with leaves that can grow to 36 inches tall, it has dramatic 18-inch-wide, crinkly, rich green leaves with red veins atop rosy red stalks. The red and pink rhubarbs are so handsome that they fit into the most sophisticated herbaceous border or flower bed. Rhubarb works well as an accent in a container or to fill a corner spot in a garden or yard. It is truly eye-catching when planted with red geraniums. Rhubarb is traditionally grown as a foundation plant or against a corner.

Rhubarb flowers bloom atop tall stalks. In warm-winter areas, cut them off as soon as they emerge, to focus the plant's energy on stalks and leaves. However, in colder climates, where the plants are so vigorous and flower plumes so decorative, let them grow and show off in summer. You may notice rhubarb planted by the corner of an old red barn, often with goatsbeard; the cream-colored plumes of both plants dazzle against the red siding.

How to Grow

Rhubarb has specific requirements: It needs at least 2 months of winter cold and is not productive in areas with very hot summers. In the high desert, plant it in partial shade for coolness in autumn as a winter annual.

Grow rhubarb in full sun in acidic, well-drained loam rich in organic matter. Mulch in spring and fall with compost or manure to keep weeds down and to feed the plant. Rhubarb has few pests and diseases. In arid climates, provide 1 inch of water a week. If placed correctly and given a modest amount of attention, a plant will last a lifetime. Three to four plants are adequate for the average family.

Unless you are growing it as an annual, do not harvest any stalks the first year. After that, harvest by gently pulling or cutting off the thickest, healthiest stalks near soil level. Harvest begins in spring and, if the plants are healthy, goes well into summer. Growth slows in hot weather, but picks up again in fall. Well-established plants tolerate an additional light fall harvest. After a decade or so, if the plant is getting crowded, dig it up and divide into three or four plants.

How to Purchase

In spring, rhubarb rhizomes are readily available either bare root or in containers from local nurseries or mail-order firms, including Burpee, Raintree, Stark Bro's, and Territorial. Look for the red cultivars 'Chipman's Canada Red', 'Cherry Red', and 'Crimson Red'. 'Strawberry' is a pink variety, and 'Victoria' a white rhubarb. Save money by offering to help a friend or neighbor divide their plant and get a division as a thank-you.

Romaine lettuce

See Lettuce

Rosa rugosa

See Rose

Rose

Rosa spp.

Effort Scale

NO. 2
Easy to grow
Processing fruits is time consuming

Zones

2 to 9

Thumbnail Sketch

Deciduous shrub
4 to 12 ft. tall
Propagate from cuttings or seeds
Needs full sun or light shade
Leaves are compound, composed of 5 to 9 leaflets, medium to deep green
Blooms in summer
Flowers are white, red, pink, or lilac, 2 to 4 in. across
Flowers are edible; harvest all season; fruits (hips) are edible; harvest in fall
Use as interest plant, barrier, or hedge; espalier or train; grow in raised bed or container

How to Use

In the Kitchen

Rose hips are small, applelike fruits. Usually red-orange, they can be yellow or deep red. Many roses produce hips (if you don't cut off the flowers), but only some are pleasant tasting; others are astringent or

'Magnifica' rugosa rose has some of the tastiest petals. Note the wrinkled leaves that give rugosas their moniker. In fall the plant is covered with orange hips high in vitamin C that are great for syrups, teas, and jellies.

pithy. Rugosa roses, the dog rose, and the Eglantine rose bear the most flavorful hips. A few others also bear nice-tasting hips; try your rose hips. Use fresh hips to make jelly, syrups, marmalade, and sauces; and dried hips for tea. Most rose hips are high in vitamin C.

Rose petals, too, are edible. To be safe, eat only those grown without chemicals. That said, a number of varieties and species produce lovely flowers that are delicious; others are unpleasant and metallic. I recommend 'Belinda', a small pink hybrid musk whose semi-double flowers are first-rate for candying; 'Graham Thomas', a yellow David Austin rose; and 'Carefree Delight', a pink shrub rose. Edible flower maven Cathy Wilkinson Barash prefers the David Austin rose 'Gertrude Jekyll'; the spicy floribunda 'Julia Child'; the hybrid teas 'Tiffany' and 'Double Delight'; and the ground cover rose 'Flower Carpet Pink', which, while not fragrant, has a delightful flavor.

Candy whole rose petals; use whole or minced petals in salads or sprinkled over cakes; and incorporate minced petals into sweet butter and serve on brioche. Boil rose petals with sugar and water, strain out the petals, and infuse the perfumed liquid into sorbets, jams, honey, and syrups. Roses also make lovely garnishes.

To dry rose hips, wash the fruits, cut open, and remove the seeds. Spread on trays and use a food dehydrator or a low oven (150°F) to remove all moisture.

Candied petals, if kept in a cool dry place in an airtight container, will keep for a year.

In the Landscape

The best rose to grow for both hips and petals is the vigorous rugosa rose, a deciduous shrub, usually 4 to 8 feet tall, with prickly, thorny branches; use it as a barrier plant. With its dense upright growth, rugosa serves as a good screen or hedge. The deep veining of its lush, dark leaves gives an almost quilted look. Most varieties have gloriously fragrant blooms—single or double, 2 to 4 inches across, and in colors ranging from white through magenta or lilac, most plentiful in late spring. Some repeat bloom, producing flowers and fruits simultaneously. In early fall, the 1-inch-long fruits are showy, followed by bonfire-bright fall foliage. Compact rugosas like 'Alba', 'Frau Dagmar Hastrupp', 'Hansa', and 'Belle Poitevine' do well in large containers.

Some species roses also produce wonderful flowers and hips. Most are big rangy plants, best suited for the back of an herb garden or planted along a country lane.

Note: Some rugosas are extremely vigorous; restrain them with a metal header. Do not plant near open fields, or birds will disperse the seeds, and the plants will take over.

How to Grow

Climate
Unlike their hybrid tea cousins, rugosas (and other species named here) can take wind, salt air, drought, and harsh winters. They grow in most of North America except in the warmest-winter parts of Zone 9 and all of 10 and 11.

Exposure and Soil
These species roses need full sun or light shade. They are highly tolerant of most soil types but prefer neutral soil. Good drainage is essential.

Fertilizing
Very little fertilizer is needed. Mulch shrubs in spring with a few inches of compost or shredded leaves. In alkaline soils, chlorosis can be a problem; apply chelated iron.

Watering
These shrubs are drought tolerant once they are established.

Pruning
For good fruit production, minimize occasional heavy pruning. Instead, prune annually in late winter or early spring for shape and size control. Do not remove spent flowers (deadhead) if you want rose hips to develop.

Pests and Diseases
Unlike hybrid tea roses, rugosas and the species mentioned here have few pests and diseases. Aphids and Japanese beetles may be bothersome in some areas. Rust is an occasional problem; treat with baking soda or compost tea. Check before using any pesticides, particularly sulfur, as rugosa foliage is easily burned.

For more information on rugosa roses, consult *Rosa Rugosa* by Suzanne Verrier and *The Rose Bible* by Rayford Clayton Reddell; for other old-time roses, *Landscaping with Antique Roses* by Liz Druitt and G. Michael Shoup.

Caution: Never use systemic rose pesticides on plants that are to be eaten.

Harvesting
Harvest flowers when they first open and remove their petals. Pick hips when they are fully colored but not over-ripe (soft and wrinkled).

How to Purchase

Purchase the roses described here bare root or in containers from local nurseries or from Heirloom Old Garden Roses, High Country Roses, or Antique Rose Emporium.

Pollinizers
Plant more than one variety for good fruit production.

Varieties
RUGOSA ROSE
Originally from Asia, *Rosa rugosa* was a popular rose in the 1800s. With the exception of 'Alba', most of these roses are old hybrids. All bloom repeatedly over a long period.
'Alba' (*R. rugosa* var. *alba*)—single, elegant, white flowers; fragrant with a spicy rose flavor; great for sorbet; 4 to 5 ft. tall; large, orange fruit.
'Belle Poitevine'—large, lilac pink, double flowers; 4 to 5 ft. tall; large, orange-red hips.
'Delicata'—semi-double, cerise pink flowers; 4 to 5 ft. tall; orange hips.
'Frau Dagmar Hastrupp' ('Frau Dagmar Hartopp')—clear pink, single flowers; 24 to 36 in. tall; large, red hips.
'Hansa'—hybrid; violet red, double flowers; blooms repeatedly; clovelike fragrance; compact, 4 ft. tall; large red hips; popular variety.
'Magnifica'—double, deep cerise flowers; fragrant; 4 to 6 ft. tall; large orange fruit.
'Rubra'—single, purple to crimson flowers; appear over long season; 5 ft. tall; growth less dense than for other rugosas; prolific, red-orange fruit.

OTHER SPECIES
Apothecary rose, *R. gallica officinalis*—medium red, semi-double flowers in early summer; to 4 ft. tall; small, orange hips.
Dog rose, *R. canina*—small, pink to white, single flowers in small clusters, spring bloom; tall rangy plant 10 to 15 ft. tall; associated with hedgerows; hips red and in clusters.
Eglantine or sweet briar rose, *R. rubiginosa* (*R. eglanteria*)—small, pink, single flowers; fragrant; apple-scented foliage; 8 ft. tall by 15 ft. wide; spring bloom; suckers readily, prune vigilantly; clusters of orange to scarlet hips.

Rosemary

Rosmarinus officinalis

Effort Scale

NO. 1
In a mild, dry climate, it almost grows itself

Zones

6 to 10; grow as annual elsewhere

Thumbnail Sketch

Evergreen woody shrub
12 in. to 7 ft. tall
Propagate from seeds or cuttings
Needs full sun
Leaves are needlelike, deep green with gray underside, ½ to 1½ in. long
Blooms in spring

Flowers are blue, lavender, or pink, small, showy

Leaves and flowers are edible; use as seasoning; harvest leaves year round

Use as bank cover, ground cover, or topiary; in herb garden, raised bed, or container

How to Use

In the Kitchen

The aromatic leaves of this well-loved herb have a slight piney taste. Rosemary is commonly used to season lamb, pork, poultry, and oily fish. Its unique flavor marries well with roasted vegetables and gives a piney flavor to casseroles, egg dishes, marinades, and vinaigrettes. A classic dish I've made for years is roasted lamb with a mustard and rosemary glaze. My favorite way to serve baby potatoes is roasted in olive oil, garlic, and rosemary. As they are cooking, the rosemary and garlic perfume the air. In the end, the potatoes come out crunchy and full of flavor. Steep rosemary leaves to add zest to fruit punch. Use the straight woody stems of tall varieties for skewering meats and vegetables *en brochette*. To preserve, dry like oregano.

The flowers—with a milder flavor than the leaves—add a little zing sprinkled on green or pasta salads.

In the Landscape

This woody shrub ranges in height from 12 inches to 7 feet, depending on the variety. The tall, upright plants make beautiful flowering hedges and lend themselves to pruning into geometric shapes and topiaries. Unpruned, use them as informal shrubs or—with their interesting, gnarled shapes—as container or accent plants. Prostrate varieties are ideal for covering banks or cascading over a retaining wall. Rosemary's strong root system is helpful in controlling erosion on hillsides in mild-winter areas. Let cultivars like 'Irene' and 'Prostratus' trail out of containers almost clinging to the sides. If you are using rosemary as a ground cover in a large area in a fire-danger zone, prune the plant back quite hard each year to reduce the fuel load and encourage new, tender, fleshy growth. All types of rosemary are well suited for herb gardens and containers.

All rosemary plants have deep green, needlelike leaves with gray undersides. These leaves handsomely set off the plentiful blooms, whether they are light blue, lavender, pink, or deep violet blue. Rosemary attracts bees, but deer leave it alone.

How to Grow

Rosemary needs full sun and slightly alkaline soil with great drainage. Most varieties are hardy down to about 5 to 10°F. Plant it in spring in cold climates, any time of year in mild-winter areas. In hot, humid climates, prevent root rot by growing rosemary in raised beds with a ½-inch mulch of sand or pebbles; water sparingly. Except when it is grown in sandy soils or in containers, fertilizer is seldom required. When growing it as a perennial, cut it back after flowering to keep it from getting too woody. Rosemary is drought tolerant, but in the desert or in clay soils, give it a deep watering once a month in summer—in sandy soils more often. Harvest branches at any time of the year.

How to Purchase

Rosemary is slow to grow from seed, so most gardeners purchase small plants. Common varieties of rosemary are readily available at local nurseries; for the many special cultivars, look to herb nurseries and mail-order catalogs, including Mulberry Creek, Nichols, Thyme Garden, and Richters.

Varieties

The following are among the many varieties of rosemary available as plants; all have a similar flavor. All but 'Arp' are hardy to Zone 7.

'Arp'—semi-upright type, 4 ft. tall; medium blue flowers; hardy to the warmest parts of Zone 6; developed in Texas; tolerates heat and humidity better than most varieties.

'Golden Rain' ('Joyce DeBaggio')—shrubby type, 3 to 4 ft. tall, with fine leaves; new growth has gold streaks; blue flowers.

'Irene'—trailing type, mounding to 18 in. tall; medium blue flowers; quite hardy.

'Lockwood de Forest'—trailing type, mounding to 24 in. tall; bright blue flowers.

'Majorca Pink'—shrub type, 24 to 36 in. tall; small leaves; pink flowers.

'Prostratus'—trailing type, to 24 in. tall and spreading to 6 ft.; lavender blue flowers; also called creeping rosemary.

'Tuscan Blue'—shrub type, 5 to 7 ft. tall; deep blue flowers; upright, woody, straight stems.

'Tuscan Blue' rosemary with its sculptural upright branches and gray-green leaves stands tall behind a birdbath. It's the perfect foil for a magenta fuchsia, as well as million bells and geraniums in containers. I cut the stems for barbecue skewers.

Sage

Salvia spp.

Effort Scale

NO. 1
Very easy to grow
Common sage should be taken indoors in coldest-winter areas

Zones

Common sage, all but South Florida and Texas Gulf regions
Pineapple sage, 9 and 10

Thumbnail Sketch

Common sage

Perennial evergreen woody herb grown as annual in coldest climates
12 to 24 in. tall
Propagate from seeds or divisions
Needs full sun; afternoon shade in desert
Leaves are gray-green, purple, gold, silver, or variegated, 1 to 2 in. long
Blooms in summer; not all varieties produce flowers
Flowers are blue, lavender, or white, small, in spikes
Leaves and flowers are edible; use as seasoning; harvest year round
Use in herb garden, flower bed, planter box, rock garden, or container

Pineapple sage

Evergreen woody herb; perennial often grown as annual
2 to 4 ft. tall
Propagate from cuttings
Needs full sun; partial shade in desert areas
Leaves bright green, underside slightly woolly, 2 to 4 in. long
Blooms in fall
Flowers are red or coral on tall, thin spikes

Leaves and flowers are edible; use as seasoning; harvest season varies
Use in herb garden, back of flower bed, or container; as accent plant or houseplant

How to Use

In the Kitchen

The aromatic leaves of common or garden sage (*Salvia officinalis*) are used as a seasoning for poultry stuffing and homemade sausage. Its earthy low notes are welcome in marinades and dressings, too. Sage adds an aromatic note to soft, mild cheese spread on crackers and, because of its congeniality with chicken, is good in the dressing used on a chicken salad. Roasted potatoes and Italian baked beans are made with olive oil and garlic, and seasoned with lots of sage—healthy alternatives to the American versions. Dry sage leaves like oregano. Spiky sage flowers are divine dipped in tempura batter and deep-fried.

Pineapple sage (*S. rutilans* [*S. elegans*]) has a pleasant pineapple flavor; the leaves are used in jellies, sorbets, and fruit salsas and compotes. The flowers make a dramatic garnish when sprinkled over a salad.

In the Landscape

These woody perennials differ sharply from each other in appearance. Common sage grows to 24 inches high and has gray-green, rough-surfaced leaves and lavender blue, pink, or white spiky flowers. It is widely used in herb and flower gardens and in containers. While some purists insist on the flavor of common sage, there is a palette of similar-tasting sages that are striking in the landscape. 'Tricolor' sage with its purple, red, and white variegated leaves or the chubby-leaved, velvet gray 'Berggarten' gives textural and color contrast to an herb border of thyme and chives. Yet another variety, 'Icterina', has green and gold foliage. Though it never flowers, it can be relied on to cast a beam of sunlight into a border of somber grays and deep greens.

Pineapple sage grows taller, is more open in its growth habit, and has brighter green, softer-looking leaves than common sage. Its late-summer flowers are clear red and grow in slender spikes that are favorites of hummingbirds, bumblebees, and butterflies. It should not be confused with scarlet sage (*Salvia splendens*), the strictly ornamental sage. Pineapple sage is a nice addition to any flower bed, toward the back because of its height. Try it with Shasta daisies, green basil, ruby chard, and red zinnias. Plant chartreuse-leaved 'Golden Delicious' in partial shade; it will not only brighten the area but also keep its color better than in full sun.

How to Grow

Common sage grows in most areas of the country. In the coldest climates, raise it as an annual. Pineapple sage is quite tender. Both sages need ordinary garden soil and especially good drainage or they develop root rots. Though full sun is best in most areas, in the desert give them afternoon shade. Neither needs much watering or fertilizer.

Both sages can be harvested at any time of the growing season for use fresh. If you plan to dry common sage, it's best to harvest before the plant flowers to ensure optimum texture and flavor.

How to Purchase

Both seeds and plants of common sage are readily available. Pineapple and the specialty sage plants are sold in containers in retail nurseries and available from Nichols, Richters, and Thyme Garden.

Common or garden sage is flanked by two popular variegated varieties: 'Icterina', at left, and 'Tricolor'. Only garden sage blooms, sending up striking stalks of purplish blue flowers in late spring. The flowers are delicious, sweeter than the leaves.

Satsuma

See Citrus

Shaddock

See Citrus

Silverbeet

See Chard

Society garlic

See Chives

Sour orange

See Citrus

Sprouting broccoli

See Broccoli and Cauliflower

Squash and Pumpkin

Cucurbita spp.

Effort Scale

NO. 3
Must be planted annually
Vulnerable to some pests
Occasional watering necessary
Some weeding necessary
Some training of vining types necessary
Need fertilizing and mulching

Zones

Not applicable

Its large bold leaves and yellow flowers make zucchini a standout in this garden, planted among petunias and marigolds for color contrast. For textural contrast, note the small-leaved tomatillo plant on the left and the dainty, yellow-flowered fennel at the top.

Thumbnail Sketch

Annuals
Bush types, 24 to 36 in. tall; vining types, to 12 ft. long
Propagate from seeds
Need full sun
Leaves are medium to dark green
Flowers are bright yellow, 2 to 4 in. across
Fruits are edible; harvest summer and fall; flowers are edible; pumpkin and some squash seeds are edible
Use bush types in herbaceous borders, raised beds, or containers; vining types on fences and trellises

How to Use

In the Kitchen

First let me clarify the distinctions between summer and winter squash, as both grow and are harvested in the summer. You pick summer squash when they are small; they are thin skinned and do not store well. Winter squash have tough skins (often called shells) and are good keepers for fall and winter eating.

Squash—both summer and winter—are kitchen staples, the foundation of my garden cuisine. Gold and green baby zucchini grilled or roasted with olive oil and garlic, zucchini frittatas with squash blossoms, and corn bread pancakes filled with grated summer squash served with salsa—all are warm-weather standards at my house. As is zucchini bread with chopped crystallized ginger to give it some zing; I make extra to freeze, then toast it and serve with cream cheese, yum! With fall comes butternut squash soup with cream and acorn squash baked with brown sugar and butter. Native squash stew with kidney beans, cumin, and chilies; and roasted butternut cubes with olive oil and rosemary are other winners. While squash plants don't grow in the winter, I can still enjoy the zucchini relish and pickles from the pantry and some of the big winter squash from the garage, and the freezer is full of squash treats. Squash is the queen of my kitchen.

Pumpkin is the quintessential fall treat; arguments rage over the best varieties for making pie. Pumpkin soup, served in a scooped-out pumpkin, is always a crowd pleaser. When I go to a pumpkin-carving party, I save all the seeds and then clean and dry them for winter snacking.

In the Landscape

Most types of squash have large, hairy, rough, ivy-shaped green leaves. Most reach a foot wide, but some, like zucchini and pumpkins, have 2-foot-wide leaves that lend a tropical look to a garden. All have yellow, cup-shaped flowers; many produce big showy blooms that last for only a few hours in the morning.

Bush-type squash are useful in herbaceous beds near a patio or front walk; interplant with dwarf zinnias and marigolds to dress them up. All do well in large containers on balconies and patios. Train vining types on low trellises and fences, or let them spill over an embankment. A few like 'Tromboncino' have vines long enough to cover a trellis. I have seen vining squash and pumpkin plants meander over large trellises and through a large flower border of sunflowers, cosmos, and morning glories. 'Jack Be Little' pumpkin is adorable on a teepee—guaranteed to entice children—or trained on a trellis.

How to Grow

All squash—whether they are called summer or winter—and pumpkins are warm-season annuals. They require full sun and very rich soil; add plenty of organic matter before planting as they are heavy feeders.

Planting

In short-summer areas, start seeds indoors a few weeks before your last frost. Move them to the garden after the weather is warm. In all areas, plant either in hills (with two plants to a mound) or singly in containers or flower borders. Provide ample water during the growing season. Fertilize monthly.

Pests and Diseases

Young plants are susceptible to cutworms, slugs, and striped and spotted cucumber beetles. In the East, squash bugs can build up to large numbers; grow the young plants under row covers until they are big enough to withstand the hoard. Remove the row covers when blossoms appear so that bees can pollinate the flowers. You can hand-pick the bugs. The squash borer, a clear-winged moth with orange markings, tunnels into stems and is a problem in the East and Midwest; choose resistant varieties like yellow crookneck summer squash and 'Butternut' and 'Sweet Mama' winter squash.

Set organic mulch over layers of wet newspaper to keep the plants from drying out, suppress weeds, and give cucumber beetles less access to the roots and squash vine borer larvae fewer places to burrow.

Mildew can be a problem on all cucurbits, particularly late in the season. Johnny's Selected Seeds offers mildew-resistant varieties, including 'Sunray' and 'Tip Top' zucchini and 'Cornell's Bush Delicata' winter squash. Mildew begins to show up when the plants are nearly done producing. By that time I've had more than my fill of zucchini, so I pull them out. There are other diseases that infect squash plants; for more information see the "Cucumber" entry.

Harvesting

Pick all summer squash when it is young and tender and the blossoms have withered, or a few days later when the fruits are less than 12 inches long and great for stuffing and shredding for zucchini bread.

Harvest winter squash and pumpkins when fully mature and the skin is hard to puncture with your fingernail. Cut the stem with a sharp knife or garden shears. Leave a few inches of stem attached. Do not lift pumpkins by the "handle" or they will break off and the pumpkin may rot. Cure winter squash and pumpkins for 2 to 3 weeks in a well-ventilated area away from direct sunlight for a longer storage life. Ideal storage temperature is between 50 and 60°F; an unheated basement is ideal.

Zucchini produce a fruit every day or two (last summer I harvested 143 green zucchini of various sizes from two 'Raven' plants in my trial garden!). Crooknecks and pattypans produce one fruit every 2 or 3 days. Winter squash produce two to six squash per plant, depending on their size.

How to Purchase

The choice of squash varieties is tremendous—hybrids and open pollinated; early-, mid-, and late-season varieties; compact or vining types; and, of course, winter and summer varieties. Seeds for some squash are available at local nurseries. Find a much greater variety from Johnny's, Nichols, Park, Pine Tree, Burpee, Jung, and Stokes Seeds. Kitazawa carries numerous Asian squash; Native Seeds and Redwood City carry Native American varieties; and Baker Creek, Seed Savers, Seeds of Change, and Southern Exposure offer many heirlooms.

Varieties

SUMMER SQUASH

The fruit is thin skinned and green, yellow, or white. All varieties are *Cucurbita pepo* var. *pepo* unless otherwise noted.

'Clarimore'—hybrid zucchini; neat-looking bush; pastel green skin, creamy texture, mild flavor; 44 days.

'Early Yellow Crookneck'—heirloom; compact bush; yellow skin, sweet flesh; 50 days.

'Golden Dawn'—hybrid zucchini; upright plant; yellow skin, mild flavor; 47 days.

'Raven'—hybrid zucchini; upright bush, fewer spines; deep green skin, pronounced flavor; productive; 48 days.

'Ronde de Nice'—hybrid zucchini; round, light green fruit; delicate flavor; 45 days.

'Sunny Delight'—hybrid straightneck squash; open semi-bush vine; flat, scalloped, yellow fruit, dense flesh, mild flavor; 40 days.

'Tromboncino' (*C. moschata*)—heirloom; very long vine; pale green fruit to 24 in. long; slightly sweet, mild flavor; resists borers; productive; 56 days.

WINTER SQUASH

Most are long vines; skin color varies.

'Burpee's Butterbush' (*C. moschata*)—butternut type; compact bush, good for containers; deep reddish orange flesh, excellent flavor; 1 to 2 lb.; 75 days.

'Buttercup' (*C. maxima*)—sprawling vine 3 to 5 ft. long; dark green, blocky, turban-shaped fruit; fiberless, rich, sweet-flavored orange flesh; 3 to 4 lb.; 95 days.

'Cornell's Bush Delicata' (*C. pepo*)—compact bush to 36 in. tall; green and white striped fruit; fine-textured, sweet, yellow flesh; 1 lb.; 100 days.

'Sunshine' (*C. maxima*)—hybrid; short vine; round shape; scarlet skin; dense, sweet-flavored, orange flesh; 4 lb.; 95 days.

'Waltham Butternut' (*C. moschata*)—sprawling vine 3 to 5 ft. long; light tan skin; sweet, orange flesh; productive; 105 days.

The size range alone is greater than for any other vegetable or fruit—from dainty 4-in. 'Jack-Be-Little' to the humongous ¾-ton 'Atlantic Giant'. All grow on long vines.

'Rouge Vif d'Etampes' ('Cinderella', *C. maxima*)—heirloom; large, flattened, scalloped, deep orange fruit, delicate flavor, use for soup; 15 to 20 lb.; 115 days.

'Winter Luxury Pie' (*C. pepo*)—heirloom; deep orange, slightly netted skin; yellow-orange flesh, makes excellent pie; 6 lb.; 100 days.

Strawberry

Fragaria spp.

Effort Scale

Alpine strawberry
NO. 2
Fertilizing and weeding necessary
Regular watering needed in most areas
Harvesting is time consuming
Dividing plants every 3 or 4 years may be necessary
Winter protection needed in some areas

Garden strawberry
NO. 3
Susceptible to some diseases and pests, including birds
Replanting necessary every 3 or 4 years
Runners must be managed
Watering and fertilizing necessary
Weeding necessary
Harvesting the large, perishable yield is time consuming
Winter protection needed in many areas

Zones

4 to 11

Thumbnail Sketch

Herbaceous perennial
6 to 12 in. tall
Propagate from seeds or runners
Alpine strawberry prefers morning sun or dappled shade; garden strawberry needs full sun
Leaves are compound; alpine, medium green; garden, deep green
Blooms in spring and summer
Flowers are white or pink, small
Fruits and flowers are edible; harvest in spring, summer, and fall
Use in flower bed, raised bed, hanging basket, or container or as small-area ground cover; alpine along woodland path and in rock garden

How to Use

In the Kitchen

Native Americans consider a red, ripe strawberry a mystical symbol of the human heart. One large, sun-warmed fruit can bring joy far

'Tristar' strawberries hanging over a wood retaining wall are safe from most slugs, snails, pillbugs, and birds. Since the fruit stays dry, diseases are seldom a problem. This tasty, day-neutral variety produces fruit from spring through early fall.

beyond its size, and a whole bowl of fragrant, succulent, homegrown strawberries with cream—that's a taste of paradise. Close behind are strawberry pie and shortcake, which dress up strawberries without masking their flavor. Scandinavians use the berries in cold soups. Strawberry jam is such an American tradition it hardly needs mentioning. All this pleasure and joy is packed with vitamin C, folic acid, potassium, and lots of antioxidants.

If you like garden strawberries, you will love alpine strawberries (the French call them *fraises des bois*). I call them strawberries with the flavor volume turned up. They're seldom sold commercially; grow them yourself and enjoy this rare treat.

As incredible as fresh strawberries are, you can get a taste of summer later in the year by making jellies, jams, fruit leather, and wine. Freeze whole berries with sugar or lay them on cookie sheets, freeze, and then package the frozen berries in freezer bags.

In the Landscape

Perky, red garden strawberries dangling from hanging baskets and terra-cotta chimney flues or out of a strawberry jar are treats for the eyes as well as the taste buds. Their leaves and small, white flowers contrast nicely with the dark color of wood tubs or a stone patio. Strawberries are also good in raised beds or to line flower borders. I always have some growing near my walk for neighborhood children to help themselves.

Alpine strawberries are star edible ornamentals. With no runners, they remain neat looking near a lawn or a walkway. The fruits are long lasting on the plant, then dry up and fall off instead of rotting, and for some reason birds usually leave them alone. And because they tolerate light shade, they are perfect to line a woodland walk combined with other shade plants like fibrous begonias.

How to Grow

Traditionally strawberries were a June celebration. The plants bloomed as days lengthened in spring, and the harvest lasted a few blissful weeks. Then breeders introduced varieties that bear an early-, mid-, or late-season crop, so gardeners planted all three types to extend their harvest. All these varieties produced a large harvest perfect for feasting and making jam and freezing. Subsequently, breeders introduced varieties that bore a spring crop, plus a few berries throughout the summer, and yet another small crop in late summer—everbearing strawberries. Today's varieties are clearly modern miracles—day-neutrals that bear a steady, sizeable harvest from May until frost stops production. Planting and care of spring-bearing, everbearing, and day-neutral strawberries are quite different, as noted in the information below.

While traditional large rows of spring-bearing varieties required much effort, today we can grow plenty of berries with ease. Choose day-neutral varieties and plant them in raised beds or large containers. Day-neutrals provide a modest harvest all summer, and the raised beds eliminate weeds as well as most pests and diseases.

Alpine strawberries are easy-care perennials with few cultural needs once established.

Climate

A strawberry variety exists for nearly every area of North America—if only as annuals. Alpine strawberries are quite hardy and grow into milder parts of Zone 4, but they do poorly in very hot climates. In cold climates, cover all types of strawberries with a heavy winter mulch before the ground freezes, to prevent the plants from heaving out of the ground during alternating freezes and thaws. In areas where summer temperatures remain above 90°F for more than a day or two, strawberries stop producing unless you mulch with an inch of straw to keep the soil cool. In low-desert climates and regions with more than 300 frost-free days, treat garden strawberries as winter annuals and choose day-neutrals.

Exposure and Soil

Grow garden strawberries in full sun, and alpine strawberries in morning sun or filtered shade from a high-branching tree. Both prefer slightly acid, well-drained, highly organic soil. With iffy drainage, plant in hills or raised beds. Strawberries do not grow well in areas with high soil salinity, like some high desert areas. Avoid soil where tomatoes have grown, as it can harbor verticillium wilt, which infects strawberries.

Alpine strawberries are petite plants with small, intensely flavored, aromatic fruit that is held above their dainty leaves. In the landscape, utilize them as a fragrant ground cover in semi-shade or as a frilly edging for a shady border.

Planting

In cold-winter areas, plant as soon as the soil is workable in spring. In mild-winter areas, plant in fall or spring. Plant spring- and everbearing varieties about 6 inches apart, in rows 12 inches apart. Plant day-neutrals 4 to 5 inches apart in staggered rows. In all cases, be sure to plant the crowns at ground level. Strawberries planted too deeply will rot; too high and they will dry out. Grow garden strawberries for only 3 years in one place as diseases build up and the mother plants stop producing.

Start alpine strawberries from seeds in early spring. Plants are also available. For best production, divide every 3 or 4 years.

Fertilizing

Apply garden compost to strawberries in spring; keep them well mulched. Avoid high-nitrogen fertilizers on spring-bearing and alpine strawberries; they create lush foliage prone to disease. Heavy-working day-neutral and everbearing varieties require more nitrogen: fertilize in spring after blossoms set and again at least once a month for the next 2 months (for a longer period in mild climates) with an all-purpose organic fertilizer. Watch all types of strawberries for symptoms of nitrogen starvation—light green or yellowish leaves; treat by applying a nitrogen fertilizer.

Watering

Keep the soil fairly moist. Avoid overhead watering, which fosters diseases that rot the berries; drip irrigation works best. Consistent watering is critical for day-neutrals and alpines.

Pruning

In the first year, pruning differs for each of the four strawberry categories. Spring-bearing garden strawberries: remove blossoms to encourage strong growth and good root development (no berries the first year). Everbearing: remove spring flowers; allow fall flowers to fruit. Day-neutrals: remove all flowers for 6 weeks. Alpines need no pruning.

If you want fruits to cascade over the side of a container, choose varieties that bear on the runners, and do not remove them. If diseases aren't a problem, use some of the rooted runners from the mother plant as replacements for older plants as they decline.

Pests and Diseases

While the following information may sound daunting, few gardeners have more than one or two of these problems. A good fall cleanup, spring mulch, and rotating your crop every few years will prevent and control many pests and diseases. If birds are a problem, use netting over the bed; secure it well to keep out chipmunks and squirrels, too.

A number of other pests bother strawberries, but chemical controls are usually unnecessary. Snails, slugs, and tarnish bugs are exceptions. For snails and slugs, occasionally move the mulch aside and handpick. Brown tarnish bugs cause deformed and dried-up berries. Control weeds in and around the plants; in severe cases, spray with pyrethrum every few weeks until under control. If weevils are a problem, grow spring-bearers, as weevils usually emerge after the harvest; after the second year, pull up the plants and put something else in that space for a few years. For tarnish bug and weevil infestations, plant day-neutral varieties and treat them as annuals, move the strawberry patch every year, or plant in large containers like wine barrels. Aphids, Japanese beetles, and mites are universal pests; nematodes are a problem in the Southeast.

Weeds easily crowd out strawberries and provide ideal conditions for slugs, weevils, and diseases. To suppress weed seed germination, apply a 2-inch-deep mulch of straw, leaf mold, or pine needles after planting.

The major strawberry diseases—verticillium wilt and red stele (root rot)—can be serious. Buy plants from a nursery that carries certified disease-free plants. Control by rotating crops and buying resistant varieties. Botrytis is a problem in cool, damp weather, rotting the fruit and sometimes infecting the buds; control by using a fluffy mulch like pine needles or straw, avoiding overhead watering, growing the plants in containers so berries dangle over the sides, and picking and destroying rotten fruits.

Harvesting

Commercial berries are bred to be firm and keep for days. Home-grown strawberries are soft and fragile; their quality declines rapidly. Pick berries at their peak—when they are fully colored, fragrant, and slightly soft; check the plants daily. Carefully pull off the berry with stem and cap attached. If you are not using the berries within a few hours, refrigerate only a few days. A mature garden strawberry plant produces about 1 pint of berries each season. Alpines produce less.

How to Purchase

Buy bare-root garden strawberries in early spring from local nurseries or from Burpee, Johnny's, Park, or Raintree. Indiana Berry and Nourse specialize in berries and have the largest bare-root selection. Alpine strawberry seeds are available from Johnny's, Nichols, Renee's, and Richters. One Green World and Raintree offer small plants of alpine strawberries.

Varieties

GARDEN STRAWBERRY, *FRAGARIA* × *ANANASSA*

Strawberries are climate specific; choose varieties well suited to your area. For a bed filled with large berries, choose spring-bearers to glory in for a month and preserve. Choose a suitable variety for freezing; some turn mushy. Most strawberries are sold bare root (often in bunches of 25 of one cultivar) in spring. Many folks choose an early variety for a big early-summer harvest if they want to preserve them and add a day-neutral variety for summer and fall harvest. For a family of four, 75 plants are ideal.

If you want a smaller but consistent harvest from May through October, choose from the list of everbearing and day-neutral strawberries for a total of 50 plants. Expect a quart of berries every few days, except in hot weather, when production drops.

Day-Neutral

Plant in spring as soon as you can work the soil; plantings after May can disappoint. Day-neutral production declines the third year.

'Fern'—medium-size fruit, good flavor; few runners; well adapted to hot-summer areas and mild, coastal parts of Canada.

'Seascape'—fairly large berries, good flavor; productive, disease resistant; hardy to about 0°F.

'Tribute'—medium-size fruit, good, tart flavor; resistant to major diseases including verticillium; does best in cool-summer areas.

'Tristar'—small to medium-size berries, great flavor; few runners, good in containers and hanging baskets; resistant to major diseases; very popular, widely adapted, hardy to –25°F.

Everbearing

'Ozark Beauty'—large berries, old-time flavor; bears only on mother plants, not runners; disease resistant; produces poorly in mild-winter climates, very hardy.

'Quinault'—large fruit, good flavor; produces quickly after planting, bears fruit on unrooted runners, great for hanging baskets.

'Redchief'—medium-size berries, good flavor; resistant to red stele and mildew; for the Southeast.

Spring-Bearing

'Earliglow'—mid-size, sweet fruit, good for freezing; early harvest; one of the best; resistant to major diseases.

'Guardian'—very large fruit, good for fresh eating or freezing; ripens midseason; resistant to many diseases; great in Michigan and the Southeast.

'Honeoye'—large berries, great flavor; early midseason, productive; disease prone; for the Northeast.

'Hood'—heavy crops of large, sweet fruit, great flavor; midseason; disease resistant, bears fruit high up so less rot; hardy to –10°F, popular in the Northwest.

'Jewel'—large, firm berries, excellent flavor; good for freezing; late midseason; hardy plants widely adapted.

'Rainier'—large, firm berries, full flavor; produces few runners; midseason; for the Northwest.

'Sequoia'—large berries, great tasting; ripens early; resistant to many diseases; for California.

'Sparkle'—medium-size, bright red fruit, flavorful; midseason; widely adapted, especially good in Mid-Atlantic, Rockies, and Great Basin regions.

'Surecrop'—medium-size fruit, good quality, good for freezing; ripens early; resistant to major strawberry diseases and drought; good for most climates and soils.

ALPINE STRAWBERRY (*FRAISES DES BOIS*), *F. VESCA* VAR. *VESCA* (*F. ALPINA SEMPERFLORENS*)

Most alpine strawberries are similar in fruit size (about ½ in. at the most) and quality as well as growth habit. Plants fruit on and off all summer. Grow four to five dozen plants for a family of four.

'Alexandria'—red fruit; intense flavor; old variety.

'Improved Rugen'—dark red berries; improved quality.

'Variegata' ('Cresta')—red berries, mild flavor; not too productive; bold green and white leaves.

'Yellow Fruited' ('Alpine Yellow Strawberry')—yellow, sweet fruit.

Sweet bay (bay laurel)

Laurus nobilis

Effort Scale

NO. 1, if informal
Some watering needed
Occasional pest problems

NO. 2, if clipped into a formal shape or grown in a container

Zones

8 to 11

Thumbnail Sketch

Evergreen shrub or tree
15 to 40 ft. tall
Propagate from seeds or cuttings
Needs full sun or partial shade

Sweet bay is a versatile plant well adapted to containers. It has a long history in formal gardens as it takes well to pruning and shearing. Since the plant is hardy to only Zone 8, many gardeners move it indoors for winter.

Leaves are deep green, 2 to 3 in. long
Flowers are insignificant
Leaves are edible; use for seasoning; harvest year round
Use as formal (topiary) or informal shrub, hedge, screen, small tree, or container plant

How to Use

In the Kitchen

Sweet bay plants yield aromatic leaves that you can use fresh or dried as a seasoning in stews, soups, corned beef, potatoes, and pickled herring as well as many dishes associated with both French and Mexican cooking.

California bay, a close relative with a very resinous flavor, was recommended for years as a sweet bay substitute. However, it does not have a USDA GRAS (Generally Recognized As Safe) designation, as it causes allergic reactions in some people.

In the Landscape

Sweet bay is a slow-growing evergreen shrub or medium-size tree. Often multistemmed, it is an excellent addition to your landscape plan. Shiny, oval, deep green leaves, 2 to 3 inches long, cover the tree year round. Flowers are insignificant, but in some climates the dark purple berries are a nice addition to the fall scenery. Sweet bay lends itself to pruning and topiary clipping. Its distinctly formal, classic appearance makes it an excellent container plant. 'Willow-leaf' (aka 'Angustifolia') bears twisted narrow leaves and has a more informal feel. In a container, sweet bay is a calming fragrant addition to an indoor landscape.

How to Grow

Sweet bay is semi-hardy, tolerates quite a bit of shade, and grows best in very well-drained, slightly acidic soil. In arid climates, give it afternoon shade, a thick application of mulch annually, and occasional deep waterings to keep it looking fresh. Except when the plant is grown in containers or very sandy soil, fertilizer is seldom needed.

In some areas of the country, sweet bay develops small, deformed, bubblelike leaf edges caused by a tiny sucking insect called the bay psyllid. Prune off and destroy any affected foliage. Scale is a problem in some areas; the minute insects are usually "farmed" by ants.

Harvest bay leaves anytime to use fresh. To preserve: Pick leaves in late summer, set them on a screen in a dark area with good air circulation, let dry for 10 to 14 days, and package in airtight containers. They keep their intense flavor for over a year.

How to Purchase

Sweet bay plants are usually available at herb nurseries, both mail-order and online. Sweet bay seeds are available only from specialty mail-order firms, including Richters, Nichols, and Thyme Garden.

Sweet marjoram

See Oregano and Marjoram

Sweet orange

See Citrus

Sweet potato (yam)

Ipomoea batatas

Effort Scale

NO. 3
Must be started from slips every spring
Fussy about soil, fertilizer, and water requirements
Susceptible to a number of pests and diseases

Zones

Not applicable

Thumbnail Sketch

Perennial tuberous vine grown as annual in most climates
Trailing, usually kept to 2 to 4 ft.
Propagate from shoots or slips
Needs full sun
Leaves vary from oval to lobed, 4 to 6 in. long
Flowers are sparse, rose to pale pink, 2 in. across

Tubers are edible, harvest in fall; leaves are edible, harvest midseason

Use in herbaceous border or containers, display on a trellis, or let spill over a retaining wall

How to Use

In the Kitchen

Call them sweets or yams, this South American sweet, yellow, white, or reddish orange tuber is delicious baked, boiled, fried, or steamed. The Center for Science in the Public Interest rates sweet potato the most nutritious commonly eaten vegetable. Though sweet, it is very high in fiber (eaten skin and all, it contains more fiber than oatmeal), so the sugars digest slowly. It contains amazingly high amounts of vitamin A and is a great source of vitamin C.

Sweet potatoes are delicious eaten plain and in casseroles, pies, and stir-fries. A southern favorite, "candied sweets" are boiled sweet potatoes cooked in a sauce of brown sugar and butter. My favorite way to prepare them is to cube, roast in olive oil with garlic and thyme (or with rosemary or minced ginger) until golden brown, and serve warm over salad greens.

In much of Asia and West Africa, sweet potato leaves are spinach substitutes in soups and stews and enjoyed as a vegetable. In the Philippines, steamed leaves flavored with vinegar and fish sauce are a breakfast favorite. In Sierra Leone, steamed leaves are seasoned with chilies, okra, and smoked fish for a hearty supper.

Can or freeze cooked sweet potatoes.

In the Landscape

Sweet potato vines are perennials usually grown as annuals that produce lovely, 4- to 6-inch-long, tropical-looking, oval to lobed leaves that spread along the ground or cascade gracefully down the sides of planters. Occasionally a pink or lavender flower like a morning glory nestles among the leaves. Combine sweet potato vines with cousin 'Marguerite', the popular ornamental with lime green foliage (its edible tubers are small and not very sweet) or with 'Purple Wave' petunias as a ground cover in front of a flower bed. Train the vines up a trellis; you'll get larger tubers as the runners of trellised plants don't touch the ground and so can't root and make mini-tubers throughout the bed.

How to Grow

Climate

Sweet potatoes are the most heat-tolerant vegetable in the United States. They need lots of heat to produce a good crop, although some produce well in northern gardens.

Exposure and Soil

Choose a site in full sun with slightly acid, very well-drained sandy loam (sweet potatoes grown in heavy clay become stringy and in alkaline soil are disease prone). In containers use a rich, light soil mix. Dig and loosen the planting area well; mix in lots of fertilizer high in potassium and phosphorus.

Planting

If you cannot obtain slips (sprouts produced by the tubers) commercially (plants can't be sent to some states because of quarantine laws), start your own: buy organically grown tubers, which have not been treated with sprout inhibitors. About 6 to 8 weeks before the weather warms up, place the tubers in a hotbed (a wooden tray with waterproof heating coils on the bottom, filled with sand). Cover the tubers with damp sand and maintain a temperature of 75 to 85°F. Pull—do not cut—the shoots off; they pull off easily with their roots.

Once the soil has warmed in spring, bury the bottoms of the slips 4 inches deep and 12 inches apart. Keep the vines fairly moist until they are well established. The plants require less moisture once they are growing vigorously.

Pests and Diseases

A number of pests affect sweet potatoes. Among them are flea beetle larvae, wireworms, and cucumber beetles, which tunnel in the roots. Fall cleanup and turning the soil help keep the populations under control. Diseases can be a problem and differ from region to region. Check with your local Cooperative Extension Service for more information; choose varieties that resist pests and diseases in your area.

Harvesting

Harvest sweet potatoes in fall when the soil is slightly moist and before a frost is expected. Handle the tubers carefully, as they bruise easily. Sweet potatoes develop their ambrosial flavor 6 weeks or more after harvesting. To cure, store them in an 80°F room with high humidity. Once the potatoes are cured, store them at about 60°F for up to 5 months.

How to Purchase

Slips are available in spring at some local nurseries and Steele Plant Company.

Varieties

'Bush Porto Rico'—heirloom; red-orange flesh, fine flavor; compact vine to 18 in., good for small areas.

'Centennial'—deep orange, rich flesh; some resistance to flea beetles; widely adapted.

'Nancy Hall'—moist and sweet; yellow flesh; resistant to soft rot.

'Vardaman'—compact vine to 18 in., good for small spaces; deep orange flesh, classic flavor; widely adapted.

Sweet potatoes are heat-loving plants with large ivylike leaves; they root along the stems creating a thick ground cover. Although most varieties taste similar, those with the most colorful flesh are more nutritious, packed with vitamin A and antioxidants.

Swiss chard

See Chard

Tangelo

See Citrus

Tangerine

See Citrus

Tea

Camellia sinensis

Effort Scale

NO. 2
Growing is experimental in most areas
Fertilizing and watering necessary
Soil must be kept acid

Zones

7 to 9

Tea is a member of the camellia family. In spring the shrub is sprinkled with small, fragrant, white or pink flowers with showy stamens. Combine it with blueberries and alpine strawberries in a shady foundation planting.

Thumbnail Sketch

Evergreen shrub
4 to 15 ft. tall; much taller if left unpruned
Propagate by grafting or from seeds or cuttings
Needs partial shade; full sun in cool, cloudy climates
Leaves are deep green, leathery, 3 to 5 in. long
Blooms in fall
Flowers are white or pink, camellia-like, 1½ to 2 in. across, fragrant
Leaves are edible; use in beverages; harvest spring through fall
Use as interest shrub, as formal or informal hedge, as espalier, or in raised bed or container

How to Use

In the Kitchen

The dried, young, tender leaves are the source of spirit-soothing tea. Despite its caffeine content, tea is considered more relaxing than activating. There are two primary types of tea for drinking—green and black. Green tea is a favorite with modern chefs, who make it into ice cream and use it as the base for fruit and alcoholic punches. Black tea is the base for many iced drinks made with fruits of all types, combined with milk and spices for chai, and in some cocktails. Tea, whether black or green, is not just a pick-me-up; a cup provides vitamins A, B1, B2, and B6, as well as powerful antioxidants.

Each type of tea—green and black—has its own curing process. There are many ways to process tea leaves to preserve them; refer to the directions that come with your tea plant or look on the Internet.

In the Landscape

The tea plant has many of the same landscaping uses as ornamental camellias. The dense evergreen shrub bears dark green, leathery leaves. Its small, fragrant, fall flowers are white or pink and single, with prominent yellow stamens. Tea plants grow slowly and take many years to reach about 5 feet. Grow them in containers, use them as informal hedges, or clip them for formal hedges or screens. Pruning for a formal hedge actually stimulates new growth that provides the tea leaves. Four shrubs are ample for a family of tea lovers.

How to Grow

Climate

Grow semi-hardy tea plants wherever ornamental camellias grow and where it rarely falls below 10°F. Provide extra warmth in Zone 7 by planting in a protected, south- or west-facing spot with heat-absorbing pavement or walls. Tea plants prefer fairly high humidity.

Exposure and Soil

Tea thrives with full sun in cool-summer areas (in hot-summer areas, provide partial shade) in acid (pH 4 to 6), sandy, or clay soil with plenty of humus and good drainage. To protect the roots, keep the plant well mulched.

Planting

Instructions for planting generally come with tea plants and seeds. When sowing seeds, place them with the "eye" face-down.

Fertilizing

Tea plants prefer cottonseed meal or an organic acidic fertilizer. Avoid overfeeding.

Watering

Keep young plants well watered; do not allow them to dry out. In arid climates, mature tea plants need an occasional deep watering during spring and summer.

Pruning

Prune to shape the shrub and to stimulate new growth for harvesting. Extensive clipping provides lots of new growth for leaf harvesting but reduces flower production.

Pests and Diseases

Tea suffers from the same pests and diseases as other camellias, namely red spider mites, weevils, and scale. In the Southeast, leaves may get leaf spot disease.

Tea planted in neutral or alkaline soil usually becomes chlorotic. Acidify the soil with peat moss and sulfur and treat with chelated iron as you would with blueberries.

Harvesting

Once the shrub is 3 years old, you can start harvesting. After the first flush of growth in spring, pluck two or three of the tender outer leaves from the top of each shoot. If the plant is growing vigorously, you can harvest three times during the summer.

How to Purchase

Seeds and plants are available from a number of mail-order nurseries, including a few that specialize in camellias, as well as Edible Landscaping, Nichols, Raintree, and Richters.

Varieties

'Blushing Maiden'—single pink flowers.
'Rosea'—single pink flowers; new leaves are burgundy.

Thyme

Thymus spp.

Effort Scale

NO. 1
Very easy to grow in all but very hot, humid climates

Zones

3 to 10; grow as annual elsewhere

Thumbnail Sketch

Evergreen shrub or mat-forming perennial
2 to 15 in. tall
Propagate from seeds, cuttings, or divisions or by layering
Needs full sun
Leaves are gray-green, very small, ¼ in. long
Flowers are lavender, white, or pink, tiny, in small spikes
Leaves and flowers are edible; use as seasoning; harvest all year
Use as ground cover, in herb garden, as edging for flower border, among stepping-stones, or in flower bed, rock garden, raised bed, or container

Some thymes are flavorful; others, like lavender-flowered woolly thyme at lower right, are strictly ornamental. The dark lavender blooms of rich-tasting English thyme and medium green leaves of zesty lime thyme contrast with woolly thyme's gray leaves.

How to Use

In the Kitchen

Except for the distinctive flavor of caraway thyme, I consider most types of thyme "go with" herbs, as they have a fairly neutral flavor that complements other herbs rather than standing alone as cilantro or basil do. Use thyme's aromatic leaves to season soups, omelets, gumbos, poultry stuffing, and sauces for fish. Add them to vegetable juice cocktails, green beans, and carrots to make them more interesting. Highlight the citrus-flavored lemon and lime thymes with lemon or lime juice or zest in vinaigrettes and marinades.

In the Landscape

These evergreen plants vary in form from the matlike growth of creeping thyme to a shrublet like common thyme growing to 15 inches tall. The leaves are very small on all types. Leaf color among varieties ranges from gray-green to dark green and includes gold or silver variegations. The tiny lavender, white, or pink flowers, which attract bees, grow on short spikes.

The variations in form add to thyme's versatility. There are at least a dozen superior culinary thymes as well as a hundred ornamental thymes, which—while not poisonous—either have little flavor or taste "off." All thyme plants, whether culinary or strictly ornamental, are equally at home in an herb garden, flower border, or container. Plant creeping thyme between stepping-stones or other areas with limited foot traffic. Thyme can fit into the smallest garden spaces, where it fades into the background, or it can be the star attraction, as when planted in a lovely container and placed on a decorative pedestal.

Chives, sage, oregano, saffron crocus, alyssum, ageratum, and small pink zinnias are among the good garden companions for any of the thymes.

How to Grow

Thyme is relatively easy to grow in most regions of the United States; its ideal growing conditions are rocky or sandy soil, excellent drainage, and full sun. In very hot-summer areas, thyme requires supplemental water; however, take care not to overwater. In parts of the South where root-knot nematodes and root rots are a problem, plant thyme in raised beds with a gravel mulch to help keep the soil cool, or grow in containers. Prune back thyme foliage in spring to keep the plant compact and lush. Harvest thyme anytime to use fresh or just before blooming to dry and preserve.

How to Purchase

Plants are available in small containers and as seeds from local nurseries and mail-order firms. One source in particular, Thyme Garden, carries a broad range of thymes—both culinary and purely ornamental.

Varieties

Types of culinary thyme are distinguished by size, scent, and other characteristics noted below. All the thymes listed here are *Thymus vulgaris* unless otherwise noted.

Caraway thyme (*T. herba-barona*)—2 to 5 in. tall; dark green leaves, rich caraway flavor and scent; rose pink flowers; good ground cover.

Common thyme—6 to 15 in. tall; gray leaves, classic flavor; lavender flowers.

Creeping lemon thyme (variegated lemon thyme, *T. pulegioides* 'Lemon')—6 to 10 in. tall; golden variegation, lemon scent and flavor; pink flowers.

Creeping thyme (*T. praecox* ssp. *britannicus* [*arcticus*])—2 to 4 in. tall; dark green leaves, bland flavor; purplish rose, purple, or white flowers; good ground cover.

English thyme—6 to 12 in. tall; upright to slightly sprawling habit; rich thyme flavor; hardy to Zone 4.

French thyme—12 to 18 in. tall; similar to English thyme; narrower leaves, slightly sweeter flavor; hardy to Zone 4.

Lemon thyme (*T.* × *citriodorus*)—4 to 12 in. tall; green leaves, citrus flavor; lavender flowers; types with leaves variegated silver or gold are available.

Lime thyme—3 to 4 in. tall; bright lime green leaves, mild lime flavor; lavender flowers.

Silver thyme (*T. vulgaris* 'Argenteus')—6 to 8 in. tall; leaves variegated silver and green, flavor similar to English thyme; good container plant, gently spilling over the rim.

Tomato

Solanum lycopersicum (*Lycopersicon esculentum*, *L. lycopersicum*)

Effort Scale

NO. 2
Must be planted annually
Tying and staking usually needed
Vulnerable to some pests and diseases
Harvest is large and ongoing

Zones

Not applicable

Thumbnail Sketch

Perennial grown as annual
Determinate types, 3 to 5 ft. tall; indeterminate types, 6 to 12 ft. tall
Propagate from seeds
Needs full sun
Leaves are compound, medium green, occasionally gray green, or variegated
Blooms in summer
Flowers are yellow, usually not showy
Fruits are edible; red, yellow, orange, white, pink, green, purple, and purple-black, often showy; harvest in summer or fall
Use in vegetable garden, flower border, hanging basket, or container; on fences and arbors

How to Use
In the Kitchen

Tomatoes need no introduction. If you've never had a freshly picked, sun-warmed, vine-ripened tomato, you've missed one of the greatest taste sensations—ever. If you have enjoyed that sensation, you understand why tomatoes are the most commonly grown vegetable (although technically fruit) in North America. Whether your favorite is a 'Sun Gold' cherry or a 'Brandywine' heirloom slicer does not matter. Once you have sunk your teeth into fully ripened tomatoes, store-bought ones seem a travesty.

There are three categories of tomatoes: cherry (good for eating fresh and cooking), paste (meaty Roma types for sauces and cooking), and slicing (best for eating fresh). Enjoy fresh tomatoes throughout their fruiting season—sliced, quartered, stuffed, or whole. Their flavors and many colors enhance all summer meals. Do not refrigerate unless they are starting to spoil; cold temperature stops ripening and can destroy flavor.

One of the great joys of tomatoes is the ability to preserve them in a number of different ways. Frozen or canned tomatoes add a high note to winter meals in stews, soups, casseroles, and pasta sauce. It is simple to freeze tomatoes whole in freezer bags. Before using, partially defrost them so the skins slip off. Squeeze the flesh to remove some of the watery juice and seeds. Drain them in a colander over a bowl, collect more juice, and you're ready to use the pulp in sauces and soups. Add the juice to sauces and drinks. Canning is a satisfying way to provide for your family out of season, making treats including pasta sauce, salsa, or various juices flavored with lemon and spices.

For me, pureed and dried tomatoes are winter staples. To dry, cut small tomatoes in half and slice large ones and place them in a dehydrator, in the oven, or in the sun (impossible in humid areas). Store in labeled freezer bags in the refrigerator or freezer. To reconstitute, dip the dried tomatoes in boiling water for about 1 minute. Work them into dressings, sprinkle over pizza, and add to soups. Or crush the bag of dried tomatoes with a rolling pin and add the crumbled pieces to soft cheeses and marinades. It's hard to imagine cooking without salsa and tomato paste.

Pickle green (unripe) tomatoes or make them into chutney. Tomatoes can also be preserved for 4 to 6 weeks by harvesting the vines before the fruit is fully ripe and hanging them—fruit and all—from the rafters of a cool garage or shed.

In the Landscape

When tomatoes were first introduced to Europe from the New World, they were thought to be poisonous. Since tomatoes belong to the nightshade family, the fruit was suspect, so they were used only as showy ornamentals. They, when proven edible, tomatoes were relegated to the vegetable garden—until now. How fickle we are!

Indeed, the bright green, lobed leaves and colorful fruits of the tomato plant are highly ornamental. Small-fruited varieties are a temptation dangling over the sides of hanging baskets. Train large vining types to cover a fence or trellis as a background for 'Avalanche Red' petunias and red peppers (leave room for a path so you can easily tie the vines and harvest). Grow extra-tall cherry tomatoes over an arbor; just imagine purple-black cherry tomatoes intertwined with white morning glories and moon vines—that's high style.

Planter boxes are excellent for growing tomatoes. In cool climates, planter boxes warm up quickly in spring. They keep disease spores from splashing up from the soil, and because the plants are elevated, rabbits can't nibble the fruit. Healthy plants are beautiful, but diseased plants look tatty and have limited use in the landscape.

How to Grow

Indeterminate tomato varieties, like their wild ancestors, are rambling vines that grow until struck down by disease or frost. They produce for months and are prized for their flavor. Determinate varieties grow between 3 and 5 feet tall and produce a concentrated crop, which ripens within a 3- to 4-week period. They are generally not the most flavorful as they are bred for commercial production. Yet short-season gardeners sing their praises because they produce quickly. And the intense harvest is perfect for cooks who want to preserve large amounts of fruit. Most home gardeners plant a few varieties of both types of tomatoes.

Climate

Tomatoes are large, semi-tropical, perennial plants—generally grown as annuals—that do best when daytime temperatures are in the 65 to 90°F range with nights between 60 and 70°F. Most tomatoes require at least three frost-free, sunny summer months.

Exposure and Soil

All tomatoes need a minimum of 6 hours of full sun a day. They thrive with plenty of organic matter and well-drained garden loam. Contact your Cooperative Extension Service for specific information on tomatoes in your climate.

Planting

Purchase plants or, for a greater choice of varieties, start seeds inside 6 to 8 weeks before your last spring frost date. After all danger of frost is over, incorporate large amounts of compost into a planting area. Apply a fertilizer rich in phosphorus and potassium with only a modest amount of nitrogen, and work it in. (Too much nitrogen fosters leaf growth instead of fruit production.) Plant your tomatoes 2 to 3 feet apart if you stake the large vining, or indeterminate, types—farther apart if you let them sprawl.

Tomatoes are one of the few plants that can grow roots along their stems. I remove all but the top two sets of leaves and then set the seedling deep into the planting hole with just the leaves showing above the soil line. Fill in with soil, gently firm it in place, make a small watering well around the plant, and water thoroughly. If cutworms are a problem in your garden, put cardboard collars around the stem.

Stake indeterminate and large determinate varieties to keep the fruit off the ground and hold leaves up and away from water-splashed soil, which can spread diseases. Staked plants also take up less space and make harvesting easier. Use 8-foot-tall wooden stakes and pound them 2 feet into the ground. (The typical funnel-shaped or cylindrical wire tomato cages are much too short and weak to hold a large vine but are fine for most determinate bush types, as well as peppers and eggplants.) If you live in a desert area, do not stake tomatoes as it exposes the foliage to hot dry winds and the fruit to sunburn. For growing tomatoes in the desert, consult *Desert Gardening: Fruits and Vegetables* by George Brookbank.

Until the plants put on new leaves, keep the soil moist, but not soaking. Cover the plants with floating row covers or another insulation to protect them if the nights are still cold, and to outwit flea beetles.

Once the tomatoes are growing vigorously, use wireless flexible ties to secure the main stem to the stake every 8 inches. When the plant reaches the top of the stake, remove the terminal growth; this controls the height and makes the plant fruit sooner. Some gardeners swear by pinching out the small side shoots that emerge from the crotch of the main stem and leaf branch (axil); others don't bother. This method—great for rainy areas and short-summer climates—controls the size of the plant, provides better air circulation, makes spraying for disease control easier, encourages the plant to produce fewer—yet larger—fruit, and makes tomatoes more accessible for harvest. It is not advised for the South or desert areas, as the fruits tend to sunburn with less foliage. After the weather has warmed thoroughly, add 3 inches of organic mulch, which prevents disease spores on the soil from splashing up onto the foliage, keeps the soil evenly moist, and helps prevent blossom end rot.

Fertilizing

Fertilize the plants with hydrolyzed fish once the blossoms have set. If the plants start to get pale, or you've had problems in the past, supplement with fish or other organic all-purpose fertilizer monthly.

Luscious 'Brandywine' has become the poster child for heirloom tomatoes. When grown in warm, humid climates, it produces the ultimate tomato experience: meaty, juicy, and out-of-this-world flavor. In cooler climes, it's not nearly so flavorful or productive.

In spring take a recycled wooden bench, fix its broken leg, and paint it red. Then build a trellis, add a few flowers, and plant two indeterminate paste tomatoes. Come summer, you'll have a colorful secluded sitting area and 80 pounds of tomatoes.

Watering

Drip irrigation is a superior way to water tomatoes, as wet leaves foster diseases. Water about an inch of water every 7 to 10 days.

Pests and Diseases

A number of pests bother tomatoes, namely cutworms, whiteflies, tomato hornworms, tobacco budworms, slugs, and flea beetles. Fortunately, few gardeners are faced with more than one or two of these, and the pests can be controlled.

Microscopic bronze mites (aka tomato russet mites) thrive in hot, arid climates. They turn the main stems a bronze color and the leaves dry and brown—from the bottom of the plant upward. Control them by dusting or spraying with sulfur every few weeks during the cool part of the day.

Tomato diseases and nematodes can be more damaging than insects as defoliation robs the fruit of its great flavor. Research proves that the more leaves per fruit, the better the taste. To ward off diseases, give the plants the best cultural conditions possible. Nematodes can be a problem in light soils. If you previously had nematodes, choose from the many nematode-resistant varieties.

Avoid planting tomatoes or their relatives in the same bed year after year. Rotate the plantings to where no tomatoes, eggplants, peppers, or potatoes have grown for 3 years. In autumn, clean up and remove all tomato debris; do not compost it. And most importantly, choose resistant varieties when possible.

In humid and rainy climates with temperatures between 75 and 85°F, early blight (aka alternaria blight) is a common problem, evidenced by small dark spots with characteristic concentric rings on leaves and fruits. Control by mulching and rotating crops. For serious infestations, apply sulfur or copper sprays.

Plant breeders have developed cultivars resistant to some of the most troublesome tomato diseases. Resistance means the plant is slow to develop the disease; by no means is it immune. Disease resistance is indicated after the variety name by the following symbols. **V** = verticillium wilt, **F** = fusarium wilt, **N** = root knot nematodes, **A** = alternaria, **LB** = late blight, and **TMV** = tobacco mosaic virus resistance.

Harvesting

Harvest tomatoes when they have fully colored and give slightly to gentle pressure. A healthy tomato plant typically produces between 20 and 30 pounds of fruit.

How to Purchase

Grow tomatoes from seeds or plants available from local nurseries and mail-order firms. Johnny's, Park, Renee's, Stokes Seeds, Nichols, and Tomato Growers carry a wide variety of tomato seeds. More and more companies offer transplants; they include Burpee, Cross Country (aka chiliplants.com), Park, Seed Savers, Seeds of Change, Territorial, Natural Gardening, and Tasteful Garden.

Varieties

The taste of the tomato is in the tongue of the beholder. Some folks swoon over sweet varieties; others prefer an acidic tang; then there are those who are rabid about fruit with what can only be called the elusive pure "tomato" flavor. The gardener-cook can choose tomatoes based on flavor and size—those best for drying, slicing, sauce, stuffing, or just popping in your mouth—and by colors that range from white to purple-black.

With hundreds of varieties from which to choose, your first consideration should be whether it grows well and produces tasty fruit in *your* climate. A number of tomato varieties, including 'Ace', 'Better Boy', 'Celebrity', 'Early Girl', 'Legend', 'Rutgers'—and 'Sun Gold', 'Sweet 100', 'Yellow Pear', 'Snow White', and all other cherry tomatoes—thrive and are flavorful in most parts of North America.

Many varieties are quite climate specific, while others are a matter of personal taste and your growing preferences.

EARLY, MIDSEASON, OR LATE

Most gardeners benefit from planting a selection of early, midseason, and late tomatoes; each has its virtues. Early varieties ripen within 52 to 68 days after transplanting but don't always have the best flavor. Midseason types mature in 70 to 80 days and are usually the main crop. Late-maturing varieties require over 80 days, tend to be large and luscious, and include many heirloom beefsteak types. In short or cool summers they may never ripen.

COOL CONDITIONS/SHORT GROWING SEASON

If you live in a cool, coastal, northern, or mountain area, look for varieties adapted to these conditions like 'Fourth of July', 'Siberia', 'Stupice'; all cherry tomatoes; and parthenocarpic cultivars like 'Gold Nugget', 'Legend', 'Oregon Spring', and 'Siletz'. (Parthenocarpic varieties can set fruit without pollination and when nights are cool—usually 10 days to 2 weeks earlier than most varieties. Ironically, they can also set fruit in hot desert areas when it's normally too hot for pollination.)

Tiny currant tomatoes (*S. pimpinellifolium*) burgeon with fruit in cool climates. Take care to plant them away from other tomatoes if you plan to save seeds, as they are promiscuous.

For tomatoes that will produce in cool areas, look for appropriate seeds from Bountiful Gardens, Cook's, Ed Hume, Johnny's, Nichols, Pinetree, and Territorial. High Altitude offers varieties selected for mountain areas—many from Siberia.

HOT-SUMMER AREAS

Among the varieties tolerant of high summer heat are 'Creole', 'Eva Purple Ball', 'Ozark Pink', 'Solar Set', 'Tropic', 'Viva Italia', and the heirlooms 'Arkansas Traveler', 'Cherokee Purple', and 'Rutgers'. For a large selection of varieties suitable for hot climates, contact Tomato Growers and Southern Exposure.

HYBRID, OPEN POLLINATED, AND HEIRLOOM

Hybrid varieties like 'Better Boy' are the stable and predictable offspring of two parents that have been selected by breeders for special characteristics such as uniformity, disease resistance, and productivity. Hybrid varieties seldom come true from seed, so gardeners do not save their seeds. By law, hybrid tomatoes are labeled hybrid or F1.

In contrast, open-pollinated varieties (**OP**) are pollinated naturally. If the open-pollinated variety has not been cross-pollinated by another variety, gardeners can save the seeds, which will grow into plants that are identical to the parent. Open-pollinated varieties that have been in cultivation for more than 50 years are considered heirlooms.

The most popular heirlooms are generally late, large, beefsteak-type varieties selected for their outstanding flavors, unique shapes, and colors. While many set the gold standard for taste and texture, they usually perform poorly in cool weather or desert heat and take too long to mature in short-summer areas. For those areas, select the small-fruited heirlooms 'Siberia' and 'Stupice'.

For tomato nirvana, choose larger varieties like luscious red 'Brandywine' and 'Mortgage Lifter', red and yellow bicolor 'Big Rainbow', purple 'Black Krim' and 'Cherokee Purple', and green 'Evergreen', and the smaller red 'Principe Borghese' for drying. Companies that specialize in heirlooms include Baker Creek, J. L. Hudson, Heirloom Seeds, Redwood City, Seed Savers, Seeds of Change, and Southern Exposure.

FOR CONTAINERS

Determinate plants are well adapted to containers (they do best in pots at least 18 inches wide and 24 inches deep—the bigger the better). They include 'Celebrity', 'Heartland', 'Legend', and 'Sugar Baby', as well as any cultivar that includes the word "bush" in its name. 'Silvery Fir Tree' is compact, and unique for its lacy silver leaves; 'Sweet Baby Girl' is a dwarf red cherry tomato; and 'Window Box Roma' is a determinate paste type.

Turkish tree hazel

See Filbert

Ume

See Apricot

Walnut

Juglans spp.

Effort Scale

NO. 3
Vulnerable to some pests, including squirrels
Raking dropped nuts and leaves is often necessary for pest and
    disease control
Harvest is large

Zones

3 to 9

Thumbnail Sketch

Deciduous tree
20 to 80 ft. tall
Propagate by grafting or budding or from seeds
Needs full sun
Leaves are compound; leaflets are 4 to 5 in. long, medium green
Flowers are in catkins, not showy
Nuts are edible; harvest in fall
Use as shade tree (in very large yard), street tree, windbreak, or screen

How to Use

In the Kitchen

There are four distinct nuts here: English walnuts, most people's favorite; butternut, with its "buttery" taste; heartnut, best known for its sweetness; and black walnuts, both Eastern and California. Enjoy any and all of them in pastries; toasted for snacking and salads—plain, sprinkled with soy sauce, or maple glazed; or ground and layered with phyllo dough for baklava. The flavor of black walnuts is quite strong; use it sparingly in cakes and ice cream. Walnuts not only add richness to food but are high in omega-3 fatty acids and vitamin E.

Walnuts, like other tree nuts, consist of an outside husk and a hard inner shell that holds the nutmeat. The husk leaves a dark stain, so use leather gloves to remove it. A strong nutcracker will free the nutmeat.

After husking, store unshelled walnuts in a cool, dark place, or shell and freeze them. Oil made from walnuts can be stored in a cool, dark place for months at a time.

In the Landscape

Walnut comprises a number of closely related deciduous trees. These stately trees, with their compound leaves and handsome branching structures, are useful for screening an unwanted view or for casting cooling shade in hot weather. Their presence enhances large lots and country lanes. Because of their size and the fact that they are often bothered by aphids, whose black sticky secretion is a problem on cars or patios, walnut trees are difficult to use in small yards. Also, throughout the growing season the trees drop catkins, leaves, and husks, which are no problem for a woodland path but are not compatible with a tailored yard or paving surfaces. In the East and Midwest, walnuts are often used as lawn trees; take care to keep the lawn at least 4 feet from the trunk to avoid injury to the trunk.

Note: Black walnuts exude an acid, juglone, from their roots that inhibits the growth of most plants. Give the trees a wide berth.

How to Grow

The most popular type is the English walnut. Its nut is the easiest to crack, the largest, and the mildest in flavor; this is the nut of commerce. A native of southeastern Eurasia, the English walnut is a large, spreading tree. Our native walnuts—black walnut and butternut—have delicious nuts, but they are small and hard to crack without shattering the nutmeats. Heartnut is a walnut relative native to Japan that bears at an early age; it produces 1-inch, heart-shaped nuts that are easy to crack.

Climate

The English walnut is the least hardy walnut mentioned here and grows best in Zones 6 to 9. An English walnut from northern Europe, called Carpathian, has proved hardy to –25°F and is grown in colder regions. English walnuts grow poorly in hot climates.

Butternut is the hardiest of the native walnuts. It grows as far north as New Brunswick, Canada, south to Georgia, and west to Minnesota. Butternut is especially prone to defoliating diseases in humid climates, so check with your local nursery to see if it's suitable for your area.

The Eastern black walnut is quite hardy; its range covers southern Ontario to northern Florida and west to Texas, as well as parts of the West Coast. In humid areas, where it suffers from numerous diseases, pecan is a better choice.

California black walnut is grown widely in California and is one of the major rootstocks for commercially grown English walnuts.

Heartnut is an extremely hardy tree that thrives in the Great Lakes region.

Exposure and Soil

These trees need full sun. Walnut trees are deep rooted and require well-drained, rich, deep loam.

Planting

Plant walnuts the same as pecans.

Fertilizing

Do not fertilize the first year. After that, if young trees put on 18 to 30 inches of new growth a year, no nitrogen fertilizer is needed. If the leaves are pale and growth slows, then apply an organic nitrogen fertilizer in the spring. Mulch walnuts with 2 or 3 inches of organic matter in spring.

Watering

For best nut production in arid climates, walnuts require regular deep watering. In rainy climates, water only during times of drought.

Pruning

Do not prune black walnuts from late winter through spring because they bleed heavily at this time. Prune as you would pecans.

Pests and Diseases

Squirrels and blue jays can consume most of the crop. Aphids, fall webworm, codling moth, walnut husk maggot, and walnut caterpillar can also be problems. To control the webworm, remove the webs you can reach and destroy them. For the maggot and caterpillar pests, try Bt (*Bacillus thuringiensis*). Spinosad spray or beneficial nematodes are recommended for severe infestations of the walnut husk fly—a particular problem in the West. The nematodes control the larvae pupating in the soil.

Anthracnose is a major fungal disease affecting walnuts. Fall cleanup is critical in controlling it. The best defense is Bordeaux mix applied after the tree has leafed out—before the leaves become infected—and then every other week for the next 6 weeks.

For information on pest and disease problems, go to the University of California at Davis website www.ipm.ucdavis.edu/PMG.

Harvesting

Harvest nuts off the ground; check daily to keep ahead of squirrels. English walnuts usually fall from their husks/hulls; if the husks are still attached, remove them immediately or they will discolor the shells and affect the flavor. A mature walnut tree produces from 50 to 100 pounds of nuts, depending on the weather and walnut variety.

Black walnut husks are usually still intact when they fall from the tree. Removing the husks is no easy task; wear rubber gloves to avoid staining your hands. An alternative is—wearing heavy shoes—to stomp the nuts and roll them out of their husks. Some people even drive their cars over black walnuts and let the tires do the job! Dry and cure the nuts in a cool dry place for 2 to 3 weeks before storing.

How to Purchase

Buy bare-root trees in late winter. Bay Laurel and Burnt Ridge carry grafted varieties of English walnut. Nolin River, Rhora's, and St. Lawrence specialize in hardy nuts.

Pollinizers

The sex life of walnuts can get a bit technical. While farmers need to know how to plan pollination for large harvests, home gardeners can consider most walnuts self-fertile unless a specific pollinizer is recommended.

Varieties

There are dozens of named and seedling black walnuts, butternuts, and Asian walnuts chosen for their ease of cracking, nut size, and, in a few cases, disease resistance. Consult the sources noted above, especially Nolin River, for the ones best suited to your climate.

Nurseries specializing in nut trees sometimes carry a number of Asian walnut species, including heartnut, *J. ailantifolia* var. *cordiformis*, from Japan; Chinese walnut, *J. cathayensis*; and Manchurian walnut, *J. mandshurica*.

ENGLISH (PERSIAN), *JUGLANS REGIA*

Carpathian walnut is best for northern climates as it is hardier than the standard English walnut. 'Hansen' bears high-quality, small nuts; the tree is smaller than average, growing to about 30 ft. tall. The tree leafs out late, so it avoids most late frosts and the spring rains that foster anthracnose infections.

The following commercial walnuts are adapted to the home garden; all are self-fertile and produce a harvest in late September. In recent decades, breeders have developed more productive varieties that bear nuts on lateral branches, not just on terminal growth like traditional walnuts.

'Carmelo'—large nuts; late to leaf out and bloom; better adapted to colder climates than most English walnuts.

'Chandler'—large, high-quality, light-colored nuts; heavy crop; bears on lateral and terminal buds; tree smaller than standard varieties.

'Pedro'—delicious nuts; two-thirds the size of a standard walnut; widely adapted; low chill, about 400 hours.

'Placentia'—thin-shelled, medium-size nuts; mild flavor; adapted to mild-winter coastal California; low chill, about 300 hours.

Watermelon

See Melon

Western sand cherry

See Plum

Wheat

Triticum spp.

Effort Scale

NO. 2
Shearing or staking usually needed for small plots
Weeding is necessary
Harvesting and processing are time consuming

Zones

2 to 9

Thumbnail Sketch

Annual
2 to 4 ft. tall
Propagate from seeds
Needs full sun
Leaf blades up to 12 in. long and ¾ in. wide, bright green
Flowers are borne on spikes, not showy
Seeds are edible; harvest in summer or fall; seed heads showy
Use in small plots with geometric shapes, to border a meadow, as background to flower bed, or in vegetable garden

How to Use

In the Kitchen

Homegrown wheat is healthful as it retains the bran (outer coating prized for its fiber) and the embryo (germ, a nutrient powerhouse). Use wheat berries whole, sprouted, or ground finely into flour. Cook whole wheat berries as you would rice, but use more water and cook about 90 minutes, or until tender. Once cooked, serve as a cereal with nuts and dried fruits. Crack the berries and cook as you would porridge, or incorporate sprouted wheat berries into entrees and salads. Of course, whole wheat bread is also popular in many households.

Store threshed whole wheat berries in insect-proof containers in a cool, dark place. Grind flour as needed. Hand grinders take a lot of effort; I prefer the KitchenAid grain grinder attachment to my stand mixer. Or buy an electric mill.

In the Landscape

Adding wheat to a landscape allows designers to use all the creative pages in their book of tricks. Of course, the size of the harvest is the first consideration. Large plots of wheat, say 1,000 square feet, while ripe for designing a meditation labyrinth, are a commitment beyond the scope of this book. Here, I concentrate on small plots of 100 square feet or so, enough for about 20 loaves of bread, and a much more manageable garden harvest. I have had success using a long bed of winter wheat, 20 feet by 5 feet, behind a flower border of boisterous cool-season annuals like larkspur and clarkia. I've also grouped wheat with barley and rye, each in its own geometric bed, and surrounded them all with salad greens and tulips.

For spring wheat, fill a border in front of the wheat with tall zinnias and cosmos. Or take a big circular area out of the back lawn and make ray-shaped beds and fill them with wheat; in the center, make a circular bed of sunflowers or put in a scarlet runner bean tepee. Wheat beds are generally very linear, but all sorts of distinct shapes work; use your imagination.

Wheat planted in small amounts is prone to lodging in stormy weather. To support it, I painted standard wooden garden trellises, attached stakes for legs, and placed them horizontally. The wheat didn't fall over, and the trellises added pizzazz.

Hard winter wheat blooms in spring, producing minute flowers filled with pollen that attracts armies of beneficial insects. Among them is this aptly named soldier beetle, a "good guy" that eats aphids.

To add all-season color to my landscape and to prevent the plants from lodging (falling over) later, I bought common prefab trellises, painted them a rich plum, trimmed the "legs" off to make a clean rectangle, and placed them horizontally over the beds with stakes to hold them up off the ground.

How to Grow

Climate
There are wheat varieties for all climates.

Exposure and Soil
Choose a well-drained bed of good soil in full sun; the richer the soil, the higher the yield. For a 100-square-foot area (5 feet by 20 feet), spread an inch or more of compost, a pound of blood meal, and a pound of bonemeal; mix in the amendments and rake the bed smooth. No further nutrients are usually needed.

Planting
Plant winter wheat in fall; it grows a small amount over winter and matures in late spring to midsummer. Harvest winter wheat in time to succession plant with bush beans or a crop of fall carrots. Spring wheat is best for the coldest-winter areas; plant it between February and April and harvest it mid- to late summer.

Broadcast wheat seeds as you would grass seeds. Use about six handfuls, or ¼ pound of seeds, per 100 square feet. Rake the seeds in to bury them to about three times their diameter to prevent lodging later. In arid climates, winter rains are often sufficient for winter wheat. Irrigate if there is no rain for more than 2 weeks. In rainy climates, average rainfall is usually enough.

Lodging can be a problem, especially in rich soil. Fallen stalks mold and are difficult to harvest. Prevent lodging by cutting the young plants back to 6 to 8 inches tall with hedge shears when they are over 12 inches high and before they start to send up stalks (feed trimmings to your chickens or add them to your compost pile). An alternative: Place sturdy stakes around the outside of the bed and weave string back and forth among the stalks to provide support.

Pests and Diseases
Ground-feeding birds easily decimate seeded plots; use floating row covers or bird netting to cover the beds. Some gardeners use metallic tape to scare birds away. Weed a young plot regularly, so weeds don't crowd out the new sprouts. Once the wheat has filled in, weeds have little chance. And, as a bonus, wheat in bloom attracts many beneficial insects.

The Hessian fly, while primarily an agricultural problem, is an introduced species whose larvae attack wheat stalks in much of the Midwest and East. Most Cooperative Extension Service websites list a fly-free date. Delay planting until then.

Harvesting
When your wheat turns brown and your tooth can no longer dent the berries, it is ready to harvest. In mild climates, you can harvest by early June; I let my crop stand awhile to make the harvest part of our Fourth of July block party. In cold-winter areas, the harvest is in summer. For more about harvesting techniques, see "Grain Gardens" in Chapter 6.

Once you have harvested the wheat berries, use hedge clippers to cut the straw off at ground level; use it to line paths or for composting. Leave the roots in the ground to boost organic matter and prevent erosion.

John Jeavons, with his Biointensive Method, reports yields of about 8 pounds of wheat per 100 square feet, while agricultural yields average about 4 or 5 pounds.

How to Purchase

New to growing wheat? Start with modern varieties that are easier to thresh and more productive. Experienced growers might consider the old varieties (einkorn wheat, *Triticum monococcum* ssp. *aegilopoides* [*T. boeoticum*] or emmer wheat, *T. turgidum* ssp. *dicoccon*) to keep a diminishing gene pool alive. For more information, visit the Heritage Wheat Project website: www.grassrootsolutions.com.

Seeds of both modern and ancient wheat and other grains are available from Bountiful Gardens and Prairie Garden. Or buy wheat berries in bulk from your natural food store.

Varieties
Durum wheat (*T. durum*)—most varieties are planted in spring and harvested in late summer; best for upper Midwest into Canada and in California; used primarily for pasta.

'Hard Red Spring' (*T. aestivum* ssp. *aestivum*)—plant at last spring frost date, matures early summer; adapted to Northwest, Midwest, and Canada; high in protein.

'Hard Red Winter' (*T. a.* ssp. *aestivum*)—plant at first fall frost date, harvest late spring; great for most of the continent; high production.

'Lavras'—heirloom wheat from Brazil; easier to thresh than most heirloom wheat.

Yam

See Sweet Potato

Opposite: Savoy cabbage, chartreuse kale, and collards thrive among ornamental red cannas and coleus.

APPENDIX A
The Big List of Edible Plants

Landscape designers and architects as well as homeowners designing their own yards generally work from lists of recommended plants in order to choose the right plants for their climate and landscape needs. Unfortunately, these sources usually include only a few edibles. For years I searched for a list that would systematically cover just about all the edible plants I could possibly put in a landscape. Since I never found one, I compiled this information for my own use. The following chart is the distillation of nearly three decades of my experience working with these plants, seeing them in landscapes and trial gardens throughout my travels, and doing extensive research on them. For each edible, I provide the following:

Common Name: This is the plant's most common name(s) as used by horticulturists, gardeners, and cooks.

Botanic (or Latin) Name: Botanic names change over time, so I included any previous names where applicable.

Cultural Conditions: Here are the basic needs of the plant— its sun/shade, soil, and water requirements.

USDA Zones: The numbers correspond to the USDA Plant Hardiness Zone Map (see the introduction to the Encyclopedia) for perennials, shrubs, and trees. Annual plants, such as spinach, and biennials or perennials usually grown as annuals,

such as tomatoes, grow in most climates, so "N/A" (not applicable) is noted in the Zones column.

Edible Part: Not all parts of the plants we consider edible are in fact safe to ingest. For instance, potato tubers are edible, but their leaves are toxic. This column lists the edible portion. For clarity, I use the precise botanic terms.

Landscape and Cooking Information: A specific description of the edible plant includes climate preferences; whether it is an annual, perennial, shrub, or tree; growth habit and eventual height when grown in the ground in its preferred climate; flower color; and how to propagate. For tropical fruits, harvest season is not included because the timing depends so much on the variety grown and the climate. I provide suggestions for each plant's use in the landscape and the kitchen. *Note:* The designation "HH," often used in seed catalogs, indicates that a plant is half-hardy (withstands light frosts with little damage). GRAS (Generally Recognized As Safe) is a term used by the FDA. When a plant on this list includes the phrase "not considered GRAS," such as some of the herbs and seasonings, it should be eaten only in small doses. For more information on GRAS, see the FDA's website under Food and GRAS or consult *The Big Book of Herbs* by Arthur O. Tucker, Ph.D., and Thomas DeBaggio.

Lavender is a favorite garden plant, but few of us think to cook with it. *Lavandula angustifolia* is the tastiest species. Here a harvest of *L. a.* 'Munstead' flowers is ready to be used in shortbread cookies, ice cream, or herbes de Provence.

COMMON NAME	LATIN NAME	CULTURAL CONDITIONS	USDA ZONES	EDIBLE PART	LANDSCAPE AND COOKING INFORMATION
Acerola (Barbados cherry)	*Malpighia emarginata*	Full sun; fast-draining soil; drought tolerant	10–11	Fruit	Large deciduous shrub. Irrigate for best fruit. Use as screen; in hedgerow or in container. Enjoy red, ribbed fruit fresh or in jellies and syrups.
Allspice	*Pimenta dioica*	Full sun; fast-draining, rich soil; average water	10–11	Leaf, fruit	Evergreen tree to 20 ft. tall. Use as screen; in container or greenhouse. Invasive in Hawaii. Propagate from seeds or by grafting or budding. Leaves give clovelike flavor to syrups; grind dried berries for baking.
Almond	*Prunus dulcis*				See "Almond" in the Encyclopedia
Alpine strawberry	*Fragaria vesca* var. *vesca*				See "Strawberry" in the Encyclopedia
Amaranth (Aztec heirlooms, Chinese spinach)	*Amaranthus* spp.	Full sun; rich soil; average water	N/A	Leaf, seed	Warm-weather annual. Upright, 3–6 ft. tall, with green or red leaves. Some grain types have spectacular magenta spikes. Use in back of border with sunflowers. Shorter Chinese types have red-veined leaves; good for mid-border or container. Propagate from seeds. Sauté young leaves; use seeds for cereal or pop for snacks.
American custard apple	*Asimina triloba*				See "Pawpaw" in the Encyclopedia
Angelica	*Angelica archangelica*	Full sun or partial shade; rich soil; average water	4–9	Leaf, seed, stem, root	Tropical-looking herbaceous perennial to 6 ft. tall. Compound green leaves; large white flower umbels attract beneficial insects. Needs cool conditions. Plant in back of herb garden or flower bed. Propagate from seeds. Use leaves in soups; seeds and roots in liquors; candy the stems.
Anise	*Pimpinella anisum*	Full sun; rich soil; average water	N/A	Seed	Warm-weather annual. Spindly, sprawling, cut-leaf plant to 24 in. tall. Small white flower umbels attract beneficial insects. Use in herb garden or container. Propagate from seeds. Use licorice-flavored seeds in soups, sausages, and baked goods.
Anise hyssop	*Agastache foeniculum*	Full sun; rich soil; average water	4–9	Leaf, flower	Herbaceous perennial to 36 in. tall. Purple flower spikes attract bees. 'Golden Jubilee' has chartreuse leaves. All do poorly in hot climates. Beautiful in border or container. Propagate from seeds. Use licorice-flavored leaves and flowers for tea, desserts, salads, and sautéed with mushrooms.
Apple	*Malus* spp.				See "Apple and Crabapple" in the Encyclopedia
Apricot	*Prunus* spp.				See "Apricot" in the Encyclopedia
Artichoke	*Cynara scolymus*				See "Artichoke and Cardoon" in the Encyclopedia

COMMON NAME	LATIN NAME	CULTURAL CONDITIONS	USDA ZONES	EDIBLE PART	LANDSCAPE AND COOKING INFORMATION
Arugula (rocket)	*Eruca sativa* (*E. vesicaria* ssp. *sativa*)	Full sun or partial shade; rich soil; average water	N/A	Leaf, flower	Cool-season annual to 10 in. tall. Short lived. Small whitish flowers. Plant in spring or fall; replant among shorter lettuces and spinach, let it fill in among edible flowers, or grow in container. Propagate from seeds. Reseeds readily. Use spicy leaves and flowers in salads and on pasta and pizza.
Arugula, rustic	*Diplotaxis tenuifolia* (*E. selvatica*)	Full sun or partial shade; rich soil; average water	9–11	Leaf, flower	Tender perennial grown as annual. Compact bright green plant. Serrated leaves to8 in. long; small yellow flowers in sprays to 14 in. tall. Use in vegetable or herb garden or container. Propagate from seeds. Very spicy leaves; use sparingly in salads, ravioli, and pizza; use flowers in salads.
Asparagus	*Asparagus officinalis*				See "Asparagus" in the Encyclopedia
Aubergine	*Solanum melongena*				See "Eggplant" in the Encyclopedia
Avocado	*Persea americana*				See "Avocado" in the Encyclopedia
Bamboo	*Bambusa* spp., *Phyllostachys* spp.				See "Bamboo" in the Encyclopedia
Banana	*Musa* spp.				See "Banana and Plantain" in the Encyclopedia
Barley	*Hordeum vulgare*	Full sun; rich soil; average water	N/A	Seed	Cool-season annual grass widely adapted. To 36 in. tall. Use in grain garden for children; as cover crop. Propagate from seeds. Use barley in soups, beer, and pilaf.
Basil	*Ocimum* spp.				See "Basil" in the Encyclopedia
Bay laurel	*Laurus nobilis*				See "Sweet bay" in the Encyclopedia
Bean, asparagus (Chinese yard-long bean)	*Vigna unguiculata* ssp. *sesquipedalis*	Full sun; rich soil; average water	N/A	Pod	Warm-weather annual vine, to 8 ft. long. Insignificant flowers. Very long (to 36 in.) green or purple beans. Use on trellis or arbor, in child's garden. Propagate from seeds. Cook like green beans.
Bean, fava (broad bean)	*Vicia faba*				See "Bean" in the Encyclopedia
Bean, hyacinth (bonavista bean, lablab)	*Lablab purpureus* (*Dolichos lablab*)	Full sun; rich soil; some drought tolerance	9–11	Leaf, pod, seed, flower	Perennial vine grown as warm-season annual, to 10 ft. long. Heat-loving, tall. Attractive purple or white flowers; purple or green pods. Use on arbor or trellis. Many cultivars; flavors vary. Common in India. Propagate from seeds. Use young pods like string beans; leaves like spinach; sprinkle flowers on salads. Boil fresh mature seeds until tender to remove toxins; use cooked beans as side dish and in curries and soups.
Bean, lima	*Phaseolus lunatus*				See "Bean" in the Encyclopedia
Bean, runner	*Phaseolus coccineus*				See "Bean" in the Encyclopedia

COMMON NAME	LATIN NAME	CULTURAL CONDITIONS	USDA ZONES	EDIBLE PART	LANDSCAPE AND COOKING INFORMATION
Bean, snap	*Phaseolus vulgaris*				See "Bean" in the Encyclopedia
Bean, winged (Goa bean)	*Psophocarpus tetragonolobus*	Full sun; average soil; average water	N/A	Seed, pod, shoot	Warm-season annual vine to 10 ft. Heat loving. Use on arbor or fence. Propagate from seeds. Prepare pods like snap beans; eat seeds fresh or roasted; cook young shoots like spinach.
Beebalm (Oswego tea)	*Monarda didyma*	Full sun; average soil; keep moist	4–9	Leaf, flower	Upright, bushy herbaceous perennial to 36 in. tall. Showy red, pink, or lavender flowers attract bees. Use in herb or flower garden. Propagate from divisions. Red-flowered varieties have best taste. Use petals to flavor herbal teas and ice cream.
Beet	*Beta vulgaris* ssp. *vulgaris*	Full sun; rich soil; keep moist	N/A	Leaf, root	Biennial grown as annual, to 18 in. tall. HH. Prefers cool conditions. Short plant with red- or gold-veined leaves. Spring or fall planting. Harvesting creates empty spaces; interplant with spreading annuals. 'Bull's Blood' is especially showy. Propagate from seeds. Use leaves like chard. Roast the roots or use in stews and salads, and, of course, in borscht.
Begonia, tuberous	*Begonia* × *tuberhybrida*	Filtered sun; rich soil; keep moist	9–11	Flower	Tender herbaceous perennial to 30 in. tall. Large fleshy leaves; big showy flowers 2–4 in. across in red, orange, pink, or yellow. Propagate from tubers. Use citrus-flavored flower petals in salads, sandwiches, yogurt, or ice cream, or as garnish.
Birch (sweet birch, black birch)	*Betula lenta*				See "Maple" in the Encyclopedia
Bitter melon	*Momordica charantia*	Full sun; rich soil; average water	N/A	Leaf, fruit	Warm-season annual vine to 15 ft. Heat loving. Handsome bright green cut leaves and bumpy fruit. Use on arbor or fence. Propagate from seeds. Harvest when immature. Much beloved in Asian cuisine. Stuff bitter fruit or slice and add to curries and soups. Stir-fry leaves.
Blackberry	*Rubus* spp.				See "Brambleberry" in the Encyclopedia
Black nigella (black caraway, black cumin)	*Nigella sativa*	Full sun; average soil; average water	N/A	Seed	Cool-season annual to 24 in. tall. Easy to grow. Finely divided leaves, wonderful pale blue or white delicate flowers and black seed heads. Use in grain garden or wildflower mix. Propagate from seeds. Use as spice in string cheese and sauerkraut, with lamb, and to flavor Indian curries and naan.
Blueberry	*Vaccinium* spp.				See "Blueberry" in the Encyclopedia
Borage	*Borago officinalis*	Full sun or partial shade; average soil; average water	N/A	Flower	Warm-season annual to 24 in. tall. Dramatic, prickly, large gray leaves; handsome blue flowers in clusters attract bees. Use in herb garden or flower bed. Can become a weed. Propagate from seeds. Add flowers to salads, float them in lemonade, or candy them.

COMMON NAME	LATIN NAME	CULTURAL CONDITIONS	USDA ZONES	EDIBLE PART	LANDSCAPE AND COOKING INFORMATION
Brambleberry	*Rubus* spp.				See "Brambleberry" in the Encyclopedia
Breadfruit	*Artocarpus altilis*	Full sun; average soil; average water	10–11	Fruit, seed	Tropical evergreen tree to 60 ft. tall. Striking cut-leaf foliage and huge fruit. Use as shade or specimen tree. Favorite in Southeast Asia. Bake or boil unripe fruit like a starchy potato; use ripe fruit in desserts; roast the seeds.
Broccoli	*Brassica oleracea* var. *italica*				See "Broccoli and Cauliflower" in the Encyclopedia
Brussels sprouts	*Brassica oleracea* var. *gemmifera*	Full sun; rich soil; average water	N/A	Leaf, flower	Cool-season biennial grown as annual. Somewhat top-heavy plant to 36 in. tall can appear raggedy by end of harvest. Use in vegetable garden or middle of border or bed. Grow like cabbage. Propagate from seeds. Cut sprouts from main stem and roast, steam, or stir-fry. Flowers good in salads.
Buckwheat	*Fagopyrum esculentum*	Full sun; average soil; average water	N/A	Seed	Warm-season annual. Triangular-leaved plant to 36 in. tall. Short lived. Small clusters of fragrant white flowers attract beneficial insects. Use in informal yard adjacent to meadow or as cover crop. Propagate from seeds. Use flour in pancakes and soba noodles.
Butternut	*Juglans cinerea*				See "Walnut" in the Encyclopedia
Cabbage	*Brassica oleracea* var. *capitata*				See "Cabbage" in the Encyclopedia
Calamint (lesser calamint, nepitella)	*Clinopodium nepeta* (*Calamintha nepeta*)	Full sun or partial shade; average soil; average water	5–11	Leaf	Spreading perennial herb to 36 in. tall. Gray-green leaves, lavender flowers. Pretty in herb garden or container. Reseeds. Propagate from seeds. Leaves contribute oregano-mint flavor to butters, marinades, and dressings. Not considered GRAS.
Calamondin	× *Citrofortunella microcarpa*				See "Citrus" in the Encyclopedia
Calendula	*Calendula officinalis*	Full sun; rich soil; keep moist	N/A	Flower	Cool-season annual. HH. To 18 in. tall; dwarf varieties available, but more prone to mildew. Reliable color mid-border or in container. Flowers attract beneficial insects. Propagate from seeds. Heirloom varieties with large flower petals best for sprinkling over salads and cooked rice. Adds saffron color and flavor.
Cantaloupe (muskmelon)	*Cucumis melo* var. *reticulatus*				See "Melon" in the Encyclopedia
Caper	*Capparis spinosa*	Full sun; fast-draining soil; drought tolerant	10–11	Flower bud, fruit	Sprawling, subshrub to 3 ft. tall, 5 ft. across Round leaves; white flowers with showy pink stamens. Good desert plant. Use in rock garden, on dry bank, or in container. Propagate from seeds or cuttings. Flower buds, and occasionally fruits, are pickled and used as flavoring or condiment.

COMMON NAME	LATIN NAME	CULTURAL CONDITIONS	USDA ZONES	EDIBLE PART	LANDSCAPE AND COOKING INFORMATION
Carambola	*Averrhoa carambola*	Full sun; good soil; keep moist	10–11	Fruit	Tropical evergreen tree to 25 ft. tall. Best in humid climates. Showy yellow fruit. Use as shade or interest tree. Keep away from paving. Propagate from seeds or by grafting. Enjoy fruit fresh in salads and desserts.
Caraway	*Carum carvi*	Full sun; rich soil; average water	N/A	Leaf, seed	Cool-season annual to 24 in. tall. HH. Lacy appearance. Decorative white flowers in umbels attract beneficial insects. Plant in spring or fall. Use in herb garden or container. Propagate from seeds. Use seeds as distinctive seasoning in breads and cabbage and meat dishes; leaves in salads and curries.
Cardoon	*Cynara cardunculus*				See "Artichoke and Cardoon" in the Encyclopedia
Carob	*Ceratonia siliqua*	Full sun; average soil; drought tolerant	9–11	Pod	Shrubby evergreen tree to 50 ft. tall. Handsome foliage and form. Use as screen or specimen. Male and female trees needed for pollination. Tree is messy and roots invasive. Use in xeriscape garden. Propagate from seeds or by grafting. Harvest pods in late summer; they contain nutritious sweet pulp used in pastries and as chocolate substitute.
Carrot	*Daucus carota* ssp. *sativus*	Full sun or partial shade; deep, rich soil; average moisture	N/A	Root, leaf	Biennial grown as cool-season annual. HH. Graceful, ferny foliage to 12 in. tall. For long, straight carrots, grow in light soil in container or raised bed. Harvested carrots create empty spaces; interplant with compact flowering annuals. Propagate from seeds. Enjoy roots raw in salads and slaws, roasted, pureed, juiced, or added to soups, curries, and stews. Use tops in soups.
Cattail	*Typha latifolia*	Full sun or partial shade; rich soil; aquatic	3–11	Shoot, rhizome pollen	Grasslike herbaceous native bog plant 4–8 ft. tall. Brown fuzzy seed heads. Use in pond or rain garden. Propagate from seeds. Use young shoots and rhizomes raw like cucumber or cook like zucchini; add pollen to flour to make baked goods.
Cauliflower	*Brassica oleracea* var. *botrytis*				See "Broccoli and Cauliflower" in the Encyclopedia
Celeriac	*Apium graveolens* var. *rapaceum*	Full sun; rich, slightly acid soil; keep moist	N/A	Swollen crown	Biennial grown as cool-season annual. HH. Upright, to 4 ft. tall. Attractive cut leaves. Limited landscaping use. Use in container or interplant with nasturtiums. Propagate from seeds. Flavor is celery-like. Enjoy raw in salads or cooked in soups and stews.
Celery	*Apium graveolens* var. *dulce*	Full sun; very rich soil; keep moist	N/A	Leaf, stem	Biennial grown as cool-season annual. HH. Upright plant to 36 in. tall. Attractive bright green, cut-leaf foliage. 'Chinese Golden' has chartreuse foliage. Use midborder or in container. Propagate from seeds. Use raw or cooked; add to soups, stews, and sauces.

COMMON NAME	LATIN NAME	CULTURAL CONDITIONS	USDA ZONES	EDIBLE PART	LANDSCAPE AND COOKING INFORMATION
Chamomile, German (sweet false chamomile)	*Matricaria chamomilla* (*M. recutita*)	Full sun; any soil; average water	N/A	Flower	Warm-season annual. Upright, branching, to 30 in. tall. Apple-scented, yellow and white, 1-in. daisylike flowers top bright green ferny leaves in summer. Lovely in bed, herb garden, or container. Propagate from seeds. Harvest flowers in summer; use fresh or dried to make calming tea.
Chamomile, Roman (garden chamomile)	*Chamaemelum nobile*	Full sun or partial shade; any soil; average water	4–9	Flower	Hardy evergreen perennial 3–12 in. tall. Upright, branching plant with small, bright green, fernlike leaves. Small, white, daisylike flowers bloom in spring and summer. Tolerates light foot traffic; excellent ground cover between stepping-stones, in herb garden, in rock garden, or along semi-shaded woodland path; also in container. Propagate from seeds or divisions. Harvest flowers in spring and summer; use fresh or dried for tea.
Chard	*Beta vulgaris* ssp. *vulgaris*				See "Chard" in the Encyclopedia
Chayote	*Sechium edule*	Full sun; rich soil; average water	9–11	Fruit, seed, shoot	Very large herbaceous vine. Use to cover arbor or fence. Start from sprouted fruit from the market. Short-day plant needs at least 4 weeks of 12-hour or shorter days; doesn't flower until well into fall and needs at least a month to produce mature fruit. Cook like summer squash; good in spicy dishes. Stir-fry shoots or use in soup.
Cherimoya	*Annona cherimola*	Full sun; average soil; average water	10–11	Fruit	Shrubby evergreen tree to 30 ft. tall. Large velvety leaves. Hand pollination usually needed. Use as interest plant or screen. Propagate by grafting or from seeds. Harvest October through May. Eat custardlike fruit fresh, or add pulp to ice creams.
Cherry, sour and sweet	*Prunus* spp.				See "Cherry" in the Encyclopedia
Cherry of the Rio Grande	*Eugenia aggregata*	Full sun; fast-draining soil; average water	9–11	Fruit	Evergreen tree to 15 ft. tall. Grow in large container; use as informal hedge or specimen. Propagate from seeds. Harvest in summer; eat sweet purple fruit out of hand or make into juice or preserves.
Chervil	*Anthriscus cerefolium*	Full sun or partial shade; rich soil; keep moist	N/A	Leaf, flower	Cool-season annual to 18 in. tall. Delicate, fern-leaved plant. Small flowers attract beneficial insects. Grow with salad greens or in herb garden, flower bed, or container. Propagate from seeds. Use leaves and flowers in salads for a slight anise flavor.
Chestnut	*Castanea* spp.				See "Chestnut" in the Encyclopedia
Chickpea (garbanzo bean)	*Cicer arietinum*	Full sun; rich, light soil; average water	N/A	Seed	Warm-weather annual. Heat loving, bushy, to 24 in. tall. Undistinguished, sprawling habit. Use in vegetable garden or large container. Propagate from seeds. Use fresh or dried; add to soups, bake, or grind into paste for hummus.

COMMON NAME	LATIN NAME	CULTURAL CONDITIONS	USDA ZONES	EDIBLE PART	LANDSCAPE AND COOKING INFORMATION
Chinese leeks (Chinese leek flower)	*Allium ramosum*				See "Chives" in the Encyclopedia
Chives	*Allium schoenoprasum*				See "Chives" in the Encyclopedia
Chocolate (cacao)	*Theobroma cacao*	Full sun or partial shade; fast-draining, rich soil; keep moist	10–11	Seed	Evergreen tree 12 to 25 ft. tall. Beautiful dark green leaves and decorative pods. Use as interest plant or in container or greenhouse. Propagate from seeds. To process the dried beans, ferment, roast, grind, and "conch" with sugar to develop texture and full flavor. Make finished chocolate into candies and sauces.
Cilantro (coriander)	*Coriandrum sativum*	Full sun; rich soil; keep moist	N/A	Leaf, seed, root, flower	Cool-season annual. HH. Graceful plant to 36 in. tall. Compound leaves; small white flowers in umbels attract beneficial insects. Usually set out in spring, but best planted in early fall to produce full-size plant. Use in herb garden, flower bed, or container. Propagate from seeds. Use strong-flavored leaves for seasoning in Chinese and Mexican dishes; roots in Thai curry; seeds in many stews and curries; flowers in salads.
Citrus	*Citrus* spp.				See "Citrus" in the Encyclopedia
Coconut palm	*Cocos nucifera*	Full sun; fast-draining, light soil; moderate water	10–11	Nut	Graceful palm tree to 50 ft. tall. Use as specimen in areas where falling coconuts will not cause damage. Propagate from seeds. Grate nutmeats and use in countless dishes, especially curries and desserts.
Coffee	*Coffea arabica*	Shade or bright, indirect light; rich soil; average water	10–11	Seed	Evergreen tree to 30 ft. tall. Handsome, shiny deep green leaves; showy, fragrant white flowers followed by small red berries. Use as screen or hedge; in container or greenhouse. Propagate from seeds or cuttings. Dry coffee beans and roast to make the familiar drink.
Collards (collard greens)	*Brassica oleracea* var. *viridis* (*B. oleracea* Acephala Group)	Full sun; well-drained, good soil; average water	N/A	Leaf	Cool-weather biennial grown as annual. HH. Stands up to summer heat. Attractive blue-green, tasty leaves. Grow like cabbage, but practically pest and disease free. Combine with other greens and annual flowers in herbaceous border or container. Propagate from seeds. Traditionally cooked with black-eyed peas and ham. Use in stir-fries, steam, or add to soups.
Coriander, Vietnamese (rau ram)	*Persicaria odorata* (*Polygonum odoratum*)	Full sun or partial shade; average soil; keep moist	8–11	Leaf	Herbaceous perennial grown as annual in cold-winter areas. Sprawling plant to 18 in. tall. Use in herb garden, container, or greenhouse. Spreads via root system; invasive in mild-winter areas. Propagate from cuttings or divisions. Use leaves to give cilantro flavor to cooked dishes.

COMMON NAME	LATIN NAME	CULTURAL CONDITIONS	USDA ZONES	EDIBLE PART	LANDSCAPE AND COOKING INFORMATION
Corn (and popcorn)	*Zea mays*	Full sun; rich soil; average water	N/A	Seed	Warm-season annual. Tall, heat-loving, broad-leaved grass to 12 ft. tall; dwarf varieties to 5 ft. tall. Minute flowers attract beneficial insects. Types of corn include sweet, grinding, and popping. Challenge to use in a landscape, but fun for children; use dwarf varieties as temporary background plants in informal gardens and to make mini-maze. Propagate from seeds. Roast or boil fresh sweet corn; pop popcorn types; grind dried seeds into meal for baked goods and mush.
Cornelian cherry	*Cornus mas*	Full sun or partial shade; average soil; drought tolerant	4–8	Fruit	Deciduous tree to 20 ft. tall. Multi-stemmed, upright. Lightly scented, small yellowish flowers in late winter. Fruit ripens midsummer; small maroon red berries attract birds. Use as screen, interest tree, or hedgerow. Propagate from seeds or cuttings. Enjoy fruit fresh or make into jam.
Costmary	*Tanacetum balsamita* (*Chrysanthemum balsamita*)	Full sun; average soil; average water	6–9	Leaf	Herbaceous perennial. Straggly, to 36 in. tall. Gray-green leaves, tiny yellow flowers. Keep trimmed; use in herb garden. Can become a weed. Propagate from divisions. Use minty-flavored leaves in liquors.
Crabapple	*Malus* spp.				See "Apple and Crabapple" in the Encyclopedia
Cranberry	*Vaccinium macrocarpon*				See "Cranberry and Lingonberry" in the Encyclopedia
Cress (wrinkled cress and upland cress)	*Lepidium sativum, Barbarea verna*	Full sun or partial shade; rich soil; keep moist	N/A	Leaf	Biennial grown as cool-season annual. HH. Small plant to 12 in. tall with ruffled green leaves. Plant in spring or fall. Short lived; use in vegetable, flower, or salad garden, or in container. Propagate from seeds. Use peppery young leaves in salads and sandwiches; stir-fry more mature leaves.
Cuban oregano	*Plectranthus amboinicus*	Full sun; average soil; average water	10–11	Leaf	Tender perennial often grown as annual. Bushy, to 36 in. tall. Succulent, spicy-scented, velvety leaves. Decorative foliage plant; variegated cultivar is striking. Keep pinched or gets rangy. Propagate from cuttings. Mild oregano flavor; use with meats, beans, or anywhere you would use an oregano.
Cucumber	*Cucumis sativus*				See "Cucumber" in the Encyclopedia
Culantro (Mexican coriander)	*Eryngium foetidum*	Full sun; good soil; average water	N/A	Leaf	Biennial herb grown as warm-season annual. To 16 in. tall, spiny. Use in herb garden as filler; in container or green-house. Propagate from seeds. Cilantro-flavored leaves are traditional Mexican seasoning. Not considered GRAS.

COMMON NAME	LATIN NAME	CULTURAL CONDITIONS	USDA ZONES	EDIBLE PART	LANDSCAPE AND COOKING INFORMATION
Cumin	*Cuminum cyminum*	Full sun; average soil; average water	N/A	Seed	Warm-season annual. HH. Wispy plant to 18 in. tall with threadlike leaves. White or pink flowers in small umbels. Fussy about conditions. Use in front of herb garden or flower bed. Propagate from seeds. Great in curries, chili, and Mexican foods.
Currant	*Ribes* spp.				See "Currant and Gooseberry" in the Encyclopedia
Curry leaf	*Bergera koenigii* (*Murraya koenigii*)	Full sun; fertile soil; average water	10–11	Leaf	Tropical evergreen tree to 20 ft. tall. Finely cut leaves. Use in shrub border, container, or greenhouse. Propagate from seeds. Fragrant leaves add flavor to curries.
Dandelion	*Taraxacum officinale*	Full sun or partial shade; rich, deep soil; keep moist	5–11	Leaf, flower, root	Perennial to 18 in. tall with rosette of long-toothed leaves; yellow flowers. Inter-plant superior varieties with greens in herbaceous border. Can become a weed (surprise!). Propagate from seeds. Enjoy young leaves in salads or cook like spinach. Use flower petals to make wine; batter-fried young flowers taste like mushrooms. Roast the roots for coffee substitute.
Date palm	*Phoenix dactylifera*	Full sun; average soil; drought tolerant	9–11	Fruit	Handsome palm tree 30–40 ft. tall. Fruit production poor in humid climates, but good desert plant. Use as shade or specimen tree. Propagate from seeds or offshoots. Use fruit fresh or dried, eat out of hand, or add to pastries.
Daylily	*Hemerocallis* spp.	Full sun or partial shade; any soil; tolerates drought or wet conditions	3–10	Flower, buds	Herbaceous perennial to 36 in. tall. Strap-like leaves; yellow, orange, or pink flowers with open trumpet shape. Use in flower border or container. Propagate from divisions. Buds have slightly sweet flavor, though not all varieties are flavorful. Use dried buds in Chinese hot-and-sour soup, fresh ones in omelets, stir-fries. Use flower petals in pancakes, frittatas, and dips, and as elegant "cup" for ice cream or sorbet.
Dill	*Anethum graveolens*	Full sun; rich soil; keep moist	N/A	Leaf, seed, flower	Cool-season annual, but tolerates some heat. Short-lived plant to 36 in. tall; compact varieties available. Ferny, threadlike foliage; yellow flowers in umbels attract beneficial insects. Best planted in spring. Use in herb garden or container. Propagate from seeds. Distinctive flavor for salads, sauces, egg dishes, and pickles.
Dragon fruit (pitahaya, night-blooming cactus, night-blooming cereus)	*Hylocereus undatus*	Full sun; partial shade in dry climates; lean, well-drained soil; drought tolerant	10–11	Fruit	Climbing succulent vine; epiphytic member of cactus family. Needs orchid soil and mild temperatures. Gorgeous, huge, fragrant white flowers at night. Two or more varieties needed for pollination. Use as interest plant; in container or greenhouse. Propagate from seeds or cuttings. Eat fruit out of hand.

COMMON NAME	LATIN NAME	CULTURAL CONDITIONS	USDA ZONES	EDIBLE PART	LANDSCAPE AND COOKING INFORMATION
Eggplant	*Solanum melongena*				See "Eggplant" in the Encyclopedia
Elderberry	*Sambucus* spp.				See "Elderberry" in the Encyclopedia
Endive, escarole, frisée (curly endive)	*Cichorium endivia*	Full sun or partial shade; rich soil; average water	N/A	Leaf	Cool-season biennial grown as annual. HH. Compact bright green leaves in rosette to 12 in. tall. Use curly and broad-leaved varieties in vegetable or flower border, or in container. Propagate from seeds. Use the slightly bitter leaves in salads; wilt in olive oil as side dish.
Fennel (sweet fennel)	*Foeniculum vulgare*	Full sun; average soil; average water	6–9	Leaf, seed, flower	Herbaceous perennial grown as annual in short-summer areas. To 6 ft. tall. Handsome, fernlike foliage; large, rounded umbels of yellow flowers attract beneficial insects. Bronze cultivar is striking. Use in back of herbaceous border. Can be invasive in mild-winter climates. Propagate from seeds. Use anise-flavored leaves and flowers in salads; seeds as flavoring in Italian foods. Seeds used as a digestive.
Fig	*Ficus carica*				See "Fig" in the Encyclopedia
Filbert	*Corylus* spp.				See "Filbert" in the Encyclopedia
Flax, culinary	*Linum usitatissimum*	Full sun; good soil; average water	N/A	Seed	Cool-season annual. HH. Spindly plant to 36 in. tall with small blue flowers. Plant in spring. See "Wheat" for landscaping uses. Propagate from seeds purchased at natural food store. Seeds are high in omega-3 oils. Use seeds in cereal and bread; sprouts in salads.
Foxberry	*Vaccinium vitis-idaea* ssp. *minus*				See "Cranberry and Lingonberry" in the Encyclopedia
Gai lon (Chinese broccoli, Chinese kale)	*Brassica oleracea* var. *alboglabra*				See "Broccoli and Cauliflower" in the Encyclopedia
Galangal	*Alpinia galanga*				See "Ginger" in the Encyclopedia
Garlic, softneck, hardneck	*Allium* spp.	Full sun; rich soil; average water	5–9	Bulb, leaf	Upright herbaceous plant to 24 in. tall. Tubular gray-green leaves. Use in flower border, vegetable garden, or container. Propagate from cloves. Uses for garlic in savory cooking are legendary.
Garlic chives (Chinese chives)	*Allium tuberosum*				See "Chives" in the Encyclopedia
Geranium, scented	*Pelargonium* spp.	Full sun; average soil; average water	9–11	Leaf, flower	Variable herbaceous plants—some upright, others vining; some with gray leaves, others variegated. Flowers red, pink, or lavender. Flavors include rose, lemon, and mint. Use in herb garden or container. Propagate from cuttings. Use leaves and flowers to add flavor to tea, jellies, butter, honey, and cakes.

COMMON NAME	LATIN NAME	CULTURAL CONDITIONS	USDA ZONES	EDIBLE PART	LANDSCAPE AND COOKING INFORMATION
Ginger	*Zingiber* spp.				See "Ginger" in the Encyclopedia
Ginkgo	*Ginkgo biloba*	Full sun; average soil; average water	4–9	Nut	Deciduous tree to 100 ft. tall with striking gold fall foliage. Female tree bears unpleasant-smelling fruit in late summer, prized in Asian cuisine. The nuts are the seeds of the fruit. Obtain seeds and plant a few to get one female plus a male or two to pollinize. Plant female tree in woodland setting or informal area. Roast ginkgo nuts (silver nuts) and eat out of hand; steam and add to rice dishes.
Goji berry	*Lycium barbarum*	Full sun; poor to average soil; drought tolerant	6–8	Fruit	Hardy shrub to 10 ft. tall. Small, bright red-orange berries in late summer to early fall. Use in shrub border or as hedge. Propagate from seeds or cuttings. Goji berries are high in antioxidants. Sweet cranberry flavor; eat out of hand or use in cereal, rice, or fruit salad.
Gooseberry	*Ribes* spp.				See "Currant and Gooseberry" in the Encyclopedia
Grape	*Vitis* spp.				See "Grape" in the Encyclopedia
Grapefruit	*Citrus paradisi*				See "Citrus" in the Encyclopedia
Ground cherry (poha)	*Physalis peruviana*	Full sun; average to rich soil; average water	N/A	Fruit	Herbaceous perennial grown as warm-season annual. Sprawling, bushy, to 36 in. tall. Fruit has a papery husk. Use in vegetable garden or container. Propagate from seeds. Harvest when fruit drops; eat fresh out of hand or make into pie and jam.
Guava, Chilean	*Ugni molinae*	Full sun or partial shade; average soil; average water	9–11	Fruit	Evergreen shrub to 6 ft. tall. Small leaves; white flowers like lily-of-the-valley. Use as foundation shrub or in container. Propagate by grafting. Eat small red to black fruit out of hand.
Guava, strawberry	*Psidium cattleianum* (*P. littorale*)	Full sun; poor to average soil; average water	9–11	Fruit	Handsome evergreen shrub or small tree to 15 ft. tall. White flowers, deep red fruit. Quite ornamental, but fruit is seedy. Use as hedge or multistemmed tree. Invasive in Hawaii. Propagate from seeds or cuttings. Eat fruit out of hand or make preserves.
Hazelnut	*Corylus* spp.				See "Filbert" in the Encyclopedia
Heartnut	*Juglans ailantifolia* var. *cordiformis*				See "Walnut" in the Encyclopedia
Hican	*Carya* spp.				See "Pecan and Hickory" in the Encyclopedia
Hickory	*Carya* spp.				See "Pecan and Hickory" in the Encyclopedia

COMMON NAME	LATIN NAME	CULTURAL CONDITIONS	USDA ZONES	EDIBLE PART	LANDSCAPE AND COOKING INFORMATION
Hoja santa	*Piper auritum*	Full sun or partial shade; average soil; average water	10–11	Leaf	Large herbaceous plant with dramatic, heart-shaped, large leaves. To 6 ft. tall, much taller in tropical climates. Use for tropical look in patio or container. Propagate from cuttings. The fresh leaves have a root beer and anise flavor; wrap them around tamale dough, fish, or meat to flavor the filling. Not considered GRAS.
Honeydew (Crenshaw melon)	*Cucumis melo* var. *inodorus*				See "Melon" in the Encyclopedia
Hops	*Humulus lupulus*				See "Hops" in the Encyclopedia
Horseradish	*Armoracia rusticana*	Full sun; deep, rich soil; average water	5–9	Root	Herbaceous perennial to 18 in. tall. Stout, wavy-edged leaves. Variegated cultivar reverts to green. Can be invasive; grow in container. Grind roots to use as spicy condiment or add to sauces. **Caution:** Pungent fumes; use protection for eyes and nose.
Huauzontle (red Aztec spinach)	*Chenopodium berlandieri* ssp. *nuttalliae*	Full sun; good soil; keep moist	N/A	Leaf bud, seed head	Warm-season annual to 4 ft. tall. with showy, bright red stems. Red seed heads in fall. Use in back of border. Propagate from seeds. Braise young leaf buds or batter-fry young seed heads. Not considered GRAS.
Huckleberry, black	*Gaylussacia baccata*	Full sun or partial shade; rich, acid soil; average water	3–8	Fruit	Handsome, low-maintenance native shrub 18–36 in. tall. Elegant, reddish, bell-like flowers in spring; black berries. Green foliage turns deep crimson in fall. Use in shrub border or woodland garden. Eat berries out of hand; make into jam or pies.
Huckleberry, garden (wonderberry)	*Solanum scabrum* (*S. melanocerasum*)	Sun or shade; rich soil; average water	N/A	Fruit	Warm-season annual. Undistinguished plant to 30 in. tall. Small white flowers; black berries. Use in vegetable garden. Can become a weed. Propagate from seeds. Harvest berries when black and dull; always cook before eating. Usually made into pies.
Jaboticaba (Brazilian grape tree)	*Myrciaria cauliflora*	Full sun or partial shade; rich, deep soil; moderate water	10–11	Fruit	Bushy evergreen tree 15–45 ft. tall. Unusual blackish fruit grows along trunk. Use in shrub border or as screen. Propagate from seeds or by grafting. Eat fruit fresh in salads, or use in preserves and sorbets.
Jamaica (roselle)	*Hibiscus sabdariffa*	Full sun; average soil; moderate water	9–11	Calyx, fruit	Woody perennial grown as warm-season annual in most climates. Lovely plant to 4 ft. tall. Reddish leaves with dark veins; small cream to pink flowers. Great in flower or foliage border, container, or greenhouse. Propagate from seeds. Use to make tangy herbal red tea, marinades, and salad dressings.
Japanese plum	*Prunus mume*				See "Apricot" in the Encyclopedia

COMMON NAME	LATIN NAME	CULTURAL CONDITIONS	USDA ZONES	EDIBLE PART	LANDSCAPE AND COOKING INFORMATION
Jerusalem artichoke (sunchoke)	*Helianthus tuberosus*	Full sun or partial shade; average soil; average water	3–9	Tuber	Herbaceous perennial to 10 ft. tall. North American native's showy sunflowers attract finches and beneficial insects. Stake to keep neat; can become invasive. Use as screen or background for large flower border. Propagate from tubers. Tasty tubers contain valuable nutrients and are easily digested. Boil or sauté like potatoes or add to soups and stews.
Jicama	*Pachyrhizus erosus*	Full sun; rich, light soil; keep moist	N/A	Tuber	Herbaceous perennial vine grown as annual, to 15 ft. long. Needs long season. Handsome foliage. Use on arbor or fence, or grow in large container. Propagate from seeds or tubers. Sweet, crunchy tubers are usually eaten raw. **Caution:** Seeds are poisonous and are used to make the pesticide rotenone.
Jujube	*Ziziphus jujuba*	Full sun; fast-draining, average soil but tolerates alkaline and salty; drought tolerant	6–9	Fruit	Semi-weeping deciduous tree from Asia, to 40 ft. tall. Attractive shiny foliage. Suckering can be a problem. Use as shade or interest tree, or grow in xeriscape or desert garden. Propagate by grafting or budding. Eat small sweet brown fruit fresh or dried.
Juniper, common	*Juniperus communis*	Full sun; fast-draining, average soil; average water	5–9	Cone	Coniferous shrub. Attracts birds. Many subspecies and cultivars grow in temperate climates. Use tall types (5–10 ft.) in shrub border, short types (around 12 in. high) as ground cover; all in woodland gardens. Propagate from cuttings. Use dried blue-black cones ("berries") to flavor gin and add to sauce for game.
Kaki (Asian persimmon)	*Diospyros kaki*				See "Persimmon" in the Encyclopedia
Kale	*Brassica oleracea* var. *viridis*				See "Kale" in the Encyclopedia
King nut (shellbark hickory)	*Carya ovata*				See "Pecan and Hickory" in the Encyclopedia
Kiwi (kiwifruit)	*Actinidia* spp.				See "Kiwi" in the Encyclopedia
Kohlrabi	*Brassica oleracea* var. *gongylodes*	Full sun; rich soil; average water	N/A	Stem	Cool-season annual. Leafy plant to 24 in. tall with bulbous main stem. Some varieties are purple. Harvesting creates empty spaces; interplant with greens and low flowering annuals. Propagate from seeds. Use swollen stem as root vegetable and in salads.
Kumquat (nagami)	*Fortunella* spp.				See "Citrus" in the Encyclopedia
Lamb's-quarter (magentaspreen, giant goosefoot)	*Chenopodium album*	Full sun; average soil; average water	N/A	Leaf	Cool-season annual. HH. Green and magenta leaves. Grow as quick salad herb or allow to grow to full height of 36 in. at back of annual border. Can reseed and become invasive. Propagate from seeds. Cook like spinach or use young leaves in salads.

COMMON NAME	LATIN NAME	CULTURAL CONDITIONS	USDA ZONES	EDIBLE PART	LANDSCAPE AND COOKING INFORMATION
Land seaweed	*Salsola komarovii*	Full sun; sandy soil; average water	N/A	Leaf	Cool-season annual. Thread-leaved, upright plant to 24 in. tall. Short lived; best for container or vegetable bed. Prefers slightly alkaline soil. Propagate from seeds. Use slightly crunchy leaves raw or cooked in salads and sushi.
Lavender	*Lavandula* spp.	Full sun; fast-draining, average soil; drought tolerant	6–9	Leaf, flower	Compact gray-green subshrubs. Purple flowers. Great for border, container. Dwarf varieties include 'Hidcote' and 'Munstead'. Culinary varieties are *L angustifolia* and *L. × intermedia* 'Provence' and 'Grosso.' Use in herbes de Provence, ice cream, baked goods, and lemonade.
Leek	*Allium porrum* (*A. ampeloprasum* var. *porrum*)	Full sun; partial shade in hot climates; rich, light soil; average water	N/A	Bulb, leaf	Biennial grown as cool-season annual, 24–36 in. tall. HH. Short, narrow leaved; handsome fanlike form. Use in flower border, vegetable garden, or container. Harvesting creates empty spaces; interplant with greens or flowering annuals. Propagate from seeds. Use bulb and leaves in soups, sauces, quiches, and stews.
Lemon	*Citrus limon*				See "Citrus" in the Encyclopedia
Lemon balm	*Melissa officinalis*	Full sun or partial shade; average soil; average water	5–9	Leaf	Herbaceous perennial to 24 in. tall. Leaves resemble mint; insignificant flowers. Use in herb garden or container. Propagate from seeds. Can become a weed. Lemony flavor for tea and salads.
Lemongrass	*Cymbopogon citratus*	Full sun; good soil; average water	9–11	Stalk	Herbaceous grasslike perennial to 36 in. tall. Grow in foliage or perennial flower border, container, or greenhouse. Propagate from divisions. Stalks give an authentic taste to Southeast Asian curries and soups.
Lemon verbena	*Aloysia citriodora* (*A. triphylla*)	Full sun; good soil; average water	9–11	Leaf	Woody, upright but rangy shrub to 6 ft. tall. Use in back of border; in greenhouse or container. Prune often. Propagate from seeds or cuttings. Use in tea and to make lemon-flavored syrup.
Lentil	*Lens culinaris* ssp. *culinaris*	Full sun; average soil; average water	N/A	Seed	Cool-season annual. Many-branched, open plant to 18 in. tall. Interesting small feathery foliage. Attractive, but tends to sprawl. Use in raised planter or container. Propagate from seeds. Enjoy in soups, salads, and dips.
Lettuce	*Lactuca sativa*				See "Lettuce" in the Encyclopedia
Licorice	*Glycyrrhiza glabra*	Full sun; average soil; average water	6–9	Root	Herbaceous perennial, upright to 36 in. tall. Attractive small cut leaves; small blue pealike flowers. Use in perennial flower border, herb garden, or container. Propagate from seeds or divisions. Has no licorice flavor. Dry the root and use to sweeten candy.

COMMON NAME	LATIN NAME	CULTURAL CONDITIONS	USDA ZONES	EDIBLE PART	LANDSCAPE AND COOKING INFORMATION
Lilac	*Syringa vulgaris*	Full sun; fast-draining, average soil; average water	3–9	Flower	Deciduous shrub to 20 ft. tall. Clusters of fragrant lavender or white flowers in spring. Use as hedge or screen. Many varieties available. Propagate from cuttings or by grafting. Use florets in soft cheeses, in ice cream, and on pastries. Not all varieties are flavorful.
Lime	*Citrus* spp.				See "Citrus" in the Encyclopedia
Lime leaf (makrut, kaffir lime)	*Citrus hystrix*				See "Citrus" in the Encyclopedia
Limequat	× *Citrofortunella floridana*				See "Citrus" in the Encyclopedia
Lingonberry	*Vaccinium vitis-idaea*				See "Cranberry and Lingonberry" in the Encyclopedia
Litchi (lychee)	*Litchi chinensis*	Full sun; rich soil; keep moist	10–11	Fruit	Evergreen tree to 30 ft. tall. Tropical, but needs some winter chilling. Handsome foliage and red fruit clusters. Use as interest or shade tree. Propagate by air layering. Eat fruit fresh or dried.
Longan	*Dimocarpus longan*	Full sun; rich soil; keep moist	10–11	Fruit	Evergreen tropical tree to 40 ft. tall. Use as interest or shade tree. Propagate by grafting or from seeds. Light brown, grape-size fruit in clusters; eat fresh or dried.
Loquat	*Eriobotrya japonica*	Full sun; average soil; average water	8–10	Fruit	Evergreen tree to 20 ft. tall. Dramatic form; beautiful woolly foliage, colorful orange fruit in late spring. Plant away from pavement. Use for shade or interest. Propagate by grafting. Enjoy fresh fruit out of hand, in fruit and green salads, and canned.
Lotus (sacred lotus, Chinese lotus)	*Nelumbo nucifera*				See "Lotus" in the Encyclopedia
Lovage	*Levisticum officinale*	Full sun; rich soil; average water	5–9	Leaf	Herbaceous perennial to 6 ft. tall. Upright form. Celery-like leaves; yellow flowers in umbels attract beneficial insects. Ornamental; good for back of perennial or annual flower garden; in herb garden. Propagate from seeds. Use celery-flavored leaves in soups and salads. Use stem as straw for bloody Mary.
Macadamia	*Macadamia integrifolia*, *M. tetraphylla*	Full sun; rich soil; average water	10–11	Nut	Evergreen tree to 40 ft. tall; handsome foliage. Use as shade tree. Propagate by grafting. Harvest nuts late fall through spring. Hard to shell; eat out of hand or use in desserts.
Mâche (corn salad)	*Valerianella locusta*	Full sun; rich soil; keep moist	N/A	Leaf	Cool-season annual. HH. Compact, short-lived foliage plant to 9 in. tall; small leaf rosette. Delicate white flowers attract beneficial insects. Slow growing. Often reseeds. Use along stone paths, in vegetable or flower garden, or in container. Propagate from seeds. Nutty-tasting leaves great in salads, soups, and sauces.

COMMON NAME	LATIN NAME	CULTURAL CONDITIONS	USDA ZONES	EDIBLE PART	LANDSCAPE AND COOKING INFORMATION
Makrut	*Citrus hystrix*				See "Citrus" in the Encyclopedia
Mandarin orange (satsuma, tangerine)	*Citrus reticulata*				See "Citrus" in the Encyclopedia
Mango	*Mangifera indica*	Full sun; average soil; average water	10–11	Fruit	Striking, tropical evergreen tree to 60 ft. tall. Colorful fruit. Use as shade tree, screen, or interest plant. Propagate by grafting. Use immature fruit in chutneys and pickles; enjoy ripe fruit in salads and ice cream.
Maple (sugar maple)	*Acer saccharum*				See "Maple" in the Encyclopedia
Marigold (Signet marigold)	*Tagetes signata* var. *pumila*	Full sun; fast-draining, average soil; average water	N/A	Flower	Warm-season annual 6–12 in. tall. Heavily flowering; fernlike leaves. Use in flower or vegetable border, or container. Attracts beneficial insects. Gem series is tastiest. Propagate from seeds. Use citrusy tarragon-flavored flower petals in salads, eggs, and rice dishes.
Marjoram	*Origanum majorana*				See "Oregano and Marjoram" in the Encyclopedia
Marsh mallow	*Althaea officinalis*	Full sun; light soil; semi-aquatic	3–9	Leaf, root	Perennial herb to 5 ft. tall. Fuzzy leaves; small pink flowers. Rangy growth. Use in back of herb border; prune to keep neat. Propagate from seeds. Use young leaves in salads or dry for soothing tea. Extracted juice from roots long used for throat conditions; dry the roots and mix with sugar and egg whites to make the familiar candy.
Maypop (purple passionflower)	*Passiflora incarnata*	Full sun; well-drained, average soil; average water	5–10	Fruit	Hardy herbaceous perennial vine to 20 ft. long, native to southeastern U.S. Dies to ground in winter. Train on fence or arbor; contain to keep from running. Pale purple flowers to 5 in. wide are showstopping; light green, egg-shaped fruit. Propagate from seeds or cuttings. Use like passion fruit.
Medlar	*Mespilus germanica*	Full sun; average soil; average water	6–9	Fruit	Deciduous tree to 20 ft. tall. Handsome large foliage, white flowers. Use as shade or interest tree. Propagate by grafting. In late fall, let the applelike fruit ripen almost to the point of rotting, then enjoy their tropical flavor and sweetness fresh.
Melon	*Cucumis melo*				See "Melon" in the Encyclopedia
Mexican oregano	*Lippia graveolens*	Full sun; average soil; average water	10–11	Leaf	Leggy evergreen shrub to 36 in. tall. Small leaves, white flowers. Use in shrub border, container, or greenhouse. This verbena relative is most common oregano in Mexico. Propagate from seeds. Use to flavor stews and salsas. Not considered GRAS.

COMMON NAME	LATIN NAME	CULTURAL CONDITIONS	USDA ZONES	EDIBLE PART	LANDSCAPE AND COOKING INFORMATION
Millet (proso)	*Panicum miliaceum*	Full sun; average soil; average water	N/A	Seed	Warm-season annual grass to 36 in. tall. Widely adapted. Plant in spring. Propagate from seeds. See "Wheat" for landscaping uses. Use in cereals and pastries; also for chicken and bird food.
Miner's lettuce	*Claytonia perfoliata*	Full sun or partial shade; rich soil; keep moist	N/A	Leaf	Cool-season annual, western native. HH. Small upright plant with distinctive round, nasturtium-like leaves atop upright stems. Tiny flowers attract native bees. Short lived; use in vegetable or salad garden, or container. Propagate from seeds. Lemony leaves good in salads, soups, and omelets.
Mint	*Mentha* spp.				See "Mint" in the Encyclopedia
Mioga ginger	*Zingiber mioga*				See "Ginger" in the Encyclopedia
Miracle fruit	*Synsepalum dulcificum*	Partial shade; average soil; average water	10–11	Fruit	Evergreen shrub with pyramidal shape, to 20 ft. tall. Fragrant, small brown flowers; small red fruit. Needs humid conditions. Grows well in container. Propagate from seeds or cuttings. Use as a sweetener; when eaten, chemicals in the fruit change perception of sour foods to sweet.
Mitsuba (Japanese wild parsley)	*Cryptotaenia japonica*	Partial or full shade; rich soil; keep moist	6–9	Leaf, seed, stem	Herbaceous perennial to 36 in. tall. Great for herb border or container. Propagate from seeds. Celery-like taste. Add sprouts to salads; use leaves and blanched stems in soups and sukiyaki.
Mizuna	*Brassica rapa* var. *japonica*				See "Mustard" in the Encyclopedia
Monstera (split-leaf philodendron)	*Monstera deliciosa*	Partial shade; average soil; average water	10–11	Fruit	Herbaceous vine usually grown as house-plant; usually less than 10 ft. long. Dramatic with huge, deep green, cut leaves; use for tropical look in large container. Propagate from cuttings. Large segmented fruit ripens in stages, has pineapple flavor; eat fresh or in sauces. **Caution:** Do not eat unripe fruit, which is high in oxalic acid.
Mulberry	*Morus* spp.				See "Mulberry" in the Encyclopedia
Mustard (mustard greens)	*Brassica* spp.				See "Mustard" in the Encyclopedia
Nashi	*Pyrus pyrifolia*				See "Pear" in the Encyclopedia
Nasturtium	*Tropaeolum* spp.				See "Nasturtium" in the Encyclopedia
Natal plum	*Carissa macrocarpa*	Full sun; average soil; average water	10–11	Fruit	Evergreen tropical shrub. Shiny green leaves; small, fragrant, star-shaped white flowers; small red fruit. Different varieties grow from 2 to 18 ft. tall. Use short types as shrubs and ground covers, tall ones as small trees. Propagate from cuttings. Use fruit fresh or make into syrups and jam.

COMMON NAME	LATIN NAME	CULTURAL CONDITIONS	USDA ZONES	EDIBLE PART	LANDSCAPE AND COOKING INFORMATION
Nectarine	*Prunus persica* var. *nucipersica*				See "Peach and Nectarine" in the Encyclopedia
Oats, hull-less	*Avena nuda*	Full sun; average soil; average water	N/A	Seed	Cool-season annual grass to 4 ft. tall. Tolerates very cold weather. Hull-less varieties easier for home gardeners to thresh than standard oats. See "Wheat" for landscaping uses. Propagate from seeds. Use in cereals and breads.
Oca	*Oxalis tuberosa*	Full sun or partial shade; fast-draining, rich soil; average water	7–9	Tuber	Herbaceous perennial to 18 in. tall, 36 in. wide. Cloverlike leaves and flowers. Use as small-area ground cover or in container. Propagate from tubers. Bake, boil, or fry tubers.
Okra	*Abelmoschus esculentus*	Full sun; rich soil; average water	N/A	Pod	Warm-season annual. Needs heat. Upright, to 6 ft. tall; dwarf varieties available. Large tropical-looking leaves; hibiscus-type yellow flowers. Some varieties have red stems and pods. Use in herbaceous border; dwarf varieties in containers. Propagate from seeds. Fry immature pods or use in gumbo and soups.
Olive	*Olea europaea*				See "Olive" in the Encyclopedia
Onion, bulbing types including shallots, multiplier, common onion	*Allium cepa*	Full sun; rich soil; average water	N/A	Bulb, leaf	Most types grown as annuals. HH. Tubular, upright (to 18 in. tall), herbaceous. Thrips can damage the gray-green foliage, making plants look dirty. Use in herb or vegetable garden, or container. Propagate bulb onions from seeds; shallots and multipliers from offsets. Can harvest at many stages. Use young as green onions; any size bulbs for cooking. For best storage, wait until foliage dies and bulbs mature fully. Onions flavor much of the world's savory cuisine.
Orach	*Atriplex hortensis*	Full sun or partial shade; average soil; average water	N/A	Leaf	Cool-weather annual. Leaves toughen and plant bolts in hot weather. Narrow, non-branching plant to 5 ft. tall. Foliage colors include purple-red, chartreuse yellow, and shades of green. Use in back of flower or herb bed or grow as baby greens in container. Readily reseeds. Propagate from seeds. Use young tender leaves in salads, or cook like spinach.
Orange, sour	*Citrus aurantium*				See "Citrus" in the Encyclopedia
Orange, sweet	*Citrus sinensis*				See "Citrus" in the Encyclopedia
Oregano	*Origanum vulgare*				See "Oregano and Marjoram" in the Encyclopedia

COMMON NAME	LATIN NAME	CULTURAL CONDITIONS	USDA ZONES	EDIBLE PART	LANDSCAPE AND COOKING INFORMATION
Pac choi (bok choy)	*Brassica rapa* var. *chinensis*	Full sun or partial shade; rich soil; average water	N/A	Leaf, flower	Hardy biennial grown as cool-weather annual; bolts in hot weather. Short lived. Vase-shaped plant has green leaves with large white ribs; resembles chard. Purple varieties exist. Great for middle of flower border, in raised bed, as baby greens in geometric bed, or in container. Propagate from seeds. Use mild-flavored young leaves as baby greens in salads; mature leaves in stir-fries and soups. Add flowers to salads.
Papaloquelite (papalo)	*Porophyllum ruderale* ssp. *macrocephalum*	Full sun; average soil; average water	N/A	Leaf	Summer annual to 5 ft. tall. Bushy growth, round blue-green leaves, purple starburst flowers. Native from Arizona to South America. Use in back of border in mild-winter areas; great in container. Propagate from seeds. Flavor related to cilantro, but heavier. Use fresh leaves sparingly in Mexican cooking. Not considered GRAS.
Papaya	*Carica papaya*	Full sun; fast-draining, rich soil; average water	10–11	Fruit	Evergreen tree to 12 ft. tall; dwarf varieties available. Large palmate leaves 24 in. across Use as specimen plant or screen. Need male and female plants and consistently warm temperatures for best fruit production. Propagate from seeds or cuttings. Enjoy fresh fruit in salads and desserts.
Parsley	*Petroselinum crispum*				See "Parsley" in the Encyclopedia
Parsnip	*Pastinaca sativa* ssp. *sativa*	Full sun; rich, deep soil; average water	N/A	Root	Herbaceous biennial grown as annual. HH. Plant in summer for winter harvest. Avoid hot conditions. Harvesting creates empty spaces; grow in container or interplant with greens. Propagate from seeds. Boil, roast, sauté, or add root to stews.
Passion fruit (granadilla)	*Passiflora* spp.	Full sun, some shade in hottest areas; average soil; keep moist	10–11	Fruit	Rampant, twining, semi-tropical evergreen vines to 20 ft. Attractive foliage and large showy flowers. Prefers humid conditions. Use on fence or arbor. *P. edulis* and *P. ligularis* have superior fruit. Others can be invasive in mild climates. Propagate from seeds or cuttings. Eat fruit fresh or add to juices, sorbets, and sauces. Pulp freezes well.
Pawpaw	*Asimina triloba*				See "Pawpaw" in the Encyclopedia
Pea	*Pisum sativum*				See "Pea" in the Encyclopedia
Pea, asparagus (winged pea)	*Lotus tetragonolobus* (*Tetragonolobus purpureus*)	Full sun; rich soil; average water	N/A	Pod	Warm-weather annual; needs heat. Short vining plant, 12–18 in. tall. Beanlike deep red flowers. Use in hanging baskets and in front of flower beds. Propagate from seeds. Enjoy whole young pods (less than 1 in.) raw in salads; cook in stews and curries.

COMMON NAME	LATIN NAME	CULTURAL CONDITIONS	USDA ZONES	EDIBLE PART	LANDSCAPE AND COOKING INFORMATION
Pea, black-eyed (cow pea)	*Vigna unguiculata*	Full sun; rich soil; average water	N/A	Seed	Warm-season annual. Sprawling, heat-loving, bushy, undistinguished plant to 36 in. tall. Use in raised bed or vegetable garden. Propagate from seeds. Cook fresh or dry the peas; use in soups and stews.
Peach	*Prunus persica* var. *persica*				See "Peach and Nectarine" in the Encyclopedia
Peanut (goober)	*Arachis hypogaea*	Full sun; light, rich soil; average water	N/A	Seed	Warm-season annual. Needs long, warm summer. Compact plant to 24 in. tall. Attractive leaves and yellow flowers. Grow as temporary ground cover or in large container. Must have light soil so flowering pegs can burrow into the ground to form "nuts." Propagate from seeds. Boil raw nuts as vegetable and serve with rice; eat roasted nuts out of hand, make into butter, or add to pastries.
Pear	*Pyrus* spp.				See "Pear" in the Encyclopedia
Pecan	*Carya illinoinensis*				See "Pecan and Hickory" in the Encyclopedia
Pepino	Pepino dulce	Full sun; average soil; average water	10–11	Fruit	Perennial tomato-like plant to 36 in. tall. Grow in vegetable garden or container. Propagate from cuttings. The 3-in. yellow- and purple-striped fruit has a melon-cucumber flavor; peel and add fresh to fruit and green salads.
Pepper, black	*Piper nigrum*	Partial shade; average soil; keep moist	10–11	Fruit	Evergreen trailing vine to 30 ft. Give warm, humid conditions; good for container or greenhouse. Propagate from seeds and cuttings. Grind dried fruit for classic seasoning.
Pepper, sweet and chili	*Capsicum* spp.				See "Pepper" in the Encyclopedia
Peppermint	*Mentha × piperita*				See "Mint" in the Encyclopedia
Perilla (shiso)	*Perilla frutescens* (*P. nankinensis*)	Full sun; average soil; average water	N/A	Leaf	Warm-season annual to 36 in. tall. Striking plant with broad, textured leaves; red and green varieties available. Use in flower, foliage, or herb border, or container. Can be invasive. Propagate from seeds. Use spicy leaves in Japanese soups and pickled ginger. Not considered GRAS.
Persimmon	*Diospyros* spp.				See "Persimmon" in the Encyclopedia
Pestle parsnip (barestem biscuitroot)	*Lomatium nudicaule*	Full sun; average soil; average moisture	6–9	Leaf, seed, root, stem	Herbaceous perennial to 24 in. tall, western native. Small yellow flowers. Plant in meadow, along paths, or with other natives. Propagate from seeds. Eat root raw or dried; spicy parsnip flavor. Cook leaves and young shoots in spring. Use leaves and stems for tea; seeds for seasoning.

COMMON NAME	LATIN NAME	CULTURAL CONDITIONS	USDA ZONES	EDIBLE PART	LANDSCAPE AND COOKING INFORMATION
Pineapple	*Ananas comosus*	Full sun or partial shade; fast-draining soil; keep moist	10–11	Fruit	Herbaceous tropical succulent. Sword-shaped leaves in rosette to 36 in. tall; dwarf available. Fruit is borne on top. Use with other bromeliads, as pine barren understory plant, in container, or in greenhouse. Propagate from leafy top of commercial pineapple. Place in damp sand; once rooted, transplant to potting soil. Takes 2 years to fruit. Eat fresh, cooked, in sauces; dry for snacks.
Pineapple guava	*Acca sellowiana* (*Feijoa sellowiana*)				See "Pineapple guava" in the Encyclopedia
Pineapple sage	*Salvia rutilans* (*S. elegans*)				See "Sage" in the Encyclopedia
Pine nut (pignoli and piñon)	*Pinus* spp.	Full sun or partial shade; fast-draining, average soil; drought tolerant	3–10	Seed	Conifers. Many pine species yield tasty nuts. Most familiar are Italian stone pine, *P. pinea,* to 60 ft. tall, and shrubby North American native piñon, *P. edulis,* to 10 ft. tall. Two trees needed for cross-pollination. Use as shade trees, as windbreak, or in xeriscape garden. Attract birds and native animals. Propagate from seeds. Roast the nuts and eat out of hand or add to salads, pesto, candies, and stews.
Pinks (clove pinks)	*Dianthus caryophyllus*	Full sun; fast-draining, average soil; average water	5–9	Flower	Herbaceous perennial to 14 in. tall. Silver leaves; fragrant pink or white flowers. Use along paths or in herb garden, flower bed, or container. Propagate from divisions. Use clove-scented flower petals in sorbets, cold drinks, and fruit salads.
Pistachio	*Pistacia vera*	Full sun; average soil; average water	7–9	Nut	Deciduous tree to 30 ft. tall. Best in areas with low humidity. Use as screen or street tree. Male and female trees needed for pollination. Roast the nuts and eat out of hand or add to ice creams and pastries.
Plantain	*Musa* spp.				See "Banana and Plantain" in the Encyclopedia
Plum	*Prunus* spp.				See "Plum" in the Encyclopedia
Pomegranate	*Punica granatum*				See "Pomegranate" in the Encyclopedia
Pomelo (pommelo, shaddock)	*Citrus maxima*				See "Citrus" in the Encyclopedia
Poppy, breadseed	*Papaver somniferum*	Full sun; average soil; average water	N/A	Seed	Cool-season annual to 36 in. tall. HH. Gray-green foliage; mauve, white, or red flowers, showy, to 3 in. across. Seedpods dramatic, illegal in some jurisdictions. Propagate from seeds. Use seeds in breads and salad dressings.

COMMON NAME	LATIN NAME	CULTURAL CONDITIONS	USDA ZONES	EDIBLE PART	LANDSCAPE AND COOKING INFORMATION
Potato	*Solanum tuberosum*	Full sun; fast-draining, rich, deep soil; keep moist	N/A	Tuber	Perennial grown as annual in most climates. Not hardy. Widely adapted and grown in most of North America. Sprawling plant to 24 in. tall. Ornamental, dark green leaves; small white or purple flowers. For vegetable garden, great in large container. Wait until foliage dies back to harvest. Propagate from tubers. Bake, boil, fry, or mash potatoes, use in soups and stews.
Prickly pear	*Opuntia* spp. *(Nopalea* spp.)	Full sun; average soil; drought tolerant	6–11	Pad, fruit	Cactus to 15 ft. tall. Thorny pads, showy yellow flowers. Use as specimen or barrier plant; good for xeriscape garden, desert garden. Propagate from cuttings. Harvest young pads in spring and fruit in summer. Remove spines from pads, slice, boil like string beans until tender, drain, and add to soups or scrambled eggs, or combine with chopped tomatoes, herbs, and lime juice. Round, red fruit is seedy with a fruity, citrusy flavor; eat fresh or use in sorbets and drinks.
Pumpkin	*Cucurbita* spp.				See "Squash and Pumpkin" in the Encyclopedia
Purslane	*Portulaca oleracea*	Full sun or partial shade; rich soil; average water	N/A	Leaf	Warm-season annual. Succulent plant to 18 in. tall. Culinary varieties related to weedy one. Use in annual bed, vegetable garden, or container. Propagate from seeds. High in omega-3 oils. Add young leaves to salads; cook mature greens like spinach.
Quince (European quince)	*Cydonia oblonga*				See "Quince" in the Encyclopedia
Quince, flowering	*Chaenomeles* spp.				See "Quince" in the Encyclopedia
Quinoa	*Chenopodium quinoa*	Full sun; average soil; average water	N/A	Seed	Warm-season annual to 5 ft. tall. Related to lamb's-quarter and grows similarly. Beautiful fall color. Use in back of border with sunflowers and amaranth. Propagate from seeds. Pseudo-grain high in protein. Cook for cereal and pilaf; grind into flour and add to bread.
Radicchio and chicory	*Cichorium intybus*	Full sun or partial shade; rich soil; average water	N/A	Leaf	Hardy herbaceous perennials grown as annuals, to 12 in. tall. Radicchio has green or red foliage. 'Chioggia' grows rosette of leaves—green in summer, red head in fall or late spring. Less familiar chicory grows upright like Romaine lettuce or has straplike leaves. Use both in vegetable or flower border, or container. Propagate from seeds. Roast leaves as side dish; enjoy slightly bitter inner leaves raw in salads.

COMMON NAME	LATIN NAME	CULTURAL CONDITIONS	USDA ZONES	EDIBLE PART	LANDSCAPE AND COOKING INFORMATION
Radish and daikon	*Raphanus sativus*	Full sun or partial shade; rich, fast-draining soil; average water	N/A	Root, flower	Cool-season annual. HH. Short, clumping plant to 12 in. tall. Plant radishes between slower-growing peppers and tomatoes, or in fall interplant with sweet alyssum and spring bulbs and harvest before winter sets in. Daikons are larger and slow growing. Plant most varieties in late summer. Propagate from seeds. Eat roots raw or add to stews and stir-fries.
Rapini (broccoli raab)	*B. rapa* var. *rapa*				See "Broccoli and Cauliflower" in the Encyclopedia
Raspberry	*Rubus* spp.				See "Brambleberry" in the Encyclopedia
Redbud	*Cercis* spp.	Full sun or partial shade; light, fast-draining soil; average water	Zones vary	Flower	Deciduous shrubs or trees. Dramatic magenta flowers in spring, handsome summer foliage, fall color. Use as specimen plants or mass in background. *C. canadensis* (to 30 ft. tall) and *C. occidentalis* (to 18 ft. tall) are native to North America. Propagate from seeds. Add crunchy flowers to salads and pasta, or float on drinks.
Rhubarb	*Rheum rhabarbarum*				See "Rhubarb" in the Encyclopedia
Rice, cultivated	*Oryza sativa*	Full sun; rich soil; keep moist; can take poor drainage	N/A	Seed	Warm-season annual grass to 36 in. tall. Growing rice in water eliminates most weeds, but many varieties don't need to be flooded. Propagate from seeds. See "Wheat" for landscaping uses. Rice is one of the world's staple foods and has hundreds of uses.
Rice, wild; annual wild rice	*Zizania aquatica*	Full sun; average soil; aquatic	N/A	Seed	Warm-season annual grass to 10 ft. tall. Must grow in running water at least a foot deep. Landscape use limited to lakes and streamsides. Usually harvested from a boat in late summer. Propagate from seeds planted in spring or fall. Use wild rice in cereal or mix with other rice types in side dish or stuffing.
Rose (rose hips)	*Rosa* spp.				See "Rose" in the Encyclopedia
Rosemary	*Rosmarinus officinalis*				See "Rosemary" in the Encyclopedia
Rutabaga (swede)	*Brassica napus* ssp. *rapifera*	Full sun; rich, deep soil; average water	N/A	Root	Cool-season annual. HH. Clumping plant to 20 in. tall. Interplant with flowering annuals. Propagate from seeds. Roast the roots or add to stews and soups.
Rye, cereal	*Secale cereale*	Full sun; average soil; average water	N/A	Seed	Cool-season annual grass to 4 ft. tall. Very hardy. Propagate from seeds. See "Wheat" for landscape uses. Grind rye "berries" for flour to use in breads and pastries. Boil whole "berries" and use for cereal or add to pilaf and grain salads.

COMMON NAME	LATIN NAME	CULTURAL CONDITIONS	USDA ZONES	EDIBLE PART	LANDSCAPE AND COOKING INFORMATION
Safflower (false saffron)	*Carthamus tinctorius*	Full sun; average soil; average water	N/A	Seed, flower, shoot	Warm-season annual. Upright to 36 in. tall. Spiny leaves, orange to yellow flowers. Use in middle of annual border or in cutting garden for dried flowers. Propagate from seeds. Use young shoots in salads; roast seeds and eat out of hand (seeds also used for oil); sprinkle flower petals over salad and rice. Not considered GRAS.
Saffron	*Crocus sativus*	Full sun; average soil; average water	6–9	Stigma of flower	Grasslike herbaceous bulbing plant to 4 in. tall. Large mauve flowers. Use in rock garden, flower border, herb garden, gravel planting, or container. Start from corms. Dry the stigmas and use as seasoning in savory dishes and with rice. **Caution:** Do not confuse true edible saffron with poisonous autumn crocus.
Sage	*Salvia* spp.				See "Sage" in the Encyclopedia
Salad burnet	*Sanguisorba minor* (*Poterium sanguisorba*)	Full sun; average soil; average water	5–9	Leaf	Herbaceous perennial to 18 in. tall. Distinctive leaves grow in a rosette; flowers insignificant. Can become a weed. Use in herb or flower garden. Propagate from seeds. Use young cucumber-flavored leaves in salads, sauces, and soft cheeses. Not considered GRAS.
Salal	*Gaultheria shallon*	Partial shade; average soil; average water	6–9	Fruit	Evergreen shrub 3–10 ft. tall. Small leaves, attractive white to pink flowers, black berries. Use as hedge or in shrub border or container. Propagate from seeds or cuttings. Harvest in summer. Cook berries, sieve, and use juice as a base for sauce for game; make into wine.
Sand cherry, western	*Prunus besseyi*				See "Plum" in the Encyclopedia
Sapote (mamey sapote)	*Pouteria sapota*	Full sun; fast-draining, average soil; keep moist	10–11	Fruit	Evergreen or deciduous tree 40–60 ft. tall. Big leaves to 12 in. long. Interesting large, brown-skinned fruit. Use as shade tree or screen. Propagate from seeds or by grafting. Enjoy fresh fruit out of hand, make into jam, or add frozen pulp to ice creams and shakes.
Sapote, black	*Diospyros digyna*	Full sun; average soil; average water	10–11	Fruit	Evergreen tree to 80 ft. tall. Glossy leaves. Use as shade tree or screen. Propagate from seeds. When ripe, fruit is greenish brown, soft, and filled with dark brown, soft flesh; eat fresh or add to desserts and smoothies.
Sapote, white	*Casimiroa edulis*	Full sun; average soil; average water	9–11	Fruit	Evergreen tree 20–50 ft. tall. Use as shade tree or screen. Propagate from seeds and by grafting. Light green fruit about 2 in. across, custardy when ripe. Usually eaten fresh out of hand.

COMMON NAME	LATIN NAME	CULTURAL CONDITIONS	USDA ZONES	EDIBLE PART	LANDSCAPE AND COOKING INFORMATION
Savory, summer	*Satureja hortensis*	Full sun; average soil; average water	N/A	Leaf, flower	Warm-season annual. Small, upright, bushy growth to 18 in. tall. Small lavender flowers. Use in herb garden, flower bed, or container. Propagate from seeds. Use leaves with beans, salad dressings, and soups; flowers in salads.
Savory, winter	*Satureja montana*	Full sun; average soil; average water	6–9	Leaf, flower	Upright, green-leaved shrub to 18 in. tall. Small white flowers attract beneficial insects. Use in herb garden or container. Creeping variety is great for container and to cascade over wall. Propagate from seeds and divisions. Use like summer savory.
Sea berry	*Hippophae rhamnoides*	Full sun or partial shade; average soil; good drainage	3–9	Fruit	Upright, weeping deciduous shrub 8–15 ft. tall. Silver foliage, dramatic clusters of gold berries. Need male and female plants for pollination. Grow in large shrub planting or as screen or hedgerow. Propagate from seeds and cuttings. Harvest in fall. Use nutritious berries for juice.
Sea grape	*Coccoloba uvifera*	Full sun; average soil; average water	10–11	Fruit	Evergreen tree or shrub 20–40 ft. tall, Florida native. Large decorative leaves and attractive fruit. Use in seaside garden or as windbreak, hedge, or interest tree. Propagate from seeds or by layering. Use berries for preserves and syrup.
Sea kale	*Crambe maritima*	Full sun; rich soil but tolerates alkaline; average water	5–9	Leaf, shoot, root	Herbaceous perennial with lovely large gray leaves to 24 in. Tolerates seacoast conditions. Use in seaside garden, perennial border, or container. Propagate from seeds, divisions, or root cuttings. Cover new shoots in spring to blanch, then harvest shoots. Steam or boil shoots and serve like asparagus. Add young leaves to salads or cook like spinach. Eat root raw or cooked.
Serviceberry (Juneberry)	*Amelanchier* spp.	Full sun or partial shade; average soil; average water	3–8	Fruit	Deciduous native North American shrubs. White spring flowers, blue or red summer fruit, great fall foliage. Varieties were selected for ornamental value, not culinary, but some (*A. laevis*, to 30 ft. tall, and *A. arborea*, to 25 ft. tall) have red or deep purple fruit delicious eaten out of hand, on cereal, or in jams or pies. Use as hedge or train as small tree. Propagate from seeds.
Sesame	*Sesamum indicum*	Full sun; rich soil; average water	N/A	Seed	Warm-weather annual. Needs long season. Upright to 36 in tall. Pleasant foliage, white flowers. Use in back of herbaceous border or large container. Propagate from organic seeds purchased at the market. Eat seeds raw or roasted; add to stir-fries, sushi, rice, and vegetable dishes.

COMMON NAME	LATIN NAME	CULTURAL CONDITIONS	USDA ZONES	EDIBLE PART	LANDSCAPE AND COOKING INFORMATION
Shungiku (garland chrysanthemum)	*Chrysanthemum coronarium*	Full sun or partial shade; average soil; average water	N/A	Leaf, flower	Herbaceous annual chrysanthemum 24–36 in. tall. Many 1-in. yellow flowers. Prefers cool to mild weather. Use in flower border or container. Propagate from seeds. Use young leaves in stir-fries and hot pot; add flower petals to salads or dry them for tea.
Silverbeet (chard)	*Beta vulgaris* ssp. *vulgaris*				See "Chard" in the Encyclopedia
Society garlic	*Tulbaghia violacea*				See "Chives" in the Encyclopedia
Sorghum	*Sorghum bicolor*	Full sun; average soil; average water	N/A	Seed	Warm-season grasslike annual to 8 ft. tall. See "Corn" for landscape uses. Propagate from seeds. Pop the seeds or use them to make a sweet syrup.
Sorrel, common (garden sorrel)	*Rumex acetosa*	Full sun or partial shade; average soil; average water	5–9	Leaf	Herbaceous clumping perennial. Grows vigorously to 24 in. tall. Sword-shaped leaves to 6 in. long; tall, nondescript brown flower spikes. Can be invasive. Use in herb garden, raised bed, container; along woodland path. Propagate from seeds or divisions. Leaves have strong sour lemon flavor; use sparingly in salads, sauces for fish, and soups.
Sorrel, French (true French sorrel)	*Rumex scutatus*	Full sun or partial shade; average soil; average water	3–10	Leaf	Semi-vining herbaceous perennial to 6 in. tall. Shield-shaped, 1-in. leaves grow along supple stems. Use in herb garden, flower bed, raised bed, container; along woodland path. Can become invasive. Propagate from seeds or divisions. Less assertive lemon-flavored leaves; use like common sorrel.
Soybean (edamame)	*Glycine max*	Full sun; average soil; average water	N/A	Seed	Warm-season annual 2–6 ft. tall. Hairy stems and leaves; undistinguished looking. Select vegetable (not field) types; green or black varieties. Good in vegetable garden or wine barrel. Propagate from seeds. Boil whole fresh pods in salted water as snack; shell and add to rice dishes, soups, and salads.
Spearmint	*Mentha spicata*				See "Mint" in the Encyclopedia
Spinach	*Spinacia oleracea*	Full to part sun; rich soil; average water	N/A	Leaf	Cool-season annual to 12 in. tall. HH. Rosette of dark green leaves—smooth or savoyed, depending on variety. Contrasts nicely with frilly lettuces, carrots, and ruffled blue-green kale. Use in salad or herb garden, or containers. Propagate from seeds. Use leaves raw in salads; cook as side dish or add to soups, sauces, and pasta.
Spinach, Malabar	*Basella alba*	Full sun; rich soil; average water	9–11	Leaf	Tender perennial vine grown as warm-season annual, to 4 ft. long. Heat loving, fleshy leaved. Green and purple varieties available. Use in hanging basket, planter box, or other large container. Propagate from seeds. Use like spinach.

COMMON NAME	LATIN NAME	CULTURAL CONDITIONS	USDA ZONES	EDIBLE PART	LANDSCAPE AND COOKING INFORMATION
Spinach, New Zealand	*Tetragonia tetragonoides*	Full sun or partial shade; average soil; average water	N/A	Leaf	Tender annual vine to 24 in. Triangular, fleshy, 2-in. leaves; insignificant flowers. Grows well in hot weather. Let sprawl along the ground or cascade from container. Propagate from seeds. Enjoy as a spinach substitute.
Squash (summer and winter)	*Cucurbita* spp.				See "Squash and Pumpkin" in the Encyclopedia
Stevia (sweet leaf, sugarleaf)	*Stevia rebaudiana*	Full sun; sandy soil; average water	9–11	Leaf	Tender perennial to 16 in. tall. Trim flowers to maintain new leaf production. Good in container. Propagate from seeds or cuttings. Contains stevioside, which is 300 times sweeter than sugar. Use leaves fresh or dried and ground as sweetener.
Strawberry	*Fragaria* spp.				See "Strawberry" in the Encyclopedia
Strawberry tree	*Arbutus unedo*	Full sun or light shade; average soil; average water	8–11	Fruit	Evergreen tree to 30 ft. tall. Attractive pinkish flowers, showy orange and scarlet fruit of variable quality. Use as screen, multistemmed tree, or interest plant. Propagate from cuttings. Harvest in fall. Seedy, insipid fruit eaten fresh or made into jam.
Sunflower	*Helianthus annuus*	Full sun; average soil; average water	N/A	Seed	Warm-season annual. Upright growth to 10 ft. tall. Giant yellow flowers; some varieties are top-heavy. Dwarf varieties to 5 ft. tall. Use in back of flower gardens. Propagate from seeds. Eat seeds raw or toasted as snacks or grind for molés.
Surinam cherry (pitanga)	*Eugenia uniflora* (*E. michelii*)	Full sun; average soil; average water	10–11	Fruit	Evergreen shrub or small tree 10–30 ft. tall. Showy red or yellow fruit. Use as hedge, screen, or multistemmed specimen. Can become invasive in Florida. Propagate from seeds or cuttings. Eat fruit raw; use in jams or juices.
Sweet bay (bay laurel)	*Laurus nobilis*				See "Sweet bay" in the Encyclopedia
Sweet cicely	*Myrrhis odorata*	Partial or full shade; rich soil; keep moist	5–9	Leaf, seed	Perennial herb to 6 ft. tall. Does poorly in hot climates. Let delicate fernlike leaves and small white flowers in umbels grace woodland path or add softness to back of shady herb border. Propagate from seeds. Add young leaves sparingly to salads; use anise-flavored seeds in pastries and liquors. Not considered GRAS.
Sweet potato (yam)	*Ipomoea batatas*				See "Sweet potato" in the Encyclopedia
Sweet woodruff	*Galium odoratum*	Full sun or partial shade; average soil; average water	5–9	Leaf, flower	Low-growing perennial to 12 in. tall. Lovely deep green leaves, clusters of tiny white flowers. Use as shade ground cover, under blueberries, or in woodland planting. May be invasive. Propagate from division or seeds. Drying leaves and flowers for 1 day develops vanilla flavor. Use lightly in May wine or custard. **Caution:** Acts as blood thinner so should be used sparingly.

COMMON NAME	LATIN NAME	CULTURAL CONDITIONS	USDA ZONES	EDIBLE PART	LANDSCAPE AND COOKING INFORMATION
Swiss chard	*Beta vulgaris* ssp. *vulgaris*				See "Chard" in the Encyclopedia
Tamarind	*Tamarindus indica*	Full sun; average soil; drought tolerant	10–11	Pod	Evergreen tree 15–25 ft. tall. Ornamental pinnate leaves and yellow flowers. Use as shade tree. Propagate from seeds or by air layering or grafting. Needs arid conditions for fruit to mature. Harvest pods in early summer and eat pulp fresh or dehydrated; the sweet acidic flavor is used in South American and Asian dishes.
Tangelo (mandarin hybrids)	*Citrus* × *tangelo*				See "Citrus" in the Encyclopedia
Taro	*Colocasia esculenta*	Full sun or partial shade; average soil; keep moist	9–11	Corm	Tropical herbaceous perennial with large elephant-ear leaves. There are two types of taros: wetland and upland. Use in foliage border, bog garden, container, or greenhouse. Can spread and be invasive near wild waterways. Propagate from corms. Serve steamed, boiled, and fried. **Caution:** Raw taro corms are toxic; cook before eating.
Tarragon, French	*Artemisia dracunculus*	Full sun; average soil; average water	5–8	Leaf	Creeping, narrow-leaved, floppy perennial to 24 in. tall. Use in herb garden or container. Propagate from cuttings (not seeds). Use anise-flavored leaves for chicken and fish dishes; for sauces, dressings, and green and potato salads.
Tarragon, Mexican (Mexican mint marigold)	*Tagetes lucida*	Full sun; average soil; average water	9–10	Leaf, flower	Upright perennial to 36 in. tall. Small, yellow, marigold-like flowers in fall. Use plants mid-border or in container. Propagate from divisions or cuttings. Use intense tarragon flavor in moderation in tea or sprinkle flower petals on salads. Not considered GRAS.
Tea	*Camellia sinensis*				See "Tea" in the Encyclopedia
Thyme	*Thymus* spp.				See "Thyme" in the Encyclopedia
Tomatillo (husk tomato)	*Physalis philadelphica* (*P. ixocarpa*)	Full sun; average soil; average water	N/A	Fruit	Warm-season annual. Upright, to 4 ft. tall. Awkward; tends to sprawl, needs staking. Propagate from seeds. See "Tomato" for landscape uses. Remove husk and cook fruit. Use in spicy green salsa, pork stew, and many traditional Mexican dishes.
Tomato	*Solanum lycopersicum* (*Lycopersicon esculentum*)				See "Tomato" in the Encyclopedia
Tree tomato	*Solanum betaceum* (*Cyphomandra betacea*)	Full sun; average soil; average water	10–11	Fruit	Evergreen shrub or small tree 10–20 ft. tall. Large leaves, colorful 3-in. fruit, but awkward form. Use in back of border, container or greenhouse. Propagate from seeds or by grafting. Eat fruit fresh out of hand or peel and add to fruit salads or stews.

COMMON NAME	LATIN NAME	CULTURAL CONDITIONS	USDA ZONES	EDIBLE PART	LANDSCAPE AND COOKING INFORMATION
Tulip	*Tulipa* spp.	Full sun; well-drained, rich soil; average water	4–9	Flower	Elegant bulbing plants. Use as accent in late-winter garden; best massed. Underplant with salad greens or pansies. Propagate from organically grown bulbs. Remove flower petals and use in salads and as appetizer stuffed with goat cheese.
Turmeric	*Curcuma longa*	Partial shade; average soil; average water	9–11	Rhizome	Tropical herbaceous plant to 5 ft. tall. Large swordlike leaves. Use like canna in tropical border or grow in container. Grow and propagate like ginger. Boil, cure, and dry rhizomes; use to color and flavor curries and mustard pickles.
Turnip	*Brassica rapa* ssp. *rapa*	Full sun; rich, deep soil; average water	N/A	Leaf, root	Biennial grown as cool-season annual. HH. Short, clumping plant to 18 in. tall. Harvesting creates empty spaces; grow in container or interplant with pansies. Propagate from seeds. Roast, bake, or boil the roots; also use in stews and side dishes. Use young leaves in soups.
Ume	*Prunus mume*				See "Apricot" in the Encyclopedia
Viola, pansy, Johnny jump-up	*Viola cornuta,* *V. × wittrockiana,* *V. tricolor*	Full sun or partial shade; average soil; average water	N/A	Flower	Cool-season annuals to 10 in. tall. Free flowering in many colors. Great in masses and containers. Propagate from seeds. Plant among greens to add color. Use flower petals in salads and candied.
Violet	*Viola odorata*	Full sun or partial shade; average soil; average water	4–9	Flower, leaf	Herbaceous perennial to 10 in. tall. Spring blooming. Great in container, but can become a weed if allowed to go to seed. Propagate from seeds or divisions. Add young leaves to salads; candy the flowers.
Walnut	*Juglans* spp.				See "Walnut" in the Encyclopedia
Wasabi	*Wasabia japonica* (*Eutrema japonica*)	Partial or full shade; rich soil; aquatic	8–9	Rhizome, leaf, stem	Upright herbaceous perennial to 18 in. tall. Handsome round leaves. Fussy about growing conditions; prefers shady, moist site with slightly running water. Can be grown hydroponically. Purchase from specialty grower. Propagate from rhizomes. Grated rhizome is used to give horseradish flavor to fish and noodles in Japan; some Western cooks add it to sauces and mayonnaise. Leaves and stems can be pickled. Not considered GRAS.
Water chestnut	*Eleocharis dulcis*	Full sun; rich, organic soil; aquatic	7–11	Corm	Herbaceous reedlike water plant to 36 in. tall. Use in decorative pond or container with no drainage. Propagate from corms from Asian grocery store in spring or order from water-plant nursery. See "Lotus" for planting and growing. Harvest corms and peel; use sweet crunchy flesh in stir-fries, salads, and soups.

COMMON NAME	LATIN NAME	CULTURAL CONDITIONS	USDA ZONES	EDIBLE PART	LANDSCAPE AND COOKING INFORMATION
Watercress	*Nasturtium officinale*	Full sun; rich, organic soil; keep very moist or in potable running water	6–9	Leaf	Semi-aquatic perennial to 6 in. tall. Attractive foliage and small white flower similar to alyssum. Landscape use limited to streamside or container with no drainage. Can become invasive in streamside habitat. Propagate from seeds or cuttings. Watercress leaves have a peppery taste; enjoy in salads, sandwiches, and soups.
Watermelon	*Citrullus lanatus* var. *lanatus*				See "Melon" in the Encyclopedia
Wheat	*Triticum* spp.				See "Wheat" in the Encyclopedia
Wintergreen	*Gaultheria procumbens*	Partial or full shade; average soil; keep moist	4–9	Leaf, fruit	Ornamental creeping woody plant 6 in. tall. Dark green, shiny leaves turn red in fall; white flowers in summer and scarlet berries in late fall. Prefers cool conditions. Use as ground cover in shade. Propagate from cuttings or rooted suckers. Use wintergreen-flavored leaves and berries in tea; fruit in jam and as flavoring for candy.
Yacon	*Smallanthus sonchifolius* (*Polymnia sonchifolia*)	Full sun; average soil; average water	7–9	Tuber	Herbaceous perennial to 5 ft. tall. Large light green leaves and small yellow daisies good in back of flower border. Harvest crispy, large storage tubers for food; save small tubers for propagation. Use sweet taste of yacon cooked in curries; peel and use raw in slaws and salads.
Yam	*Ipomoea batatas*				See "Sweet potato" in the Encyclopedia
Yerba buena	*Satureja douglasii*	Full sun; afternoon shade in warm climates; average soil; some drought tolerance	7–9	Leaf	Ground-hugging tender perennial. Non-invasive, mint-flavored herb native to West Coast. Use in herb garden, as ground cover, or let drape from a hanging basket. Propagate from rooted runners. Popular tea herb. Not considered GRAS.
Yucca	*Yucca filamentosa*	Full sun; average to sandy soil; drought tolerant	4–10	Flower	Hardy evergreen perennial to 36 in. tall, with swordlike leaves to 18 in. Creamy white flowers along single tall stem that rises above foliage in summer. Use as specimen plant in border, rock garden, or container. Propagate from seeds and offshoots. Sauté flower petals for garnishes or to add to salads and soups.

Edible Plants for the Small Garden

The chart below lists edible plants that I recommend for small gardens. I chose varieties that are the most manageable, are compact, or produce the largest harvest in the least amount of space. Many of these edibles are ideal for containers. More information about these plants can be found in the Encyclopedia and Appendix A.

NAME	FORM	EXPOSURE	FOLIAGE SIZE	ESPALIER OR TRAIN ON A FENCE	RECOM- MENDED SIZE	PATIO TREE	MINIMUM CONTAINER SIZE*	RECOMMENDED VARIETIES OR TYPES
Almond	Tree	Full sun	Medium	Espalier	Dwarf	Yes	Large	Dwarf varieties
Apple	Tree	Full sun	Medium	Espalier	Dwarf, semi-dwarf, columnar	Yes	Large	Dwarf, semi-dwarf, and columnar varieties
Apricot	Tree	Full sun	Medium	Espalier	Semi-dwarf	No	Large	Semi-dwarf varieties
Artichoke	Tender herbaceous perennial	Full sun, partial shade	Large	No	All	No	Large	All varieties
Avocado	Tree	Full sun	Medium	No	Dwarf	Yes	Large	'Gwen' and 'Don Gillogly'
Bamboo	Perennial evergreen grass	Full sun, partial shade	Medium to large	No	All	No	Large	All types; dwarf varieties for containers
Banana	Tender herbaceous perennial	Full sun	Very large	No	Compact	Yes	Large	'Dwarf Cavendish', 'Dwarf Red Jamaica'
Basil	Annual/ tender perennial herb	Full sun, partial shade	Small	No	All	No	Small	All varieties
Bean	Annual vegetable	Full sun	Medium	Train (pole types)	All	No	Large	All types
Blueberry	Shrub	Full sun, partial shade	Small	Train (rabbiteyes)	All	No	Large	All varieties; 'Tophat' miniature; 'Sunshine Blue' compact
Brambleberry	Biennial canes	Full sun, partial shade	Small to medium	Espalier or train	All	No	No	'Black Satin' blackberry easiest to control
Broccoli	Annual vegetable	Full sun, partial shade	Large	No	All	No	Medium	All varieties
Cabbage	Annual vegetable	Full sun, partial shade	Large	No	All	No	Medium	All varieties
Caper	Shrub	Full sun	Small	No	All	No	Medium	All varieties
Cauliflower	Annual vegetable	Full sun, partial shade	Large	No	All	No	Medium	All varieties

* Small—6-in. diameter and height; Medium—12-in. diameter and height; Large—24-in. diameter and height

NAME	FORM	EXPOSURE	FOLIAGE SIZE	ESPALIER OR TRAIN ON A FENCE	RECOM-MENDED SIZE	PATIO TREE	MINIMUM CONTAINER SIZE*	RECOMMENDED VARIETIES OR TYPES
Chamomile	Annual/perennial herb	Full sun, partial shade	Small	No	All	No	Medium	All types
Chard	Annual vegetable	Full sun	Large	No	All	No	Medium	All varieties
Cherry	Tree	Full sun	Medium	No	Compact	No	Large	'North Star' (dwarf sour cherry), 'Sweetheart' (sweet cherry)
Chives	Perennial herb	Full sun, partial shade	Small	No	All	No	Small	All types
Citrus	Tree, shrub	Full sun, partial shade	Medium	Espalier or train	Dwarf	Yes	Large	Dwarf varieties need constant pruning to keep compact
Cranberry	Shrub, woody vines	Full sun, partial shade	Small	No	All	No	Large	All types
Cucumber	Annual vegetable	Full sun	Medium	Train (some varieties)	All	No	Medium	All vining cukes on fence; 'Bush Pickle', 'Spacemaster', and other bush types best for containers
Currant	Shrub	Full sun, partial shade	Small	Espalier or train	All	No	Large	All varieties
Eggplant	Annual vegetable	Full sun	Medium	No	All	No	Medium	'Fairy Tale' and 'Dusky' excellent for very small spaces
Endive	Annual vegetable	Full sun, partial shade	Large	No	All	No	Small	All varieties
Fig	Tree	Full sun	Large	Espalier	Semi-dwarf	No	Large	'Violette de Bordeaux', 'Hardy Chicago', and 'Texas Everbearing' most compact; all can be kept small
Ginger	Tender perennial	Partial or full shade	Small	No	All	No	Medium	All types
Gooseberry	Shrub	Full sun, partial shade	Small	Espalier or train	All	No	Large	All varieties
Grape	Woody vine	Full sun	Large	Espalier or train	All	No	Large	All varieties
Hops	Perennial vine	Full sun	Large	Train	All	No	Large	All varieties
Kale	Annual vegetable	Full sun, partial shade	Large	No	All	No	Medium	All varieties
Kiwi	Woody vine	Full sun, partial shade	Medium	Train	All	No	No	All varieties
Leek	Annual vegetable	Full sun, partial shade	Medium	No	All	No	Medium	All varieties

NAME	FORM	EXPOSURE	FOLIAGE SIZE	ESPALIER OR TRAIN ON A FENCE	RECOM-MENDED SIZE	PATIO TREE	MINIMUM CONTAINER SIZE*	RECOMMENDED VARIETIES OR TYPES
Lettuce	Annual vegetable	Full sun, partial shade	Large	No	All	No	Small	All varieties; for very small areas use 'Bibb', 'Tom Thumb', 'Deer Tongue'
Lingonberry	Shrub	Full sun, partial shade	Small	No	All	No	Large	All types
Lotus	Herbaceous perennial	Full sun	Very large	No	All	No	Large	All varieties
Marjoram	Perennial herb	Full sun	Small	No	All	No	Medium	All types
Melon	Annual fruit	Full sun	Medium	Train (small-fruited varieties)	Midget varieties	No	Large	'Minnesota Midget' canta-loupe, icebox watermelon varieties
Mint	Perennial herb	Full sun, partial shade	Small	No	All	No	Small	All types
Mustard	Annual	Full sun, partial shade	Small to very large	No	All	No	Medium	All types
Nasturtium	Annual herb	Full sun, partial shade	Medium	Train (vining types)	All	No	Medium	All varieties; dwarf varieties best for small areas and containers
Natal plum	Shrub	Full sun	Small	Espalier or train	Small and dwarf varieties	No	Medium	'Fancy' and 'Tuttle' (dwarf)
Nectarine	Tree	Full sun	Medium	Espalier	Dwarf, semi-dwarf	No	Large	Dwarf and semi-dwarf
Okra	Annual vegetable	Full sun	Large	No	Dwarf	No	Medium	Dwarf varieties
Oregano	Perennial herb	Full sun	Small	No	All	No	Medium	All types
Parsley	Annual herb	Full sun, partial shade	Small	No	All	No	Small	All species
Pea	Annual vegetable	Full sun, partial shade	Small	Train (some varieties)	All	No	Large	Bush varieties in contain-ers, vines for fences and trellising
Peach	Tree	Full sun	Medium	Espalier	Dwarf, semi-dwarf	No	Large	Dwarf and semi-dwarf
Peanut	Annual vegetable	Full sun	Small	No	All	No	Large	All types
Pear	Tree	Full sun	Medium	Espalier	Dwarf, semi-dwarf	Yes	Large	Dwarf and semi-dwarf
Pepper	Annual vegetable	Full sun, partial shade	Medium	No	All	No	Medium	All types
Pineapple guava	Shrub, tree	Full sun, partial shade	Small	Espalier	All	Yes	Large	All varieties

NAME	FORM	EXPOSURE	FOLIAGE SIZE	ESPALIER OR TRAIN ON A FENCE	RECOM-MENDED SIZE	PATIO TREE	MINIMUM CONTAINER SIZE*	RECOMMENDED VARIETIES OR TYPES
Plum	Tree	Full sun	Medium	Espalier	Dwarf, semi-dwarf	No	Large	Dwarf and semi-dwarf; 'Weeping Santa Rosa'
Plum, bush	Shrub	Full sun	Small	No	All	No	Large	All varieties
Pomegranate	Shrub, tree	Full sun	Small	Espalier	All	Yes	Large	All varieties
Quince	Tree, shrub	Full sun	Medium	Espalier	All	Yes	Large	All types
Rhubarb	Perennial vegetable	Full sun, partial shade	Large	No	All	No	Medium	All varieties
Rose	Shrub	Full sun	Medium	Espalier or train	All	No	Large	All varieties
Rosemary	Shrub	Full sun	Small	No	All	No	Medium	All varieties
Saffron	Corm	Full sun	Small	No	All	No	Small	All varieties
Sage	Perennial herb	Full sun, partial shade	Small	No	All	No	Medium	All varieties
Salal	Shrub	Partial shade	Small	No	All	No	Medium	All varieties
Sorrel	Perennial herb	Full sun, partial shade	Medium	No	All	No	Small	All types
Spinach	Annual vegetable	Full sun, partial shade	Medium	No	All	No	Small	All varieties
Spinach, New Zealand	Annual vegetable	Full sun, partial shade	Small	No	All	No	Medium	All varieties
Squash	Annual vegetable	Full sun	Large	No	Small varieties	No	Large	Bush winter varieties ('Cornell's Bush Delicata', 'Burpee's Butterbush'); all varieties of summer squash
Strawberry	Herbaceous perennial	Full sun, partial shade	Small	No	All	No	Medium	All types
Sweet bay	Tree, shrub	Full sun, partial shade	Small	Espalier	All	Yes	Large	All varieties
Sweet potato	Annual vegetable	Full sun	Medium	No	Small varieties	No	Large	'Bush Porto Rico'
Tea	Shrub	Full sun, partial shade	Medium	Espalier	All	No	Large	All varieties
Thyme	Shrub	Full sun	Small	No	All	No	Small	All types
Tomato	Annual vegetable	Full sun	Medium	Train	All	No	Large	Most varieties suitable; 'Patio' and 'Sweet Baby Girl' cherry for containers
Water chestnut	Corm	Full sun	Small	No	All	No	Medium	All
Watercress	Annual vegetable	Full sun	Small	No	All	No	Medium	All

Planting and Maintenance

Although this book's focus is landscaping rather than gardening, I wanted to include some basic gardening information. There are glories and pitfalls in gardening; none of us can ever know it all because there is always something new to be learned—that's nature. Here I cover the most up-to-date basics of establishing and caring for an edible landscape.

Before You Plant

Everyone is understandably eager to start planting and enjoying a garden's growth, beauty, and bounty. However, to ensure a great garden, there are a couple of things you must do beforehand. Before putting in a single plant or sowing any seeds, it is absolutely necessary to work your soil into tip-top condition: soft, well aerated, fertile, and well drained, with plenty of organic matter and a proper pH (acid-alkaline) balance. If the soil is not adequately prepared, plants simply cannot thrive.

And along with—or even before—churning and enriching the soil, start making compost, because it will become your permanent resource for plant nutrients, humus, and weed control. Besides the fun of creating something valuable out of plain old garbage, home composting helps reduce our stream of municipal waste.

Composting

Just as the three things you need to know about real estate are "location, location, location," in edible landscaping they are "compost, compost, compost." Organic materials decompose whether or not they are in a compost pile; the breakdown into humus takes place continuously under every tree, shrub, and flower on earth. The objective of a composting system is to centralize and speed up the decomposition of kitchen waste, tree leaves, and/or lawn clippings in a convenient space for collection and distribution.

I am a firm believer in composting. Some municipalities collect compostable materials, such as leaves, twigs, and grass clippings, from homeowners on a regular basis and compost them. The finished compost is available at little or no cost—you just pick it up at the facility. It is gratifying that some municipalities do that, but I want to know what is in my compost—and what is not—like pesticides and herbicides from lawn clippings, weed seeds, and other things I don't want. So I make my own compost.

Composting can be as simple or as complex as you wish—no need for complicated recipes or a fancy tumbling composter. Use whatever method you want, but *do* compost. It's the best possible thing you can do for the health of your plants. Compost is full of wonderful microorganisms that help get nutrients—vitamins, minerals, and organic matter—from the soil to the plant through its rootlets. For more information, I recommend the great standard, *Let It Rot! The Gardener's Guide to Composting* by Stu Campbell. Visit howtocompost.org for all you'll ever want to know.

LOW-PRODUCTION SYSTEMS

I have a low-production composting system that is simplicity itself. I pile all disease-free garden clippings and any fruit and vegetable wastes that don't go to the chickens, as well as coffee grounds and eggshells and banana peels. I don't add any weeds that have gone to seed, as my pile isn't hot enough to render them non-aggressive. Since I rarely turn or water the pile, microbial action is slow; some nutrients leach out before reaching the garden. Yet a huge amount of organic matter that would have gone to a landfill stays in my yard as soil-building humus. In warm weather, the composting action is much faster than in cold. I cut up or shred large twigs or branches (or put them in a different pile), as they take much longer to break down.

You can speed up a low-production system by occasionally turning the pile, adding some form of nitrogen now and then, and watering once in a while. The point is that composting does not have to be a big deal; everyone can and should "just do it."

HIGH-PRODUCTION SYSTEMS

A well-designed, high-production compost pile creates an environment in which the organisms that decompose organic matter can thrive. The keys for such a system are good aeration (turn the pile so that eventually all parts get exposed to the air); keeping the pile lightly moist, not wringing wet; and maintaining a good balance of materials so that the microbes have sufficient food.

There is a lot of technical information available about topics like the optimum ratio of available carbon to nitrogen. But it is enough to know that you will have successful compost if you build a pile with alternating layers of fresh green material (lawn clippings, kitchen waste, and healthy green leafy garden matter), dry brown material (twigs, dried leaves, and weed-free straw), and thin layers of soil, and occasionally add some nitrogen (manure, alfalfa meal, or blood meal) if the pile is not heating up.

VERMICULTURE: WORM COMPOSTING

A great technique for small spaces (you can do it in the kitchen) is to let worms do the work. Red wiggler worms readily convert kitchen waste and garden scraps into rich, earthy-smelling worm castings perfect for garden beds and containers. I've had an outdoor worm bin for years; it really is one of the easiest ways to compost. To start, all you need are some plastic tubs, shredded newspapers, worms, and kitchen scraps. My favorite compost guide is the classic *Worms Eat My Garbage: How to Set Up and Maintain a Worm Composting System* by Mary Appelhof. If you don't want to make your own worm bins, garden supply houses offer kits; see Gardener's Supply Company, GREENCulture, Harmony Farm Supply and Nursery, and Peaceful Valley Farm & Garden Supply in Sources and Resources.

WHAT TO DO WITH YOUR COMPOST

Once the organic matter is fully transformed to rich "black gold," apply it to the garden. The importance of compost cannot be underestimated. Here's how to use it:

- Mix it into the soil when planting edibles.
- Use it as mulch to provide nutrition for major fruits and most vegetables (even lowly rhubarb benefits from a compost mulch).
- Add it to soilless potting mixes to impart microbial action and nutrition.
- As noted in Chapter 2, use it to modify soil pH, hold moisture, and benefit all soil types.

If I'm not ready to use it, I put my finished compost in old garbage cans or cover it with a tarp to prevent nutrient loss (leaching into rainwater or evaporating).

Preparing the Soil

I believe that we all have an obligation to turn soil that has been abused by compaction or chemicals or stripped of its organic matter back into living, healthy, productive garden space. That is the legacy we leave for the planet.

The key to a healthy, beautiful garden is proper soil preparation. Poor soil is difficult to improve once plants are established. If you are just adding a fruit tree to a corner of the garden or herbs among existing shrubs, all you need is well-drained soil and compost for mulch. However, if you are redoing large beds or a whole yard, more thought and effort are in order.

In Chapter 2, you learned about soil and how to deal with acidity, alkalinity, salinity, drainage, and hardpan. Once you have taken measures to correct any such soil problems, you are ready to prepare the ground for planting.

CLEAR IT UP

Whether planning a new border or a whole landscape, it's important to start with a clean slate. There are a few ways to accomplish this, depending on the starting point. For a lawn,

remove small areas of sod with a spade and use the sod to repair any areas that may need it. For large areas, rent a sod cutter and compost the rolled turf. For an overgrown or neglected area, first remove large rocks. If you want to get the garden going quickly, weed-whack tall weeds and then pull or dig up the rest of the plants.

If you have several months, wet the area and cover it with black plastic; use bricks or stones to weigh down the sides and corners. Let the heat of the sun kill the weeds. Depending on the temperature, this may take as little as 6 weeks or as much as 3 months. *Note:* This process solarizes the soil, too, killing off any pests or diseases in the top few inches of soil—as well as any beneficial organisms.

Plan far enough ahead, and you can get away with less work using the "no-till" method that Pat Lanza espouses in her *Lasagna Gardening* books. In early fall, set down two or three layers of wet cardboard on the intended garden. Cover them with 3 to 6 inches of wet newspaper. Then alternate layers of compost (raw or finished) or grass clippings and shredded leaves, wetting each layer as you go. It will end up about 18 inches high and shrink down by about half over the winter. In spring, you now have new raised beds ready for planting annuals. In a few years the newspaper and cardboard will break down and you can put in perennials and plants with more extensive root systems.

DIG IN

Many people inherit soils deficient in humus because the area has been extensively walked on, a lawn has not been aerated or top-dressed with compost, or "weed and feed" and other chemicals have been applied for years. Those commercial fertilizers build up salts that destroy microbe populations, so the soil is badly in need of rejuvenation.

Double-digging (see John Jeavons's book *How to Grow More Vegetables* for details and an explanation of his Biointensive Method) is a good idea when starting a garden from a lawn or otherwise uncultivated area. I'm the first to admit that it does involve a lot of strenuous work and copious amounts of organic material in the preparation stage, but the end result is worth the extra effort. After the first year, I veer from John's Biointensive Method, as I don't see the necessity to double-dig each year. To me, it's unnecessary work and taxing to the soil—artificially changing the layers just when the millions of organisms in the soil are getting settled in their rightful places.

If you are not double-digging, rototill or spade over the area when the soil is not too wet; then cover it with 4 to 6 inches of compost and 1 to 2 inches of well-aged manure and mix it in. Add more compost if you live in a hot, humid climate (heat burns the compost at an accelerated rate) or if your soil is alkaline, very sandy, or very heavy clay. Most edibles grow best in neutral to slightly acidic soil; adjust the pH depending on your soil test results.

If the soil test results indicate nutrient deficiencies, these formulas represent the amount (by weight) of major nutrients to apply per 100 square feet of average soil: *nitrogen*—2 pounds of blood meal or 2¼ pounds of fish meal; *phosphorus*—2 pounds of bone meal; *potassium*—kelp meal according to package directions (in acidic soils, 1½ pounds of wood ashes help to raise the pH while adding potassium). Sprinkle the amendments over the soil and mix everything thoroughly by turning the soil over with a spade, working it all into the top foot. If the garden is large or the soil hard to work, use a rototiller. Finally, grade and rake the area. It's not necessary to add so many nutrients in subsequent years if you mulch well with compost, rotate plantings, and use cover crops.

At last it's time to turn your design into reality by forming the beds and pathways. Keep the beds less than 5 feet wide so you can easily reach into the middle to weed and harvest. Install the paths so they are wide enough for a wheelbarrow or garden cart—2½ to 3 feet across. All the materials you added will elevate the beds, which helps drainage. Slope the sides of the beds so that loose soil will not easily wash or be knocked onto the paths. Some gardeners outline the beds with an edging. Cover the paths with gravel, brick, stone, or mulch to keep them from getting muddy and to forestall weed growth.

Planting

For many gardeners, planting is the most rewarding part of the gardening process.

It All Starts with a Seed

It is easy to grow most annual vegetables and many herbs from seeds. Yet you may well ask, "Why bother?" Because it saves lots of money, it's a joyful activity to share with children, and the selection of varieties is vast compared with the plants available (even online). You can start seeds indoors in flats or other well-drained containers, outdoors in a cold frame, or—depending on the time of year—directly in the garden.

Although the cultural needs of seeds vary widely, one basic rule applies: when started in the ground or in a container, seeds require loose, water-retentive soil that drains well. Otherwise, waterlogged seeds get root rot, also known as damping-off.

STARTING SEEDS INDOORS

Starting seeds indoors gives seedlings a safe start away from slugs and birds and allows gardeners in cold or hot climates a jump on the season. Start cool-loving vegetables (broccoli, cauliflower, and many greens, including kale and spinach) in spring 4 to 6 weeks before your last frost date; transplant into the garden as soon as the soil is workable. These vegetables do not do as well and tend to bolt in high temperatures. If started indoors in mid- or late summer, they are ready to transplant outdoors in early fall, when cooler weather begins.

In cold-winter areas, start heat-loving plants like tomatoes, peppers, and basil 8 to 10 weeks before your last frost date so they are ready to go into the garden when the weather and soil warm—well after the last frost date.

Start seeds in flats or other containers with good drainage. I use cardboard milk cartons (cut each carton in half lengthwise and punch holes in the bottom for drainage) or recycle plastic cell packs from the nursery. Whatever the container, the soil needs to be at least 2 to 3 inches deep; any shallower and the growing medium dries out too quickly and doesn't provide ample space for root growth. Use a sterile seed-starting mix; the quality varies greatly from brand to brand, so try different ones to see what works best. I add worm castings to the soil as a bioactivator to add microbial life to the relatively inert soil. Follow the seed packet directions for planting depth. I find that most seed-starting mixes lack nitrogen, so I water with a weak solution of hydrolyzed fish when I sow the seeds and again a week later. Use a pencil to write the plant name, variety, and date on a plastic or wood label. Place the container in a warm place like on a commercial heating mat or atop the refrigerator.

Once the seeds germinate, move them to a quality source of light; otherwise the new seedlings will grow spindly and pale. A greenhouse, sun porch, or south-facing window with no overhang will suffice, provided it is warm. Or use fluorescent lights (the full-spectrum types sometimes called "grow lights" are best); hang them no more than 3 to 4 inches away from the tops of the plants, adjusting them as the plants grow. If the weather is above 60°F, I put seedling trays outdoors in the sun, protected with bird netting, and bring them in at night. Keep seedlings lightly moist. If they are crowded, thin them with small scissors so there is about an inch between plants.

SOWING DIRECTLY IN THE GARDEN

Smooth the soil and plant the seeds according to the seed packet directions, the listing in the Encyclopedia section, or the advice in books such as *The New Seed Starter's Handbook* by Nancy Bubel. Pat down the seeds, and water gently so that the seedbed is moist but not soggy. Use a pencil to write the plant name, variety, and date on a plastic or wood label. Protect the area with floating row covers or bird netting. If slugs and snails are a problem, circle the area with hardwood ashes or diatomaceous earth.

Transplanting

Do not transplant seedlings until they have at least a second set of true leaves; the first are seed leaves (cotyledons) that look different from true leaves. If the plants are frost tender, wait until all danger of frost is past before setting them out. Don't put heat-loving tomatoes, peppers, eggplants, or basil out until the weather has warmed and is stable.

Harden plants off by gradually acclimatizing them to differences in temperature, humidity, and air movement. Start by putting them outdoors in a partly shaded, sheltered area for several hours. Over a period of a week to 10 days, keep them outside for a longer time and move them into more sunlight each day until they remain out overnight.

Transplant on a cloudy day or in late afternoon to prevent transplant shock. Gently remove each plant along with the soil from its container. Be careful not to detach roots from the soil. If the roots are matted, slice off a third from the bottom so the roots can stretch out into the soil. Set each plant in the ground at the same depth at which it was growing in the container, fill in with soil, pat lightly into place, and gently water in. Space plants so they will have ample room when they mature; plants grown too close together are prone to diseases. Install drip irrigation if you are using it, and mulch with a few inches of organic matter at least 2 inches away from the stems.

If the weather is hot, shade each plant with a shingle or piece of wood. Keep transplants lightly moist—but not soggy—for the first few weeks.

Planting Annuals

Incorporate plenty of organic matter into the top 4 to 6 inches of soil, as most annual edibles have shallow root systems, are heavy feeders, and need soil that is both light and high in organic matter. Sow seeds following packet directions, or set out plants. Transplant tomatoes and cabbage family members a bit deeper into the ground than they were in the container so they will root more strongly. Refer to individual Encyclopedia entries for specific planting information.

Planting Perennials

Prepare the soil as described above and incorporate a moderate amount of organic matter into the top foot of soil. Add fertilizer if needed and mix it into the bottom of the planting hole. Plant so that the top of the root crown is at ground level; backfill with soil and gently firm in place. Make a small watering basin if needed; water in well. For asparagus, see the Encyclopedia for specific planting instructions.

Planting Shrubs and Trees

Remember to test for drainage first; trees and shrubs will not grow in poorly drained soil. Dig the planting hole and fill it with water. If the water has not emptied out within 4 hours, refer to Chapter 2 for methods of dealing with poor drainage.

Dig a hole one and a half times as deep as the root ball and three times as wide. If you are planting more than one fruit tree in the same hole make the hole much wider to allow about 2 feet between trees. Roughen the sides and bottom of the hole with a border fork or shovel. Loosen the removed soil so it is as finely textured as possible. Replace one-third of the soil

and—only if specifically recommended—mix in fertilizer. Gently loosen the soil around the root ball (tease or cut matted roots as necessary), set the plant in the center of the hole, and adjust the soil level so the soil line on the plant is at ground level. Backfill with native, unamended soil; water gently when the hole is half filled, then again when completely filled. Form a watering well at the drip line. Add several inches of organic mulch beyond the drip line; keep the mulch at least 6 inches from the stems or trunk. For more information and photos of the planting process, visit the Dave Wilson Nursery website (www.davewilson.com) and click on "How to Plant Trees" in the home fruit tree grower section.

BARE-ROOT SHRUBS AND TREES

Many deciduous plants are dug up while dormant and sold bare root—without soil on the roots—in nurseries and garden centers as well as by mail-order and online sources.

As soon as you get a bare-root plant home, unwrap it and soak the roots and base of the stem overnight in cool water. If you can't plant right away, rewrap in lightly moist newspaper, put in a plastic bag, and refrigerate or set in a cool (35 to 45°F), dark place for up to a week. If you must delay planting longer, heel in the plant in a trench of well-drained soil in a cool, shady area: lay the plant down at an angle, cover it with damp compost or loose soil so only the very top is aboveground, water, and keep lightly moist for up to 6 weeks.

Before planting, prune off any broken, withered, or overlong roots. Dig a hole and make a cone of soil in the bottom. Set the plant so it rests a little high in the hole; gently straighten and position the roots over the cone. The object is to plant it so the original soil line on the trunk is just above the new soil level (it will settle when watered and firmed into place). Cover half the root zone with soil; press gently into place and water. Add more soil, filling the hole completely. Don't cover the graft (the bulge on the lower trunk) except on roses in cold-winter climates. Tamp down the soil firmly with your hand.

Create a watering basin and fill it several times. To protect young fruit tree trunks from sunscald, paint them with light-colored latex paint diluted with an equal amount of water. An alternative is to temporarily wrap the trunk with burlap or other material. If rodent damage is a potential problem, wrap the trunk with chicken wire or flexible plastic tree wrap. If you are planting one of the weak-rooted dwarf trees or you live in a windy location, stake the tree with sturdy supports and use a flexible tying material that will not choke or bind the trunk. One final step: add a 4- to 6-inch layer of mulch outside the watering basin.

CONTAINER-GROWN SHRUBS AND TREES

Nurseries sell evergreen and some deciduous plants in the containers in which they grew—often in light, porous planting mix.

Dig a hole at least twice as wide as and 6 inches deeper than the container. When planting in heavy soil, create a transition zone between the growing mix and the garden soil. Rough up the sides of the hole with a shovel; a smooth, straight-sided hole thwarts root penetration. Fill the first 6 inches of the hole with native soil mixed with any necessary amendments. Carefully slip the plant out of the container. Examine the root zone. If there is a mass of roots on the outside and bottom, use a knife or sharp spade to make four 1-inch-deep slashes (from top to bottom) equally spaced around the root mass and loosen the roots. Set the plant in the hole; if you want to turn the plant in the hole, gently lift it up and reposition. Fill the hole three-quarters of the way with native soil, water in well, and fill the rest of the hole. Tamp the soil in place with your hands. Make a watering basin and water deeply. Stake if necessary, and mulch as described for bare-root shrubs and trees.

Fertilizing

As a group, edible plants are heavy feeders. Refer to Chapter 2 for specifics on different fertilizers. Follow these guidelines:

- Whenever feasible, use sustainable materials like compost and manure.
- Keep the soil pH between 6 and 7 so plants can make better use of soil nutrients.
- Avoid nitrate or nitric forms of nitrogen fertilizers.
- Maintain a high level of organic matter in the soil to encourage the microbial action that makes nutrients more available to plants.
- Incorporate fertilizer into the top few inches of soil so it doesn't blow away or evaporate.
- Apply fertilizers where they will be used; tree feeder roots are concentrated from 5 or more feet outside the drip line to within 2 feet of the trunk.
- Water fertilizer in well, but avoid flooding the area, which washes it away.
- Don't apply any organic nitrogen fertilizer if the soil temperature is below 40°F, as the microbes that break it down into a usable form will be dormant.

Major Fruits

All the major fruit trees—as well as most young nut trees, gooseberry, fig, blueberry, strawberry, pomegranate, and brambleberry—need annual feeding. Apply 3 to 4 inches of compost around the drip line in spring.

When gardening in an area with acid soil, add lime every 2 years if the soil is loamy, annually if the soil is light and sandy.

Other Trees, Shrubs, and Perennials

Once the following plants are established in average soil, they usually require little or no supplementary fertilizer: caper, chives, Jerusalem artichoke, jujube, maple, marjoram, olive, oregano, pine, prickly pear, rosemary, sage, sweet bay, and thyme.

Annual Vegetables and Fruits

Annual vegetables and fruits are hard-working plants that typically are heavy feeders. In vegetable gardens, cover crops such as alfalfa, winter wheat, and rye are a valuable source of nutrients. In areas where cover cropping is not feasible, add plenty of organic matter to the soil. Supplemental nitrogen is usually needed, particularly for leafy vegetables. Tomatoes often need extra calcium and phosphorus, and root vegetables require extra potassium.

Mulching

As discussed in Chapter 2, mulching saves time, effort, and water. Mulch's attributes are many: it conserves soil moisture, prevents erosion, controls weeds, minimizes soil compaction, and moderates soil temperature. When the mulch is an organic material, it adds nutrients and organic matter to the soil as it decomposes, making heavy clay more porous and helping sandy soil retain moisture. In addition, mulch gives the garden a finished look.

A spring application of several inches of organic mulch keeps most vegetables healthy. Unlike a soil additive or fertilizer you work into the soil, nature—in the form of microbes, earthworms, and insects—slowly works the mulch into the soil. Use your own finished compost, mushroom compost, or one of the many agricultural by-products like apple or grape pomace. I have mulched my garden with compost and chopped leaves for more than 20 years. The soil structure and texture have changed so much that I can easily plunge my arms down into what was once rock-hard clay soil. My plants now grow with few problems.

Keep mulch at least 6 inches away from tree trunks to avoid burrowing mice, voles, and fungi that can rot the trunk. (To avoid rodent problems altogether, enclose the trunk with chicken wire or flexible plastic tree wrap.) If the mulch covers the scion (the fruiting wood above the graft or bud union) of a grafted tree, roots could develop above the graft, turning a dwarf tree into a full-size one. Gardeners in very moist climates need to guard against major slug infestations and avoid mulching near succulent young transplants and leafy greens so that slugs don't have a place to hide.

Weeds

What makes a plant a weed? For our purposes, a weed is any plant that is growing where it is not wanted. Weeds aren't "bad" plants; most have some positive attributes. In fact, three persistent weeds—dandelion, purslane, and lamb's-quarter—are among the most nutritious edibles you can grow. Some deep-rooted weeds bring up nutrients from far down in the soil. And weeds on bare ground or a slope prevent erosion. Yet, because weeds compete with our chosen plants for space, water, nutrients, and sunlight; because they make the garden appear unkempt; and because some are quite invasive—we weed. And dealing with these ubiquitous plants can be time consuming.

For more information on weeds, refer to *Just Weeds: History, Myths, and Uses* by Pamela Jones; *The Gardener's Weed Book: Earth-Safe Controls* by Barbara Pleasant; and *Weedless Gardening* by Lee Reich.

Prevention

From reading garden blogs, it seems to me that weeding is the biggest deterrent to beginning gardeners, taking the most time (or they anticipate it will). In actual fact, when you prevent weeds in the first place, weeding becomes a minor part of gardening.

Even with the best mulching, one or two weeds slip in. I use weeding time to advantage; I'm close to the ground so I can see what's happening in my garden, checking for plant damage, snails and slugs, signs of insects or disease, plant crowding, and soil moisture.

MINIMIZE SOIL DISTURBANCE

Gardeners love to dig in the soil. However, a lot of digging isn't necessary. Digging or rototilling the soil brings up dormant weed seeds from deep down. Exposed to light, they germinate, producing a healthy crop of baby weeds practically overnight. Perform enough initial soil prep in new beds to remove stones, debris, grass, and weeds, but once that's done, leave the digging tools in the shed—unless you're planting.

MULCH

Many weed seeds need light to germinate; a 3- to 4-inch application of mulch immediately after disturbing the soil will keep seeds in the dark. Since my compost pile is not hot enough to kill off seeds from the food scraps I add, the finished compost may contain tomato or other vegetable seeds that can sprout. So when I mulch with my compost, I top it off (top-dress) with a ½-inch layer of pine needles, composted sawdust, or other favorite weed-free mulch.

Control

When I was a new gardener I had a yard full of crabgrass, purslane, bindweed, and spurge. I spent hours pulling weeds and in my naivety left the pulled weeds on the bed. When I went back a week later I saw that, like the proverbial phoenix, some weeds had risen from the dead. Some had rerooted, and the purslane had dropped seeds so there were soon 50 baby plants. I'm a quick study; I now pick up weeds as I go, and remove them when they are small and cannot yet reproduce.

WEEDING

I take two buckets or tubs into the garden, one for trimmings that go into the compost pile and one for seedy or invasive weeds that go into the trash. I try not to put weeds in my compost; most home compost piles don't generate enough heat to kill the seeds.

If weeds sprout, hoe or pull them out as soon as they are identifiable, as they're much easier to remove when they are small. Weeding, especially removing larger, more established weeds, is less challenging when the soil is moist—a day or two after a rain or irrigation.

NATURAL WEED-CONTROL METHODS

Over the past decade, the garden industry has introduced less toxic herbicides—with more available each year. Instead of petroleum-based chemicals, look for new products, such as post-emergent herbicides made from lemongrass oil. Try these controls:

- Boiling water. For isolated large weeds or those between bricks and pavers, boiling water is a quick and easy solution. Cut the foliage down to an inch or so, and pour boiling water on the base of the plant. It kills effectively with no side effects.
- Corn gluten. A broad-spectrum suppressant, often labeled as a pre-emergent or weed blocker, corn gluten prevents any seeds from germinating for up to 6 weeks. Use it around existing plants or before transplanting—not when sowing seeds.
- Flaming. Using a propane torch to flame young weeds, especially stubborn ones between bricks or pavers is effective. Stating the obvious, do not use a flamer where it would be a fire hazard, and always have a water hose handy.
- Foliar sprays. Natural weed killer foliar sprays contain ingredients such as clove oil, cinnamon oil, acetic acid, and citric acid. Take care to apply to weeds only on a still day.

Watering

Unfortunately, there is no easy formula for the right amount or frequency of watering; proper watering takes experience and observation. The needs of a particular plant usually depend on the type of plant as well as soil type, wind conditions, humidity, and air temperature. Learn how to water, how much to water (too much is as bad as too little), and how to recognize water stress symptoms (often a dulling of foliage color along with the obvious symptoms of drooping leaves and wilting). Follow these guidelines for more efficient watering:

- Water deeply. Most plants benefit from infrequent, deep waterings rather than frequent light sprinklings (except shallow-rooted blueberries and cranberries).

How Much Water Can You Save?

You can be much more water efficient and still have a great-looking property by following these tips from the Environmental Protection Agency (EPA). The figures following the suggestions for water savings are based on what the average homeowner experiences:

- Water the lawn only when it needs it. Step on the grass; if it springs back, do not water. *Saves 750 to 1,500 gallons a month.*
- Avoid watering the sidewalk, driveway, or gutter. Adjust sprinklers so that water goes only on the lawn or garden where it is needed. *Saves 500 gallons a month.*
- Water in the early morning when it is cool as too much water is lost to evaporation in the heat of the day. Late afternoon or evening watering can leave the grass damp all night and lead to fungal diseases. *Saves 300 gallons a month.*
- Put a 3-inch layer of organic mulch around trees and other plants to prevent water evaporation from the soil. *Saves 750 to 1,500 gallons a month.*
- Do not water on windy days; too much water is lost to evaporation. *Wastes up to 300 gallons in one watering.*
- Adjust or deactivate automatic sprinklers so you don't water in the rain. *Saves up to 300 gallons each time.*
- Set lawn mower blades one notch higher. Longer grass means less evaporation. *Saves 500 to 1,500 gallons a month.*
- Xeriscape. Replace lawn and high-water-using trees and other plants with less thirsty ones, especially drought-tolerant types. *Saves 750 to 1,500 gallons a month.*

- To ensure good absorption, apply water slowly enough to prevent runoff.
- Test your watering system regularly to make sure coverage is optimal.
- Use methods and tools that conserve water.

The entries in the Encyclopedia include plant-specific information on water requirements.

Irrigation Systems

Many folks quickly tire of dragging hoses around for watering. Plus it is difficult to deliver the right amount of water to the right places and have it well absorbed if you only aim a hose around the yard. And those old-fashioned back-and-forth sprinklers that children love to run through on hot summer days are very inefficient because they lose moisture to evaporation and wind drift and often overshoot the selected area. However, if you decide to use a manual sprinkler, consider a Noodlehead. This sprinkler is good for odd-shaped areas, whether they are long and narrow or even free-form; it has a dozen pliable spaghetti-like strands with nozzles on the ends that can be directed exactly where water is needed.

To make watering far easier and more effective, a variety of irrigation systems have been developed, many of which are quite affordable and pay for themselves in water savings and bigger harvests. Among the benefits of irrigation systems are that different stations in the network allow varied watering to meet the needs of specific plants.

If you are highly organized in your gardening, you can control the irrigation system manually. But if you are like most of us, an automated system will produce the best and most water-saving results.

AUTOMATED SPRINKLER SYSTEMS

Automated systems provide easy control over irrigation timing for overnight or early-morning watering and allow watering while you're on vacation. Rain sensors eliminate unnecessary watering when there is ample moisture.

To save water, most automated systems are sophisticated enough to water an area for 5 minutes at a time, shut off and allow the water to soak in for 20 minutes, and then go on again for 5 minutes, repeating the cycle until the proper amount of water has soaked into the soil. This prevents the runoff that 20 minutes of straight watering could produce, particularly on a slope.

However, automatic systems are not "set and forget" devices. I have seen more overwatered than drought-stricken plants when clients forget to reset the systems for the changing seasons.

DRIP IRRIGATION

As a designer and gardener, I recommend a drip irrigation system wherever feasible, mainly because it is more efficient than furrow or standard overhead watering. It delivers water to its precise destination one drop at a time through spaghetti-like emitter tubes or plastic pipe with emitters that drip water onto the root zone of each plant, or through small spray heads. Because of the time and effort involved in installing the emitters for each plant, a drip system works best in permanent plantings. A drip system has many benefits:

- Delivers water slowly, preventing runoff
- Waters deeply, encouraging deep rooting
- Eliminates many disease problems
- Reduces weed growth because so little of the soil surface is moist
- Has the potential to waste a lot less water

There are two basic ways of applying irrigation water directly to the soil around plants: drip-type systems, which include solid distribution lines with emitters, mini-sprayers, or laser-cut holes situated every 6 or 12 inches along flexible tubing; and ooze tubing, also called leaky or soaker hoses, which apply water along an entire flexible porous hose. Both work well with annuals and herbaceous perennials. Drip systems are generally pressure compensated so the water flow is even throughout the length of the tubing. High-quality brands have a built-in mechanism to minimize clogging and are made of tubing that doesn't expand in hot weather and consequently pop off its fittings. Porous hoses, which are usually made from recycled tires (it's your choice on using that), come in two sizes: 1-inch-diameter—great for shrubs and trees planted in a row—and ¼-inch tubing that easily snakes around beds of smaller plants. Neither is pressure compensated, so plants nearest the water source get more water than those at a distance, and they don't work well on a slope.

Install drip irrigation once the plants or seeds are in the ground so you know exactly where you need the water. Ground staples hold everything in place. An anti-siphon valve at the water source is a must to prevent dirty garden water from being drawn up into the drinking water. Also required is a filter to prevent debris from clogging the emitters. Installing the system requires some thought and time. You can get a kit from a home improvement center or nursery, or you can visit your local plumbing or irrigation supply store. I've found that plumbing supply stores offer professional-quality supplies, usually for less money than kits. Also, they are professionals who can help you lay out irrigation tailored to your garden.

Bring with you a rough drawing of the area—with dimensions, location of the water source, any slopes, and, if possible, the water pressure at the water source. Let them walk you through the steps and help pick out supplies that best fit your site.

In cold-winter areas, where the temperature goes below 32°F for any length of time, winterizing a drip irrigation system is a must. For detailed instructions on preparing for winter, visit www.dripworksusa.com/store/freeze.php.

Pruning

The best way to learn how to prune is to watch someone who knows what he or she is doing. If you have lots of trees and shrubs, a course on pruning is well worth taking. Some Cooperative Extension Services offer classes; all have up-to-date pruning information and can recommend local classes. There are many good books on pruning, including Lewis Hill's *Pruning Made Easy* and Lee Reich's *The Pruning Book*.

Like cooking, pruning is both an art and a science. Your climate and the type of plant determine when and how to prune. Many universities have great websites, but their Cooperative Extension Service links are more relevant to home gardeners. Look at the home fruit tree grower section of the Dave Wilson Nursery website (www.davewilson.com).

Use the right tool: hand pruners (secateurs) for twigs, loppers for small branches, and pruning saws for large branches. Keep tools sharp. When removing diseased wood, between each cut sterilize your tool in a 10 percent bleach solution or in straight rubbing alcohol or Lysol to prevent the transfer of disease from one part of the plant to another.

Summer Pruning: Tough Love Keeps It Small

Ed Laivo of Dave Wilson Nursery is the most enthusiastic and down-to-earth pruning instructor I've ever met. Much of the following is from his "Backyard Orchard Culture" practices. Most professional pruning information has been aimed at commercial orchardists with the goals of efficiency, maximum production, and low cost. However, most of us are not trying to grow trees that produce 200 pounds of fruit per tree.

Small fruit trees make everything easier—from pruning to harvesting—because you can reach it all. A mature fruit tree should be no higher than you can reach with the tips of your fingers when you raise your hands over your head (no tippy toes). Ed suggests imagining the tree you want to grow—as a bush, with a low canopy. And above all he advocates summer pruning. Here are his tips for fabulous fruit that you can pick without a ladder:

1. Before planting a bare-root tree "cut it off at the knees"—the height of your knees—or in spring choose a container-grown tree with well-spaced branches. Starting low on the trunk, trim back the entire tree by one-third to one-half; leave plenty of foliage so the main branches and trunk do not sunburn.

2. After the next flush of growth, cut back the new growth by one-half to two-thirds.

3. In the second year, cut back the spring flush of growth by one-half to two-thirds (depending on how vigorous the tree is); if there is any fruit, thin and remove 75 percent of it; after the next flush of growth, cut back the new growth by one-half to two-thirds.

4. In subsequent years, thin the fruit at the same time as spring pruning. Cut back the spring flush of growth by one-half to two-thirds. Remember how much of the fruit you actually used in past years and thin to leave that amount, or simply remove 75 percent of the fruit (whichever you can remember more easily). Leave a huge amount of space between fruits—two to three fists wide. After the harvest, cut back the summer flush of growth by one-half to two-thirds. Repeat until the tree reaches your ideal height, and then prune to keep it there.

Central leader, the strongest pruning form, is characterized by a single main trunk, or leader. Secondary branches grow off this trunk in decreasing length as you move up the tree. This is the preferred training system for many nut trees (including hickory, pecan, and most walnuts) and is occasionally used for some fruit trees, especially in windy areas.

Open center, or vase shape, is used for apricot, peach, nectarine, plum, sour cherry, almond, and filbert. The center of the tree is open for good air circulation, ease of spraying, and increased fruit production. The tree is shorter overall and easier to harvest than trees produced by the central leader system.

Fruit and Nut Trees

There are different schools of thought about how to prune fruit and nut trees. All agree that you cannot let a tree just grow on its own and expect it to produce a healthy, tasty, and bounteous crop.

Most deciduous fruit and nut trees come as unbranched bare-root plants called "whips." When planting, head them back (shorten to between 24 and 30 inches). Most mail-order nurseries do that critical first pruning before shipping the tree, and they include detailed drawings of how to continue training the tree.

For the next 2 or 3 years, the goal is to form the tree's permanent framework by selecting three to five main branches that are evenly distributed around the trunk. Although the natural tendency of the tree is to grow upward, select somewhat horizontal branches to let good light and air circulation into the center of the tree. There are two major training systems used by most fruit and nut growers: central leader and open center (also called vase shape). See the accompanying illustrations for a comparison of the these two training systems.

After the first 3 to 5 years, with proper pruning fruit and nut trees have developed a permanent framework and begin to bear. Prune most trees annually to shape them and to encourage fruit and nut production. Apples, pears, cherries, and most nut trees require little annual pruning to encourage fruiting; prune to control size. Peaches and nectarines require severe pruning yearly to encourage fruiting and to control fruit size and quantity. Apricots, sour cherries, Japanese plums, and filberts fall between apples and peaches in the amount of pruning needed. See individual Encyclopedia entries for specific pruning information.

Fruiting Shrubs

Remove old, diseased, or dead wood at any time. For the first few years, prune shrubs lightly to shape them. Once a shrub is established, thin up to one-third of the branches to promote fruiting, improve air circulation, and give a more pleasing shape. If fruits on blueberries and elderberries seem particularly small, tip-prune by pinching out the last three or four buds. See the individual Encyclopedia entries for more information.

Protecting Plants from Cold

Low temperatures can damage tender plant tissue, and alternating freezes and thaws can heave plants right out of the ground. A freeze can be a temporary situation, for instance, when you need to protect tomato plants from an early freeze or briefly protect borderline-hardy plants from a cold snap. By contrast, for gardeners in very cold climates, freezes are a standard part of their gardening consciousness throughout the year. The USDA Plant Hardiness Zone Map (see the introduction to

Floating Row Covers

Among the most valuable tools for plant protection are floating row covers. The heavy versions, sometimes called frost blankets or cold blankets, protect against cold. The lighter ones, called summer-weight or insect barriers, can be used to guard against pests (particularly squash bugs, vine borers, aphids, leaf miners, and cucumber, asparagus, flea, and bean beetles); as they create little heat buildup, they can also be used to shade new transplants.

To protect bedding plants, crops, and compact perennials against both cold and pests, lay the fabric over hoops made of saplings or PVC pipe or drape it loosely over the soil or plants, where it "floats" in place. In both cases, anchor the sides with bricks, rocks, or ground staples so the fabric won't blow away or let pests in. Use the heavy versions to protect against frost. Either lay them over beds when cold threatens or cover tender perennials such as citrus and hold the blankets in place with spring-type clothespins.

A fabric covering has both advantages and disadvantages.

Advantages
- Protects plants from most songbirds, but not crafty squirrels and jays
- Raises humidity around plants—a bonus in arid climates, but not in humid ones
- Extends spring and fall seasons by protecting plants from freezing
- Protects young seedlings from sunburn in hot-summer and high-altitude gardens

Disadvantages
- Keeps out pollinating bees; should be removed when squash, melons, and cucumbers bloom
- Unattractive for front yard gardens unless you like a Halloween look
- Covers made from petroleum products destined for the landfill; best to get newer cotton covers
- Heavy versions cut down on much light and keep in humidity, thus encouraging some diseases

Given the many uses of lightweight and heavy row covers, many gardeners keep both types on hand throughout the growing season.

---

the Encyclopedia) shows the average range of low temperatures for your area. For your last spring frost date and first fall frost date, contact your local Cooperative Extension Service or visit www.victoryseeds.com/frost. For a detailed study on how frost affects plants and how to protect them, including a listing of the frost tolerance of common vegetables, see Philip Harnden's book *A Gardener's Guide to Frost*.

Outdoor Cold Protection

Let's start with temporary cold protection. In late summer and early fall, if an early frost is predicted, cover sensitive plants (tomatoes and other tender vegetables like peppers, eggplants, cucumbers, beans, and tender herbs not quite ready for harvest) with old blankets or floating row covers—preferably before dark (it's hard to hold a flashlight and work with only one hand). Remove covers in the morning after the temperature rises above 40°F.

A different short-term situation can arise in spring, and in some regions even in summer—an unexpected late frost. Some young vegetable seedlings and all tender transplants are vulnerable to frost. Cover the young plants with old bedsheets or floating row covers. The insulation is more effective and less apt to damage small plants if you use hoops or other bracing materials to keep the fabric from touching the plants.

If you live in a cold-winter climate or are in a warmer-winter area but stretching your climate zone a bit, start thinking about freeze damage in August by avoiding fertilizing and

pruning, both of which stimulate new growth that will be sensitive to frost.

A full-blown winter problem is when plants heave out of the ground due to alternate freezing and thawing. Avoid this situation by adding at least 6 inches of mulch after the ground starts to freeze in autumn. Mulching too early keeps the soil warm; you want it to stay cold and frozen. In the coldest climates, select the hardiest varieties and mulch the graft in a grafted fruit or nut tree to protect it from hard freezing; remove the mulch when the coldest part of the winter has passed.

Overwintering Tender Plants Indoors

Citrus, tender herbs, and most subtropical and tropical edibles are not very cold hardy; in fact, a number cannot tolerate any frost. To grow them for more than a short summer season, they need warmth and brightness—indoors.

A few weeks before the first expected frost, prune plants back, check for pests, treat any infestations, and move the plants into a shady spot for a week to acclimatize them to limited light before bringing them indoors. Just before moving them inside, wash the foliage and spray the leaves with a prophylactic dose of insecticidal soap and rinse off.

Choose a place indoors with at least 6 hours of direct sun a day and temperatures around 60°F. If a sunny window or greenhouse is not available, set up an area with fluorescent lights about 6 inches from the tops of the plants and run them for 12 hours a day. If the air in the house is very dry, raise the humidity by filling a shallow tray with pebbles and placing the plants on it. Add ½ inch of water every few days. Water the plants only when the soil surface starts to dry out. Fertilize monthly with a half-strength fertilizer solution. Keep an eye out for pests; if they appear, immediately isolate any infested plants and either treat or discard them.

In spring, after all danger of frost is past, rejuvenate the plants by washing them down well to remove any dust and cobwebs. Soak the container in tepid water for a few hours to flush out any salts. Prune the canopy back by a quarter or more and remove any dead or damaged leaves. To renew the roots, run the blade of an old, dull knife around the inside of the container and pull the root ball out. With a sharp knife, cut off the bottom inch of roots and score the sides in three or four places. Add new potting soil to the bottom of the container, repot the plant, add some all-purpose organic fertilizer, and water well. Before putting the plants out in the sun for the summer, acclimatize them by setting them in a shady spot outdoors for a few weeks and gradually moving them into more light.

Container Gardening Basics

Years ago I grew some pretty sad-looking plants in my containers. Through years of trial and error, I now possess some hard-won solutions that I share here. In addition to a fairly sunny spot, edible container gardening requires quick-draining soil in fast-draining pots.

Containers

Let's begin by taking a look at the containers themselves and how to choose them. You'll find containers varied enough to fit any landscape style. Plant dwarf citrus in a classic Italian urn or fill an informal wood crate with marigolds and eggplants. Day-neutral strawberries in hanging baskets produce fruits for 3 months while staying dry and out of the reach of slugs. A trellis in a planter with Armenian cucumbers, pretty as any ivy, plus a few pots of herbs are guaranteed to delight the cook in the household.

A good place to find containers is your local nursery. Other options: look online, at garage sales, and in secondhand stores. Don't forget to search the garage and attic for containers to recycle like large olive oil cans, old leaky buckets, and baskets.

The biggest challenge in container gardening is keeping the roots moist but not soggy. Even in rainy-summer areas, containers need regular irrigation, as rain does not fall evenly or regularly and plant roots cannot seek water in the depths of the earth. The sun heats one side of the container (wood less so than most other materials); in the hottest climates it kills the roots on the hot side. To offset water loss and mitigate the heat, choose the largest containers feasible for the space or use self-watering containers.

Container Types: Pros and Cons

Type	Pro	Con
Fiberglass	Lightweight Wide range of designs	Limited colors
Glazed pottery	Highly decorative Tremendous range of colors and patterns	Heavy when filled Glaze can chip off
Plastic	Lightweight Can be placed inside a more decorative pot	Can be unattractive
Terra-cotta	Natural, earthy look	Dries out quickly Heavy when filled Fragile; can break if left outside in winter
Wood	Natural material Can be painted any color	Rots with age
Self-watering	Minimizes watering Allows a vacation from watering	Heavy when filled

Not all containers need a bottom. Bottomless containers, such as recycled terra-cotta drain pipes, chimney flues, and bottomless wooden boxes, accommodate plants with vigorous root systems, vary height levels in a group of plantings, and help avoid drainage problems. However, they are not portable.

Soil/Potting Mix

Container gardening requires quick-draining soil. Garden soil by itself is generally too heavy and compacts too much to use in containers, but you can make your own mix or buy ready-made potting soil. Commercial potting soils, also called potting mixes, contain ingredients that retain water, provide nutrients, prevent compaction, and facilitate drainage. Despite the word "soil" used on the packaging for many products, real soil is rarely an ingredient in the mix. Some form of peat, coir (coconut husks), or ground bark holds water. Manure, a chemical fertilizer, or a supplemental mineral provides nutrients. Vermiculite (a natural mineral that is expanded by heating), coir, or perlite (a volcanic glass) prevents compaction.

Potting mixes are not all created equal. In an attempt to ensure quality and provide gardeners with safe and environmentally sound products, the Mulch & Soil Council certifies and randomly tests products. For more information, visit www.mulchandsoilcouncil.org.

Buy in bulk or look for mixes in bags made from recyclable plastics, corn, or paper products. Also check for the Mulch and Soil Council certification on the bag. Look for these ingredients in commercial mixes, or use them to make your own mix:

- ◆ For bulk: perlite, coir, forest products including leaf mold, aged sawdust, and ground bark
- ◆ To increase the microbe population: bioactivators like worm castings and compost
- ◆ For nutrition: manures and meals (blood, bone, kelp, feather, and fish)

Avoid the following:
- ◆ Peat moss unless you are planting blueberries, cranberries, lingonberries, ginger, or tea
- ◆ Potting soils that contain imidacloprid, a systemic pesticide used to control sucking insects and beetles (found in many Bayer potting soils)
- ◆ Gel polymers made from plastics; instead add your own corn-based gels
- ◆ Commercial chemical fertilizers, including urea
- ◆ Bargain brands as they may contain subsoil or sawdust made from questionable wood sources and may have skimped on nutrients

Folks ask if they can reuse potting soil season after season. Unless your plants were diseased, don't refill your containers with new potting mix every spring; it's a waste of money that can be better spent on plants. To keep my container plants going like the Energizer bunny, I mix in lots of compost and worm castings that are not high in salts (commercial fertilizers and manures are); use drip irrigation so any salts are continually washed out of the soil; and mulch with compost and renew it regularly to keep organic matter in the mix. I keep the mix in my pots for years. If I do decide to empty the pot, I add the mix to the compost pile. This works regardless of your climate—even cold-winter ones.

Drainage

Good drainage is critical in containers. Air pores in fast-draining potting soil provide oxygen, which plant roots absorb for respiration. If plant roots are flooded for more than a day or two, the roots in effect suffocate. Soggy soil also provides ideal conditions for fungi that cause root rot. Therefore, it is very important to provide drainage holes in containers and to use a fast-draining potting soil.

Before planting, cover the drainage holes with a piece of window screen to keep the soil in and slugs and other pests out. The notion of using potsherds at the bottom of containers is a throwback to the days of the grand English gardens with huge pots that had big holes through which the soil could run out; old broken pots were heaped in the bottom to keep the soil in place. Studies have found that potsherds can in fact block the holes.

Since drainage water stains decks and concrete, use saucers under the planters. Place a few handfuls of stones or marbles in the saucer to raise the container up so the roots don't get soggy. All but self-watering containers need sufficient drainage holes.

Large containers—over a few feet wide or deep—have inherent drainage problems, which I discovered when the plants in my 3-foot-diameter whiskey barrels began to look stressed and turned yellow. The soil compressed under its own weight, the plant roots suffocated, and anaerobic bacteria were able to thrive. I raised the issue with a number of soil experts and was given two suggestions: place a 12-inch-deep pile of sticks and twigs in the bottom of the barrel to provide plenty of air space and fast drainage or use a soilless light mix made mostly from perlite and vermiculite. I opted for a pile of twigs, and it worked very well in my patio garden. I've since spoken to many gardeners who grow plants successfully in soilless mixes. However, these lifeless mixes do not hold fertilizer, so unless you add some compost to the mix, frequent feeding is essential.

Watering

Although a challenge, maintaining the correct moisture in containers is vital for growing quality edibles. Plants in small or porous terra-cotta pots or in hot, arid, or windy locations dry out fast; plants in large containers, especially in cool, humid, or shady places, dry out less quickly. Similarly, a large plant in a small pot needs watering more frequently than a small plant in a large pot.

Unfortunately, you can't always trust rain to water containers as it often does not penetrate the umbrella of foliage above the soil. I've dried out so many plants in my time that now I'm fanatical about using only fairly large containers—ones big enough to accommodate healthy root systems and hold ample soil so that constant watering isn't necessary.

Knowing *how* to water a container-grown plant is as important as knowing *when*. Avoid giving plants a quick sprinkling because such shallow watering causes the roots to grow toward the sides of the container, forming drainage channels through which water is lost. Experience has shown that premoistening the soil (filling up the area between the top of the soil and the rim of the container with water) pays off. Although water starts running out the bottom, I know that if I don't fill the container with water at least twice more, chances are the soil in the middle of the pot will remain dry.

Although plants in containers are water hungry, there are ways to keep your water use low. Before you plant the container, mix water-holding granules, such as Zeba (made from cornstarch; I avoid synthetic moisture-absorbing polymers made from petroleum), into the potting mix; they hold water like a sponge, releasing it to the plants over several days. Since containers are likely to be near the house, connect a rain barrel to the gutter system and use free rainwater.

To cut water use even more, install automatic drip irrigation. I never realized how much better container plants grow when they are slow watered daily. The dripping action soaks the entire root ball every night and, unlike me, it never forgets to water. And it prevents salt buildup from irrigation water, which damages the roots. I don't use the irrigation kits offered at home improvement stores and nurseries; generally they don't fit the area well, clog easily, and are expensive. Instead, I visit my local plumbing or irrigation supply store. Bubblers and Shrubblers with variable adjustments or micro spray heads on stakes give the best coverage and are the least apt to clog. The staff helps me figure out how many feet of distribution tubing and flexible piping and how many fasteners I need. I attach my system to an automatic timer. While most irrigation system timers need a household electrical source to tap into, there are battery-operated timers that are perfect for a container line. Dripworks, Peaceful Valley Farm & Garden Supply, and the Urban Farmer Store (has lots of DIY information) are good suppliers.

Consider, too, self-watering containers like EarthBox, which provide the exact amount of water the plants require with no overwatering. *Incredible Vegetables from Self-Watering Containers* by Edward C. Smith gives detailed information on soil and water capacity, how-tos for several DIY self-watering containers, and directions on how to best grow edibles in these containers. Gardener's Supply Company carries an ever-growing selection of plastic self-watering containers—from window boxes to wine barrels.

Fertilizing

A key to successfully growing edibles in containers is to fertilize them frequently, as nutrients leach out of the potting mix every time you water. To fertilize my plants, I apply a dry, balanced organic fertilizer or liquid hydrolyzed fish—carefully following the package instructions. Both are slow-release fertilizers that provide a steady source of nutrients. If the plants turn pale, I apply fish emulsion to get a fairly quick response.

If you do not use a drip system, salts from water and fertilizers eventually accumulate as whitish deposits along the bottom and sides of the pots. Before you fertilize, water thoroughly five or six times to flush out these accumulated salts.

Winter Protection

In freezing weather, most terra-cotta containers crack and the exterior layer flakes off glazed pots, so bring them inside. (Some high-fired, very expensive terra-cotta containers can withstand freezing temperatures.) On the other hand, plastic, fiberglass, faux materials, and wood containers usually come through unscathed. Drain drip irrigation systems and bring battery-operated timers inside.

Protect perennial plants as their roots are exposed to the cold in a pot. As a rule, choose varieties that are two zones hardier than your actual zone. For example, a blueberry variety that is hardy to Zone 5 in the ground will be hardy only to Zone 7 in a container. For extra protection, mulch the plant with 3 to 4 inches of straw or compost, wrap the container with Bubble Wrap or many layers of burlap, or dig a hole and sink the container into the soil to its rim and then mulch.

When edible plants are the main elements in a landscape, it's not enough for them to be tasty—they have to look good, too. That's why making sure your plants are healthy and well maintained is key to a successful edible landscape.

Pests and Diseases

As a nation of gardeners emerging from the "chemical era," we are starting to get a handle on controlling pests and diseases by preparing the soil properly, choosing the appropriate plants for our particular location and conditions, and maintaining a balanced garden ecosystem. We know that it is much more important to prevent a problem in the first place than to correct it.

That said, this appendix covers the pests and diseases that can affect a range of plants in different parts of the country. Problems specific to only one or two plants are covered in their individual entries in the Encyclopedia. Once you identify the problem (see the books and websites noted in "The Garden Ecosystem" for more information), look at the ways I offer for controlling it. I emphasize those with the least impact on the environment, and I recommend only a few commercial controls.

Garden Pests

There are really only a few types of insects that "bug" us. Most insects in our gardens pollinate our edibles, clean up debris, devour pest insects, or are food for other critters. In a balanced garden ecosystem, beneficial insects—those that devour pest insects—plus birds and toads are in charge of pest control.

The Garden Ecosystem

I was introduced to the concept of a balanced garden ecosystem when we purchased our house in the early 1970s. For years the previous owner had a pesticide service, which she assured me was safe—all the neighbors used it. Hesitantly, I signed up. Watching the pesticide fog settle over the yard the first time gave me the willies; I worried about my children and soon canceled the service. The company warned that I would have problems. Indeed, in no time aphid honeydew dripped from the ivy, the bentgrass lawn was patchy with fungus, whiteflies moved in, and spider mites were everywhere.

One of my new neighbors, an entomologist, diagnosed the problem: a classic case of pest resurgence. She explained that pesticides never kill *all* the pest insects; some survive and

Top 10 Ways to Prevent Pests and Diseases

Follow these tips for healthy plants. Remember that the key is healthy soil. Feed the soil and it will feed your plants. Soil rich in organic matter is full of life. Plants growing in healthy soil get the nutrition they need to be vigorous and are less vulnerable to pests and diseases.

1. *Use reliable, quality seed and plant suppliers.* The old adage is true: you get what you pay for—especially when investing in a tree or shrub.

2. *Select the right plant for the right place.* Check the cultural requirements of a plant before purchasing it. Proper light, air circulation, water, soil type, and climate help avoid and control diseases. For instance, if you have poorly drained soil and can't sufficiently amend it, then choose plants that thrive in that kind of soil or grow in containers.

3. *Choose disease-resistant varieties when available.* This is especially important if you live where spring and/or summer is humid—the perfect climate for fungal diseases.

4. *Inspect plants for pest or disease symptoms before purchasing.* Avoid plants with leaves that are discolored, have dark or light spots, or look powdery. Tap the leaves to see if anything flies off.

5. *Provide good air circulation and sufficient sunlight.* Giving plants room to grow is crucial. Don't put plants that are susceptible to diseases or pest insects (especially whiteflies) up against solid surfaces where air does not circulate. Prune trees and shrubs so air can move through the branches and sunlight reaches all parts of the plant. Sunlight is nature's disinfectant.

6. *Practice crop rotation.* Change the location of disease-prone annual plants (and their relatives) every year to cut down on the buildup of pests and diseases in the soil.

7. *Mulch to prevent splashing water from contaminating leaves of susceptible plants.* Soil can house disease organisms. A good layer of mulch acts as a barrier, preventing these organisms from bouncing up from the soil onto lower leaves during heavy rain or overhead watering.

8. *Eliminate overwintering pests and diseases with fall cleanup.* Tidying up every fall is essential. Discard diseased vegetable plants—roots and all. Pick up diseased or insect-infested fruits and pull them off the tree; rake up diseased leaves. Discard the debris; do not compost it.

9. *Do not work around plants when they are wet.* When you brush against a wet plant that has a fungal disease, you pick up spores that transfer easily to healthy plants.

10. *Disinfect tools that have been used on infected plants.* Dip pruners in a 10 percent solution of bleach or in straight alcohol or Lysol after each cut and again before putting pruners away.

It's easy for me to stay in touch with my plants on a daily walk through the garden with my morning cup of tea. It is a relaxing time for me and doesn't feel like a chore.

reproduce very quickly. Since their natural enemies (beneficial insects that consume the pest insects) are absent—also killed by the pesticides—pest populations explode. The natural enemies reproduce more slowly; in time, if I did not spray, they would catch up and take control. It took 18 months, but they did.

By the summer of 1981, my garden was thriving and I was finishing the first edition of this book. Enter the State of California, which dropped malathion (a broad-spectrum insecticide) on our county to stop the Mediterranean fruit fly (medfly), which was threatening the state's agriculture. Malathion killed the medfly, as well as billions of other insects. Nights were eerily still without katydid and cricket songs. Within months, there were no mockingbirds singing, either; we were having our own "silent summer." What a dramatic example of an ecosystem out of balance—and not just my own this time. As pest insects began to return, I witnessed all sorts of new problems. Sadly, I pulled out most of my vegetable garden, concentrated on washing down my fruit trees repeatedly, and waited for the return of the "good guys." It took 2 years to approach normal—3 years before I heard a cricket again.

As you can see, it's paramount to know which insects play for which team—the black hats or the white hats. For general control of garden pests, I recommend Barbara Pleasant's *The Gardener's Bug Book*. To aid identification, I recommend *Garden Insects of North America: The Ultimate Guide to Backyard Bugs*, by Whitney Cranshaw, and *The Organic Gardener's Handbook of Natural Insect and Disease Control*, edited by Barbara Ellis and Fern Bradley, both of which contain color pictures of pests and beneficials in all stages of development.

For photos of beneficials, visit these websites: Cornell University (www.nysaes.cornell.edu/ent/biocontrol) and the University of California at Davis (www.ipm.ucdavis.edu/PMG). For photos of pest insects, go to a different part of Cornell University's website (www.gardening.cornell.edu/pests).

Natural Controls: Beneficial Creatures

To have a sustainable organic edible landscape, it's essential to create a garden that attracts a diversity of beneficial creatures—from barely visible parasitic wasps to songbirds. This is an ongoing process, and one of the first steps is learning to recognize beneficial insects. A good hand lens is key to identifying who's who out there. Many beneficial insects go through four stages in their lives: egg, larva (called nymph or maggot in some insects), pupa, and adult. Adults and larvae (young) rarely look at all alike. Often adults consume only nectar or pollen; larvae are the pest insect eaters. Many beneficials are quite tiny.

Two main types feed on other insects: predators and parasitoids. Like predatory lions stalking zebras, predatory insects hunt and eat plant feeders like aphids and mealybugs. Some predators, praying mantids, for example, consume any smaller insects that they find—pests as well as beneficials like ladybugs.

Other predators, such as syrphid fly larvae, consume only plant feeders.

Parasitoids provide the most effective insect control because they are specific, developing in or on the bodies of other insects. Most parasitoids are tiny, non-stinging wasps or flies whose larvae eat other insects from within. Some are small enough to live within an insect egg. Or one wasp egg divides into thousands of identical cells, each of which develops into a mini-wasp; all together, they consume an entire caterpillar.

The following describes some of the most common beneficials, which pests they control, and how to encourage their presence in the home garden.

AMPHIBIANS

All amphibians are predators; sadly, their populations are in decline worldwide. We can do our bit to save them by adding a small water garden to attract frogs and by providing overturned containers as cool, moist hiding places for toads.

BENEFICIAL NEMATODES

Nematodes are common microscopic worms that live in the soil. Some nematodes are parasitic, feeding on plant roots; others, however, eat decaying matter and are predators of some pest insects. Organic supply houses carry specific beneficial nematodes to control pests that spend part of their life cycle in the soil. *Heterorhabditis* controls most pest beetles when applied during the beetles' larval stage. *Steinerema* controls caterpillars, like those of cutworms and root weevils. Apply to moist soil.

FLIES

Snipe and robber flies are rapid-flying predators that often capture their prey on the fly. Adults consume other flies, beetles, and moths; larvae (maggots) prey on soil-dwelling insects. Tachinid flies are parasitoids. Adults look like colorful, bristly houseflies; their larvae eat moths, butterflies, beetles, grasshoppers, and wasps.

GROUND (CARABID) BEETLES

These fairly large black beetles with grooved wings (Carabidae family) scurry away when you uncover them. Encourage them by giving them places to hide like low-growing herbs and perennials or a compost pile. Both larvae and adults are predators of armyworms, asparagus beetles, cabbageworms, codling moths, and slugs.

LACEWINGS

Lacewings (*Chrysoperia* spp.) are highly effective and beautiful insect predators. Adults are small, green or brown, gossamer-winged insects that mainly eat nectar and pollen. Larvae resemble little tan alligators—fierce aphid predators that also prey on

Attracting Beneficial Insects

Adult beneficial insects, most of which are very small, seek out clusters of tiny flowers that offer easy access to plenty of nectar and protein-rich pollen. Many are drawn to members of the large aster family (Asteraceae), which comprises favorites like yarrow, goldenrod, cosmos, coreopsis, marigold, chamomile, feverfew, and a host of plants referred to as "daisies." Although some flowers appear to be large, look closely; the centers consist of tiny flowers.

The carrot family (Apiaceae), which includes the popular herbs parsley, dill, cilantro, and fennel, as well Queen Anne's lace, offers an abundance of umbels (umbrella-shaped flowers) made up of tiny flowers. The parts of some edible plants fly under the radar as attractants, like wheat flowers and corn tassels. Sweet alyssum (cabbage family, Brassicaceae) bears a profusion of tiny floral offerings. At the end of the season, let broccoli, mustards, and cauliflower flower to provide lots of nectar and pollen.

mealybugs, mites, thrips, and eggs of many pest caterpillars. When purchased and released at the right time, green lacewings, unlike ladybugs, stay around.

LADYBUGS

Adult ladybugs, also known as lady beetles (many types, in a variety of colors except green, all Coccinellidae family), are the best-known predator insects. Yet, when I pass around the alligator-shaped, black and red larva at lectures, few people recognize it. Both adults and larvae eat aphids and other small pest insects. Most purchased ladybugs fly away when released. Attract native ladybugs by growing many native flowers.

SPIDERS AND PREDATORY MITES

Spiders and mites are arachnids. All spiders are predators; some trap prey with a web, others hunt down their victims, and a few ambush their quarry. Spiders are valuable as they fill many niches left empty by insect predators. Despite our innate fear, most spiders are harmless to humans.

Predatory mites are similar in appearance to their prey—spider mites—and are effective at controlling pest mites and thrips.

SYRPHID FLIES

Also called hoverflies or flower flies, syrphid flies are very common predators that distinctively hover over flowers. Many species have yellow and black stripes, resembling small bees. Larvae are small green or tan maggots that look like little pointy-headed caterpillars and live individually on plants, eating small pests including aphids and mites. Attract syrphid flies by growing plants with lots of tiny flowers, like sweet alyssum and Queen Anne's lace.

WASPS

Unfortunately, the few large predatory wasps that sting give wasps in general a bad name, yet all wasps are either insect predators or parasitoids. Look for big predatory wasps, such as hornets, flying stealthily among garden plants seeking prey. Tiny parasitoid wasps, which are hardly noticeable, do not sting. Parasitoid adult females lay their eggs in or on other insects, and the developing larvae devour the host. Some parasitoid wasps create aphid mummies (hardened dead aphids that look like minute brown Ping-Pong balls), which act as protective cocoons for the developing wasps.

OTHER BENEFICIAL INSECTS

Big-eyed bugs and *minute pirate bugs* are valuable predators of small, soft-bodied, destructive pests like thrips, aphids, and mites. Both are blackish, small, and oval to square. Vase shaped with small heads, most *assassin bugs* and all *damsel bugs* and *ambush bugs* are predators of plant-feeding insects. *Tiger beetles*, *soldier beetles*, and *rove beetles* are a varied-looking lot that feed on root maggots, aphids, and other insects and their eggs.

SONGBIRDS AND BATS

Many native songbirds devour countless pest insects. In addition, some gardeners are lucky enough to have resident bats to help control night-flying moths, beetles, and, of course, mosquitoes. For a valuable primer on bats and how to bring them to your garden, visit Bat Conservation International at www.batcon.org.

Mixed Blessings

Unfortunately, a few creatures that are usually beneficial may cause an occasional problem when they appear in the wrong place or in large numbers. I include ants, earwigs, and sowbugs in this category.

ANTS

On the plus side, ants are scavengers that remove dead matter from the garden; their nest-building activities help aerate the soil; and some ant species are natural enemies of termites. However, many ants feed on the honeydew exuded by plant-sucking aphids and scale, actually "farming" these pests and protecting them from predators.

Control: To protect a tree or arbor, wrap the trunk or support with masking tape, and cover with Tanglefoot, Stickem, or other sticky substance. Make sure you completely block off the ants' approach to the plant. If they continue to be a problem, try orange oil spray. Or place ant bait containing boric acid at the base of the plant.

Red fire ants are a problem in the South and Southwest; their sting is painful, and a swarm can make life miserable. **Control:** Look for botanical insecticides that contain orange oil as the main ingredient. A number of fire ant baits now contain spinosad.

EARWIGS

Earwigs are fierce-looking brown insects with large pincers in the back, but they are harmless to humans. In the Southeast, two native species prey on pests. Also, earwigs are thought to be valuable scavengers. However, in some parts of the country, European earwigs can be a problem, eating young vegetable seedlings and ripe fruits.

Control: Earwigs are nocturnal, so observe them at night with a flashlight. If you determine that they are eating your vegetables or fruits, trap them by laying rolled-up newspaper, bales of bamboo stakes, or corrugated cardboard around the garden. Earwigs hide in these materials; shake the collectors over a container of soapy water to dislodge the earwigs.

SOWBUGS

Sowbugs are not insects but crustaceans. Some species like pillbugs roll up into a ball when they are disturbed. They prefer to eat decaying material. On occasion I have seen sowbugs eating young lettuce, bean seedlings, and tomato or strawberry fruits.

Control: Sufficient dry mulch under vulnerable crops helps prevent damage. There is good evidence that these critters are secondary feeders; other insects, snails, or slugs likely cause the initial plant damage. Controlling the primary pests is the key to managing sowbugs.

Major Plant Pests

Some common pests of many different edible plants are described below. Pests specific to a plant in the Encyclopedia are discussed in its entry.

APHIDS

Aphids are small, pear-shaped, soft-bodied insects—in various colors, including green, black, pink, and gray—that produce many generations in a single season. They suck plant sap and exude honeydew (a sticky, sweet, nutrient-rich substance), which forms a shiny, sticky film on the leaves below. Sooty mold can grow on the honeydew, turning the leaves black and blocking sunlight. (Treat the mold by spraying a mixture of 2 tablespoons of dishwashing liquid in a gallon of water; rinse with fresh water.) In large numbers, aphids weaken a plant, especially young fruit trees; some spread viral diseases.

Control: Aphids are the major food source for many beneficial insects, so a few are usually not a problem. They often show up in large numbers in early spring before the predatory and parasitic insects appear. However, if the population increases rapidly, look for aphid mummies and other natural enemies. If beneficials are not present, a strong squirt of water from a hose will drown aphids. In a balanced garden, most aphids should be gone in a few weeks. If there are few flowering plants in the area, incorporate more to attract beneficial insects.

A sizeable outbreak later in the growing season can indicate that a plant is stressed. Make sure it is properly fertilized, mulched, and watered, and that it gets enough sunlight. Always start with the simplest remedy. Hose affected plants with a strong stream of water; repeat two or three times if needed. If aphids stick tightly, spray with insecticidal soap; it will kill aphids on contact. Spray thoroughly—tops and bottoms of leaves and the growing tips. Spray woolly and other waxy aphids once and then again 24 hours later. Do not spray when temperatures are above 80°F. Rinse the plant with clean water 24 hours after the soap application. Conventional pesticides are generally not necessary.

If aphids are a continuing problem on woody plants, make sure ants are not farming them (see "Ants").

BORERS

Borers, the larval stage of various insects, damage plants by boring through stems and trunks. The first sign is wilted foliage or sawdust around a hole on the stem or trunk. Even one or two borers can be fatal to young fruit trees, pecans, and raspberries.

Control: Inspect young fruit tree trunks often in summer and early fall; look for holes or oozing sap, particularly near the base of the tree. Prevent borers by wrapping the trunk with newspapers or tar paper 24 inches up from the ground and tied at the top. Cut off damaged branches, twigs, and leaves. When borers are in the main trunk, use a wire to reach up into the tunnel to pull them out. Beneficial nematodes help control some borers. To protect the main stems of young squash plants from the squash vine borer, wrap aluminum foil around the stems. If the plant is infested, cut off affected stems below the entry holes. Grow resistant varieties.

CATERPILLARS

Caterpillars are the larval stage of butterflies and moths. Some species, such as tomato hornworms and cabbageworms, are notorious for eating leaves or burrowing into fruits and vegetables.

Control: Handpick. Cover young cabbage family plants with floating row covers to deter cabbageworms. On older plants, inspect the undersides of leaves every few days; look for tiny white eggs the white cabbage moth lays. For large infestations of all types of caterpillars, unless the larvae are inside the fruits, spray with *Btk* (*Bacillus thuringiensis* var. *kurstaki*).

CUCUMBER BEETLES

Cucumber beetle is the common name for various types of ladybug-like, greenish yellow beetles with black stripes or spots. Their larvae, which look like small segmented worms, feed on squash family plants and corn roots. Adults eat cucumber and squash plants as well as other vegetables and flowers, and they can transmit disease.

Control: Protect seedlings of cucumber family members with floating row covers; to allow pollination, remove the cover when the plants begin to bloom. Handpick beetles early in the day. Neem spray kills the beetles. Beneficial nematodes control the larvae.

CUTWORMS

Cutworms are the larvae of certain small night-flying moths. During the day cutworms rest just below the soil surface, curling up into a ball when disturbed. At night they feast upon succulent seedlings. Cutworms can be a problem on newly planted vegetable and grape transplants, chewing off the stem at the soil line.

Control: Use cardboard collars or bottomless food tins around the plant; sink the collar 1 inch into the ground with 1 to 2 inches aboveground. Carefully probe the soil near damaged plants for larvae and dispose of them. Control severe infestations with *Bt*.

EUROPEAN CODLING MOTHS

European codling moth larvae are often the "worms" in wormy apples and pears. Nationwide, it is the key pest of apples, pears, and walnuts. Adult moths are small with gray and brown wings. They lay their eggs singly and their larvae (pinkish white caterpillars with dark heads) are visible for only about 24 hours and then burrow into the fruits to feast; the blackened entry hole is a sign of infestation.

Control: Monitoring is the first step; visually inspect your trees regularly for female moths, eggs, and larvae; destroy any you find. When fruits are the size of Ping-Pong balls, thin to two per cluster; to be super safe, cover the fruits with protective bags made from old stockings or order fruit covers online. Continually remove and destroy damaged fruit on or under the tree. Supplement visual inspection with pheromone traps, which release female sex attractant to trap males. Monitor their numbers and time spraying to kill larvae before they enter the fruit.

Spray lightweight or summer horticultural oil if you see only a few dozen worms. Spinosad and *Btk* (*Bacillus thuringiensis* var. *kurstaki*) give some control.

GRASSHOPPERS

Grasshoppers are occasionally a problem, particularly in grassland areas in dry years.

Control: Use bait containing the parasitic protozoa *Nosema locustae*, which will kill grasshoppers but will not harm other insects, people, pets, or plants.

JAPANESE BEETLES

Accidentally brought to America in the early 1900s, Japanese beetles are now a serious problem in the East and are moving westward, having crossed the Mississippi. Metallic green beetles with coppery wings chew their way through leaves and flowers of most edible plants. The larval stage is a whitish grub that feeds on the roots of turfgrasses.

Control: Milky spore, a naturally occurring disease in the soil (*Bacillus popilliae*), can be purchased to control the larvae. It can take 4 years to get established, yet can live in the soil for more than 25 years. Chemicals applied to the lawn will kill the milky spore. Beneficial nematodes (specific for Japanese beetle grubs) are more immediately effective, as they actively seek out the grubs. Both controls work best if neighbors also treat their lawns. It is also effective and satisfying to go out in early in the day and knock the beetles into soapy water.

MITES

These arachnids are so small you need a hand lens to see them. While most mites are either predators or benign, a few are pests, reproducing in great numbers and sucking on the leaves of citrus, apples, and strawberries—among other plants. Leaf stippling and dried-looking silvery leaves are signs of mite infestation. Mite infestations often indicate drought or insufficient fertilizer; they can also be caused by sprays of a broad-spectrum pesticide that killed off beneficial predators.

Control: Mites thrive on dusty leaves in dry, warm weather. Wash and mist the foliage of susceptible plants. In spring, when mite populations on citrus can explode, mist every 2 weeks (if fungal diseases are not a problem). Young stages of many predators are natural enemies of mites.

PARASITIC NEMATODES

Parasitic nematodes attach themselves to roots, stunting the plant's growth. They are most prevalent in light sandy soils. Symptoms include small swellings or lesions on the roots and sometimes stems. Many herbs and vegetable crops, as well as figs and brambleberries, are particularly susceptible to parasitic nematodes.

Control: Prevent damage by planting trees grafted onto nematode-resistant rootstocks and tomato varieties that are labeled nematode resistant. Rotate annual vegetables with less susceptible varieties. Plant contaminated beds with a blanket of marigolds such as 'Nema-gone' (*Tagetes* spp.) for a whole season. Keep your soil high in organic matter to encourage biological controls. If all else fails, grow susceptible edibles in containers.

SCALE

Scale insects are plant suckers that are usually covered with a shell or waxy coating. Adult females shed their legs and antennae to permanently attach themselves to a leaf or branch; they lay their eggs so the young hatch beneath the female's protective covering.

Control: Ladybugs and mini-wasps attack scale. If needed, spray lightweight oil late in the dormant season, just as the buds begin to swell and unprotected young scale crawlers are susceptible. Ants often protect scale to collect the honeydew. If ants are present, control them first (see "Ants").

SNAILS AND SLUGS

These mollusks (cousins of clams) are indiscriminate feeders, eating most commonly grown vegetables and citrus leaves. They feed at night and can go dormant for months in times of drought or low food supply. Seedlings are especially vulnerable.

Control: Hand-collect snails and slugs when it's dark, ideally after a rain or irrigation, when they are most active, spotting them with a flashlight. I use a long-handled grabber with suction cup ends. Only repeated forays provide adequate control.

Slugs hide in many places and burrow in the ground for protection. I get some slug control by laying a shingle near affected plants. By midmorning slugs have gathered underneath, and I scrape them into a jar of soapy water.

Pelletized iron phosphate bait, such as Sluggo, is effective if applied to dampened soil around young seedlings. Baiting the entire garden once or twice a year is the most effective strategy. Start in early spring, when slugs and snails are most active, and repeat in late spring before breeding season starts. Consider a late-summer application if you have a heavy infestation or populations have built up.

WEEVILS AND CURCULIOS

The adults (long-snouted beetles) feed on leaves and lay eggs inside flower buds and developing fruits and nuts. The larvae (legless grubs) feed inside, withering the buds and infesting the fruits and nuts; some types enter the soil and feed on roots. East of the Rockies, the plum curculio makes growing some fruits, especially plums, apricots, apples, and peaches, daunting. A few insects are not problematic, but they typically show up in large numbers.

Control: Scrupulously clean up any dropped fruits and nuts all season long. If you see adult weevils or curculios, place sheets under fruit or nut trees, strike the branches with a padded pole daily to dislodge the beetles, and dispose of them. Neem may be worth a try. Get information from your local Cooperative Extension Service on controlling these pests.

WHITEFLIES

Especially attracted to tomatoes, eggplants, lettuce, and citrus, whiteflies can be a problem in mild-winter areas and in greenhouses. In cool weather, whiteflies slow down production.

Control: In the garden, *Encarsia* wasps and other parasitoids usually control whiteflies. If infested plants are too near fences or walls, or growing too close together, move them to an area with good airflow. Look under leaves for the scalelike, immobile nymphs and pupae. Hose them off with a strong spray of water; repeat daily for 3 days. Insecticidal soap and light horticultural oil sprays are effective.

Wildlife Pests

Be careful what you ask for: in our enthusiasm to attract wildlife to our gardens, we attract some creatures that are not conducive to a productive garden—for us.

The most effective way to protect your edible plants from two- and four-legged critters is to put a physical barrier between them and the fruit or vegetable. Fences—usually the most effective control for most animals—and netting for birds are both time-honored controls. The English construct decorative berry houses that look like screened gazebos—complete with entry doors and mesh large enough for the bees to fly in and out to pollinate the flowers—and plant them with currants, blueberries, and strawberries. In some settings, electric fences can be very effective. Protect small plants from squirrels, dogs, and other critters with wood-frame boxes covered with small-diameter wire mesh placed over the plants; secure to the ground with irrigation stakes.

Other controls: Cover fruits with small fruit bags to deter some birds and all insects; sprinkle hot chili pepper powder on foliage to deter raccoons and squirrels; attach metallic tape to scare away birds; spray with strong-smelling and -tasting chemicals, such as predator urine or products that smell of rotten eggs or contain hot sauce, to repel deer (this only works if they are not starving).

The following are some of the most common pest critters you may encounter and how to thwart them.

BIRDS

Some birds, especially starlings, catbirds, mockingbirds, crows, and finches, can be major pests of berries and cherries.

Control: Cover dwarf trees and bushes with black nylon bird netting; wrap tightly and thoroughly. You need about 24 square feet to cover an 8-foot-tall tree. Netting is usually sold in 14-foot-wide pieces; lace them together with plastic ties. Use a rake to ease the netting over the tree and secure it to the ground with concrete reinforcing bar, making sure that it is sealed at ground level or the birds will get in. Remove the netting after harvest. Wrap smaller plants, such as short blueberry plants, from the bottom to the top with netting so you can open it to harvest; secure the netting with spring-type clothespins. Other deterrents—hanging metallic strips or aluminum pie pans in trees, and scarecrows—are somewhat effective, but use them just before harvest, or birds become desensitized to them.

DEER

Deer are rapacious vegetarians with ever-increasing populations and ever-decreasing forage lands, so it's no wonder they are the scourge of many gardens. Some edibles that deer usually do not eat include artichokes, cardoon, cucumbers, garlic, rhubarb, squash, fig, and the herbs chives, mint, fennel, lavender, oregano, peppermint, rosemary, sage, and thyme.

Control: Try spraying with a repellent; reapply after each rain and when the odor starts to wane. In winter the odors of repellents are ineffective, and it is in winter that deer problems are more severe. In some areas, a fence at least 8 feet high (or a shorter fence within a fence or an electric fence) or a trained dog may be the only option. For more information, you can visit www.gardening.cornell.edu and www.ext.colostate.edu.

GOPHERS

Gophers are rodents that live underground, where they burrow and eat roots and plants.

Control: Plant trees and shrubs in wire baskets with the top of the basket a few inches above ground level. Buy the baskets or form them yourself from fine-mesh aviary or chicken wire. Grow vegetables and herbs in raised beds lined with small-mesh hardware cloth that goes at least 2 feet below ground. A good dog can really help, and you can always trap gophers.

MOLES

Contrary to popular belief, moles don't eat plant roots, but they do disturb them while tunneling through the soil looking for earthworms, and they can make a mess out of brick-on-sand paving.

Control: Trapping is the best bet, or try one of the repellents containing castor oil.

RABBITS

Bunnies love to eat new growth, young vegetable plants, and fruits.

Control: Surround raised beds with rabbit wire—2-foot-wide mesh set 6 inches into the ground. Or grow vegetables in tall containers. Spraying plants with hot pepper wax formulated for rabbits and squirrels sometimes works. (Hot pepper wax formulated for insects does not repel most mammals.)

RACCOONS

These smart animals have an innate sense of when fruits and vegetables are just ripe—and beat you to the harvest.

Control: Two-foot-high, solar-powered electric fences help keep raccoons (and woodchucks) out of garden beds. Discourage them by sprinkling large amounts of hot chili powder (buy it in bulk in Mexican grocery stores) on the ground, or use hot pepper wax formulated for mammals.

RATS, VOLES, AND MICE

These rodents are known to gnaw on the bark of fruit trees in winter and may eat the fruit.

Control: Surround trunks with plastic or metal rodent guards (or use chicken wire or plastic trunk wraps—at least 6 inches from the bark). Keep mulch at least a foot away from trunks so there is nowhere to hide. Trapping helps.

SQUIRRELS

Omnivorous eaters, squirrels pose a serious and hard-to-control problem for many gardeners.

Control: Completely covering fruit trees with bird netting may help. Use hot pepper wax formulated for mammals. Hunting or trapping and killing them is allowed in some areas; check with your local Cooperative Extension Service.

Plant Diseases

Diseases and disorders caused by nutrient deficiencies or excesses are covered in Chapter 2. This section deals with diseases caused by organisms such as fungi, bacteria, and viruses.

These types of plant diseases are potentially far more damaging to your edibles than most pests. Diseases are particularly difficult to control once they have begun; therefore, most disease-control strategies feature prevention rather than cure. Check individual Encyclopedia entries for specific cultural information so you can keep your plants healthy and fend off diseases.

The most common diseases of edible plants, how to prevent them, and their controls, if any, are described below. See "Recommended Products" later in this appendix for precautions concerning suggested control materials.

ANTHRACNOSE

A fungal disease (caused by *Colletotrichum* spp., *Glomerella* spp., and fungi specific to certain plants), anthracnose occurs primarily in the eastern and central United States. The disease spreads readily in warm, wet, or humid weather and overwinters in the soil and on debris. Affected plants include tomatoes, grapes, and berries. Fruits and leaves develop sunken, circular, watery spots that darken and enlarge with age.

Control: Anthracnose can be seedborne; don't save seeds from infected crops. Choose resistant varieties and disease-free seeds. Plant and prune for good air circulation, practice 3-year crop rotation, avoid overhead irrigation, mulch well, and carry out a thorough fall cleanup. Bordeaux mix, sulfur, lime sulfur, Serenade, and neem-based sprays give some control.

BROWN ROT

Monilinia fungus causes brown rot, which is evidenced by browning blossoms, soft or rotten sunken areas called cankers on twigs, and fruit rotting (just as fruit ripens, round brown spots appear that eventually affect the entire fruit). Unless removed, fruits stick tightly to the branches; dried-up, diseased fruits are known as "mummies." The fungus overwinters in mummies and infected twigs; it thrives in mild, wet weather.

Control: Plant resistant varieties, thin the fruits for good air circulation, clean up dropped fruits, and avoid planting in lawns, where conditions are humid. If the disease develops, remove and destroy all spoiled fruits. Prune out and dispose of infected twigs. If the spoilage level is intolerable on apricots and cherries, spray with micronized copper immediately after bloom. For peaches, nectarines, and plums, spray with lime sulfur or micronized copper, timed according to package directions.

DOWNY MILDEW

Downy mildew is caused by a variety of fungi—each specific to a particular plant, including lettuce, grapes, roses, and cucumber and cabbage family members—that thrive in damp, cool weather. The fungi enter through pores on the undersides of leaves, creating a yellow spot on the top and a fuzzy patch below. Fruits of infected plants may be tasteless; badly infected plants die.

Control: Select resistant varieties. Site and prune the plants so they have plenty of sun and good air circulation. Practice crop rotation. Avoid overhead watering or water in early morning so leaves dry off before nighttime. Immediately pinch off and dispose of infected leaves. If the infection continues, apply Bordeaux mix, Serenade, or neem.

FIREBLIGHT

Fireblight is a serious disease of fruit trees caused by the *Erwinia amylovora* bacterium; pears are highly susceptible, while quinces and apples are prone to it. Blossoms and succulent growth are especially vulnerable. The blight moves fast with symptoms that can resemble scorching: blossoms and leaves turn brown; shoots turn black and wilt. A tan liquid awash with bacteria can ooze from cankers on twigs or branches. The disease is most prevalent in spring when it is rainy, temperatures are about 65°F, and trees are in bloom. Water, bees, and garden tools spread the bacteria.

Control: Choose fireblight-resistant varieties when possible. Avoid high-nitrogen fertilizers, which encourage tender, susceptible new growth. Check blossoms, twigs, and leaves frequently—especially in spring—for any signs of scorched-looking brown leaves, shepherd's crook twigs, or blackening shoots. Immediately cut off diseased tissue—at least 6 inches into healthy tissue. Sterilize tools between cuts in a 10 percent solution of bleach or in straight rubbing alcohol or Lysol. Prune in winter when the disease is dormant. Agrimycin, an antibiotic registered for preventing fireblight in pears and apples, is available in some states. Serenade may provide control.

Disease Resistance

Agricultural research on plant diseases has led to new varieties like mildew-resistant grapes and fireblight-resistant pears. If a particular disease is a problem in your area, choose resistant varieties if possible. I include disease-resistant varieties in the Encyclopedia section. Be aware, however, that plant diseases adapt to new conditions, so a disease-resistant variety may work for a while, but then you may have to change to a new variety. For some edibles, such as raspberries, strict inspections help ensure that certified disease-free plants are clean.

FUSARIUM WILT AND VERTICILLIUM WILT

Soil-dwelling fungi cause similar diseases that enter plants through the roots, move up through water-conducting tissues, and cut water flow to the upper portions of the plant. This causes yellowing leaves, wilting, individual stem die-off, and eventual death of the plant. Cross sections of the stem show the typical rings of darkened tissues.

Fusarium wilt (*Fusarium oxysporum*) is prevalent in warm temperatures (75 to 85°F) and is especially a problem on members of the cabbage and tomato families. Verticillium wilt (*Verticillium* spp.) is a cool-weather disease (55 to 65°F) brought on by cold, wet spring weather and poorly drained soil. It affects a wide range of plants, including cabbage and tomato family members, strawberries, raspberries, plums, and cherries.

Control: If the disease is a problem in your area, seek out resistant varieties when possible (F = fusarium resistant, V = verticillium resistant). In general, apples, asparagus, beans, citrus, figs, pears, walnuts, and certain tomatoes and strawberries are naturally resistant to verticillium wilt. Crop rotation does not work as these fungi live too long in the soil. Pull up vegetables that are diseased and destroy them. Sterilize your tools in a 10 percent bleach solution or in straight rubbing alcohol or Lysol.

LEAF SPOT FUNGI

A number of fungal diseases (among them alternaria and shot hole fungus) cause leaf spots and are associated with warm, wet weather. On tomatoes, *Alternaria* species cause early blight diseases (which, despite the name, occur throughout the growing season); they attack leaves, stems, and fruits, starting on lower leaves, causing small round spots with concentric, targetlike rings. In cabbage family plants, alternaria leaf spots begin as small black dots that enlarge to brown spots—also with a targetlike appearance. Shot hole disease, which affects almonds, apricots, and peaches, begins with small purple spots that develop ¼-inch holes in the center.

Control: Plant resistant varieties. Allow for good air circulation. Rotate vegetable crops on a 3-year basis. Avoid overhead irrigation. Clean up and destroy diseased leaves and fruits. Dispose of plants seriously affected with early blight. Do not compost infected plants or save seeds from infected fruits. Serenade may provide control.

POWDERY MILDEW

Caused by plant-specific fungi, powdery mildew is aptly named: it appears as a gray powdery dust on leaves and stems of a wide variety of plants. Unlike other fungal diseases, powdery mildew can thrive in semi-arid climates and establish itself in morning dew. In severe cases on highly susceptible plants, such as cucumber family members and roses, leaves dry out and die; grape clusters wither and rot. Plants rarely die from this disease.

Control: Prevention is the first line of control: plant resistant varieties, prune to allow for plenty of air circulation, clean up diseased leaves in fall, and train fruit trees to an open vase shape. Sprays of baking soda, neem oil, lightweight horticultural oil, liquid sulfur, or Serenade can be effective. Be sure to spray the tops and bottoms of leaves. Spray grapes with liquid sulfur four times—once every 10 days—beginning when the new shoots are a foot long. Never spray oil and sulfur at the same time; always allow at least 2 weeks if switching between these products.

SOILBORNE FUNGI

In poorly drained soil, certain fungi become active and attack plant roots—especially in warm weather. *Pythium* species are notorious for causing damping-off in seedlings; *Phytophthora* fungi cause root rot in many plants nationwide. In the West, *Armillaria* (oak root fungus) is associated with warm, wet soil.

Control: Keep seedling trays lightly moist, not drenched. Before planting fruit trees, make sure drainage is excellent. Always keep mulch several inches away from trunks, and do not mulch too thickly.

VIRUSES

Virus-infected plants often show symptoms of deformed or mottled leaves and stunting of the whole plant. Cucumber beetles and certain aphids transmit several mosaic viruses, including tobacco mosaic (TMV), which attacks tomato family plants, and cucumber mosaic virus (CMV), which affects cucumbers, melons, and squash. Grapes, raspberries, figs, and strawberries are particularly virus susceptible.

Control: Buy virus-resistant plants whenever possible. There is no cure for viruses; destroy plants that show symptoms. Do not save seeds from infected plants.

Natural Products for Pest and Disease Control

Good cultural techniques and a balanced ecosystem that includes natural enemies are essential for pest and disease control. As you become more in tune with how natural controls operate, you'll find you use fewer purchased products.

Timely Tips

No matter what kind of natural products you use, they will be most effective and safest when you adhere to these tips:

- Follow package directions to the letter.
- More is not better.
- Wear protective clothing such as goggles and rubber gloves when spraying any pesticides, including organics.
- Keep pets and children inside when applying any pest or disease control.
- To avoid drift, spray when the air is still.
- To protect honeybees, spray in the early morning or very late in the day (before and after bees are active).
- Never spray when the temperature is over 80°F or risk burning the leaves.

And remember, it is always better to avoid using sprays and other control products.

Recommended Products

Take time to read labels completely before purchasing a pest or disease control product. Look for selective products that affect the target pest or disease and allow natural enemies to survive. Avoid those that are harmful to bees—or to fish if you are near water. Of the available materials, the most selective are not chemicals but microorganisms such as *Bt*, which affects only the target pest. If a selective product is not available, use one of the more benign pesticides, such as horticultural oil, baking soda, or insecticidal soap.

BAKING SODA SPRAY

Baking soda is the main ingredient of a simple anti-fungal spray you can make at home. To 1 gallon of water add 3 tablespoons of baking soda, 1 tablespoon of dish soap (not antibacterial), and 1 tablespoon of vegetable oil. Shake vigorously to mix. Spray the tops and bottoms of leaves of plants susceptible to or suffering from powdery mildew (remove diseased leaves first). The baking soda changes the pH on the leaf surface just enough to discourage fungal growth. Do not spray in bright sun. Reapply every 7 to 10 days. Keep unused spray in a cool, dark place.

BORDEAUX MIX

A century-old treatment for fungal diseases, especially grapevine fungus, this sprayed mixture of copper sulfate and hydrated lime works on anthracnose, downy mildew, and other fungi. Caution: Copper can leach and contaminate waterways. Follow directions carefully; misuse of Bordeaux mix can damage plants.

BORIC ACID

Boric acid is available as ready-to-use ant bait stations or as a liquid. Worker ants bring the bait back to the colony and feed it to the larvae and the queen. Although it eventually eliminates that colony, often another ant family will move into the same area, which you will have to treat.

BT

Bacillus thuringiensis is a naturally occurring bacterium used as an insecticide for larvae, but it works only if the organism ingests the bacteria. Spray early or late in the day; it degrades in sunlight. You may need to reapply weekly. There are several strains of the bacteria. *Bt* var. *kurstaki* (*Btk*), which controls assorted leaf-eating caterpillars, is marketed under numerous trade names, including Dipel and Thuricide. **Caution:** *Bt* is indiscriminate; it will kill any butterfly or moth larvae. Look for other insect-specific strains, such as *Bt* var. *san diego*, which targets Colorado potato beetles, and *Bt* var. *israelensis*, which comes in the form of mosquito dunks that float in standing water to kill mosquito larvae.

COMPOST TEA

Compost tea is a solution that used to be made by soaking a bag of well-aged compost and/or worm castings in an old trash can or large bucket filled with water. For safety sake, I recommend aerating the water while brewing (a fish-tank pump works well) and using the tea within a day. Spraying the compost tea prevents some fungal diseases and is excellent for foliar feeding. Do not use compost tea on developing fruit (including tomatoes) or leafy greens. Research on compost tea is changing quickly, including concerns about *E. coli* contamination. Look online for the latest information.

DIATOMACEOUS EARTH

Also known as DE, diatomaceous earth is the naturally occurring fossilized remains of hard-shelled phytoplankton called diatoms. Microscopic, sharp protuberances act as an irritant barrier to pests, especially slugs and other soft-bodied critters. Purchase DE labeled for garden use, not for swimming pool filters, and use it dry. Wear a dust mask when spreading it around plants.

HORTICULTURAL OILS

Petroleum-based oils smother certain deciduous fruit tree pests: the overwintering eggs of aphids, mites, pear psylla adults, red spider mites, scale, and whitefly nymphs. Spray dormant oil only in winter or early spring when woody plants are dormant or you will burn the buds and leaves. Use lightweight or summer oil throughout the year. Never spray oil and sulfur at the same time; always allow at least 2 weeks between application of these products.

HOT PEPPER WAX

Hot pepper wax is made with food-grade paraffin wax and capsaicin from cayenne peppers. Capsaicin, the chemical compound that gives the heat to all hot peppers, acts as a lethal metabolic stimulant to soft-bodied insects. The wax makes the spray stick to aphids, scale, spider mites, and thrips—killing them on contact and repelling them for up to 3 weeks. The capsaicin isn't absorbed into the plant tissues; a rinse in warm water gets rid of any on the outside. To repel mammals, look for hot pepper wax formulated for animals such as rabbits and squirrels.

INSECTICIDAL SOAP

A staple for organic gardeners, insecticidal soap is derived from potassium salts. A direct spray smothers and desiccates insects, including aphids, mealybugs, and scale, as well as spider mites. However, it is not pest specific; avoid spraying near beneficials. Be sure to spray the tops and undersides of leaves; do not spray leaves in full sun or they will burn.

LIME SULFUR

Lime sulfur is one of the most effective fungicides for brown rot, peach leaf curl, scab, and other fungal diseases. If horticultural oil has been used, wait 2 to 3 weeks before spraying lime sulfur. Wear safety goggles and gloves, as this material is caustic and can seriously injure eyes and skin. Do not spray or let drift onto evergreens, or on wood or painted surfaces.

MICRONIZED COPPER

Finely ground copper sulfate such as Microcop is used to fight brown rot, fireblight, and scab on fruit and nut trees. All copper products are toxic to humans and other mammals and are highly toxic to fish. Wear protective clothing, goggles, and a respirator. Spray in early spring, early in the morning on a dry day; do not apply after pink bud stage or when trees are in leaf, as injury to the leaves may occur. Let the tree dry before touching it.

NEEM EXTRACT

A botanical insecticide extracted from the tropical neem tree's seeds, neem has been used for centuries in Asia. Azadiractin, the active ingredient, suppresses feeding and prevents breeding and metamorphosis. Spray neem to control caterpillars, cucumber beetles, the Japanese beetle, parasitic nematodes, thrips, and weevils; it can harm beneficials.

NEEM OIL

Neem oil is a broad-spectrum insecticide and miticide that is sprayed on aphids and other soft-bodied insects as well as mites to suffocate them. As a fungicide, the spray thwarts diseases, including anthracnose and powdery mildew, by preventing fungal spore germination and killing fungi on the leaves.

PHEROMONE TRAPS

Containing species-select, synthetic female sex hormones, these traps lure and catch the males, thus disrupting the mating cycle. Use them to monitor pest populations, too. Currently, species lures are available for the cabbage looper, codling moth, cucumber beetles, olive fruit fly, and peach twig borer. Store unused, unopened lures in the freezer.

PYRETHRUM AND PYRETHRINS

Use pyrethrum or pyrethrins as a last resort when nothing else works. Both come from the pyrethrum flower (*Chrysanthemum cinerariifolium*); pyrethrum is the crushed, dried flower heads, while pyrethrins are the extracted natural ingredients of the flowers. Both have a "knock down" that stuns flying insects and an "exciter" that irritates insects to come out of hiding into contact with the spray, so they work against most insects—pests and beneficials. Pyrethrum and pyrethrins break down quickly in sunlight, so apply them in the evening. Because both have a short residual effect, repeat applications may be necessary. Both are toxic to fish. Used inappropriately, both can trigger secondary pest outbreaks. Avoid any product containing pyrethroids, which are synthetic and even more toxic, especially when piperonyl butoxide has been added.

SERENADE GARDEN DISEASE CONTROL

Serenade is an OMRI-listed, living microbial made from a strain of *Bacillus subtilis* that penetrates and destroys disease spores without harming beneficial insects or wildlife. It is a wettable powder that is sprayed on. Serenade is listed to control anthracnose, bacterial leaf blight, black root rot/black crown rot, black spot, botrytis, gray mold, powdery mildew, and walnut blight. It suppresses bacterial spot, downy mildew, early blight, fireblight, late blight, leaf spot fungi, and scab.

SPINOSAD

This pesticide, derived from fermentation of the naturally occurring *Saccharopolyspora spinosa* bacterium, is also a last resort. A nerve and stomach poison, spinosad is a new alternative to *Bt* for caterpillar control that is also toxic to leaf miners and thrips. To lessen damage to beneficials, apply it very late in the day, when they are not active.

SULFUR

Sulfur is a broad-spectrum insecticide and fungicide that is easiest to use in liquid form. Its submicronized particles have a strong adhesive quality that allows them to stick to the plant despite adverse weather. Use it on fruit trees for anthracnose, brown rot, powdery mildew, mites, rust, scab, and thrips; and on grapes for powdery mildew. Never spray oil and sulfur at the same time; always allow at least 2 weeks if you switch from one to the other.

Remember, appropriate plant care and maintaining a healthy garden ecosystem will keep pest and disease problems to a minimum. A balanced ecosystem will reward you with many hours to enjoy the garden and to feast on its bounty.

Sources and Resources

Now that I've shared my enthusiasm for edible gardens, it's only fair that I share the many sources and resources I've personally used over the years—and that gardening friends around the country whose opinions I trust have used and found invaluable. So in this section you'll find directories of reputable mail-order seed and plant suppliers as well as innovative companies that carry the latest earth-friendly garden products. You'll also find contact information for many organizations devoted to edible plants and preserving the environment and a list of exceptional gardens with edible plants that you can visit for inspiration.

How to Obtain Plant Materials

Plants are available from many sources: a gardening neighbor, horticultural organizations, supermarkets, and discount stores as well as local, mail-order, and online nurseries. From your neighbors and horticultural societies you can get seeds, transplants, tubers, and divisions. Commercial sources supply seeds, transplants, tubers, and bare-root or container plants. Every plant mentioned in this book is available from at least one of the sources listed here.

Sharing and Saving

One of the great joys of gardening is sharing your bounty with others. Whether you give or receive, you have the satisfaction of knowing that these edible plants are acclimated to your area, are proven successful, and may be a variety no longer available commercially. The extra seeds from an old-time bean that Aunt Polly grew or budding stock from an out-of-fashion fruit tree adds diversity to a garden. Some edible plants need to be divided, so there may be opportunities to pick up an artichoke plant, Jerusalem artichoke tubers, or a banana pup.

Many edible plants set enough seeds that gardeners are happy to share them. Remember that plants designated as hybrid or F_1 hybrid on the seed package cannot reliably reproduce themselves. Other plants to avoid when saving seeds are corn and members of the cucurbit family (cucumbers, melons, pumpkins, and squash). Unless planted in complete isolation, these plants cross-pollinize and produce strange second generations.

Open-pollinated varieties come true from seed; save these and resow them the following year. You can save seeds of some herbs, beans, peas, and carrots as well as select varieties of many other vegetables. If you have a favorite, share it and cherish it. Some seed companies specialize in heirlooms; others provide both hybrids and open-pollinated varieties.

To save money, you can grow fruit and nut trees from seed. They take a few years longer to bear and will give a variable product—sometimes better than the parent, sometimes worse, and sometimes the same. Or grow a seedling tree and graft wood from a known cultivar onto it. Joining the fruit and nut societies named in this guide is well worthwhile.

Caution: No matter what the form of the shared crop—seeds, cuttings, or divisions—be sure the source is disease free. Virus-infected bean seeds or strawberry roots with nematodes are no bargain. If you save your own seeds, learn to identify virus symptoms in plants, and discard seeds from affected plants. When trading seeds, ask if the plants had any particular disease problems.

Horticultural Organizations and Seed Exchanges

These organizations are excellent sources of antique and unusual edibles. Membership is usually required, but dues are minimal and the advantages many. Besides offering uncommon seeds and scion or bud wood, they usually share information online; some have newsletters and offer cultural and historical material on plants of interest.

Another popular way of obtaining seed is through various seed exchanges—published lists of gardeners willing to share their seeds. Some of the sources listed offer this service (Seed Savers Exchange is the best known), as do some gardening magazines and organizations devoted to different aspects of food growing. An Internet search on "seed exchanges" will yield many more sources of seeds.

State Forestry and Agricultural Departments

Many states have programs to encourage tree planting and provide young trees for reforesting woodland areas at a nominal fee. Inquire at your local Cooperative Extension Service to see if there is such a program in your area. This service is aimed at homeowners who need a number of trees to help control erosion, establish woodlands, or create windbreaks.

Cut-Rate Plants

In general, the plants sold at national chain discount stores, groceries, and hardware stores cannot be considered good buys. They have usually been given sporadic care, with minimal attention to their light requirements and pest problems. Salespeople in these stores generally cannot provide advice on care or suitability.

These stores sometimes carry inferior seeds and fruit tree varieties better suited to other climates. In plants, as in other things, the old adage holds true: you get what you pay for.

Nurseries

Nurseries—local, mail-order, and online—reflect the people who run them; some are honorable and very well informed, but others are not. Most are operated by people who love plants and want your garden to be successful.

LOCAL RETAIL NURSERIES

Well-informed local nursery people often know the best varieties for your area—plants resistant to diseases or that have been bred for local soil conditions—take pride in their knowledge, and sell superior products. Many take courses to keep current and often proudly display their credentials. A good local nursery is your most valuable plant source because it enables you to choose plants and products yourself. Check for the following when visiting a new nursery:

- Do the plants look healthy?
- Does the nursery sell plants for the wrong season? For example, is it selling marigold or pepper plants a month before frost is due? (Seeds are seldom sold for a particular season; usually seeds for all seasons are sold at one time.)
- Will the nursery special-order plants or merchandise for you?
- Can the nursery person give you information about the plants you buy?
- Does the nursery push chemical pesticides and herbicides?

The majority of local nurseries carry deciduous fruit trees and a few perennial vegetables, such as strawberries, asparagus, and artichokes, bare root during late winter and early spring and the most popular edibles in containers throughout the growing season. When you find a good nursery, frequent it and appreciate it.

MAIL-ORDER AND ONLINE NURSERIES

Mail-order and online nurseries and seed companies offer a much larger selection of plants than any local nursery can provide. Many are generalists and carry vegetables, herbs, and flowers, while others specialize. Most have websites that give information on how to grow and harvest their plants; many sell helpful specialized products such as cranberry rakes, tree trunk guards, and pheromone traps.

Go online to see what fruits and vegetables are offered and when possible look for companies that are geographically close to you. And do your homework. Be leery of "miracle plants." A few nurseries seem to hire fiction writers to compose their catalogs. Sadly, there are no climbing strawberries. And the "egg tree" is really just a white eggplant!

Most catalogs come out in winter; some of the companies that specialize in edibles offer plants only in spring while they are still dormant. Start your research in fall so that you can take advantage of bare-root shipping if possible and to be assured of the best and most complete selection of varieties.

Note: To help control pests and diseases, many states have laws covering the importation of plants. Some plants, such as currants, are banned altogether in a few states. Inspection requirements or agricultural crop protection in a state determines if a nursery can ship what you want. Read catalog and web pages carefully; they usually tell what can be sent where. Most seeds and small plants are sent out by first-class mail; the majority of large plants and trees are sent parcel post.

Mail-Order Sources for Seeds and Plants

The following companies carry a number of the plants and a few of the supplies mentioned in the text. Most have a website and a toll-free number. Since web addresses and phone numbers may change, if you can't find one of these companies from the information listed here, look for it by entering the name into your favorite search engine.

Acorn Springs Farms
3418 FM 1252 W.
Kilgore, TX 75662
903-660-2636
www.acornsprings.com
Pomegranates, olive trees, dwarf citrus, bananas, and herbs; garden merchandise

Adams County Nursery
26 Nursery Rd.
PO Box 108
Aspers, PA 17304
717-677-8105
www.acnursery.com
Large selection of fruit trees; books on fruit, tree trunk guards, and online month-by-month cultural information

American Blueberry Co.
7E Shawnee Bypass
Muskogee, OK 74403
866-985-2247
www.americanblueberrycompany.com
Blueberry specialist; also carries blackberries and daylilies; website offers valuable growing information about blueberries

Ames' Orchard and Nursery
18292 Wildlife Rd.
Fayetteville, AR 72701
501-443-0282
Disease-resistant apples, pears, grapes, and raspberries; other fruits for the South

Antique Rose Emporium
9300 Lueckemeyer Rd.
Brenham, TX 77833
800-441-0002
www.antiqueroseemporium.com
Specializing in antique roses; roses that thrive in milder-winter climates and resist diseases

Apple Art Espalier
498 Pepper Rd.
Petaluma, CA 94952
707-795-0919
www.appleart.com
Apples, pears, and other fruit trees trained as espalier

Applesource
1716 Apples Rd.
Chapin, IL 62628
800-588-3854
www.applesource.com
Apples for tasting; buy a sampler of unusual varieties to help you decide which ones to grow

Baker Creek Heirloom Seeds
2278 Baker Creek Rd.
Mansfield, MO 65704
417-924-8917
www.rareseeds.com
Huge selection of heirloom vegetable, flower, and herb seeds

Bamboo Giant Nursery
5601 Freedom Blvd.
Aptos, CA 95003
831-687-0100
www.bamboogiant.com
Many species of bamboo; bamboo products

Bamboo Sourcery
666 Wagnon Rd.
Sebastopol, CA 95472
707-823-5866
www.bamboosourcery.com
Many species of bamboo; bamboo products

Banana Tree
715 Northampton St.
Easton, PA 18042
610-253-9589
www.banana-tree.com
Banana rhizomes; Asian vegetable, herb, and pepper seeds

Bay Laurel Nursery
2500 El Camino Real
Atascadero, CA 93422
805-466-3406
www.baylaurelnursery.com
Fruit trees for the Southwest and California

Blossomberry Nursery
2662 Hwy. 21
Clarksville, AR 72830
479-754-6489
Seedless table grapes and muscadines

Bountiful Gardens
18001 Shafer Ranch Rd.
Willits, CA 95490
707-459-6410
www.bountifulgardens.org
Open-pollinated vegetables; herbs, flowers, grains, and green manures; supplies for biointensive gardening

Brite Leaf Citrus Nursery
480 CR 416 S.
Lake Panasoffkee, FL 33538
352-793-6861
www.briteleaf.com
Specializing in citrus

Burgess Seed & Plant Co.
905 Four Seasons Rd.
Bloomington, IL 61701
309-662-7761
www.eburgess.com
Seeds, bulbs, perennials, annuals; also ornamentals

Burnt Ridge Nursery & Orchards
432 Burnt Ridge Rd.
Onalaska, WA 98570
360-985-2873
www.burntridgenursery.com
The usual fruits plus raspberries, nut trees, mulberries, pawpaws, and persimmons

Burpee
300 Park Ave.
Warminster, PA 18974
800-333-5808
www.burpee.com
Vegetable, herb, and flower seeds; some plants in spring

C & O Nursery
1700 N. Wenatchee Ave.
Wenatchee, WA 98807
800-232-2636
www.c-onursery.com
Great source for many types of fruit trees

Camellia Forest Nursery
620 Hwy. 54 W.
Chapel Hill, NC 27516
919-968-0504
www.camforest.com
One of the few sources of tea plants in the United States

ContainerSeeds.com
204 Morris St.
Blossburg, PA 16912
570-638-2524
www.ContainerSeeds.com
Fruit, herbs, and vegetable seeds suited to growing in containers

Cook's Garden
PO Box C5030
Warminster, PA 18974
800-457-9703
www.cooksgarden.com
Vegetable, herb, and flower seeds; some organic and heirloom varieties

Cox Berry Farm and Nursery
1081 Hwy. 818
Clarksville, AR 72830
479-754-3707
www.coxberryfarm.com
Blackberries, blueberries, and raspberries

Cross Country Nurseries
PO Box 170
199 Kingwood-Locktown Rd.
Rosemont, NJ 08556
908-996-4646
www.chileplants.com
Great selection of chili and sweet pepper, eggplant, and tomato plants in spring

Cummins Nursery
1408 Trumansburg Rd.
Ithaca, NY 14850
607-227-6147
www.cumminsnursery.com
Custom-grown apple, pear, cherry, and plum trees

D. Landreth Seed Co.
60 E. High St., Bldg. #4
New Freedom, PA 17349
800-654-2407
www.landrethseeds.com
Oldest seed house in the United States; heirloom vegetables and flowers; potatoes; container and small-space garden plants

Dave Wilson Nursery
800-654-5854
www.davewilson.com
Wholesale breeder and grower of major fruits; website is a great resource for fruit tree information for home gardeners; look for their plants in your local nursery

Dixondale Farms
PO Box 129, Dept. WP09
Carrizo Springs, TX 78834
877-367-1015
www.dixondalefarms.com
Onion and leek plants

Durio Nursery
5853 Hwy. 182
Opelousas, LA 70570
337-948-3696
www.durionursery.biz
Very large selection of pomegranates

Ed Hume Seeds
PO Box 73160
Puyallup, WA 98373
253-435-4414
www.humeseeds.com
Vegetable seeds for short seasons and cool climates

Edible Landscaping
361 Spirit Ridge Ln.
Afton, VA 22920
800-524-4156
www.ediblelandscaping.com
The best selection of attractive fruits, berries, vines, nuts, and herbs

Evergreen Y. H. Enterprises
PO Box 17538
Anaheim, CA 92817
714-637-5769
www.evergreenseeds.com
Asian vegetable and herb seeds

Fall Creek Farm & Nursery
39318 Jasper Lowell Rd.
Lowell, OR 97452
541-937-2973
www.fallcreeknursery.com
Blueberry specialist, wholesale only; website offers valuable growing information about blueberries; look for their plants at your local nursery

Fedco Seeds
PO Box 520
Waterville, ME 04903
207-873-7333
www.fedcoseeds.com
Bare-root, hardy fruit trees and shrubs available only January through March; vegetable seeds available through summer

Filaree Farm
182 Conconully Hwy.
Okanogan, WA 98840
509-422-6940
www.filareefarm.com
100 varieties of garlic; green manure seeds

Forestfarm
990 Tetherow Rd.
Williams, OR 97544
541-846-7269
www.forestfarm.com
Shrubs, perennials, bamboos, and medicinal plants

Four Winds Growers
www.fourwindsgrowers.com
California-based online source of dwarf citrus trees and information on growing citrus; look for their plants at your local nursery

Garden of Delights
14560 SW 14th St.
Davie, FL 33325
800-741-3103
www.gardenofdelights.com
Specializing in tropical fruits

Goodwin Creek Gardens
PO Box 83
Williams, OR 97544
800-846-7359
www.goodwincreekgardens.com
Herbs; plants to attract beneficials

Gourmet Seed International
HC 12 Box 510
Tatum, NM 88267
575-398-6111
www.gourmetseed.com
Herb and vegetable seeds, many Italian specialties; gardening supplies

Greenfield Citrus Nursery
2558 E. Lehi Rd.
Mesa, AZ 85213
480-830-8000
www.greenfieldcitrus.com
Specializing in citrus

Gurney's Seed & Nursery Co.
PO Box 4178
Greendale, IN 47025
513-354-1492
www.gurneys.com
Vegetable seeds and plants, flower seeds, berries, and fruit and nut trees

Harris Seeds
355 Paul Rd.
PO Box 24966
Rochester, NY 14624
800-544-7938
www.harrisseeds.com
Large selection of vegetable, flower, and herb seeds

Hartmann's Plant Co.
310 60th St.
Grand Junction, MI 49056
269-253-4281
www.hartmannsplantcompany.com
Many berries and small fruits, especially blueberries; wholesale and retail

Heirloom Old Garden Roses
24062 NE Riverside Dr.
St Paul, OR 97137
503-538-1576
www.heirloomroses.com
Large selection of new and old roses

Heirloom Seeds
www.heirloomseeds.com
Online source of heirloom vegetable, flower, and herb seeds; many southern favorites

Henry Field's Seed & Nursery
PO Box 397
Aurora, IN 47001
513-354-1494
www.henryfields.com
Vegetable seeds and plants, fruit and nut trees, and garden supplies

Henry Leuthardt Nurseries
Montauk Hwy.
PO Box 666
East Moriches, NY 11940
631-878-1387
www.henryleuthardtnurseries.com
Apple and pear espaliers, fruit trees, and berry plants

Hidden Springs Nursery
170 Hidden Springs Ln.
Cookeville, TN 38501
931-268-2592
www.hiddenspringsnursery.com
Organically grown bare-root fruit trees and berries

High Altitude Gardens
PO Box 596
Cornville, AZ 86325
928-649-3315
www.seedstrust.com/has/highaltitudeseeds
Heirloom vegetable seeds and bulk wildflower seeds adapted to cold climates and short seasons

High Country Roses
PO Box 148
Jensen, UT 84035
800-552-2082
www.highcountryroses.com
Hardy old rose varieties

Hortico Nurseries
723 Robson Rd., RR #1
Waterdown, ON, Canada L0R 2H1
905-689-6984
www.hortico.com
Heirloom and new roses; perennials, shrubs, and aquatic plants; ships worldwide

Indiana Berry & Plant Co.
5218 W. 500 S.
Huntingburg, IN 47542
800-295-2226
www.indianaberry.com
Asparagus, rhubarb, horseradish, and many small fruits

Ison's Nursery & Vineyards
6855 Newman Hwy.
Brooks, GA 30205
800-733-0324
www.isons.com
Fruit and nut trees, blueberries, brambleberries, and grapes

Italian Seed & Tool Co.
HC 12 Box 510
Tatum, NM 88267
575-398-6111
www.italianseedandtool.com
Wide selection of herb and vegetable seeds, especially uncommon Italian varieties

JD Andersen Nursery
2790 Marvinga Ln.
Fallbrook, CA 92028
760-723-2907
www.jdandersen.com
Tropical fruits and many banana varieties

J. L. Hudson, Seedsman
PO Box 337
La Honda, CA 94020
www.jlhudsonseeds.net
Seed bank helping to preserve botanical diversity; many heirlooms and natives

Johnny's Selected Seeds
955 Benton Ave.
Winslow, ME 04901-2601
877-564-6697
www.johnnyseeds.com
Large selection of vegetable varieties for short-season gardeners; herbs, flowers, and cover crops

John Scheepers Kitchen Garden Seeds
23 Tulip Dr.
PO Box 638
Bantam, CT 06750
860-567-6086
www.kitchengardenseeds.com
Vegetable, flower, and herb seeds

Johnson Nursery
1352 Big Creek Rd.
Ellijay, GA 30536
888-276-3187
www.johnsonnursery.com
Antique and disease-resistant fruit trees and small fruits; orchard supplies

Just Fruits and Exotics
30 St. Frances St.
Crawfordville, FL 32327
850-926-5644
www.justfruitsandexotics.com
Fruits, nuts, and herbs

Kitazawa Seed Co.
PO Box 13220
Oakland, CA 94661
510-595-1188
www.kitazawaseed.com
Asian vegetables and herbs

Lewis Bamboo
877-796-2263
www.lewisbamboo.co
Nursery based in Oakman, Alabama, carrying many varieties of bamboo

Lilypons Water Gardens
6800 Lily Pons Rd.
Adamstown, MD 21710
800-999-5459
www.lilypons.com
Catttails, water chestnuts, taros, and a variety of lotuses; water gardening supplies

Logee's Tropical Plants
141 North St.
Danielson, CT 06239
888-330-8038
www.logees.com
Tropical edibles, including tea, bananas, dragon fruit, numerous citrus, passionfruit, and many others suited for container culture in cooler climates

Mid City Nursery
3635 Broadway St.
Napa-Vallejo Hwy.
American Canyon, CA 94503
707-642-4167
www.midcitynursery.com
Broad range of fruits, nuts, berries, and grapes; ships only in January and February

Miller Nurseries
5060 W. Lake Rd.
Canandaigua, NY 14424
800-836-9630
www.millernurseries.com
Fruit and nut trees

Mulberry Creek Herb Farm
3312 Bogart Rd.
Huron, OH 44839
419-433-6126
www.mulberrycreek.com
Herb plants shipped only between April and June

Native Seeds/SEARCH
526 N. Fourth Ave.
Tucson, AZ 85705
520-622-5561
www.nativeseeds.org
Southwestern Native American and Mexican vegetable seeds, some for desert conditions

Natural Gardening Co.
PO Box 750776
Petaluma, CA 94975
707-766-9303
www.naturalgardening.com
Certified organic tomato, eggplant, and pepper seedlings in spring; vegetable and herb seeds; and organic products

Nature Hills Nursery
3334 N. 88th Plaza
Omaha, NE 68134
402-934-8116
www.naturehills.com
Fruit and nut trees, small fruits, and some organic seeds

New Dimension Seed
PO Box 1294
Scappoose, OR 97056
503-577-9382
www.newdimensionseed.com
Asian vegetable and herb seeds; garden supplies

Nichols Garden Nursery
1190 Old Salem Rd. NE
Albany, OR 97321
800-422-3985
www.nicholsgardennursery.com
Wide selection of vegetable and herb seeds; garlic bulbs; plants of herbs, mioga ginger, and olives

Nolin River Nut Tree Nursery
797 Port Wooden Rd.
Upton, KY 42784
270-369-8551
www.nolinnursery.com
Grafted nut trees, persimmons, and pawpaws

Nourse Farms
41 River Rd.
South Deerfield, MA 01373
413-665-2658
www.noursefarms.com
Asparagus as well as strawberries, blackberries, raspberries, and other small fruits

Oikos Tree Crops
PO Box 19425
Kalamazoo, MI 40019
269-624-6233
www.oikostreecrops.com
Fruit and nut trees

One Green World
28696 S. Cramer Rd.
Molalla, OR 97038
877-353-4028
www.onegreenworld.com
Unusual fruits, berries, and nuts—some from eastern Europe;
rootstocks

Pacific Farms
PO Box 223
Florence, OR 97439
800-927-2248
www.freshwasabi.com
Wasabi rhizomes

Park Seed Co.
1 Parkton Ave.
Greenwood, SC 29647
800-213-0076
www.parkseed.com
Vegetable, herb, and flower seeds; some fruit plants

Pepper Gal
PO Box 23006
Ft. Lauderdale, FL 33307
954-537-5540
www.peppergal.com
Wide selection of pepper, tomato, and herb seeds

Petals from the Past
16034 County Rd. 29
Jemison, AL 35085
205-646-0069
www.petalsfromthepast.com
Citrus, blueberries, Asian pears, and antique roses

Peterson Pawpaws
PO Box 1011
Harpers Ferry, WV 25425
www.petersonpawpaws.com
One of the few pawpaw nurseries in the United States

Pine Island Nursery
16300 SW 184th St.
Miami, FL 33187
305-233-5501
www.tropicalfruitnursery.com
Tropical fruits, avocados, and mangos

Pinetree Garden Seeds
PO Box 300
New Gloucester, ME 04260
207-926-3400
www.superseeds.com
Flower, herb, and unusual and cool-season vegetable seeds

Plants of the Southwest
3095 Agua Fria Rd.
Santa Fe, NM 87507
800-788-7333
www.plantsofthesouthwest.com
Specializing in vegetables, herbs, cover crops, and trees (including
native plums) for the Southwest

Prairie Garden Seeds
PO Box 2758
Humboldt, SK, Canada S0K 2A0
306-682-1475
www.prseeds.ca
Legumes, greens, and grains for cool, short summers; ships to the United
States

Raintree Nursery
391 Butts Rd.
Morton, WA 98356
360-496-6400
www.raintreenursery.com
Fruits, nuts, berries, and unusual edibles

Redwood City Seed Co.
PO Box 361
Redwood City, CA 94064
650-325-7333
www.ecoseeds.com
Heirloom and unusual vegetable, chili, and herb seeds

Reeseville Ridge Nursery
512 S. Main St.
Reeseville, WI 53579
920-927-3291
www.wegrowit.com/Reeseville/ReesevilleRidgeCatalog.htm
Native trees, shrubs, and perennials

Renee's Garden
6116 Hwy. 9
Felton, CA 95018
888-880-7228
www.reneesgarden.com
Flower, herb, and vegetable seeds; online and in retail stores;
information-packed website

Rhora's Nut Farm and Nursery
R.R. #1
32983 Wills Rd.
Wainfleet, ON, Canada L0S 1V0
905-899-3508
www.nuttrees.com
Nut trees; unusual fruit trees and shrubs; ships to the United States

R. H. Shumway's
334 W. Stroud St.
Randolph, WI 53956
800-342-9461
www.rhshumway.com
Vegetables, herb, and flower seeds; fruit and nut trees

Richters Herbs
357 Hwy. 47
Goodwood, ON, Canada L0C 1A0
905-640-6677
www.richters.com
Huge selection of herb seeds and plants; ships to the United States

Rolling River Nursery
PO Box 332
Orleans, CA 95556
530-627-3120
www.rollingrivernursery.com
Container-grown fruit trees, shrubs, and vines—sustainably grown

St. Lawrence Nurseries
325 State Hwy. 345
Potsdam, NY 13676
315-265-6739
www.sln.potsdam.ny.us
Fruit and nut trees for northern climates; some rootstocks

Seed Savers Exchange
3094 N. Winn Rd.
Decorah, IA 52101
563-382-5990
www.seedsavers.org
Heirloom vegetable and flower seeds, seed exchange; some plants in spring

Seeds of Change
888-762-7333
www.seedsofchange.com
New Mexico–based company offering organically grown vegetable and herb seeds; apple trees, strawberry plants, and garlic bulbs

Southern Exposure Seed Exchange
PO Box 460
Mineral, VA 23117
540-894-9480
www.southernexposure.com
Herb and heirloom vegetable seeds, especially for the Southeast

Southmeadow Fruit Gardens
PO Box 211
Baroda, MI 49101
269-422-2411
www.southmeadowfruitgardens.com
Huge selection of heirloom and European apples, rare heirloom fruits, and hardy native fruits

Stark Bro's Nursery
PO Box 1800
Louisiana, MO 63353
800-325-4180
www.starkbros.com
Fruit and nut trees; berries

Steele Plant Co.
202 Collins St.
Gleason, TN 38229
731-648-5476
www.sweetpotatoplant.com
Sweet potato starts and onion sets

Stokes Seeds
PO Box 548
Buffalo, NY 14240
800-396-9238
www.stokeseeds.com
Large selection of vegetable, herb, and flower seeds

Stokes Tropicals
4806 E. Old Spanish Trail
Jeanerette, LA 70544
866-478-2502
www.stokestropicals.com
Banana, pineapple, and ginger plants

Strawberry Store
107 Wellington Wy.
Middletown, DE 19709
302-378-3633
www.thestrawberrystore.com
Seeds and plants for dozens of alpine strawberry varieties

Tam's Tropical Trees
1900 Al Don Farming Rd.
Clewiston, FL 33440
800-704-6637
Tropical and exotic fruits, nuts, and spices

Tasteful Garden
973 Country Rd. 8
Heflin, AL 36264
866-855-6344
www.tastefulgarden.com
Online source of pepper, tomato, vegetable, and herb plants in spring; garden supplies

Territorial Seed Co.
PO Box 158
Cottage Grove, OR 97424
800-626-0866
www.territorialseed.com
Organically grown vegetables, herbs, cover crops, and grains; some plants in spring

Thyme Garden Herb Co.
20546 Alsea Hwy.
Alsea, OR 97324
541-487-8671
www.thymegarden.com
Organically grown herb plants, seeds, and hop bare-root divisions

Timpanogos Nursery
TJK Enterprises
284C E. Lake Mead Pkwy. #204
Henderson, NV 89015
800-822-6164
www.timpanogosnursery.com
Goji berry and stevia plants; ships March though May only

Tomato Growers Supply Co.
PO Box 60015
Fort Meyers, FL 33906
888-478-7333
www.tomatogrowers.com
Extensive selection of tomato, pepper, tomatillo, and eggplant seeds

Trade Winds Fruit
PO Box 1102
Windsor, CA 95492
www.tradewindsfruit.com
Seeds of tropical fruits, peppers, tomatoes, vegetables, and unusual edibles

Trees of Antiquity
20 Wellsona Rd.
Paso Robles, CA 93446
805-467-9909
www.treesofantiquity.com
Heirloom fruits and berries

Tripple Brook Farm
37 Middle Rd.
Southampton, MA 01073
413-527-4626
www.tripplebrookfarm.com
Eastern natives, figs, cranberries, blueberries, hardy kiwis, and bamboo

TyTy Nursery
4723 U.S. Hwy. 82 W.
PO Box 130
TyTy, GA 31795
229-388-9999
www.tytyga.com
Fruit and nut trees, grapes, and berries

Van Ness Water Gardens
2460 N. Euclid Ave.
Upland, CA 91784
800-205-2425
www.vnwg.com
Water garden plants and information

Vesey Seeds
PO Box 9000
Calais, ME 04619
800-363-7333
www.veseys.com
Canada-based company offering organic vegetable and flower seeds, especially for short seasons

Waters Blueberry Farm
925 Bainbridge Rd.
Smithville, MO 64089
816-718-5948
www.watersblueberryfarm.com
Some of the best blueberry varieties

Well-Sweep Herb Farm
205 Mt. Bethel Rd.
Port Murray, NJ 07865
908-852-5390
www.wellsweep.com
Herb plants and seeds

Willhite Seed
PO Box 23
Poolville, TX 76487
800-828-1840
www.willhiteseed.com
Vegetable seeds, especially for hot-summer areas

Willis Orchard Co.
PO Box 119
Berlin, GA 31722
866-586-6283
www.willisorchards.com
Fruit and nut trees, berries, and grapes

Sources of Garden Supplies and Equipment

The following companies carry non-plant garden supplies. Some specialize in drip irrigation or carry a range of organic pest controls; others carry an assortment of environmentally friendly garden supplies from worm bins to organic fertilizers. Most pride themselves on offering "green" products. In many cases, they sell some products in bulk, making them less expensive, and they offer a much wider selection of materials than most local nurseries and home improvement stores.

Contech Electronics
800-767-8658
www.contech-inc.com
Products to deter deer, pests, and pets from the garden

Dripworks
190 Sanhedrin Circle
Willits, CA 95490
800-522-3747
www.dripworksusa.com
Micro- and drip irrigation supplies

Gardener's Supply Company
128 Intervale Rd.
Burlington, VT 05401
888-833-1412
www.gardeners.com
Extensive selection of basic garden tools and products, including rain barrels, self-watering containers, and pest controls

Gardens Alive!
5100 Schenley Place
Lawrenceburg, IN 47025
513-354-1482
www.gardensalive.com
Organic pest controls and fertilizers

GREENCulture
32 Rancho Circle
Lake Forest, CA 92630
877-204-7336
www.composters.com
Composting equipment, push reel mowers, and rain barrels

Green Spot
93 Priest Rd.
Nottingham, NH 03290
603-942-8925
www.greenmethods.com
Biological pest controls and integrated pest management products and information

Harmony Farm Supply and Nursery
3244 Hwy. 116 N.
Sebastopol, CA 95472
707-823-9125
www.harmonyfarm.com
Excellent source of drip irrigation supplies; gardening tools; large selection of biological controls, seeds, and food preservation and storage accessories; informative catalog

Peaceful Valley Farm & Garden Supply
PO Box 2209
125 Clydesdale Ct.
Grass Valley, CA 95945
888-784-1722
www.groworganic.com
Most extensive selection of organic gardening supplies, including drip irrigation, fertilizers, pesticides, and many specialized products; main print catalog is an invaluable resource for organic food growers; also seeds and plants carried in spring available through mail order

Planet Natural
1612 Gold Ave.
Bozeman, MT 59715
800-289-6656
www.planetnatural.com
Natural pest controls, push reel mowers, organic fertilizers, and composting supplies

SimplyArbors.com
Online source offering more than 400 arbors, trellises, pergolas, and accessories in a variety of materials

Urban Farmer Store
2833 Vicente St.
San Francisco, CA 94116
415-661-2204
urbanfarmerstore.com
Irrigation, lighting, water-garden supplies, and much information online

Organizations

Many organizations are steeped in gardening knowledge, and some of them specialize in edible plants. Others are critically interested in preserving the environment. In addition to the following associations, your local Cooperative Extension Service can tell you about local groups, including native plant societies, horticultural societies, and botanical gardens.

American Horticultural Society
7931 E. Boulevard Dr.
Alexandria, VA 22308
800-777-7931
www.ahs.org
Society whose mission is to educate and inspire people to become successful and environmentally responsible gardeners; members have access to a seed exchange and online seminars with national horticulture experts

California Rare Fruit Growers (CRFG)
The Fullerton Arboretum, CSUF
PO Box 6850
Fullerton, CA 92834
www.crfg.org
Group devoted to experimenting with and spreading information about unusual fruits; valuable growing information through publications, annual meetings, and website

Culinary Vegetable Institute (CVI)
12304 State Rte. 13
Milan, OH 44846
419-499-7500
www.culinaryvegetableinstitute.com
Learning center for chefs and growers committed to sustainable agriculture

Ecological Landscaping Association
1257 Worcester Rd., #262
Framingham, MA 01701
617-436-5838
www.ecolandscaping.org
Association that advocates environmentally responsible landscaping and horticultural practices by professionals and the public

Herb Society of America
9019 Kirtland Chardon Rd.
Kirtland, OH 44094
440-256-0514
www.herbsociety.org
Society devoted to promoting the culture of herbs

Home Orchard Society
PO Box 230192
Tigard, OR 97281
www.homeorchardsociety.org
Group that promotes modern and heirloom fruit varieties through demonstration orchard, newsletter, and classes on growing fruits

International Dark-Sky Association (IDA)
3225 N. First Ave.
Tucson, AZ 85719
520-293-3198
www.darksky.org
Organization whose mission is to preserve and protect the nighttime environment through environmentally responsible outdoor lighting

Kitchen Gardeners International
3 Powderhorn Dr.
Scarborough, ME 04074
207-883-5341
www.kitchengardeners.org
Group dedicated to empowering people to achieve greater food self-reliance through kitchen gardening, home cooking, and sustainable local food systems; information-packed online newsletter

Midwest Fruit Explorers (MidFEx)
PO Box 93
Markham, IL 60428
www.midfex.org
Organization of amateur backyard fruit-growing enthusiasts (many in the Chicago area) interested in special, superior, and unusual fruits—regardless of their appearance or commercial appeal

National Audubon Society
225 Varick St., 7th Floor
212-979-3000
New York, NY 10014
www.audubon.org
Society devoted to the study and preservation of birds and other wildlife and their habitats

National Wildlife Federation
11100 Wildlife Center Dr.
Reston VA 20190
800-822-9919
www.nwf.org
Organization whose mission is to inspire Americans to protect wildlife for our children's future

North American Fruit Explorers (NAFEX)
1716 Apples Rd.
Chapin, IL 62628
217-245-7589
www.nafex.org
Group that shares ideas in a quest to grow superior fruit varieties; quarterly newsletter and mail-order library available to members

Northern Nut Growers Association
PO Box 6216
Hamden, CT 06517
www.nutgrowing.org
Excellent resource for nut growing; experts answer questions; quarterly newsletter and mail-order library available to members

Permaculture Institute
PO Box 3702
Santa Fe, NM 87501
505-455-0514
www.permaculture.org
Institute that promotes sustainable living skills through education, networking, and demonstration projects

Plants For a Future
www.pfaf.org
Online databases (for U.S. and U.K.) of edible and useful plants

SafeLawns.org
110 Maryland Ave. NE, Suite 203
Washington, DC 20002
202-544-5430
SafeLawns.org
Group that promotes environmentally responsible lawn care and gardening

Seed Savers Exchange
3094 N. Winn Rd.
Decorah, IA 52101
563-382-5990
www.seedsavers.org
Group dedicated to saving vegetable gene pool diversity; extensive membership network of gardeners saving and exchanging seeds

Sierra Club
85 Second St., 2nd Floor
San Francisco, CA 94105
415-977-5500
www.sierraclub.org
Environmental organization that works to protect local communities and wild places and to find smart energy solutions to global warming

Slow Food USA
20 Jay St., Suite 313
Brooklyn, NY 11201
718-260-8000
www.slowfood.com
Organization founded to counteract fast food and disappearing local food traditions, and to support seasonal and locally produced foods

Urban Wildlands Group
PO Box 24020
Los Angeles, CA 90024
www.urbanwildlands.org
Group dedicated to the conservation of species, habitats, and ecological processes in urban and urbanizing areas

WaterSense
www.epa.gov/watersense
Partnership program sponsored by the U.S. Environmental Protection Agency; information for adults and children on ways to save water in the home and landscape

Gardens to Visit

The majority of public gardens feature exotic ornamentals, historical plantings, and woodlands to explore but include few edible plants. The gardens listed here are exceptions; they glory in fruits, vegetables, and herbs and are wonderful places to get specific information on edibles as well as inspiration for your landscape.

Bakersville
Baker Creek Heirloom Seeds
2278 Baker Creek Rd.
Mansfield, MO 65704
417-924-8917
www.streetsofbakersville.com
Ozarks pioneer town featuring 6,000-square-foot heirloom seed store and farm; monthly garden festivals with nationally acclaimed speakers, tastings, and music

Brooklyn Botanic Garden
1000 Washington Ave.
Brooklyn, NY 11225
718-623-7200
www.bbg.org
Urban horticultural resource with children's garden, formal herb garden, home composting exhibit, and more; classes and demonstrations year round

Callaway Gardens
17800 U.S. Hwy. 27
Pine Mountain, GA 31822
706-663-2281
www.callawaygardens.com
Resort encompassing 13,000 acres—gardens, and golf; 7½-acre Mr. Cason's Vegetable Garden; many workshops covering varied garden subjects

Chanticleer
786 Church Rd.
Wayne, PA 19087
610-687-4163
www.chanticleergarden.org
Former estate, now a public garden; includes vegetable garden, potager, orchard, and serpentine; open April through October

Cheyenne Botanic Garden
710 S. Lions Park Dr.
Cheyenne, WY 82001
307-637-6458
www.botanic.org
Volunteer-based, solar-heated and -powered botanic garden and municipal nursery operating on a philosophy of sustainability since 1977; classes available

Chicago Botanic Garden
1000 Lake Cook Rd.
Glencoe, IL 60022
847-835-5440
www.chicagobotanic.org
385 acres with 26 theme gardens; edible landscape at the Regenstein Fruit & Vegetable Garden; Garden Chef cooking classes on Saturdays and Sundays in summer

The Cloisters
99 Margaret Corbin Dr.
Fort Tryon Park
New York, NY 10040
212-923-3700
www.metmuseum.org/cloisters
Magnificent medieval-style cloistered gardens, including formal herb garden

Colonial Williamsburg
PO Box 1776
Williamsburg, VA 23187
757-229-1000
Colonial restoration of the former capital of Virginia; major tourist attraction with numerous gardens and homes to visit; special events and tours year round

Cornell Plantations
1 Plantations Rd.
Ithaca, NY 14850
607-255-2400
www.plantations.cornell.edu
200 acres on Cornell University campus; Pounder Heritage Vegetable Garden and Meunscher Poisonous Plants Garden of special interest

Denver Botanic Gardens
1005 York St.
Denver, CO 80206
720-865-3500
Premier American garden; specialty areas include the Kitchen Garden, Herb Garden, Birds and Bees Garden, and Water-Smart Garden; classes and special events year round

Fairchild Tropical Botanic Garden
10901 Old Cutler Rd.
Coral Gables, FL 33156
305-667-1651
www.fairchildgarden.org
In Miami area, the place to see tropical edibles; classes and special events, including rare-fruit weekend and mango celebration

Festival Hill
248 Jaster Rd.
Round Top, TX 78954
www.festivalhill.org
200 acres with a series of stunning herb gardens; annual herbal forum

Fruit and Spice Park
24801 SW 187th Ave.
Homestead, FL 33031
305-247-5727
www.fruitandspicepark.org
Tropical botanical garden with more than 500 varieties of fruits, vegetables, and spices

Fullerton Arboretum
1900 Associated Rd.
Fullerton, CA 92831
714-278-4791
fullertonarboretum.org
Subtropical rare fruit grove, including papayas, guavas, kiwis, and citrus varieties

Genesee Country Village & Museum
1410 Flint Hill Rd.
Mumford, NY 14511
585-638-6822
www.gcv.org
Living history museum with authentic nineteenth-century buildings, farms, and gardens

Hakone Estate and Gardens
21000 Big Basin Wy.
Saratoga, CA 95070
408-741-4994
www.hakone.com
Oldest Japanese and Asian estate garden in the Western Hemisphere, on 18 acres overlooking Silicon Valley; the place to see bamboo

Huntington Botanical Gardens
1151 Oxford Road
San Marino, CA 91108
626-405-2100
www.huntington.org
Magnificent rose (including an antique rose collection), herb, and desert gardens on 207 acres in the Los Angeles area; special events and classes year round

Longwood Gardens
100 Longwood Rd.
Kennett Square, PA 19348
610-388-1000
www.longwoodgardens.org
Philadelphia-area estate garden covering 1,000 acres; edibles in the Idea Garden and Estate Fruit House; Bee-aMazed Children's Garden; classes year round

Minnesota Landscape Arboretum
3675 Arboretum Dr.
Chaska, MN 55318
952-443-1400
www.arboretum.umn.edu
More than 1,000 acres near Minneapolis; six different herb gardens and home demonstration gardens; special events and classes year round

Missouri Botanic Garden
4344 Shaw Blvd.
St. Louis, MO 63110
800-642-8842
www.mobot.org
79-acre former estate; Kemper Center for Home Gardening has 23 demonstration gardens; special events and classes year round

Monticello
931 Thomas Jefferson Pkwy.
Charlottesville, VA 22902
434-984-9822
www.monticello.org
Thomas Jefferson's historic gardens, including 1,000-foot-long garden terrace, home to 330 vegetable varieties, and two orchards in which Jefferson grew 170 fruit varieties

Montréal Botanical Garden
4101, rue Sherbrooke Est
Montréal, QC, Canada H1X 2B2
514-872-1400
www2.ville.montreal.qc.ca/jardin/en
185-acre garden with must-see First-Nations Garden and Economic Plant Garden

The New York Botanical Garden
200th St. and Kazimiroff Blvd.
Bronx, NY 10458
718-817-8700
www.nybg.org
National Historic Landmark founded in 1891 consisting of 250 acres with 50 display gardens; Home Gardening Center encompasses the vegetable garden and compost demonstrations as well as herb, children's, and family-oriented gardens

Old Sturbridge Village
1 Old Sturbridge Village Rd.
Sturbridge, MA 01566
508-347-3362
www.osv.org
Living history museum; vegetable and fruit displays typical of an 1830s rural New England town; fall harvest festival with heirloom vegetables

Old Westbury Gardens
71 Old Westbury Rd.
Old Westbury, NY 11568
516-333-0048
www.oldwestburygardens.org
Long Island estate garden with exemplary children's and herb gardens

Powell Gardens
1609 NW U.S. Hwy. 50
Kingsville, MO 64061
816-697-2600
www.powellgardens.org
Kansas City–area botanical garden featuring the Heartland Harvest Garden with edible landscapes, classes on growing, and cooking demonstrations

Seed Savers Exchange
3076 N. Winn Rd.
Decorah, IA 52101
563-382-5990
www.seedsavers.org
890-acre organic Heritage Farm; displays of endangered vegetables, apples, grapes, and an ancient breed of cattle; open April through December

Stone Barns Center for Food and Agriculture
630 Bedford Rd.
Pocantico Hills, NY 10591
914-366-6200
www.stonebarnscenter.org
Carved out of the Rockefeller estate, culinary center featuring Blue Hill restaurant and an herb and vegetable garden designed by Barbara Damrosch; tours and classes year round

United States National Arboretum
3501 New York Ave., NE
Washington, DC 20002
202-245-2726
www.usna.usda.gov
Living museum and botanical research and education center; National Herb Garden with ten theme gardens, including Asian, culinary, Native American, and beverage gardens

Bibliography

The books listed here include ones that reside on my shelves as well as those I used while researching and writing this book. They include classics in addition to more recent publications. Some of the older titles may be a bit hard to find, but you won't regret the effort; try searching for them online or at your local library. You may find that there is a newer edition of a book I've listed, but I cited the version that I've found indispensable. If you have the opportunity to compare editions, choose the one that most appeals to you.

Alexander, Rosemary, and Karena Batstone. *A Handbook for Garden Designers*. London: Cassell, 2008.
Each stage of the garden design process explained; many tips for the amateur

Appelhof, Mary. *Worms Eat My Garbage: How to Set Up & Maintain a Worm Composting System*. Kalamazoo, MI: Flower Press, 1997.
The most comprehensive book on vermiculture

Ashworth, Suzanne. *Seed to Seed: Seed Saving and Growing Techniques for Vegetable Gardeners*. Decorah, IA: Seed Savers Exchange, 2002.
The basics of seed saving; a must for heirloom vegetable growers

Bailey, L. H., and staff. *Hortus Third: A Concise Dictionary of Plants Cultivated in the United States and Canada*. New York: Macmillan, 1976.
Once the basic reference book for horticulturists; still valuable but superseded by more updated references

Bales, Suzy. *Suzy Bales' Down-to-Earth Gardener: Let Nature Guide You to Success in Your Garden*. Emmaus, PA: Rodale, 2004.
Author walks you through her garden and shares her sophisticated yet down-to-earth way of gardening with nature

Barash, Cathy Wilkinson. *Edible Flowers: From Garden to Palate*. Golden, CO: Fulcrum Publishing, 1995.
Well-researched combination cookbook and gardening guide showcasing 67 edible flowers; the most reliable book on the subject

———. *Taylor's Weekend Gardening Guide to Kitchen Gardens: How to Create a Beautiful and Functional Culinary Garden*. Boston: Houghton Mifflin Harcourt, 1998.
Numerous ideas for kitchen garden designs, from formal potagers to informal gardens

Bartholomew, Mel. *All New Square Foot Gardening*. Franklin, TN: Cool Springs Press, 2006.
New edition of the classic book that shows how to produce food efficiently in a small area with a minimum of effort

Bartley, Jennifer R. *Designing the New Kitchen Garden: An American Potager Handbook*. Portland, OR: Timber Press, 2006.
Ways to weave vegetables, fruits, herbs, and flowers together in a classic formal but productive design, resulting in a delightful change from the typical vegetable garden

Belanger, Jerome D. *Raising Small Livestock: A Practical Handbook*. New York: Dover Publications, 2005.
Valuable collection of information about raising small domesticated animals

Bell, Michael. *The Gardener's Guide to Growing Temperate Bamboos*. Newton Abbot, UK: David & Charles, 2003.
Complete guide for selecting and growing bamboo species; includes propagation, problems, sources, and A to Z listing of species

Better Homes and Gardens, eds. *New Complete Guide to Landscaping*. Des Moines, IA: Meredith Corp., 2002.
All-inclusive book that covers the nitty-gritty aspects of landscape planning and construction from seeding a lawn to building a pond (with how-tos)

Bradley, Fern Marshall, Barbara W. Ellis, and Ellen Phillips, eds. *Rodale's Ultimate Encyclopedia of Organic Gardening: The Indispensable Green Resource for Every Gardener*. Emmaus, PA: Rodale, 1997.
The most practical organic information collected from garden experts nationwide; a must-have for the organic gardener

Brickell, Christopher, and H. Marc Cathey, eds. *The American Horticultural Society A to Z Encyclopedia of Garden Plants*. New York: DK Publishing, 2004.
Reference text for ambitious gardeners ever on the prowl for new plants to grow

Brickell, Christopher, and David Joyce. *The American Horticultural Society Pruning and Training*. New York: DK Publishing, 1996.
Detailed encyclopedia for pruning most standard ornamental and edible plants; includes photos and illustrations as visual guides

Brookbank, George. *Desert Gardening: Fruits & Vegetables: The Complete Guide*. Tucson: Fisher Books, 1997.
Invaluable for food gardeners living in this challenging climate; covers everything from protecting citrus from sunburn to starting tomatoes in January to avoid the heat

Brookes, John. *Room Outside: A New Approach to Garden Design*. Woodbridge, UK: Garden Art, 2007.
Revised look at Brookes's original supposition that the garden should be an extension of the home—a design idea that is perfect for the edible gardener

Bubel, Nancy. *The New Seed Starter's Handbook*. Emmaus, PA: Rodale, 1988.
Comprehensive how-to for starting most vegetable and herb seeds; a classic that is valuable to both novice and experienced gardeners who are eager to try new edible plants

Campell, Stu. *Let It Rot! The Gardener's Guide to Composting*, 3rd ed. North Adams, MA: Storey Publishing, 1998.
Valuable text on composting basics, making it easy for the beginner to understand

Capon, Brian. *Botany for Gardeners*. Portland, OR: Timber Press, 2004.
Revised edition is a must-have for gardeners with more than a passing interest in plants; knowing some basic botany helps head off plant problems and troubleshoot if they come

Carson, Rachel. *Silent Spring*. Boston: Houghton Mifflin, 1962.
Groundbreaking book that awakened Americans to the hazards of many common pesticides; still well worth reading today

Carucci, Linda. *Cooking School Secrets for Real World Cooks*. San Francisco: Chronicle Books, 2005.
Great for the serious cook but also valuable for a beginner; covers the chemistry, tools, and techniques for preparing and presenting great food

Cathey, H. Marc, with Linda Bellamy. *Heat Zone Gardening: How to Choose Plants That Thrive in Your Region's Warmest Weather*. Alexandria, VA: Time-Life Books, 1998.
Identifies different heat zones in North America and details the summer heat tolerances of many common plants

Cox, Jeff. *From Vines to Wines: The Complete Guide to Growing Grapes and Making Your Own Wine*. North Adams, MA: Storey Publishing, 1999.
Title says it all; details all the steps for making your own great wine

Cranshaw, Whitney. *Garden Insects of North America: The Ultimate Guide to Backyard Bugs*. Princeton, NJ: Princeton University Press, 2004.
One of the best insect identification resources for the home gardener

Creasy, Rosalind. *Blue Potatoes, Orange Tomatoes: How to Grow a Rainbow Garden*. San Francisco: Sierra Club Books for Children, 1994.
Beautifully illustrated gardening book for children

———. *Cooking from the Garden*. San Francisco: Sierra Club Books, 1988.
Showcasing 17 theme gardens and cooks; details on how to grow and prepare a wide variety of fresh foods

———. *The Edible Asian Garden*. Boston: Periplus, 2000.

———. *The Edible Flower Garden*. Boston: Periplus, 1999.

———. *The Edible French Garden*. Boston: Periplus, 1999.

———. *The Edible Heirloom Garden*. Boston: Periplus, 1999.

———. *The Edible Herb Garden*. Boston: Periplus, 1999.

———. *The Edible Italian Garden*. Boston: Periplus, 1999.

———. *The Edible Mexican Garden*. Boston: Periplus, 2000.

———. *The Edible Pepper Garden*. Boston: Periplus, 2000.

———. *The Edible Rainbow Garden*. Boston: Periplus, 2000.

———. *The Edible Salad Garden*. Boston: Periplus, 1999.
Series of highly illustrated books on specific vegetables and herbs, each featuring an ethnic or gardening theme, with recipes

———. *Rosalind Creasy's Recipes from the Garden*. North Clarendon, VT: Tuttle Publishing, 2010.
A compendium of favorite recipes using garden-fresh ingredients

Creative Homeowner, eds. *Smart Guide: Home Landscaping*. Upper Saddle River, NJ: Creative Homeowner Press, 2008.
General guide to the basics of landscaping and gardening

Cutler, Karan Davis. *Burpee: The Complete Vegetable & Herb Gardener*. New York: MacMillan, 1997.
If you only have one vegetable and herb reference book, this should be it; covers extensive information on how to grow and choose cultivars for common and uncommon edibles

———. *Starting from Seed*. Brooklyn, NY: Brooklyn Botanic Garden, 2001.

———. *Tantalizing Tomatoes*. Brooklyn, NY: Brooklyn Botanic Garden, 1997.

Damrosch, Barbara. *The Garden Primer*, 2nd ed. New York: Workman Publishing, 2008.
Must-have for beginning gardeners; packed with practical advice from landscape design basics to composting—all information delivered in an engaging style

———. *Theme Gardens*. New York: Workman Publishing, 2001.
Original edition was the inspiration behind many of my edible theme gardens; this revised edition is sure to help even more readers see gardening in a new way

DeBaggio, Thomas. *Growing Herbs from Seed, Cutting & Root: An Adventure in Small Miracles*. Loveland, CO: Interweave Press, 1995.
One of the best texts on herb propagation; includes countless how-tos and tips from a pro

Denckla, Tanya L. K. *The Gardener's A–Z Guide to Growing Organic Food*. North Adams, MA: Storey Publishing, 2004.
Great reference on vegetables, herbs, fruits, and nuts with much modern information on organic controls

Dirr, Michael A. *Manual of Woody Landscape Plants: Their Identification, Ornamental Characteristics, Culture, Propagation and Uses*. Champaign, IL: Stipes Publishing, 1998.
The major reference book for woody plants in temperate climates; covers some edibles such as maples, pecans, walnuts, amelanchier, roses, and a few woody herbs

Druitt, Liz, and G. Michael Shoup. *Landscaping with Antique Roses.* Newtown, CT: Taunton Press, 1992.
One of the first modern books about old garden roses; a great resource for gardeners who want to grow roses with ease and few chemicals

Ellis, Barbara W., and Fern Marshall Bradley, eds. *The Organic Gardener's Handbook of Natural Insect and Disease Control.* Emmaus, PA: Rodale, 1996.
A to Z look at up-to-date organic solutions for many pest and disease problems

Erhardt, Walter, Erich Goetz, Siegmund Seybold, and Nils Bodeker. *Zander: Handwörterbuch der Pflanzennamen (Dictionary of Plant Names).* Stuttgart, Germany: Eugen Ulmer, Gmbh & Co., 2002.
An international standard for botanical nomenclature; used for many of the botanic names in this edition

Facciola, Stephen. *Cornucopia II: A Source Book of Edible Plants.* Vista, CA: Kampong Publications, 1998.
Jam-packed source of botanic information on hundreds of edible plants; includes suppliers

Fisher, Joe, and Dennis Fisher. *The Homebrewer's Garden.* North Adams, MA: Storey Publishing, 1998.
How to grow hops, barley, and other grains; includes the basics of beer brewing

Fizzell, James A. *Guide to Illinois Vegetable Gardening.* Knoxville, TN: Cool Springs Press, 2008.

———. *The Midwest Fruit and Vegetable Book: Michigan Edition.* Knoxville, TN: Cool Springs Press, 2001.

———. *The Midwest Fruit and Vegetable Book: Wisconsin Edition.* Knoxville, TN: Cool Springs Press, 2001.
Collection of books with climate-specific advice on growing edibles in the Midwest

Flores, Barbara Jeanne. *The Great Book of Pears.* Berkeley, CA: Ten Speed Press, 2000.
Everything you wanted to know about growing and purchasing pears

Flores, Heather Coburn. *Food Not Lawns.* White River Junction, VT: Chelsea Green Publishing, 2006.
An activist's look at producing food in the yard instead of creating lawn clippings

Gertley, Jan and Michael. *The Art of the Kitchen Garden.* Newtown, CT: Taunton Press, 1999.
All you need to know to create a kitchen garden, complete with history through the ages

Gibbons, Euell. *Stalking the Wild Asparagus.* New York: David McKay Co., 1962.
Complete guide to edible plants in the wild; truly a classic

Goldman, Amy. *The Compleat Squash: A Passionate Grower's Guide to Pumpkins, Squashes, and Gourds.* New York: Artisan Books, 2004.

———. *The Heirloom Tomato: From Garden to Table.* New York: Bloomsbury USA, 2008.

———. *Melons for the Passionate Gardener.* New York: Artisan Books, 2002.
Series of books, each a comprehensive look at open-pollinated varieties complete with recipes, fascinating history, and information on how to grow, including seed saving

Gothein, Marie-Luise. *A History of Garden Art*, Vols. I and II. New York: Hacker Art Books, 1966.
Important work that details the history of landscape design

Griffiths, Mark. *Index of Garden Plants: The New Royal Horticultural Society Dictionary.* Philadelphia: Trans-Atlantic Publications, 1994.
An international standard for botanical nomenclature; used for many of the botanic names in this edition

Haeg, Fritz. *Edible Estates: Attack on the Front Lawn.* New York: Metropolis Books, 2008.
Provocative book questioning Americans' love affair with the lawn and including a number of authors' philosophical views; prototype edible gardens were documented for the book

Hagy, Fred. *Landscaping with Fruits and Vegetables.* Woodstock, NY: Overlook Press, 2001.
A landscape architect's look at designing with edible plants; includes many drawings of plants and plans as well as lists of edibles for various landscaping uses

Harnden, Philip. *A Gardener's Guide to Frost.* Minocqua, WI: Willow Creek Press, 2003.
Fabulous book for understanding all sorts of weather—not just frosty conditions; information on protecting plants

Hatch, Peter J. *The Fruits and Fruit Trees of Monticello.* Charlottesville, VA: University Press of Virginia, 2007.
Written by the Director of Gardens and Grounds at Monticello, and illustrated with old drawings as well as old and new photographs; the book that brought Jefferson and his gardens to life for me

Helyer, Neil, Kevin Brown, and Nigel D. Cattlin. *A Color Handbook of Biological Control in Plant Protection.* Portland, OR: Timber Press, 2003.
Photos and information covering the life cycle of both pest and beneficial insects from egg to adult; descriptions of the pests' natural enemies and plant damage

Hemenway, Toby. *Gaia's Garden: A Guide to Home-Scale Permaculture*, 2nd ed. White River Junction, VT: Chelsea Green Publishing, 2009.
Philosophical look at landscape design that includes powerful arguments for using more earth-friendly techniques and plants

Hill, Lewis. *Fruits and Berries for the Home Gardener*. North Adams, MA: Storey Publishing, 1992.
Great all-around fruit-growing book for the East Coast; includes extensive cultural information and identifies diseases and pests

Huxley, Anthony. *An Illustrated History of Gardening*. New York: Lyons Press, 1998.
Scholarly look at the history of gardening

Ingels, Chuck A., Pamela M.Geisel, and Maxwell V. Norton. *Home Orchard: Growing Your Own Deciduous Fruit and Nut Trees*. University of California, Agriculture and Natural Resources, 2007.
Primarily written for California gardeners, but a valuable resource for most fruit growers because of the many photographs, diagrams of propagation techniques and pruning, and up-to-date information on organic and non-toxic pest management practices

Jacke, Dave, with Eric Toensmeier. *Edible Forest Gardens: Ecological Vision and Theory for Temperate Climate Permaculture*, Vol. 1. White River Junction, VT: Chelsea Green Publishing, 2005.
Like a number of books, covers the basic tenants of permaculture—but also stresses the importance of planting trees, shrubs, and herbaceous plants to fill many niches in an ecosystem

Jaynes, Richard A., ed. *Nut Tree Culture in North America*. Hamden, CT: Northern Nut Growers Association, 1981.
Timeless and valuable resource for serious nut growers

Jeavons, John. *How to Grow More Vegetables (and Fruits, Nuts, Berries, Grains, and Other Crops) Than You Ever Thought Possible on Less Land Than You Can Imagine*. Berkeley, CA: Ten Speed Press, 2006.
Classic primer on the biodynamic/French intensive method of organic horticulture

Johnson, Hugh. *The Principles of Gardening*. New York: Simon & Schuster, 1997.
Thorough look at gardening from design through planting; a basic text for serious gardeners

Jones, Louisa. *The Art of French Vegetable Gardening*. New York: Artisan Books, 1995.
Inspiring look at traditional French edible gardens and their unique aesthetic

Jones, Pamela. *Just Weeds: History, Myths, and Uses*. Boston: Houghton Mifflin, 1994.
Covers the many uses of weeds and helps the reader understand their place in the ecosystem

Katz, Sandor Ellix. *Wild Fermentation: The Flavor, Nutrition, and Craft of Live-Culture Foods*. White River Junction, VT: Chelsea Green Publishing, 2003.
Must-have for slow- and healthy-food advocates; a how-to for homegrown edibles from cider to sauerkraut

Kent, Douglas. *Firescaping: Creating Fire-Resistant Landscapes, Gardens, and Properties in California's Diverse Environments*. Berkeley, CA: Wilderness Press, 2005.
Basic how-to for designing a yard that can better survive a wildfire

Kingsolver, Barbara, with Steven L. Hopp and Camille Kingsolver. *Animal, Vegetable, Miracle: A Year of Food Life*. New York: Harper Perennial, 2008.
Best seller that got people thinking about eating local and growing their own food

Kourik, Robert. *Designing and Maintaining Your Edible Landscape Naturally*, 2nd ed. East Meon, UK: Permanent Publications, 2009.
Classic primer including soil preparation, how to choose suitable edible plants, and numerous cultural techniques

————. *Drip Irrigation for Every Landscape and All Climates,* 2nd ed. Occidental, CA: Metamorphic Press, 2009.
Comprehensive guide to drip irrigation

————. *Roots Demystified*. Occidental, CA: Metamorphic Press, 2007.
Explains roots' many functions and encourages gardeners to foster healthy roots—critical for edible plants

Lang, Susan, and Jeff T. Williams. *Water Gardens*. Menlo Park, CA: Sunset Publishing, 2004.
All the information needed to install a water garden

Lanza, Patricia. *Lasagna Gardening: A New Layering System for Bountiful Gardens: No Digging, No Tilling, No Weeding, No Kidding!* Emmaus, PA: Rodale, 1998.

————. *Lasagna Gardening for Small Spaces*. Emmaus, PA: Rodale, 2002.

————. *Lasagna Gardening with Herbs*. Emmaus, PA: Rodale, 2004.
Series of books on a method of gardening that is amazingly simple and successful

Larkcom, Joy. *Creative Vegetable Gardening*. London: Mitchell Beazley, 2006.
Thorough and inspiring look at "fancy" vegetable gardens and potagers; a classic.

Logsdon, Gene. *Successful Berry Growing*. Emmaus, PA: Rodale, 1974.
One of the best books on organic methods for growing small fruits; primarily for eastern gardens

Long, Jim. *Making Bentwood Trellises, Arbors, Gates & Fences*. North Adams, MA: Storey Publishing, 1998.
Great how-to book for folks who love the rustic look of bentwood outdoor furnishings or just want to recycle their yard prunings.

Lowenfels, Jeff, and Wayne Lewis. *Teaming with Microbes: A Gardener's Guide to the Food Web*. Portland, OR: Timber Press, 2006.
Details microbial life in the soil; provides many soil-improving techniques

MacCubbin, Tom. *The Edible Landscape*. Oviedo, FL: Waterview Press, 1998.
Great resource for Florida gardeners growing edible plants

Madison, Deborah. *Vegetarian Cooking for Everyone*. New York: Broadway Books, 2007.
Tenth-anniversary edition of a classic cookbook

McCloud, Kevin. *Choosing Colours*. London: Quadrille Press, 2005.
Primarily a guide for using color schemes in the house, yet many of the color combinations and theories are applicable in the garden

McGee, Rose Marie Nichols, and Maggie Stuckey. *McGee & Stuckey's The Bountiful Container*. New York: Workman Publishing, 2002.
The major resource for edible container gardening; includes hands-on methods along with an extensive list of vegetables, herbs, and dwarf fruit trees

Meredith, Ted Jordan. *Bamboo for Gardens*. Portland, OR: Timber Press, 2001.
Covers culture, climate, varieties, and landscape considerations as well as ways to harvest and use bamboo in the kitchen

Merrill, Richard, and Joe Ortiz. *The Gardener's Table*. Berkeley, CA: Ten Speed Press, 2004.
The ultimate no-nonsense guide to cultivating and cooking from a kitchen garden; a must-have for edible gardeners

Mollison, Bill. *Permaculture: A Designer's Manual*. Tyalgum, Australia: Tagari Publications, 1996.
By one of the co-founders of permaculture; details the primary concepts and design methods, and includes many ecologically friendly gardening techniques

Nash, Helen, and Marilyn M. Cook. *Water Gardening Basics*. New York: Sterling Publishing, 1999.
Walks the reader through site planning and installation to a finished pond

Ogden, Ellen Ecker. *From the Cook's Garden: Recipes for Cooks Who Like to Garden, Gardeners Who Like to Cook, and Everyone Who Wishes They Had a Garden*. New York: Morrow Cookbooks, 2003.
The title says it all

Ogden, Shepherd. *Straight-Ahead Organic: A Step-by-Step Guide to Growing Great Vegetables in a Less Than Perfect World*. White River Junction, VT: Chelsea Green Publishing, 1999.
Incredible source of knowledge based on cold-climate growing methods; filled with technical information

Ortho Books, eds. *All About Citrus & Subtropical Fruits*. Des Moines, IA: Meredith Corp., 2008.
Thorough look at how to grow citrus and other tender fruits—in the garden and indoors

———. *All About Growing Fruits, Berries & Nuts*. San Francisco: Ortho Books, 1987.
Classic well worth searching out; one of the best for growing information around the country

———. *Complete Guide to Vegetables, Fruits, and Herbs*. Des Moines, IA: Meredith Corp., 2004.
Basic information from A to Z on vegetables, fruits, and herbs

Otto, Stella. *The Backyard Berry Book*. Maple City, MI: Ottographics, 1995.

———. *The Backyard Orchardist*. Maple City, MI: Ottographics, 1995.
Complete how-to guides for growing temperate-zone berries and fruit trees in the home garden

Page-Roberts, James. *Wines from a Small Garden: Planting to Bottling*. New York: Abbeville Press, 1995.
Great resource for the beginning winemaker

Pennington, Susan J. *Feast Your Eyes: The Unexpected Beauty of Vegetable Gardens*. Berkeley, CA: University of California Press, 2002.
Thorough history of how edible plants have been used in ornamental plantings

Phillips, Michael. *The Apple Grower*. White River Junction, VT: Chelsea Green Publishing, 2005.
Best source available on growing apples organically

Pleasant, Barbara. *The Gardener's Guide to Plant Diseases: Earth-Safe Remedies*. Pownal, VT: Storey Publishing, 1995.
A gardener's best friend, covering many of the most common plant diseases and giving preventive measures and solutions

———. *The Gardener's Weed Book: Earth-Safe Controls*. North Adams, MA: Storey Publishing, 1996.
Practical how-tos for controlling weeds

Pollan, Michael. *Food Rules: An Eater's Manual*. New York: Penguin Press, 2009.
Simple, straightforward rules for how to eat well, with an emphasis on fresh foods and a variety of cuisines

———. *In Defense of Food: An Eater's Manifesto*. New York: Penguin Press, 2009.
Pollan's call to action—"Eat food. Not too much. Mostly plants."—could also be the call to creating an edible landscape

———. *The Omnivore's Dilemma: A Natural History of Four Meals*. New York: Penguin Press, 2007.
Powerful look at how America eats and the ramifications on our health and the environment

Proulx, Annie, and Lew Nichols. *Cider: Making, Using & Enjoying Sweet & Hard Cider*, 3rd ed. North Adams, MA: Storey Publishing, 2003.
Great for gardeners with dreams of lots of apples; covers variety selection through brandy making

Reader's Digest, eds. *The Garden Problem Solver*. Pleasantville, NY: Reader's Digest, 2004.
Valuable diagnostic tool for the most common vegetable, fruit, and ornamental plant pest and disease problems

Reddell, Rayford Clayton, and Robert Galvean. *The Rose Bible*. San Francisco: Chronicle Books, 1998.
Comprehensive look at roses available today; many photos for identification

Reich, Lee. *Landscaping with Fruit*. North Adams, MA: Storey Publishing, 2009.
Valuable information on growing most of the major fruits in a landscape

———. *The Pruning Book*. Newtown, CT: Taunton Press, 2010.
Excellent resource for pruning edible and ornamental trees

———. *Uncommon Fruits for Every Garden*. Portland, OR: Timber Press, 2008.
Guide for the adventurous fruit gardener

———. *Weedless Gardening*. New York: Workman Publishing, 2001.
Includes techniques for cutting down on weeds in the garden

Rice, Graham. *All-in-One Garden: Grow Vegetables, Fruit, Herbs and Flowers in the Same Place*. London: Cassell Illustrated, 2007.
Photos and text for inspiration; practical information for designing a lovely English-style edible garden

Rieger, Mark. *Introduction to Fruit Crops*. Binghamton, NY: Haworth Press, 2006.
Scholarly text covering the most popular fruits and nuts; includes taxonomy, nutritional benefits, cultural needs, and harvesting information

Rombough, Lon. *The Grape Grower*. White River Junction, VT: Chelsea Green Publishing, 2002.
Guide to organic viticulture; A to Z of grape growing in North America and the tropics, including wine, juice, and table grapes

Rosengarten, Frederic, Jr. *The Book of Edible Nuts*. Mineola, NY: Dover Publications, 2004.
Re-publication of a classic; great look at the natural history of about 40 nut species

Rubatzky, Vincent E., and Mas Yamaguchi. *World Vegetables: Principles, Production, and Nutritive Values*, 2nd ed. New York: Springer, 2007.
For the serious vegetable grower

Sanchez, Janet H., and Hazel White. *The Edible Garden*. Menlo Park, CA: Sunset Publishing, 2005.
Comprehensive and informative overview of the major fruits, herbs, and vegetables; cultural information and many helpful diagrams, photos, and techniques

Saville, Carole. *Exotic Herbs*. New York: Henry Holt & Co., 1997.
For the passionate herb connoisseur, covering about 60 exotic culinary herbs

Schneider, Elizabeth. *Uncommon Fruits & Vegetables: A Commonsense Guide*. New York: Harper & Row, 1998.
Enlightened book on the vast selection of fruits and vegetables grown worldwide; encyclopedic format includes selection, care, and a few choice recipes

———. *Vegetables from Amaranth to Zucchini: The Essential Reference*. New York: William Morrow, 2001.
Seed-to-table exploration of more than 350 common and uncommon vegetables listed with common, botanic, and market names; includes recipes

Schultz, Warren. *The Chemical-Free Lawn*. Emmaus, PA: Rodale Press, 1989.
How to grow a great lawn without polluting the environment

Skelsey, Alice, and Gloria Huckaby. *Growing Up Green: Parents & Children Gardening Together*. New York: Workman Publishing, 1973.
One of the best books on children's gardening; includes lots of easy projects and ideas

Smith, Edward C. *Incredible Vegetables from Self-Watering Containers: Using Ed's Amazing POTS System*. North Adams, MA: Storey Publishing, 2006.
How to build and use self-watering containers; great ways to grow vegetables using less water

———. *The Vegetable Gardener's Bible*. North Adams, MA: Storey Publishing, 2000.
Primer for growing great vegetables

Smith, J. Russell. *Tree Crops: A Permanent Agriculture*. New York: Devin-Adair Publishing, 1987.
Classic text that lays the philosophical groundwork for many aspects of permaculture

Smith, Shane. *Greenhouse Gardener's Companion: Growing Food & Flowers in Your Greenhouse or Sunspace*. Golden, CO: Fulcrum Publishing, 2000.
Great reference for growing edibles in a greenhouse; revised and expanded edition

Solomon, Steve. *Gardening When It Counts: Growing Food in Hard Times*. Gabriola Island, BC, Canada: New Society Publishers, 2006.
Founder of Territorial Seed Company shares years of experience and numerous techniques for improving yield

Southern Living, eds. *Southern Living Garden Book*. Birmingham, AL: Oxmoor House, 2004.
Comprehensive reference book including more than 5,000 plants for southern gardens

Stangler, Carol A. *The Craft and Art of Bamboo: 30 Eco-Friendly Projects to Make for Home & Garden*. New York: Lark Books, 2009.
Revised and updated book with valuable information on bamboo projects

Staub, Jack. *75 Exceptional Herbs for Your Garden*. Layton, UT: Gibbs Smith, 2008.

———. *75 Exciting Vegetables for Your Garden*. Layton, UT: Gibbs Smith, 2005.

———. *75 Remarkable Fruits for Your Garden*. Layton, UT: Gibbs Smith, 2008.
Beautiful and very informative series of books; author has a poetic way of sharing his many years of gardening experience

Stell, Elizabeth P. *Secrets to Great Soil*. North Adams, MA: Storey Publishing, 1998.
Great primer on preparing soil for hard-working edible plants

Sunset Books, eds. *National Garden Book*. Menlo Park, CA: Sunset Publishing, 1997.
Reference book with detailed information on over 6,000 plants; invaluable resource for all aspects of landscaping

———. *Western Garden Book*. Menlo Park, CA: Sunset Publishing, 2007.
Comprehensive western plant encyclopedia, with its own zones; popularly known as the "bible of West Coast gardening" with some 8,000 plant identifications and 1,300 photos

———. *Western Garden Book of Edibles: The Complete A to Z Guide to Growing Your Own Vegetables, Herbs, and Fruits*. Menlo Park, CA: Sunset Publishing, 2010.
Great resource for western gardeners detailing most of the major edible plants with information on where they grow best

Tallamy, Douglas W. *Bringing Nature Home: How You Can Sustain Wildlife with Native Plants*. Portland, OR: Timber Press, 2009.
Updated and expanded guide for including more native plants in the landscapes

Toensmeier, Eric. *Perennial Vegetables*. White River Junction, VT: Chelsea Green Publishing, 2007.
Information about many perennial vegetables—from asparagus and artichokes to walking onions and edible cactus—for a rewarding and fairly low-maintenance, edible garden

Toogood, Alan, ed. *American Horticultural Society Plant Propagation*. New York: DK Publishing, 1999.
Comprehensive text for propagating the most popular plants—edible or just ornamental

Tucker, Arthur O., Ph.D., and Thomas DeBaggio. *The Big Book of Herbs*. Loveland, CO: Interweave Press, 2000.
Must-have for gardeners interested in growing herbs; covers every aspect of herbs, from their active oils to their uses in the garden

Tukey, Paul. *The Organic Lawn Care Manual*. North Adams, MA: Storey Publishing, 2007.
For anyone who owns and maintains a plot of grass, the only book needed to grow lawn beautifully in an earth-friendly manner

Underhill, J. E. *Wild Berries of the Pacific Northwest*. Seattle: Superior Publishing, 1974.
Helpful information on edible and poisonous berries, including many unusual species

Verrier, Suzanne. *Rosa Rugosa*. Richmond Hill, ON, Canada: Firefly Books, 1999.
Detailed information on this most valuable and culinary species of rose

Walheim, Lance. *Citrus: Complete Guide to Selecting & Growing More Than 100 Varieties for California, Arizona, Texas, the Gulf Coast & Florida*. Tucson: Ironwood Press, 1996.
Beautifully illustrated book covering all aspects of citrus growing, including indoor culture

———. *The Natural Rose Gardener*. Tucson: Ironwood Press, 1994.
Includes great techniques for maintaining a rose garden with few chemicals

Waters, Alice. *In the Green Kitchen: Techniques to Learn By Heart*. New York: Clarkson Potter, 2010.
The founder of famed restaurant Chez Panisse emphasizes fresh, local, and organic ingredients in recipes collected from world-class chefs

Weaver, William Woys. *Heirloom Vegetable Gardening: A Master Gardener's Guide to Planting, Growing, Seed Saving and Cultural History*. New York: Henry Holt, 1999.
One of the most comprehensive books on the history and characteristics of heirloom vegetables

Wilson, Jim. *Landscaping with Herbs*. Boston: Houghton Mifflin, 1995.
Primer with ideas and ways to design herbs into your landscape

———, and Walter Chandoha. *Homegrown Vegetables, Fruits, and Herbs: A Bountiful, Healthful Garden for Lean Times*. Upper Saddle River, NJ: Creative Homeowner Press, 2010.
Excellent for beginner and intermediate gardeners, especially those who don't have the experience of growing edibles, written by one of the most esteemed gardeners in America; a good companion for this book

Xerces Society. *Pollinator Conservation Handbook*. Portland, OR: Xerces Society, 2003.
Valuable text that speaks to the importance of pollinators and how to bring them into your landscape

Index

Page numbers in **boldface** type refer to plant entries in the Encyclopedia or Appendix A; page numbers in *italic* type refer to photos and/or illustrations.

About the Author

Rosalind Creasy is a landscape designer, garden writer and photographer, and leading authority on edible landscaping. She is the author of eighteen books, including two best-selling titles for Sierra Club Books: the groundbreaking original edition of *Edible Landscaping* (1982) and *Cooking from the Garden* (1988), which were both Garden Writers Association award winners. She has written for countless national publications, including *Country Living Gardener, Fine Gardening, Garden Design,* and *Organic Gardening,* and has also produced a syndicated food column for the *Los Angeles Times.* Creasy lectures extensively and serves on the board of directors of the Seed Savers Exchange. She lives in Los Altos, California.